KINDERGARTEN
AND
EARLY SCHOOLING

KINDERGARTEN AND EARLY SCHOOLING

Second Edition

Marguerita Rudolph

Dorothy H. Cohen

PRENTICE-HALL, INC., Englewood Cliffs, N.J. 07632

Library of Congress Cataloging in Publication Data

Rudolph, Marguerita.
   Kindergarten and early schooling.

   Rev. ed. of: Kindergarten and early schooling /
Dorothy H. Cohen, Marguerita Rudolph. c1977.
   Includes bibliographies and index.
   1. Kindergarten—Methods and manuals. 2. Education,
Preschool—Curricula. I. Cohen, Dorothy H. II. Cohen,
Dorothy H. Kindergarten and early schooling. III. Title.
LB1169.R75 1984   372'.218   83-8684
ISBN 0-13-515338-7

Editorial/production supervision: Colleen Brosnan
Cover design: Diane Saxe
Manufacturing buyer: Ron Chapman

© 1984, 1977, 1964 by Prentice-Hall, Inc., Englewood Cliffs, New Jersey 07632
(1964 edition entitled: KINDERGARTEN—A YEAR OF LEARNING)

Photo Credits

From Bank Street College of Education, New York City. For the cover photo and the photos
on pages 45, 119, 127, 141, 173, 205, 237, 245, 287.

From the Bureau of Child Development and Parent Education of the New York State
Department of Education, Albany, N.Y. For the photos on pages 9, 39, 41, 48, 52, 71, 92,
108, 113, 165, 182, 193, 217, 218, 313, 324, 326, 330, 335, 370.

From the filmstrip series "Beginning Concepts," photographed by Tana Hoban, produced by
Scholastic Magazines, Inc. For the photo on page 227.

From the filmstrip series "Five Families" and "Five Children," photographed by Ken Heyman,
produced by Scholastic Magazines, Inc. For the photos on pages 19, 393.

From Pacific Oaks College and Children's School, Pasadena, Calif., photographed by Gail
Ellison. For the photo on page 60.

Printed in the United States of America

10 9 8 7 6 5 4

ISBN 0-13-515338-7

Prentice-Hall International, Inc., *London*
Prentice-Hall of Australia Pty. Limited, *Sydney*
Editora Prentice-Hall do Brasil, Ltda., *Rio de Janeiro*
Prentice-Hall Canada Inc., *Toronto*
Prentice-Hall of India Private Limited, *New Delhi*
Prentice-Hall of Japan, Inc., *Tokyo*
Prentice-Hall of Southeast Asia Pte. Ltd., *Singapore*
Whitehall Books Limited, *Wellington, New Zealand*

To the memory of Agnes Snyder,
a great educator and influential friend of both authors.

Contents

7

THE MEANING OF PLAY IN CHILDREN'S LIVES   92

8

PLAY IN THE CURRICULUM   108

9

EXPLORING THE ENVIRONMENT   119

12

THE IMPORTANCE OF ART FOR ALL CHILDREN   205

13

MUSIC AND RHYTHM IN SCHOOL LIFE   227

14

EXPOSURE TO LITERATURE   245

15

READING AND WRITING   287

16

MATHEMATICAL EXPERIENCE IN EARLY CHILDHOOD   313

17

PROBLEMS AND PLEASURES OF OUTDOOR PLAY   324

18

CLASSROOM MANAGEMENT   342

19

THE MEANING OF DISCIPLINE   370

20

PARENTS AND TEACHERS CAN LEARN FROM EACH OTHER   393

Foreword

Dorothy Cohen and I were friends and colleagues for the last six years of her life. We shared concerns about our students and the courses we taught, and we argued about ideas and strategies.

Dorothy Cohen may have been the busiest person at Bank Street College but she always had time to look up a reference, to ponder a suggestion for an interesting class session, or to interpret an experience. Often she would embellish her communication with vivid anecdotes from her long history of work with children, parents, teachers, students. No question was too trivial for her attention because no colleague, child, teacher, or graduate student was unimportant. A teacher to her core, she exemplified the possibilities of teacherhood: the vitality, the energy, the courage, the productivity. Even while she battled with cancer, she was training junior colleagues to teach her courses.

To be Dorothy Cohen's friend and colleague was neither restful nor comforting because she always expected that we, too, would stretch our capacities to the utmost. But she showed us all what it meant to care.

The same qualities of care, enthusiasm, and unstinting energy that characterized Dorothy Cohen's teaching also characterize her writing. In *Kindergarten and Early Schooling* she shares her commitment to humane and developmental education for children and their teachers and shows us as well the liveliness and the intellectual challenge of the profession of early childhood education.

Dorothy W. Gross
Until recently, faculty member
of Bank Street College
of Education, New York.
Currently, Parent Counselor
in Portland, Maine.

Preface

This book was begun by Marguerita Rudolph as an outgrowth of many years' work in early childhood education and previous writing in the field. The book evolved into final form as a result of creative collaboration with Dorothy Cohen, who enhanced the original manuscript with her special rapport with teachers and regard for research, her insight into childhood, and her power of communicating knowledge and feeling. The authors were pleased with their achievement and the reception of the first edition, *Kindergarten—A Year of Learning,* published in 1964.

A revised edition, published in 1977, required considerable updating since all the scientific-social-political changes occurring during that time were reflected in trends and practices in education, including early schooling. The authors brought to this edition, *Kindergarten and Early Schooling,* their experiences of continuous activity in the field, including professional writing, as well as the benefit of their previous collaboration. Thus the new book acquired a livelier cover, contemporary photographs of children in action, and new material.

Much of this new material reflected Dorothy Cohen's considerable scholarship, especially pertaining to reading and academic learning in the early years. At the same time, however, the authors retained the initial conviction that educational needs of young children must be met in relation to developmental needs of the whole child. They believed that the years of early schooling do not consist of mere preparation for later academic achievement but are in themselves a significant period of human experience and creative (not simply acquisitive) learning.

Soon after Dorothy Cohen's death in 1979 the publisher ascertained the need for a second revised edition of *Kindergarten and Early Schooling,* and the question of co-authorship loomed. How simple it would be if the co-authors were still working together: dividing chapters, going over and sometimes changing each other's writing, using anecdotal records from experiences of each. But reality has no "ifs." As the remaining author could not possibly accept the expediency of a substitute co-author, the revision became her responsibility alone.

Fundamentally, this revised edition is still a collaboration and contains all the important input of Dorothy Cohen as well as the combined work of both co-authors. Inevitably, however, some changes in style evolved, in the process and progress of the revision, as a result of the now one author's approach. Greater responsibility resulted in more critical attention, and thus in simplifying, condensing, or deleting some paragraphs and sections. Some changes in content were of course inevitable, due to the lapse of time since the mid-seventies and to the author's judgment. New material had to be added in a few areas—such as contemporary children's literature, studies in writing-readiness, and focus on the changing family.

Kindergarten and Early Schooling is not, nor should it be, completely up to date. Some old material here (including literary classics) remains valuable irrespective of age, and the preponderance of current "innovations" could not all be examined or considered.

Acknowledgments are due to the following persons for help, encouragement, and special contributions:

Alicia Kaufmann, my daughter and former student of Dorothy Cohen, for her indispensable professional assistance as sympathetic and patient editor and as practical critic; and for sharing in the many tiring chores of preparing this edition, as well as being uncomplainingly on call.

Sally Cartwright, a teacher who has been influenced by Dorothy Cohen, and who has contributed a number of unpublished records of children in her school which illustrate brightly many educational principles.

Bank Street College of Education faculty members who expressed an appreciation of the book and interest in the new edition, including Barbara Biber who had words of confidence and encouragement when I first began the revision; and, very importantly, Pearl Zeitz who read selected portions of the manuscript with constructive, professional criticism.

Louis Cohen, who had concern for the continued importance of his late wife's co-authorship and gave his serious editorial attention to the content and nuances of the completed work.

xxi *Preface*

Eleanor Fitchen and Janet Fitchen, grandmother and mother of Sylvia, who shared with me Sylvia's "Litel Girl Story" which is reproduced in this edition.

Appreciation is due also to the following people for their reviews and helpful comments on this book: Dr. Jacqueline Blackwell, School of Education, Indiana University; Prof. Steven H. Fairchild, Department of Elementary and Early Childhood, James Madison University; Dr. James L. Hoot, Elementary, Early Childhood, Reading and Special Education, North Texas State University; Prof. Millicent Savery, Center for Curriculum and Instruction, University of Nebraska–Lincoln; Prof. Loraine Webster, School of Education, University of South Dakota.

It is hoped the book will provoke discussion, and even win favor!

M.R.

1 Kindergartens Have a Long History

EARLY BEGINNINGS

Early childhood education has a generally complex history, but the kindergarten as a unique educational entity has its own traceable origin. Like most of us Americans and many of our institutions, the kindergarten came here from another country; it is an immigrant from Germany. It was started there in 1837 by Friedrich Froebel, a philosopher and educator with reverence for the spirit and nature of childhood and a high regard for the capacity of the young to engage in active learning. Froebel's first teachers were men—women were admitted to the profession after Froebel married.[1]

[1] Bernard Spodek, *Teaching in the Early Years* (Englewood Cliffs, N.J.: Prentice-Hall, Inc., 1978), p. 18.

EMERGENCE AND GROWTH
OF KINDERGARTENS IN AMERICA

The Froebel kindergarten, with its special organization, materials, and teacher training, won favor and influence among liberal elements in Germany. It was transplanted to America in 1856 by Mrs. Carl Schurz, a student of Froebel, who started a kindergarten in her new Wisconsin home for her own young children and those of relatives and friends. This first kindergarten in the United States was conducted in German.

In time, a New England educator, Elizabeth Peabody, became enchanted with the idea and opened the first English-speaking kindergarten in Boston in 1860. Peabody publicized the movement widely and helped organize the first teacher training center for kindergarten teachers.[2] The original German name, *Kindergarten* (children's garden), was kept. It was a good name, with focus on children, implication of growth, and a whiff of idealism—all in one word!

The carefully thought out Froebelian teaching methods and materials gathered adherents throughout the United States. The U.S. Commissioner of Education, Henry Barnard, was an enthusiastic proponent, spreading the good word while editor of the *American Journal of Education.*[3] Not surprisingly, all this interest led to the establishment of a kindergarten in the public school system of St. Louis in 1873.

NATURE OF THE FROEBELIAN KINDERGARTEN

The Froebelian kindergarten, reflecting the philosophical influence of the time, combined a religious philosophy of striving for unity of Man with God with a belief in the purity of the child's spirit as an inner force for development. Froebel believed that children needed the kind of careful guidance and nurturing that are neither available at home nor provided in formal schooling later. Thus Froebel's kindergarten included the following elements: play, considered important for self-development; special games and songs, which served to enhance learning; construction with materials that had symbolic meaning as well as manipulative value; practice at various tasks, especially gardening, that served to build character; and nature study, which Froebel considered uplifting. An important component of the Froebelian kindergarten was "creativity," which was assumed to occur through imitation followed by construction and production. Another component was active physical involvement with play materials.

[2] Evelyn Weber, *The Kindergarten: Its Encounter with Educational Thought* (New York: Teachers College Press, Columbia University, 1969).
[3] Ibid.

SPREAD OF KINDERGARTENS
IN THE UNITED STATES

Kindergartens became a definite part of American society during the last decades of the nineteenth century. They were regarded as corrective for affluent children, who were presumed to be indulged at home, and as beneficial for lower-class children, who were presumed to be sufficiently hurt by street influences to need the orderliness and social morality of the kindergarten.

Although the spread of kindergartens in the public schools was slow, there were hundreds of them in the schools by the 1880s. In this era of rising social conscience, a number of settlement houses in the big cities incorporated kindergartens into their programs for the education of the mothers as well as the benefit of the young children. A kindergarten department was even added to the Women's Christian Temperance Union "to lay the foundation of moral strength in the young." In general, toward the end of the nineteenth century great value was placed on the education and upbringing which took place in the kindergarten.

INEVITABILITY OF CHANGE

Inspiring as the Froebelian kindergarten was, it was inevitable that its idealistic goals should clash with practical reality. For example, Kate Douglas Wiggin's free Silver Street Kindergarten was housed in a squalid tenement in San Francisco, and "Though the rooms had been planned as an inspiration to cleanliness and courtesy, the ideals were not readily imparted,"[4] for the teachers had great difficulty extending the Froebelian law of love to the squabbling children, and they "found direct washing a necessity."[5]

On another level, challenges arose that ultimately shook the Froebelian kindergarten at its foundation. The prescribed materials and their rigidly sequential use proved not to be in tune with the liberal thinking influencing education at the time. By 1892, the International Kindergarten Union emerged as an organization of largely American educators, psychologists, and philosophers who were eager to influence the growth and development of the kindergarten. Their meetings were by no means harmonious, but they led ultimately to important changes.

CLAMOR FOR REFORMS

As the International Kindergarten Union grew and branched out across the country, its membership increased and the discussions of educational principles and classroom practices became more intense. The issues that were raised in the first decades

[4] Ibid., p. 43.
[5] Ibid.

of the twentieth century reflected a conflict between the mystic and spiritual values of Froebel and the scientific thinking of such students of child behavior as G. Stanley Hall. The Montessori system, too, was examined, and its structured pedagogical procedures and materials were evaluated and criticized. What won out was a pragmatic philosophy, with which John Dewey was associated: a scientific approach to child study and a child development point of view about curriculum. It was an exciting struggle, even though painful.

One of the outstanding innovators to emerge from this early period of conflict was Patty Smith Hill, from 1906 to 1935 a professor at Teachers College, Columbia University. In her differences with the Froebelians, she was guided by principles of democracy and respect for individuals. She argued for freedom and initiative for children, as well as a curriculum relevant to children's lives. It was she who originated large-muscle equipment and materials suitable for climbing and construction, a departure from the prescribed small-muscle activities of the Froebelians.[6] Patty Hill also urged unification of kindergarten and first grade, but her objective was not to start five-year-olds on first-grade work, as we today might readily assume. Rather, her emphasis was on giving six-year-olds the opportunity for independent, creative activities before embarking on the three R's.[7] Her ideas colored the approach to kindergarten curriculum right through the mid-1960s, when the emerging civil rights struggle and the antipoverty programs raised new questions and offered new solutions to old problems. By that time, there were other criticisms too, because the once progressive kindergarten movement had settled into its own rigidities and limitations.

The history of the kindergarten movement in the United States rings with the commitment, intelligence, and hard work of many devoted practitioners and theoreticians, most of them women of high idealism and strength. The story of some of them and of their movement is told in detail by Agnes Snyder in her book, *Dauntless Women in Childhood Education, 1856-1931.*[8] Both this effort and Evelyn Weber's overview cited above are worth reading, for they acquaint us with the unique features of American education, particularly in the area of the kindergarten.

NATIONAL FOCUS ON YOUNG CHILDREN

Until the 1960s, the early struggle notwithstanding, the world of the kindergarten existed in a quiet backwater of noncompetitive timelessness as far as its position in the large educational establishment was concerned. Kindergarten teachers knew

---

[6] In the same period, Caroline Pratt named the unit blocks she developed "free materials" in reaction to the rigid, didactic Montessori and Froebelian materials prevalent in her time. See Elizabeth Hirsch (ed.), *The Block Book* (Washington, D.C.: National Association for the Education of Young Children, 1974), p. 53.

[7] Patty Smith Hill, *Kindergarten,* The American Educator Encyclopedia (*Also,* Washington, D.C.: American Association for Childhood Education, International, 1942, 1967).

[8] Agnes Snyder, *Dauntless Women in Childhood Education, 1856-1931* (Association for Childhood Education International, 3615 Wisconsin Avenue N.W., Washington, D.C. 20016, 1971).

how important kindergarten was for later schooling, but above the kindergarten level there was a general lack of empathy in school circles for little children's special styles and needs. Kindergarten teachers did, however, appreciate being left to their own devices as they worked at enabling the children to enjoy an unpressured pre-academic period of satisfaction in many areas of learning and growing. In that fast disappearing past, kindergarten teachers saw themselves as warm, loving, devoted practitioners whose skills were focused on children as total human beings and not on children as academic achievers. Their interest in the larger issues of education tended not to stray too far from the specifics of interesting new equipment, games, or activities for their classes.

But in the 1960s, the problems of the country as a whole stimulated forces both within and outside the world of education to seek causes for the devastating failure in school and society of a large segment of the nation's children. Technology made employment increasingly dependent on skills associated with school learning; pressures for educating all children, but especially the children of the uneducated poor, grew more marked. Changes that were long overdue in the approaches to children of poverty could not now come fast enough. Simultaneously, it was recognized that if changes in attitudes and skills related to school learning were to take place at all, children and families must be reached as early as possible.

Inevitably the spotlight turned on the beginnings of learning, and on the preschool and kindergarten years. Thus, the kindergarten, long separated from the problems and anxieties of the total school community, was jolted out of its isolation to face new conceptions of children and new demands for children's learning. The kindergarten came under pressure from all sides to "change with the times."

KINDERGARTEN AT THE CROSSROADS

Contemporary feelings about what is right or wrong in the education of young children run as strong and deep in this latter part of the twentieth century as they did at its beginning. The social implications of education are perceived in ever-widening areas, and a relation between early childhood education and later schooling is today readily accepted outside the early childhood field. While few disagree on the sociopolitical urgency of tackling and resolving the problems of illiteracy and potential joblessness, there is less agreement on which course to follow to achieve this desired end. A good deal of research on cognition since the 1960s indicates a relationship between the lack of certain kinds of preacademic experience and academic failure. But no research to date has shown a relationship between specific preacademic experiences and academic success, and contradiction and controversy abound as the debate continues. The kindergartens, which fought long and hard for a curriculum based on play and which eschewed academic training for four- and five-year-olds, are now called "traditional." Montessori schools, British infant schools, Bereiter-Engleman behavior modification approaches, and a host of other "innovative" experiments including some reflecting current technological advances, all different from each other, have claimed to hold the key to formal school success.

It is hard to be a student of early childhood education at a moment of confrontation and challenge within one's chosen profession. Yet, crises in the field are not new; as far back as the 1870s, there were those who fought to spread the kindergarten influence upward into the grades instead of allowing kindergarten to become a literal and mechanical preparation for first grade. In our time, that struggle has taken an odd twist. The first grades have become generally informal, whereas the kindergartens are in places being transformed into copies of traditional first grades. The meaning of play was argued and even its value disputed during the first years of this century, and they still are today, when play is not yet understood in depth even by its proponents.

Yet a time of change can offer much that is promising. Outmoded ideas and habits can be sloughed off and new concepts and ideas tested in the reality of living. What we need to guard against is too rapid change brought about by anxiety and haste rather than careful analysis, because sound thinking can affect children's education and their future in ways that are helpful, while panic will do so with unfortunate consequences.

The kindergarten of today is being beckoned in two opposite directions. To some it seems that kindergarten can and ought to be strengthened in the direction of supporting more effective total learning and growth for young children in ways that matter to children yet are significant in the eyes of adults. This approach does not focus on specific academic skills but supplies the ground for them. To others it seems appropriate to hasten children's entry into formal skill learning by borrowing from the grades and turning the kindergarten into a watered-down version of first grade. Ironically, as we have indicated, this is happening at the same time that the first grades are at last taking on the more relaxed features of the traditional kindergarten without giving up their historic focus on the skills.

Which way kindergarten will go will depend on how carefully the coming generation of teachers and administrators studies the implications of the different directions proposed. They need to scrutinize the present avalanche of programs and materials which claim to be "new," "nonsexist," "cognitive," and "creative," and which are presented in ever more enticing "packages." The student as well as the practitioner of early childhood education must learn to recognize what is redundant, intrusive, and questionable. In any case, the contemporary student of early childhood can no longer settle for the pleasure of concentrating on stories to read, songs to sing, and games to play with the children he or she loves and enjoys, although these remain important aspects of his or her work. A teacher is expected not only to become a good practitioner but also to do so out of genuine competency in the theoretical considerations of why what is done is done. The early childhood teacher must grow as a thoughtful, professional person if the education of young children is to be vital and meaningful.

KINDERGARTEN AS AN OPPORTUNITY

The child under six goes to school as a matter of special advantage rather than legal requirement. Yet, the special ways in which kindergarten is beneficial for all children are recognized by more and more educational leaders; and although not compulsory, public kindergartens now exist in every state of the union. Moreover, their number is growing significantly. According to the latest study of the United States Census Bureau "in 1980 almost 96 percent of all 5-year-olds in the country were attending kindergarten, compared with 85 percent in 1965."[9]

In our present kindergartens there is great variation in goals and standards from state to state and district to district. Even within one district there are considerable differences from school to school. Throughout this book we will look at different kindergartens, meet different teachers, and try to recognize what makes them good or bad. We will begin by focusing on the children.

REFERENCES AND FURTHER READING

ALMY, MILLIE. *The Early Childhood Educator at Work.* New York: McGraw-Hill, 1975.

Association for Childhood Education International, Washington, D.C., 1966. *Toward Better Kindergartens.*

CALDWELL, BETTYE. "On Reformulating the Concept of Early Childhood Education—Some Why's Needing Wherefore's," *Young Children,* 22, 6, September 1967. To be found also in Anderson, Robert, and Shane, Harold (eds.), *As the Twig is Bent.* Boston: Houghton Mifflin, 1971.

DOWLEY, EDITH M. "Perspectives in Early Childhood Education," in Anderson and Shane (eds.), *As the Twig Is Bent.* Boston: Houghton Mifflin, 1971.

EDWARDS, ESTHER. "Kindergarten Is Too Late," in Anderson and Shane (eds.), *As the Twig Is Bent.* Boston: Houghton Mifflin, 1971.

EVANS, ELLIS D. *Contemporary Influences in Early Childhood Education,* 2nd ed. New York: Holt, Rinehart and Winston, 1975.

HILL, PATTY SMITH. *Kindergarten.* The American Educator Encyclopedia. *Also:* Washington, D.C.: Association for Childhood Education International, 1942, 1967.

HYMES, JAMES L., JR. *Early Childhood Education: An Introduction to the Profession.* Washington, D.C.: National Association for the Education of Young Children, 1975.

KILPATRICK, WILLIAM H. *Froebel's Kindergarten Principles Critically Examined.* New York: The Macmillan Company, 1916.

LAZERSON, MARVIN. "Social Reform in Early Childhood Education," in Anderson and Shane (eds.), *As the Twig Is Bent.* Boston: Houghton Mifflin, 1971.

Montessori in Perspective. Publication No. 117, NAEYC Publications Committee, Lucille Perryman, chairperson. Washington, D.C.: National Association for the Education of Young Children, 1966.

[9]Carey Adina Sassower, "Kindergartens Finally Becoming Universal," Winter Survey of Education, *New York Times,* January 10, 1982, p. 41.

SASSOWER, CAREY ADINA. "Kindergarten Finally Becoming Universal," Winter Survey of Education, *New York Times,* January 10, 1982, p. 41.
SNYDER, AGNES. *Dauntless Women in Childhood Education.* Washington, D.C.: Association for Childhood Education International, 1972.
SPODEK, BERNARD. *Teaching in the Early Years.* Englewood Cliffs, N.J.: Prentice-Hall, 1978.
WEBER, EVELYN. *The Kindergarten: Its Encounter with Educational Thought in America.* New York: Teachers College Press, Teachers College, Columbia University, 1969.

2 Relation of Early Childhood Experience to Later Schooling and Life Itself

THE WORLD OF TODAY'S CHILDREN

At no time in history has it been more necessary that the average citizen be a well-educated person. Technical knowledge has increased man's leisure time and brought the far reaches of the earth close to the eyes and ears of the ordinary citizen. Concepts of time and space shift faster than all of us can adjust to easily. Although further advanced than ever, knowledge about human beings, of the earth they inhabit, and of the space in which the earth whirls becomes outmoded at a more rapid pace than ever before.

There is more about the world in which children are growing up that we must consider too. All kinds of values are undergoing change, and it is not as easy to pass on a cultural heritage as it once was. The attitude toward work and leisure; the roles of men and women, separately and in relation to each other; the rejection of authoritarianism in favor of more democratic relationships at every level—all these are being examined and altered. The growing list of endangered species of animals; the increasing scarcity of natural products in the world, such as wood and wool; the estimate that we are running out of water and of traditional sources of energy; and the replacement of physical reality by images—these are all factors in the environment in which children learn and teachers teach. No one has yet fully assessed the full impact of these changes. Undoubtedly they affect the normal development and life of children as we have understood this process in the past.[1]

In such a world there is no question of the need for increasing areas of factual information and the corresponding need for flexibility in coping with new ideas. Children need more than facts; they must learn to think and to continue learning in order to cope with expanding knowledge. They will also need to be socially and emotionally mature to withstand the challenges of their adulthood. Such an educational goal is not really new.[2] But our past understanding of how to achieve this goal is being subjected to critical analysis as we learn more about what affects the learning process itself. It is this relatively recent insight into how learning takes place that makes us say that both the base on which school learning flourishes and the groundwork for original thinking and scientific problem solving needed in our time are laid in the preschool years.

ENVIRONMENTAL INFLUENCE ON LEARNING CAPACITY

Careful observation has shown that what happens to children long before they dream of entering school markedly influences their capacity to grow in school.[3] Relationships with adults, opportunities for varieties of experience, health and sickness, nutrition, space and crowding are among the many factors involved.[4] Consider the implications in this regard of the following studies.

Knoblock and Pasamanick[5] tested some three hundred children, half black, half white. They found no difference in intelligence scores between white and nonwhite babies at forty weeks of age. But when tested again at age three, the environmentally less-favored black children showed less responsiveness and curiosity; their language intelligence scores were as much as sixteen points lower than those of the white children with whom they had been on a par at ten months. On the other hand, Irwin[6] persuaded a group of mothers whose husbands were unskilled, semi-

[1] See Dorothy H. Cohen, "Children of Technology: Images or the Real Thing," *Childhood Education,* March 1972, and, by the same author, "This Day's Child in School," *Childhood Education,* October 1974.

[2] John Dewey, *Experience and Education,* Kappa Delta Pi Lecture Series, 1938 (New York: Collier Books, The Macmillan Company, 1963).

[3] Jerome Hellmuth, ed., *Disadvantaged Child,* Vol. I (New York: Bruner/Mazel, Inc., 1967).

[4] Eleanor Pavenstedt, ed., *The Drifters* (Boston: Little, Brown and Company, 1967).

[5] Hilda Knoblock and B. Pasamanick, "Environmental Factors Affecting Human Development Before and After Birth," *Pediatrics,* August 1960.

[6] O. C. Irwin, "Infant Speech: Effect of Systematic Reading of Stories," *Journal of Speech and Hearing Research,* 3 (June 1960), pp. 187–190.

skilled, and skilled workers to read to their children ten minutes a day from the time they were one. Not only were the mothers, who ordinarily would not have read to their children, amazed to find a strong interest in books among their little ones, but Irwin found a measurable difference in the speech development of these children as compared with that of a control group of similar background. And this difference showed up when the children were as young as twenty months. Or consider Esther Milner's study[7] of three groups of black first-graders. This study revealed a definite relationship between children's ability to read in the first grade and two factors, (1) the warmth of affectional relationship (parents and children chatted at meals together) and (2) the degree of intellectual stimulation (not only were there books in the house but even the punishment was *verbal*). The work of Hess and Shipman[8] has revealed that the very different ways mothers have of teaching their children influence the children's style of learning. Most dramatic, and reading like a fairy tale, is a study by Skeels[9] in which children sent as preschoolers to an institution for the retarded responded so well to the loving care of the adolescents in the institution that their true potential was revealed, they were adopted, and they grew up to lead productive lives.

What does all this mean? That learning, which consists of inborn curiosity and adaptiveness to new, changing phenomena, can be encouraged or extinguished much earlier and more easily than we have ever believed. The life condition of young children must offer stimulation and interest within an emotional climate of love and support, or they will not grow in capacity to learn. Or in the words of Bronfenbrenner

> In order to develop, a child needs the enduring, irrational involvement of one or more adults in care and joint activity with the child. . . . What do I mean by irrational involvement? Somebody has got to be crazy about the kid.[10]

Some researchers believe that lack of opportunity in early childhood and its resultant damage cannot be overcome. But others are inclined to the view that if a stimulating environment counteracts this void in the early years much can be done to reverse the downward trend. The fact that environment can play so dramatic a role in children's capacity to learn, and the frighteningly early stage at which children can show the effects of inadequate experience, point up the responsibility of the teacher of young children in a way we have not fully recognized before.

---

[7]Esther Milner, "A Study of the Relationship between Reading Readiness in Grade 1 School Children and Patterns of Parent-Child Interaction," *Child Development,* 22 (June 1951), pp. 95–112.

[8]R. D. Hess and V. Shipman, "Maternal Influences on Early Learning," in R. D. Hess and R. M. Bear (eds.), *Early Education* (Chicago: Aldine Press, 1968).

[9]H. M. Skeels, *Adult Status of Children with Contrasting Early Life Experience* (Chicago: Monograph of the Society for Research in Child Development, No. 31, 1966).

[10]Uri Bronfenbrenner, "Who Cares for American Children?" Address delivered at Pace University, New York, and printed in *The Month of the Child,* Frederick Bunt (ed.), (New York: School of Education, Pace University, June 1976).

Kindergarten, the earliest school experience for large numbers of children, is strategic in relation to future educational progress.

LEARNING FIRST FROM LIFE
AND THEN FROM BOOKS

Under ordinary circumstances of daily stimulation and affection, children are capable of learning and growing intellectually long before they can read from books. Yet the common conception of learning assumes that it begins with books and therefore with reading. Educators must revise their conception of learning to recognize that whether ideas are gleaned from books, films, discussions, or firsthand observation, the major consideration is that a mind is at work and insights are deepening. To assume that only reading can offer information and provoke thought is a fallacy that underestimates the capacity for factual learning, generalization, problem solving, and cause-and-effect thinking of the preschool child. Young children may be illiterate but they have minds and hearts. Indeed, the amount of learning many children do before they come to school, about customs, people, animals, natural phenomena, the industrial world they live in, and the more abstract conceptions of what they may or may not do, is enormous. Of course, books do in time become a major source of learning. But they are secondary sources which cannot be used beneficially at this stage without suitable and adequate preparation in firsthand, or sensory-motor, learning.

TRANSITION FROM SENSORY EXPERIENCE
TO BOOK LEARNING

What children learn on their own, if the opportunity is there, is real enough. But without adult guidance what they learn may be inaccurate and inadequate. Misconceptions and misinterpretations are then inevitable. Children need adults if their natural bent for wanting to know is to be rooted in a solid base of accurate facts and clear concepts. A child, for example, learns at the beach that sand can crumble into seemingly endless grains, pack into a specific shape when wet, be scattered by the force of water, absorb water and change color, be soft, dry, and warm as the sun shines on it, and cold, wet, and clammy when it is in the shade of rocks. But adults teach children that sand is made up of disintegrated rock, and geology beckons.

Or a child notices in a drawer the transformations of a familiar piece of bread into a strangely colored and textured object that is both repelling and fascinating. The adult tells the child what molds are and may acquaint him or her with an illustrated book.[11]

---

[11] Robert Froman, *Mushrooms and Molds,* Grambs Miller, illus. (New York: Thomas Y. Crowell, 1972).

Naturally, the knowledge an adult presents to children should be comprehensible to them and at their maturity level. The important thing here is that the child's own learning from life serves as an introduction and springboard to the accumulated heritage stored in books. It is this relationship between "natural" learning and "book" learning that makes the kindergarten experience so valuable for later school learning.

Although a very young child can be taught to recognize words and, theoretically, to read, no child can become a *reader of books* unless he or she can use the skill of recognition to absorb the ideas that the symbols represent. For this a child must have lived a while in order to be ready to share ideas and communicate through symbols, verbal as well as written ones. It is no accident that there is a high correlation between language facility (verbal intelligence) and school learning. But language facility means having something to talk about and knowing how to say it. This depends heavily on opportunity to experience, and experience is what kindergarten is about.

Kindergarten must be seen as a significant aspect of school life in its own unique way, stretching the minds of children but holding off on the tools for book learning, developing the broad qualities necessary for scholarship but not demanding the specific skills that will eventually enhance scholarship.[12]

Kindergarten is the time to find out that wanting to know is exciting, stimulating, and fulfilling. It is a time to ask questions, seek answers wherever they are to be found, and exchange ideas, knowledge, and impressions; it is a time to learn that mistakes and confusions can be turned into clarification and enlightenment. The kindergarten teacher makes it possible for the children to explore, examine, test, and understand that which is reality to a young child. Only in this way, by building understanding of what their senses contact, will children truly be ready for the symbolic learning that will come in time.

KINDERGARTEN'S ROLE IN MENTAL HEALTH

There is beginning to be evidence that the school plays its part, for good or for bad, in the mental health of children too.[13] We have long known that early childhood experiences throw a far shadow, although not an unchangeable one, over later behavior. While it is true, of course, that the home plays the primary role in this regard, school is the next single greatest influence in any child's life, and school begins before the first grade. For many children, kindergarten can be a strategic emotional experience, as well as the strategic intellectual one pointed out earlier.

Understanding the world in which they live does more for children than strengthen their intellectual powers. There is a tremendous sense of security in

---

[12] See Chapter 15 for further development of this position.

[13] Minuchin, B. Biber, E. Shapiro, and H. Zimiles, *The Psychological Impact of School Experience* (New York: Basic Books, 1969).

understanding what goes on around one, a sense of security not too easily won by a child in our highly complex, industrial, and increasingly computerized civilization. This idea may be seen more clearly if we think back to the life of a young child in our agricultural society of one hundred years ago. Reality stared such a child in the face. Children of both sexes observed the step-by-step procedures by which mothers and fathers arranged for the basic necessities of food, clothing, and shelter. From the first plowing of the earth through seeding, weeding, and harvesting, children saw the cycle that a product followed from field to table. They saw animals born, reared, and slaughtered for food; they saw clothing cut from cloth, and perhaps cloth itself made first. With their own eyes they saw the cutting of trees, the planing of wood, the construction of barns and houses. The five-year-olds in that economy suffered the gaps in comprehension of all five-year-olds at any time. But they understood the one-to-one relationships that they saw—fruit on a tree to fruit in a jar, lamb to chops, hen to eggs, and cow to milk. They might not have been able to say it, but they knew just how people depended upon the earth's resources for survival. This *knowing,* this comfortable feeling of comprehension about the processes of life, unfinished to be sure, was nevertheless a solid under-pinning to what we call security.

Let us contrast this with the situation of young children in our complex way of life. They do not see firsthand one original source of the things they learn to identify from their earliest days. Water, which they so enjoy, comes from a tap; light and dark are effected by buttons and switches; bread is taken from a plastic wrapper; telephones are just there, like trees; and to top it all, a world of people they cannot touch, voices they cannot answer, and actions they may not compre-hend are an integral part of their home life through television. We would not go back to the simpler way of life for the sake of the children in society, but we must remember that today's children need the same sense of knowing and understanding that offers comfort and security as did children in a simpler society. The kindergar-ten teacher, in making the reality around them comprehensible, is helping to clear away some of the confusion so likely to appear in our apparently more sophisti-cated, but somewhat overwhelmed, preschoolers. This *is* a contribution to mental health.

The comfort that comes from understanding one's environment is itself only part of a total feeling of security, albeit an important part. Life includes people as well as processes and things, and interaction with people calls for a variety of emo-tional responses. Much research and observation have gone into our understanding of the part emotions play in living and learning. The child who feels unlovable acts unlovable; the child who feels inadequate acts inadequate; the child who is afraid withdraws from the challenge of trying. By five, attitudes affecting one's relations with others and one's capacity to cope with what life offers (even with a good kin-dergarten program) are indicated in fairly clear trends. By five, the potential misfit can often be spotted by the astute teacher.

But kindergarten children are still tender and pliable—they still respond to adults whose affection and approval are eagerly awaited. Even the predelinquent can still be steered into another course if he or she is only five. And the "normal" child, whose responses to life can be strengthened to become more healthful and positive, is certainly amenable to direction toward good mental health.

Unrestricted by a precise course of study, the kindergarten teacher has a clearer and more direct involvement with the development of human beings than is apparent in the upper grades of school. Children's emotions are not yet concealed behind poker faces and polite formalities. The many admonitions from home and community that "good children do not behave that way" have made kindergarten children aware of what adults approve and disapprove of, but they have not closed off entirely the relatively uninhibited expression of feeling, including the "unacceptable," in social behavior. Kindergarten children show their anger, jealousy, hate, pique, fury, envy, rage, and bitterness. They also show tenderness, loyalty, affection, admiration, respect, and compassion. The teacher concerned with mental health has an opportunity in the kindergarten, not to hasten the suppressing of emotional responses earlier than ever, but to help children know where and when feelings, their own and others', are fitting; and to guide them toward techniques of social behavior that preserve the honesty of their feelings but also take into account other people's feelings. This is not easy, but it is very important.

KINDERGARTEN IS REAL SCHOOL

It becomes apparent then that the role of the kindergarten teacher is truly professional in scope. It is not enough to be charmed and intrigued by the wide-eyed naïveté, the trust and dependence on adults, and the unexpected independence and even cockiness of the four- to six-year-old. It is not enough to be loving and kind and offer friendship and activity. The possibilities for social and intellectual development of these youngsters call for careful study of their capacities for comprehension and behavior, and for just as careful decision as to which aspects of the environment will be built into curriculum. These may well be different for different groups of children and based as much on their intellectual needs and interests as the curriculum in the first grade. Some children have been to one or another form of child care center; some have been to private nursery schools and play groups; some have been to Headstart programs; and some are entering group life for the first time. Their experiences will differ as to awareness of organization, openness to materials, sensitivity to adults, and even familiarity with certain stories and songs. Such variations among children distress teachers who have fixed ideas about program content and cannot accept the fact that no group of children is ever the same as any other group, much less homogeneous. Building curriculum that is sufficiently varied to be relevant to most, if not all, children is what every kindergarten teacher must do.

The kindergarten teacher needs many skills. She or he is called upon to know more about human behavior and learning than personal experience yields, and more than is required at other levels of schooling which are subject-matter based and grade oriented. The teacher is responsible for children who are at a particularly impressionable stage of growth and still quite susceptible to change. Growth in both the intellectual and emotional areas is basic to children's adaptation to the more formal demands of grade school and the ability to cope with life itself.

DIFFERENCES BETWEEN KINDERGARTEN AND FIRST GRADE

There are educators and parents who are not at all sure that kindergarten has true merit. In these times of anxiety about the future, there is a feeling of urgency on the part of some educators and parents about rushing children into school and "real" learning. Although it has been well established that early childhood years *are* very important for learning in the basic, most general sense, the common concept of school is frequently that it starts with Grade 1. As a result, the kindergarten may be regarded as a preliminary of debatable necessity, a year spent pleasantly enough in games but adding little to what the child has already had at home or in some cases in nursery school. Therefore, there are parents who believe that if a child could somehow skip kindergarten and go directly into the first grade, or if kindergarten could do what first grade has already done, children would not be losing a whole year. This was how Mrs. Albert, mother of five-year-old Robert, reasoned, and her husband agreed. Robert would be only two months short of the required age for first grade and could therefore be tested for first-grade readiness—that was the local law.

Mrs. Albert presented her case to the principal, who acknowledged her claim for promotion but advised her to observe the kindergarten and then make up her mind about skipping it. Mrs. Albert went along with the suggestion.

Walking the length of the corridor, Mrs. Albert had an uneasy sense of confinement and officialdom—a characteristic of big public schools. She felt relieved when, on opening the kindergarten door, she found herself in a large, cheerful room, bright with children's work on the walls. She responded warmly and with curiosity to the liveliness of various activities, the informal, audible conversation between teacher and children, and the friendly, casual greetings she received. One child asked her to button his smock, another showed her drawings made by several children; she watched a small group of boys and girls experimenting with magnets and discussing their findings and opinions in a lively and intelligent way. With equal earnestness and imagination another group was managing a family dinner in the well-equipped housekeeping section of the class. Two were thoughtfully "reading" books taken from a well-stocked book rack. The teacher circulated among the children and was easily accessible to them, at that time being in charge of a word-and-picture game which fascinated the group engaged in it. Everybody in the room was working with zest, and as far as Mrs. Albert could see, without being told what to do or make.

She thought of her son, always so full of ideas, and felt sure that he'd not be overlooked in this kindergarten class where the children's activities and interests seemed so important to the teacher.

"How big these children are!" Mrs. Albert said to the teacher. She was thinking that Robert was smaller than any of them.

"Oh, they do grow during the year—in every way," the teacher answered. "Besides, there is a ten-month age spread, so some of them are already six and are bigger." Mrs. Albert was now visualizing next year and hoping that Robert wouldn't be the smallest in kindergarten. Her notion of skipping was giving way to a desire to protect her child during his first year in the "big school" as he was already referring to it.

As Mrs. Albert looked closer at the play materials in the room and the children's use of them, she could see that more than "just play" was going on. A girl and a boy at a table were playing with a set of wooden pieces and plastic screws called Bilo. The boy was fitting pieces together by trial and error, while the girl was explaining what a plastic gear was for. The boy put the gear on his structure and asked the teacher for a rubber band to put around two wheels. He showed the girl how the rubber band enabled the two wheels to turn at the same time and said gleefully, "A rubber band is something like energy."

In the elevated sandbox, a child was using real measuring cups and filling two halves to make a whole. At the other end of the sandbox, a little girl had dug a tunnel in a mound. After smoothing the passage with her hand, she told the teacher she didn't want anyone to break it.

"How will you stop them?" the teacher asked.

"Make a sign!"

"What will the sign say?" the teacher prodded.

"Keep off!" was the little girl's answer. And although there was such a cardboard sign already made, the little girl proceeded laboriously to copy the two printed words. She became so involved in the writing that she seemed to forget the tunnel.

Mrs. Albert was impressed.

"Do they learn to read and write in the kindergarten?" she asked the teacher.

"That depends on the children," the teacher answered. "They are in an in-between stage of readiness. They grow ready for writing during the year and want to do it when it is important to them. A very few are ready to read. Most haven't the patience to work at it just yet."

Mrs. Albert noticed that many children read the sign in the sandbox. The teacher explained that that was part of the readiness she was talking about. "First you have to know that print stands for something."

On the way home, this mother continued thinking of her still impulsive and impatient Robert, whose interests shifted frequently and who couldn't really sit still for long. And she decided that the flexible kindergarten would give him needed time to mature, give him a year to grow and learn in a stimulating class, and provide a sound start for "real" learning.

REFERENCES AND FURTHER READING

Association for Childhood Education International. Washington, D.C. *Early Child-hood: Crucial Years for Learning.*

BRONFENBRENNER, URI. "Who Cares for American Children?" Address de-livered at Pace University, New York, and printed in Frederick Bunt (ed.), *The Month of the Child.* New York: School of Education, Pace University, June 1976.

BURGESS, EVANGELINE. *Values in Early Childhood Education* (2nd ed.). Washington, D.C.: NEA, Dept. of Elementary-Kindergarten-Nursery Educa-tion, 1965.

COHEN, DOROTHY H. "Children of Technology: Images or the Real Thing," *Childhood Education,* March 1972.

COHEN, DOROTHY H. "This Day's Child in School," *Childhood Education,* October 1974.

DEWEY, JOHN. *Experience and Education,* Kappa Delta Pi Lecture Series, 1938. New York: Collier Books, The Macmillan Company, 1963.

FROMAN, ROBERT. *Mushrooms and Molds,* Grambs Miller, illus. New York: Thomas Y. Crowell, 1972.

HELLMUTH, JEROME, ed. *Disadvantaged Child,* Vol. I. New York: Brunner/ Mazel, 1967.

HESS, ROBERT, and SHIPMAN, VIRGINIA. "Maternal Influences on Early Learning" in Hess, R. D., and Bear, R. M., eds., *Early Education.* Chicago: Aldine, 1968.

IRWIN, O.C. "Infant Speech: Effect of Systematic Reading of Stories," *Journal of Speech and Hearing Research,* 3, June 1960, pp. 187–190.

KNOBLOCK, HILDA, and PASAMANICK, BENJAMIN. "Environmental Factors Affecting Human Development Before and After Birth," *Pediatrics,* August 1960.

MILNER, ESTHER. "A Study of the Relationship between Reading Readiness in Grade 1 School Children and Patterns of Parent-Child Interaction," *Child De-velopment,* 22, June, 1951, pp. 95–112.

MINUCHIN, P., BIBER, B., SHAPIRO, E., and ZIMILES, H. *The Psychological Impact of School Experience.* New York: Basic Books, 1969.

PAVENSTEDT, ELEANOR, ed. *The Drifters.* Boston: Little, Brown, 1967.

SKEELS, H. M. *Adult Status of Children with Contrasting Early Life Experience.* Chicago: Monograph of the Society for Research in Child Development, No. 31, 1966.

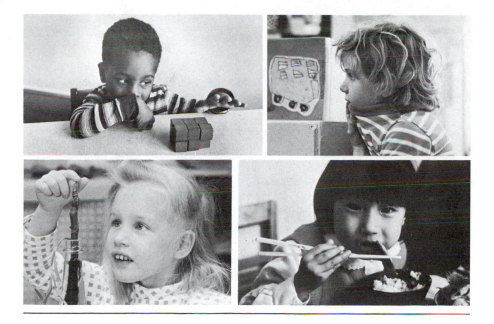

3 What Are Kindergarten Children Like?

KINDERGARTEN CONSISTS OF INDIVIDUALS

They Are Unique

Teachers inevitably appreciate the unique charm of children's faces, so open and expressive, so free of the masks and pretenses which all too many adults wear. In growing numbers of instances, this uniqueness is heightened by a variety that is something special and even exciting, as children of different ethnic and racial backgrounds come to school together from changing communities. Here is a class in a large city housing development. A lively little girl with tiny gold earrings is draping a flowing scarf around her shoulders. She does not look black, yet she isn't quite like many of the "white" children either. She moves snappily, arm in arm with a blond companion, talking in blurred English. She is from Central America, one of the Hispanic groups in our multiracial population, quite familiar in appearance and

(Photos by Ken Heyman)

language to many teachers and parents. The black children are shades of soft brown or warm tan with a variety of features and hair styles. The oriental children come with dark glowing eyes, flat black hair, and delicate differences of complexion. The white children are fair-complexioned foils for the deeper tones of their non-Caucasian peers, thus sharpening the teacher's perception of their unique differences. They too have varied complexions, eyes of different colors, and great variety of color and texture in their hair.

The children cluster in small, intimate, active groups and show no concern for racial identity. The visitor, however, cannot fail to be impressed and moved when four hands of different colors grab the mound of pale play dough, squeezing and kneading it to desired consistency amidst chuckles of delight. These children are like children everywhere, teasing and testing, physically active and exploring, having sudden bursts of tears, and giving in to abandoned laughter. Of a distinct ethnic background, the special individuality of each child shines clearly through the skin coloration and the ethnic features. They are children first of all, and kindergarten children in this particular class.

They May Be at Different Levels of Maturity

All kindergarten children are young children but not all who attend kindergarten are the same age chronologically or in terms of maturity. The chronological age for entry may be anywhere from four to six depending on the district laws, the child's birthday, or the type of school. A kindergarten teacher is thus just as likely to start in September with children not yet five as to have sixth year birthdays in February. She may expect to encounter occasional wet pants among the fours and fives or toothless gaps in the smiles of the sixes. Furthermore, there are tremendous individual differences in development even among children of the same chronological age. Thus Jackie, five years and two months, can hang by her heels from a jungle gym and is striving to accomplish more advanced tricks, while Jimmie, the same age, exerts caution and effort in slow climbing and steady descent, happy to land with both feet on the ground. Hector, not yet five, is wearing size six clothes, while Mary, the same age, is comfortable in size four. Ruthie picks up scissors and uses them matter-of-factly, while Angel is hesitant and helpless in using such a tool. Jean speaks fluently and freely at five-and-a-half but is sometimes hard to understand, as her *r*'s and *k*'s do not come through; Debbie, two months younger, enunciates very clearly although she does not have as much to say.

They Have Common Characteristics

Despite the wide range of individual differences so common at this and all ages, there are some characteristics kindergartners share that are worth bearing in mind. The contrasts in behavior are the most startling. These children are no longer babies, as they will tell you in no uncertain terms; yet they need affection and support and will break down under excessive stress as though they *were* babies. They are eager for information, yet they cannot concentrate for too long on any one area.

Kindergartners may use such advanced technical terms as *infection,* and of course space- and computer-age vocabulary; yet they may also use such baby words as *boo-boo* to denote a bruise or *pee-pee* for urinate. Frequently they will use big words or refer to adult concepts and not know what they mean. "We have a whole solution of enemies on this planet," shouted Ky as he dashed across the yard. "What does that mean?" asked his teacher. "I don't know," Ky answered cheerfully, "but I meant a lot."

Kindergarten children are creatures of feeling, and they laugh and cry with remarkable ease. Yet they love to be philosophical and attack such weighty concepts as the meaning of life and death. They are concrete, direct, and full of lusty humor, yet not always sure of the difference between reality and make-believe in the grown-up world. Children of this age are also very limited in experience and may lack knowledge which is commonplace to adults.

The teacher in a class of four-and-a-half- to five-year-olds told the children that she would be leaving them because she was going to have a baby. After she had gone out of the room for a few minutes and returned, some of them asked her, "Did you have the baby?" Practically all of them had younger brothers or sisters and supposedly knew that it takes a while for a baby to be born; also, the teacher had stated that it would take a while after she stayed home and "got ready," and until the baby grew big enough inside her to be born. Yet the children's lack of experience, their sense of immediacy in important matters, and their limited concept of time at this age made it natural for them to ask this question.

They Are Physical

We cannot help noticing that physical activity is the first characteristic of healthy young children. They are always ready to run and climb and reach and grasp and shout. Watching them in the playground, we marvel at their energy as they race at full speed, climb over self-imposed obstacles, and screech with delight when propelled into the air.

We sedate adults must remind ourselves that five-year-olds are not only excited by their own power but actually unaware of its full strength. When they push a large crate with their arms and chest, they surprise themselves by causing the crate to turn upside down. Their coordination is still to be refined. They therefore find it necessary to do a great deal of practicing of such interesting skills as jumping from or over moderate heights, suspending vertically by hands or by feet, or climbing swiftly up and slowly down. Kindergarten children often choose to do something the hard way just to give themselves interesting exercise!

They Love to Talk

With their keen ears, good memory, and flexible tongues, four-, five-, and six-year-olds grow astonishingly in language power and in vocabulary. At this age they can pick up a foreign language, they can use accurate intonations and inflections when portraying a certain character in dramatic play, they can learn many verses of a song, and they delight in acquiring new words, especially appealing ones like *infinity, dinosaur,* or *trillion.*

To exercise their expanding speech power, kindergarten children need to experiment and be inventive with language, to engage in rhyming, and to indulge in joking. They need to have opportunity for easy conversations with each other and with teachers, to do some arguing, and to express their ideas.

They Are Eager Learners

Intellectual growth in kindergarten children is in evidence throughout the school year—their constantly increasing power of reasoning, their deep and often unanswerable questions, their love of guessing games or riddles, their absorption in problem solving, their fascination with a variety of mathematical concepts, and their spontaneous interest in symbols. These children need and want a chance to exercise their fast-growing minds. Yet they do not learn primarily by passive attention to the teacher or mere listening to information. Exercise of the mind at this age comes about as part of the total activity of the child and is accompanied by a sense of urgency to find out *now, on the spot.*

Tony is typical of kindergartners as he says excitedly and earnestly, "I have an idea, I have an *idea.* If one of us could sit in the wagon and hold the milk, then the milk won't spill. Okay?" Observe the concentration of a little girl digging to the depth of a root and calling excitedly, "I see how far it goes, I see it!" Or look at the attention to detail with which a group of five kindergartners are playing bus. They are oblivious to all other activity in the room and are concentrating on the proper bodily positions of the "passengers," on representing the bus itself by sounds of the engine and wheels, on portraying the driver by appropriate movements of shoulders, arms, and hands, on keeping track of the people getting on and getting off the bus, on the financial transactions involved, and on the definite and rhythmic calling out of the stations. Or see what happened the day Regina brought lemons to school for making lemonade and the children at once began to investigate the lemons intently by smelling them and fingering the skins. They speculated on the color and quantity of juice. When the teacher cut the lemons and let the children squeeze them with ordinary hand squeezers, there was excitement over the special muscle in the palm of the hand which had to be put to use.

"See how my muscle works!"

"I am squirting out a *lot* of lemon juice!"

"Let me squeeze the juice out with my muscle without the squeezer."

Then those four-and-a-half- to five-year-old children enjoyed tasting the plain lemon juice and the bitter rind.

"Look at Johnny making a sour face!"

They added a measured amount of water and the right amount of sugar. They judged and differentiated among degrees of sweetness and sourness and noted how grimacing reflected taste sensations.

"I don't make any face—you want to see?"

They Love Feeling Grown-up
and Enjoy Being Helpful

Young children also want to experience being trusted with responsibility. They want the chance to practice some "real grown-up" work. That is why they appreciate going on errands, helping the teacher with responsible tasks, using proper tools, taking a legitimate part in such grown-up work as cooking, cleaning, shopping, or suggesting solutions to practical problems.

Emerging from the storage house in the yard Barbara has something "dangerous" to report.

"There's a nail sticking out!" And she asks for a tool to remove the danger.

Although we are apt to take for granted young children's egocentricity and social immaturity, they can, in a suitable group environment, be of actual help to each other, and enjoy such experience. Help with materials, with winter clothing, with food, with empathy toward humans and animals—however incidental—does occur. When noticed and encouraged by the teacher, such helpfulness brings satisfaction to the child and attains importance for the group.

The psychologist Jerome Bruner contends in an interview that children do indeed have the ability to be helpful and to take part in classroom management and that the proper environment for encouraging helpfulness is not excellent facilities or techniques but adults' continued subtle and intelligent guidance.[1] That kindergarten teachers, with their unique opportunity for observing and their sensitivity to children, play an important role in nurturing helpfulness is also expressed by Janet Black. While there are many theories—including observations by Piaget—concerning egocentricity in young children and their inability to act altruistically, there is growing evidence that this is not always so. "Children from at least the age of one have a capacity for compassion and various kinds of prosocial behavior."[2]

They Experience Personality Growth

The emotional growth and personality development of kindergarten children are not as obvious as their getting bigger, stronger, and smarter. You can easily see the increases in height and weight, and the loosening teeth. But if you look closely, you will also see that a kindergarten child develops noticeably in personality too. He or she may change from a youngster who seems to have no initiative and who only imitates what another child does into a child who asserts preferences, expresses ideas, and carries them out so that both teachers and children have a genuine respect for him or her.

Cleon, according to his teacher, "became a different child in six months." He seemed frightened and confused at first, hitting children impulsively for no ap-

---

[1] Elizabeth Hall, "Schooling Children in a Nasty Climate," Interview with Jerome Bruner, *Psychology Today*, January 1982.

[2] Janet K. Black, "Are Young Children Really Egocentric?" *Young Children*, September 1981, 51.

parent reason and disturbing other children's work. His classmates referred to him as "the bad boy." In the course of the year he learned to be constructive and satisfied with many materials. He made contributions to the children's play. Although he still demanded extra attention from the teacher once in a while and still had occasional outbursts of destructiveness, the teacher and class, including Cleon himself, knew that he had changed. Kim, too, changed. For months no one knew she was in the class at all, because she was so quiet and unobtrusive. But as she came to know the situation well, Kim moved in to offer some real leadership, which all the children accepted.

GROUP SIZE AFFECTS THE EXPERIENCE
OF THE INDIVIDUAL

Clearly, education in a democratic society puts primary emphasis on the worth of the individual. But children attend school in groups, and there's the rub. A group may consist of fifty, which can seem like a herd, an undifferentiated mass, and the teacher finds it difficult to maintain contact and give guidance on an individual basis to the Tommys and Marys who make up the fifty. Studies confirm that the quality of interpersonal relationship suffers with increased class size, as we might expect.

It is easy to see the educational and human advantages of smaller kindergarten classes,[3] and theoretically that is our national goal. But money for education does not always follow in the wake of knowledge about what is desirable, and large kindergartens still exist. Although they cannot be as effective, teachers must try to reach the individual child even under the adverse conditions of overlarge classes.

An Individual Child Need Not Be Overlooked
in a Crowded Class

Here is a public school kindergarten with forty-nine children in the class. Mrs. Rand, the teacher, is frustrated by the limitations that such crowded conditions impose on her and on the children, but she is more concerned with reaching each individual child. What does Mrs. Rand do?

First, whenever possible she avoids speaking to the children en masse. She does not have an entrance line into class nor does she say one impersonal "Good morning, children." Instead, she allows informal arrival by groups and individuals and therefore has the opportunity for informal, spontaneous greetings and pleasantries, even if these are reduced to a wave of the hand and a smile for some. Although this takes a few more minutes of her time each day, it gives her in return some measure of genuine communication with each child and a chance to notice any special needs.

[3] Dorothy H. Cohen, "Dependency and Class Size," *Childhood Education*, September 1966.

Later in the session, when the children are settled into work activities, attending independently to painting, clay, building, puzzles, housekeeping play, and other activities, Mrs. Rand resists the temptation to bury herself in clerical tasks and keep only a perfunctory eye on the free play. Instead she often works on a special private project with one, two, or three children, such as sewing, carpentry, storytelling by the children, or reading by the teacher. The ten minutes of such meaningful, fully personal attention coming regularly, albeit not often enough for each child, helps to establish a sense of the worthiness of the individual which is readily appreciated by the children.

You may think that Mrs. Rand—so dedicated and seemingly tireless—is too good to be true. However, this being a true account, Mrs. Rand, though admittedly not a frequently encountered kindergarten teacher, does really represent the professional teacher, as we will see.

In many other situations Mrs. Rand shows her awareness of the children's feelings. While reading a story one day she was called out of class on official business. The children had to wait for her return to hear the end of the story. When Mrs. Rand did return she included all in her glance as she said warmly and sincerely, "Children, you were wonderful to wait quietly so long while I was talking on the telephone. I know it was hard." And it *is* hard for any kindergartner to exercise such control. Despite the size of the class, Mrs. Rand's honest pleasure and her understanding of the strength of the achievement helped each child feel appreciated for his or her efforts. This pervasive understanding, growing out of a teacher's knowledge of the age group, becomes particularly important when not enough attention can be given to individuals.

In another crowded class the teacher confides cheerfully that she looks forward to days when winter colds and spring epidemics cut her class of fifty to practically half. On those days she makes a point of establishing closer contact with the children present, and especially of getting to know the overlooked ones who were previously lost in the shuffle. Somehow teacher and children are never strangers to each other after that.

In still another crowded class the teacher evolves his special system of attending to individual children; each day when the forty children are distributed in about six working groups, he spends twenty minutes or so with one working group. Thus he concentrates one day on the children who draw, then on those who build, or on those who fingerpaint. By focusing on small groups he increases his knowledge of individual children.

The teacher working under crowded conditions must strive to reach each child and not be discouraged by only partial success. This can be done in the following ways: keeping the program and routines informal so that advantage can be taken of every possible opportunity for communication ("informal" does *not* mean without socially established controls against chaos); speaking to children personally and separately as much as possible; listening to at least some individuals every day; discerning individuals within small groups; concentrating on ways of encouraging independent behavior so that in time more individuals can be worked with because so many more children can be trusted to function without continuous need for the teacher's attention. Rules and regulations that help group movement and interaction must be clear and unequivocal (for example, no running inside the classroom; all tools must be put away).

Individuals Are More Easily Seen in a Group of Reasonable Size

When the enrollment in a kindergarten group is in the neighborhood of twenty or twenty-five children, with a sufficiently large room and adequate equipment, the teacher has many opportunities to know and enjoy each child, to help each one in different ways, and to communicate knowledge and appreciation of each child. When the organization of the classroom materials and program is flexible enough to meet particular children's interests and needs, the teacher can focus even more effectively on individuals and small groups.

Here is a teacher of 24 five-year-olds in a child care center reading to the children at the end of a long, rainy day. All nineteen children present want to hear the story and sit on the floor in front of the teacher. First the teacher tells the children that this particular book (*The New Pet*)[4] was especially chosen from the library because it is about babies and about pets and looking at the close, friendly circle of faces, "because Carlos and Jésus have new babies, and because Walter told us about his pets." Information about additional pets is promptly added by other children, and the teacher gives full recognition to that. During the story some details from the book are related to individual children and some situations to the experiences the children have had. The teacher speaks to them without sentimentality or even endearments, yet brings personal and individual considerations into the ordinary process of reading a book. Each child feels the teacher's interest and devotion.

Some Children Stand Out in Any Group

In any group, whether large or small, one is always conscious of the dramatically different child. A teacher of a class of fifty speaks readily about Glenn because "he is extremely bright and can answer any question quicker than anybody else in the class." Another teacher in a class of twenty-five tells how Bobby is the "biggest challenge; he is very aggressive so that other children always have run-ins with him." A teacher in a class of forty is aware of Roslyn, who has defective muscular coordination, yet "sticks to her work and is so cheerful!" No teacher can overlook Reuben, whose overabundance of energy, constant mobility and activity, exciting ideas and lively talk, and the unique zest with which he does everything are magnetic points of focus.

[4] Marjorie Flack, *The New Pet* (Garden City, N.Y.: Doubleday & Co., Inc., 1943).

Some Children Must Be Sought Out

But what about the less demanding, the not so aggressive, not brilliant, not dramatically attractive child? What about the overlooked "good" child about whom the teacher will say to an inquiring mother, "She is getting along just fine, Mrs. Smith."

Let us look at two children who are not easily distinguished from the group. Are such children as uninteresting as we might at first glance assume? Jill, almost five, is a seemingly placid child who takes school for granted, complies with routines, and busies herself in the doll corner or with materials. She is never heard in the room nor is she distinguished by any special contribution. Jill allies herself with only a few children and takes her place matter-of-factly among the others for group games or projects. She is also merely on looking terms with the teacher: looking when the teacher reads a story, looking when she carries on some communication with other children. One day the teacher realizes that for the past week Jill has been insisting stubbornly on wearing a special little wool hat with a bow in the back while indoors; if she is persuaded to remove it and place it in her cubby, she invariably gets it back on her head later during the morning. So the teacher asks about it.

"This is a pretty hat, Jill—is it new?" Jill laughs gleefully at this and makes a sweeping motion with her hand at the teacher's absurdity.

"It's not new. It's my *mommy's* hat."

"Oh?" the teacher raises her eyebrows.

"She even gave it to me . . ." (whatever the word *even* means). Now the teacher is surprised and curious about Jill; she watches Jill's motherly and managerial play in the doll corner, her independent kind of conversation, and her relations with the other children. And perhaps responding to the teacher's new notice of her, Jill herself begins to confide in the teacher. Other times Jill dares to test the teacher's authority and thus commands the teacher's further attention. Jill has come alive.

André, just five, simply blends into the group. One not only does not hear André, but one does not see him. A small child, he usually works quietly by himself, smiling amiably when approached by the teacher and looking on casually at the livelier children and activities in the room. The only time the teacher really becomes aware of André is when a sliding block bruises his ankle during clean-up time. André then becomes frightened and clings silently to the teacher for protection and comfort, looking up at her appealingly. So the teacher becomes aware of André's baby quality but she knows practically nothing about André as a growing, active schoolchild.

Then Nina, in many ways also a gentle child, suddenly notices André and goes after him—literally. "Will you build with me, André?" André nods. "I want to sit next to André," she tells the teacher at snack time, and André smiles at this—clearly a smile of being favored. "Let's wrestle!" she proposes to André outdoors and the two of them (similar in size and with similar spirit of fun) push and pull each other and laugh and fall to the ground, rise and chase each other all over the yard. The teacher, thanks to Nina, at last sees André's humor, his physical power, his ingenuity with materials, his tractability, and certainly his response to friendship and affection.

ACCEPTING CHILDREN AS THEY ARE

Appreciating individual children means appreciating them not only for what the teacher or the parents *want* them to be or are helping them to become ("more mature," "better skilled," "more outgoing"), but for what they are *at present.* For example, when Marilyn went to kindergarten she worked valiantly to produce various daily prescribed constructions from boxes and cardboard and paper. However, she was not as handy as some other children with those constructions and thus disappointed the teacher and herself. The teacher unfortunately had no opportunity to know how skillful and responsible Marilyn could be with other activities. Marilyn complained philosophically at home. "The teacher wants us to *make things* all the time. I like nursery school better 'cause in kindergarten it's only what you make that counts; but in nursery school, it's what you are that counts." It is of basic importance to children to be recognized for what they are as individuals.

How does a teacher come to realize this uniqueness? By closely observing each child's own way of reacting to life.

Physical Appearance and Movement

The most striking first impression of any child is given by his or her outward appearance and quality of movement. Closer observation without prejudice reveals not only how different children are in looks, but how different children *are.* See how a first look at their outward appearance led to further consideration of the behavior of the following children.

In the first month of school, the teacher noticed that Sammy was different physically from the other children. He had a heavy, sluggish walk and a slight stoop; his hands hung down idly most of the time. With his rather small face and thin mouth, he looked like a little gnome. There seemed to be a minimum of inflection in Sammy's speech and never any shouting. How different from the other boisterous four-and-a-half-year-olds! His glance shifted uncomprehendingly from one object to another and his smile in response to the teacher or children was not fully formed. The teacher felt impelled to discuss Sammy's rate of development with his mother and was not too surprised to learn that he had been slow in developing. This knowledge served her well as a teacher to this little boy, who, in spite of his slowness, wanted very much to come to school, liked being among the children, and responded to the teacher even if in a limited way.

The same teacher noticed Paul, conspicuously big in size, with a heavy, middle-aged type of figure which was most obvious when he wore long pants and a tight belt that revealed his bulges. His mother said with a mixture of pride and worry that he wore size eight clothes. When Paul entered the room even at the middle of the year, when he surely ought to have felt comfortable enough, he stood hesitantly by the door. He often sat lonely and apart, with discouragement revealed in the curve of his little boy's mouth. When the teacher and the mother talked together, the teacher learned that when Paul cried or acted naturally babyish, there was always someone who said, in a shaming tone, "A big boy like you!"

What can being big mean to Paul, the teacher asks herself as she assures Paul that she is on his side, that he does not have to act big for her or be ashamed of his occasional babyishness.

In the same class there is Lenny, also a young five, a handsome, dark-skinned little boy with curly black hair, sunny brown eyes, a quick, expressive face, and an agile body. He is of average height and all his movements show fine strength and zest, but he looks quite thin when he removes his padded snow pants and heavy sweater—revealing a predominance of knees and elbows. Lenny's grandmother complains about his being "so skinny," and tells Lenny's mother to "fatten him up." The teacher tells the mother that Lenny shows plenty of strength and energy and alertness in school, so that she *must* have succeeded in feeding him pretty well after all. "I'll tell that to his grandmother!" the mother jokes with evident pleasure. The teacher watches Lenny some more. He has a ravenous appetite at snack time, stuffs his mouth with as many crackers as he can grab in his hands, and picks up the scattered crumbs from the basket on the table. Lenny usually has something in his mouth that he chews on, such as a mitten, a thumb, a wad of paper, sometimes the upper part of his shirt. Yet his attention is always on some activity, building or woodworking, or construction with table materials. Lying on the floor for a rest, Lenny is almost perpetually wiggling, stretching, or drawing himself up to different positions. When sitting on a chair, he always either tips the chair or taps or scuffs his feet. Yet with all this bodily activity that seems so distracting, Lenny concentrates fully on the task at hand. The teacher is impressed by his simultaneous bodily mobility and busy mouth, the wealth of interest and feeling shown in his face and his constant mental activity. There is much more to Lenny than his elbows and knees.

Ernest is a child who usually avoids participation in group exercises or games. His movements are jerky and unsteady. He walks down steps with both feet on each step. He runs with feet wide apart and claps in an uneven rhythm with fingers open, blinking his eyes tightly each time he claps.

In a game of following the leader through different movements, Ernest stays at the outer edge of the group. He watches intently, his body poised to move, but does not actually do anything. Finally the leader swings her arms around, making a large circular movement backwards. Ernest tries to follow. His arms are bent in a tight angle, his fists are clenched, and he moves his hands up and down rather than around, his eyes blinking tightly with each move.

And there is Katie, a charming, well-built youngster who has worn a hearing aid since she was two. Her intense, focused stare and slightly tilted head as she listens to those around her and her impulsive jumble of still somewhat awkward language are the only vestiges of an otherwise fine adjustment to the world of people and sound.

In a busy classroom it may take weeks, and sometimes months, to get that closer look that gives each child distinction. It is helpful to a teacher to focus in this special way on at least one child every day.

Observing the Child's Behavior in Routines

The time when all children in the class do the same thing according to the teacher's plan is during routines: getting on outer clothing before going out; cleaning up after work period; washing hands; preparing for a snack; settling for rest. In spite of the sameness of procedure, this is a good place to notice individual behavior, especially at the beginning of the year.

During dressing time the teacher can observe that some children are helpless and give up easily, others are independent to the last stubborn button, and still others are able and happy to help friends with sleeves and scarves and attend to themselves as well. Fearfulness, shyness about the body, or excessive fastidiousness are not infrequent among young children when you observe them in the bathroom; a child may even resist using the toilet at all in school. Nevertheless most five-year-olds are matter-of-fact about toileting.

When it comes to cleanup, the children are especially apt to show differences of behavior. There are always children who show resistance in varying degrees. Some may simply refuse to take any part; some will invent devices to get out of work; some will cooperate only on a minimum level. Yet other children the same age will respond to cleanup with gusto, loading their arms with blocks from the floor, swooshing a brush across a table, stuffing the wastebasket to capacity. And some child will become so fascinated with removing wetness with a sponge that he or she will squeeze the sponge out over the table in order to do the work over again several times. Observing the children's individual behavior at cleanup enables the teacher not only to plan routines realistically, but to assess the capabilities and the needs of each child more concretely.

Observing Individual Responses to Children and Adults

A child's way of approaching and responding to others is such an important indicator of human strength and growth that we are devoting a separate chapter to the subject. Our immediate concern is the teacher's observation of any child's behavior with others, for a better understanding of the child as an individual and to be able to guide her or him more wisely.

Although kindergartners are by and large sociable beings who need and seek each other out, a teacher can readily see tremendous individual differences in the way they do it. Within a kindergarten group there may be some who pick fights and push others around. The teacher might well ask: What do these children want? What could make them happy? What and whom do they like? The teacher could ask too about the fearful child who gets pushed around, who does not dare stand up for his or her rights yet may go into the midst of the rougher children and *prefer* playing with the very ones who abuse him or her. What does this child really want? What are his or her *strengths*?

A quiet child who usually chooses to play alone comes to school one day with a package of bubble gum and offers it to the four most aggressive and extroverted children in class. The next day some charm trinkets are distributed to the same potential friends. "This is bribery," the teacher thinks, feeling impelled to tell Sandy: "This is not the way to make friends." Yet apparently this is the only way that gives Sandy the confidence to approach others and actually win friends.

Many children have difficulty getting along with others their own age and at the same time are able to get along beautifully with older children and adults. They do not hesitate to approach a visitor in the room, and they love to play host; they speak politely and well to adults and are content in adult company.

Finally, there may be a child in the class who can be characterized as a "goody." Among candid, outspoken, impulsive preschoolers a "goody" is a pathetic phenomenon. He or she does everything to please the teacher, is conspicuously polite, uses adult phrases, even clichés ("I always eat vegetables—they are *good* for you"), and is ridiculously righteous ("I *never* cry"). A veritable apparition in the midst of flesh-and-blood four-, five-, and six-year olds! Yet some teachers encourage "goodies" by citing their behavior as exemplary. One sometimes confuses "goodiness" with straightforward goodness. The one shows watchful currying, and even fearful response to adult appraisal. The other is friendly, cooperative, positive, and natural with adults.

Thus individual children reveal themselves in many different ways. Their appearance and quality of movement tell us some things about them, their responses to people and objects tell us other kinds of things. Each child responds to life in a totally idiosyncratic way. A sensitive teacher notes the details that add up to a fuller understanding of the individual.

CHILDREN WITH SPECIAL PROBLEMS

Occasionally there will be a child whose behavior seems to go just a shade beyond the normal expectation, who does not respond to teacher guidance and support, and who seems unable to learn from experience. Teachers then wonder whether to ask for further help for such a child, and if so, how to report their concerns. In the July 1975 issue of *Young Children,* three authors organized certain behaviors into "categories that are critical for the analysis and prediction of academic, social and psychological difficulties."[5] While these are not all-inclusive, they are helpful to kindergarten teachers as an aid to observing and recording behaviors that would be useful to any diagnostic team. We reproduce these categories with permission of the authors.

[5]Larry M. Raskin, William J. Taylor, and Florence G. Kerckhoff, "The Teacher as Observer for Assessment: A Guideline," *Young Children,* 30, 5, July 1975, 339–44. Reprinted by permission from *Young Children.* Copyright ©1975 by National Association for the Education of Young Children, 1834 Connecticut Ave., N.W., Washington, D.C. 20009.

Visual

1. *Eye movements:* Do the child's eyes seem to work as an integrated pair? Do they point in different directions or do they seem to move independently? Does the child have trouble converging his or her eyes on a close-in object, or have difficulty keeping both eyes on a fixed or moving target?
2. *Winking:* Do some children have difficulty closing their eyes when asked, either both at once or one at a time? An inability to wink by five years of age should be noted.
3. *Distance and position from work:* Does the child continually hold dolls, puzzles, or pictures less than seven inches away from his or her eyes? Also, does the child hold his or her head to one side when looking, or lean the whole upper trunk in one direction? Does the child avoid table work that requires looking and moving materials at less than an arm's length away, or is there a tendency to hold things far away from the body in an apparent attempt to see more clearly?
4. *Signs of irritation:* Have you noticed that the child rubs his or her eyes frequently, or the eyes are red-rimmed or runny? Does the child blink excessively when looking from the teacher to table top and back again, and soon stops looking at what is going on?
5. *Visual-motor control:* Does the child do puzzles only by feeling whether the pieces fit, or have trouble throwing a beanbag into a large opening, or never seem to be able to keep a flashlight on target? These may be signs that more than poor vision is involved.

Motor Behavior

1. *Strength:* Is there a general lack of physical strength in comparison to others about the same age? This may show up in either small motor activities such as operating a wall light switch with the index finger or such large motor activities as hanging from a pull-up bar. Can the child sustain a leg lift for five seconds while lying on his or her back?
2. *Agility:* Does the child stumble and fall often or seem to avoid jumping, running, climbing, rhythm, or balancing tasks? Are both arms used as aids in balancing and running? Has the child failed to master the leg movements used in pumping while on a swing? Can the child jump with both feet off the floor simultaneously? Is an apparent lack of good judgment displayed when climbing or running? Stepping off the top of a high place or other dangerous behaviors should be noted.

Use of Writing Instruments

1. *Handling:* Does the child still hold the crayon, paintbrush, or pencil in his or her fist by about three and a half years of age, rather than between the thumb and forefinger or other fingers?
2. *Copying:* Is the child able to imitate or copy simple lines, e.g., vertical or horizontal, without frequent overstroking or whorling, by three years of age? Is s/he able to reasonably reproduce such geometric shapes as a circle, cross, and square by five years of age? (Triangles and diamonds are more difficult and not usually accomplished until about age seven.)

3. *Drawing:* Are spontaneous pictures barren of details or composed of simple outline shapes? Do drawings of human figures include such major parts as head, eyes, nose, mouth, a distinct body, and legs by five years of age?

Looking, Listening, Remembering, and Doing

1. *Remembering and doing:* Can the child remember and follow three-part directions such as "After you have put away your blocks, you may wash your hands and come for juice"?
2. *Shutting out distractions:* Does the child shut his or her eyes in order to listen better, or cover the ears to watch better?
3. *Distractibility:* Does the child remember and return to the task at hand following interruptions by five years of age?

Social-Emotional

1. *Attitude:* Does the child continually rely upon stubborn, negativistic, or extremely independent behavior when interacting with adults or other children?
2. *Is the child destructively hostile?* Are materials smashed, attacked without apparent cause, and the child's own productive work destroyed? Does the child cause physical or psychological harm to herself or himself or others? Is she or he excessively aggressive with little or no provocation?
3. *Cyclical behavior:* Does the child have successions of good days and then bad days? This should be recorded over at least a three-week period.
4. *Withdrawal:* Does the child answer questions clearly and directly when asked? Does the child avoid all contact with the teacher and classmates, possibly sitting alone in a corner?
5. *Extreme attachment:* Does the child have difficulty separating from the teacher or parents to start new activities or begin the day? Often a young child shows dependence through a predisposition to touch or hold the parent or teacher and takes every opportunity to be near them. During free-play activities the child will follow the teacher or if engaged in an activity, will frequently ask for help in order to remain at the task.

OBSERVING THE CHILD'S USE OF MATERIALS

As the children choose and use the materials made available by the teacher, getting whatever help and guidance they may need, the teacher has the opportunity to observe the individual child's approach to materials and the quality of performance with them. The teacher can observe one child's hesitation and tentativeness with everything new. She or he sees the emergence of confidence in another child as he or she gains experience with some material. In still another child she or he may see the complete assurance and skill that comes with success. The teacher may also notice in the class a child who is so attracted to new things that he or she rushes and grabs them, and the child's haste indeed makes waste, or even causes damage. Teachers soon learn to keep an eye on such a child and to help him or her learn healthy caution, whether with water at the sink or with a saw at the workbench.

The teacher will also observe that some children may use school materials as if they were weapons; they hit with the crayons on the paper, they jab the paintbrush on the easel, they pick up a building block as if it were a gun. She or he may squirm inside at first, but if the jabbing painter operates with paintbrush on paper and even compares the sharp strokes with the large curly ones or little squiggly ones of nearby friends, the teacher simply watches and learns. The teacher may be wary of the block gun but if the "soldier's" attention is shifting to construction of a jet-port or barn (just as likely as a fort) and if the activity invites participation of others, the teacher again watches and learns about the individual child.

The teacher notices also the difference in the way children regard the results of their work. Some want to make sure that their names are properly affixed to their paintings; some are concerned about taking home anything they make; some are eager to produce as large a number of objects as possible. "I did *six* paintings, didn't I, teacher? And I am going to make more!" Although children generally enjoy the results of their work, some child may find a building or clay work inadequate and wish to destroy it. The teacher then encourages that child to try again. Still other children may appreciate the work of others even more than their own. Any given child may show modesty, nonchalance, concern, pride, or possessiveness in the results of his or her efforts. But all children will reveal their own unique style.

Here, for example, are two five-year-olds using clay in their own special ways:

Bill watched the teacher slowly and carefully when she announced a clay time, and ambled phlegmatically to where the children were lining up for their clay allotment. He was the last child in line and the last to find a seat at the table. He held the clay in his hand casually, looking from side to side at the other children and staring at their pieces of clay. Suddenly he blurted out, "I'm not making a snake!" He seemed to come to life, his agile fingers breaking, poking, and manipulating the tiny pieces of clay with great speed and meticulousness. He paused and stared at the clay, muttering to himself, "I made a man." His piece had two tiny legs and a round head and body and did indeed look like a man. Unemotionally, he took it apart, rolled it deftly and moments later came up with a tadpole, again tiny and delicate. As he worked, his tongue was often between his lips, rubbing back and forth over them. He looked up at the teacher and showed her his tadpole, then immediately rolled it up and made a hippopotamus. The hippopotamus was again small and precisely made, with four legs and a head. Now, moving more animatedly, the clay became a door. "I'm going to slam the door," he gloated. Then it became a sea-monster "with a long tail." Bill's face seemed more cheerful now, as with a slight, crooked smile he held up his monster for the teacher to see. His body became more involved in his activity as he pounded the clay noisily onto the table, saying excitedly, "Fe, fi, fo, fum, here comes the dinosaur" in an artificially deep, growling voice. He seemed increasingly involved with the material, now standing and swaying slightly from side to side and pounding the whole blob of clay aggressively onto the table.

Aileen is on her knees at the low clay table where Maribel is also working. Aileen sing-songs, "I'm the mommie and I am making breakfast," as she busily flattens out a piece of clay with a spatula. Smash, smash, smash!! Next she takes a roller out of the clay tools container and grunts and moves back and forth on her knees as she rolls the clay out into a smooth round shape. "See, just like mommie," she says to herself happily. She again takes the spatula, scrapes up the clay, and with a quick movement she throws the clay into the air. The clay flips once and Aileen catches it flat on the spatula. "I like pancakes!" she crows. She repeats this action three more times. Maribel looks up and watches, then begins to make a flat piece similar to Aileen's. Aileen in the meantime is busy hand-rolling six thin pieces. She sets each of these with care on top of the "pancake." "Now I have a birthday cake with six candles," she tells Maribel. Maribel looks up and begins to roll out some skinny pieces also. "Miss D., come to my party!" Aileen calls to the teacher. She reaches for the clay tool container and dumps it over. Maribel jumps at the noise. Aileen begins to cut her cake. "Whose birthday, Aileen?" asks the teacher. "Somebody's," comes the reply. Aileen cuts the cake into pieces, moving the knife across the complete circle, in one direction and then in another. With the knife she picks up each piece and arranges it in a circle around the outside of the tray. Carefully she slides one hand under the tray and pops up onto her feet. "Take two, Miss D.!" she offers. "Hm, what delicious cake," says the teacher. Going toward Mrs. V., Aileen says cordially, "Have a piece." "Why, Aileen, this tastes delicious!" obliges Mrs. V. "OK, now you can put it back," directs Aileen. She moves toward Miss D. and asks, "Are you finished? Then put it back. I'm going to dry my cake and paint it. Then it will fit together." And she carefully walks into the other room carrying her cake.

To merely say of these two children that "they played with clay today" would tell us practically nothing, while in a carefully observed recording of their activity, their feelings about themselves and their environment come through.

There is an increasing number of children who do not seem able to get involved with materials. These are children who may prefer to watch others, or who hesitate to try, or who barely touch materials and then with a lackadaisical, noncommittal attitude. It may be that these are children who have learned to be passively entertained by television and have never learned to do for themselves; or they may be children whose parents do not value play and push them toward academic achievement too early. They may be children whose standards for themselves are too harsh—who would rather not try than fail—or who are afraid of getting dirty. Whatever the reason, the teacher has to help such children to use materials constructively by sitting with them and using materials herself in order to model the process (not the product!) and encourage the children to stay with the materials longer so as to be productive. The experience of being personally productive, focused, and attentive is an important groundwork for all future tasks, including academic ones, and therefore much too important to be overlooked by teachers of young children.

A CHILD'S BEHAVIOR VARIES

A teacher may find that a child is assertive in one situation and quite different in another. Thus, big, boisterous, and bold Howard, who intimidated several smaller children in class, surprised the teacher during a trip to the neighboring firehouse.

While the other children, including the quieter, more cautious ones, were excited by the adventure of touching the shiny equipment and ringing the loud bell, Howard was too scared even to go in.

In another class Liza, a silent, uncommunicative, tense child who refrained from using materials most of the time, joined some children one day at the work-bench where there was a big coconut which the class had been trying to open for several days with the teacher's help. The teacher soon came over to the three children who were taking turns whacking the coconut with a hammer. To the teacher's surprise, Liza grasped the hammer forcefully and, warming up to the activity, this normally passive little girl became genuinely excited. As part of the outer hard shell of the coconut broke off, a layer of very tough, brown, hairy fiber was revealed. The other children were fascinated with snipping "the hair" off the coconut with scissors, but Liza was determined to get hold of "the hair" and pulled it hard. She actually succeeded in pulling off a wad of the tough fiber. "There! I am pulling the skin off!" she exclaimed eagerly and squealed, "Ooh, ooh, ooh!" Noting that Liza really enjoyed such rough materials and work, the teacher encouraged her to try the tools at the workbench, which she had hitherto shunned.

CAREFUL LISTENING AND LOOKING

Young children like to talk, and a teacher can take their comments as clues to knowledge about individuals. Enid says to the teacher, "I'll better not have any milk and cookies because I'm going to have dinner at my grandmother's! She is going to wait for me!" On another day Enid exclaims: "You know what my mother and I did? *We* made a cake together. I'll even bring some to school." And again, "Guess who is coming for me today! My daddy—yes. You don't believe it, but he is!" It is easy to see how important family life and family members are to Enid and she to them.

Minimal Interpretation

Alive and responsive to children, a teacher is often intrigued by the different personalities in the class. It seems only human to indulge in interpretations of the causes for children's behavior or misbehavior on the basis of one dramatic episode. It is easy to label a thumbsucker insecure or to conclude that a child who does not like painting is inhibited. And it seems especially easy for teachers to "diagnose" a questioning child as an attention-seeker and a whiner as spoiled. It is also not uncommon for a teacher to misjudge an entire group. When some children stray from the line the teacher tells them all: "I guess you don't care about going out—so get back to your seats." Quick judgments may prove quite wrong after a more careful look. We must learn to see children in many different kinds of activities and situations in order to understand their abilities and their limitations.

Ways of Perceiving the Individual

The warm, perceptive kindergarten teacher will get to know the individual children by observing each one in a variety of situations. He or she will notice the different expressions, the individual features, the distinguishing gait, the particular pace, and the quality of mobility or passivity. He or she will see the different sizes, stamina, and physical skills, and be moved by the many kinds of beauty among children. The perceptive teacher will look beyond external appearance too, observing the caution in approaching materials on the part of one, the hostile use of the same materials by another, and the happy, easy way of a third. He or she will observe each child's way of approaching others, of settling differences, and of sharing and exchanging ideas. He or she will be conscious of the special way each youngster responds to life, what causes frustration, and what gives satisfaction, and will get as full a picture as possible of each child's patterns of response as they appear under differing conditions. And the teacher will refrain from hasty interpretations and judgments, recognizing that each child is a growing, changing human being at a point in time. Knowing children better, the teacher can be more useful in guiding their growth and in gaining their confidence.

INVITING CHILDREN'S TRUST

Children can sense the feelings teachers have about them. They know when a teacher accepts them as they are or when she or he likes only certain kinds of children. It is perfectly true that no teacher can love all children equally. Children are different, and teachers are human. But all children should feel they have an equal chance in the eyes of the teachers, and this they will feel if each one is accepted for what he or she is without judgment or prejudice.

When the teacher is genuinely friendly in talking to children and working with them, this invites their trust and encourages their friendship. When he or she makes it a practice to listen to them every day as well as to speak to them, even the shy ones will want to talk. When the teacher makes only the promises he or she intends to keep ("We will go to the farm next Wednesday if it doesn't rain," or "The five children who missed the trip will be the ones to bake the cookies tomorrow"), the children will believe and trust their teacher.

A teacher of young children should be a responsive person—warm, caring, attentive. Yet a teacher must not expect the same response and devotion from the children as a parent would receive. Because kindergartners can be helpless and dependent, a loving teacher may become possessive and speak strongly of "*my* children." The teacher may even compete with a parent for status with the child. The teacher must never forget that the children are not his or hers; devotion is expressed through service to them, not possession of them; concern as their teacher is shown by building security and promoting learning in the children. Teachers can derive great satisfaction from fulfilling such a role without taking full possession.

The most loving teacher, however, is definitely not a paragon. She or he may at times be tired and cranky or too busy to hear a child out or may face realistic interferences and fail sometimes to notice something important. But if the teacher is basically friendly, the children will readily forgive. And she or he can try to compensate for a failure. ("I didn't come over to see your building yesterday when you asked me to, but I will today. I was too busy with the woodworking.") In such a teacher the children will not lose their trust. Knowing the teacher is on their side, they continue to have faith in her or him and accept her or him as a fellow human being with human foibles. This mutual acceptance sets the tone for an emotional climate in which good relationships can flourish.

REFERENCES AND FURTHER READING

COHEN, DOROTHY H. "Developmental Aspects of Five-Year-Olds, Including Learning Style," Chap. 3 in *The Learning Child.* New York: Pantheon, 1972, and Random House, Vintage Books paperback, 1973, pp. 50–71.

COHEN, DOROTHY H., STERN, VIRGINIA, and BALABAN, NANCY. *Observing and Recording the Behavior of Young Children.* New York: Teachers College Press, 1958; revised ed., 1983.

DAVIE, R., BUTLER, N., and GOLDSTEIN, H. *From Birth to Seven,* the Second Report of the National Child Development Study. London: Longman Group Limited and the National Children's Bureau, 1972.

FRAIBERG, SELMA. *The Magic Years.* New York: Charles Scribner's Sons, 1959. Especially Part IV, "Three Years to Six."

HAVIGHURST, ROBERT J. *Developmental Tasks and Education* (3rd ed.). New York: D. McKay, 1972.

ISAACS, SUSAN. *The Social Development of Young Children.* London: George Routledge and Sons, Ltd., 1948.

ISAACS, SUSAN. *Intellectual Growth in Young Children.* New York: Schocken Books, 1972.

JENKINS, GLADYS, SCHACTER, HELEN, and BAUER, WILLIAM. *These Are Your Children* (4th ed.). Glenview, Ill.: Scott, Foresman, 1975.

KLEIN, JENNIE. "Mainstreaming the Preschooler," *Young Children,* July 1975, pp. 317-26.

PIAGET, JEAN. *The Child's Conception of the World.* Totowa, N.J.: Littlefield, Adams, & Co., 1972.

STONE, L. J., and CHURCH, J. *Childhood and Adolescence* (3rd ed.). New York: Random House, 1973. Chapters on the preschool child.

4 Kindergarten Children Need Each Other

Just as kindergarten children are ready for all kinds of experiences, they are ready for each other. They are hungry for companionship and will go to any length to seek it. "He hasn't anybody to play with," a common complaint one hears from parents, is actually an important reason for registering children at kindergarten. At three years of age a child can take or leave the companionship of others. But by five the ability to identify with the world beyond one's immediate self, curiosity about others, readiness to share, and diminishing dependence on adults for direction and companionship make children indispensable to each other. Although the road to balanced give-and-take is not smooth and friendships bloom and wither with amazing rapidity, five-year-olds are able to appreciate and gain strength from group membership.

Teachers often say that when the kindergarten class has fewer than fifteen children in it life seems dull. To satisfy the continuing experimentation in relationships, twenty to twenty-five children seems to be a good number. This offers sufficient opportunity for each child to choose friends, enlarge the circle of companions, or change partners. The other children in class are an important reason why kindergarten children like school so much.

THE IMPORTANCE OF FRIENDSHIP

Andy, just five years old, was invited to visit the kindergarten after he had registered. He spent almost twenty minutes in the class touching different materials on tables and floor, finding himself in the midst of playing, working children. To his surprise he noticed Bob, a neighborhood friend, in the class. "Hi," Andy said, somewhat shyly but gleefully. To his joy, Bob responded.

At home that evening Andy's father, mother, and older sister were eager to hear about the kindergarten visit. Andy answered "yes" or "no" quite casually to various questions, but reserved his enthusiasm for "And you know what—I saw Bob there, and I said 'hi' to him, and he said 'hi' to me." He repeated this information several times. The parents were perplexed. They regarded their son as quite a bright and perceptive child. Yet here, on a first visit to the kindergarten, to the "big school," as he had been referring to it, the most important thing to him was seeing his friend Bob there. Why should that be so important?

When Andy entered the kindergarten room for the first time, he was interested in seeing familiar toys and materials, and he did notice the teacher. But he could not unify and relate the brief experience to give it personal meaning. What made the strongest impression on Andy was to see Bob, whom he knew well, perfectly at ease there in the kindergarten—doing things, speaking to people, responding with a "hi" to him. So kindergarten was a place where you could speak to friends and do what they do! This concrete promise of being able to maintain or to create relationships was of first importance to Andy, as it is to many others.

Creating relationships in class requires opportunities to practice different techniques of winning friends and coping with opponents, opportunities for actually helping others, for choosing and changing friends, and for forming different alliances.

AN EXPANDING PATTERN OF INVOLVEMENT

In any kindergarten class several stages of social development are usually present. The intimacy of one friend at a time is all some children can manage, at least for a while. Little twosomes play in the doll corner, chat at the swings, crayon together, or play dominoes. Three to five children join together in other parts of the room or the outdoor play area, sometimes staying together as a unit, sometimes forming and reforming around one central dominating figure or strong pair. Relations within these larger units range all the way from the smoothest kind of cooperative effort applied to the completion of a commonly agreed upon task to constant bickering and quarreling over every detail.

Still larger than the groups of three, four, or five which may be forming (often along sex lines) is the unit of the entire class. To this larger unit each child must somehow make reference and within it find a niche. At first the size of the class can be quite confusing. But in time identification with the class as a whole gives a child the assuring comfort that feelings are universal, and with that the special sense of power that comes only from being one of many who are tied in common interests. Children who have experienced intimacy with a friend for the first time and enrichment of play interests among a group of friends feel that they belong to something that is part of a big world indeed. "That's my teacher," they say with pride. "Those kids are in *my* class."

What about a child who is different and not quite acceptable to the group? An observant teacher will sense that and, realizing how important it is for such a child to have a role, will use authority and guidance to include him or her.

HANDICAPPED CHILDREN NEED TO BE INCLUDED

While being included serves a vital need for any child by nurturing self-confidence, it is uniquely important for handicapped children whose social contacts are limited. Yet until recent times a child with a handicap, in spite of a capacity for development and learning, was generally not admitted into the mainstream of American education. Instead, such a child was either placed in special education classes or her or his educational needs were ignored. Thus the term *mainstreaming* came to denote admission of some handicapped children into regular classes of ordinary, "normal" students.

The principle of mainstreaming—and it is the law of the land[1] —is that every child have access to all the schooling and cultural advantages there are, even if, due to a particular handicap, the child can derive only partial benefit. Moreover the presence and acceptance of handicapped children benefits other children and adults by adding to their understanding of human needs and to their feelings of compassion.

From our point of view, the kindergarten year and the years of early schooling in general constitute an unusual opportunity for mainstreaming, since those early years of growing and of learning social values are also years when external differences in people can be more readily accepted and when experiences may have a lasting influence. Later in the chapter we will present an experience of mainstreaming.

EXPERIMENTATION WITH FRIENDSHIP

When children work together in small groups, there is spontaneous conversation, exchange of ideas, acquaintance with one another's interests and performances, and the experience of liking others and of being liked. Special friendships or lasting attachments may thus be formed. There are also clashes, conflicts, and differences that have to be resolved. A teacher has to be aware of the children's need to *practice* relating.

Three five-year-old girls are at a table with play dough. Jeannie, for no *apparent* reason, snatches pieces of dough from the other girls; she does not heed their demand that she return their dough, and to make sure that the two girls do not get it back by force, Jeannie throws it on the floor and steps on it. When Jeannie persists in trying to snatch more dough from the table, one of the two girls, Carmen, restrains Jeannie by grasping and pinching her shoulder. Jeannie's defiance weakens, and she bursts into the classic face-saving song:

> It-doesn't-even-hu-urt,
> It-doesn't-even-hu-urt.

---

[1] U.S. Congress. *Education for All Handicapped Children Act* (P.L. 94–142), 1975. Subsequently implemented by state and federal programs.

As she sings she keeps pulling away. Now there is a triumphant expression on Carmen's face as she magnanimously stops pinching Jeannie and says, "Well, if it doesn't hurt, why do you try to get away?" Jeannie shrugs, then just as magnanimously gives all the dough back to the other two girls!

Sometimes kindergarten teachers arbitrarily stop arguments, forgetting that arguments can be a satisfying way of getting to know another person as well as a way of testing language power. An argument can be quite as civilized among children as among adults. And surely learning to resolve disagreements plays an important part in becoming friends. The best friends in the kindergarten often have the most arguments.

To be able to argue well, or to dare to argue at all, a child needs a chance to practice good techniques. A teacher would do well then to listen to and appraise a verbal dispute before arbitrarily stopping it out of fear that it will get out of hand and to remember that children's arguments, quarrels, and fights are short-lived and not as dangerous as they may appear.

PREPARATION FOR ESTABLISHING RELATIONSHIPS VARIES

Some kindergarten children are still very dependent on grown-ups and unable to make decisions on their own. Such children can hardly have the best relationships with other children if they are not sure of their own likes and wants. Others have been so indulged by adults that they are startled and unbelieving when they are crossed. Children make short shrift of those who think they are entitled to special consideration as a matter of course.

Children between four and six already have some concept of their inner worth, and this affects their relationships with others. It never occurs to some children that someone will not like them, because people have always liked them. Approaching others with an expectation of friendly response, they get it more often than not. Other children are not so fortunate. Scolded and berated too often at home, they may be on the defensive and attack without provocation simply because they do not trust people. Still others have been overprotected with constant admonitions, such as "be careful," "you'll fall," "watch out," to the point where they no longer trust themselves to act, and they approach all situations with an anxious fear that something will go wrong if they do act. How can they abandon themselves to the carefree, physical activities of their peers if they are so afraid?

Experiences differ for children, of course. But some have far more to share or contribute than others. The "idea" person in the group is frequently sought out. The child who can see the sense in a variety of play themes is better off than the one who thinks playing ball is the only form play can take.

The causes of the very normal difficulties involved in forming relationships are many, among them the stage of development of the children, or in the case of a handicapped child, relative isolation and deprivation. But experience with other

children, relative independence from adults, concept of self, and scope of general experience all play their part too. The poignancy of how much some children have to overcome before they can finally make contacts that eventually lead to good relationships is clearly seen in the year-end report below.

Writing about five-year-old Randie, his teacher became strongly aware of how he had struggled to be noticed and accepted and how he had rejoiced after winning recognition. A painfully shy child, he spent weeks of schooltime clinging to his mother, then more weeks standing stiff and silent in one spot most of each day. He shrank whenever approached by teacher or children. Then Randie began watching the teacher, especially the way she dealt with children; after that, watching the children themselves. Every day he seemed to move closer to where action was taking place. Although he didn't speak out, and replied to others with a mere motion of the head, Randie soon began using a word here and there with continuous daily contact.

In his way, Randie was learning everything he could, physically and psychologically, *from* the children; learning about pleasures of action, surprises of interaction, usefulness of different materials. After four months he was not only taking part but excelling in activities: climbing in an intricate way to the highest rung of the jungle gym, constructing a complicated building, defending himself effectively. Randie changed from being a loner to becoming a joiner, and his language progressed from single-word utterances to braggadocio.

As Randie found himself and his activities acceptable in the eyes of others and as he spoke his thoughts, a change took place. In what looked like an attempt to raise his importance in the eyes of classmates, he bragged, "We have trees in our yard too. Bigger ones." And again, "My dog is even stronger than that." When shouting was in order as part of an outdoor game originated by a group of children, Randie shouted the loudest. During the last three months of the school year he felt so happy and so much a part of school that he told his mother, "I wish I could live in school—all the time."

THE GIVE-AND-TAKE OF PLAY IN A SMALL GROUP

After our concern with the effect of the group and of the teacher's guidance on one child over a stretch of time, it is interesting to look in on a scene of play by a small group of preschoolers. The children come from a community where trucks play an important part in daily life.

> Windy built a truck with large hollow blocks. He climbed up and sat royally in the driver's seat, steering with a curved (unit) block. Ty came over, eyeing him jealously, and said in an attempted one-upmanship.
> "I'm Spiderman!"
> "No, I'm Spiderman!" Windy swiftly retorted. They argued with some heat until Sharity, who was baking a lovely cake on the back of Windy's truck (!) intervened.
> "For goodness sake, you're both Spiderman! Would you like some cake?" Thereupon Ty asked.
> "Do you need a helper, Windy?"
> "Yes, get your shovel and fill my truck with more gravel."
> "That's not gravel, it's cake!" put in Sharity. But Ty went off and got an armful of different shaped unit blocks for a horn, lights, tire pump, clutch and throttle pedals and a brake lever (also used as the dumping lever). The two boys added these accessories with much comment on their use, each learning (I thought) from the other. Todd came over with a bit of rope for hose, and filled their tank with gas. Fuel had not occurred to them.
> "You might need oil, too," Sharity said, removing her cake to a safer oven.[2]

We've heard arguments, accommodations, responsiveness to others, testing knowledge with words and deeds—all taking place without a teacher's direct intervention, though of course with her or his support, of which children are unquestionably aware.

Sally Cartwright gives this account of the same group:

> Even rest and story times are enhanced by group experience:
> Rest time was quiet, relaxing, and (I felt) held together by a warm sense of companionship and group unity, after a morning of shared work. Group feeling continued into the story time (which follows rest every day). "Gilberto and the Wind" by Marie Hall Ets, had every shining pair of eyes glued to the pictures—eleven kids in rapt attention, sharing each other's earnest involve-

---

[2] Sally Cartwright, "Group Endeavor Can Be Valuable Learning" (report to Community Nursery School parents, Tenants Harbor, Me., 1980).

ment. When the dust blew in Gilberto's eyes, Brent put his hand to his own eye and said, "oooh," softly.[3]

The "group unity" Sally Cartwright describes, that came about in a small group "after a morning of shared work," may not be a common occurrence in a large class with a greater variety of children. Yet friendships are sought through shared activities in any group.

FORMING FRIENDSHIPS CAN BE A STRUGGLE

Donald is a good example of how awkward some children are in forming friendships. At first he appeared to have little zest for any activity or interest in any children. Then suddenly he singled out a little girl for attention. But she did not respond to his direct "Will you play with me?" After a while he tried something different; he followed her and aped whatever she was doing—puzzles, clay, water play. But Nancy remained indifferent to his efforts. Still Donald did not give up. He tried another method of gaining response. He gave her a poke—affectionately, perhaps, but still a poke. Well! He got a negative response, but at least it was a response. The teacher saw that Nancy could cope with this and did not interfere. Donald, however, delighted that Nancy was at last responding, continued to follow his exciting pursuit. He went on talking, persuading, poking, showing preference (when passing cookies, he passed them to Nancy first), inviting her to look at a book with him, and sometimes disrupting her building. He persisted in this difficult relationship until he finally met with some success and satisfaction. At the same time he began to respond to an approach from another child, a little girl full of initiative and adventure. Donald rather lacked those qualities himself, yet stimulated by Kathy, he gained courage. Through Kathy's leadership, Donald engaged in exuberant physical activities, including wrestling; in joyful and experimental use of different materials; in seeking new ways of cooperating and of testing relationships. The two were sharing various delights not only with each other but with others, now including Nancy. Through his relationship with one, then finally with several children, Donald grew in his interests, developed initiative, and began to express humor. His relationship with others gave meaning to the word *school.*

Some Children May Not Know How to Make Friends

Kindergarten children are eager for friendships outside their families. There are good reasons why it is hard for them to develop these smoothly, as they are still inexperienced in the art of relating. During the first two or three years of their lives they were on the receiving end of affection and attention. Whatever they have learned of giving was learned primarily in response to and in imitation of the grown-

[3] Ibid.

ups who showered them with love. Even their feelings for siblings are still mixed, and rarely do they take the same tender and protective view of little brothers and sisters that their parents do. *Their* feelings are far more important to them than anyone else's. Indeed, they are not too certain about the nature of other people's feelings, although they are carried away by their own. Yet as growth proceeds, they inevitably plunge into relationships with eagerness, but they may not know what to do. An adult, after all, recognizes that a child is "only a child" and makes concessions. But no child can see another child with the eyes of an adult in the early years. Concessions to someone else will carry overtones of unwanted deprivation to one's self. Experience teaches children to barter, and trial and error gives them further techniques. Necessary as this trial and error learning is, it is certainly not easy, nor is there always an opportunity to practice it in the classroom.

A Teacher's Help in Developing Relationships

A kindergarten class houses a group of human beings unquestionably aware of each other, and constantly relating on different levels. It is therefore important that the routines not require too much waiting, unnecessary getting in line, and needless silence, which reduce the children's time for relating and the teacher's time for genuine attention.

When young children are noticed by the teacher, they feel they have a place in the class that makes it worth coming to school. When they have an opportunity to be heard by the teacher and other children, each child feels the security of being among friends. When they enjoy others' responses they do not hesitate to take part in activities or to try again if they fail. On the other hand, fear of a bully can inhibit participation, and a teacher's indifference can squelch a child's fresh enthusiasm for school.

The teacher's role in helping children form relationships must be based on reality. A teacher must have neither overly idealistic expectations of children's behavior nor fear direct action when necessity calls for it. What is needed is help without didacticism, and the nature and extent of that help must be different in each situation. Above all, the teacher must be aware of the constant challenge to stimulate and guide the growth of positive human relations in the classroom and must offer reassurance, support, and suggestions for specific techniques. There is a point, with young children, in creating a social climate that stresses kindness and helpfulness. This is achieved more by the teacher articulating what is expected— "You do not have to be friends, but you do have to be friendly" or "You really helped—I knew you would!"—than by putting up a printed slogan (sometimes read in chorus) such as "We are always kind to each other."

Of course, adults who are themselves helpful and considerate provide a basic model. But since, realistically, there is a good deal of indifference to human need in our society, it is necessary to state such values clearly as support to our actions and to create a climate of mutuality and cooperation even while we remain sympathetic to the individual child's conflicts and struggles. Since children who struggle for acceptance are sometimes scapegoated by other children, scapegoating too must be clearly discredited in a classroom. Children will accept teacher direction in these regards. Indeed, they expect and welcome it.

CHILDREN NEED HELP IN UNDERSTANDING THEMSELVES AND OTHERS

Children's motives are as varied as adults' but are more readily apparent. Young children feel strongly, with an either-or approach that sometimes makes them seem quite stubborn and unreasonable. The saving grace is that feelings pass quickly and four- to six-year-olds do understand a teacher's guidance in the handling of their feelings. The basic human emotions motivate children—they love or hate; they admire freely and envy easily; they are tender to each other and jealous too. They are afraid of being put upon but enjoy leadership. Above all it is important to them to save face; self-esteem is vital. As the following episode shows, it is completely possible for a teacher to appeal to kindergarten children for understanding in time of troubled relationships.

Victor had worked painstakingly on a "skyscraper" building when Charles inadvertently caused it to collapse by removing a box next to it. Victor was enraged and quickly reached out to hit Charles. Unaware of any wrongdoing, Charles felt the sting of injustice even more than the hurt of Victor's punch. He retaliated in kind. Stepping right into the battle the teacher called for an immediate cease-fire. But he did not leave it there; he called each child to account and challenged each to think. "Victor," he asked, "why are you so mad at Charles?"

"He made my building break down! Don't you know?" Victor answered.

"No," the teacher explained, "he only took the box which was near and empty; Charles didn't realize you needed it for support." Victor thought this over.

"And Charles," the teacher continued, "why are you so mad at Victor?"

"He got after me *first!* "

"But you can understand why Victor was upset," the teacher said, clarifying the matter without scolding.

"Yes, his building broke. But I just took the box. I didn't know the building would crash," Charles explained.

"Explain that to Victor," the teacher advised confidently. Charles did this gladly and graphically. After talking a bit, both boys even saw something funny in the episode.

The teacher recognized that indirectly there *was* an implication of apology on the part of Charles and an expression of silent understanding on the part of Victor. More than a truce had been established between the children. Helped to understand each other's motives, the two boys furthered their friendship.

INDIVIDUALS AS PART OF A GROUP

Our interest in individuals must not allow us to forget that individuals need to find satisfaction in being contributing members of a group. Young children need much help in becoming identified with a group. It is not easy for them to deny themselves in favor of others or to see themselves as one of many when their every instinct cries out, "See me! See me!" Yet we do not serve children well if we carry our concern for them as individuals to the point where we unwittingly nurture narcissism and fail to stress concern for others.

In societies where the group is recognized as an important unit, even preschool children act with regard for the group, without harm to their individuality. Furthermore, the acceptance of each other gives to children an extraordinary sense of security about their own abilities. Thus our ready focus on the individual must be balanced by an equal concern for the individual as a member of a group. This is especially relevant now, in an era of extraordinary social changes: greater influx of people of diverse races and cultures, common incidence of single- or multiple-parent families, and regular school admission of children with various handicaps. Yet with a teacher's positive approach and effort the group can be enriched by diversity and each child strengthened by being part of a group.

THE TEACHER AS PART OF A GROUP

Sometimes the teacher participates in the children's activities. At snack time Miss Wayne does not merely serve the children efficiently but partakes of the snack herself and often joins in the children's conversation and humor. "I didn't have any milk. See, my glass is empty," says Ramon, clanking onto the table a freshly emptied milk glass. His lively companions restrain themselves from correcting him. They are bursting to know what the teacher will say; maybe Ramon really fooled Miss

Wayne. To their great delight she goes along with the joke: "Oh, poor Ramon, you must be so thirsty! Pass Ramon the milk pitcher, Annie!" The children all burst out laughing at this, and although they reveal the truth to Miss Wayne, another child immediately repeats the same prank. Everybody laughs together once again. The children have a close feeling with this teacher who is able to share their kind of fun.

Similar participation by the teacher is appropriate in many activities. "Watch out, watch out, Mr. Bell," commands a kindergarten bus driver while "steering" from a pile of large hollow blocks. "Oh goodness," says the teacher jumping out of the way. "Want a ride, Mr. Bell?" The driver motions to a "seat" and Mr. Bell actually perches for a minute. As he gets off to attend to other business, the driver waves with one hand, keeping the other on the steering wheel. The teacher's sharing in class activities and going along with their imagination is rewarding for him or her and fun for the children. But some delicacy, diplomacy, and restraint are necessary if the potentially good relationship is not to deteriorate into one in which the teacher replaces the child leader. And of course the teacher is always firmly rooted in reality. He or she may agree to "be put in jail" by an eager jailer, but on no account should the ropes be real in a misguided effort to prove his or her sincerity to the children. In joining children's play a teacher never compromises his or her basic freedom to attend quickly to some real teacher task.

PARENTS CAN HELP TEACHERS
AND CHILDREN TO UNDERSTAND OTHERS

Mrs. U. had already learned that her daughter Elizabeth, blind from birth, would need extra time for adjustment to preschool, and especially to interaction with sighted children. In addition, the mother was prepared to actually help out in the classroom as needed. The teacher, although experienced, had never known a blind child. Fortunately, she was flexible and willing to learn from a parent, along with the children, how a blind child manages and learns with senses other than sight.

On the first day of school, when the teacher handed a cookie to Elizabeth, she did not react. So Mrs. U. said "Elizabeth, the teacher has a cookie for you." Instantly, Elizabeth thrust her hand out to get the cookie, and all the children understood the need for verbal directions.

At the beginning they all felt strange when Elizabeth went up to them and started fingering their hair, hands, and body; and when she upset cups and plates while moving her hands during a tea party, the children yelled, "No, Elizabeth!" So then and there the mother explained to the children what "seeing with her hands" meant to Elizabeth. She suggested that they too try to see with their hands by closing their eyes. Later the children's favorite game was to be blindfolded and to identify different objects on a table by touching. Of course Elizabeth excelled at this game; and in the playing, they were all on the same level.

Thus the year in preschool proved to be successful not because everything worked smoothly all the time, but because the teacher accepted honest reaction from children, the necessity for help, the needed time for the children to learn to get along and to grow in understanding of others, even when others are very different.

GOOD RELATIONSHIPS
FOSTER LEARNING

Good relationships in class provide both incentive and stimulation to good learning. Whether good relationships are developed and maintained in a classroom depends heavily on the teacher, not only on what she or he does, but on what she or he does not do as well. The teacher's relationships with individuals must be matched by the support and latitude given to children to learn from each other. Adults often underestimate how much children can gain from each other's experiences and responses. Teachers who respect children's need for each other will work in indirect as well as direct ways to build good human relationships. Their knowledge of what is going on will be as full as their powers of observation.

REFERENCES AND FURTHER READING

DANOFF, JUDITH, BREITBART, VICKI, and BARR, ELINOR. *Open for Children.* New York: McGraw-Hill, 1977.
READ, KATHERINE, and PATTERSON, JUNE. *The Nursery School and Kindergarten, Human Relationships and Learning* (7th ed.). New York: Holt, Rinehart and Winston, 1980.
SUNDERLIN, SYLVIA. *The Most Enabling Environment: Education Is for All Children.* Washington, D.C.: Association for Childhood Education, 1979.
ULRICH, SHARON. *Elizabeth.* Introduction and commentary by Selma Fraiberg and Adna Adelson. Ann Arbor, Mich.: University of Michigan Press, 1972.

5

Scope and Variety in Language Learning and Use

THE HUMAN URGE FOR EXPRESSION
THROUGH SYMBOLS

The philosopher Susanne Langer[1] has advanced a theory now supported by new theories in linguistics, namely that human beings are born with an urgent biological need to talk, draw, paint, sculpt, act, dance and make music because they need to deal with the meaning of their experience in symbolic form. By converting experience into some kind of symbolic representation, whether words or art, people set their experience off at some distance from themselves so they can examine it and thereby come to understand it beyond the mere experiencing of it. That is why talking often clears up a problem, or listening to music can change a mood. Sym-

---

[1] Susanne K. Langer, *Philosophy in a New Key* (Cambridge: Harvard University Press, 1942).

bolic representation allows us not only to clarify our own experience, however, but to share and exchange it with others. The capacity to symbolize is the key to human socialization and learning, the key to civilization.

Nonverbal and verbal forms of symbolic representation tend to serve different purposes. For example, we have all had feelings that could not easily be put into words. And we have all found that nonverbal symbols sometimes express our moods and feelings exactly; a particular color in an item of clothing is just right for some moods and not for others; a particular piece of music releases us for gaiety or introspection that we could not otherwise quite capture; a look, a gesture reveal exactly the meaning we wish to convey. Yet, if we want to reason or build a series of arguments to show relationships between cause and effect, we are better off with words. In fact, for most of our activities, we do express ourselves in words and are constantly seeking better ways of making our words clear and meaningful to others.

LANGUAGE LEARNING IS INCOMPLETE
BY KINDERGARTEN

Young children use nonverbal and verbal expression with equal freedom, but they do more learning through nonverbal forms such as play and use of play materials and the handling of objects than through words. Although kindergarten children talk with sense, their talk is very much a matter of social communication rather than an exchange of ideas or concepts. It is far easier for a young child to draw a picture of a man or woman than to describe a man or woman, far easier to show with body movement and gesture how a jet plane takes off or a tree reaches into the air than to explain these acts in words. The reason for the apparent shortcoming lies in the miracle of language itself. A remarkable, endless, flexible tool, language allows for continuous creativity in its use and for unlimited deepening and broadening of its possibilities for expressing thought and feeling. Thus, although kindergarten children display an impressive facility with language, there is much they still need to learn, and they are conspicuously ready for such learning.

LANGUAGE DEVELOPMENT
IN KINDERGARTEN CHILDREN

By the time children are four to five years old, unless they have suffered physical defects like deafness or brain damage, their grasp of their native language is remarkably good, even if not yet quite complete. They have appropriate vocabulary and know the correct relationship of words to each other in a sentence. They never fail to put the subject before the verb and the complement after it. For example, they say "I have a bike," never "A bike have I," an achievement we take for granted but which is no mean feat.[2] By age four, children have not only learned the words of

[2] Jean Berko, "The Child's Hearing of English Morphology," *Word,* 14, 1958, 150–77.

their native language but how to fit the words together in countless ways to make sense in countless situations. They have learned the structure, that is, the grammar and syntax of their language, and it is this which allows them to put words into fresh combinations every time they open their mouths. Miraculously, this happens in every language, yet no one teaches children to speak. They learn vocabulary by listening carefully, noting associations, and asking, "What's that?" And they ferret out the rules of grammar for and by themselves (a real miracle) showing their grasp of these rules by following them unerringly. They generalize rigidly from *play—played, walk—walked,* and so on to *buy—buyed;* and from *house—houses,* to *mouse—mouses.* This grasp of rules at kindergarten age may actually reflect an advanced state of progress. What children have yet to learn is that in English there are not only rules to follow but exceptions to the rules, and that's what they will be learning, informally and formally, in the years ahead.

Understanding Adult Speech

Children have some real problems understanding and using oral language. For one thing, many words that sound alike have more than one meaning, such as *pair, pear,* and *pare.* Words such as these have to be differentiated and interpreted only by context, which depends on experience and without the visual aid that spelling gives. Pronouns are another source of difficulty because their reference can so easily be ambiguous. In "Laura thinks she knows everything," *she* can refer to Laura or to someone else. Other problems which may not be so obvious to teachers stem from children's general expectation of how a noun and a verb should relate to each other. Once children have extracted the rules from the language they hear, they expect them always to work the same way. Thus, they understand perfectly when someone says, "Jason hit Whitney!" But when children overhear one teacher saying to another that "Whitney was just hit by Jason," they are nonplussed. As far as they are concerned, the name they have heard first (Jason) refers to the *doer* and the name that follows the verb (Whitney) is the one *done to.* So they are not sure what the teacher means when she turns it all around. They often need to hear this type of construction a second time in order to think their way through to the meaning.[3]

Common Ambiguities

A different type of structural ambiguity kindergartners struggle with is illustrated in the sentence, "John is easy to see." Carol Chomsky has found that such a sentence (so simple to us) is heard by young children as though *John* is the subject of *see,* that is, as though the sentence meant "John sees easily." The true focus, "To see John is easy" (a form we seldom use), is not perceived until some time between the ages of five-and-one-half and nine.

Some sentences with the verbs *ask* and *promise* are also ambiguous and con-

---

[3]Carol Chomsky, *The Acquisition of Syntax in Children Five to Ten,* Research Monograph No. 57 (Cambridge, Mass.; London: The M.I.T. Press), 1969.

fusing to young children. According to Chomsky's research, when four-year-olds hear "John promised Bill to go," they assume that Bill (not John) will go because *Bill* is the noun closest to the verb *go*. Similarly, when they hear "John asked Bill what to do," they assume that Bill has to do something. Chomsky found that such ambiguities persisted among some children until the age of nine or ten. We are explaining these possible misinterpretations in some detail because kindergarten teachers (and parents) often assume willfulness or stupidity in children who are simply confused. For example, sometimes a child is requested to ask another child about something and gives what seems like a totally irrelevant answer, as in the following exchange:

TEACHER: Martha, please ask Mimi where she put the scissors.
MARTHA: I didn't see.
TEACHER: I know you didn't, but ask her where she put them.
MARTHA: Maybe she lost them.

Martha is reacting to the demand as though the request were addressed to *her*. She has trouble separating the *request to ask* from the *message of what to ask*. Yet, saying, "Martha, please tell Mimi to bring back the scissors," produces a firm and authoritative "Mimi, Miss Lewis wants the scissors back," from the same child.

Confusing "Ask" and "Tell"

Frank Kessel[4] investigated the confusion between *ask* and *tell* by comparing children's responses to pictures and sentences in which these verbs were used to describe a boy and a girl involved in some action. In half the pictures, either the boy or the girl *tells* the other child what to do; in the other half, either the boy or the girl *asks* the other child what to do. In one of the pictures the action has to do with a child feeding a bird and the children in the study were directed to find the picture that illustrates the sentence, "The boy asks the girl which bird he should feed." In a response typical of 5 to 7 year olds, one little girl stated, before choosing the pictures, "The boy *asks* the girl which bird *she* should feed." Then she chose the picture which showed the boy *telling* the girl which bird to feed. The experimenter asked her why she had chosen that one.

CHILD: 'Cause she said this one (points to the bird in the *tell* picture).
EXPERIMENTER: What were the words in the sentence? (Experimenter repeats, "The boy asks the girl which bird he should feed.")
CHILD: The boy asks the girl what bird she's gonna feed.
EXPERIMENTER: She's gonna feed or *he's* gonna feed?
CHILD: She.
EXPERIMENTER: What would she say?

[4] Frank S. Kessel, *The Role of Syntax in Children's Comprehension from Ages Six to Twelve*. Monograph Series No. 139, 35, 6, September 1970 (Chicago, Ill.: Society for Research in Child Development).

CHILD: I want to feed the bird, feed this bird.
EXPERIMENTER: What's happening in this other picture? (where a child is *asking* what to do).
CHILD: The girl asked the boy what bird he should feed.

The reason for this kind of confusion is not low intelligence but uncertainty about the relationship between content and form. That relationship is not always too clear to egocentric young children for whom the meaning of what they want to communicate far outweighs their concern with correct form, as all teachers know.

Nevertheless, we must not underestimate the significance of what children of four and five have learned. This is clear if we compare the human potential for symbolic representation of experience through language with the way an animal responds to symbols. It will then be possible to see how remarkable a tool language is and what it needs to feed on in order to grow.

Language as "Sign" or "Symbol"

One can teach an animal to understand that a word, or perhaps an object, stands for something else. Thus, when one says "bath" to a dog it scurries under the nearest bed, and one can guess that it has learned to associate the word *bath* with the experience of being washed. Similarly, holding up a leash for it to see will cause it to run eagerly to the front door. Again it has associated a sign of some kind with an actual experience. Babies do this too. When a mother holds a bottle in front of a baby of several months, the baby reacts with excitement and pleasure at the prospect of eating. The baby has come to associate the bottle with the satisfying of hunger. One might say that the word *bath* and the objects *leash* and *bottle* are all symbols used to indicate the occurrence of a particular experience. They are not used for communication beyond their value as a sign pointing to something specific.

The animal will never be able to use the word *bath* to discuss its meaning conceptually. It cannot compare bathing practices in different cultures, describe the kind of bathing it enjoys, or add any comments on how it would like the procedure conducted. Neither does the bottle have meaning for a baby beyond its immediate application to a specific, associated experience. But the baby, being human, will learn to use the word *bottle*, instead of the object itself, to express anticipation and desire. Moreover, as the baby's experience broadens, the word *bottle* will conjure up different meanings—a memory of weaning, cola, a whiskey advertisement, or a perfume dispenser. The growing person will be able to conceive of *bottle* as something breakable or plastic, something manufactured, a utensil, or an art object. Even though the baby, like the animal, uses symbols first as signs—she or he will in time be able to say, "Let's go for a walk," without pointing to the street or bringing a hat and coat to her or his mother.

Language is thus more than a way of communicating wants and needs. It can become a means for expressing cumulative experience—impressions, feelings, facts, events, and concepts. Obviously, the more experience a child has the more he or she will have to express. That is why the first and most basic support for good language development in early childhood is *experience,* accompanied, of course, by the adults' use of appropriate language that defines, describes, names, asks questions about, or even challenges the meaning of the experience.

IMPORTANCE OF SYMBOLIZATION
IN THE LEARNING PROCESS

The urge to express thought and feeling and the power to do so are uniquely human and are essential aspects of growth and development. The animal, in using symbols as signs for specific objects or events, remains locked within the confines of specific, therefore limited, comprehension. But humans can abstract the essence of an experience and give it symbolic form. With symbols they can generalize from their experience: *they can think.* That is why symbolic representation is the basis for socialization and learning. Both the intellectual and emotional effects of experience demand clarification if a person is to find meaning in life. The symbolic expression that aids clarification represents the uniqueness of experience as each individual recreates it in an effort to understand it. Yet a common sequential development runs through the process: comprehension precedes speech; speech precedes writing; and writing is grasped before reading.

LANGUAGE DEVELOPMENT
FOLLOWS UNIVERSAL LAWS

Despite the vast array of languages that exist, all children everywhere follow an invariant progression in learning the language of their culture. They babble at a few months, utter a first word at about ten to twelve months, begin to combine words at between eighteen and twenty-four months, and have the basic structure and syntax of their language pretty well assimilated at between four and five years of age. All human beings learn to speak a language if they hear one; only the deaf or criminally neglected fail to develop speech. In the case of the deaf, current methods of early detection and diagnosis allow even a congenitally deaf child to hear some sounds with amplification, bringing the possibility of speech within the range of many more deaf children than was once thought possible.

Children Speak the Language They Hear

The language children hear in their early years is the language they will reproduce, whether that be English, Spanish, Swahili, Arabic, Urdu, French, or whatever. In a country like ours, although English is the language spoken by the majority, immigration has always brought us substantial groups who speak languages other than English. In addition, regional differences and educational levels present a variety of English-language dialects as models to children, so that there may or may not be homogeneity of language spoken in kindergarten classes in many parts of the country. There has also been a steady increase of immigrants into this country in recent years, bringing different languages and affecting homogeneity of language in the kindergarten.

It is therefore important that teachers understand the linguists' conception of language rather than the traditional, ethnocentric one. The traditional view assumes that English is superior to all other languages and standard English is superior to nonstandard. Linguists do not rank languages as superior or inferior. From their careful analyses of many different languages, they have come to the conclusion that all human beings develop and learn languages, and that every language is structurally complete for the purposes of the community that uses it. Thus, people can be friends, argue, exchange commodities or money, reason, exercise judgment, measure, narrate stories, or spread rumors in every language. When linguists say that every language is complete for its own purposes, they mean that every language is a reflection of the history, economy, and culture of the people who use it. Eskimos have a dozen words for snow because their lives for countless centuries depended upon detailed, differentiated, and quick identification of snow in its varied states. As technology has advanced all over the world, many words describing now dated processes have disappeared from the languages and new words have taken their place. Thus, in English, cooper and wainwright are archaic, whereas computer and astronaut are recent additions. However, both old and new reflect the history, economy, and culture of their time.

There Is No One Best Form of Speech

Understanding the linguist's outlook frees teachers to relate the children from many different backgrounds in our pluralistic society without feeling pressured into making all children conform to speech patterns the teacher considers the most desirable. This is important because the language with which children come to school is the language of their parents, and to repudiate their language is to reject their parents and home environment. This is neither necessary nor desirable in terms of respecting variety of human style.

The Place of Standard English

Granting, however, that every language serves the purposes of its users, we must also concede that schools, the press, and the government in our country all use standard English. There is therefore a unifying value in every citizen's ability to relate to and to use standard English as a matter of course. For this reason, teachers must be concerned about standard English, but not because it is "better." Standard English is likely to be the first language for most children, but the existence of an equally expressive other language for many others can add to the teaching challenges. It need not, however, seriously interfere with the children's ability to relate to the teacher or to each other. Young children have a way of transcending words and getting down to basics. Yet some teachers may have to include some training in English as a second language in their kindergartens in ways suitable for young children if all Americans are to participate with comfort in the larger world beyond school. Before discussing special ways of handling such second-language learning among young children, let us first discuss what is common to all children in their own primary learning, because this information affects the heart of kindergarten life.

TALKING IS SPONTANEOUS AND SOCIAL

Four-, five-, and six-year-olds are great talkers. Their vocabulary and experience are sufficient to carry on all normal social amenities (and sometimes animosities), to make pertinent (and sometimes impertinent) inquiries, to answer reasonable questions, and to understand important commands. They use speech to greet the teacher, to speak with friends, to select materials, to change activities. They make use of language when making complaints, whispering secrets, responding to a joke, and singing a song.

Kindergarten children love working in groups, and that involves constant talking: discussion of what they are building or dramatizing, determining areas of responsibility, and stating agreement and disagreement with the common scheme. When seated around the snack table or working in small groups with art media, they can carry on fascinating conversations sharing personal news, making observations of social happenings, and listening and contributing to the ideas of others. Spon-

taneously, enjoyably, kindergartners frequently just chat with each other in class—provided, of course, that talking is not a forbidden activity!

In all these conversations one can discern the children's quality of thought, their powers of communication, and the array of feelings that accompany the verbal outpourings.

Let us listen in on a number of actual conversations of four- to six-year-olds and see the variety of scope and purpose in their use of language.

LANGUAGE CLARIFIES THOUGHT AND ACTION

Young children often use language to clarify their connectedness with the outer world by accompanying their actions with speech that is not necessarily addressed to anyone but seems to be defining what they are doing and what they intend to do, as though that makes the process clearer. Listen to this five-year-old mixing sand in the sandbox and working out the organization and sequence of her actions:

> Put 'em in a bowl (mixing). . . . Make a circle (pressing both palms together to make the tapering edge of a round enclosure). . . . Put the chop meat in (sprinkling sand in the middle). . . . Now broil the meat . . . Now we flatten the meat down (making a patting motion with her palms).

LANGUAGE REFLECTS PERSONAL EXPERIENCE

Five-year-old Maria, tugging eagerly at her teacher, seeks the precise word she cannot recall, and demands, "What do you call that . . . when you wear all that," indicating with gestures what might be a veil, "and you get a name but it's not getting

married? What do you call that? Sansuration?" The teacher is perplexed at first, but realizing Maria's difficulty with *k*'s and *f*'s and knowing her religious background, she guesses: "Confirmation?" Maria: "Yes! Yes!" and she runs off to tell the others.

The following reflects both personal experience and the acceptable language of the community:

> Todd and Emily start building a lobster boat with large hollow blocks. (Most of our fathers are fishermen.) The children make a good, pointed bow (for once!), a cabin, pretend winch to haul traps, helm, depth finder, lobster crates and traps, etc. Their building attracts a good many crew members, whose mingled voices come through: "Get aboard!" "We're going fishing!" "Did you bring lunch?" "It's in that basket." "Can't get this engine started, damn it." "Well, you've over-choked it and she's flooded." This from Travis, our mechanic, of course. "Rrmmm, rrmmmm! Going now. Cast off, you guys." "Untie those lines!" "What lines?" "The ropes to the dock! What are you, a farmer?" This from Noah, who goes out fishing with his dad.
>
> "Hey! Big seas ahead!" "Look at those waves! Gigantious!" "Wow! Put on your lifejackets!" "Got yours?" "Yup."
> "My God, Mary! Phew, what a stink!"
> "Why?"
> "You're standing in my bait barrel!"[5]

LANGUAGE INCORPORATES ATTITUDES FROM THE ADULT WORLD

Two boys, aged five and six, do remember the exact words that reflect an experience they are absorbing and use them appropriately. They have set up a party, but before pouring anything from a pitcher, they give it a stir, put their legs up on the table, and say to an accommodating little girl nearby, "Pour me a Scotch. I'm exhausted." Some four- and five-year-olds planning a space trip to the moon also incorporated some earthbound attitudes along with technological patter as they made plans, arranged props, and got ready for the "countdown" and "lift off." At the crucial moment, a girl approached, wanting to join the moon journey.

"Girls don't travel in a space rocket," the boys informed her.
"Why?"
"They're not supposed to."
"I want to go," the girl persisted.
"No. We don't need girls."
Undaunted, the girl insisted. "That's not true!"
This was apparently thought-provoking, because one of the boys said, "Yeah. A girl can go in a space rocket to serve meals!"

---

[5]From an unpublished report by Sally Cartwright, Director, Community Nursery School, Tenants Harbor, Me.

Yet, as though in refutation of this conventional relationship of women to men, in another classroom, where a group of children were arguing, a little girl's voice could be heard high above the others', "I am going to quit if we don't have *equal rights!*"

Language Reflects a Total Way of Life

Obviously, as children learn the language of their elders, they are learning the culture and mores of their society. They also pick up value judgments, attitudes, information, and emotional coloration, all of which they promptly make their own, albeit at different stages of comprehension. This happens inevitably, because language does not exist separately from people and life; it feeds upon experience. Most important, what looks like the imitation of words ends as a fresh and individual way of formulating what a person is thinking, assessing, feeling, or otherwise responding to. All human beings are born with the capacity to use the pattern of the language they hear in babyhood in fresh and original combinations to suit every new situation all their lives, even as they engage at the same time in the effort to grasp the reality around them.

Language Reveals Level of Thought
and Helps Strengthen Thinking

From infancy onward, children reach out to the world to try to understand it. Their first grasp is undifferentiated, impressionistic, and personal. As they grow in the capacity to differentiate, their perception of people, objects, and events becomes more realistic. They become less influenced by what they feel or want and more by what may be true for others as well as for themselves. They grow in the power to be logical. Such growth in logic is seen in a discussion by kindergartners struggling to break down their generalized awareness of "buying" into *reasons* why people might not buy. They had been listening to the story *Caps for Sale.*[6]

"Maybe they didn't like any of those colors he had."

"Maybe they didn't have much money."

"Maybe fifty cents was too much money for the caps."

"Maybe people already had a cap they bought before."

A discussion at this level would not be possible with three-year-olds, although they too would enjoy the story *Caps for Sale.* Threes are quite unable to speculate about why nobody is buying caps. But kindergarten children are likely to be ready to think more about reasons behind actions because the human mind continues to grow—provided that it is fed well both nutritionally and experientially.

[6] Esphyr Slobodkina, *Caps for Sale* (Reading, Mass.: Addison-Wesley, 1973; Scholastic Book Services, 1976).

LANGUAGE AND THOUGHT DEVELOP TOGETHER

The growth of the mind is in large measure dependent on the process of differentiation which goes on all our lives and allows us to integrate new knowledge at ever fresher levels of understanding. Consider, for example, that when children first learn to speak, they ask for the name of everything in sight and make easy generalizations based on their new information: All four-legged creatures are dogs (or cats). Gradually, the details that differentiate a dog from a cat (as well as from a cow, pig, or horse) become clear enough so that children recognize individual animals for what they are even though they have characteristics in common, that is, all have four legs, a tail, and teeth. Breaking down a first global perception into detailed specifics is a thought process that obviously extends vocabulary. It is also a basic process that eventually affects learning to read, a discovery made by Ames and Walker when they studied a group of suburban children from kindergarten to fifth grade. In kindergarten, they gave the children a Rorschach test, one part of which happens to measure how well children differentiate. Later, in fifth grade, they matched good and poor readers of similar I.Q. and compared the reading scores with the kindergarten Rorschach scores. The poor readers had not been as competent at differentiation in kindergarten, although their I.Q.'s were the same as those of the good readers.[7]

Using General to Specific Concepts
to Stretch Thought and Language

The role of differentiation in young children's learning is an important guideline to kindergarten curriculum. For example, it is a stretching experience for children to differentiate the commonplace, personal understanding of *house* (the house *they* live in) into such variations of house as cottage, igloo, log cabin, high-rise apartment house, farmhouse, and so on. If a teacher pushes on to even greater distance, from house as a dwelling to house as a shelter for things, and introduces variations like schoolhouse, firehouse, boathouse, or outhouse, the children's concepts stretch from their original, purely personal associations with the word *house* to include a reality beyond themselves.

The cognitive style of the children toward continuous breakdown from the general to the specific suggests a horizontal approach to content in the kindergarten. That would mean reaching out, in survey fashion, *across* an area of content rather than delving deeply into increasingly subtle meaning of the same content, as would be true for older children, who might examine housing styles over the centuries from cave to palace, or the relation between economics, technology, and housing. But in the kindergarten, if the study is to be of trucks, boats, stores, or food, the children are ready to learn about the variations and functions of trucks,

---

[7]Louise Ames and Richard Walker, "Prediction of Later Reading Ability from Kindergarten Rorschach and I.Q. Scores," *Journal of Psychology*, 55 (December 1964), 309–12.

boats, stores, or food, but not to go deeply into historical origins or technical information.

Recently a visitor brought a bunch of daisies from a neighboring field to the kindergarten. All the children wanted to hold "the flowers" and put them in water. To the surprise of the teacher, none of the children identified them as daisies, although they were all familiar with them. But as the children handled the daisies and put them in cans of water, they differentiated the white petals, the slim stems, and the difference in appearance between a single daisy and a bunch of them. The kindergartners were learning, personally, the features of a particular flower—without pretensions to botany.

Abstracting Similarities in Dissimilar Objects

Kindergarten children can also learn that things can be unlike in appearance and function yet be similar in nonconcrete attributes. For example, a fur coat, a kitten, and a toy rabbit all have the unseen characteristic of *softness* despite differences in appearance, size, or shape. Thought and language will develop together in a well-guided curriculum where language constantly supports concrete sensory experience in new areas of experience.

Diversity of Differentiation

Listening to children, one can literally hear them think aloud. Touching on subjects which they have picked up here and there, they exchange views and search for the understanding of reality. One major effort of this search involves the distinction between fantasy and faith on the one hand and factual reality on the other, such as in this episode:

RONNIE: I saw Santa Claus yesterday at the department store.
JOAN: There is no such thing as Santa Claus! Your mother and daddy buy you presents. Santa Claus is make-believe.
RONNIE: (torn between the evidence of his eyes and the logic of reason) I *know* it. But this was a *real* one.

Along the same lines of trying to understand the real and the not real, two youngsters engage in casual conversation while leafing through a book.

RICHARD: Why are the trees little?
ROBERT: Maybe they are far away. That's why they look little.
RICHARD: And maybe they are little because they are not real. Sometimes things are *not* real in a story. Just like in *Curious George,* he didn't really do all those things.

And children love talking and speculating about the ultimate: the *tallest* building, the *oldest* animal, the *farthest* star. "Is it as big as the sky?" children often ask, sometimes meaning the universe and not just the immediately visible sky. ". . . *infinity*. Infinity years—that's how old the sun is." "There is no such thing as 'infinity *years.*' It's just infinity."

Levels of Thought

Now listen in on this conversation in which differences in capacity to deal with more than one attribute at a time, so clearly a function of stage of mental development, come through in the language of four-year-old Billy and five-year-old Kami, who were waiting with Billy's grandmother for the school door to be opened.

"Pluto is a dog," Billy said matter-of-factly, pointing to his grandmother's dog.

"Pluto is a *boy* dog," Kami informed him.

"No, he is a dog, not a boy," Billy protested.

"He is a *boy* dog," Kami persisted, annoyed.

Grandmother, involving herself in the conversation, says, reassuringly, "Yes, Billy, he's a dog."

"But he's a *boy* dog, he's not a *girl* dog, right?" Kami insisted further.

"We won't discuss that with him," said Billy's grandmother after a pause. "He's just a dog."

But Kami was not to be silenced. "But he's got to be a boy or a girl, right?"

To be able to deal with *two* variables at once, that is, that a dog can be a dog and a male or female, is hard for a great many kindergarten children to grasp, although many are on the verge of doing so. The language of children reveals their level of thought and gives clues to the teacher as to the kind of experiences that might help the mental processes (and, incidentally, language) grow stronger. These experiences would not be planned as language lessons, but when language unfailingly accompanies experience, language development is supported as the mind grows.

As mental capacity proceeds toward increasing differentiation and relationship thinking, it can result in some genuinely profound insights, as in this poem by six-year-old Noel:

Poem

There is always
            a starting
And there is always
            an ending.
It happens in a story,
It happens with people:
            In starting they are born,
            At the end they die.
And with cars:
            The cars start getting made
            And end with breaking down.
And an apple at the start
            is fresh,
But when you forget it,
            it ends rotten.

Interests and Concerns

The ongoing search to make order out of the world is also apparent in discussions that have important emotional implications, such as family life has for young children. As Stevie got to school one morning, he began at once to deal with his concern.

STEVIE: My mother is still in the hospital and guess what, she had a baby and the baby is not big enough to come home yet.
TEACHER: That's good news, Stevie! Is the baby a boy or a girl?
STEVIE: It's a boy, it's a *brother*. I wanted a sister; next time we'll have a sister. But this one is a brother and I'll be a big brother to the baby—just like my brother is a big brother to me.
TEACHER: So your family is bigger now.
STEVIE: We have . . . *five* in the family now: my father, my mother, my big brother Jim, and me, and my name is Stevie, and my baby brother Edward Dennis!

Making order out of the world can take children far afield from everyday concerns too. The following conversation touches on history, death, and resurrection. It is the day after Lincoln's birthday. Several children are working with clay at the table. They are using their hands and talking calmly.

". . . Lincoln died."

"He was shot—by a soldier."

"But you can have a birthday (she meant a birthday celebration) after you are dead."

"God doesn't die ever."

"Oh, yes. He died once, and came to life again."

"Jesus was nailed on a cross and he looked horrible with blood coming out."

Can we doubt that this is both language and thought?

EXPRESSING FEELINGS VERBALLY

Putting feeling into words comes harder to young children than describing concrete experiences or even defining a concept they are trying to clarify. Feelings have no objective criteria and, in early childhood, feelings often control actions. It is an indication of maturing powers of control when children do put their feelings into words. Sometimes the feelings are intense and expressed in physical ways, as in this incident.

Chanell is examining a box of beautiful seashells with a friend, handling, fingering, looking, touching, and even listening. She takes a choice one and confides to her friend, "Ooh, I like it so much I could break it up." Then slowly she puts it down as the two friends exchange understanding glances.

Tact and diplomacy may take second place to honesty and directness when feelings are involved.

"Are you my friend, Wayne?" asks Luis.

"No," Wayne answers without any note of unfriendliness in his voice.

"Why? You were my friend yesterday."

"But today I don't like you."

At the same time, children's growing capacity to identify with others leads to expressions of tenderness and compassion, as one can see in this next record.

Coming into the classroom from outside, Dale immediately sizes up the tense situation of her friend Brent, who is sprawled on the floor in a screaming tantrum, with the teacher nearby, guarding and guiding. Dale looks over the scene without asking questions of either Brent or the teacher, then leans over Brent and says simply and understandingly, "I know how you feel. I feel this way myself sometimes."

Unusual, but it does happen!

Preschool children frequently replicate versions of the following conversation, a beautiful example of their effort to merge feeling and thought.

"My mother had a birthday. She is thirty years old now."

"My mother is thirty-*one*!"

"Well, my daddy is thirty-five."

"And my daddy is a hundred!" a little boy said with conviction in his voice and a sense of the ultimate.

The children were hardly conveying chronological or statistical facts; rather, they were expressing the immensity of their parents' importance to them, using newly discovered numbers to symbolize their need to publicize that impressive relationship.

Young children can be so free in their comments about their families that we must add a brief caution here. In their spontaneous conversations children often reveal information which the bystander, in this case the teacher, may find embarrassingly intimate. In such cases tact and discretion constitute the wisest response to childish innocence.

Verbal Humor

Play on words can be very funny to four-, five-, and six-year-olds, and makes for good joking. "If it's a dandelion, it must be a lion—ooh, I am afraid of it!" "You said this tree is a sycamore. If it's sick, you should call the doctor!"

There are language theorists who believe that children's playfulness with words represents a growing awareness of the structure of language, even if at a very simple level, and this awareness represents a precondition for literacy. The playfulness best remembered by adults occurs closer to age seven or eight, when children delight in puns and double-meaning jokes (e.g., moron jokes). Preschoolers enjoy incongruity of content more, and five-year-olds are able to figure out simple riddles and love doing so. See how the children in this episode played with words in direct contradiction of meaning:

JAMIE: Where is Marjie?
TEACHER: She has the chicken pox and couldn't come to school.
RAFAEL: I had the chicken pox last year.
JAMIE: You had the chicken pox! Then you are a chicken!
RAFAEL: (earnestly) Oh, no, I am a boy. Once you are a boy, you stay a boy.

(Next Day)

LISA MAE: Where is Marjie?
TEACHER: She has the chicken pox, but she'll be back in a few days.
RAFAEL: If you have the chicken pox, then you are a chicken! Isn't it funny? *And,* if you have the rooster pox, you are a rooster!

Body References and Humor

Children often laugh uproariously as they tell jokes of simple mishaps and mistakes and misplacings, or of some preposterous physical happenings; ". . . and there was somebody on the roof, and he slipped and fell and *smashed to pieces.*" This is just the punch line to cause an outburst of laughter. Or, ". . . and she couldn't eat her nice lunch because she didn't have any fork, and she didn't have any knife, and she didn't have any spoon, so she took a great big broom from the kitchen, and she *swept* her lunch from the plate!" That joke was so good it had to be repeated.

But unlike adult jokes, which are mostly heard and then passed on, children's jokes are told ad lib; they are completely spontaneous and original, and it seems that spontaneity is part of the humor, since it surprises and amuses the teller as well as the listeners.

Somewhat like grown-ups, kindergarten children love to tell "dirty jokes." What is more, there seems to be no distinct sex difference among children in the enjoyment of such jokes, which are most often an exaggerated and rather sly tale, told with lascivious expression, about parts of the body or functions of the body, the point or purpose of the tale being to shock or at least surprise the hearer and to enjoy a good laugh together with one's comrades, who appreciate a good dirty joke when they hear one! Thus, the subject is any part of the body conventionally concealed by clothing, sometimes extending to conventionally concealed clothing itself, such as underwear. The functions are all gastrointestinal and told with sound effects. But the manner of telling, when the general conversation gets a bit dull perhaps, and the laughter imply delight in the social subversiveness of the joke, and make it analogous to adult dirty jokes. One is wise to divert or otherwise redirect this kind of conversation before it reaches a state of uncontrolled contagion, which it can do. It goes without saying that the children need not be made to feel that there is anything wrong in joking about bodily processes. They probably feel pretty cocky about their present state of knowingness when a few short years earlier they could not control their body processes by themselves at all. The humor could well be a declaration of victory tinged with some still lingering feelings of anxiety about the stability of their control. And not to be overlooked—in the kindergarten—is the sex-related vocabulary that now permeates verbal expression in every stratum of our society. Coming into the classroom a little girl is eager to relate the latest happening: "You know what? On the bus Janie showed us sexy pictures! She had such sexy pictures . . . you know." Clearly, "sexy" is both a daring and an accepted word—whatever it means.

MISCONCEPTIONS

In the preceding spontaneous conversations, the teacher did not try to clarify or question beliefs or exaggerations which were of an emotional and personal nature. If she had, she might have spoiled the spontaneity and there would not have been true conversation. There are times indeed when a teacher ought to speak only when spoken to. At other times, however, a teacher may need to enter a conversation to help resolve an argument or clarify confusion, as in the following instance, where the teacher clearly overheard the subject of discussion among a small group of four-year-olds. It was tonsils.

"Tonsils are in the mouth, where the tongue sticks," one child explained, indicating with a finger poking past the tongue.

"No, it's in the throat; and tonsils give you a sore throat, my mommy says."

"But how do you get the tonsils out?" the first child asked. The teacher was listening as a third child, Rickey, gave a serious and graphic explanation.

"I know! The doctor cuts off the head!" Rickey demonstrated a drastic incision with a finger under the chin while several more children gathered around him and listened without any questioning. "Then he takes the tonsils *out* (again agile finger demonstration) and puts the head back on again." None of the other children could think of a better explanation of a tonsillectomy, and although the teacher's authority was not consulted, she nevertheless took advantage of the children's intense attention and explained convincingly: "When my brother had his tonsils out, the doctor used a special instrument which he put in the open mouth. Then he quickly snipped the tonsils off—just the tonsils, nothing else."

So often logical thinking is bogged down in sheer lack of information!

THE TEACHER'S ROLE IN STRENGTHENING
LANGUAGE POWER

Teachers play an important part in the development of language in young children. Not only do they act as models by simply talking to and with the children, but by the very nature of their interaction and by their decisions about activities, they can encourage and support the extension of language in children at every level of expressiveness. Such extension includes increasingly complex syntax as well as extension of vocabulary. To do this with good judgment and appropriateness, teachers must be clear about realistic, reasonable expectations in kindergartners' language development and about what constitutes developmental lag. They must also be clear about the differences between a mediocre and a rich language environment, know how language is best extended in young children, and know how best to deal with the children for whom English may be a second language. We will look at each of these in the next chapter.

REFERENCES AND FURTHER READING

BERKO, JEAN. "The Child's Hearing of English Morphology," *Word,* 14, 1958.

CAZDEN, COURTNEY B. *Child Language and Education.* New York: Holt, Rinehart and Winston, 1972.

CHOMSKY, CAROL. *The Acquisition of Syntax in Children Five to Ten,* Research Monograph No. 57. Cambridge, Mass.; London, England: The M.I.T. Press, 1969.

CHUKOVSKY, KORNEI. *From Two to Five.* Berkeley and Los Angeles: University of California Press, 1966.

EVERTTS, ELDONNA (ed.). *Dimensions of Dialect.* Champaign, Ill.: National Council of Teachers of English, 1967.

KESSEL, FRANK S. *The Role of Syntax in Children's Comprehension from Ages Six to Twelve,* Monograph Series No. 139, 35, 6 (1970). Chicago: Society for Research in Child Development.

MACGINITIE, WALTER, and HOLDEN, MARJORIE. "Children's Conceptions of Word Boundaries in Speech and Print," *Journal of Educational Psychology,* 63, 6, December 1972.

MONTESSORI, MARIA. *The Absorbent Mind.* New York: Holt, Rinehart and Winston, 1967.

SCHWARTZ, JUDITH I. "Children's Experiments with Language," *Young Children,* July 1981, 16.

TOUGH, JOAN. *Talking, Thinking, Growing.* New York: Schocken Books, 1974.

WINSOR, CHARLOTTE (ed.). *Dimensions of Language Experience.* New York: Agathon Press, 1975.

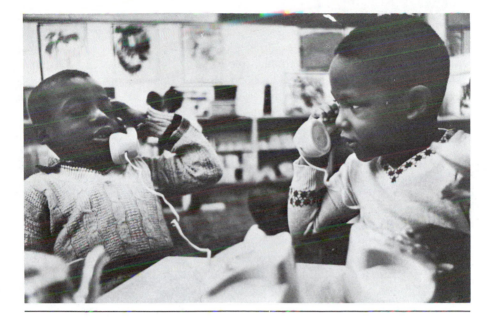

6 Language Environments

Language is so related to experience, to thinking, to evaluation of self and others, that it can be influenced by many factors. Children's vocabulary, for example, can be extensive or meager as a result of rich or limited verbal experience at home. Although the syntax of a language offers possibilities for infinite variations of expression, not all people have varied things to say. A rich language environment in early childhood is one in which experience is supported by freely flowing language that defines, labels, questions, analyzes, and compares these experiences.

A kindergarten can thus have a poor language environment despite ample equipment and much activity if the teacher's major use of language is to give commands and make demands: "Put your things away" "Where are your boots?" "Be sure to bring your milk money to school." There are classrooms where teachers do not often speculate with their children on matters of real interest: "I wonder why the gerbil isn't eating?" "What would happen if we all tried to get our coats on at the same time?" "How did that spider spin its web?" In far too many classrooms discussions about ideas are few and far between. This one took place during a reading of *Veronica* by Roger Duvoisin,[1] because the children felt strongly about the issues the story raised and the teacher responded.

"They shouldn't put Veronica in jail. They were mean," said one child, protesting the injustice.

"Why did they decide to put her in jail?" the teacher asked the children, calling their attention to some facts of the story.

"She *stole* the vegetables" (saying the apparently new word carefully).

"And she parked the wrong way!"

"Yes, she parked *herself* because she was like a car."

"She was a hippocar!" one boy contributed enthusiastically, repeating a word he had actually invented listening to the earlier part of the story.

"Veronica's too big to fit in the jail."

"She's too wide to get through the door."

"The policemen can't make her—the hippo can step on their toes!" (laughter from some children). "She'll *squash* them!"

"But in the story Veronica is made to go through this jail door. Do you have an idea what happens next?" There were lots of ideas judging by the eager hands, expressive faces, and bright eyes.

"She is strong, she can knock the door off with her nose."

"A hippo's nose can't knock—it can rub though, hard."

"*I* know: she can push the jail walls with her body, and that's heavy. She's a heavy hippo!"

"Yes, she's a heavy hippo," said the teacher.

Then a little girl said rather timidly: "Maybe her family, her mother and father and everybody, will find Veronica and *they* would help her get out of jail." And just as the teacher was thinking that the fifteen-minute discussion had provided enough expression and stimulation, a child spoke up: "Finish the story! Let's hear it!"

In examining the discussion we see that it served several purposes. It crystallized the children's feelings, directly for those who spoke and vicariously for those who listened, focused feelings of sympathy for a fellow creature in a predicament, expressed feelings of resentment toward punitive laws, and helped define their knowledge about violating the law, especially the traffic law. Also, it provided a medium for the expression and sharing of ideas about the solving of a mechanical problem having to do with forcing, fitting, and breaking.

Since this discussion just happened in the midst of reading, it will be interesting to examine another, deliberately planned one to support the point about rich verbal environments versus barren ones.

---

[1] Roger Duvoisin, *Veronica* (New York: Alfred A. Knopf Inc., 1961).

PLANNING A DISCUSSION

By early spring, when she was planning her program for the rest of the year, Miss Santino became increasingly aware that of all the educational materials they had in the class, of all the interesting items they had constructed, nothing held the children's attention as much as the various animals they had had in class from time to time. Nothing aroused as much feeling and curiosity and provoked as much comment as did the animals. Some project, therefore, of a zoological or biological nature seemed right and worthwhile. At the same time she learned at a staff meeting that an incubator for hatching chicks was available from an educational supply company.

She decided to discuss the project with the children and brought in the incubator and some fertilized and unfertilized eggs. From this discussion she hoped to find out the extent of the children's interest, the level of their comprehension, and therefore the value of undertaking the project at all. She believed that the discussion would give the children an introduction to biological beginnings, for they would observe and handle the concrete items, see pictures, and talk about them. She believed that the discussion would also stimulate the children to further observation and thought. She realized while thinking about it how little she knew herself, and she was nervous about having to answer the children's questions. However, she reminded herself that this was to be a learning discussion, not a teaching lecture. "We have something special to talk about today," she said as the children slid into a circle on the floor. Immediately they noticed the eggs in the two bowls.

"We have eggs at home!" "Where did you get these eggs?" "Are we going to eat them?"

"I have different kinds of eggs here," the teacher replied. "These come from the store and these Mrs. Gregory brought from a farm."

"The farm eggs are brown," said one child. The teacher realized that the child, in true preoperational style, was concluding that all eggs coming directly from a farm are brown and all store eggs are white. How was she to correct that?

"Well," said the teacher, "some chickens lay brown-shelled eggs and some lay white-shelled eggs. But only the color of the shell is different; the inside is the same. Here, you can see for yourselves."

The teacher let one child break a white egg into a bowl and one a brown egg. The children noticed the hardness of the shell, the "yellow part," the "wiggle" of the white; the teacher could tell by their comments that the error was corrected, and she put aside the bowls with eggs for the time being.

"Let me tell you about these eggs from the farm. They are special because a baby chick can grow from them," the teacher said. Some children smiled pleasantly; others stared in puzzlement. One child asked, "How?" The teacher realized that her information was too remote and the children had nothing to say or to think on the subject. She brought the five unbroken eggs and said:

"See these eggs."

"Let me see."

"Let me feel one."

So the teacher let each child hold an egg, look at it, turn it, feel its weight, and rub its surface, always being careful and even mysteriously quiet while beholding the egg. When the eggs were safely placed back in the bowl, there were many comments.

"It's heavy. Maybe there is a baby chick in it already." Other children wanted to respond to this so the teacher held off her comment.

"But how could the baby chick *fit* inside an egg?"

"And how would it get air?"

"It couldn't see anything . . .!"

"Then how would it find food?" The teacher listened to all these expressions of faith, skepticism, and practicality.

"Yes," she answered, holding an egg in her own hand, "it is quite heavy. It has that white part for the baby chicken's body to grow from, and the yellow part is the baby chick's food while it is growing inside. But there is no baby chick in the egg yet."

"But when will the baby chick grow?"

"To make a baby chick start growing inside the egg, we will have to do something to the egg."

"What?" the children asked eagerly, all eyes big, eager, and hungry for knowledge.

"First, it has to be kept very warm—warmer than your body. Then it has to be turned over once in a while. When that's done day after day after day, a baby chick will grow and peck its way out." The expression on the children's faces clearly said: "What wondrous things can happen," but pragmatic thinking was expressed by others.

"Can we do *that* . . .?"

"On some farms," the teacher explained, "the mother hen sits on the eggs most of the time for twenty-one days and keeps the eggs warm that way and she turns them with her body and feet."

"Birds sit on their eggs in the nest," contributed one child. There was a relevant exchange of information about the phenomenon of birds hatching eggs. The teacher used the word *hatch* repeatedly. Then she added:

"But we can keep the eggs properly warm without a hen, and that's what they do on many farms, too. We can do it in this incubator with a little electric bulb; and the eggs can hatch in *it* after twenty-one days, just as with the mother hen." The incubator was very interesting to the children, but the teacher thought that the discussion, though unfinished, should terminate before the children got restless. Then a little girl made an important request: "I want to hold the egg again." Other children did too, so the teacher brought the eggs back. The little girl looked at the egg, then put it up to her ear. "I could *hear* the chicken a little bit," she confided to the child next to her. Immediately the other children put the eggs to their ears and they too "heard" the chick. Not wanting to intrude on their imagination, yet remembering that she was offering the children accurate knowledge, the teacher said:

"There is no chicken there yet," and she let the child break open the egg to see a familiar raw egg. "But there is a beginning of a chick in *this* egg and in the other egg we broke." The teacher placed both bowls in the center on the floor and pointing to the fertile spot said, "This little spot means the egg is fertile; a baby chick can grow from it."

"If you keep it warm and everything," came an appropriate qualification from a child.

"Can we eat the broken egg in the bowl?" With that practical comment the teacher terminated the half hour discussion, deferring to another time the showing of embryological pictures and the construction of a calendar for marking the passing days.

This was a vital discussion and it took a good deal of emotional and intellectual energy. Most valuable for the teacher was the realization that it is difficult for young five-year-olds to comprehend the abstract, the potential, the future, but that they have very intense concern with the immediate, the egg in the hand. They perceived all the attributes of the egg they were holding and readily endowed it with life. She realized that more direct experience with egg hatching, more time to make individual observations, and more group discussions were needed by the children to learn some of the biological concepts involved in the hatching of eggs.

Language used as it was in these discussions is deeply satisfying to children and adults because it is so integral to their common interests and feelings. At the same time, thoughtfully led discussions stretch the capacity for language, first because fresh thinking often demands fresh vocabulary, and second because language is learned best by using it actively for a range of serious purposes, serious, that is, to children. Research shows that personal involvement affects communication in childhood.[2] Compare the language of a five-year-old child who was asked first to describe a picture arbitrarily chosen for him and then to describe a picture he selected himself.[3] About the first picture, he said:

> That's a horse. You can ride it. I don't know any more about it. It's brown, black and red. I don't know my story about the horse.

About the second, self-chosen picture, he said:

> There's a picture of my tree that I climb in. There's—There's where it grows at and there's where I climb up—and sit up there—down there and that's where I look out at. First I get on this one and then I get on the other one. And then I put my foot under that big branch that are strong. And then I pull my face up and then I get a hold of a branch up at that place—and then I look around.

---

[2] E. C. Mueller, "An Analysis of Children's Communication in Free Play." Ph.D. dissertation, Cornell University, 1971, as reported in C. Cazden, *Child Language and Education* (New York: Holt, Rinehart and Winston, 1972).

[3] T. E. Strandberg, and J. Griffith, "A Study of the Effects of Training in Visual Literacy on Verbal Behavior," Eastern Illinois University, 1968, as quoted in C. Cazden, *Child Language and Education,* p. 207.

Teachers would do well to ask themselves, as Strandberg and Griffith suggest, "How often, when we seek a child's attention, are we responding to him, and how often are we intruding on his mental life with some interest of our own?"[4]

An Unplanned Discussion

A teacher in an after-school program in a suburban school district provides the following account of an impromptu discussion among children:

> A small group of kindergarten and first grade children gathered to hear an announcement from the teacher. Before she could begin, they began talking with a sense of excitement, urgency, drama.
> "I know," said one. "The school is going to close!" And the others followed:
> "Yeh, we won't have any school . . ."
> "That's because the king died!" a child added with authority. Another elaborated:
> "Because someone *shot* him . . . shot the king!"
> "No, he wasn't a *real* king—that was just his *name* . . ." someone clarified.
> Then others joined in, reflectively:
> "But he was a very good man, and someone *bad* shot him . . ."
> "That was a long time ago . . ."
> "Yeh, and now it's his birthday."
> (There was a moment of silence while they tried to puzzle that out.)
> "But he's *dead* now, so how can it be his birthday?"
> "It's just so we can remember him . . ."

Somehow the children worked this all out by themselves, with only minimal interjections from the teacher, who while listening attentively, was reluctant to interrupt the flow of ideas. In the end, however, she did clearly establish the identity and importance of Martin Luther King, and the idea of a commemorative birthday.

What an excellent, natural opportunity it was for the teacher to shed some light on a complicated historical event for the questioning children! And although a teacher generally has to be ready to intervene in a children's discussion in case of hopeless confusion or misinformation, in this case the children were providing answers themselves. Thus, by not intruding, the teacher gave the children an opportunity to express their own thoughts, and listening, she could assess their level of comprehension and the nature of their interest.

LITERATURE AS LANGUAGE ENVIRONMENT

A rich language environment in the kindergarten is fed through literature. Good stories for children use language that is provocative and colorful, vivid or poetic; it is noticeably different from the language of daily usage. It can be found in well-known classics as well as in modern titles. For example, in *In the Forest* the adven-

[4]Ibid.

turous character says simply, "I spied a rabbit behind a tall weed."[5] Yet, how pic-
turesque and descriptive the sentence is! And how expressive when Max, in *Where the Wild Things Are,*

> . . . came to the place where the wild things are
> they roared their terrible roars and gnashed their terrible teeth
> and rolled their terrible eyes and showed their terrible claws
> till Max said "BE STILL!"[6]

Such literary rhythm and imagery, such grotesqueness and even horror (wel-
comingly exciting rather than frightening) and the powerful effect of two ordinary
words "BE STILL!" contribute significantly to the language environment in a classroom.

Literary language stretches the imagination and understanding by giving us
more words to conjure images with than are normally used. As children listen to
stories they can respond to emotionally and grasp conceptually, the language of the
books is absorbed in the same way language was first absorbed at home in babyhood—through the ears![7] Even if all the words heard are not actively used, there is
a gain. They remain part of the much larger passive vocabulary that enriches our
reading and deepens our understanding all through life.

Literature need not be confined to the story a day, although that is basic.
There is much good poetry available for young children (see the chapter on literature), and rhymes and chants also support language learning.

For most children, the expansion of language simultaneously with thought is
sufficiently served by a combination of varied and interesting experiences accompanied by verbal naming, questions, and comment supported by regular discussions
and regular story listening. For children whose initial language is poor to begin with,
however, or who must learn English as a second language, further steps are necessary. Before discussing what to do, let us look more closely at the children who
might need more help. They are not all alike by any means.

CHILDREN OF LIMITED LANGUAGE POWER

By limited language power we mean shorter sentences than most children the same
age use, more limited vocabulary (e.g., not knowing all kinds of commonplace
names for things), and fewer syntactical variations than others their age use. Since

---

[5] Marie Hall Ets, *In the Forest* (New York: The Viking Press, 1961).

[6] Maurice Sendak, *Where the Wild Things Are* (New York: Harper & Row, Publishers, Inc.), 1963. Reprinted by permission of Harper & Row, Publishers, Inc., and The Bodley Head Ltd.

[7] Dorothy H. Cohen, "Effect of a Special Program in Literature on the Vocabulary and Reading of Second Grade Children in Special Service Schools," *Elementary English*, February 1968.

language is learned at home, there may be good reasons in the home life style for these limitations. Families vary in the degree to which they rely on language to relate to each other, and this can affect even the mode of disciplining children. For example, all children misbehave, but some parents "give a look," some give a slap, some shout "stop that!" and some explain when they want to curb their children. Children whose mothers say, "I'd rather you buttoned up tightly when you go out because it's cold today," are hearing that their mother has a point of view, a preference, in "I'd rather"; and they learn *degree* in the word *tightly; time orientation* in *when; causal relationship* in *because,* and *time definition* in *today.* The child whose mother says repeatedly only, "Put on your coat," is missing all of these nuances. Language has quality as well as quantity and can be sophisticated even on a kindergarten level.

The study by Milner[8] (see Chapter 2) showed how quality and quantity may go together. She found a correlation between the amount of conversation around the supper table and children's success in reading in first grade. It also turned out that parents who held conversations with their children at the table were the ones most likely to read to their children, take them on excursions, and discipline them verbally. Carried to its ultimate logic, this seems to mean that children who are talked to and reasoned with hear and respond to more variation and complexity in language than children whose parents give them brief commands and seldom answer their questions, never read to them, or never have discussions with them. Both kinds of children come to school, however, and the teacher's style of verbalizing and choice of story material to read to her class will have to be tempered by the reality of her children's different experience. Her goals would be the same, but the material and procedures for the children with poor language power need sharper focusing and tighter organization.

Limited language power often reflects a total syndrome of inadequate adult-child relationships, and focus on language alone may not be enough for such children. They are likely to need introductions to many experiences other children take for granted. They may need help in differentiating and focusing on objects, events, and people along with the stimulation and encouragement to be curious. They probably also need better self-images, courage to try new things, and faith to stick to what they try. An all-inclusive approach to such children is well described in *The Drifters,* a study of children from multiproblem homes.[9]

CHILDREN WHO SPEAK A DIALECT OF ENGLISH

Children who speak a dialect of English are not necessarily children with poor language power, a common error made by many teachers. According to the linguists, dialects of English have more in common with standard English than differences

---

[8] Esther Milner, "A Study of the Relationships between Reading Readiness in Grade One School Children and Patterns of Parent-Child Interaction," *Child Development,* 22, 1951, 95–112.

[9] E. Pavenstedt (ed.), *The Drifters* (Boston: Little, Brown and Company, 1967).

from it. Nonstandard English dialects have consistent rules of grammar which differ from standard English in specific respects. The largest single dialect in the United States is black English, a dialect that has for too long been misunderstood and derided, encouraging teachers to humiliate black children and scorn their speech as "sloppy" and "lazy." Careful study has revealed how unjust the accusations have been, and black dialect is now recognized as rooted in the black experience, as all language is rooted in the experience of its people. It is as full and rich a language as standard English. It is of interest to note, in passing, that historically, the standard in any country has been a factor of who uses the language, not the language itself. Standard English has been and continues to be used by people who have status and so it, too, takes on status.

Children who use black dialect learn it as all children learn language, from intimate association in their family circle. It serves them well until they come to school, where standard English is the language. Children brought up on a dialect are thus in need of learning standard English in order to participate in and enjoy the wider opportunities available in the mainstream of society. They must learn it, however, not as a replacement for their dialect, but as a second language at their disposal, to use when appropriate. Approaches continue to be sought to teaching standard English as a second language, and there are contradictory attitudes and methods in use at the present time. A most creative study by Dorothy Strickland[10] showed that kindergarten is a most favorable time for such learning, if it is done wisely. Strickland recognized that repetition and practice are important factors in second-language learning but that young children become bored with uninteresting repetition and practice. She therefore developed a two-part program that encourages children to imitate and repeat standard English in a natural, childlike context. First, all teachers in the experiment were asked to read to the children regularly from books that used the criteria suggested by the Cohen study cited earlier—that is, stories that permitted emotional identification and comprehension. Then teachers of the experimental classes were trained to follow the story readings with such oral language activities as creative dramatics, choral speaking, puppetry, and role playing, in which the language used by the characters in the stories would be repeated exactly as heard. It was an ingenious idea, and it worked.

For generations children have learned mathematical concepts and words from countless repetitions of the phrases in "The Three Bears": "the *big* chair is for the Papa bear, the *middle* chair is for the Mama bear, and the *littlest* chair is for the baby bear." Why shouldn't dramatic repetition of "Who's been eating *my* porridge?" stamp in the standard form without in any way denying the validity of "Who be eatn' mah porridge?" The kindergarten children in Strickland's study made significant progress in their assimilation of standard English without ever feeling humiliated or ashamed of the language of their parents. They continued to use black dialect at will, and their teachers accepted it without ever "correcting" them. Yet

[10]Dorothy Strickland, "A Program for Linguistically Different Black Children," in *Research in the Teaching of English, 7, 1* (Spring 1973), pp. 79–88, *Bulletin of the National Council of Teachers of English*, Urbana, Illinois.

their knowledge of standard English grew markedly. Experience has shown that children who come to school using a dialect that is frowned upon by the authorities quickly learn not to speak in class. From this the myth has arisen that black children do not have language strength. Current evidence shows that there is no necessary correlation between dialect and language development.

One of the major investigators in this area, William Labov, told an audience at an early childhood conference of the way in which he discovered that young black children were not at all language poor.[11] He entered a kindergarten classroom and showed a picture of a street and houses to some children, and asked them to describe what they saw, the conventional psychologist's approach. He got words and fragments in reply, the conventional finding. But then he tried something different. He showed the children a rabbit he had brought with him and explained that the rabbit was a nervous rabbit who felt better when people talked to him. He put the rabbit in a separate room with three of the children from the kindergarten class and left his tape recorder going while he stepped out. The flow of language from the same children who had given stilted responses to the "test" was full of complexity, good thinking, reasoning, and colorful expression. Labov had discovered once and for all that if you put children from a minority culture into a situation that has meaning for them, their language flows as naturally and easily as it does for the majority children of equal experience and intelligence.

Teachers need to face the fact that children who come to school speaking a dialect but hearing standard English learn quickly to decode and interpret what they hear. See how black and Appalachian children understood their teacher's meaning and reworked her words to fit their own more familiar structure:

> TEACHER: The children go to bed.
> APPALACHIAN CHILD: The children goes to bed.
>
> TEACHER: She cleans her teeth with a brush.
> BLACK CHILD: Her cleans her teeth with a brush.

Yet teachers in the same situation complain that they cannot understand the children. Surely one must ask why children can learn two dialects, but teachers remain limited to their own? Does willingness to listen and learn have anything to do with it?

Children who speak one or another dialect of English often come from minority groups whose customs may not quite be the same as that of the majority culture, and in this regard, too, teachers must be sensitive to the ways in which these cultural modes clash during conversation. For example, Apache Indians teach their children that too much talking is foolishness; Navaho Indians avoid direct, open-faced looking when talking to someone; Puerto Rican children are taught to lower their eyes when talking to someone in authority.

[11] William Labov, *Language in the Inner City* (Philadelphia: University of Pennsylvania Press 1973).

Teaching children whose culture and dialect are different from our own is not always easy. But children seek meaning always, rather than form, and they will respond to teachers who respect them for what they are, try to understand their communication, and treat them with fairness under all circumstances.

CHILDREN WHO KNOW LITTLE OR NO ENGLISH

Sizable and growing numbers of children in different parts of the United States are born into Spanish-speaking families, and, in the way of language learning, learn Spanish as a first language. Efforts to teach such children to read English in the first grade have resulted in failure that should have been foreseen, since print, after all, is only the symbolic rendition of oral language. If a child does not understand the oral version of the print he or she is being taught to decode, no amount of sounding it out will help.

In schools which once served the melting pot tradition, this rather obvious difference between learning a symbol system for a known language and learning a new language orally is at last being clarified. Kindergarten teachers whose child population is totally non-English-speaking must be at least partially bilingual in order to help the children take on a new language in its oral form first.

The goal of learning a second language is to speak it fluently and appropriately, even to think in that language. This is entirely possible but does not happen when the mechanics are abstracted and separated from the life of the children and presented as meaningless exercises performed to please the teacher and easily forgotten.

The issue of bilingual education is larger than can be dealt with here, but we urge a basic approach that combines two kinds of knowledge: (1) that language is best learned in a context of experience and meaning, and (2) that a range of interests meaningful to young children must be combined with the concrete style of learning so typical of preschoolers in any programs developed for them. Although such programs are still experimental the best ones reflect the principles we are urging.[12]

Demand for bilingual programs constitutes a public educational concern of the 1980s, since there are 7.6 million children in the United States for whom English is not a native language.[13] Although the concern has to do chiefly with the academic progress of school-age children to whom English is a foreign language, bilingualism (use of native *and* secondary language) is also a reality in the kindergarten. This presents a unique language environment in which the second language in the kindergarten may be Spanish or some East European or oriental language.

---

[12] *Un Marco Abierto: An Open Framework for Educators* (High Scope Educational Research Foundation, 600 North River Street, Ypsilanti, Michigan 48197). Institute for Urban and Minority Education, *Alberta, A Bilingual, Multicultural Early Childhood Curriculum* (New York: Teachers College, Columbia University).

[13] Janet Gonzalez-Mena, "Program for English Experiences: English as a Second Language for Pre-school and Kindergarten" (Silver Spring, Md.: Institute of Modern Languages, 1975).

Mrs. L., who taught kindergarten for many years in a suburban community, found that practically a third of her 1981 enrollment consisted of recently arrived Japanese children. The first part of the year those children communicated mostly with each other in their native language, while the local children heard, or were at least aware of, a foreign language and learned the Japanese names. But through the many daily activities and contacts on the part of all children, with the common-sense guidance of the teacher and while living in an English-speaking community, the Japanese children had acquired sufficient command of English by spring to continue progress on their own. Thus while these immigrant children remained bilingual by continued use of their native language at home, English became their dominant oral language in school.

The chief elements of the language environment of that kindergarten were the mutual acceptance of the linguistically diverse groups of children and the *communication* on different levels between children of similar age and common interests.

To non-English-speaking children, as to all children, communication means first and foremost a meeting of minds and hearts. Whether this is through gestures, pictures, miming, or whatever, positive, nonverbal communication is basic to children's acceptance of the teacher's more formal language lessons. What a teacher must rely upon is the children's own will and desire to be able to communicate better with representatives of the majority culture. Self-motivated children are generally willing learners; they cannot be coerced. The bilingual teacher, like all teachers, must never forget that she is dealing first of all with young children, and secondly with young children who have a particular need. To the degree that she is a supportive, enabling person, children will gladly accept her guidance. This principle is clearly evident when a school serves a community where use of two languages is a way of life.

When a group of about twenty-five children gathered in a private bilingual kindergarten in a Mexican town with a large number of U.S. residents, the atmosphere seemed distinctly bilingual. Some children were speaking to each other in English, others in Spanish. There was no dominant language, and language was not an obstacle to the children's spontaneous communication, their use of materials, or their taking part in any activities. The teacher, being bilingual of necessity and by education, helped the children appreciate the difference between the languages—through songs, games, reading, and conversation. She focused on the expressiveness or usefulness or unique meaning of the Spanish or English. Meanwhile, the children themselves, without formal teaching, were learning from each other as well as from the teacher the use of two languages in the context of two cultures, the experiences of everyday life, and close relationships.

LANGUAGE AND THE POTENTIAL FOR LEARNING

There is no indication that children of families who do not use language richly or children who speak a dialect or children whose first language is not English are less capable than children who are facile with standard English. All such children, however, probably require a special, more consciously focused approach to their further language development than a spontaneous, natural environment could offer them. This is so because they are long past the beginning thrust of language learning in babyhood, when they were wide open to seeking out the rules of language as a matter of developmental stage. By four, five, and six, other things are on their minds, and other goals beckon. They need help in refocusing anew on language beginnings in a second language. Such refocusing calls for their active participation, because language is best learned by using it, especially in one-to-one style. An interesting deterrent for some children is the fact that teachers, without meaning to, tend to talk more to the children who talk to them. As a result, the less expressive, quiet, or more self-conscious children can easily be lost in a school environment in which language occurs only spontaneously and naturally and is not deliberately fostered in those who need it. If the children in need of help then do not learn, they are often labeled uneducable, whereas the problem is, more likely, that the teaching method and attitudes are inadequate to the need.

FOCUSING ON LANGUAGE IN A SPECIAL WAY

A first environmental requirement for all children who need more than spontaneous interaction is *full and total acceptance by adults of who and what the children are as people,* regardless of their skill in the English language or the reasons why they are not as skilled as others. A second major requirement is trust in their capacity to learn, which will involve helping them build their own belief in themselves as learners. It is the child's task to take the language rules out of the experience-plus-language environment, not the adult's task to *impose* the rules. In planning special experiences for children who need them, all the reasons why a child will want to respond must be built in. These reasons may have nothing to do with learning language from the child's point of view; the situation must allow for that as a by-product of what matters to the children as a whole. Frances Hawkins, whose work with deaf children is a testimony to the powers of children to learn when they are approached as whole human beings and not in terms of their handicap alone, has something to say about language learning which is completely applicable here.

> When the art and skill of using language is marked off and delimited as a special "subject," the powers of an early learner are correspondingly enfeebled.[14]

Her view is consonant with that of Shari Nadler, whose ten years of experimentation with several bilingual programs for young children led her away from an early, mechanical approach to language learning as an isolated phenomenon into a program of orderly sequence that aims to help children internalize the second language, not merely to mimic it.[15] Easily understood, concrete activities like cooking,

[14] Frances P. Hawkins, *The Logic of Action* (New York: Pantheon Books, 1974), p. 28.

[15] Shari E. Nadler, "Explorations in Teaching English as a Second Language," *Young Children*, 30, 6 (September 1975).

the use of puppets, and much singing of songs (mouthing words helps to make them one's own) are good; finger plays (rhythmic beat of "Where is Thumbkin?" helps establish its difference from "Where Thumbkin?") and modeling standard English phrases when suitable in a lotto game (e.g., "Who has the ring?" to counter "Who got . . ."); games that call for questions and answers (e.g., "Whose shoes are red?"); and constant readiness by the teacher to respond to the content of what a child is saying—all these enrich the environment of children who need more than the usual. Most important, *language must be elicited from children,* not merely modeled for them and imitated by them. Some will need help in articulating what they would like to say, that is, using imitation in the service of the child's own thought, as in the following situation, when a student teacher offered to help children write notes to an absent child:

> When Spanish-speaking Madeline came to the table, the student teacher greeted her warmly and started to write "Dear Michael" on the paper. He turned to Madeline and said, "What shall I put down next?" Madeline, however, was mute, her eyes looking downward, her only movement the rhythmic activity of her tongue sliding back and forth in a space in her mouth where a tooth had recently fallen out. The student teacher made little headway and finally he tried, "Would you like to tell Michael about losing your tooth?" Madeline nodded shyly, and the student teacher said, "O.K. Tell me what to say." Muteness again. "Well, what is in your mouth now where the tooth used to be?" "A hole." "O.K., let's tell Michael there's a hole where your tooth used to be because the tooth fell out." . . . Silence. The student teacher persisted in trying to get Madeline to say what she had to say in her own way, but Madeline couldn't seem to. Finally the young man urged her to repeat the rather complicated sentence, "There is a hole in my mouth where my tooth used to be," in direct imitation of himself. After several tries, Madeline repeated the entire sentence alone, "There's a hole in my mouth where my tooth used to be." She grinned, the student teacher grinned back and wrote the sentence down with conspicuous attention to its articulation.

This little girl, who had learned enough English in preschool to carry her past the first hurdles of communication, found it difficult to use present and past tenses together, an indication that her knowledge of English, after a year and a half at school, was not as sound as her proud teacher thought it was. Without the ability to use somewhat more syntactical devices than the simple present tense expressed in, "I need the scissors," or "I want the stapler," Madeline, and others like her, will be handicapped in their school learning. So it is important to help children say what they need to say in the best possible way, not with pressure, and hardly all in one day. But attention must be paid to the child who cannot yet manage alone. It is important, for example, in the case of the child who always says, "I want dat," no matter what the object, that a teacher respond with an explanation of his desire— "Oh, you want the box of crayons on top of the shelf," or "You want to try on my ring,"—and then give the desired object to the child. But, as trust increases (you *will* give him the desired object), try urging the child past the rut-like "I want dat," toward expressing his or her wish. "Tell me its name. I don't know what you want," or "There are many things over there. Which one is the one you want?" This requires patience and the building of trust, both of which take time. Children who are not reasonably at home with the syntax and vocabulary of the English language by kindergarten age need words and structures put into their mouths so they can try them on for size.

COMPREHENSION VERSUS PRODUCTION
OF LANGUAGE

Concern about children's *production* of language often blinds teachers to the part played by comprehension in the progress *toward* productivity. Early language learning begins with comprehension; studies of reading and language development also show that children listening to stories can understand a more difficult reading level than they would be capable of reading themselves. Kindergarten teachers, engrossed in extending children's language, may not realize that a first step in children's language learning at school is their comprehension of the teacher's language as well as the teacher's comprehension of theirs.

When Teachers Talk to Children

In communicating with children, teachers need to recognize the children's limitations. For example, language can be structurally simple or complex and still state essentially the same thought. Thus, a teacher can ask her class, "Who needs paper?" or "Does anyone need paper?" Or she can ask, "Is there anyone in the class who is working on a project for which paper is necessary?" In most kindergartens, the last question would be hard to follow. "Who" and "anyone" stretch most five-year-olds' egocentric "I" and "me" about as far as they can comfortably accommodate. Yet the capacity to follow and reproduce complex sentences does increase, primarily with age, but only when appropriate models are present in the language environment. It is from such models that children themselves pick up the exceptions, variations, and irregularities in the language. It is not at all accidental, therefore, that kindergarten children of highly educated parents are more comfortable with complex speech sooner than others, nor is it surprising that there is a 75 percent correlation between the spoken language errors of children and those of their parents.[16]

Above all, a teacher's language must be comprehensible in concept. No talking over children's heads! Neither concepts nor specific words need be at an artificially low level to be understood by kindergarten children. Neither are habitual endearments necessary. A teacher saying, "I want to show you something, Yvonne," is communicating in a friendly, personal, yet dignified manner. But when she uses

[16]D. L. Noel, "A Comparative Study of the Relationship between the Quality of the Children's Language Usage and the Quality and Types of Language Used in the Home," *Journal of Educational Research*, 47, *63* (November 1953), 161–167.

"sweetheart" or "honey" instead of the child's name, the communication becomes sentimental and impersonal, despite friendly intonations. But unfamiliar concepts and words do need the underpinning of concreteness and illustration (which, incidentally, is also true for adults who tackle new areas of learning).

The capacity to grasp concepts depends partly on one's stage of development (e.g., what can the concept of "democracy" mean to a preschooler?) and partly on experience (seeing enough insects leads to a concept of insect). Children are bound to be confused about many things a teacher takes for granted, but watching for the responsive signs of comprehension allows teachers to make necessary adjustments.

No Condescension!

A teacher's language must also be free of patronizing clichés or tricky phrases like "You are letting your golden moments go by," "Take the key and lock your lips," or "Put on your thinking caps," once standard clichés used with young children. They do not make sense. Some teachers also used to think that it was necessary to change their voices by adding a pinch of saccharin or adopting a condescending tongue-in-cheek tone in talking to children. Unhappily, one often perceives a condescending attitude and tone of voice on children's radio and television programs. This merely perpetuates the stereotyped notion that an adult cannot speak sincerely and simply to young children but must use extra and artificial endearments to communicate with them.

Talk to Children Eye-to-Eye

In talking to young children it is an act of courtesy for a kindergarten teacher to remember that she or he must find ways to be more nearly face-to-face with the children in order to speak to them directly and personally. Sometimes sitting on low chairs, and sometimes stooping when conversing with a particularly small child are both helpful. It is much more meaningful for children when a teacher makes it possible for them to talk face-to-face rather than face-to-legs.

Comprehension of Children's Speech

Equally important with being clear is the effort a teacher must make to understand what children are trying to say, no matter how inarticulate they may be. This reciprocity is not a mere matter of courtesy but the basic vehicle for language learning in childhood. Children assimilate language most easily when it is used interactively for the exchange of thought, feeling, information, or whatever, especially in reference to what interests *them*. They do not learn language well enough to use it creatively when content is subverted to mechanics and mechanics are unduly stressed. Language is a tool, and the usefulness of the tool is grasped early by children because they are so eager to understand the world. They value being involved with adults who relate to them around the issues that concern them. Look for every clue—facial expression, body posture, gestures, and quality of voice—to help inter-pret their words.

PRODUCTION OF LANGUAGE

Children tend to be highly motivated by their own emotional involvement in what they experience. Consequently, what they express may be a mere fragment of what the adult sees, a small part of the whole, or a distorted perception of what is actually there. The results of children's expressions, therefore, cannot be evaluated by adult standards. Children can only express meaning that is comprehensible to them in the light of their limited understanding and personal emphasis. Thus, the Maine lobster-man's child, who sees a picture of a lobsterman, says, "He hauls like m'dad." A slum child in the housekeeping area says, "You be the daddy and be the tough guy." A little girl asks her teacher, "Why do you wear earrings?" A five-year-old boy sings, "Thoughts in my head are moving," to describe his dreams. All are attempting to understand the meaning of their experience: What is the essence of *lobsterman?* Of *daddy?* Of *teacher?* What does *dream* mean? Kindergarten is a good place for enriching meaningful speech, but it must be done with good sense and respect for children. One small but vital part of the process is help in *extending* speech. A child says, "I found a button," and the teacher replies, playfully, perhaps, but pointedly, "A tiny red button with two holes is what you found." Or she plays games of de-scription. "I see something which is round and flat and black. It has a white circle in the middle of the black and there are letters printed on the white. There's a tiny hole inside that, at the very middle. What do you think it is?" (A record, if you didn't guess.) Children need to hear and be encouraged to pronounce extended, more precise, and better modified expression of their meaning.

Equally vital is the fact that language development is as dependent on chil-dren's having something to say and being urged to say it as it is on their hearing good models of language. The teacher's role in encouraging children to express thoughts and feelings, speculations and hypotheses, generalizations and questions, comments, observations, and evaluations is thus very important. If an adult's major responses to a child's work and comments are casual observations like "That's nice" or "Very good" and the spirit of relating is not really there, the children will see beneath the words to the absence of caring, and they will withdraw from mean-ingful communication. Having said all this, let us return to an earlier topic, the dis-cussion, since it is an orderly, often organized way of developing children's capacity to engage in reciprocal exchange of experience and thought with others.

TECHNIQUES IN DEVELOPING DISCUSSION

Unless they occur spontaneously, discussions should be regularly initiated and have a specific purpose, such as the planning of a program, the introduction of a project, orientation for a trip, summation and clarification of experience, or further probing.

Sometimes the discussion follows a topic that came up during a story, a question raised by a child, or an experience shared by all. The nature of the teacher's questions and his or her handling of the discussion will reflect the teacher's purpose.

The chief responsibility of the teacher, after making sure that the subject of discussion is interesting to the children and one to which they can contribute, is to lead children through thought processes by raising challenging questions. The teacher does *not* always give the answers! Sometimes he or she throws the children's own questions back to them in Socratic fashion if it is felt they are capable of working out the answer. Obviously, the teacher does not expect children to know facts which they have never learned. But relating facts to each other to form new understanding is something they can do with the teacher's help. Letting the children answer each other's questions and comments encourages exchange of ideas and genuine communication.

Since success of a discussion depends so much on the value the teacher places on its use in the curriculum and on the children's interest and capacity for expression, no formula can be offered that is suitable for every discussion. It helps to remember, however, that young children easily go off on tangents. One unimportant comment can trigger a long sequence of personally interesting but actually diverting episodes or comments, and drawing children back to the discussion at hand has to take feelings as well as logic into account. Furthermore, children do not always listen as enthusiastically as they talk, and teachers must keep the flow as interesting as possible to all. Children talk best and most effectively when they can discuss what they have seen, felt, heard, tasted, or smelled.

Whether it is for remembering together, straightening out misconceptions, thinking one's way to new questions, planning an experience, or just socializing, a teacher must know his or her purposes. Children need to use language in different ways, and discussions are a means of group communication that is a very necessary aspect of our group-centered learning.

There are several useful techniques for handling discussions. On the physical side, the children should be able to see and hear each other well, stretch their limbs, or move a bit. Sitting on the floor is sometimes less confining for them than a circle of chairs. Children known to have difficulty concentrating are best seated near the teacher. Putting together at the far end of the circle those children who are most likely to become restless is to ignore reality. At all times a teacher is conscious of the individual children, looking at each and referring to individuals by name as part of the conversational mood. Since young children tire easily from physical inactivity, which happens during discussion, a discussion period should not last too long. From ten minutes to about twenty minutes, depending on the particular children and the time of the year, may be considered a suitable duration. After the children mature more and their discussion skills are better developed, the discussion periods can be a little longer. The rules of taking turns, raising hands when the group is large, listening until a person has finished speaking, and keeping to the subject of the discussion are introduced one or two at a time at the beginning and are learned by practice and patient reminders from the teacher and children throughout the year. Some really courageous teachers have been known to help kindergartners carry on a discussion without any hand-raising. The fives of whom we speak learned to listen for cues and await their turn with much more sensitivity to each other than we usually assume such young children to have.

"What do you think of Ashton's idea, Betty Ann?" "Why did Molly think that, William?" "Did that ever happen to you, Lila?" "And then . . . and then . . ." Sometimes discussions are started by helping children remember what they experienced with their senses. "What did you hear?" "What did you smell?" "What did you see?" Or they can be started by summing up the high points of an experience and encouraging the children to discuss its meaning in other connections, developing relationships with other areas of knowledge or pinning down what else they now need to know.

TECHNIQUES IN STIMULATING
CREATIVE LANGUAGE

Teachers who listen note that four-, five-, and six-year-olds are still young enough to use spontaneous rhythmic chants and refrains. In the housekeeping corner a little boy or girl may accompany tender attention to a doll baby with repeated sing-song words which the teacher may jot down and then recall to the child later. The child may then want to enlarge such a fragment of a lullaby into a fuller composition, and the teacher or the child could recite it to the class. Or a group of children may use effective, repeated chants or refrains as part of dramatic play. The teacher could present the children's own rhythmic refrain as a beginning or an idea for a story or a play. Five-year-olds, being talkative and sociable, will not infrequently be heard saying: "Guess what happened!" or "You know what!" in a tone of newsy promise. They may then proceed with a lively accounting, engaging the attention of several children. The teacher may write down only the opening phrase and the highlights of such an account and then use these later as a spontaneous start for creative writing. Every nursery school and kindergarten teacher hears some original expressions, apt descriptions, and delightful poetic phrases which can be shared with friends. Such phrases, fragments, and fun words written down by the teacher and brought to the attention of children as creative language can serve as a start for creative writing—dictation, really.

The teacher can initiate creative writing by focusing the children's attention on sensory language. For example, one teacher said to the class, "Somebody told me that something was 'easy as pie'! Do you think pie is something easy?" Several comments about pie were offered, none indicating its "easiness." Then the teacher asked: "What do you think is easy?" And many thoughtful, original expressions and concepts of *easy* were offered by the children (easy as breathing, smiling at a friend, jumping, eating ice cream). The teacher wrote down the brief lines and the result was an "Easy Poem" that was continually edited by the children. A similar group literary expression might be achieved with: "What do you know that is little?"

or "Have you seen the dark?" The brief responses from children can be truly poetic and expressed in original words.

The teacher can also use as literary material an exciting event, such as fire engines speeding and clanging by, an injured or dead bird which the children found and examined, perhaps the capture and the caging of a beetle, or a local snowstorm that made working parents stay home. Suggesting an account of such an event will stimulate children to practice real narration and description.

Writing a letter or a report in connection with an interesting trip is also a good technique in practical composition that can at times become creative.

There will be many times when attempts at creative writing produce a great deal of repetition, dullness, or straying away from a set subject. Such failures or inadequacies need not be at all discouraging to the teacher, for better results may certainly come at another time under different conditions or with a different mood. Besides, this may be the time when editing which is not too strict is in order. Repetitions, unless they are poetic or patterned, should be eliminated ("You said that already"), dull or bare phrases can be amplified ("Tell me, Johnny, *why* Peter went home"), and straying can be redirected ("*That* will be another story; now you are telling about the airplane pilot").

Reading children's compositions back to them gives them real satisfaction and pride and stimulus for further composition. The fact that the teacher finds the children's creative writing worthy of reading to the group as regularly as books is often an incentive to further effort. If a teacher has mimeographing facilities a "book" may be compiled of selected group and individual pieces from the class to send to all the parents and thus further encourage practice by showing respect and giving status to the children's creative writing.

What is particularly cherished by preschoolers after their interest in creative writing has been established, is to have individual scrapbooks in which children secure their own poems and stories, attach individual decorations, and often add fitting original illustrations. Such a book of collected works will have deep personal meaning to the creator and will give the kind of satisfaction from tangible expression with language that contributes to maturity and learning. When a similar book is made of the group's expressions which the teacher has recorded and duplicated, each child will take home a valued part of herself and himself as a member of a group, and that, after all, is the meaning of communication.

REFERENCES AND FURTHER READING

CAZDEN, COURTNEY B. *Language in Early Childhood Education*. Washington, D.C.: National Association for the Education of Young Children, 1972.

CAZDEN, COURTNEY, JOHN, VERA and HYMES, DELL, eds. *Functions of Language in the Classroom*. New York: Teachers College Press, Teachers College, Columbia University, 1972.

COHEN, DOROTHY H. "Criteria for the Evaluation of Language Arts Materials in Early Childhood," New York: Early Childhood Education Council of New York, 1971.

COHEN, DOROTHY H. "Effect of a Special Program in Literature on the Vocabulary and Reading of Second Grade Children in Special Service Schools," *Elementary English*, February 1968.

COHEN, DOROTHY H. "Word Meaning and the Literary Experience in Early Childhood," *Elementary English*, 46, 7, November 1969.

CULLINEN, BERNICE E., JAGGER, ANGELA M., and STRICKLAND, DOROTHY. "Language Expansion for Black Children in the Primary Grades: A Research Report," *Young Children*, January 1974.

FASICK, ADELE MONGAN. "Television Language and Book Language," *Elementary English*, January 1973, 125–31.

GONZALEZ, PHILIP C. "Beginning English Reading for E.S.L. Students," *Reading Teacher*, November 1981, 154–62.

GONZALEZ-MENA, JANET. "Program for English Experiences: English as a Second Language for Pre-school and Kindergarten," Silver Spring, Md.: Institute of Modern Languages, 1975.

HAWKINS, FRANCES POCKMAN. *The Logic of Action* (rev. ed.). New York: Pantheon, 1974.

MANDELBAUM, JEAN. "Creative Dramatics in Early Childhood," *Young Children*, January 1975.

MATTICK, ILSE. "The Teacher's Role in Helping Young Children Develop Language Competence," *Young Children*, February 1972.

MILNER, ESTHER. "A Study of the Relationships between Reading Readiness in Grade One School Children and Patterns of Parent-Child Interaction," *Child Development*, 22, 1951.

NADLER, SHARI E. "Explorations in Teaching English as a Second Language," *Young Children*, 30, 6, September 1975.

NOEL, D. L. "A Comparative Study of the Relationship between the Quality of Children's Language Usage and the Quality and Types of Language Used in the Home," *Journal of Educational Research*, 47, 63, November 1953, pp. 161–67.

STRICKLAND, DOROTHY. "A Program for Linguistically Different Black Children," *Research in the Teaching of English*, 7, 1, Spring 1973. (Official Bulletin of the National Council of Teachers of English.)

WILSON, R., *et al.* "Bilingual Academic Curriculum for Navaho Beginners," Los Angeles: Consultants in Teacher Education, 1969.

7 The Meaning of Play in Children's Lives

Susan Isaacs, British educator and psychoanalyst, once made the following very penetrating statement about play:

> If now we compare . . . the more adaptable and intelligent animals with the less, for instance, the reptiles and fishes with the mammals, we notice something which throws much light on human childhood—viz. the fact that the animals which are able to *learn* more are also able to *play* more. Those with fixed and inherited instincts play not at all; the young behave as the old from the beginning, and there is nothing to add to the wisdom of the species. But the playing animals, and in proportion as they play, gain something of an individual wisdom. They are the curious, the experimental animals. The young lamb skips, but only for a short time, and soon settles down to sheep-like stolidity. Whereas the kitten plays on, and tries its way about the world with playful paw and nose, long after its size might lead us to expect a sober maturity. Those animals nearest of all to ourselves, the monkeys and the ape,

are like us in keeping the will to play even into maturity; but no animal young play so fully, so inventively, so continually and so long as human children.[1]

In the years since Susan Isaacs made that observation, there has been much evidence from careful studies in the wild and controlled laboratory research that she was right about the importance of play in the early growth of complex living creatures. Young primates initiate play without the encouragement of adults, spend much time and energy at play, and always stimulate peers to join in. Their play is frequently complex and appears to be significant for learning. Much of it is repeated over and over again and is usually pleasurable, although at times, as with children, it incorporates tension as well as pleasure. Significantly, there are no extrinsic rewards.[2]

Biologists tend to agree that play among primates is preparation for adult life and that lessons for the human child can be inferred. Among those who believe this is Harry Harlow, who has concluded that "no play makes for a very socially disturbed monkey" and that "monkeys (and children) need playmates to become functioning members of a social unit." Harlow is convinced that "play provides behavioral mechanisms by which activities for adult social functioning can be initiated, integrated, perfected."[3]

The existence of a biological base for the urge to play among "higher level" animals is affirmed for humans by cross-cultural studies of children. At every level of societal development, preliterate, or industrial, children play in startlingly similar ways that suggest a sequence of stage-related, self-initiated tasks and fantasies that may differ in detail but not in kind. " 'Playing house' is a rehearsal for adult roles by children round the world," says anthropologist Eleanor Leacock,[4] who describes how, as she watched little African girls pouring water and dirt back and forth in cans, she was reminded of a statement in the Nuffield Math Project. Originally written for and about children in highly industralized Western societies, the statement was just as apt for these African children.

> From the point of view of mathematical concepts, water play is important in establishing a basis of experience which will lead to the eventual and true understanding of volume and capacity. The children will be filling three-dimensional space and discovering relationships between containers.[5]

[1] Susan Isaacs, *The Nursery Years* (New York: Schocken Books, 1968).

[2] Frank A. Beach, "Current Concepts of Play in Animals," republished from *American Naturalist, 79, 785* (1945), pp. 523–41, in R. E. Herron and B. Sutton-Smith, eds., *Child's Play* (New York: Wiley, 1971).

[3] Stephen J. Suomi and Harry F. Harlow, "Monkeys at Play," *Natural History,* December 1971, pp. 72–75.

[4] Eleanor Leacock, "At Play in African Villages," *Natural History,* December 1971, p. 60.

[5] Margaret Read, as quoted by Leacock, "African Villages," p. 63.

Leacock draws on Margaret Read, another anthropologist working in an African village, for a description of dramatic play which sounds very much like the children we know.

> A perennial amusement among Ngoni boys of five to seven was playing at law courts. They sat around in traditional style with a chief and his elders facing the court, the plaintiffs and defendants presenting their case and the counsellors conducting proceedings and cross-examining witnesses. In their high, squeaky voices, the little boys imitated their fathers, whom they had seen in the courts, and they gave judgments, imposing heavy penalties and keeping order in the court with ferocious severity.[6]

Compare this with the play of urban children in an American kindergarten. Their models were different, but not the way they used the adult styles of meting out justice in their society as they saw it.

> Several boys are playing a game. Terence has all five boys with their backs to him and their hands up on the fence as if in a police lineup. Terence's face is grimly set and his teeth are hidden behind his scowl.
> "Put your hands up. Don't make a move."
> His hands moved down the children's sides, first their right sides and then their left. The boys squirmed in protest, but they did not move from the designated spot.
> "Keep still!" Terence's voice mocked some television, or perhaps real-life, police voice.
> "I didn't do nothin'," Gary whined in protest. "You can't arrest me."
> "Shut up!" Terence barked out, still not smiling. "Turn around, but keep your hands in the air." The five boys did as they were told. As they passed by the teacher, Rolando said to her.
> "Ms. Bly, we're being taken to jail. Help us," Rolando smiled faintly, enjoying his game.
> "What did you do?" the teacher asked, curious and bemused.
> "We robbed a bank," said Rolando.
> Meanwhile Terence had been behind them all, with his fingers pointed and ready to shoot if necessary. His face did not look as stern as it had previously. Perhaps he just wasn't able to keep his normally smiling face stern for too long a time.
> "Keep on walking till we get to the jailhouse!"
> When the children reached the cement turtle at the end of the playground, Terence held each one for Dwight to photograph. The apparatus was simple. All it comprised was an eye and Dwight's right hand. The prisoners sat patiently waiting for their turn to be photographed. Terence looked back at them every minute to make sure they didn't escape.
> All at once Juan jumped up from the bench and ran toward the other side of the playground. Terence looked taken aback. His face blew up. His mouth opened in astonishment, his eyes bulged outward and his tongue made an appearance.
> "He escaped. All officers go catch him. Catch him!"
> At this moment Terence himself took after Juan, forgetting all the others.

[6]Ibid., p. 61.

They got up laughing and started running all over the yard, shouting, "Catch me!"

The jailhouse episode ended and a game of tag began with Terence as the first "it."

THE NATURE OF PLAY

Play has, of course, long been considered a natural part of childhood. But "child's play" has tended to be a term denoting something trivial, not to be taken seriously, or at best, a way of releasing energy. Careful examination, mostly in this century, has revealed a meaning and depth in play that kindergarten teachers would do well to understand and interpret to the public.

Almost from the beginning of professionally serious child study, children's play has been investigated both by educational philosophers and psychologists. Depending on biases they may have had toward emotional or cognitive development, or the amalgamation of both, such investigators uncovered a variety of functions in play, none of which contradict each other and many of which overlap. The significant findings from our own viewpoint are the interrelatedness of physical, emotional, and intellectual aspects of play.

Susan Isaac's extensive observations and analyses, which appeared in two books in the 1930s, related play to total growth. She saw physical, intellectual, and social-emotional meaning all interlocked in children's play, and her classifications point to three major functions: (1) Play leads to discovery, reasoning, and thought; (2) play is a bridge to social relations; and (3) play leads to emotional equilibrium.[7] In our country, Hartley, Frank, and Goldenson formulated eight functions of play from their hundreds of observations: (1) to imitate adults, (2) to play out real-life roles in an intense way, (3) to reflect relationships and experiences, (4) to express pressing needs, (5) to release unacceptable impulses, (6) to reverse roles usually taken, (7) to mirror growth, and (8) to work out problems and experiment with solutions.[8]

All of these authors reflected a strong interest in children's inner lives, that is, in what children were feeling and thinking. They saw play as the way children worked through problems and conflicts and came to understand the things that concerned them. They studied play to learn more about children so as to give appropriate guidance to children and to those who worked with them.

Piaget is another major contributor to our understanding of play, but from a different perspective. Although Piaget realized the unity of the mental and emotional (cognitive-affective), his primary interest in children's mental development

---

[7]Susan Isaacs, *Intellectual Growth in Young Children* and *Social Development in Young Children* (London: Routledge & Kegan Paul., Ltd., 1930, 1933, rspt., and New York: Schocken Books Inc., 1972).

[8]R. Hartley, L. Frank, and R. Goldenson, *Understanding Children's Play* (New York: Columbia University Press, 1952).

determined his focus on the relation of play to cognitive growth. Piaget underscores that play is a basic means by which children strengthen their thinking capacities in several important ways. It was he who recognized that children are constantly trying to make order out of their environment by organizing and reorganizing it into patterns, or *schemas,* that make sense to them. Since they are constantly absorbing new information and experience, they are always in the process of altering these schemas, a process Piaget defines as learning.

Piaget discerned two aspects in the process: the one by which children conform to outer reality he labeled *accommodation*; and the other, by which information gained by adapting to reality is incorporated into already existing systems of thought, he labeled *assimilation.* These two aspects of a common dynamic he saw as reciprocal and often almost simultaneous in occurrence. When accommodation is in the ascendancy, play is imitative; when assimilation is ascendant, children are creatively involved in original use of information, that is, in dramatic play. Careful observation by teachers reveals the truth of this simultaneous and dual character of play. Without imitation, children would lack content for their play. But without creative imagination in using content, play does not become the children's own in the unique and personal way that acts as a spur to further learning.

Piaget also helped us understand the importance to learning of children's capacity to substitute one object for another as they play. This capacity to let something stand for something else Piaget calls *symbolic play* and regards it as the basis for imagination and learning.

Other psychologists who have pursued the matter of symbolic functioning for its own sake, unrelated to play, have arrived at the conclusion that play is in fact a means of resolving problems, because children set up "as if" situations and try out solutions until they find comfortable ones. Such work supports the early findings of Ruth Griffiths. One such psychologist interested in the symbolism of language writes

> The importance of imaginative play in a child's cognitive development is that it readily expands into exploratory and constructive play which, as it presents him with successive problems, demands the exercise of reasoning. . . . For instance, in playing with water, he explores its physical properties and is confronted with problems which he may try to solve.[9]

Piaget has made other important contributions to our understanding of play in the young child. For one thing, he points out that by playing with companions at their own stage of growth, children are forced to take into account the positions taken by others if they want to continue playing. Their egocentric views are thus challenged, and they are pushed toward understanding that there are perceptions of reality other than their own. Piaget considers this broadening of social perspective an important cognitive experience at the kindergarten stage.

[9]M. M. Lewis, *Language, Thought and Personality* (New York: Basic Books, Inc., Publishers, 1963), p. 126.

The psychoanalyst Jung was concerned with the relation between play and creativity. He wrote

> The dynamic principle of fantasy is play, which belongs also to the child, and as such it appears to be inconsistent with the principle of serious work. But without this playing with fantasy no creative work has ever yet come to birth. The debt we owe to the play of imagination is incalculable.[10]

It is a common belief among scientists and philosophers that playfulness is a prerequisite to creative thinking in any field. Philosophers and teachers know that an excess of imitation and conformity in childhood is likely to lead to conformity in adults. From all this it should be clear that the play of young children is far more than a release of energy or a waste of good time that could be spent more productively. Play is productive. It is the means by which children come to grips with reality, both of the external, objective world, and of their feelings and relationships. It affects their total development, and because it tends to be so physical and motoric, serious consideration is now being given to the effect of this physical activity on neurological development.

It has always been obvious that children climb and jump, tumble and roll, hop and skip for the sheer joy of movement and that they have a strong impulse to touch and manipulate materials. But neurologists and physical education specialists are now telling us that bodily control gained in play underpins the neurological integration essential for learning to read.[11]

So when children laughingly swing and chase each other, climb to the tops of structures and crow, leap from high surfaces, roll clay in their hands or hammer nails into wood, they are strengthening the neurological structures they will in time need for the less physical, academic learning our society values so much. Play is a totally integrating experience, and one that teachers of young children must take seriously. It is not accidental that children love to play. Play is in their own best interest.

Satisfying Many Needs

Let us now look at the way in which children's natural desire to play can be incorporated practically into the curriculum. We will use Susan Isaacs's classifications of the functions of play as baselines because, as a teacher of young children and a psychoanalyst, she had a rare combination of psychological insight into children's emotional and social needs and an appreciation of materials and activities that extend intellectual growth. Her formulations are particularly helpful to teachers and worth repeating: (1) Play leads to discovery, reasoning, and thought; (2) play is a bridge to social relations; and (3) play leads to emotional equilibrium. We shall explore the implications of each in turn.

[10] As quoted in *Natural History Magazine,* December 1971, p. 77.

[11] Matthew Kleinman, "A Central Role for Physical Education in Early Childhood," *N.Y.U. Education Quarterly,* Spring 1975, p. 22.

PLAY AND DISCOVERY, REASONING, AND THOUGHT

As children play they reach out to all materials available (whether natural or manufactured) and examine them, handle them, observe changes and possible uses, pull
things apart, and put them together again. How does this lead to discovery? Let us
take the simple, common experience of playing with water, referred to by others
earlier. Every youngster loves to dabble in water. Both boys and girls spend more
time at the sink than efficient washing calls for, splash in puddles with a fine disre-
gard of clothes, poke fingers into the opening of the faucet to see what will happen
to the flow, pour water back and forth into containers of different size and shape,
add ingredients to it, suck it up with a straw, and luxuriate in a tubful of water
when tired of floating toy boats and ducks on its surface. This is all play, truly
childlike play. But what does a child discover? He or she discovers the properties of
water; it can flow and take on the shape of any container, it can act with force and
push things away, it has weight and some things can rest on it comfortably while
others cannot, it can be mixed with some ingredients to make substances of different colors or textures, it has no color by itself but appears to be blue or green when
you see lots of it in some settings, it can form little drops or spread flat over a surface. Is not this discovery in an important sense? Do not all children learn this
without adult help through play? How many other discoveries they make in this
way depends of course on the number of things they may observe, touch, and
experiment with.

Let us see what happens beyond discovery in the play with water. On a little
mound of sand or dirt a child carefully pours a bit of water. It runs downhill.
Another time she or he spreads water just as carefully at the base of the mound,
and it spreads out and away or remains in a puddle. It does not go upward. The
child learns not only to recognize this as a phenomenon but to reason that water
apparently does not have an inner force of its own to carry it upward. After a few
attempts the child no longer expects that it will go up. Through trial and error and
experimentation, she or he arrives at a conclusion; the child reasons.

Normally any child will have a good deal of experience not only with water
but with other fluids as well. He or she pours milk or watches it being poured; or
spills it and mops it up. At some time or other, as every mother knows, a child
plays with it; makes bubbles in the glass, pours it from a small glass to a large one,
and puts a probing finger into the little milk puddle on the table and makes designs.
Or exploring elsewhere, a child pretends to be a painter and stealthily slips a brush
into her or his father's can of paint and quickly dabs at an empty spot on the wall;
she or he helps an older brother make lemonade for an outdoor stand, adds sugar
and watches it dissolve, and cautiously pours lemonade into a paper cup and sells it.
The child is playing all the time, but generalizations begin to form. Apparently
many things flow, take on the shape of their containers, can be mixed with other
ingredients, will spill, and so on. The child learns to generalize about fluids, without
even knowing the word *fluids*. She or he learns how to handle fluids for maximum

efficiency and begins to admonish younger children to be careful. Children *know* from their experience, and they can think and talk about what they know.

Here are records of play taken by kindergarten teachers in which one can clearly see discovery, reasoning, and thought taking place.

Darleen, who sat talking to her doll and handling her, reasoned out her problem, which was to dress the doll.

> She pulled some hats out of a box and searched in the box, looking, it soon became apparent, for turquoise shoes to match the dress of the doll she was playing with. She found two shoes, matched them together (for left and right), then searched under the doll bed. (They were apparently both for the same foot.) She banged her head against another child accidentally but continued to look under the doll bed.
>
> "I see it," she said to no one in particular, and she matched the shoe with another one to see if they were a pair. Apparently she was satisfied, because she began dressing the doll.

Sometimes reasoning emerges from needs developed during play, rather than out of the manipulation of materials. Here are two such episodes. In the first the reasoning went on even when it seemed to go underground.

> Axel dropped abruptly to his knees, saying enthusiastically to Julio, "Let's pretend this is the deep water all around. The shallow water is up here," showing with his hand on his chest how deep the water would be on him. Then, boastingly, "I once made a wooden raft and it could float." There was no response from Julio, who was lying prone on his back. Axel asked quizzically, "Are you sleeping or dead, Julio?" No answer. "What, are you in a graveyard?" No answer. But a moment later, Julio sat up and said, affirming a conviction, "I don't believe you could ride on your raft."
>
> "No, no," Axel reassured him. "It was a toy raft."

The second episode shows some really original use of known information among some four-year-olds who were playing near a tall block structure.

> Child on top: "I'm the teacher. If we play nursery, there has to be *one* teacher. You can't climb up here. You have to be babies."
>
> Second child, climbing up: "I'm the student teacher. They're grown-ups too!"

PLAY AS A BRIDGE TO SOCIAL RELATIONS

Much of the preceding dealt with play from the point of view of individuals who may or may not be involved with other children as they play with water or a wagon, stones and sticks, cans, or paper plates. But eventually a child wants children to play with because only children can communicate within the same dimension of thought that is meaningful to them. Only another child can see dishes in walnut shells or coffee in the seeds of wild flowers; only another child can understand that a big rock or an empty box is obviously a boat, or a plane, or the top of the tallest building ever built. The world of imagination and make-believe can only be peopled by members of the same generation.

The world of make-believe has an almost real quality for children, and they can pretend within a wide range of possible behavior. They can wish themselves anything they like, and play that it becomes a reality. They can pretend to be big, powerful, and authoritative, even if they really are only little children with very little power indeed. They can pretend that they are angry tigers, growling dogs, and fierce monsters or robots, even if in reality they are gentle and well-mannered boys and girls. They can try on for size the feeling of being a mother, a father, a street cleaner, or a truck driver. They can go back to babyhood or forward to adulthood, they can frighten others or be the thing they are themselves afraid of. This inner life of children we call their fantasy life and it represents an integral part of children's efforts to comprehend themselves and the world around them.

One case that beautifully illustrates the combining of inner need and outer reality is that of Freddie, who in a short span of time had to understand two very different environments—the Nazi Germany of his babyhood and the democratic America to which he came at age four. Freddie had the inner need to feel big and important, a leader and a force. His play reflected this effort to understand his environment in terms of his personal need. He would roll a piece of paper, toot-toot forcefully into it, and march around and around. Or he would take a long block, place it across his shoulder, raise his chin, and with undeviating glance march, march, march. One day, with a few children following him, he suddenly stopped before a keg and stood upon it. Then with a commanding glare he laid down his "gun" and made a short bombastic speech. Abruptly he climbed down and resumed marching.

After several months at an American school and the acquisition of some English vocabulary and American values, Freddie expressed that inner need in new terms.

"Look, I am so big now!" said Freddie with pride and purpose in his bigness. He stretched his body and placed one hand on his hair to indicate his height. He made a line on the teacher's waist, just where his head reached. Finally, to explore still further his own size, he stood back-to-back then nose-to-nose with other children to see how much bigger he was than they.

"I am a big boy now, yes," he reiterated.

"Next month when I am big," he said, tiptoeing and stretching his hands as high as possible, "so big, then—I be a father."

Yet to Freddie even being a father was not all. He was reaching out for other concepts of manliness.

"I am strong," said Freddie, flexing his muscles on arms and legs. "See?" There was a new look in Freddie's eyes now as he expanded his chest, held his head high, and smiled. "I am Joe Loui." He made heroic gestures with his arms and body. "I am Joe Loui."[12]

---

[12] Joe Louis, the heavyweight boxing champion of the 1930s and 1940s.

This drew an immediate response from two other boys. "And I am Joe Loui!"

"Me, too. I am strong." And all three Joe Louises walked around with powerful steps.

It was brave and good to be Joe Louis. The children carried chairs on their heads and tried to carry some protesting children. Finally they moved a couple of tables in preparation for lunch. "I carry it! I carry it myself," said Freddie. "I am strong. I am Joe Loui."

Freddie's concepts of American heroes and men challenged even Americans of longer standing than Freddie. He was successively Santa Claus, truck driver, and "union man." But the most significant thing occurred the day after Lincoln's birthday. Freddie came to the school yard and immediately made an announcement: "I am Lincoln."

He poked with his foot in the snow, contemplated a while, and was ready for action. He picked up a stick lying nearby and began digging in the snow with it, saying, "I am Lincoln. Lincoln is working now."

In due course this stick became a gun. Freddie put the gun across his shoulder and began marching briskly with it, saying, "I am Lincoln. Lincoln is a soldier." There was seriousness in his face, but lightness and change were in it too.

When the soldiering was done the "gun" was transformed into a "banner." Gaily now, Freddie carried it in front of him singing "Happy Birthday." His air of festivity and pleasure made the other children join him. They all sang "Happy birthday, dear Lincoln."

An hour later, inside the large nursery school room, a teacher was at the piano with the children gathered about. "I want to sing happy birthday, happy birthday to Lincoln," Freddie demanded loudly and confidently.

There was joy on his face as he listened to the music, to the children's chorus, to his own lusty voice. "Happy birthday, dear Lincoln," he sang.

The Lincoln idea grew as the day progressed. Before settling down for a nap, Freddie warned, "Don't call me Freddie. No. My name is Lincoln. Abraham Lincoln." The earnestness in his voice made one not dare to do otherwise.

When everything became quiet in the sleeping room, Freddie lifted his head and confided in an audible whisper, "Lincoln was a very good man. I am Abraham Lincoln."

Developing Friendships Out of Need

Working out fantasies through play is extremely important to preschool children. But they need each other to be most effective. How can a child feel like a "real" parent without a "real" baby? How can a child be a "real" pilot without passengers? How can a child feel powerful if there is no one to intimidate or subject to one's power? Thus the search for playmates begins, and the play is often a hodgepodge of different children's fantasy needs meeting, crossing, conflicting, or merging into the ideas of the theme they are pursuing. This is the crucible in which children learn to see others' points of view, but it is sometimes a painful pursuit, especially at the beginning of the school year, as it was for Ronald. As his teacher was observing the children so she could know them better, she caught sight of Ronald.

> He ran awkwardly, with pigeon-toed steps, to the far corner of the yard where the big red wagon was. He walked mechanically in two large circles around the yard, pulling the wagon, a determined, somber expression on his face, cheeks sucked in. He approached a boy, ran off, and then stood meditatively, eyes staring ahead, arms swinging back and forth. He approached two other boys, asking agreeably, "Want a ride?" They were busy climbing on the jungle gym and shook their heads. Ronald made several more large circles around the yard, pulling the wagon, occasionally sucking one or two fingers. Cautiously he observed a noisy, excited group that was involved in a large traffic jam of tricycles tied together. With a suppressed grin, he shouted, "Hey, I've got an idea. I'll traffic-control the place." He gave orders in a loud, high-pitched voice, but as the teacher moved in at this point to disentangle the traffic jam, nobody reacted to his suggestion.
>
> Five minutes later, Ronald was standing in great excitement behind a step structure which he and another boy were pretending was a police station. In a high-pierced shriek he said to Igor, one of his best friends, "I won't let you in because you wouldn't come to my house yesterday." Igor moved threateningly to come in anyway, and Ronald ran off waving his arms while Igor taunted him: "Scaredy cat."
>
> Ronald: "I'm not scared. I'm just trying to see if you can catch me."
>
> At this point, Igor went into the structure, with Ronald watching from a healthy distance. Igor lost interest and moved off. Ronald wandered alone, blinking his eyes and shuffling his feet. He picked up a jump rope, handled it, and shook it. The teacher asked him whether he would like to try jumping. His immediate response, with a sly smile, was, "I can't. I tried once." He ambled to the basketball net, where a teacher and two boys were throwing balls. His eyes followed their activity, moving quickly, his hands hanging limp. At the end of the outdoor play, he was again slowly and mechanically pulling the wagon around in large circles, and obediently he put it back in its corner when the teacher asked the children to clean up.

Ronald was going to need a lot of help from his teacher, and of course in time he got it.

In Harry, who needed help of a different kind, we see a child at another stage of the effort to play with others. He has succeeded in entering the play but struggles with maintaining it.

As Harry tries to incorporate children into his play ideas, he faces frustration because of his inept tactics and must finally modify the form but not the essence of his relationship with the children. At first Harry pushes and shoves several children who scream and attract the teacher's attention. She discovers three children cornered behind a table and box in the housekeeping area, pleading to her in a chorus of complaint. Harry, standing guard over them, is now on the defensive.

"But they are in *jail*—I have to keep them in jail!" Harry asserts. The teacher must see both sides, including this jailer's.

She says to Harry, "When you want to play jail, get people who *want* to play jail with you," and she watches Harry carry out this advice as he continues his game. He promptly turns to the imprisoned children in a matter-of-fact manner:

"Do you *want* to be in jail?"

"No," they answer grumblingly.

"Let's let them out then," says the teacher, and together with Harry she pushes the table and box away and releases the victims. Harry continues playing jail and follows the teacher's suggestion for a way of obtaining prisoners. He comes over to every active group of children in the different areas of the room as well as to Brad, a released prisoner who is working on a puzzle by himself, and asks:

"Do you *want* to go to jail?" And the children, scattered as they are in the room—some painting, some building, some listening to a story—all hear Harry's question and answer definitely, "No." Harry is finding out that other people have interests and wishes as well as he.

"They all don't want to go to my jail," he says to the teacher. The teacher looks interested. "Should I ask them again?" Harry asks. As he goes around canvassing the room this time, Harry changes his approach. He adds an appealing note to his voice and manner and qualifies his question with an implied promise: "Do you want to go to jail? *It's nice.*" Though not as decisively this time, the children still decline—all except Anita. She is such an easily led person that she cannot say no. Harry grins with a sense of victory as Anita looks hesitant but follows him. When she gets to the jail area, however, she suddenly changes her mind, turns around, and escapes from jail before even entering it! Harry is now really distressed; after all that work—defeat. He makes a plea to the teacher and they face reality together.

"Nobody wants to be in jail," the teacher points out simply. "Why don't you ask them to play something else?" she suggests, since it is apparent that Harry has an urgent need to play with a group of children and to lead them in some way. He cannot manage such social activity himself and accepts the teacher's help.

"Okay," Harry agrees promptly, "I'll ask them to be cowboys on my ranch."

"Fine!" The teacher is very hopeful about Harry.

"Who wants to be a cowboy?" he asks, with confidence in his voice and an appropriate swagger. Nickey and Billy and Johnny promptly come up with a "Yippee!" And Harry shouts "Yip-pee!" swatting an imaginary horse and leading the others to the ranch, which is on the site of the former jail and is indeed the same structure slightly altered.[13]

The Ongoing Pursuit of Friends

One of the reasons kindergartners change their friendships through the year has to do with their outgrowing old needs and discovering new ones for which different companions are suitable. Thus Marie, who was content to be Binney's baby for weeks, wants very much to be mother. If Binney agrees, they reverse roles. But if Binney still must be mother, Marie goes off to find a willing baby. When Jack no

---

[13] Marguerita Rudolph, *Living and Learning in Nursery School* (New York: Harper & Row, Publishers, 1954), pp. 53–55 (out of print).

longer feels the need to prove his strength by bossing timid children, he finds the courage to share ideas with other strong members of the group and changes his choice of play partner. As Mercedes gains confidence from her relationship with a compassionate and gentle Cora, she extends her friendship to include Lavonia, who is more brusque but stimulating in her relationships.

Thus, by sharing both their outer and inner lives in play and by exchanging ideas about the world as well as acting out feelings about their place in the world, children learn from each other. They become sensitive to how far they may go with different children; how much of their own needs they give up for the sake of holding on to companions; which techniques work and which do not. In short, their play inevitably leads them to people and to ways of getting along with people. That is why Susan Isaacs described play as a "bridge to social relations," and Piaget pointed out that play helps to decrease children's egocentric view of the world.

PLAY AND EMOTIONAL EQUILIBRIUM

Few adults remember in detail the play experiences of early childhood. But most do remember the play of their middle childhood years. In this period, the self-directed, unsupervised play of childhood leads to the same sense of well-being and satisfaction that it does earlier.

Elementary school children are eager for a change when they leave their school, and it is important that they have an opportunity to achieve this change through play. The play may consist of traditional games with strictly observed rules, or dramatic play reflecting a particular culture and time, or some inventive activity incomprehensible to an adult. Typically, such play represents children's own choice and initiative and has a physical as well as emotional component. The exact form of the play may well depend on the opportunity of the day, as in the following:

A small group of boys and girls on their way home from school stopped to peer through the fence around the playground of an afternoon preschool still in session.

"Those kids are lucky—they can play!" said a third grader to the teacher who came over to greet them. Since the teacher was about to take the class inside, she allowed the "big kids" to come in and use the playground for a while. She could see from the window with what boundless energy and enthusiasm the children played!

They used the slide with outstretched arms and legs; they constructed a high-rise building with boards and hollow blocks; one sifted sand attentively by himself; another operated an imaginary steering wheel on a "truck"; and two embarked on a distant journey in an old row boat. They were obviously doing "what comes naturally." Although they were reluctant to leave when this special play time was over, there was unmistakable satisfaction in their relaxed and cheerful good-byes.

Their uninhibited play, whether exuberant or quiet, was a needed change from sitting still, following directions, doing what you are supposed to. Their play was a relief and an expression of imagination and feeling.

This is what happens to younger children, too. Of course they argue and become upset as they work things out with others. But in general there is release of tension and a deep sense of satisfaction as they succeed in leading, planning, arguing, sharing, demanding, giving, hating, and loving.

Emotions are an integral part of learning, whether the learning takes place through play or through formal lessons, whether feelings are positive or negative. Margaret Lowenfeld, like Susan Isaacs, addressed herself to the emotional aspects of play on the basis of her observations of children. She wrote

> Without adequate opportunity for play, normal and satisfactory emotional development is not possible. . . . [Play is an] essential function in the passage from immaturity to emotional maturity. . . . Any individual in whose early life these necessary opportunities for adequate play had been lacking will eventually go on seeking them in the stuff of adult life.[14]

Even Piaget, the master of the cognitive experience, respected the importance of emotional development.

> Affective life, like intellectual life, is a continual adaptation, and the two are not only parallel, but interdependent, since feelings express the interest and value to actions of which intelligence provides the structure.[15]

Only as teachers recognize that no one grows or learns without some kind of emotional involvement will they be able to recognize when emotional factors impede or support learning.

PLAY AND PERSONAL NEEDS

Sometimes the connection between a specific need and the way in which it is worked out in play is fairly clear. This was the case with Linda.

Linda's teacher was aware that there were complications at home for Linda and that the family had moved recently. The following play episode came as no surprise.

One morning while no one was in the housekeeping area, Linda came in and took charge. First she very busily pretended to cook some fried eggs on the stove and told another child who came in, "You've *got* to eat them. You eat it all up." The other child first complied, but soon refused and finally escaped from the scene. Linda then pulled at the teacher, saying, "*Sit* down and eat those eggs—I cooked them for you." Her eyes blazing with power, she was flinging her arms and snatching things up in a managerial fashion. "We've got to move," she suddenly announced, "get everything out of the house." And with considerable strength she

---

[14]Margaret Lowenfeld, *Play in Childhood* (New York: John Wiley & Sons, Inc., 1967) pp. 321–22.

[15]Jean Piaget, *Plays, Dreams and Imitation* (New York: W. W. Norton & Company, Inc., 1962), p. 205.

began pushing furniture into the room proper, throwing boxes and doll clothes after them. Everyone in the classroom stopped to look at the unusual commotion in that area, and the teacher approached Linda with words of restraint: "Don't take everything out. It will be hard for us to put it all back." But Linda's zeal and imagination were in full operation as she answered: "I said everything out—this is moving. Everything is coming out and I am not putting it back!"

Several other children promptly, almost automatically, came to Linda's aid and support. "Let's get going with the moving, men," came from Larry and Peter as a bed was carried out. "I see," the teacher said, "I'd better get the broom and mop ready to clean as everything is moved out." The teacher and the children commented on the completeness of the moving. "Linda did it." "Linda wanted to move." "It's a real moving day." While the teacher was helping with the cleaning, the movers were at work bringing furniture back into the housekeeping corner. Alice became particularly interested in a different distribution of furniture, and some other children gave advice on where to put things. Linda took some part in the arrangement of pots on the stove but without much interest. Her special play, her particular satisfaction, came from having *done* the moving, for she had at the same time done something about a deep concern.

PLAY AND EMOTION

Just as play makes healthy use of emotional content, so when emotion overwhelms a child because it is too much to understand or too strong to express, the play can be unimaginative or even nonexistent. Some light was thrown on the relation between play and emotions during World War II, when large numbers of displaced and orphaned children were studied for their responses to deprivation.[16] In one residential nursery in England, a fairly young child, both of whose parents had been killed in a bomb shelter, was placed under the care of a warm and friendly matron. The child did very little, did not speak, and betrayed no emotion in his facial expression for eighteen months. One memorable day, after tentative play with building blocks, he constructed a bomb shelter. Suddenly he ceased his building activity and turned to the matron to speak at last. "Does it hurt to die?" he asked, at long last able to deal with his shock and pain.

It is not often that a child is overcome by such tragedy that he loses all capacity for expression, even the normal urge to speak and play. But it does happen that children who are distressed beyond the ordinary find it hard to lose themselves in the world of children and materials outside themselves. Absorbed with their inner problems, they either do not play or tend to play out repetitively the one theme which absorbs them so fully. Where the problem is obviously not paucity of experi-

---

[16] Anna Freud and Dorothy Burlingham, *Infants without Families* (New York: International Universities Press, 1944); *War and Children* (New York: International Universities Press, 1943).

ence, which can also lead to nonplay or poor play, and where sufficient time has elapsed to assume that the lack of play is more than a cautious adjustment to a new environment, the careful teacher does well to note which of the children in the kindergarten are participating only minimally or not at all in the play activities. This is often a major clue to maladjustment, which can only be better understood by further observation of the child and examination of his or her life situation outside of school. But a more common challenge for us adults is to be sensitive to all children's need for play and to provide the time, suitable safe materials, and accepting atmosphere for play as part of the daily life.

NOTE

For *References and Further Reading* see those listed at the end of Chapter 8.

8 Play in the Curriculum

PLAY REFLECTS THE DIMENSIONS OF EXPERIENCE

Symbolic play enables children to transform the world, as it were, in a manner they find self-satisfying because it fits their level of understanding at a given point of their experience. If their experience is limited, they will have little to play about. If it is full, their play can be rich. Note, for example, how well three five-year-olds in this inner-city public school have caught the essence of a common childhood experience. The children are in the house corner.

> Mary Lou, standing at the stove, says to the two girls playing with her, "Gimme the plates, y'all. Gimme the plates." Her two "babies" are crawling around on the floor, making infant noises "baaa/paaa . . . mamamamama." Mary Lou crouches down and talks to the babies: "Go and get your coats." Then she "fusses" with the dishes at the stove. The babies, ignoring the command, continue to crawl around. She takes milk bottles (wooden) from the

refrigerator and gives them to the "babies" who begin to drink from them. By this time, one baby is in the high chair and the other is still on the floor.

The mother says to baby 1: "What do you want to be?" Baby 1: "I want to be the baby." Baby 2 says: "I don' wanna play" and goes away.

The "mother" sits down to eat at the table, putting plates and cups on it. Baby 1 joins her. Mother begins to eat and baby 1 says, "You have to *give* me food. I'm too little."

Mother moves closer to the baby and begins to feed her with a spoon. Baby grabs the spoon and, in true one-year-old fashion, fist clenched around the spoon, begins to feed herself. When the mother wrests the spoon from her, she begins to "cry," face contorted and wailing loudly. The baby then slips off her chair, crawls around angrily under the table, flailing her arms and banging on her mother's knees and lap with her fists. She then retreats under the table again and crawls away, out of the mother's sight.

The mother, during the baby's misbehavior, shows signs of annoyance and resignation on her face. Her body is still, she neither chases the baby nor attempts in any way to restrain her. "I ain't playing," she announces, finally, to the air. At this point, the baby peeks from around the cubby into the mother's line of sight, and mother says, resigned, "This is the last time I give in to you. Now what you doin'?" Baby: "I want to be the baby. I go to sleep."

Children Who Do Not Play

But not all children play this way, adapting their life experience to their own understanding. In today's kindergartens, there are likely to be several children who wander aimlessly or get into one aggressive episode after another, who can't, or won't, or don't settle down to play. Two major causes will be suggested for the inability of some children to play constructively and imaginatively as children need to play in order to develop socially, emotionally, physically, and intellectually.

Limited Experience

The first cause, inadequate variety of life's experience, occurs when the parents live somewhat limited lives. In most instances this results less from lack of normal intelligence or lack of love for the children than from a cultural style in which life revolves almost exclusively around the everyday facts of survival. This happens when extreme necessity leaves no room for anything else; or continues as habit where necessity is no longer the major factor. Such people may never have had the opportunity or impetus to stretch beyond their survival needs for daily activities. When they become parents and their own lives, for whatever reason, are limited, they often find their children's questions a source of irritation rather than an incentive to teach them new things. Such parents can be seen on the streets, buses, and subways shushing their curious children but neglecting to answer their questions. Without meaning to, they pass on to their children the same heritage of repressed curiosity, the same lack of development of a wide range of interests that they suffer from themselves. Children of such parents can be serene or troubled, pleasant or obnoxious, well-fed or malnourished. What characterizes them in kindergarten is the meagerness of their ideas, a meagerness which is reflected both in conversation and in play. Often, too, they are unable to concentrate for too long on any idea or to see the development of an idea through to several levels in play activity. Or their play may be confined to a few familiar themes or materials. They are most likely to prefer physical activities, such as climbing, running, riding tricycles, or swinging, which do not demand much mental or emotional input. Their imaginative play, when it does occur, is likely to be repetitive and simple, a narrowly circumscribed rendition of a narrowly circumscribed life style.

In one kindergarten, where the teacher had finally stimulated curiosity and interest in a number of such children, a mother who preferred an inactive "good" child, came to complain. "What have you done to Lisa?" she said bitterly. "When she first started school, she would come home and go sit in front of the television set. Now all she does from the time she comes home till late at night is ask questions, questions, questions. She's such a pest I have to put her to bed a half-hour earlier."

Should such a parent come your way, invite her or him in to join the activity in your classroom so she can be stimulated along with her child.

Our Technological Life Style

The other major cause of inadequate play, one that affects children of all socioeconomic classes, is the as yet little-understood impact of television on children's play. Research has thus far given us only the obvious information that TV cuts into children's playing time. But many teachers who have been in kindergartens over a span of years have noted changes in the quality of children's play that they attribute to the effect of television. Teachers have complained to the authors that many children do not know how to develop ideas of their own in play, that they use television characters for leads to play which more often than not consists of aimless running around and violent gesturing. Kindergarten classes differ, of course, and so do individual children. But it is perhaps not coincidental that a loss of imagination among children has been mentioned by teachers at all levels of schooling. It is not unreasonable to assume that the inability to make believe is related to the amount of time children spend being entertained passively rather than entertaining themselves. The habit of drawing on one's own resources to set up "as if" situations doesn't seem to get started if there is excessive exposure to watching others acting out. And we do know that young children watch TV anywhere from two to seven hours a day weekdays, and even longer on Saturday.

Be that as it may, there seem to be more children than ever who need help from their teachers in developing ideas through play and play materials. Teachers now seem to need techniques for stimulating play when it is not forthcoming. They can no longer, in most instances, simply provide materials and let the children go to it, as was once the case.

Here is how one teacher tackled the problem when a group of four- and five-year-olds from a child care center returned from seeing the seals at the zoo and failed to work through their understanding by playing it out dramatically and symbolically:

> To start the children off, the teacher sang songs she made up about swimming and diving seals. She encouraged the children to climb onto chairs and dive from them to the "pool" (the floor). The songs she sang dictated the action— to swim, dive, use flippers, bark, catch fish and so on. The children were hap- pily involved in this dramatization of what they had seen, but were not them- selves inventive.
>
> The second time they played the game, a few days later, was at the request of one child. It was again highly directed by the teacher with mostly a repeti- tion of the first actions. Two days after that, when a child requested the seal play, the teacher was deliberately less directive than during the two previous times and found that the children were able to carry out quite a bit of play themselves, differentiating the seal's movements, rolling, sliding, barking, sleeping, eating, balancing and doing "tricks."
>
> One child, who was a constant "hitter" in the class, hitting in toddler fashion at anyone and everyone who happened to brush by, did not once hit anyone during any session of playing the "seal game." Involved in the role and the action, he quite forgot to be himself, or possibly got closer to his true self.
>
> The class goody-goody, replete with ring curls which her mother finger- twisted every morning, took on the role of the "mean seal," barking, bump- ing, grimacing and threatening all the others. On the other hand, the two most aggressive, acting-out girls in the class sat limp and passive through all the "seal games"—one on the teacher's lap as she sang, the other on the assis- tant teacher's lap. By acting as a spur, this thoughtful teacher stimulated the children to deal with their thoughts and feelings.[1]

The same teacher, on many another occasion, dealt imaginatively with the need of the children for help as she guided their play about powerful, wild things into constructive channels. Here are her notes on what she did in one such instance:

> Monster play often took place outdoors. One child would be the monster and walk like Frankenstein after the other, who screamed and ran away. After a few minutes, those chased away would come back for more chasing by the monster. It was a game that was played very often.
>
> Sometimes I read *The Giant Story*[2] after we came indoors, and that seemed to give the children the opportunity to switch their strong feelings from ac- tive play to the book (an attempt on my part to stimulate their ability to symbolize). I also read "The Three Little Pigs," which seemed to have a lot of meaning for them in situations of this kind.
>
> In December, the children got into *Wild Dog* play, which in some way be- came a vehicle not only for the expression of deep feelings, but for the forma- tion of a subgroup. One day, Rosemarie, D'André and Will were racing and chasing one another in the room. I asked Will, "What game is that?" He said, "I don't know." I asked Rosemarie. "He's the dog," she said, pointing to D'André.

---

[1] Courtesy of Nancy Balaban, Bank Street College of Education.

[2] Beatrice de Regniers, *The Giant Story* (New York: Harper & Row, Publishers, 1953).

I tried to structure their thinking. I made a "house" for the dogs and suddenly there were three instead of one dog—it was too crowded. The "dish" I provided got thrown in the general melee of tumbling "dogs."

So I got a roll of string and told Rosemarie that she could take her dog for a walk and teach him to obey—to sit, to listen to her, to do peepee outside. I tied a string to D'André's belt. Soon everyone wanted to be a dog or an owner.

Neil was James's dog (sometimes out of bounds). Cleon was Debbie's dog (he is afraid to go out at home because of a neighborhood dog!). Anna Marie (the goody-goody, bad seal) was Jane's aggressive acting-out dog. (Anna Marie was a bad dog and Janie a good owner.)

Denise did not get involved until nearly the end of the play when Anna Marie's dog ran away from Jane and Denise replaced her until she (Anna Marie) "reformed." (It was Denise who cried real tears when a strange dog came into our play yard this morning.)

All owners walked their dogs—some petted, some instructed them. General peace and total absorption describe this spontaneous group activity, which went from chaos to involvement in three minutes. There was a total tone change in the room.

I was saying things like "Feed your dog," "Teach your dog to roll over, to walk," etc. General control was exhibited as if this was the major fact of life at that moment. One could not always tell the controller from the controlled because there was an emotional merging of roles.

After some moments of walking, etc., I felt that the group needed more with which to contrive the play. (This might not be the case in a more middle-class type of group.) I took the book "Dogs, Dogs, Dogs" and the flannel board I had made to accompany it. I tried to organize a dog show. No go. So on to the book. (Anna Marie sat in my "reading chair"—refused as a bad dog to let me sit there.)

I used the book and the flannel board for children to speak and imitate the actions of the dogs. They were very involved.

The story was over, but everyone was still "doggy."

I decided to sing—"I got a dog, you got a dog, all God's chillun got dogs . . ." This way the action kept going—rolling over, sitting up, lying down, etc.

Time grew short. I told the children the dogs would have to turn into children to go home. We took off the "leashes" but Debbie wanted to take hers home even though she was an owner, not a dog.

It seemed to me that the play dealt with several ideas and feelings:

1. Dogs are scary but controllable;
2. A real dog came today and scared some kids;
3. The child most fearful was unable to play;
4. Many were playing out their own four-year-old struggle with controls —their own and in dealing with others;
5. This connects in some way with the high group interest in "The Three Little Pigs," "The Three Bears," and "The Three Little Kittens," all of which deal with fear—of the wolf, of the bears (of tampering with the bears' forbidden world), or of the thwarting of authority (losing mittens). They deal with elements *of control*: (Pigs run away and are safe in a sturdy brick house, Goldilocks escapes, the kittens assuage their mother's rage by washing their mittens.) Control of the wolf, the bears, the mama is accomplished by different means. Catharsis is the reward. The play was deeply satisfying to many children at once.

ENCOURAGING VARIETY IN CHILDREN'S PLAY

Quality of play, then, is a reflection of the quality of experience children have undergone. To the watchful teacher the themes that crop up and the way in which the themes are developed in play give clues to two important aspects of curriculum development: one, what the children are interested in, how much understanding they have, and what confusions and misconceptions they reveal; and two, what leads there are to teacher planning of trips, stories, pictures, accessory materials for play, discussions, and use of human and other resources in the community to further and enhance their knowledge and understanding.

Children in the kindergarten have been noted to base their play on as wide a variety of topics as their communities and contacts embrace. Typical themes include house, doctor, cowboy, space travel, trains, ships, planes, buses, circus, zoo, dentist, store, rabbi, going to church, weddings, parents' meetings, animals, fire fighters, sanitation workers (whom children still call "garbagemen"), and innumerable others. Lack of variety, meager content, conventionality, and endless repetition are signs that children need more exposure to firsthand experience that is comprehensible to them.

Children take from their environment what they are ready for, absorb it, and then give it back through play in the form they best understand. The essential fact for teachers to realize is that unless children's feelings and thoughts cover a reasonably wide range, there will not be much to express. A dramatic illustration of this was given many years ago in the experience of a New York City nursery school teacher who left her job among children of professionals, artists, and business people to work with the children of Tennessee mountain folk, whose lives were spent within the narrow confines of their meager shacks in an impoverished community. She came with materials and ideas that had proven useful with the city children. But she found that the mountain children were not as responsive to the materials, not as richly imaginative in the themes of their play, and not so intensely and eagerly involved in play as the city children had been. Although they were friendly children and loving to each other, their play remained locked within a few simple themes of the comings and goings of adult preoccupations.[3]

The teacher's role in developing play is thus not a minimal one, even if not direct and controlling. It is the teacher who makes it possible for the children to play at all by allowing time for it in the program, providing space indoors and out, and supplying materials and aid to the children in carrying out their ideas. We must therefore reconsider the common connotation of a "free-play" period being somewhat on a par with recess in the grades, and being of lesser importance than teacher-directed or "educational" activity. The free-play period in the kindergarten program is educational in the full meaning of the word, since it fosters growth and learning and serves as a guide to the teacher. Free play for children is not a free time for the teacher, although it may provide him or her with a change of focus and even with diversion.

HELPING CHILDREN'S PLAY
TO BE MEANINGFUL

The role of the teacher in guiding and stimulating children's play is subtle and intricate. On the one hand, teachers must be sensitive to the children's capacity to direct their own play, because too much direction by an adult tends to constrict children's imaginativeness. On the other hand, teachers must also be sensitive to children who have somehow never learned to develop or use their own inner resources and who need to be stimulated and encouraged to the point where they can carry on by themselves. Such procedures might have to be repeated many times in different play situations until the children learn how to play.

To support and nurture the kind of inner growth that allows a child to set up the "as if" situations so basic to the resolution of conflicts, ambiguities, and problems, three things are necessary. First is the careful selection of appropriate experiences which young children can understand and from which they can gather the necessary details they need for their play. Much of what goes into such experience

[3]Claudia Lewis, *Children of the Cumberland* (New York: Columbia University Press, 1946). This book is out of print but worth looking for in libraries.

is described in Chapters 9 and 11 of this book. The second is to supply the kinds of materials and props that allow the children the latitude they need to develop their play along lines that make sense to them. For example, children of minority ethnic backgrounds need a housekeeping corner that reflects their life style in such matters as utensils, arrangements, food (fake), and other props that support the adult working roles familiar to them.

And the third is the awareness of the teacher as to how to use himself or herself as a resource—whether consciously refraining from intervening as a matter of policy, intervening cautiously and intermittently as necessary, or practically stepping in in full force to direct and guide children who cannot yet cope by themselves. All three aspects of the teacher's role can bespeak sensitive responding, provided the major goal, in all approaches, is that the children shall ultimately be self-directed in their play.

"Play," says Lowenfeld, "is the fitting of the half-formed concept in the child's mind with a garment, not of words, but of representation."[4] This is the child's task, not the adult's, because it supports the child's internal growth.

Harriet Cuffaro, writing in *The Block Book*, clarifies this further.

> Dramatic play requires the child to: (1) create the context for play rather than finding it; (2) deal with reality and scale in translating ideas to the medium; (3) gradually step outside of self to a symbolized self in play.[5]

THE ROLE OF MATERIALS

For children to be imaginative, they need materials that are not too complete in form and function. They need materials that do not demand prescribed answers to prescribed questions, but allow them to perform mental operations as they use the materials in order to exercise their capacity to think. Materials that can be manipulated, shaped, or altered allow children to impose their imaginative conceptions of reality and relationships on them as they process their own steps to understanding. Such materials have an inner dynamic that needs to be sensed by adults (children sense it well). For example, wood, paper, pebbles, leaves, sand, twine, fabric, leather, plastic, tri-board, water-based clay, plasticine or plaster of paris all lend themselves to different uses because their malleability, density, weight, volume, or fragility are all different. Teachers also need to be aware that children come to materials at different levels of readiness for the potential the material itself holds. For example, some can only rip cloth but others can cut it straight; some nail random pieces of wood together, whereas, others visualize cutting specific sizes and shapes

[4] Margaret Lowenfeld, *Play in Childhood* (New York: John Wiley & Sons, Inc., 1967), p. 158.

[5] Harriet Cuffaro, "Dramatic Play—The Experience of Block Building," in *The Block Book*, ed. Elisabeth Hirsch (Washington, D.C.: National Association for the Education of Young Children, 1974), p. 72.

to make a preconceived whole; some sift sand through their fingers in exploratory fashion, whereas others shape it into a series of tunnels and mounds; some glue pieces of plastic together to form an accidental shape, whereas others use a coping saw to give plastic a new outline of their own.

Materials can be unstructured, like clay; semi-structured, like blocks; or totally structured, like a puzzle. There is room for all in the kindergarten, but teachers need to understand the possibilities in each. Certainly, the value of any play material is not in its cost, nor in its attractiveness to adults, but in the extent to which it allows children to put their own stamp on it.

Before closing the topic, we wish to stress that in this age of automation and highly developed technology, the choice of materials for young children and the encouragement of their imaginative play are especially significant. Technological progress is not necessarily good for young children's learning. A cautionary note comes from an authority on environmental design, K. Izumi, who points out that "the use of plastics to simulate wood, metal and leather, cloth and even plants sets up an element of doubt in our sensory perceptors that is inconsistent with what we instinctively feel the environment ought to be, creating an unconscious tension with our own technology."[6]

As a second caution, we note that young children have listened so often to the message of television commercials that there is always an easy way to do things (if you use the right cleanser, toothpaste, or whatever), that many are reluctant to exert energy in the service of developing their ideas. It is commonplace now that kindergarten children often seek the easiest way to do anything (or not to do anything). The matter of finding the *best* material or the *best* tool for a job, rather than the *easiest*, becomes an important aspect of the teacher's support of children's development in competence beyond the power to press electronically controlled buttons. For example, many teachers have allowed children to use the stapler indiscriminately instead of paste because the stapler is "easier" and less messy. Yet the use of paste helps develop an eye-hand coordination that grows sensitive to how much is a little and how much is too much, an understanding that enhances concepts of differentiation. As they select materials teachers must ask themselves whether they really mean to limit children's experiences in differentiating texture, form, weight, and so on by giving them mechanically "easy" tools that encourage a trend to push-button, remote-control power; or whether they mean to help children find their potential strength of body and mind by getting them to grapple with problems set by materials that will not do their bidding unless the children exercise some genuine control by their physical and mental involvement in the task. However, we do accept the practical usefulness of good tools, including staplers, scissors, hole punchers, rulers, pencil sharpeners (both handheld and attached) which kinder-

---

[6] K. Izumi, "Some Psychosocial Considerations of Environmental Design." Two lectures at the University of Waterloo, Waterloo, Ontario. Quoted in *An Introduction to Environmental Psychology,* eds. Ittelson, Proshansky, and others (New York: Holt, Rinehart and Winston, 1974), p. 6.

gartners can easily master. These should be available in class for controlled use relating to imaginative play.

If we could learn to trust children's instincts to play and help those whose instincts have been distorted, we would realize how play supports later academic learning. In all the decades of kindergarten classes when reading and prereading activities were not deliberately taught, teachers of the grades recognized that something was happening in kindergarten that was effective, because children who attended kindergarten learned better in the grades than children who did not.[7] The contribution of play in this connection cannot be overlooked. As Erik Erikson put it

The playing child advances forward to new stages of mastery.[8]

REFERENCES AND FURTHER READING

ALMY, MILLIE, ed. *Early Childhood Play*. New York: Selected Academic Readings, 1968.

ALMY, MILLIE. "Spontaneous Play: An Arena for Intellectual Development," *Young Children,* 22, May 1967.

BIBER, BARBARA. "Premature Structuring: A Deterrent to Creativity." New York: Bank Street Publications, 1959.

BIBER, BARBARA. "Play as a Growth Process," Publ. No. 4. New York: Bank Street Publications, 1959.

COHEN, DOROTHY H. "Children of Technology: Images or the Real Thing?" *Childhood Education* (March 1972).

COHEN, DOROTHY H. "Continuity from Pre-Kindergarten to Kindergarten," *Young Children* (May 1971).

COHEN, DOROTHY H. "Is TV a Pied Piper?" *Young Children* (November 1974).

COHEN, DOROTHY H. and STERN, VIRGINIA. *Observing and Recording the Behavior of Young Children* (3rd ed.). Chap. 4 on materials. New York: Bureau of Publications, Teachers College, Columbia, 1983.

CUFFARO, HARRIET. "Dramatic Play—The Experience of Block Building," in *The Block Book,* ed. Elisabeth Hirsch. Washington, D.C.: National Association for the Education of Young Children, 1974.

DE REGNIERS, BEATRICE. *The Giant Story*. New York: Harper & Row, Pub., 1953.

ENGSTROM, GEORGIANNA, ed. *Play: The Child Strives Toward Self-Realization*. Washington, D.C.: National Association for the Education of Young Children, 1971.

ERIKSON, ERIK. "Toys and Reason," Chap. 6 in *Childhood and Society*. New York: W. W. Norton & Co., Inc., 1950.

FRANK, LAWRENCE K. "Play Is Valid," *Childhood Education,* 44, 6 (March 1968).

---

[7]Willis E. Pratt, "A Study of the Differences in the Prediction of Reading Success of Kindergarten and Non-Kindergarten Children," *Journal of Educational Research,* 42 (March 1949), 525–33.

[8]Erik Erikson, *Childhood and Society* (New York: W. W. Norton & Co., Inc., 1950), pp. 194–95.

GRIFFITHS, RUTH.   *A Study of Imagination in Early Childhood and its Function in Mental Development.* London: Routledge & Kegan Paul, Ltd., 1935.

HARTLEY, RUTH E., FRANK, LAWRENCE K., and GOLDENSON, ROBERT M. *Understanding Children's Play.* New York: Columbia University Press, 1952.

HERRON, R. E., and SUTTON-SMITH, BRIAN. *Child's Play.* New York: John Wiley, 1971.

ISAACS, SUSAN. *Intellectual Growth in Young Children.* New York: Schocken Books, Inc., 1972.

ISAACS, SUSAN. *The Nursery Years.* New York: Schocken Books, 1968.

ISAACS, SUSAN. *The Social Development of Young Children.* London: George Routledge & Sons, Ltd., 1948.

JAMESON, KENNETH, and KIDD, PAT. *Pre-School Play.* New York: Van Nostrand, Reinhold, 1974.

LIEBERMAN, J. N. "The Role of Play in Cognitive Development," *Young Children* (September 1967).

LOWENFELD, MARGARET. *Play in Childhood.* New York: John Wiley, 1967.

McVICKAR, POLLY. *Imagination: The Key to Human Potential, #130.* Washington, D.C.: National Association for the Education of Young Children, 1972.

MILLAR, SUSANNA. *The Psychology of Play.* Baltimore: Penguin, 1968.

MOFFITT, MARY W. "Play as a Medium for Learning," pt. 3 of *Leisure Today, Journal of American Association for Health, Physical Education & Recreation,* Washington, D.C. Special issue on *Research and Thought about Children's Play,* 1972.

PERRYMAN, LUCILLE. "Dramatic Play and Cognitive Development," *Journal of Nursery Education,* 17, 4, September 1962.

PIAGET, JEAN. *Play, Dreams and Imitation.* New York: W. W. Norton & Co., Inc., 1962.

"Play: A *Natural History Magazine* Special Supplement," *Natural History Magazine* (December 1971).

RUDOLPH, MARGUERITA. *Living and Learning in Nursery School.* New York: Harper & Row, Publishers, Inc., 1954.

SCARFE, N. V. "Play Is Education," *Childhood Education, #39, 3* (November 1962).

SMILANSKY, SARA. *The Effects of Sociodramatic Play on Disadvantaged Children.* New York: John Wiley, 1968.

SPONSELLER, DORIS, ed. *Play as a Learning Medium.* #306. Washington, D.C.: National Association for the Education of Young Children, 1974.

STONE, JEANNETTE G. *Play and Playgrounds.* #123. Washington, D.C.: National Association for the Education of Young Children, 1970.

Films

PLAY AND CULTURAL CONTINUITY—4 films: "Appalachian Children," "Mexican-American Children," "Southern Black Children," and "Montana Indian Children." Sara H. Arnaud, Ph.D., Project Director. Campus Film Distributors, 14 Madison Ave., Valhalla, N.Y. 10595.

9 Exploring the Environment

Curious and ready for information, kindergarten children stop to stare at everything on their way to and from school as though trying to capture the essence of the civilization that surrounds them. Inside the classroom they dramatize signs of the outside world in their play. Their spontaneous conversation is concerned with people and materials in the environment they know.

Kindergartners are constantly seeking answers to the question *"How?"* "How does it work?" "How did it get there?" "How do you know?" Some of the answers they uncover by themselves, some come to them through television, and some are given by parents. The haphazard character of finding answers is considerably decreased in the kindergarten classroom, where the teacher consciously answers children's questions, reads them a story that gives answers, shows them a picture, or takes them to see the actual thing or person they are curious about.

A good kindergarten curriculum inevitably makes wanted or needed information accessible to children. Although the best way to do this is by offering opportunity for firsthand investigation, this is not always possible or necessary, and vicarious experience must be substituted. In either case any source of information to which a teacher deliberately exposes children must be simple, clear, and of course, accurate. Firsthand experiences in gathering information, such as trips and personal contacts, or vicarious experiences such as pictures and books, must be carefully chosen and developed so that they are completely comprehensible. Otherwise these sources will not prove useful in the special learning style typical of young children described in the chapters on play. Children must be able to pinpoint details, apply the knowledge learned in their play, and deepen their understanding through exchange with others.

THE IMPORTANCE OF TRIPS

As children leave the classroom to see the actual processes by which workers perform their tasks and as they recognize the distinctive uniforms or other marks of a trade, they use in their play the bits and pieces they pick up, digesting, assimilating, and raising further questions once they understand simple beginnings. The more obvious the nature of a person's performance the more dramatically fascinating it is to a young child. Imitable, it therefore can become comprehensible. This is why kindergarten children pretend to be mechanics, drivers of all kinds, or doctors rather than lawyers, judges, or accountants. From the nature of the play, a teacher can gauge how much children actually understand and can plan for further intake experience which leads to further dramatization through play and thus to an increasing comprehension of the world.

STARTING WITH CHILDREN'S INTERESTS

The first thing that concerns the teacher in planning trips is the range of children's interests and preoccupations. There must be some evidence to show which things the children themselves might want to know, and which they would enjoy if their attention were attracted.

A teacher learns to know this about the group by listening and watching. The children's comments and questions offer direct leads to possibilities for further exploration. But these direct comments and questions point only to areas children are articulate about. Dramatic play offers less direct but equally potent clues to children's interests, degree of knowledge, and concerns. Together, the direct and indirect forms of expression serve as prolific sources of ideas for curriculum enhancement through trips or similar projects. Groups differ of course in the number and quality of their interests. Sometimes a teacher quite deliberately takes the lead of the more advanced children as a starting point for pursuit of knowledge. Sometimes she or he may cater to two or three dominant interests in turn. Kindergartners on the whole are not usually likely to remain vitally interested in one topic (boats, trains, rodeo, farm, zoo, firefighters) for more than one week, so it is possible to enlarge their horizons in many directions.

Since we are suggesting that kindergarten curriculum should be influenced in large part by children's interests and needs, we should like to consider here one added factor in their growth that affects these, namely, the emerging sex roles that tend to divide some groups of five-year-olds into areas of interest that society labels masculine or feminine. This will vary with different geographic areas or regions, but the coming years may well reflect the influence of the growing liberation from stereotyped roles of both sexes. Teachers still find that in many communities girls generally play "house," while boys act out "manly" occupations. But as society's concept of what is masculine and what is feminine changes, boys and girls will probably play house together and share several hitherto "masculine" or "feminine" roles. For instance, recently in a suburban kindergarten, after an absorbing time with an intricate block structure, a tall energetic boy came over to the housekeeping area and proceeded casually yet imaginatively to pour, stir, and vigorously mix the contents of two pots on the play stove. Before long he was drying dishes and deciding on their right place in the cupboard.

As traditions change in the wake of social and legal changes, women will more frequently be seen as doctors, dentists, engineers, architects, police officers, letter carriers, builders, sheriffs, taxi drivers, and bosses. And men of suitable inclination are growing freer to enter the serving professions (traditionally "feminine"), including the teaching of young children.[1] Children understandably ape grown-ups; they accept the division of labor that they see and pick up the climate of change without being explicitly told. Thus, teachers are beginning to see boys who are interested in jump rope, who want to play the role of mother in dramatic play, or who enjoy prancing about in smocked dresses or other articles of clothing that society has labeled "feminine." In no way do these little boys seem confused about maleness. They may at other times play television "machismo" characters or practice karate. But the changing adult environment is giving them the freedom to try to feel what *girl* or *woman* means without any threat to their masculinity. Little girls have for a long time felt free to try out some male roles and modes.

We can be glad that today's boys and girls are growing up into far more fluid social relationships than those of their grandparents or even parents. Girls as well as boys need to have a good deal of the same kinds of socially useful information. A teacher might well ask, "But which of these many lines of interest shall I develop?" The answer is, as many as possible. It is important, however, that ideas gleaned from the children develop along lines of concern for society's needs and how these are met, rather than along the narrower lines of which sex does what job.

The first task of the teacher is to know what interests, misconceptions, and misinformation the children have. The next task is to decide the best way of satis-

---

[1] Shirley R. Rausher and Teresa Young, eds., *Sexism, Teachers, and Young Children* (New York: Early Childhood Education Council of New York, 1974). This 33-page booklet discusses different social areas and lists 85 references. Also see Barbara Sprung, *Guide to Non-Sexist Early Childhood Education* (New York: Women's Action Alliance, 1974).

fying interests, clarifying misconceptions, and correcting misinformation. Since children do learn best from the evidence of their own senses, trips planned to allow them to see, listen, smell, and perhaps touch become a significant means by which their horizons are extended.

TAKING A TRIP

At this point let us accompany a class on a trip and see just what happens. Here is a class of four-and-a-half-year-olds, quite excited about a train trip, an unusual experience these days. They are driving a short distance from school to a suburban railroad station, buying tickets, and traveling about fifteen minutes to a familiar neighboring town. How did it come about? What made the teacher decide on this particular trip?

According to her notes, Mrs. W. noticed Elliot's special interest in playing with the interlocking wooden trains and asking questions about the caboose (an intriguing word to children). The teacher's response to Elliot attracted several other children, which in turn prompted the teacher to show the class pictures of trains and of a caboose. This stimulated Shari to tell the group about her visit to the station to meet her daddy. The interest in trains mounted over a period of days, so that the whole class was talking and thinking about trains. The teacher brought in pictures of trains which were inspected by many of the children. Songs about trains and cabooses which the teacher had selected from her music books were especially enjoyed.

Two side interests developed. There was a thoughtful group discussion about transportation in general; this is a universal concern of children. They mentioned and commented on various vehicles including the hydrofoil and supersonic plane. There was also personal talk about the way daddies and mommies go to work.

So it was logical enough for the teacher and the children to decide on an actual train trip. The teacher realized that many children today have never ridden in a train, although they may ride in cars or school buses, be familiar with taxis, and have had experience with plane travel. Some of the children in the group knew that their fathers or mothers traveled to work on the train, and this added to the enthusiasm.

As a matter of expediency and out of consideration for the ticket seller, Mrs. W. purchased all of the tickets herself, but the children all watched her intently. If this had been an older group, closer to six perhaps, it would have been wise to take enough time for all or several of the children to have the experience of buying the train ticket—to transact business with the ticket seller.

The children in Mrs. W.'s class observed the entire station with care, and Tina exclaimed, looking at the telephone booth, "That's where my daddy calls my mommy to say which train he is taking."

"Where are the tracks?" Danny asked anxiously, since they were still in the station building and no tracks were visible.

Waiting on the train platform the children continued their scrutiny of the surroundings.

"I think that man is waiting for a train."

"And we are waiting for a train, too."

"There is the station."

"And there is the bridge we came over."

"When is the train coming?"

"I see the track!"

"Do you know what all those signs are?" the teacher asked.

"Advertisements," Tina answered immediately.

"Oh! Here comes the train!"

Now the nineteen children boarded the train excitedly and each wanted to sit by the window in order to have the double pleasure of knowing what goes on inside and not missing anything passing on the outside. Luckily the midmorning suburban train was quite empty, and it was possible to accommodate the children. Through the windows they were pointing to and identifying schools, lumberyards, and parks. Then Donald shouted, "I just passed my friend's house." Whereupon Danny started looking not only for *his* friend's house, but also for his friend. He finally conceded, "My friend isn't out playing today."

Elliot asked the teacher, "Why does a train whistle?" And he listened seriously as she explained the signal.

A group of them sitting together watched the conductor's gestures and expression delightedly as he punched tickets.

"Where are you going?" he asked the group.

"To Port Washington!" the children answered in chorus, and Shari asked the conductor:

"Is the next stop ours?"

When the class of small children and their two teachers arrived, the conductor helped each one step off the train onto the platform, and this pleased the children greatly. As they stood on the platform, they all waved heartily and smiled at the conductor, impressed with him as a real person, a specialized worker, and a representative of the responsible, orderly, safe, and fascinating grown-up world.

THE WAY CHILDREN SEE THINGS

It is hard for teachers to resist making a trip a thoroughly academic experience, telling the children in advance what to look for and pointing out the important things to see when they are actually at the site. Yet this is neither necessary nor completely effective. Children are eager learners, but they learn at their own pace what is important to them. For example, children tend to see what is on the ground, to which they are physically closer than we are; in general, they concentrate on what is at their own eye level. Children are interested in the active and dramatic;

adults tend to be sober and formal. Children have a limited capacity for absorption; adults have a far wider grasp.

Given their own orientation and their unique backgrounds, they may not see at all what the more sophisticated eye of the adult recognizes as important. How often has a group of young children been taken to see something "significant" and remembered only a kitten that they played with on their way! For this reason it is wisest to let the children learn in their own style and at their own pace. If subsequent discussion or the content of the dramatic play reveals that they have missed important aspects, then the trip can be taken a second time and even a third, for the children will see more and different things each time if they are really ready to absorb what is there waiting for them.

Learning cannot be forced, and real understanding has to be directed toward something a child already knows. It is better for children to learn a little at a time than to be overwhelmed with too much and to be anxious about pleasing the teacher as well. Fortunately, the kindergarten curriculum can be largely a self-stimulating, creative experience for every class and teacher.

In the following thank-you letter sent by a teacher after a trip to an agricultural school farm, notice the differences in what adults and children chose to stress as a result of the same trip, and the differences in their mode of expression.

Dear Mr. C.:

Our class trip to the Farm last Wednesday was enormously interesting and pleasant to *all* of us—the twenty children, two parents, two teachers and one student teacher. I'd like to mention some of the things that were especially impressive and were talked about. First and most impressive was Jimmy, the high school student guide whom you assigned to us. His natural enthusiasm about every aspect of farming, and his knowledge about the soil, the fields, the trees, the orchard, the planting, the harvesting, every bit of machinery and even the costs and all the agricultural timing were fascinating! He answered every question—and we were asking them all the time! His friendly way with all the small children, and his tender yet practical regard for the animals were very important to the children. The grown-ups were very impressed with Jimmy's concern with cleanliness and order on the farm.

The children certainly enjoyed coming back to school laden with stalks of rye, handfuls of colored chicken feathers, and most especially, with the freshly laid, still warm egg which every child felt. Everybody also appreciated tasting little chunks of asparagus which Jimmy cut for us. "Tastes like raw peas," one of the children said.

The next day we were, of course, talking about the farm, and what each person liked. These were the children's comments:

"I liked the rooster best."

"I liked to see the bunny—he was sleeping."

"I liked the horses."

"Remember the horses' teeth!" (Jimmy's explanation of how *healthy* the horse Bill's teeth were in spite of the grass stains, was very interesting and amusing! Jimmy had obligingly pulled the horse's lip up so the children could see the large teeth.)

"The horse has such a long tail."

"I remember the great big tree-bush with the roots. The boys had to dig it up to plant it" (referring to a transplanting job that was in progress and which Jimmy had explained to the children).

I told the children I was going to write a letter to the farm and they said, "Tell the farmer that we are going to *eat* the egg we brought from the farm— we'll have it hardboiled and cut up into little pieces."

"You should say in the letter 'thank you for the egg!' "

They all had fun playing with the feathers, brushing and tickling each other and themselves with them. So you see that for these four- and five-year-old children, who have not seen and handled farm products on a farm, this was a very tangible and stimulating experience. We are all grateful to you for your kindness and interest in having us. Please convey our thanks and cordial greetings to Jimmy.

TRIPS SERVE SPECIFIC PURPOSES

Although it is common practice to take children on trips, attention must be paid to the kind of need any trip is meant to fulfill. Obviously, one major purpose for going on a trip would be to seek answers to the direct questions of how, why, what, where. There are many things which are commonplace to grown-ups but full of mystery and novelty to children, and which they would do well to see for themselves.

On the other hand, children may often have been so involved in a personal experience, such as getting a haircut or seeing the doctor, that they were too close to the situation to be objective. Taking a fresh look from the vantage point of a school trip can really broaden the perspective of preschoolers and give them content for their play.

Lucy Sprague Mitchell gave serious thought to the relation of trips to children's understanding of their environment. She was especially concerned with the development of geographic concepts: ". . . If the trips are planned with reference to the functioning of the community around them, and if the schoolroom furnishes them with proper tools for play, their play will evolve and spontaneously take on aspects of human geography, and their floor play with blocks and bench-made products will show true beginnings of map making."[2]

Another purpose for taking a trip is to examine the *processes* underlying many activities that are taken for granted in our lives. How is a house built? How is bread baked? How is milk bottled? How is merchandise brought to town? In our industrial civilization there are so many steps between the sources of food, clothing, and shelter and ourselves that it is not until a heavy snowstorm or a similar emergency paralyzes transportation, power lines, and communication that we get a sense of the mysterious doings behind the neat packages we buy ready-made.

Still another purpose might be to see behind-the-scenes people or operations related to familiar, everyday things. Another is to get something needed by the class or a group of children to accomplish some special task. It may just as well be a trip

---

[2] Lucy Sprague Mitchell, *Young Geographers* (New York: Bank Street College of Education, 1971), p. 22.

to the lot for stones to weigh as a trip to the store for a pumpkin for Halloween. If needed materials and supplies are available only outside the classroom, the teacher and her class go out to get what they need.

One more reason for going on a trip, and one not to be slighted, is for fun and adventure. Learning may indeed occur, but it is incidental to the initial purpose. A picnic, a walk to smell the first spring smells, a trip to the park for some good running—these are important to a program and should not be neglected. One must be sure, however, that the fun envisioned is the kind young children enjoy and that the adults in charge are able to control when necessary.

COMBING THE COMMUNITY
FOR SUITABLE TRIPS

Once it has been decided that a particular trip can best serve the needs of a class, a teacher must uncover the opportunities available in any given locale.

Within the school building itself there is much to intrigue children and clarify impressions for them. Where is the source of the heat? Who cleans up after school, and where are the supplies kept? What is a principal, and where can he or she be found? Where are the older children's rooms, and what staircases do they use for getting to their classes? All this comes under the heading of orientation to be sure, but to children it is pure adventure and discovery. And how reassuring it is when one knows what is really going on in one's immediate environment.

Every community and neighborhood has its resources or its special places to provide exciting trips for children. It may be a lone, old-fashioned bakery with white-aproned, high-hatted workers handling stretchy dough and producing hundreds of delicious-smelling loaves; or a modern bakery with sophisticated machinery and identical loaves coming down the conveyer belt with precise timing; or a busy pizza place, so popular with children. It may be a shoe repair shop with black-aproned men handling hundreds of worn shoes, hammering and polishing and finishing them off with the help of noisy machines. Children notice the little mounds of leather and synthetic scraps and the special smells pervading the shop. On such a trip perhaps one or two children can have their shoes repaired while waiting, or the children can purchase shoeshining materials to use in class the next day.

Another kind of trip can be taken when there is road construction or pavement repairs or work on some underground pipes or cables going on within walking distance from school. A trip to such a place provides real adventure for four- to six-year-olds. The children see big men with powerful tools, elaborate and diverse instruments, performing fascinating operations—causing hard pavements to split, the earth to open, and huge caverns to become closed. Men wearing dark goggles equipped with wires descend into mysterious depths in the midst of drowning, drilling noises and come up again safely. Heavy rocks, enormous pits, and deafening roar and clatter are all interesting, and as the children watch and ask questions, touch and hold with their own hands bits and pieces from the construction, there is

a dawning of comprehension, and some of the mystery that lies beneath the streets is cleared.

In some neighborhoods there may be a pet shop or a veterinarian's office where special kinds of workers provide food and care, protection and cure for different kinds of animals. Other neighborhoods are near ferries or fishing activities, major highways and bridges, or a network of transportation lines. It is a good idea for the teacher to walk around the school neighborhood before the term starts to see what the possibilities are.

In the words of Lucy Mitchell again

> [A teacher] gathers this information in order to place the children in strategic positions for making explorations, in order to plan trips which will lead to significant discoveries, in short, in order to use her environment as a laboratory. Of course, she will impart information even to the youngest. But it will be as an enrichment to a firsthand investigation on the part of the children rather than as the chief method of learning. If she follows this method, she will soon realize that what children and grown-ups alike find in the environment depends upon what they bring. She will not expect a four-year-old who brings a largely self-centered world to find social significance in crowded city traffic. She will be content to let him take the traffic lights as an experience for itself. She will not expect a six-year-old who brings a world full of concrete, individual experiences to generalize on how a city gets its food. She will be content to let him play how the city gets apples and lumber and milk, which are the particular things which he has seen coming into New York. When he is ready he will generalize.[3]

[3] Ibid., p. 26.

It may be unavoidable for children who explore the environment not to become aware of the evidence of pollution and the destruction of nature. Excessive refuse in city streets or unsightly dumps in the midst of a country landscape may inspire some constructive action on the children's level. With the initiative and interest of teachers, children can carry out a project of diminishing their own volume of refuse: They can collapse discarded cans and cartons, limit the use of paper goods, even control the use of nondestructible plastics. They can be drawn into the war on waste, especially if there is a recycling center or depot in the community or nearby that would offer a useful trip or continuing contact. Children can appreciate the sorting process involved in separating the stacks of newspapers; the piles of flattened metal cans; the separate baskets of green, brown, and clear-colored bottles. Though kindergartners may not understand the scientific processes of recycling, they will sense the value in doing something about such quantities of pure waste. An interesting approach was tried by a teacher who proposed that her group make an inventory of items in the wastebasket. Ten different items were identified and carefully counted that morning, a broken crayon was retrieved, and it was decided to use both sides of drawing paper from then on. Teachers interested in such approaches to the study of the environment will enjoy *Teaching for Survival* by Mark Terry.[4] Among children's books that have a practical and creative approach to environmental protection, and which would be of equal interest to teachers, are Enid Bloome's *The Air We Breathe*[5] and *The Water We Drink*[6]. Distinguished by clear, concise writing and easy appeal to children for helpful participation, the books also reflect the author's background as a kindergarten teacher.

PLANNING AND ORGANIZING A TRIP

Early in October, when Mrs. Barnes's class had been in session only a few weeks, she decided to take a trip to the produce market to purchase pumpkins. "It is nice weather now, and I have parents to help me, so I will take a class trip early," she reasoned. But although there were three adults to supervise the trip, walking six long blocks each way in a crowd (twenty-five preschool children is a crowd) proved to be tiring and distracting. Since this was early in the year, the children did not know each other well, they were not settled as a group, and they were testing each other's powers and reactions as well as the teacher's authority and patience. At the crowded market scattered children had to be collected, guarded, and hastily steered back to school. The trip proved to be an ordeal for all, and the major feeling of the teacher was that of relief that it was over safely.

[4]Mark Terry, *Teaching for Survival* (New York: Ballantine Books, Inc., 1971).

[5]Enid Bloome, *The Air We Breathe* (New York: Doubleday & Co., Inc., 1971).

[6]Enid Bloome, *The Water We Drink*. Illustrated with photographs. (New York: Doubleday & Co., Inc., 1971).

Functioning as a Group
before Trips Are Undertaken

Children enter kindergarten as separate individuals, each with different preparation for group life and group functioning. It takes a while for them to know each others' names, for the many individuals to respond as one to a suggestion or command made to all, and for the disparate interests to merge into any one common task or goal. Yet on a trip outside the building it may become necessary to demand and expect immediate and absolute obedience if any emergency should arise. Children have to be prepared to respond to a teacher in that way even if seldom called upon to do so.

The children must experience a sense of belonging, a group consciousness that will cause them to stay together and not be drawn off into individual pursuits. A kindergarten teacher in a low-income area, where children are quite accustomed to independence on the streets, returned from a trip to the nearby zoo with two of the five-year-olds unaccounted for and missing. She was in tears and kept repeating: "They simply disappeared. I can't understand it." Before a general alarm could be sent out the two missing youngsters strolled blithely into their classroom. "Where were you?" the teacher, principal, and children shouted at them. The two raised their eyebrows in surprise. "We know the way home. We don't need no teacher to show us how to get back!" This degree of individualism, commendable in some ways, needs channeling before so responsible a group action as going somewhere together can be undertaken. Children who have shifted considerably for themselves find it hard to learn group controls. On the other hand, overprotected children may be afraid to try anything so new as an excursion away from the familiar classroom. Since groups differ so markedly, a teacher has to look for the telltale signs in daily living that reveal enough cohesion for a trip. Are the routines fairly well carried out by most of the children? Is the communication between teacher and class such that the teacher really feels he or she can reach them whenever it is necessary? Is there enough contact among the children in play? Only if there is something resembling esprit de corps, is the class ready to take a trip. For some kindergartens, this may be true in early October, for others not until April or May. Teachers who sense this happening may say, "My class has jelled. You can *do* things with them."

Time of the Trip and Distance from School

The attention span of kindergarten children, as we have indicated elsewhere, is not too long. In addition, susceptibility to fatigue and overtension is high. Trips must be planned to capitalize on the best concentration period and to avoid the unpleasant aftermath of tired, overwrought children. Actual viewing time can be held safely to one half hour except in situations that include opportunities for free running around and release from tension, or where attention is obviously keen and high. Little children have lots of growing time ahead of them and do not have to get everything in at once. A trip down the hall to see the fire extinguisher might only last seven minutes yet be very meaningful to the children and therefore considered successful. Most walks in the neighborhood can thus be nicely managed under an hour, from the time of leaving to the time of return. If it is desirable to travel with the children and arrangements for buses or cars can be made, travel time should be no more than twenty minutes each way. Of course, when one plans a picnic or a stay in the park, the time can be extended but should include some restful activities, such as a story or quiet game.

When to Take Trips

If weather conditions are suitable, it is advisable to go on a trip at a time in the day when the children are fresh and rested. Obviously, a trip should not be preceded by an active rhythms or game period. Since children become quite excited over the prospect of any excursion, it is wise to plan to leave soon enough in the day to avoid exhaustion from sheer tension.

Previewing and Adding Final Touches

A careful teacher knows exactly where the class will be going ahead of time, and may even make an advance visit. In some cases a short chat ahead of time with the people the class will see helps brief these adults on what to expect from kindergartners. Most adults are happy to welcome visiting children, but some feel they owe children long, involved explanations. Some are afraid that the very things children enjoy most are too banal, and others worry excessively about the children getting hurt. The teacher can know better what to include and what to avoid if she or he looks the scene over without the children present. The teacher may also find that some hours are better for a visit by a whole class or that something special is going to occur at a certain hour. It is wise to know ahead of time if the children will have good vantage points for observation, considering their height and numbers, and where any danger spots may be. It always helps to know where the nearest bathroom facilities are since at least one child will surely have to use the bathroom.

A box of tissues and some Band-Aids in the teacher's purse are proven items of usefulness. With all this it is also necessary to have the parents' permission and notify the principal. Transportation arrangements must be fixed and definite well in advance. It is imperative to have more than one adult with any group of children, and safest to have at least three. There is always one child who needs help at a bathroom or comforting of one kind or another. There are always stragglers who need watching by an adult who brings up the rear. There may be cause to pursue a special line of inquiry that arises unexpectedly. And of course, one has to keep counting heads, which is more reliably done when several do it together. Consequently, efforts must be made to involve parents or older youngsters as aids. In most communities, unless all the mothers are working or tied down with infants, there is little problem in enlisting parental assistance on trips.

Necessary Controls

The safety of the children on a trip calls for appropriate group techniques which are probably not necessary in a simple one-adult–one-child excursion. Staying together with no wandering off is a must. Adults strategically placed at the front, middle, and end of a group can supervise the entire group quite comfortably, especially if each adult is responsible for a small cluster of six to ten. Conversation is part of the pleasure and value of doing something together, and children should be permitted to talk to each other freely. However, because of the nature of the experience, it may at some point be necessary for an adult to communicate with all children at once, and here is where a teacher's original rapport, the agreement on a preplanned signal, and the cohesion of the group become important. It is not necessary to keep children constantly quiet in order to have them available for possible instruction, but they must know what it means to stop talking and listen to the teacher when she or he has something important to say. Instructions need to be broken down into comprehensible units and made very specific. "When the first people reach that lamppost we are going to stop and wait for the others." "Hold each other's hands and do not talk at all when we cross the street." "Does anybody have a question to ask?" Young children actually have no idea of how to behave in large groups and no comprehension of the possible consequences of thoughtless behavior. Teachers, especially responsible ones, are often so worried about possible consequences that they fail to enlist the children's understanding and cooperation as aids. In trying to do the whole job alone, they often defeat their purposes. You cannot go anywhere with a group of children as fast as you can go alone. Build the extra time for straggling and awkwardness into the planning; be reasonable and realistic about the demands you consider necessary, and try to enjoy the trip with the children. In crossing streets you will find police officers most cooperative, but if there is no police officer at the crossing, have an adult stand out in the middle of the street to stop traffic while the children cross with the other adults. Most adults in the community, including motorists, feel protective and kindly toward little children and will not resent your expectation of help from them.

HOW MANY TRIPS TO TAKE

There is no mechanical answer to the question of how many trips are suitable for a kindergarten class. If the trips grow out of the children's needs, as we indicated earlier, then the number and kinds of trips will be completely related to the total curriculum development. The quality and rapidity of the group's socialization, which is so dependent on the maturity of the individuals in the class, will also play a part in determining how many trips can be made in the course of the school year. The backgrounds of the children are equally a determining factor, as is the availability of suitable places to visit. For example, there may be an excellent zoo not too far from school which the children have visited on innumerable occasions with their parents. A trip to this zoo for such children would hardly have the significance it could have for another group to whom it would be a novel and eye-opening contact with animals so far seen only in picture books, unless one were following a specific interest or going to focus on a specific procedure, such as the milking of the cows or the feeding of seals. Trips have to be regarded as a teaching method and should be used when that particular method is the best one for accomplishing a curriculum goal. For example, if there is a building construction or renovation taking place nearby, the teacher would do well to provide for several consecutive trips to the site to note the work in progress; and if a trip for the whole class presents difficulties, perhaps a trip can be arranged for a few children at a time who will then become reporters. Or a trip can take place at harvesttime in a rural community, incorporating the experience into the curriculum.

In Chapter 10 we will discuss how neighborhood trips followed by block building resulted in a rich social studies project on an early childhood level. Cartwright[7] lists eighteen trips she took in a six month period.

GROUP TRIPS DURING PERIOD OF STUDY

Date	*Trip*
11/3	Dock and river: freighter and liner docked, ebb tide current; all climbed in whale boat on dock.
11/11	Pony stables: watched feeding and watering; all rode ponies.
11/14	Hardware store and pony corral (to give note of thanks to Barney, who owns ponies).
11/19	Car and truck garages with ramps and elevators. Children rode elevator; saw cables, pulleys, counterweight.
11/24	Fire station. Children saw, touched, climbed over most everything.
12/9	Trucking and river traffic.
12/16	Warehouses and truck loading. Children climbed into cab of enormous diesel tractor with trailer, identified much freight, watched fork lifts, talked with friendly driver.
12/18	Grocery store to buy items for Christmas party.
1/7	Grocery store to buy beans for bean bags.
1/13	Hardware store to replenish nail supply, pulleys, and cord. Looked at different kinds of buildings.
1/20	River to see heavy winter ice.
1/27	Paper scrap company—bailing machines, fork lifts.
2/6	River to see ice float down stream.
2/18	Garbage disposal plant.
3/12	Construction work on new police station.
4/16	Morton St. Pier, tugs, barges, MV Rotterdam.
4/20	Hudson Street open trench for telephone cable. Children climbed into backhoe, watched all operations: noise and action.
4/28	River to see "France" come by. Tug crew waved to us. Much river traffic.

BRINGING THE OUTSIDE WORLD IN

Another way of acquiring basic learning about the grown-up world of work can take place right in school or even in the classroom if the teacher is alert to it. The nurse who lets the children listen to the hearts of others through her stethoscope;

[7]Sally Cartwright, "Trips and Blocks: A Study of Five-Year-Old Learning" (Unpublished Master's Thesis, Bank Street College of Education, New York, 1971), p. 27.

the cook who demonstrates the enormous pots and ladles, mashers and grinders; the custodian who shares the mysteries of his cavernous quarters; the principal, clerks, school bus drivers—all these people can help to interpret the world and the way it works to the youngest members of the school family.

A worker commonly in sight in a school building or a classroom is the repairperson. Too often taken for granted or ignored, a repairperson is of great interest to children and can offer much understandable, practical knowledge about work. The children are fascinated by the jangling tools at the repairperson's side and by the skill and confidence with which they are used. Jessie Stanton, one of the early specialists on preschool education, used to tell a story about a little boy who watched with the greatest admiration a grimy plumber operating a rubber plunger. With a sense of awe and envy in his voice, the little boy asked: "Mister . . . did you get that thing for Christmas?"

Most kindergartners are more sophisticated than that, but not too much more. One group of five-year-olds watched a carpenter repairing a wooden enclosure under the sink. They said this about him when he left: "A man came. He is a carpenter. He had a saw and an electric saw. He made lots of noise. He plugged in the plug and he buzzed so much noise, we had to close up our ears. He made a square hole." A precise account. The teacher arranged for the children's further observation and discussion of squareness and dimensions and depths of holes.

Children are indeed fascinated by workers of all kinds coming into the classroom—plumbers, porters, photographers, window washers, doctors, and so on—and a little teacher guidance can add significantly to their knowledge of these adults as both workers and people.

Contributions of Invited Visitors

Sometimes a visitor to the class can provide adventure, bringing in the outside world in an importantly personal way. The visitor must, of course, have a significant reason for coming, and the visit must bear relation to the children's interests.

When Mr. Morrow heard the children's argument about the name of the friendly traffic policeman on the corner, he suggested to the children that they invite him to visit in their class.

"Would a policeman come to our *class?*"

"Will you be scared, Adam?"

"What will he tell us?"

"What should we say to him?"

Mr. Morrow had no doubt that the visit would not only be interesting but exciting. When the visitor came, it was a memorable experience. Although the children had seen the policeman daily, had watched him respectfully and admiringly, and had responded to his smile, the contact had been prescribed and routine. As hosts and hostesses in their own class, the children talked to him face-to-face and watched him sit on one of their small chairs and eat the same kind of cookie they were eating. They heard his hearty laughter when a child asked if dogs could be put in jail, and they listened to him tell them about his baby at home. They tried on the policeman's hat and counted his shiny buttons. The most daring ones touched the holster. Mr. Morrow was sure that this informal visit of a formal guardian of the law gave security to the children's experience within their society.

Mrs. Dillon, on the other hand, was not sure how to handle a visitor and almost spoiled a valuable experience for her class. Learning that the mother of one of her children was a professional pianist and believing it to be advantageous both for home-school relations and the cultural advancement of her class, she invited the mother to give the children a "little concert." Unfortunately, Mrs. Dillon was so concerned about the children's behavior that she embarrassed the sensitive woman. Mrs. Dillon promptly called the class to attention and gave the modest visitor an extravagant introduction.

"And now, children," Mrs. Dillon stated admonishingly, "show our guest, Mrs. Genovese, how quietly you can do your work, and how quickly you can clean up so we can sit down and hear the *concert,* which I am sure you will all enjoy." The children proceeded with constrained movements and surreptitious glances at each other, but did attend to their routine tasks with unusual dispatch. With equal dispatch they settled on the floor in exact places and looked (some of them unmistakably smugly) toward the teacher, expecting praise. Mrs. Dillon did hand out words of praise and said to the visitor, "See how wonderful they are, Mrs. Genovese," as if implying, of course, that this was how she had trained them. Mrs. Genovese played three short, lively, appealing pieces. But anxious Mrs. Dillon could not wait for the children's response. She initiated clapping at the end of each piece and made forceful comments *for* the class. "Wasn't that simply beautiful, children?" The children did not have a chance to ask questions or show their own reaction and the visitor was therefore not able to communicate her special skill fully. The whole experience was of limited benefit.

Resources of a worthwhile kind are frequently available among the children's families. One kindergarten class had visits during the year from a tympanist father who brought six different drums for the children to test for loudness and timbre, a ten-year-old brother who brought three snakes in a pillow case and talked about them, and an African visitor in colorful costume.

SELECTED CURRENT NEWS

Up to now we have been considering direct, firsthand experiences and contacts with people and work processes interesting to young children. But appropriate secondhand contacts can also be impressive, stimulate the imagination, and enlarge children's knowledge of their environment.

If one looks for them, one can find newspaper and magazine picture stories of fire fighter's rescues, of farmers' herds and harvests, of grandparents at school, and of people in far parts of the world producing goods for us right here. Stories of builders, hunters, fisherfolk, stories of merchants and pushcart peddlers are all quite newsworthy, authentic, and appropriate for young children. And stories of ferryboats, trolley cars, and trains are as dramatic to today's children as stories of the latest supersonic plane, the launch of a spacecraft, or the successful flight of a sun-powered plane.

PICTURES AS RESOURCES

Another resource teachers can utilize to stimulate and extend children's experiences is pictures. Every kindergarten room has wall space or separate bulletin boards for pictorial displays. Building up a classified file of pictures is not a difficult task but does demand constant examination of magazines, newspapers, display materials, industrial advertising, and so forth. Today there are also available commercial sets of pictures published especially for classroom use. Pictures must, of course, fulfill certain criteria to be useful. It is important that they be large and clearly printed so as to be easily "read" by young children. Naturally, they must be mounted at the children's eye level. Aside from the clarity and size ($9'' \times 12''$ is a good average), details must be accurate and true to life. As with trips, pictures also can serve several purposes in the kindergarten.

Giving Information

The first of these purposes is of course informational. This means that any picture that appeals to the general range of young children's interests or illustrates some aspect of adult work processes has a place on the kindergarten bulletin board provided it is clear and easily comprehended. Coming after a trip, following a discussion, or put up to add meaning to some theme developed in dramatic play, such pictures bring added content into children's lives.

Illustrating the Familiar

A second purpose is to give children the opportunity to recognize something familiar and known, and thus feel the glow of identifying their world. "Look! They are fixing the street—that's the sign!" "That lady's pushing a shopping cart like my mommy does." "There's a dog like Butch!"

Releasing Emotions

A third purpose is to allow children to identify with situations and scenes common to their lives, not only with the pretty pictures that show smiling, clean, good children but also the range of real experience, good and bad, known to every child. Such pictures may include the child and adult in the pleasant circumstance of storytelling or a picnic, and also the envious little fellow who watches his daddy toss the baby and is not sure he likes it; the child who successfully rides the high end of the seesaw as well as the child who lands with an ignominious bump at the foot of the slide; the child who is an eager and cooperative helper along with the child who creates a mess or breaks something; the proud child with the missing front tooth and the child in tears at the receiving end of an injection needle. Pictures put up for emotional identification can free children to express the range of their feelings and often stimulate discussions in which a teacher can be very helpful and reassuring. There is much the teacher can learn about individuals in the class as a result of reactions to pictures that capture a typical childhood experience.

Bringing the Adult World Closer

Then, of course, there are the pictures illustrating some event occurring in the environment and of interest to young children, the kind of happening of which they seem to have an uncanny awareness: a coming holiday, new president, a new structure in the community, an abundant harvest in the state, the latest efforts at fighting pollution, the graphic results of an electric power failure, a nearby flood or volcanic eruption. Children are naturally concerned about any much-talked-about occurrence ("little pitchers have big ears" is an apt saying). Sometimes newsworthy events may be distressing to children as well as to adults, as, for example, when they hear about a big fire or children harmed at Halloween. Facing up to and sharing distress over events in the environment can often clarify confusion and prove reassuring.

Not all pictures need have social or cognitive significance. A teacher may choose pictures purely for aesthetic pleasures: a colorful design, a painting, a seasonal nature illustration, or anything else that is lovely in and of itself regardless of the specific content.

Before any picture goes up on the wall, however, a teacher should ask herself, "What does this picture say? Do I want to say this to these particular children?"

WAYS OF HANDLING PICTURES

Pictures should be changed frequently enough that the children do not learn to ignore the displays as part of the fixtures. Pictures can be a live and meaningful experience to children if they are thoughtfully chosen and regularly changed.

Illustrations cut and mounted can be filed according to a classification system, for instance, animals, wild and tame; workers; transportation; children's activities; holidays; machinery. The right picture will then be readily available as it is needed. Some libraries and museums also have picture files from which teachers may borrow. Many of the big industrial companies supply pictures as part of their public relations program when requested on school stationery.

A last essential prerequisite for any meaningful picture in a kindergarten room is that it capture a bit of life rather than depict a posed, highly romanticized, sentimental portrait. The question raised before, "What does it say?" is a good one to remember.

MOVING PICTURES, FILMSTRIPS, AND RECORDS

The application of technology to the picture and story does not alter the basic approach to their use. "What does this picture say?" is still a valid question when applied to a series of pictures or to pictures accompanied by sound.

Moving pictures, filmstrips, records accompanying books, records unaccompanied by visual aids have all grown in popularity and are very much a presence in the kindergarten. Many of these teaching tools were first conceived as ways of helping hard-pressed teachers reach more children on an individual basis. Valuable as mechanical aids might be, it must be pointed out that overreliance on them adds to the dangers that come with excessive television viewing. Images instead of real people and things are fast becoming the significant environment to many children. Excessive use of audiovisual aids cuts down the interaction between children and people, children and objects, children and living situations. While there is, of course, plenty of such interaction still going on in the average kindergarten, the warning must nevertheless be sounded, because situations like the following have already begun to develop. In a funded preschool program amply stocked with mechanical aids, one of the authors observed that during a full hour, the four adults working with the eleven children present made exactly three comments to the children: "Sit up" "You are sitting very nicely" and "Line up." For the rest, the children's entire communication was one-way with the expensive array of mechanical aids except for a few brief, unproductive interactions among the children. The room was quiet, orderly, and controlled as every child was shunted from one audiovisual aid to another, and the four adults were a useless crowd.

Obviously, this was an extreme, and it might have happened without mechanical aids. But the uncritical reliance by three licensed teachers and a paraprofessional on the efficiency of technology as a teaching tool actually fostered this sterile environment in which interaction between adult and child hardly took place. Piaget's view about present-day reliance on visual and audiovisual materials in place of first-hand experiences and the child's own involvement is worth taking seriously if we really want children to grow and learn as human beings. He wrote

> It appears that many educators, believing themselves to be applying my psychological principles, limit themselves to showing the objects without having the children manipulate them, or, worse still, simply present audio-visual representations of objects (pictures, films, and so on) in the erroneous belief that the mere fact of perceiving the objects and their transformations will be equivalent to direct action of the learner in the experience. The latter is a grave error, since action is only instructive when it involves the spontaneous participation of the child himself, with all the tentative gropings and apparent waste of time that such involvement implies. It is absolutely necessary that learners have at their disposal concrete material experiences (and not merely pictures) and that they form their own hypotheses and verify them (or not verify them) themselves through their own active manipulations. The observed

activities of others, including those of the teachers, are not formative of new organizations in the child.[8]

Piaget is thus reinforcing the observation of Montessori that children learn through the use of their senses and of Dewey that children learn by doing. Obviously, imitation has a role in learning. So does identification with others, and so does analogy. But the problematic question in the face of the barrage of audiovisual materials and devices remains the *ratio* of active involvement with physical reality to passive observation of the image of reality.

Pictures, filmstrips, moving pictures, and the like help clarify experiences already learned in the old fashioned way, *through all the senses,* not just those of sight and sound. Touch is an extremely important sensory tool for young children, because touch allows for manipulation and differentiated perception in a way that eyes and ears do not—at least, not between ages four and six. Since children do begin to learn some things by analogy at this stage, secondary sources can be useful provided the experiences offered this way are carefully chosen to be consistent with their comprehension. However, when secondary sources become the main instrument of learning, something is lost—the power to learn and think independently. No amount of rote repetition of facts learned secondhand can begin to compensate for the loss of *learning how to learn by oneself,* nor can it restore one's inner belief in one's competence.

TELEVISION AS AN ENVIRONMENT

Like all audiovisual techniques, television has limitations as well as potential. They are the kinds of limitations which have serious meaning for the development of young children who are just putting their world together and learning who they are. Television is inevitably a two-dimensional experience, although a very attractive one. While two-dimensional learning has genuine possibilities for expansion of experience (obviously, not all things are learned firsthand), the ratio of two-dimensional to three-dimensional experience in early childhood must be examined. All studies of young children point to the sensory style of their learning and to their need to have many concrete experiences in order to form adequate concepts about reality. They must touch, taste, see, hear, and smell to get the feedback they need for increasing a comprehension of what surrounds them.

Thus, although TV can bring a much broader environment to all of us than we ever imagined possible, the young child approaches that fast-paced, broad environment in such a way that too much exposure can have the effect of *interfering* with learning rather than enhancing it. To utilize television's real potential, we must

[8]Milton Schwebel, ed., *Introduction to Piaget in the Classroom* (New York: Basic Books, Inc., Publishers, 1973).

assess it critically and not merely accept the popular notion that as long as it is "educational" it is helpful. As a total environment for children, it lacks an extremely important basic ingredient—there can be no feedback or interaction. A child can be only a passive recipient, not an active participant, in the experiences encountered on the television screen. Passivity is what we had in traditional education for centuries. We now know better, thanks to much research in child study. We must not be mesmerized into thinking that passivity is not damaging to learning because the teacher (television) can perform marvelous tricks. The process of how children learn remains the same.

By the phrase "exploring the environment" we mean discovering the environment of three-dimensional reality. Understanding and participating in this environment gives children the security of knowing what the world is about. Subjecting them to an environment of images alienates children from that which is truly real—from people, nature, and the objective world. We must be conscious of how we use our many audiovisual aids.

REFERENCES AND FURTHER READING

BRONFENBRENNER, URI. "Who Cares for America's Children," *Young Children* (January 1971).
BUSCHHOFF, LOTTE K. "Going on a Trip," *Young Children* (March 1971).
COHEN, DOROTHY H. "Children of Technology: Images or the Real Thing?" *Childhood Education* (March 1972).
COHEN, DOROTHY H. "Is TV a Pied Piper?" *Young Children* (November 1974).
ISAACS, SUSAN. *Intellectual Growth in Young Children.* New York: Schocken Books, Inc., 1972.
LANDRETH, CATHERINE. *Education of the Young Child.* New York: John Wiley, 1952, pp. 179–86.
MITCHELL, LUCY SPRAGUE. *Young Geographers.* New York: Bank Street College of Education, 1971.
OREM, R. C. (ed). *A Montessori Handbook.* New York: Capricorn Books, 1966.
RAMSEY, MARJORIE, and BAYLES, KATHLEEN. *Kindergarten Programs and Practices.* St. Louis: C. V. Mosby Co., 1980.
ROBISON, HELEN F., and SPODEK, BERNARD. *New Directions in the Kindergarten.* New York: Teachers College Press, 1965.
SINGER, JEROME, and SINGER, DOROTHY. *Television, Imagination and Aggression: A Study of Preschoolers.* Hillsdale, N.J.: L. Erlbaum Associates, 1981.
WARD, MURIEL. *Young Minds Need Something to Grow On.* Evanston, Ill.: Row, Peterson & Co., 1957 (out of print but worth looking for in library).
WINN, MARIE. *The Plug-In Drug.* New York: Viking, 1977.

Nonsexist Books for Children on Occupations

GOLDREICH, GLORIA, and GOLDREICH, ESTHER. *What Can She Be?* New York: Lothrop, Lee & Shepard, 1973.
GOODYEAR, CARMEN. *The Sheep Book.* North Carolina: Lollipop Power Inc., 1972.

KAUFMAN, JOE. *Busy People and How They Do Their Work.* New York: Golden Press, 1973.

LASKER, JOE. *Mothers Can Do Anything.* Chapel Hill, N.C.: Concept Books, 1972.

REAVIN, SAM. *Hurrah for Captain Jane.* New York: Parents' Magazine Press, 1971.

WOLDE, GUNILLA. *Tommy Goes to the Doctor.* Boston, Mass.: Houghton Mifflin, 1972.

10 The Many Purposes of Block Building and Woodworking

How can a set of wooden blocks that children simply play with have an important place in a kindergarten curriculum? And why should scraps of wood and dangerous tools be considered suitable curriculum materials? These two questions, though not articulated, are often in the minds of many teachers. In fact, the usually noisy and often exciting block play is quite distracting to some teachers, whereas to others the clutter and noise that accompany woodwork simply seem obstacles to orderliness. Yet both blocks and woodworking are among the long-recommended curriculum materials for kindergarten and first grade in bulletins issued by state departments of education and in Headstart programs during the late sixties. Nevertheless, far too many kindergartens and Headstart programs today have meager supplies of blocks and no woodwork at all. There are also instances where the materials themselves are in good supply, but no rewarding use of them is made. Could one reason for the failure of blocks and woodwork to take hold be that kindergarten teachers are so often women, and women *traditionally* do not have an affinity for woodworking or building? If so, can we hope that women's liberation from stereo-typed roles and the entry of men into the profession will stimulate participation and enjoyment of both building and carpentry in preschool classrooms?

Blocks and wood are so essential to a good program for young children—girls and boys alike—that we will analyze their functions in detail. However, although block building and woodwork depend on the same basic material, they are quite different in meaning and use, and we shall discuss them separately from here on. Let us begin with the blocks.

WHAT KINDERGARTEN BLOCKS ARE

When we speak of building blocks for the kindergarten class, we mean the large set of standard unit blocks, made of hardwood and distributed by educational equip-ment companies, that were designed by Caroline Pratt half a century ago, when she started the City and Country School in New York City.[1] Miss Pratt never bothered to put her name to her design, so that now blocks sometimes bear the name of the manufacturer or distributor, or are simply referred to as floor or unit blocks. By definition, a unit block is twice as wide as it is thick, and twice as long as it is wide; all other blocks are either multiples or divisions of the unit or related to it in width, thickness, or length. In most sets a unit block measures $1\frac{3}{8} \times 2\frac{3}{4} \times 5\frac{1}{2}$ inches.

When first introduced, these blocks were an instant success with children. They have remained unendingly popular ever since.

STUDIES OF BLOCK BUILDING

The first basic and thorough study of block building in the 1920s was made by Harriet Johnson,[2] who noted that children go through developmental stages in handling this material, in the construction process itself, in understanding of build-ing principles, in freedom of artistic expression, and in skill of elaboration. She pointed out, "The really dramatic quality about these young builders is not their mastery of techniques, but their attitude toward the material. It is essentially that of the artist. Even when they do representative building, it is the essence, not the bald form, that they make alive."

Hartley, Frank, and Goldenson,[3] who studied hundreds of records of block building by preschool children, observed the value of blocks for emotional release and for personality development. Constructing block buildings of their own design

[1]Caroline Pratt, *I Learn from Children—An Adventure in Progressive Education* (New York: Simon & Schuster, Inc., 1948). (Out of print but available in many libraries.)

[2]Harriet M. Johnson, *The Art of Block Building,* Bank Street College Publication (New York: Bank Street College, 1962 reprint), p. 35.

[3]Ruth E. Hartley, Lawrence K. Frank, and Robert M. Goldenson, "In the Block Corner," Chap. 4, *Understanding Children's Play,* 9th ed. (New York: Columbia University Press, 1959).

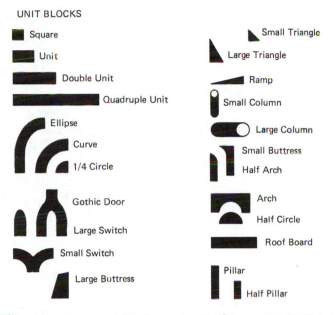

UNIT BLOCKS

Sometimes different names are used for the same units, for example, "cylinder" instead of "column," "floorboard" instead of "roof board," and so on.

and with their own bodily effort gives children a feeling of strength and security. Seeing how high they can build and balance a precarious structure gives children a satisfying sense of adventure and risk which they can enjoy with safety, as when a shaky structure is stabilized and a collapsed building built up again. The authors point out that block building can serve aggressive children by calling on their initiative and energy, and it can help shy children by allowing them individual, uncompetitive activity which brings them solid results. For both kinds of children, blocks bring the opportunity for recognition and even pride. For the inexperienced, blocks allow solitary and gradual participation and afford a natural contact with a neighboring builder. For children who are experienced with the medium, block building is an opportunity for advanced cooperative planning and working.

There are many practical effects of blocks in the kindergarten. Block building calls on the builders' coordination, involves their mathematical judgments, helps them gain concepts of space and direction, and makes use of other materials in combination with the blocks. Furthermore, children's building reflects their experiences: two boys build a bridge "over the Ohio River," and a girl builds a "bowling alley where people bowl."

A tribute to the enduring value of blocks was freshly formulated with contemporary insights in a recent volume called *The Block Book*, edited by Elisabeth Hirsch.[4] The seven chapters by experienced early childhood educators clarify the

[4] Elisabeth S. Hirsch, ed., *The Block Book* (Washington, D.C.: National Association for the Education of Young Children, 1974).

exciting potential for science, social studies, and mathematics inherent in the dramatic play associated with block building. Through photographs, diagrams, and helpful advice, the art of guiding good block building becomes a reality.

APPEAL OF BLOCK BUILDING

Although the attention and respect given to block building varies among teachers, there is no doubt of the special popularity of this medium with children themselves. Hartley and her colleagues[5] found that children choose blocks more often than paint, clay, or other materials generally available in the classroom and that only dramatic play approaches blocks in general popularity. It is easy to be convinced of this if one enters a classroom populated with four- and five- or five- and six-year-olds, for whom blocks, floor space, and ample time have been provided.

In the first classroom, Joey, not yet five, hurriedly peels the sweater sleeves off his arms and stuffs the garment, inside out, into his cubby without looking at it. With a deft skip and a slide he lands in front of the well-stocked block shelves, clanks down several piles of blocks, and possessively slaps the smooth surfaces of the top ones. Joey's gestures and facial movements all bear an expression of appetite for those blocks. The teacher is obliged to make a restraining comment. "You may not need any more blocks, Joey; start your building first, then you'll see," she says, the way a mother restrains a child who is gorging himself on a favorite food. Joey's teacher is just in time with her restraint, for several children surround him with accusations of greed. When they appeal with their need for heavy blocks for the bottom of a garage and long ones for a new road, and "a lot of blocks" for a wall, Joey understands them well and responds.

In the second classroom the teacher is asking for a show of hands in choosing activities for the session. When blocks are mentioned, hands are not merely lifted from the elbow but raised vigorously from the shoulder, sometimes one hand holding up the other for firm support and the palm of the raised hand shaking with the demand to be noticed. The potential builders make a rush for the small block corner in the large, crowded room. "I got them first," claims one child, guarding three large curves from other eager hands. Dispute is reconciled with little help from the teacher, for the children are so anxious to get their hands on the blocks and begin building that they are ready to make concessions. These energetic, bright five-year-olds know what is in store for them. One can tell that they know by the way they survey the blocks, select their workplace, measure the space, speculate on height, and however crudely, lay out the plan. One can tell by the vigorous gestures, the satisfying physical exertion, the delight with the rhythm and the sound of block building which attract the nonbuilders, that this activity rates!

[5] Hartley, Frank, and Goldenson, *Children's Play.*

HOW BLOCKS HELP CHILDREN
TO UNDERSTAND THE WORLD

Blocks can offer a variety of learning opportunities for children. Let us first look at this unique medium to consider its significance in furthering intellectual growth among young children. We can do no better than to examine the early records of block play described by Jessie Stanton in the long out-of-print *Before Books*.[6] The section we are quoting is from the chapter "Block Building, Third Week in January." The time is the 1920s; the place, downtown New York City. The episode of block building followed a number of trips in the immediate environment.

> On Monday, after a discussion of our trip, Meta said she wanted to build the Statue of Liberty. I asked her where she would put it and she said "in the bay." Albert said he would make Governors Island. Sonia said she would make Battery Park and the Staten Island Ferry House "at the bottom of New York." I asked the children in what part of the room the bay should be and they pointed correctly to the southern end. Then I asked what lay to the east of New York, and when they said the East River, I drew two chalk lines on the floor, repeating this on the West to make the Hudson.
>
> As soon as the rivers were outlined, Florence said she would make the Sixth Avenue elevated in New York, and Fred that he would make his apartment house on Sixteenth Street. Edna decided to build the Lackawanna Railroad in New Jersey. Sonia wanted to make Staten Island, so I asked her where it should be and at her direction drew a chalk line to represent it in the extreme end of the room.
>
> Both Albert and Meta used blocks laid flat to represent the small islands they were making. Both felt the form of the islands enough to make them circular, not square in shape. Meta began Bedloes Island on the same side of the bay as Governors Island, but she corrected this after I had suggested that she look at the map. She built the pedestal and placed a doll on top of it. The doll stood erect with one arm in the air, the hand being covered by a small clay jar which suggested a light. This fell down repeatedly and finally she took a Statue of Liberty drawn by Richard, and thumbtacked this to two blocks, so it would stand erect.
>
> Opposite her, across the bay, Albert worked absorbedly on Governors Island, building two lighthouses and a round pile of blocks suggesting a fort.
>
> Sonia made the Aquarium in Battery Park, with five small enclosures for fish. In one she placed Albert's clay walrus, in another Richard's duck. Then she ran for the peg lock fences (made by the children for the farm play in November and December) and made a little enclosure to represent the park, with one lone tree and a little grass in it. Below this she built the ferry house. She made a narrow entrance which led to the ticket office, a small square enclosure with a small window through which tickets could be purchased. She put two dolls inside at a table, and made strips of tiny red and blue tickets, "red for grown-ups and blue for children." Beyond this she made a ticket box

---

[6]Caroline Pratt and Jessie Stanton, *Before Books* (New York: Adelphi Company, 1926). Reference to this pioneering work is also made in the chapter entitled "Social Studies and Self-Awareness' in Hirsch, *The Block Book.*

and seated a doll beside it to watch it. Next she made the ferry slip and the ferry.

Florence, meanwhile, was working on the Sixth Avenue elevated. This ran South in the center of Manhattan Island and curved over to the East just as the real "El" does. One signal was placed at the curve, arranged just as we had seen the signal on our trip, and another was placed just in front of the Battery Park Station. Elaborate stairs led down to the ground level.

Fred made a large six-story apartment house, "my apartment house on Sixteenth Street." His interest was well sustained. Celia made the *Leviathan,* using triangular blocks to form a pointed bow. It was not so large as the liners built by the boys last week, but in shape it was quite accurate.

Edna started the Lackawanna Railroad in New Jersey. The space to work in was limited and she did not progress far with it.

[On Tuesday] Fred and Sonia ran at once to the ferry boat, on which Fred's dolls had been waiting since the day before, and pushed it down the bay past the Statue of Liberty, past Governors Island into its Staten Island dock. Fred ran for his red lantern and gave this to Sonia to set on the end of the pier, to represent the light we had seen on the trip. He took his dolls off the boat and let them look at the freight trains, but Sonia soon called "Twelve o'clock now, the ferry's going," so Fred rushed his dolls on board for the return trip. Sonia made a clock of blocks as soon as she reached the New York pier, so that she would know when to run the ferry. Fred then took his dolls to the elevated station and asked where to buy tickets. Florence said she would make a ticket office and tickets which she did. Then the dolls were put on the train. Meta told me at this juncture that she did not want to play with her house on Staten Island, so I suggested that she help Florence as the latter needed a station at Fourteenth Street for Fred's family, who were on their way to Sixteenth Street.

On Thursday, Albert built a dredger in the bay, and Fred did the same, after some play with his house. Marie, who had been absent for ten days, joined Sonia in the construction of a motion picture theatre, which was very completely worked out, with a stage on which Sonia's own pictures were shown, an orchestra of dolls "playing music," and rows of seats, on which all the available dolls were placed.

On Friday, owing to wet weather, our usual trip had to be postponed. The children, having laid out Twelfth Street and the adjacent streets and avenues, built the school, the hospital across the street, the jail on Tenth Street and Greenwich Avenue.

The reader may think that the children in Miss Stanton's class, both girls and boys, are intellectual geniuses and the program of trips and block building guidance too ambitious for kindergarten. Of course we must remember that children of the 1920s lived in a more stable era, without constant technological changes. However as one teacher observed recently, even the vicarious experience of television viewing may contribute to the content of block building; when she asked the child building "the White House" if he had taken a trip to the capital, he said, "No, I saw the White House on TV." In reality, average children this age, of whatever decade, are curious about their environment and ready to learn all kinds of concrete details, including directions and names of places if they go and *see for themselves.* Average children dramatize their experiences while block building if they have usable content that lends itself to dramatization.(See Chapters 7, 8, 9 on trips and play.) The Stanton records show quite clearly that block building that develops around themes that have intellectual implications (i.e., their fulfillment depends on inquiry and retention of information) leads to *reasoning* (In what part of the room should the bay be?), *problem solving* (How do you build the stairs down from the station?), *generalization* (Traffic needs a police officer), *thinking in terms of relationships* (Where do you place the Statue of Liberty in relation to Governors Island?), and *concept-formation* (geographical layout of a city).

MATHEMATICAL CONCEPTS GAINED FROM BLOCK BUILDING

The distinct mathematical activity in the handling of building blocks is also intellectual learning. Children have experience with quantity when they ask for "many *more*—for this big building," or complain of "not nearly *enough* for me and Jerry and Jane," or resort to hoarding a particular kind of block. Since kindergartners have some personal awareness of numbers from their actual experience (fingers, toes, TV channels, address and telephone numbers), using blocks for different kinds of construction enables them to test and put into practice quantitative concepts of numbers.

When making "a double track" or "a two-lane road," young children make the general concept of *two* concrete. They gain a clear notion of four sides when they construct a rectangular enclosure, although they may not know the word *rectangular*. Here is an interesting illustration from a classroom record.

Clara, not yet five, is putting away blocks with her teacher. The teacher hands her a pile, saying, "Here is a pile of three for you." Clara puts them away on a shelf where they go three high. The teacher hands her two more piles of three, without saying anything, but with a rhythmic gesture corresponding to Clara's own. Then Clara says, "I want to get my own pile of *three*, and you put away the long ones." She proceeds, stacking up a dozen piles of three without any error, then calls to the teacher seriously, "I need two more, I need two more—there is only *one* in this pile."

To achieve measurable, correct height, Clara is spontaneously practicing subtraction *and* addition, even though this is not the isolated process it will become in the grades.

The related *shapes* of the blocks constitute another mathematical aspect that interests young children. "Look," says Bernard rolling a small and a large cylinder block simultaneously. "These are the same, only this one is bigger." And Warren, running out of single unit blocks for his barn, picks up a couple of triangles and turns them around in his hands experimentally, trying perhaps to see if they would do in place of the rectangular piece he needs. Then a light of discovery shines on his countenance as he beholds a definitely four-sided block of the right size "born" of two triangles placed next to each other. This magic of two triangular pieces combining to produce a rectangular one is so fascinating that Warren abandons the completion of his barn and keeps working on his discovery for the rest of the session. Nor does he forget about it the next day.

When a teacher uses the correct names for the block shapes, the children automatically use the correct terms to express learned concepts of shapes, as we can see in the following scene.

Vivian and Erminio are painting on adjacent easels. Vivian says, "I made a *triangle.* Now I am going to blue the triangle." Indeed she has painted a triangular shape pretty much in the center of the paper and carefully fills it in with blue paint. Erminio glances, nodding approvingly, apparently understanding Vivian's experience of triangular shaping. When the triangle is completed to Vivian's satisfaction, she says, talking both to herself and to Erminio, "Now I'll cover the triangle with a square." And she does this surprisingly accurately. Although Vivian usually did purely artistic work when painting, the deliberation, calculation, and precision of this particular experience in painting showed her interest in geometric concepts gained from block building, as she had used the terms *triangle* and *square* freely.

This kind of mathematical conceptualization, based on concrete experience, is far more effective for ultimate mathematics learning than the rote repetition of names of shapes identified on two-dimensional cards so popular in recent years. The latter pleases the teacher but does not lay a proper foundation for understanding mathematical principles.[7]

SCIENCE LEARNING IN THE BLOCK CORNER

According to the thinking of early childhood educators, and observations of both authors (indicated throughout the book), block building in the early years of schooling offers children unique opportunities and stimulation that have bearing on science. Since the subject of science is covered in the next chapter, we are discussing it here only briefly. The very presence of blocks in appropriate arrangement automatically teaches *order* and *classification.* In building, the children are immediately confronted with *differentiating* size and shape in relation to process. With such a structured, solid material as unit blocks, children inevitably make use of the relationship of *parts to the whole.* Not infrequently, either the builder or an observer can *notice an error* (the road isn't straight, the roof doesn't reach) and has to either figure out how to make a correction or obtain help. No less important is the opportunity that blocks afford for experimentation and even fooling around (under safe conditions) which can result in sudden and delightful discoveries. A graphic demonstration of the serious intellectual involvement during block building can be seen in a film directed by Mary Moffitt.[8]

---

[7]Kristina Leeb-Lundberg, "The Block Builder Mathematician" in Hirsch, *The Block Book.*

[8]*"BLOCKS" . . . A Medium for Perceptual Learning,* FOUNDATIONS OF LEARNING SERIES, Campus Film Distributors Corp., 14 Madison Avenue, Valhalla, N.Y. 10595.

THE MEANING OF BLOCK BUILDING
TO A CHILD

We can best see the meaning of blocks to a particular child by looking in on the experiences of Billy, a wiry little five-year-old who loves to be big.

Billy takes out large piles of the heavy, long blocks, and hopping and skipping and stepping around them, he lays out what looks like a base. Then he labors, using the largest blocks as well as the various units of them, erecting a structure on the base. He then develops and shares ideas pertaining to technique or purpose. "I need *two* doubles here to *hold* the floor." "No, it won't work. I tried it." "But it's not going to be a house now. It's going to be a skyscraper." With such an ambition for a superstructure in size and importance, Billy has a great deal to do to keep the towering structure from leaning dangerously. He is intent on reaching the desired height. The higher the building, the more tiptoeing and the more care in placing the blocks properly. Soon the building becomes beyond reach of his stretching body and hands, and after a moment of thoughtful looking around, Billy uses a chair to achieve the needed elevation. The determined, self-directed, strenuous work and the fast growth in the height of the building are now replaced by a physical slowdown, by an inventiveness in design and a happy regard for decoration and beauty. He makes a top story of the "skyscraper" with triangular blocks, producing a mosaic effect. He then inserts slender, rising cylinders in an area otherwise flat and low. Painstakingly he places small colored cubes in such a way that it makes the building look lively, lighted, and altogether charming. There is a roof on the building now and a final traditional topping with a chimney. Billy's eyes and teeth flash in a smile of pleasure. Ah, but there is a gleam of further creativeness in his eyes. He hops from the chair, dashes over to the shelf with small wooden animals and plucks a little red rooster. He wants to place him on the "tippy top." But he cannot reach from the chair and prefers not to entrust this ultimate task to the teacher. And so he pleads with her for relaxation of the rule against standing on tables. Winning that and standing on the table, Billy raises himself to sufficient height, gingerly places the rooster in just the right spot, then jumps off the table with a whoop and a whirl and an expression of satisfaction with the entire work.

Would Billy take down such a laboriously and proudly completed structure when it is clean-up time? "Not just yet," he pleads and reasonable allowance is given. However, the reality of the situation demands that blocks be put back on shelves for use by the afternoon session. Billy's need to show his strength and bigness comes into play again. "Look, I can carry more than five." "Watch out, watch out, I am steering this tug to the dock," he says, as on his hands and knees he pushes a heavy pile of blocks into place.

It is easy to see that to Billy playing with blocks means full bodily activity, with both general and small motor coordination, resulting in a relaxation of tension; it means organizing, arranging, measuring, and counting; it means striving for bigness, persevering with an idea, exercising control and patience; at one point compromising, at another point agreeing with adults (dismantling a building), and practicing cooperation and orderliness in putting blocks away.

But could block building mean something else to another child?

Parading around her building almost in awe of her creation, Liz declares, talking out loud to herself, "I'm going to make a school. This is where the four's are, this is where the five's are, and this where the three's are." With gentle, timid, hesitating movements, she places three fat cylindrical blocks on the top block. "These are chimneys: one for the four's, one for the five's, and one for the three's." After taking all the trouble to get them up there, Liz very carefully removes two of the three cylinders. With intense, eager determination, she says to the teacher, "I'm going to make another one."

After the structure is completed, Liz walks up to the teacher and says, almost in a delirium, "I think my sister will know which one I made. She will walk up to this one (pointing to building 2) and say, "Lizzie made this!" The teacher is completely dumbfounded by the intensity of Liz's remark and does not respond. Liz is not concerned at all with getting a response and moves quickly to another part of the block area and begins her third building.

After struggling very patiently and unsuccessfully to balance an intricate structure, Liz looks up at the teacher and says quietly, "I think I'll do something that won't fall down," and immediately chooses the right block to replace the short one. With more ease in her movements, Liz builds up her structure. This time, it's only two levels high, and with some very delicately balanced blocks placed on each level. Then she creates a little supplementary building attached to the larger one. Pointing to the upper level, she informs the teacher clearly and with excitement, "This is where the wolf sleeps," and pointing to the bottom, "This is where Mommy sleeps," and pointing directly to the building outside, "Here is the three little pigs. This is my house."

Running back to look at each of her buildings, Liz, filled with pride, says, "I made this one and this one and this one," and struts around the teacher. "I thought you said you didn't like blocks, Lizzie," the teacher says, laughing at her incredible excitement and satisfaction. "Well, *I* didn't know I could do this!" Liz exclaims in joyous defense. "I used to copy Ricky's, and his was always better," she adds, making a wave with her hand (an adult gesture meaning—oh, how silly of me, or, wasn't that silly!).

BLOCK BUILDING, SOCIAL RELATIONSHIPS, AND COOPERATION

As the children gain skill and satisfaction from individual expression and discovery of the uses of blocks, they also gain interest in building with others in larger group projects. Cartwright points out

Block building invites children to work together. Rather than relying on suggestions from the teacher, the discipline of construction itself asks for cooperative effort. When the children are keenly interested and intent on creating a building together, they may seek each other's help and learn to tolerate, even to employ difference.[9]

[9]Sally Cartwright, "Blocks and Learning," *Young Children* (Washington, D.C.: National Association for the Education of Young Children, March 1974), p. 143.

Thus, entering a large kindergarten of thirty children, one observes that the most conspicuous part of all the productivity and activity is an extraordinarily large block enclosure that occupies a substantial portion of the room. It is about eleven feet square and the walls óf carefully laid blocks are about fourteen inches high. Three girls and two boys are busily adding to the structure, a model of their classroom begun by the three girls several days before. The toilet has just been added in an L-shaped area complete with separate stalls, and enclosed within walls of its own. The opening and closing of the single-block door by admiring children threw the walls down several times, but someone patiently rebuilt them each time. Some of the children were hanging "lights" on the walls, small wooden beads on string taped to the walls. There was much conversation and camaraderie as the project proceeded, both within the enclosure and across the room. The building was a class endeavor, and many had participated although the teacher had not initiated it. Not only were the children building, but they were also organizing, giving commands, arguing, deterring intruders, claiming credit for success, and disclaiming guilt for mishaps!

Equal Opportunity

Many of the records in this chapter indicate that boys and girls are equally interested in blocks. They respond equally to the concreteness of the material, the intellectual challenge of construction, and the enjoyment of social interaction. It is not uncommon, however, to see the block-building space in many classrooms dominated by boys. It is true that the hardness, toughness, and aggressive possibilities of blocks seem to appeal especially to boys and to challenge their energies; the teacher readily sees the meaning of blocks to the boys and may unthinkingly let it be a boys' activity. Thus the block area may become established as the boys' domain; the boys feel and act possessively about the blocks and, directly or indirectly, exclude the girls. Some girls, seeing that there is little chance for them in the area, do not even bother fighting for a chance. Other girls counter such discrimination by rushing into a free block corner "before the boys get there" and then enjoy building with their own kind of social involvement. Teachers must make it a point to provide the opportunity for the girls when this occurs, and to go even further by drawing them into mutual play with the boys when this seems possible. Teachers settling in the block area themselves seems to discourage male domination by making the blocks neutral territory.

Writing in the *Guide to Non-Sexist Early Childhood Education*[10] Harriet Cuffaro gives several suggestions to teachers on involving girls in block play.

1. Make block activity one of the activities constantly mentioned to girls, as it is usually offered to boys . . . girls might be approached with, "What would you like to build together?" or "I'll come and help you get started!"

[10]Barbara Sprung, *Guide to Non-Sexist Early Childhood Education* (New York: Women's Action Alliance, 1975), pp. 56–58.

2. Once girls get started in building, both boys and girls must be helped to accept the situation.
3. Teacher-led sessions that help extend block play must include girls through questions, comments, posing problems and drawing them into the group situation.
4. Make the effort to plan trips that include exciting, challenging female roles in the real world, roles that girls can emulate, such as women taxi drivers, doctors, plumbers, police officers, ticket sellers, etc.
5. Choose accessory block materials to include examples of women and minority members in a variety of tasks.

THE SATISFACTION OF PHYSICAL ACTIVITY IN BLOCK BUILDING

When children think about and discuss plans for projects, or conceive ideas about the special structure and function of a building, it is urgent for them to use their bodies and muscles immediately to execute the plan. They cannot hold plans and ideas in their heads too long; they must get to work and make the abstract ideas or theoretical notions concrete. *Action* is one of the essential characteristics of young children, and it is therefore worth giving attention to the purely physical aspects of block building. Should there be "hyperactive" children in class, this activity may serve as a constructive outlet for them. Of course, such children require help in focusing, which takes a teacher's time. But if they run around aimlessly, that intrudes on a teacher's time, too.

When children spend a full forty-five to seventy-five minutes in block building, they get a good deal of physical exercise, bending and straightening, lifting and carrying, carefully placing and replacing heavy blocks, and using special coordination of eye and limb muscles in the process. First, before the actual building, there is the need to remove the blocks from the shelves. Whether this is done by taking blocks one by one, in twos, in stacks of five, or in piles reaching from hand to chin —depending on the child's style or plan of building—the physical involvement is immediate. This preparatory process is itself often enjoyed by the children for the sheer muscular satisfaction. In one particular classroom there was a tall cabinet, rather than open low shelves, where the blocks were kept. The two highest shelves required standing on a chair to reach, but this in no way deterred the children. They removed blocks from the high shelves with swinging, energetic rhythm and loaded up the chairs as if they were wagons. When one chair was fully loaded, one boy called importantly, "Someone come help me!" "Okay," replied a co-worker, "I will!" and together the two pushed the loaded chair carefully to the middle of the area, really exerting strength. Then, like real workers, they dumped the load, supplying material for construction, and went back for another load. This loading up and transporting with their own muscular power, getting the load to a destination, and releasing all that weight with proper racket seem very satisfying to little children.

They also enjoy accumulating piles, stacks, or even mounds of blocks preparatory to building. This operation sometimes serves to stimulate building ideas, but the teacher needs to guard against the possibility that the possessive piling of blocks in mere preparation for building does not go on for too long. Some children may need a little push at this point.

At putting-away time, children naturally turn from self-structured, purposeful activity with blocks to a freer, noisier kind of activity. They knock blocks down; push and scoop them together with hands, feet, and whole body; stack them; slide piles into "ports" and load up "barges" as they experiment with methods of conveying blocks to the shelves. They manage to do a great deal of physical exercise—twirling on their own seats on the floor, sliding on stomachs, spreading arms and contracting legs while in practically prone or in sitting positions on the floor—but they do put blocks away!

Looked at this way, the physical activity of block-building sessions may be seen as a supplement to the otherwise inadequate opportunities for exercise in programs limited by time, space, and long periods of poor weather. Not to be overlooked is the value of physical activity for teachers when they are needed as helpers, that is, when they participate in rather than oversee putting blocks away.

ORGANIZING BLOCKS FOR CLASSROOM USE

Sufficient Blocks, Work Space, and Shelves

The teacher should request from the management of the school (whether it be a public school principal or a committee of parents) a sufficient quantity of blocks for his or her class—approximately 700 to 1,000 unit blocks composed of 17 to 25 different shapes, or as close to this number as is practically possible. A large enough area needs to be designated for building activity so that unnecessary limitations and frustrations will not inhibit the children's development in the use of blocks. As Elisabeth Hirsch tells us,

> The block area should be large enough to provide room to build for all children who wish to do so. It is also desirable to have this area open, visible from other parts of the room. Fascinating patterns of interaction can develop between dramatic play areas, table-toy areas, science areas, and the block corner.
> In selecting the best area for blocks, the total traffic pattern needs to be considered. Block areas should be away from cross traffic caused by the proximity of entrance doors or the bathroom.[11]

The teacher must also see to it that enough shelves of proper depth are available on which to keep the blocks in an orderly arrangement. Seeing blocks placed by type, children can better appreciate the distinct shapes and can enjoy putting

[11]Elisabeth Hirsch, "Block Building: Practical Considerations for the Classroom Teacher," in *The Block Book,* p. 89.

blocks back into their proper places. When the teacher respects the blocks as a medium, this discourages children from stepping on them while building, dumping them from shelves, or marring the wood. It encourages the children to remove stains and scratches with sandpaper, and in general it keeps the blocks clean and the block shelves dusted periodically.

Safety Rules

Together with the children the teacher will need to institute rational safety rules, for impulsive, strong five-year-olds with blocks in their hands and anger in their souls may have too powerful and effective a weapon at their command. Thus, using blocks as building and playing material *only* might be one logical safety rule. Sometimes demolition seems as attractive to young children as construction, but destroying another child's building can be disastrous in more ways than one. Also, demolition of a block building with children nearby can cause pain and injury. Here again a logical rule concerning efficient and safe dismantling of buildings could be instituted and observed by the children. However, for the occasional child to whom the deliberate crashing of his or her own building may have some urgent significance, *understanding,* rather than punishment for breaking a rule is the better road to eventual control. It is important to remember that although rules are a necessary security, applying them rigidly without occasional exception can be unfair and even retard learning. In one classroom, for example, to avoid dangerous crashing, a rule was made that buildings be erected no higher than a child could reach by standing. But then the smallest child in the class designed a tall building that required standing on a chair in order to reach the top and test a theory of balance. Realizing the importance of that particular building, the teacher and the other children cooperated in guarding both the building and themselves on that occasion.

Accessories Enliven Buildings

Excellent as blocks are as building material, children soon find blocks alone insufficient and may by themselves seek supplementary objects. Because children are creative, building to them is not only definite, mechanical structuring but calls also for elaboration, decoration, and items that symbolize action. We saw in Miss Stanton's records how children constantly used figures of people, transportation toys, and clay objects as properties in their block play.

The basic accessories for block play in a kindergarten are transportation toys, such as cars, trains, boats, planes, or whatever else is familiar or interesting to children in this age of transport; simple, even abstract figures of people and of animals, wild and domestic (these can be wooden, rubber, or plastic); and a few boxes of colored cubes which children use so charmingly for decorative and symbolic functions. Besides adequate supplies of these for the size of the group using the block area, each teacher can purchase or collect block building accessories of different kinds. One teacher kept on the block shelves a few pails of selected beach stones which the children used for roof decorations, chimneys, cars, and farm products in connection with block play. Another teacher advised the children to keep sticks they had collected on a trip to use as block accessories. Cut to approximately even size and stacked in a low box, the sticks looked like cords of firewood and were favorites with the children when they needed cargo at the dock or wood in a lumberyard. Still another teacher collected a few dozen empty thread spools from the parents, painted them and placed them in a box marked "for block building." The important thing to remember with homemade accessories is that they must be safe and sturdy, have uniform design, and be in sufficient quantity to be useful in a class.

TEACHER GUIDANCE OF GROUP PLAY

Interesting group play with blocks does not just happen. It takes real nurturing, at two levels, by a perceptive teacher. At one level is the *broadening* of children's horizons, the introduction of content, and the supplying of raw material which, if suitable, the children will seize eagerly. At the second level is the help in *human relationships* involved in group thinking and planning. Kindergarten children are quite dependent on teachers for both types of guidance.

In the Stanton records, the children painstakingly reproduced details of the life of the society around them with such realism that we, of a later generation, can feel quite nostalgic reading the records. But they could not have done this if their teacher had not given them the opportunity to see for themselves the comprehensible aspects of life beyond the street they lived on. From this they dramatized what could be expressed dramatically. And how creative their mutual work and play with blocks became! Clearly, this type of play, as suitable today as fifty years ago, will flounder if not fed by continuing information and redirection. The teacher's interest and efforts on the children's behalf are not only supportive, as when block building is *allowed*, but this activity must be *continuously nurtured* through trips, books, accessories and discussion if the maintenance and development of good group block building are to proceed with increasing intricacy.

On rereading Miss Stanton's records, we also see dynamic relationships and absorbing social dramatization constantly developing through the use of blocks. Children learn to appreciate how contributions from various group members fit into the integrated scheme and to recognize how interdependent the children are in the fulfillment of their ideas. All this occurs with the teacher's full awareness and carefully gauged intercession. Other portions of the Stanton records clearly show the value of teacher-encouraged interdependency. For example, when Fred's apartment house was completed and ready for occupancy, he was eager to have people move right in. But Faith and Celia had meanwhile built a church, installed a minister in the pulpit, and shepherded all the people to the service. So the people were "right in the middle" of a sermon when Fred wanted them, and the teacher helped Fred understand the use of both the apartment house and the church by the same people; this required concession and cooperation, and led, subsequently, to more meaningful play among all the builders involved. Or, when Sonia builds an aquarium, using animals and fences made by other children, a ticket office with a doll attendant, and separate tickets for grown-ups and children, Miss Stanton reports that "she was ready to weep because no one had come to see the aquarium, so Fred said all his family were coming." After that the two children work together, and, with the aid of dolls, they make full and proper use of the ticket office, tickets, and entrance into the aquarium to enjoy the sight. The right question, an appropriate suggestion —and the children can go on.

Using Judgment

Sometimes it is difficult for a teacher to decide when to let the children carry out their own ideas and when to influence them by direct intervention. Perhaps we can understand the problem better by looking in on several more teachers.

During a work period in Miss Howard's kindergarten, a conspicuous building is being erected with the large, hollow, outdoor blocks in a central part of the room. The children are piling the blocks energetically, and practically instantaneously they put up a house some four feet high. Miss Howard notices that although the children improve the building somewhat as they go along, the play in this hastily constructed and crude structure tends toward a repetitious going in and out of the building, and with undertones of giddiness developing fast. Miss Howard says, in the spirit of offering a better alternative, "Let's put these blocks away now, so you can have time to use the others today, too." Agreeably, the children put away the large blocks and proceed to make completely different use of the clear space in front of the shelves. Building with the smaller, more adaptable unit blocks, they are confronted with new challenges—*what* to make, *which way, how* things could fit and to what *use* the building could be put. The children are now thinking—of design, of structure, of function. Knowing her children, Miss Howard is able to recognize when they are at a dead end and need direction toward a more fruitful activity.

In Miss Cameron's kindergarten class, however, a group of four (and later seven) children are quite involved in rebuilding and operating a "farm" saved from a previous day. Care of the distinctly domestic animals and their placement and replacement in the barn and pasture seem to be the chief concern. Then one child finds an elephant (a large rubber animal, bigger in size than the farm animals) in their midst, "and an elephant doesn't belong!" So with a view to protecting the farm animals, the children not only drive the intruding "wild" elephant out but try to "shoot him," actually striking him with block "guns." The teacher does not see this as violence, but rather as the children's regard for the farm animals and their ability to distinguish domestic animals from wild ones. Not all of them were able to do this in a discussion a few days back. She therefore says nothing, but at the same time she realistically and unobtrusively protects the "wild elephant."

On another day the same teacher notices the children building docks and boats and arguing. She knows that all the children in class have either been on or seen different boats, and she feels that they could have an intelligent discussion.

She asks the children what the boats carry and which way each one is going. When she sees that they are not sure, yet are eager to know, she produces a book on boats. The children leave the block building for a moment and pore over the pictures in the boat book, examining minutely the details of the various boats and promptly applying the knowledge by correcting the structures, shapes, or dimensions of their boats.

What makes teachers decide at one time to step in with suggestions and help for the block-building children, and at other times not to interfere? There are several reasons for both actions.

When the children's building consists mostly of repetitious stereotyped play, the teacher, with knowledge of the children's interests, can suggest a new idea, offer different accessory materials, add stimulating information on the type of building, or question the children on the nature and purpose of the building. Any of these may liberate the children from a stilted position. A proper length of string, for instance, can make a vague reference to cables and change the block play to active dramatic building as the securing and supporting of the cable is engineered. Or a piece of earth-brown or grass-green paper may give direction and stimulation to an overdue plane landing.

Sometimes a building project, though stemming from a good initial idea, can come to a standstill because the children do not have the necessary information to develop the play. By supplying the information the teacher is helpful to the planning and later to the execution in detail of the children's ideas.

When, perhaps as a result of fatigue, tension, or even bad weather, the children's behavior becomes silly and uncontrolled, the teacher's help becomes urgent. She or he will need to redirect the children's attention and perhaps change the responsibilities of particular children.

Violation of safety is a major reason for a teacher's prompt intervention in block building. A wobbly structure may not be noticed by children close to it; unless it is made secure, it can literally crash on their heads.

Interference with other children's rights may also be a good reason for a teacher to step in and guide the children toward a fair disposition of a social problem.

Still another reason for a teacher's active help is a child's inability to get started or to get finished. The help may be physical (getting particular kinds of blocks or suggesting a good place), or it may consist of verbal encouragement ("I think *you* are a good builder, too!"). Or it may be more support in the form of a sympathetic glance or an approving smile.

A teacher should not interfere when the children are working well by themselves on a problem they encounter in block building or when they need time to correct their own mistakes. Knowing the children in her class, the teacher may judge that a relatively simple building is as much as the children can do at this point in their experience, and that leaving them alone is necessary for their development.

Thus, knowing when to give and when to withhold help in block building is not easy. Each situation requires subtle understanding and sensitive action. When giving help, a teacher must not give too much, so that the children can carry out *their* ideas and build on their own level. When not interfering, the teacher must not neglect or ignore the builders. Perhaps concern for both the lively children and the lively art of block building can help in making wise decisions.

BLOCKS AS A MEDIUM FOR PLAY

Although children will often use blocks in a less accomplished and seemingly less constructive way than in the preceding accounts, the building process which engages them, and which they invest with energy and feelings, will nevertheless reveal their particular experiences to an observant teacher.

Following is a record of quite typical block play of urban children in which a teacher tries to direct the play with occasional comments but is met with indifferent response:

CURTIS (to Norman): You wanna play blocks?
NORMAN: What do you wanna build? A police station?
CURTIS: I'll get the car for it.
NORMAN: I've got two good cars.

Curtis goes across the room and gets a large (one-foot-long) red car with a light on the hood and "Fire Chief" on the side. Norman gets two small, green trucks.

CURTIS (to Norman): Let's get building.
NORMAN (calling to Justin): Justin, help me build 'cause Neil doesn't want to.

Curtis begins to build with Justin, then stops and watches Justin, who very efficiently and quickly builds a roofed enclosure of double-unit blocks. He places two large switches on top (archlike), which he bridges with a flat block, then puts three large curves across the top. Norman and Curtis look on. Justin seems to know exactly what he wants to do. Justin puts a "one-way" sign and other traffic signs near his building.

NORMAN (handing Curtis and Justin each a wedgie): Here's your man, Curtis. Here's yours (to Justin).

Curtis' wedgie is some kind of uniformed man.

JUSTIN: Someone has to guard.

Curtis retrieves his Fire Chief car, puts his "man" on top of it, and starts moving them around, making motor sounds. He moves his Fire Chief car through the arch (a switch) at the side of the enclosure and, holding his wedgie, says something about "secret agent . . . the other night . . ."

CURTIS: I'll guard it.

Curtis puts his wedgie in the front of his parked car, then at one side of the building.

JUSTIN: I'm guarding here.
CURTIS: Who'll guard in the day?
NORMAN: I'll guard in the day.
CURTIS: Who'll guard in the night?

This sounds like the dialogue of a play which they have all seen and are repeating.

CURTIS (to Justin): It's morning now. You have to guard. It's morning.

Justin takes his wedgie out of the building.

CURTIS (immediately): It's not the morning anymore. It's the day, so I have to guard.

Curtis puts his wedgie in the Fire Chief car. He has some trouble fitting it in. Somebody says something about "robbers." Curtis moves his car around rapidly on the floor, making motor sounds of various kinds.

TEACHER: Do you need some signs for your building?

Justin says something about "hospital." . . . Teacher makes a hospital sign. Curtis says something about "secret agent" and the teacher adds "secret agent" to the sign.

CURTIS: He stole the food. He stole the food.

Curtis puts his name on the sign the teacher has made. There is now a conversation among Curtis, Justin, and Norman.

CURTIS (yelling in his high voice): Help, help!

The teacher asks the children if they know what a hospital is.

JUSTIN: Where they keep you well.

NORMAN: If you have a broken leg, they fix it.

Some more is said about bandages and casts and the difference between them.

TEACHER: Could you build a hospital that looked more like a hospital— make part of it more open so you can put beds in it? See if you can build it so you can play with it.

Justin and Curtis talk but do not, however, change their building.

JUSTIN (referring to a round, flat construction he has made out of curves): It's an automatic opener.

CURTIS: My man last night was in a crash.

Then speaking for his "man," Curtis says, "Where am I? It's the daytime. What happened?" Curtis then takes the wedgie out of the car and parks the car in the building.

CURTIS: Pretend he fainted, pretend he fainted.

Norman now has Curtis' Fire Chief car and is moving it around. Curtis sits and watches Justin, who is making different kinds of sounds.

JUSTIN (still building): Pretend I'm the robbery.

CURTIS (to Norman): *You* build a trap. *I'll* build the jail.

Curtis takes four double units from the block shelf.

NORMAN: *You* build the trap. *I'll* build the jail.

Curtis stands four double units up on end close to each other, forming a minuscule enclosure. He puts two brick blocks on top. It is a carelessly put together construction. He asks the teacher for a sign saying "Police Station."

NORMAN (protesting): Then the robbers will find it.

CURTIS (taking the sign): Then the robbers *won't* be able to find it!

On first observation the preceding block play may appear scattered, unfinished. Yet the children's talk of guards and secret agents, jails and robbers, in the context of their play, showed them trying to deal with their experiences, bringing in elements from their family life, their environment, or their television viewing. We might therefore say, in the words of Barbara Biber, that the play served ". . . two different growth needs . . . learning about the world by playing about it (realizing reality) and finding an outlet for complex and often conflicting emotions (wherein reality and logic are secondary)."[12]

STIMULATION TO BUILD

We cannot leave a discussion of block building without bringing up, at least briefly, a commonly heard complaint from teachers: "My class just doesn't seem interested in block building. They hardly ever take them out." Or "I don't have very good block building in this class." To answer such a complaint, we would advise the teacher to see if the blocks are properly and attractively arranged so that they look *inviting* to children, and to share her or his observation with the children. The different units may be mixed up, or some may be so tightly stacked that there is no room for a hand to pull them out. In our experience, children's participation in the proper placement of blocks, which requires concentration on dimensions and on related shapes, usually arouses curiosity about using the blocks. Other reasons for lack of building may be insufficient floor space, in which case another area may be found for at least temporary, if not permanent, use; or a lack of supplementary playthings to enliven or decorate a building.

If there is a particular child who appears to avoid or refrain from building, a teacher may be concerned that the child is missing something. The teacher would of course not urge the child (overtly or subtly), but she or he might want to experiment. The teacher might make a tentative flat or vertical building using a minimum of blocks and ask the child for a suggestion on how to proceed. The reluctant child may then become involved and wish to make a building. However, the average boy or girl, even if indifferent to blocks at the beginning, for whatever reason, will become challenged by their many possibilities, and the teacher's interest will be encouraging enough without special intervention.

WOODWORKING IN THE KINDERGARTEN

In spite of the general recognition by educators that woodworking is a valuable activity for preschool and young schoolchildren, there is not much literature on the subject, and standard textbooks give only perfunctory accounts of its place in a

---

[12] Barbara Biber, "The Role of Play," in *As The Twig Is Bent; Readings in Childhood Education,* eds. Robert H. Anderson and Harold G. Shane (Boston: Houghton Mifflin Company, 1971), p. 102.

kindergarten curriculum. Yet when preschool children come for the first visit before school, the woodworking bench in the classroom invariably makes the strongest impression on them.

"Look, mom!" a child exclaims, touching the rough bench tentatively, and when nails and a hammer are offered in response to the child's curiosity, his or her face lights up with excitement and pride. The child's satisfaction is unmistakable to both teacher and mother. Many a supervisor or teacher who has observed children's woodworking speaks of their insatiable desire for this activity. The most frequent comment one hears is "They can't get enough of it," and "they" means all children of both sexes. Women kindergarten teachers, however, rarely feel secure and knowledgeable about supervising woodworking, and so children miss some excellent opportunities for learning.

What Woodworking Is

Is woodworking primarily a "work" activity, completely apart from intellectual interests, something a child would do with a parent at home and only a "frill" subject in school? Does facility at woodworking preordain a child to become a good worker in the manual sense only? Or is woodworking to be regarded as an "artistic" activity along with block building, painting, drawing? Is there perhaps a scientific aspect to woodworking? Or is woodworking most important for providing preschoolers with opportunity for blowing off steam? What could be a better way of getting rid of some aggression than whacking soundly with a heavy hammer and cutting into lumber with a noisy saw, and then, relieved and relaxed, returning to quieter activities?

George Fuller, an experienced woodwork teacher, writes

> The learning ramifications [of woodworking] extend to such areas as relating parts to wholes, understanding cause and effect, understanding spatial relationships, problem solving, making sustained effort, sharing with others, coping with success and failure, and developing sound standards and values.[13]

As with everything else, however, there are tremendous individual differences in children's interest and approach to woodworking.

Children derive sensory pleasure from handling wood, and they not only construct representative, utilitarian objects such as airplanes, trucks, tables, and doll beds, but also create abstract and fanciful structures out of wood.

They learn the elementary mechanics of fitting, fastening, connecting, and cutting; they learn physical properties of different materials—roughness, softness, sharpness; they learn about the grain of wood and the source of sawdust.

But some children like woodworking for the purely physical exercise and would just as soon pound in as many nails as they can get, as long as they can use

---

[13] George Fuller, *Woodworking with Children* (New York: Bank Street College of Education, 1974), p. 1.

the hammer. Or they move the arm back and forth with a saw until they are exhausted from sheer physical exercise. Other children find great fascination in just using sandpaper to smooth and smooth a piece of wood, while still others may be determined to make a truck on wheels that move or a big barge with a smokestack to use with block buildings. One four- or five-year-old may find the sawing of endless short lengths off a long board completely satisfying, while another child wants to figure out how to make a table with four legs that requires measuring, marking, sawing, sanding, nailing, and perhaps gluing and painting. All these children will require various amounts of help from the teacher, but all need an equal degree of recognition.

Strong Appeal to Children

Children are fascinated with the transformations that take place in woodworking. One long piece of wood can, with effort and the use of a tool, become four short ones. Two separate pieces can be fused into one completely whole piece with the use of a particular tool and definite technique. An ordinary box, four unattached wheels, simple washers, and nails of a certain length can, through systematic steps with only a hammer as a tool, be transformed into a "real wagon." When the wagon is further refined by being sanded, brightly painted, and then given a handle of string attached at the front with a staple, a cup hook, or a metal eye, it becomes a treasured wagon—treasured because the child produced all the transformations by himself or herself.

As with other media, children need to master this one on their own terms in the early stages; the aids given must be technically accurate but geared to allowing a child to accomplish his or her own ends, if these are practical. Having the whole class carry out instructions for making a preplanned item is not the same thing at all.

Teachers can and should be helpful, but obviously they need to know something about wood and tools themselves. While some women do have a feeling for craft, this is not yet typical among American women. As a result, this highly satisfying experience for young children (and older ones, too) goes by the board for want of training among the women and a paucity of men among the teachers of the young. The techniques are not at all difficult and do not call for extraordinary strength. If there is no one who can teach an aspiring kindergarten teacher, we suggest a look at some older children's books dealing with the subject. George Fuller's clear and explicit booklet[14] for adults and a well-illustrated practical article, "Carpentry for Young Children,"[15] are good sources for the uninitiated.

WOODWORKING MATERIALS AND METHODS

Woodworking requires its own unique materials. Principally these are a workbench with simple but good hand tools; a sufficient quantity and variety of suitable wood; nails, sandpaper, and such accessories as string, spools, wire, or scraps of cloth and

[14]Ibid.

[15]Marijane Brandhofer, "Carpentry for Young Children," *Young Children* (October 1971).

leather in proper containers. It also requires a clear introduction of the activity to the children and careful guidance and supervision of the special techniques to insure physical safety as well as positive outcomes. We will take up the various points separately.

Workbench

This simple, sturdy object is the first item to be obtained. It may be an expensive and good commercial workbench with easily adjustable vise, roomy drawer, and ample shelf or two underneath—a workbench made to last through many years of hard use. It may also be a homemade one (made with the help or at least advice of an experienced carpenter or skillful handyperson). It may be a more crude one, made of a discarded door or even a heavy packing box, but properly reinforced and with a firmly attached clamp and conveniently placed shelves or drawers for supplies. Or it may even be a temporarily installed but durable pair of sawhorses with a heavy board secured across them so there will be no tipping. Any one of these offers a suitable place for woodworking. The very designation "workbench" suggests serious activity and may instill respect. A workbench is often a place where things are taken to be fixed—a rough spot on a block gets sanded, a loose handle on a pail gets attached, and a jar lid is taken to the workbench to have air holes punched in it for a captive insect in a jar.

The location of the workbench must naturally be such that two to four children around or in front of it have room to move their hands and arms safely without touching anyone else. It is best to place the bench where other children will not be passing too often and where the necessary woodworking noise is not a serious disturbance to others. If there is a nearby separate shoproom or workroom, even in the basement, where a few children with an adult can work undisturbed, that can be an advantage.

Wood

In this age of plastics and alloys, we are almost unaware of the properties of wood—its density, its graining, the fact that it is cut in widths of different thicknesses (e.g., 6 inches wide by ¾ inches thick) and is more or less splintery, according to origin and type. Only when we buy furniture do we become aware of the quality of wood, and then with different criteria than for the children's use. Children need raw wood, unfinished and unpainted, and of a density that will challenge them but not defeat them when they saw or hammer. It is good to have to exert effort in conquering wood, but it must be conquerable to young hands. Plywood, for example, is unsuitable because it is too hard; fir is unsuitable because it is too splintery; soft pine is about right.

Obtaining and storing the wood presents special chores and problems to the teacher, but these are worth the effort. There are many ways of getting wood. At any lumberyard in the neighborhood or community, a quantity of several sizes of white pine can be bought. White pine is particularly soft and smooth to work with, both for hammering and sawing. Balsa, poplar, and basswood are also good soft woods, but not as suitable for sawing and hammering. If the right kinds of scraps are available free, so much the better. Often lumberyards will give away scraps up to 12 inches long. Make sure the thickness is suitable, however. There may also be a furniture factory or repair shop in your locality which has discarded but useful pieces of wood. Here it is important not to take pieces of such hardwoods as oak, maple, or birch, which are very difficult for children to penetrate with nail or saw, although interesting small pieces may be used for gluing in connection with wood-working. Some teachers still manage to procure wooden boxes (fruit and liquor boxes with solid ends, as well as occasional small packing boxes) and remove usable boards free of nails and splinters. Teachers need to find their own sources of wood close to school or home and may perhaps secure the cooperation of other teachers or parents (even friends and family, as some teachers do) in getting wood for their kindergarten classes. Once in the classroom, the wood must be placed in a recep-tacle—a sturdy carton perhaps, a wide barrel, or an empty oil drum. The receptacle must not only be sufficient to hold the wood, but the children should be able to see the pieces in it.

Tools

Woodworking tools constitute a most interesting item to children, although they may at first make teachers ill at ease. For the sake of both the children and the teacher, only the basic tools should be made available to kindergartners. These in-clude four to six hammers of different weights and kinds: perhaps three flatheaded, 10- or 13-ounce hammers, which are most secure for beginners; some hammers with claws for pulling out or redirecting nails; and a full-size, heavy, adult hammer. One number 8, 12-inch, sharp, crosscut saw for straight cutting is necessary, although some tall children can use 14- or even 16-inch ones. There can be two saws if there is provision for two children to saw at the same time. A rasp is a good, safe tool for children to handle and use for smoothing a rough or splintered edge against the grain, and for such shaping of the wood as rounding a corner. This tool also has an interesting name (no doubt a new word to the children), representing the raspy sound it makes. Later in the year, when the children are more experienced and responsible with tools, a 10-inch smoothing plane and a hand drill may be added to the supply of tools. The plane not only makes an amazing change in the surface edge running with the grain but also produces delightful curly shavings. As for the drill, the holes in the wood produced by different size bits are endlessly intriguing to make and to use.

A one-foot rule (that includes metric measurements), a folding ruler, a yard-stick, and either a regular pencil or a flat carpenter pencil will be necessary for mea-suring and marking wood. In addition, pliers are handy to have and to know about, as are large scissors for cutting string or wire or sandpaper. Still another tool is a brace and bit, which does the work of the drill in a more complex fashion. This should be introduced late in the year, when kindergartners operate it with eagerness and delight. Although screwdrivers are often found among kindergarten woodwork-

ing tools and used with screws or for prying or splitting, a screwdriver is really not as safe in the hands of inexperienced five-year-olds as is assumed. It is unwise to have this tool available to children, especially at the beginning.

The other indispensable material to be obtained from the hardware store along with tools is a supply of different size nails. There must be the broad-headed ones (such as roofing nails), 1 to 1½ inches long, for crude and easy hammering; steel nails with sharp points that go in easily and do not split wood, ranging from 1 to 2 inches; nails of different lengths and thicknesses to fit the wood and the purpose—in short, enough variety of nails for the child to exercise selection, discrimination, and judgment. Necessary, too, is sandpaper of different grades of roughness.

Having selected, obtained, and paid for the best kinds of tools, a teacher must think about their care, for if not cared for they can become worthless in a few days, and the whole woodworking area can turn into mess and ruin. The saw left lying on ledges is dangerous for the child and harmful to the saw; hammers may soon be missing and lost if not regularly put back in place; nails become very easily scattered; and sandpaper can turn up inside pockets, books, and wastebasket if proper places for it are not provided. On the other hand, nothing is more attractive and inviting than tools that are cared for and in their proper place, and once order is rationally instituted, it is reasonably easy to maintain. A special place on a wall, or a tool board, is therefore a must. On such a board an outline of each tool can be made and appropriate hooks, nails, or holding gadgets put in; then children and teacher can easily get into the habit of putting tools where they belong, and they will consequently have no trouble finding them. A drawer or two and some shelves in or near the bench are also important for tools and materials. Sandpaper blocks with handles can be kept in a drawer or in a marked box on a shelf. Saws should be professionally sharpened once or twice a year, oiled and wrapped in newspaper when put away for the summer, then cleaned in the fall. If a hammer or saw handle becomes loose or damaged, it must be removed and repaired or replaced, for broken tools create low standards and low morale, and, of course, they are not safe.

Although mixed up and scattered nails can be the worst looking mess of all, keeping nails in assorted plastic jars, tin cans, or wooden bins is really fun. Just to look at a whole series of separate, uniform, and suitable containers, each holding a particular kind of nail, is a real pleasure to children, adding interest to the challenge of finding just the right size nail that will not come through unwanted and will not split the wood. A fascinating way of picking up nails from the floor is, of course, with a magnet, which should also be kept in a prescribed place and put back after use.

Accessories

The kind of extra materials a kindergarten class will have at the workbench depends not only on what is available but also on the imagination and sophistication of the class members, including the teacher. These could include

METAL GADGETS: cup hooks, metal eyes, and staples (for coupling), wire on a spool or roll (for fastening or decorating), paper clips, thumbtacks, small tin cans for expected and unexpected uses, and the tiny, silvery coasters that normally go into chair legs but which make wonderful headlights on trains.

STRING: a ball of twine and string of several different thicknesses. These have innumerable uses.

RUBBER: rubberbands and pieces of rubber or vinyl that can be cut from an old inner tube or discarded galoshes (children will surely find interesting uses for these).

WOOD: spools of different sizes, small wheels of different sizes which can be bought from educational equipment companies, doweling of different thicknesses, cheese boxes, cigar boxes, tongue depressors (all useful to inventive, constructive children). Synthetic "wood" may have usefulness as an accessory, too.

LEATHER: scraps from a shoe repair shop or pieces of discarded leather belts or shoe tongues make good hinges and handles when needed.

CLOTH: needed sometimes for sails on a boat or upholstery for furniture.

To use the various accessories, other tools and materials will be needed besides the scissors already available on the tool board. These include glue, a big needle and thick thread kept in a well-labeled box on a shelf or in a pocket on the board, and a sturdy wastebasket with dustpan and brush—all marked "woodworking" and kept in a specially designated place. A box of labels may also be useful to keep in a special drawer. (Children soon teach themselves and each other to distinguish the designation on the label.)

INTRODUCING CHILDREN TO WOODWORKING

Obtaining the workbench, tools, wood, and accessories, putting everything in place, and establishing the time of day for the activity does not necessarily mean that woodworking can then start right off, as the children usually think it must. There must first be some introduction, usually a few weeks after the school year commences. When the teacher and children have achieved a reasonably good rapport and an understanding of each other, when general routines, safety rules, and the need for taking turns have been established, introduction to the woodworking activity and all its fascinating sidelines are in order.

The inexperienced teacher may feel worried about putting real tools into the hands of some of the energetic children, or she or he may feel all thumbs; therefore, experimenting a bit without the children watching is a very sensible precaution. When tackling the job, the teacher may have the entire class or half of the class at a time for an initial session of explanation, discussion, inspection, and testing of the equipment. It will not suffice to say, "This is a nice strong bench." Instead, the children, one or two at a time, will need to knock on it or try to lift it to determine the strength or weight of the bench. And it will not be enough merely to admonish, "This saw is very sharp and dangerous, so don't fool with it." It would be more effective to allow children to feel with their fingers the flat side of the teeth, inspect the thin sharp points, feel with their own hands the hardness of wood, see and hear the teeth of the saw cut into the wood. The teacher must give a graphic and instructive demonstration of the movements of the arm in sawing—gripping the handle firmly, one pushes *down* with emphasis and comes *up* easily. The teacher should also explain the definite rules for safety—where to keep each hand, how far away from the saw other children must be, and how the saw is taken off, put down and put away.

The weight and function of the hammer can be demonstrated and tested by some children to dramatize for others its crashing power on an empty carton or perhaps on a tin can or rock. Then the tentative blow followed by the resounding, firm whack on the nail can be demonstrated and the hammer's place on the tool board pointed out. Fuller tells us

> Hammering is a most delicious activity for young children and it is most rewarding when it results in successfully and firmly fastening two pieces of wood together. For a small child this is a great achievement, as there are various things that can go wrong in the course of that simple operation. The nail

may bend, the wood may split, or the child may simply have great difficulty in controlling the hammer and hitting the nail.[16]

On a recent visit to a kindergarten, one of the authors observed two boys engaged in good whacking with a hammer on a rock. One could infer by their facial and bodily expressions that they were certainly aware of the strength of the hammer, the hardness of the rock, and the pleasure of exercising their muscles in using a hammer. Just hammering was indeed attractive and satisfying—although there was not much to show for the effort.

The other tools can also be touched, inspected by each interested child, called by the right name and tried out or at least demonstrated to the children. To emphasize correct techniques the children can be allowed to take turns using the tools right then and there. Just a demonstration will do to convince them of the necessity of putting the tools where they belong and of keeping materials and nails in proper containers. Orderliness is really fascinating to children, as long as the teacher cares about orderliness without being rigid. Since the chief difficulty will be the assignment of turns (probably no more than three children at a time can use the workbench), a decision will have to be made as to how long the turn should last—whether it should be twenty minutes, half an hour, one hour, or as long as interest and energy last. It is a good idea to prepare a calendar with an alphabetic list of the children so that at each woodworking session the children know who the workers are. (This is a good way for children to learn to recognize their names and the date(!), and even read the word "woodworking.")

Supervision for Safety and Satisfaction

Even with an interesting and effective introduction to woodworking, and the children *saying* they know the rules and can handle tools, the teacher must always realize that with their strong impulses, curiosities, and energies, kindergartners must be supervised and guided while acquiring skills and controls for satisfying woodworking activity. Although four- to six-year-olds normally respect the need for caution with a tool and will refrain from abusing it, lack of such respect is not uncommon. Children of this age do not really appreciate the cutting power of a saw that is too close to a friend's gesticulating hand. They may make sudden friendly but unsafe movements toward a child with a tool or make a quick grab at a sharp object which would be perfectly safe to pick up slowly. An erupting argument with tools in hand is potentially dangerous and children need prompt cautioning: "If you have to argue, put down the tools. That's a rule, remember." Without intimidation or nagging, safety rules must be articulated by the teacher on all appropriate occasions to assure that the rules are understood by the children.

When, after several sessions, the teacher feels secure about the children handling themselves and the tools safely at the workbench, it may not be necessary to give them close attention, and merely keeping an eye on them (one of the many

[16]Fuller, *Woodworking*, p. 14.

eyes a kindergarten teacher is mysteriously equipped with) provides sufficient supervision. The children remain free, of course, to ask for help or advice. Safe and independent woodworking will give them added opportunity to develop responsibility. There actually do exist properly equipped woodworking areas in classrooms, which children use with no more supervision than, and with as much responsibility as, is required with heavy blocks, spilly paints, or messy clay. Children need good direction to reach this point.

Good supervision in woodworking not only guards the children's safety but allows them interesting individual experiences, discoveries of their own powers, strengthening of techniques, and much exciting learning. But it gives a great deal to the teacher as well. It can reveal children's traits which were never suspected: dainty looking little girls enjoying a turn with the rough work; a boy who is usually hopping from one thing to another staying attentively put with a sawing task until completion; children asking searching questions about wood and simple mechanics during active physical involvement. The teacher also learns the nature of children's difficulty with planning through this activity. Though older children are encouraged to have a plan before starting work, kindergarten children may not know at all what they want to do or to make until they look and touch and try something first. Often they make a decision only after responding to the materials actually available or to the activity of another child. They may also get a brand-new idea while already working on something and insist on changing a project from the original idea. It is therefore important to allow children to evolve their own plans rather than to give them a ready-made plan and a set design for a product or to insist that they have a blueprint before they start.

PRACTICAL RELATION OF WOODWORKING
TO OTHER ACTIVITIES

Woodworking is not only popular as a separate activity with individual children, but it also serves in a practical way to further other classroom pursuits. Children may make vehicles, furniture, traffic signs, and other imaginatively conceived and easily constructed objects to use in block play. In one class several children collected the wood shavings which resulted from planing, took them to the housekeeping corner, and filled a pot with "spaghetti." Similarly, sawdust was collected for use as "cereal." In one class, where paintbrushes were often lost or missing, a boy who was especially fond of drilling thought up a secure device for keeping brushes from straying and for allowing them to be easily counted. This consisted of a narrow wooden shelf with as many small holes drilled into it as there were supposed to be brushes. Attached to the wall near the painting activity, this device not only eased checking on brushes during clean-up but also stimulated interest in painting.

When air holes are needed in a closed jar to keep a captured bug alive, the jar lid can be taken to the workbench and easily punctured with nail and hammer. Should a cutting board be needed in cooking, one might find just the right piece of wood to make one at the workbench. If pails are needed for collecting things or for the sandbox, holes can be punched into empty milk cartons or cans and string or wire handles attached. If nails are loose in the roof of the playhouse outdoors (apt to be discovered by a child), the teacher may take a claw hammer from its place and either pull them out or hammer them in as an emergency measure.

"The packing box has splinters—look!" a child calls. The teacher answers, "What do you think can be done about it?" The child thinks a minute. "I know! Get sandpaper from the workbench drawer and rub it smooth!" No sooner said than done.

Another time children are arguing about who is taller, until one remembers the use of a ruler in woodworking. That same ruler is now used to measure the height of the children against the wall, and with the teacher's help the argument is rationally resolved. Such practical uses of the woodworking equipment on the part of children and teacher will lead to freer and more meaningful activity and unexpected learning.

VALUE OF WOODWORKING PRODUCTS

Not all the children's products are worth keeping or even preserving with paint. To kindergarten children, the pleasure of the process is quite often as significant as the pleasure in the product.

When children make something that they (or the teacher) feel should be preserved or decorated, it should be possible for them to use paint and beautify the product as they see fit. Watercolor paints are sufficient to begin with in painting wood, but the color fades and rubs off onto hands. "Fixing" the color with shellac is somewhat messy for kindergartners, so that inevitably the time comes when "real" paint seems the best thing to use.

It is necessary to set up a place for this supplementary activity of painting wood products. What will be needed are old newspapers on which to work and enamel paint in a secure container with special brush. Water-based paints now make clean-up quite simple. If poster paints are used instead, then after the paint is dry, shellac should be applied with a brush of its own. Shellac brushes must be cleaned in denatured alcohol. Since the importance of painting wood products depends on the children and the kind of work they are doing, the teacher will supervise and guide this activity accordingly. Sometimes restriction may be necessary, as when a child is so fascinated with painting wooden surfaces that he or she would use up half of the available wood if not stopped. In one such case the teacher told Darryl, "You can paint wood only after you make something with it and it *needs* to be painted," whereupon he very quickly and crudely constructed an airplane and logically and justifiably demanded a right to paint it. When the teacher realized that it was painting and not woodworking that mattered to Darryl, she gave him a big, old, cardboard crate to paint.

Kindergarten children can be quite responsible, and the possibility of spilling should not be a deterrent to trying materials. But four- to six-year-olds are not grown-up, and it is unfair to expect more skill from them than they have. They will be cautious and respectful of paint, shellac, and turpentine. But an adult must be close at hand, especially if more than one child is working with these materials.

Woodworking does indeed satisfy many needs of young children. Perhaps the phrase heard most frequently from children in connection with woodworking is "It's real." Thus although block building is sometimes perceived as play, woodworking is usually regarded by children as real work, requiring "grown-up" tools, and it can bring immense satisfaction to small children. In addition, woodworking in the kindergarten will acquaint the children and teachers with various characteristics of wood, leading to appreciation of its source in nature.

REFERENCES AND FURTHER READING

BIBER, BARBARA. "The Role of Play," in *As The Twig Is Bent; Readings in Early Childhood Education,* eds. Robert H. Anderson and Harold G. Shane. Boston: Houghton Mifflin Company, 1971.

BRANDHOFER, MARIJANE. "Carpentry for Young Children," *Young Children* (October 1971).

BRODY, CHARLOTTE. "Social Studies and Self Awareness" in *The Block Book,* Elisabeth Hirsch, ed. Washington, D.C.: National Association for the Education of Young Children, 1974.

CARTWRIGHT, SALLY. "Blocks and Learning," *Young Children* (March 1974).

CARTWRIGHT, SALLY. "Trips and Blocks: A Study of Five-Year-Old Learning." Unpublished Master's Thesis, Bank Street College of Education, 1971.

CUFFARO, HARRIET K. "Dramatic Play—The Experience of Block Building," in *The Block Book,* ed. Elisabeth Hirsch. Washington, D.C.: NAEYC, 1974.

FRANKLIN, ADELE. "Blocks: A Tool of Learning," *Childhood Education,* 26 (January 1950), 209–13.

FULLER, GEORGE. *Woodworking with Children.* New York: Bank Street College of Education, 1974.

HARTLEY, RUTH E., FRANK, LAWRENCE K., and GOLDENSON, ROBERT M. *Understanding Children's Play.* New York: Columbia University Press, 1959.

HIRSCH, ELISABETH S., ed. *The Block Book.* Washington, D.C.: NAEYC, 1974.

JOHNSON, HARRIET M. *The Art of Block Building.* New York: Bank Street College of Education, 1962 (reprint).

LEEB-LUNDBERG, KRISTINA. "The Block Builder Mathematician," in *The Block Book,* ed. Elisabeth Hirsch. Washington, D.C.: NAEYC, 1974.

LEVITT, JEROME. *True Book of Tools.* Chicago: Children's Press, 1955.

MOFFITT, MARY W. "Children Learn about Science through Block Building," in *The Block Book,* ed. Elisabeth Hirsch. Washington, D.C.: NAEYC, 1974.

MOFFITT, MARY W. *Woodworking for Children.* New York: Early Childhood Education Council of New York City, 1976.

PRATT, CAROLINE. *I Learn from Children: An Adventure in Progressive Education.* New York: Simon & Schuster, 1948.

ROCKWELL, ANN. *Toolbox.* New York: Macmillan, 1974.

Films

"Blocks . . . A Medium for Perceptual Learning," FOUNDATIONS OF LEARNING
SERIES, Campus Film Distributors Corp., 14 Madison Avenue, Valhalla, N.Y.
10595.
"The City Builders," Campus Film Distributors Corp., 14 Madison Avenue, Valhalla,
N.Y. 10595.

11 Science Experiences for Children and Teachers

FUNDAMENTAL EARLY SCHOOL EXPERIENCES

Twentieth-century children live in a world where science determines their way of life to an extraordinary extent. Every citizen must be, if not a scientist, at least appreciative, reasonably knowledgeable, and even critical of scientific developments. The kindergarten is not too early to start nurturing such enlightened citizens. Many kindergartens and some nursery schools have science programs as formal parts of the curriculum or as special projects carried out by the teacher or science specialist. Most kindergartens have a "science corner," a "science table," or a display of some sort. Yet there is real need for self-clarification on the part of teachers as to what science is, how it is learned by young children, and what the teacher's role in supporting an interest in science can and should be.

A commission of the American Association for the Advancement of Science dealt with these questions in some detail. Its panel on kindergarten–grade three, after considering the characteristics of the five- to eight-year-old child and the nature of the school environment, concluded that the early school years are "a time of building scientific readiness" and that "pre-science" is a more appropriate description of the activities of young children than "science." Young children's natural activities of manipulation, exploration, and lively finding out are not, in the judgment of the panel, "really the formalized enterprise of scientific investigation," but they do indicate scientific readiness and must receive encouragement, since it is such readiness, if responded to, that is the basis for later formal science learning and teaching.[1]

The following is a vivid demonstration of such lively finding out in a young child's self-initiated activity:

> After watching a gardener digging out shrubbery roots, four-and-a-half-year-old Darius found a sharp stone and proceeded to "dig for roots." "Look—here is a root," he said excitedly, holding a stringy grass root in one hand and his stone-shovel in another. He became so preoccupied doing it that he was reluctant to leave for lunch and talked about "different kinds" of roots.
>
> Later, after coming home from the beach, Darius immediately went into the backyard to resume digging, but this time he preferred to use a shovel. He kept digging laboriously, until he succeeded in making a sizable hole and another discovery. He rushed into the house with an announcement: "I found a lot of ants in my hole!" He continued watching the ants with absorption and amusement for the rest of the afternoon.
>
> In the house, the subject of roots was still on his mind.
>
> "What are roots for?"
>
> "To hold the plant in the ground. Roots are strong."
>
> "Yes! Roots *are* strong. I had to pull and dig hard to get them out."
>
> After supper Darius went to digging again, and again the first thing the next morning. Impressed and satisfied with the depth and dimension of a hole, Darius this time asked for water to make mud. How good the mud seemed to him! With it his fervor cooled; he relaxed; his intellectual-physical passion seemed spent.

Darius's play was no formalized scientific investigation. Yet in his concentration in digging for roots, for revealed space, and for crawling ants, he dug a path toward science, and he knew how to relax from his intense efforts, the way many children do.

In the sense that children are so ready to manipulate, explore, and find out, they can be called "natural" scientists. They learn with their senses; they are propelled by curiosity and the temptation to test; they are capable of observing, classifying, identifying, and describing. They are interested in solving problems and arriving at conclusions. But they will need years to practice these and other skills, and above all, they need time to internalize all that they take in. Hopefully, they will retain in adulthood those characteristics they have in common with scientists,

---

[1]*Panel on Kindergarten–Grade Three,* appointed by the Commission on Science Instruction, American Association for the Advancement of Science (Directives to the Summer Writing Conference at Stanford University, Palo Alto, California, 1963).

especially their curiosity. In the words of the panel, "The young child needs not only to learn skills but to have his or her curiosity, which is after all the embryo of intellect, encouraged and magnified."[2]

USING COMMON ENCOUNTERS WITH NATURE
TO TEACH SCIENCE

A first step for the teacher is to recognize and value children's curiosity and the possibilities for science learning in spontaneous situations. For example, in a group of five-year-olds playing outdoors in freezing winter weather, several children find little islands of brittle ice on the ground. They squash it with their feet, splinter it with sticks, and characteristically pick up pieces to suck surreptitiously. Observing them, the teacher wonders: What do they *know* about ice? Can she find out from their free play and comments? Using the children's activity as a starting point, she explores these questions.

"Where do you think this ice comes from?" she asks Sasha and Perry, who are both chopping away at it.

"It comes from the ground," says Sasha, looking at the ice on the ground.

"It comes from the cold," says Perry, feeling a piece in his hands.

"How do you get ice cubes at home?" The teacher is curious about how well children understand cause-and-effect relationships.

"We get it from the freezer part of the refrigerator."

"From the ice cube tray."

There is no sign of recognition that ice is the same substance whether it is in large lumps in the schoolyard or small cubes served at the table. Nor do the children seem to see the connection between water, freezing temperature, and the formation of ice, whether caused naturally outdoors or by electricity indoors. Here then is an opportunity to help the children see the relationship—within their own experience.

"Let's make some ice cubes," the teacher offers. There is an immediate response and some puzzlement from the whole group.

"In the refrigerator?"

"No, outdoors. It's cold enough now." The children are more curious and puzzled.

"You need an ice cube tray," Vicki offers.

"All right. I'll bring one." And the teacher obtains an empty ice cube tray from the school kitchen.

"There is nothing in it," a child observes.

"We'll have to fill it up then," the teacher says.

"Will you fill it with ice?" Vicki asks.

"*I* won't put the ice in it . . ." The teacher cannot resist sounding a bit mysterious. "But I'll fill the tray with something. Or you can fill it."

[2]Ibid.

"Fill it with water," several children say, and everybody runs inside, coming back with paper cups of water and filling all the spaces in the sectioned tray.

"Now put it in the refrigerator," says Sasha automatically. No one challenges that.

"Why in the refrigerator?" the teacher questions.

"To make ice cubes."

"Yes, the water in the tray would freeze in the refrigerator. You know that. But *it is freezing cold* outdoors. Do you want to see if there will be ice cubes in the tray after we leave it in the freezing cold, outdoors?" An enthusiastic, unanimous "yes" is followed by concern for the protection of the tray against tipping and being blown, and an appropriately heavy covering is secured.

"Will there really be ice cubes in the tray?" several children ask unbelievingly. "When? When?"

"If it doesn't get much warmer there will be ice in the tray by tomorrow," the teacher answers.

The children now watch the outdoor thermometer with serious concern. The next day when there actually are ice cubes, these sophisticated five-year-olds, who speak readily about jet flights and spaceships and dinosaurs, show astonishment and jubilation about water freezing. Each child in the group reports the exciting event of making ice cubes to the parents. Several children want to make their own ice cubes and do. There is testing of, and inquiry about, conditions and results. Will a big and little dish of water freeze the same way? Will a rock freeze in the water? Unexpectedly, there is the discovery that ice makes objects adhere. There is repeated questioning about the time required for freezing and for unfreezing. When, on a day with thirty-five degree temperature the water in the ice tray remains liquid, the children see the connection. "It's not freezing cold to make ice."

When a Clue Is Not a Clue

Not every situation offers fruitful possibilities for science learning, and teachers who do not understand that science readiness involves the pursuit of curiosity more than the accumulation of facts for their own sake can make some awkward, unsuccessful attempts to get children to learn.

Let us look into a kindergarten where a conscientious teacher, always ready to offer information and give advice, always ready to promote "science learning," did not quite hit it off.

A group of six children are playing ship on a sturdy indoor jungle gym. This ship has people on it, but more important, it has cows. And the most distinguishing characteristic of a cow, according to the actions of the children, is the deep but rather loud mooing. As the mooing improves with practice, it also becomes too noisy, and Mrs. Bascom approaches the cattle ship cheerfully. Since the group went on a farm trip a week ago, she is glad to see them playing cows. "Good," she says approvingly, "but how much do cows really moo?" The children admit that the cows at the farm did not moo much. After a short while, however, the cows on the jungle gym are again mooing with unrestrained and noticeable frequency. It is apparent that this play is reflecting the children's feelings and impressions of mooing rather than the actual reality that they observed.

Mrs. Bascom once again comes over to remind the children that the cows really did not moo much on the farm.

"But this is a *ship*," answers a little boy, defending and explaining the cows' distressing mooing.

"But what else do cows do?" the teacher prods, hoping to add scientific content to the game.

"They milk," respond the children. Whether "milk" means independent action on the part of cows or passive service is not clear.

Left alone again, the children continue playing cows aboard ship but in a quieter manner, since they are now "milking," as can be gathered by the stage asides, vague squatting postures, and manual motions intended to symbolize this procedure. Before long it becomes apparent from the conversation that the bulls are getting milked as much as the cows. The teacher hears this and calls the entire crew and cattle to attention. "Just a minute, children. Do you know what bulls are?"

"A bull is a daddy," a child answers.

"Right! And do daddies give milk?" These bright, articulate five-year-olds who talk so easily are now at a loss for an answer.

"Well," the teacher persists, "does your daddy give milk?"

"Yes," one little boy answers in a straightforward manner. "My daddy gets milk, too," says another child with complete assurance. The teacher immediately corrects the children's misinformation by saying, "No, only mommies give milk." In her eagerness to inform and give scientific facts, conscientious Mrs. Bascom has failed to hear what the children are saying and thinking. These modern five-year-olds have of course seen daddies giving milk. Daddies have given a bottle to the baby or a glass to the child, and they have been observed to get milk from the store or the refrigerator. The children are clearly not thinking of lactation and breast milk, as Mrs. Bascom is, which would have been clear to her had she listened.

After clean-up, when the children gather for a discussion period on the floor, Mrs. Bascom recalls the earlier game of cows and the children's trip to the farm. She holds up a picture showing a cow family with bull and calf. The children point to the similarities in looks of each member of the family and one child says, "On our ship we had a grandpa and a daddy bull." The teacher acknowledges this with a nod and then tells the children about cows giving milk, pointing to a picture of a cow's udder. Continuing with the subject, the teacher asks the children, "And what makes good milk?" One child answers promptly, "A lot of cream makes good milk!" This time the teacher tries to clarify her question by changing the wording: "What does a cow have to *do* to make good milk?" The answer this time is "Eat grass." This pleases the teacher, and she terminates the lesson. But has it really been science learning? Was this dramatic play the right occasion for pushing facts? It is doubtful that the children learned what Mrs. Bascom taught. To an observer, it was a language exercise in which both children and teacher showed continued misunderstanding.

CONCEPT LEARNING

The first episode—the ice in the school yard—was successful because the teacher realized by observing and listening to the children that the bright, healthy five-year-olds in her class didn't know that ice comes from water, that it was difficult for them to understand the process of freezing, and that therefore they could not anticipate the change. Despite their experience with ice cubes, the phenomenon of water becoming ice was a big surprise which the children wanted to *verify* themselves, a true characteristic of the scientific approach. They also became interested in the reverse process of ice turning to water as they came indoors and watched ice slowly thin and turn to liquid. Patient observation is also a characteristic of the scientific approach.

All children can be taught to memorize facts, and in science, teachers often find it easy to state the facts and expect them to be remembered. But facts make sense only when the children can relate them to experience, idea, or intent. Furthermore, in the words of a panel on science instruction, "Premature memorization and reliance on telling and describing may deprive a child of a basic formulation for his future learnings. If this is so, the primary years of five to eight assume a crucial position."[3]

Before presenting classroom activities and materials to prepare children for science readiness, let us stop for a moment to consider the basic distinction between familiarity with facts and development of concepts.

FACTS VERSUS CONCEPTS

The confusion in teachers' minds lies in their mistaking *facts* for *concepts*. Traditional schooling has for centuries been based on the acquisition of facts, and our present uncertainty about how to teach concepts is understandable. Yet facts unrelated to each other or to general principles become isolated items that by themselves may not lead to thinking at all. Science learning and especially scientific thinking are heavily dependent on the understanding of concepts. Facts are included in concepts, but they are not the same. Let us clarify this.

A fact is a statement that is regarded as true, accurate, final, and therefore unchangeable. The sun rose at 5:32 is a fact; the rising of the sun is a concept. Two and two make four is a fact; addition is a concept. A fact is objective, but a concept is an abstraction formed out of the essentially common features of a class of objects, events, or situations that may even appear dissimilar. Sometimes a concept is close to the phenomenon represented, as in the example of the rising sun. Sometimes concepts are difficult to relate to the concrete world, such as the concepts of morality, dependency, democracy. A concept is not necessarily accurate, final, or even true. A concept is flexible and subject to change. It also depends on facts and, for a

[3] Ibid.

young child, pretty much on observed events in the concrete world. But although facts and concepts are interrelated and interdependent, they are not the same and are not taught in the same way.

An excellent case study of a preschool child by John Navarra makes clear the gradualness of concept formation, which involves a number of irregular stages of limited comprehension, some erroneous thinking and self-correction, acquisition of reliable pieces of knowledge, and finally, expression of scientific principles as all of it comes together.[4]

It is true that some things have to be taken on faith by children and learned by rote. But there must be a conscious effort to keep such rote learning to a minimum, especially in science, if a love and appreciation of the significance of science in our lives is to result. Children learn best by concrete and firsthand experience. With a little thought, a teacher can discover concrete applications for a surprising number of scientific concepts, such as the relation of parts to the whole, as in the human body; the transforming of matter from one physical state to another, as in ice and water; the relation of speed of an object in motion to the surface on which it travels. Let us take as an illustration the scientific concept of change, which may at first seem remote and abstract. Yet one teacher recognized the concept when an unexpected occurrence in her classroom made it possible for the children to draw the desired conclusion themselves.

ABSTRACT CONCEPTS

A bottle of milk left over from snack time in a kindergarten class was discovered on the sunny windowsill the next morning. The teacher told the children that the milk was not fresh any more for drinking. "Let's see it 'not fresh,'" said one child. The teacher poured some milk into a bowl, but the child could not tell that this milk was different by either looking at it or smelling it. Another child volunteered to taste it; the teacher did too, pronouncing it "a little bit sour." She might have left it at that, but instead she put the bottle with spoiled milk back on the windowsill to really become sour and thick, "so we can make cheese from it."

"Cheese?" This did not make much sense to the children, as they could not visualize without previous experience how liquid milk could possibly change into soft but solid cheese. Many of the children were curious enough to make sure an adequate sign was placed on the souring milk bottle to protect it from being thrown out by another class or by the cleaning man. In a few days, distinct curds appeared in the milk, and a distinct and repellent odor emanated from the bottle when the lid was removed. Practically all the children were curious to see the sour milk and to observe any evidence of cheese, although none of them really expected anything the least bit edible to come from it.

---

[4] John G. Navarra, *The Development of Scientific Concepts* (New York: Columbia University Press, 1955).

"Smell it—pe-euw!"

"I'm not going to eat that!"

"Me neither."

The teacher had made cheese with other city-bred children before, and this was the reaction that she anticipated. But she also counted on these four- to five-year-olds' genuine interest in the origins of familiar things. Does cheese really come from milk? How? They would see, she promised them. She then heated the lumpy soured milk to complete the curds and whey separation and provided a cheesecloth bag for draining off the whey. The children were surprised at the name "cheesecloth." (Some of them identified the cloth as polishing cloth.) Several brave children followed the teacher's example and drank some whey; they said it was a little like lemonade. The mechanical process of squeezing the cheese bag between boards, finding heavy objects to facilitate the squeezing (blocks, stones, and filled cannisters), and obtaining appropriate receptacles for collecting the whey drainage was fascinating to all the children. There was, of course, constant curiosity to see if the curds had already turned to cheese. When in about an hour and a half the cheese bag was emptied into a bowl and the children took turns stirring it with a little seasoning and salt and a touch of cream, everyone was curious to taste it. When the cheese was served on crackers with a dot of red jelly, it was a proven success. Even those children who did not want to eat it because they had remembered the smell of the soured milk or because they felt hesitant about any strange food were interested in the whole process and enjoyed vicariously the other children's pleasure in eating. When later in the year a new student-teacher in that class remarked, "Don't shake the milk when you are carrying it—it might turn to cream," the children who heard her answered: "Oh, no. Milk doesn't turn to cream. Milk turns to cheese after you keep it on the warm window."

Change in taste, change in shape, change in substance, change in color, and change in volume can be carefully observed by children in their concrete forms. A quart of moist, firm, leafy spinach, when cooked a few minutes in a glass pot, can diminish to a cupful of juicy, limp pulp before the children's eyes. And children see that heat releases water from broken vegetable fibers. Conversely a cupful of rice will swell to a potful when cooked with water. And here children see that heat causes expansion. Seeing a dripping wet shirt become perfectly dry hanging on a line in the sunshine is good preparation for children's learning the concept of evaporation later. Sometimes children make note of these things themselves; sometimes phenomena need focusing. Maggie, watching a crayon on the warm radiator cover, may have to be helped to see the cause of its gradual change from a hard, cylindrical crayon to a soft, shapeless thing, and finally to a colored liquid. A discarded apple section observed to change from white to brown may lead to curious questioning. How did it happen? Why? Would any apple change in color? In the refrigerator? If you cover it up, would it still change? Questioning is a first step to exploration, and exploration is the true basis of scientific learning. We might say that any concept that can be illustrated in concrete terms can be understood by a child.

Some concepts, however, cannot be made concrete. Government, democracy, liberty are among these, and it is not until long after kindergarten that children can understand such concepts. But many other concepts that seem as abstract actually can be illustrated in ways children can see, hear, touch, taste, or smell. We shall see this later in the chapter.

In teaching any fact a teacher must always ask, "What concepts must the children understand in order to realize the significance of this fact?" In teaching concepts one asks, "What facts underpin and support this concept?" These ideas will become clearer as we illustrate the concrete experiences through which children learn.

DISCRIMINATION AND CLARIFICATION
IN SCIENCE LEARNING

We can see what a profound challenge there is to a kindergarten teacher who wants children to enjoy scientific knowledge. She or he must learn how much knowledge the children already have, help correct misconceptions, and then plan on the basis of children's interests and available sources to extend their knowledge. The variety of backgrounds and environments in kindergarten classes make a precise guide or specific formula much too limiting.

A first approach to science teaching is exploratory, one that says "Let us find out." A second uses children's observations to heighten their powers of discrimination and strengthen their ability to classify data. Children have a natural propensity to learn this way in any case. The teacher's job is to provide opportunities and encouragement. Scientific effort in a classroom may begin with some collection of natural objects—an arrangement of autumn leaves, an assortment of acorns and nuts, a collection of rocks, or a display of differently shaped seashells. Feathers, birds' eggs, and seeds are some of the more unusual collections. The scientific validity of any collection in the kindergarten lies not only in the perfection of specimens or in their variety but also in their meaning to children. A dazzling collection of pinned butterflies behind a glass, prepared by the teacher, is hardly better than a picture to be passively admired, a decoration. But a collection that children can inspect and handle is alive with possibilities. A box of shells brought in by one teacher was not a scientific collection in the technical sense; it was made by the teacher chiefly on the basis of eye appeal and appreciation of the shells' abundance and variety. The shells were familiar to the children, since most of them had had seaside vacations; yet gathered in an open box and brought by the teacher for the children, the shells aroused considerable interest and inspired further contributions. Several children brought additional collections, and as a few children at a time played with the shells, arranging them as to size or shape, they began to differentiate them. "What kind is this purplish shell?" "A mussel," the teacher answered.

"This one looks like a saucer; I want to drink out of it," said Joyce.

"Oh, I saw millions of those," said Harley. "What do you call them? I forgot."

"Clam shells," the teacher said helpfully and allowed Dina to use them for "tea" in the housekeeping section.

"What's the name of this one? That's a beauty!" Harley asked the teacher, showing her an intricate snail shell.

"Let me look in the book to make sure," the teacher answered.

"Let me look, too. I want to see the picture." The teacher opened a picture book, *Beachcomber Bobbie,*[5] and Harley promptly identified the picture of his shell, observing both the shape and the special "eye" design in the middle; he laid the shell directly on the picture. Three more children followed suit and picked up moon shells and scallops and clams and cockles. They were particularly impressed with the similarity between the actual starfish shell and the picture of it. For a few minutes the children used the book with studious concentration, the way one uses a laboratory manual. A majority of the twenty-two children that year showed curiosity about the shells, sometimes pocketing a few, breaking some, or using them for dishes or as a block-building decoration. A few children referred to the pictures of shells constantly, asked about names, and inquired about the whereabouts of the former inhabitants of the shells.

[5]Florence Bourgeois, *Beachcomber Bobbie* (Garden City, N.Y.: Doubleday, Doran & Company; out of print, may be available in libraries). A book with similar pictures is Glenn E. Blough's *Who Lives at the Seashore,* illus. Jeanne Bendick (New York: McGraw-Hill Book Company, 1962). See also, Bernice Kohn, *The Beachcomber's Book* (New York: The Viking Press, 1970).

A collection of stones can provide an analogous experience in investigation through observation, touch, and feel, and can lead to practical and intellectual inquiry. Using a heavy stone and finding out how its crushing weight cracks an especially hard black walnut, a child wants to know: "Can one stone break another stone?" And he spends considerable time testing the stone for size and weight, hardness and durability. Another child becomes fascinated with the doughnut shape of a stone in the collection and stimulates several other children to speculate on the causes of its odd shape. The teacher accepts the children's own imaginative and spontaneous names for the stones, such as "potato stone" because of its shape and color, or "hand stone" because it fits especially nicely in a child's hand. This kind of spontaneous personal naming of stones sharpens the children's observation and perception. There are, however, occasions when the teacher can appropriately introduce correct names, which not only builds a scientific vocabulary but arouses further interest. The teacher must judge at which point to say: "This rock you hold (or this tree you see) has a real name," thus introducing the children to the rock or the tree.

"I saw this shiny kind of stone before," said Delma, inspecting a find on a brief excursion.

"It has a name," said the teacher.

"What?" Delma asked as another child joined them.

"It's called *mica*."

"Mica," Delma repeated.

"And what about this one?" Another child took a crumbly stone out of his pocket.

"Hm . . . this must be *shale*." Now other children wanted to know the names of their stones, and unable to identify them herself, the teacher promised to look them up.

Physical contact with natural phenomena is apt to stimulate curiosity and questioning on the part of children, which in turn may encourage the teacher to learn something about the topic that interests the children. Books and magazine articles written for children can often make scientific material accessible and interesting to adults as well, and they can give the teacher of four- to six-year-olds reliable basic information to guide young children's quest for knowledge (see bibliography at the end of the chapter). After going through such books, the teacher can read parts with the children and certainly look at the illustrations together with them.

RELATING TO BIOLOGICAL PHENOMENA

A boy of four-and-a-half, playing with a can full of acorns that he has collected on the way to school, decides to poke one acorn open to see the nut inside. The teacher encourages him by advising the use of a hammer at the workbench. Instead of finding a nut inside the shell the boy finds the acorn full of soft, dry, brown matter and some small, pale, grubby worms.

"Look!" This is news indeed. Not only the boy who discovered the acorn worms but also everyone in the class becomes fascinated with the looks, movements, diet, and family life of the worm. Every child grabs an acorn and eagerly hammers or cracks it open, looking for worms. For days the children collect acorns, excavating the worms and giving them acorn meat to eat. How disappointed Donna is when her three acorns prove empty, and she begs for a worm from "lucky" J. W., who has a "whole bunch." Thus, opening acorns can bring an unexpected benefit.

Feeling Possessive and Protective toward Living Things

A similar excitement about finding something alive and a similar regard for a small creature are shown by a group of six-year-olds in a play group in a city park. Benji finds a furry, yellow caterpillar on a milkweed plant.

"Look what I found!" He picks it up as if it were a treasure. Immediately there is a cluster of boys and girls around him.

"Oh, look at the black feelers."

"Let him come on me!" Then one little girl pats the caterpillar as if it were a kitten.

"Don't. You might squash him," Benji cautions. "He needs a good twig to hold onto so he can spin a cocoon." And Benji finds a large enough forked twig. When the caterpillar is securely placed on it, Benji carries the twig around. Several children follow him wanting to know, "What's the caterpillar going to eat?" "Milkweed leaves," says Benji, and adds enthusiastically to the teacher, "I saw him eating it before and I know it's milkweed because when I broke it off there was milk in the stem!"

"Where, where? Show me!" children ask eagerly, and Benji shows the children the milkweed. Then he sticks some leaves on the twig for the caterpillar's meal. A little later one boy notices that a few leaves are floating in a shallow puddle. "They look like ducks swimming in the water," he says with amusement. Then he gets an idea. "Hey! If I make a little boat then your caterpillar can have a boat ride in the water here. Right, Benji?" Benji is concerned about the effect of wetness on his pet, but somehow a boat is constructed with scraps of wood and string and launched with the caterpillar aboard. Before long, the adult who was with the children rescued the caterpillar and placed it on a twig in a jar, so that the children could see the miracle of metamorphosis.

Drawing Living Creatures into Personal Experience

In one class the teacher accepted three yellow baby ducks for Easter as a present from a parent. She kept them partly in the classroom and partly in the adjacent yard. The children loved watching the ducks huddling together; they noticed particularly the shape of their feet and commented on the ducks' rapid growth and on how they sit and swim. As they watched the yellow-turned-white ducks in the large tub, the children observed the water rolling off the ducks' backs as they splashed around; one child deliberately poured cold water on the ducks' feathered bodies to see the water rolling off. The children observed minutely as the ducks ate, drank, and excreted. They loved having the ducks as their own and requested that the teacher include the ducks in the attendance record as rightful members of the class. Thus, Lucky, Ducky, and Charlie provided a social experience as well as a scientific one. After a month, the hygienic difficulties of caring for the animals in the confines of a city classroom became too much, and the teacher gave them away to a farm in spite of the fact that this was cause for some sadness.

In another school children from several classes came in daily contact with a mother rabbit and her five tiny babies residing in a cage in the corner of the school lobby. The children noticed how at first the mother protected and concealed the babies, and they were quickly convinced by the mother not to touch them. Next they saw how some of the babies "peeked around" and others hopped on big soft feet across the cage. They then noted when the rabbits were old enough and strong enough to be allowed by their mother to be taken out and to "play alone." The greatest satisfaction came a few weeks later when the rabbits were old enough to graze in the yard and to eat from the children's hands.

FACTS OF LIFE AND DEATH IN THE CLASSROOM

A teacher who allows the children experiences with living creatures must be prepared for consequences that may not always be pleasant but are entirely possible.

Mrs. Clark could not resist some baby chicks which were available in the local pet shop. She bought six of them and installed them in a proper wire cage. After attention to food and shelter, several children had an enjoyable discussion about naming them, and finally decided upon Chicky, Nicky, Ricky, Picky, Squeaky, and Petunia. After only two days there was an unexpected loss. One chick died, possibly from cold. After an inspection it was established that there was a draft in the classroom. The maintenance man was consulted, and an electric bulb was attached to the cage to provide warmth, which the children understood was necessary for baby chicks' health. "It's a good thing the electricity works," one child observed. And with the interest in providing vital warmth for the five lively, growing chicks, the death of the sixth did not arouse more than passing concern. Then another loss occurred, which provided a different science lesson. Picky became droopy and would not eat. The children had watched the chicks so closely that they quickly noticed that "something is wrong with this one." This time another member of the school staff, who had had experience on a chicken farm, was consulted, and her advice of isolating the sick chick so that others would not succumb was promptly followed. The next day there was intense interest in preserving the health of the four chicks and also in observing the dying chick, which could no longer run or rise or take the eagerly proffered drinks of water.

Before the chick stopped breathing, the children made plans for burying him.

Richard took a box and put it next to the chicken to see if he would fit in it. The children on the whole were quite matter-of-fact about the death and burial of Picky. They did, however, seem extra watchful and more protective toward the others than they had been before. But one emotional little girl, five-year-old Helen, was upset by the chick's death, cried a little in class, and watched the other chicks anxiously, saying frequently, "I hope *they* don't die." During that week she dreamt of another of the chicks dying and conveyed her worry to her family. The teacher assured Helen that the other chicks were healthy and would receive good care; she kept herself from becoming sentimental and from contributing to Helen's distress. Helen soon became particularly happy and devoted to the four remaining chicks, who grew to be fast-running young chickens and were transferred to a large enclosure outdoors. There they provided endless entertainment by trying to take worms away from one another. Before the end of the year, the surviving chickens were returned to the pet shop owner as originally agreed.

Were the deaths a shocking exposure to the children? And should the teacher have concealed them or at least prevented the children from observing dying animals? This teacher herself was not shocked by the incident of infant mortality among baby chicks, and she felt confident that reasonably good care was provided for the animals. It seemed to her that the natural death of an animal does provide children with important facts of life and that handling such a situation as it occurs, without denying the feeling of loss or regret, will provide a wholesome rather than a morbid or worrisome experience for children. The reader may consult other books describing classroom experiences with the death of animals,[6] and may also check the children's books dealing with death in Chapter 14 of this book.

If a pair of animals is in school long enough to grow, mature, and breed, this provides an opportunity for a true biological study for the kindergartners. Animal parents are both protective and destructive of their young, and children need help in assessing such behavior as it appears. A teacher must be prepared for all eventualities, ready to tackle with clarity and honesty the children's questions and observations.

SELECTING "LIVESTOCK"

How can a teacher select the kind of animal that offers most to children, one that requires relatively simple care yet is of value in the science program?

Perhaps the general answer would be that any animal can be worthwhile if it can be safely cared for and if it evokes no revulsion on the part of the teacher. Classroom pets will invariably stimulate scientific observation and provide infinite pleasure as well. Hamsters, guinea pigs, and mice are small enough to be cared for in

---

[6]Marguerita Rudolph, *From Hand to Head: A Handbook for Teachers of Preschool Programs* (New York: Schocken Books, Inc., 1977) and Marguerita Rudolph, *Should the Children Know?* (New York: Schocken Books, Inc., 1978, Schocken Books Paperback, 1981), chap. on animals.

a cage in class and are easy to feed and clean. What is also important is that their breeding cycle is short enough for four-, five-, and six-year-olds to be able to observe in its entirely. This is also true of rabbits, who train easily to use cat litter and can enjoy the freedom of the room for longer periods of time.

Large turtles and especially tortoises are probably the most enduring of any pets, and in spite of their hardness and clumsiness seem both fascinating and endearing to children. Their slowness of locomotion, deliberateness in eating, and struggle in turning right side up invite patient observation from the often impatient children. To obtain a turtle one may try not only a pet shop, but also a restaurant which has fresh turtle soup on the menu, frequently featured in Chinese areas of some large cities. Getting a turtle from such a place will bring a double benefit: acquiring an interesting pet and (heroically) saving a creature's life! Snakes, too, are possible pets if teachers can accept them. Garter snakes will eat earthworms and fish, alive or not, and are easier to keep than one would think. In addition, they, and other animals of prey, will provide a takeoff point for children to begin thinking about the food chain on which we all depend.

In this age of environmental protection and growing appreciation of the wild, we must consider what happens to the animal when it is taken from its natural habitat and brought into a confining, people-managed room. We need to be aware that when an animal is captured in a field or stream or woods we must provide for it an environment as closely resembling its own as possible. Then, after reasonable acquaintance, we should make a plan to release it in a suitable place. If the animal is a hibernating kind, it is important that it be released before fall so that it can have time to look for winter quarters.

In the classroom the children can have the satisfaction of patting or holding the animals; they can take the responsibility of giving them food and water and can observe their anatomy and particular style of family life. Of course, teachers cannot rely on children to carry this responsibility out without some reminders and supervision. But they do grow in responsibility, and this experience is too rewarding to miss.

Animals can be obtained from pet shops or laboratories. Advice and information concerning their care is usually offered in pet shops, zoos, museums of natural history, or the library either under titles concerning the single animal or in larger volumes dealing with care of small pets. An especially informative book on the subject is simply entitled *Pets* and deals with the care and understanding of all kinds of pets—caged pets, wild creatures, farm animals, with advice on feeding and maintaining a healthy and safe companionship.[7] It includes forty-one different pets!

Uninvited Guests as Subjects for Study

Valuable as it is to provide particularly suitable animals to care for and to enjoy and study in the classroom, no less valuable is it to welcome or take notice of living creatures that may appear uninvited.

[7]Frances N. Chrystie, *Pets,* 3rd ed. (Boston: Little, Brown and Company, 1974).

A young mother brings her four-year-old Michelle to school and notices with horror that the child tries bare-handed to catch a lingering autumn fly.

"Don't you touch that dirty fly! Go wash your hands right away," she says, before leaving.

The teacher, seeing how completely fascinated Michelle is with the fly, allows her to capture it and helps Michelle place it in a jar. Michelle feeds it, watches it wash itself, listens to its droning sound, and examines its wings. The teacher explains to Michelle and the other children why flies are unsanitary and objectionable. She makes it clear that they must be kept away from food and homes. Several children promptly attest to flies' unpopularity. But, the teacher adds, in a jar at *school* a fly can be watched safely.

When a mouse appears in the wastebasket the teacher at first has an impulse to dispose of it, but seeing the children's interest, she transfers the animal to a cage. Soon the children name it "the little grey school mouse—because it came to school." They also observe that it is "too big to be a baby mouse . . . and it's too little to be a mommy mouse." They then conclude that just as they are children, this pet has to be "a child mouse." Furthermore, when the children watch it in a cage they quickly notice that this child mouse likes doing the same things they like doing—running, climbing, jumping, and eating cheese and crackers. The little grey school mouse, the child mouse, makes such an impression on the children with its agility, speed, and bright-eyed expression, that the teacher, other staff members, and parents all catch some of the children's appreciation. When later the cage is taken outdoors and the mouse disappears, the children remember and reminisce about it the rest of the year.

Part-Time Visitors

Children feel enriched by acquaintance with an animal and the sense of kinship that comes from caring for it. This can be true when an animal comes to the class for a much shorter time than the "child mouse," as long as the animal is in the children's midst and they have an opportunity for individual contact, spontaneous reaction, and observation. When a freshly-caught green frog was brought to class and the children watched it sitting on a lily pad and met it face to face, feeling it on their hands, or on the tips of their fingers—even a week's visit was profoundly impressive. (The frog eventually escaped from an outdoor tank.) "Hoppy has soft claws," Michael observed. How true, and it was independently discovered with his own sensitive hand.

And when a neighbor's goat, Josephine, came to visit the class for only one hour, practically all of the twenty children spoke about her to their incredulous parents. The animal's size in relation to the children, its manner of eating (they loved feeding it), the feel of its hide (they patted and rubbed it), the goat's face and separate features, the tail, and the detailed anatomy under the tail were not overlooked by the young investigators.

The Scientific Approach

The value of having animals in the classroom depends very much on the teacher's own willingness and ability to take advantage of the learning possibilities which living creatures offer. Overcoming squeamishness is a major first step, but only a first step. Beyond that must be the unimpeachable honesty of genuinely scientific inquiry, which may just as often lead to unforeseen and even unexpected results as to predicted ones. Here is an account of the adventure in science that was experienced by a group of handicapped young children because their teacher brought an honest spirit of inquiry into her classroom. What happened was as amazing to the teacher as to the children.[8]

> I teach in the Upper Preschool group at Lowman School. The children range in age from four-and-a-half through five-and-a-half. The group is made up of five girls and eight boys. Five of the children spend a large part of the time in wheel chairs. Eight of the children are cerebral palsied and the others have other orthopedic handicaps.
>
> Because of their physical handicaps, many of these children have not had the opportunity to observe and enjoy the everyday things we too often take for granted. Bringing such experiences into the classroom is particularly important.
>
> Our room is equipped with jars and small improvised cages for more than the usual number of crawling and wiggling things.
>
> One day our attendant found two snails on the ground near the bus ramp and brought them into the room. We put them down on the floor and the children crowded around to see. With their noses close to the floor—and to the snails—they observed:
>
> > The slowness of their movements.
> > The shell into which each disappeared when touched or when there was a loud noise.
> > The set of what looked like feelers on each side.
> > The mucus left as they moved along the floor.
> > Their habit of crawling over something rather than around it.
>
> Even the children who usually sat in wheel chairs were placed on the floor on their stomachs so they could see for themselves. All of the youngsters touched the shell and the retractable horns but only a few wanted to touch the soft "foot" part. At the end of the period, the snails were reluctantly put into an open jar with a few leaves.

Second Day

> The jar was empty! We had a "snail hunt," crawling around on our hands and knees until both snails were found, attached to the underside of the small table where the jar had been left. One of the children said, "Let's let them race again." We watched and a child said, "He's a slow-poke."
>
> I asked the children if they thought it was easy to move along that way. There were different answers of "yes" and "no."

---

[8] Rose Engel, "Learning about Common Everyday Things: Snails," *Journal of Nursery Education*, 16, *1* (1960–61).

I suggested that we find out and asked one young fellow to lie on the floor on his stomach and, without using his hands and feet, to move along the floor. Of course it was slow. Several other children wanted to try it so we had our own snail race with much wriggling and laughter and very little progress across the floor.

Third Day

On this day the Harriet Huntington book, "Let's Go Outdoors,"[9] was left opened to the section with pictures of snails. The children noticed the pictures when they came in.

I read the section and we looked at the pictures and the snails themselves. We talked about what they needed to stay alive and added a few drops of water to the jar. Some of the children said they would bring leaves to feed them. The findings of the first day's close examination were strengthened by the information in the book. Some of the children continued their watching and discussion among themselves. We set up a circle of chairs so neither the children nor the snails would be stepped upon by children engaged in other activities.

Fourth Day

Craig, a young fellow who is always bringing in leaves (which I suspect he has picked from the bushes near the bus ramp), brought a plastic bag with a "surprise" to share. "I brought a fresh snail," he said. The plastic bag also contained a few leaves. When I said that we had better keep the bag open, he informed me that plastic bags are dangerous and that is why he had made holes in the bag so the snail could breathe.

We came into the room and Craig went to put his snail into the jar. At this time we met two problems. The jar was empty again. The children began immediately to crawl around to look under the table and there they found our wandering pets again attached. The second problem was not so easily solved. The corner of the snail page in the Huntington reference book looked as if it had been chewed. The holes went through five pages, becoming smaller on each page.

We wondered what had caused this. One of the children suggested that perhaps one of the younger children in the morning class had chewed it. This idea was rejected by the rest of the group.

When an attendant came to pick up one of the children for therapy, the child pointed out the book damage. She asked what had happened and the children told her that we didn't know. She suggested that it might be a mouse. This idea was rejected also, as the book had been propped up on a table and the children thought no mouse would go there when the shelf holding other books was so close to the floor.

I felt sorry that the book had been damaged and put it back in the closet. Then I found another book entitled *Look* by Zhenya Gay, which has a snail picture on the cover. The children watched as I turned the pages until we found the same snail picture on the inside. One of the children set this book near the jar of snails.

[9]Harriet E. Huntington, *Let's Go Outdoors* (Garden City, N.Y.: Doubleday & Co., Inc., 1959).

Fifth Day

I was the most surprised of all when we found the new pages had been damaged in the same ways—as if they had been sandpapered. But this time there were some telltale glistening marks around the holes. We examined the markings and I asked the children what might have left a shining trail like that. Most of them knew that it was the snail but it seemed as incredible to me as to them that snails would eat paper.

Friday is our day to visit the library. I told the children I would look in the reference books there to see if snails were known to eat paper. In the meantime we put a cover over the jar to keep our wandering, gnawing snails out of the books—should they be the guilty ones.

While at the library I searched the encyclopedias and other references but found nothing indicating that snails eat paper.

We returned to the room still faced with the problem. In discussing the situation with the children, we came to the conclusion that we wouldn't take the chance of letting the snails out to see if they would "chew" any more books, but we could put some paper in the jar and see what might happen. So we put a sheet of regular writing paper into the jar, covered it with cardboard and left it over the weekend.

Sixth Day

On Monday we had our solution. The sheet of paper was our proof. It had a large half circle eaten away. We took out the sheet and put in a new one. While we watched we saw one snail edge its way slowly up the sheet of paper and eat a hole through the center. In a short time he had made a hole large enough that his body was all the way through and the shell section hung on the opposite side. He certainly looked odd suspended on both sides!

Seventh Day

I searched in our home encyclopedia and found a picture of a snail's mouth highly magnified, and some information on its file-like construction. But there was no mention of the paper diet. Several of the children were interested in the picture. They also found a picture of a snail hanging over the edge of a razor. I had a cutting knife with a razor blade, used for art work.

We tried this experiment and found the foot of the snail tough enough that he could hang over the sharp edge without injury. After this there was less interest in the snail. Almost a week later, during lunch, one of the children said he was going to take his paper napkin to feed the snails. He put it into the bowl but the snail didn't seem to like it as well as the other kind of paper. The children examined the napkin later and decided that the snail had tasted it because there were a few tiny holes but it seemed to prefer writing paper.

It is now four weeks since the snails were brought to our room. They are still living in the jar on a diet of paper and a few drops of water daily. Believe it or not!

Even a very simple animal drew from children—and handicapped children at that—sustained interest, persistent inquiry, careful observation, and exciting, independent discovery. Inquiry, observation, gathering data, and formulating conclusions from evidence are clearly scientific approaches and techniques. It should be obvious that it was the teacher's interest and sensitivity to the children's experience (see Chapter 17) that played an important part in that learning drama without in any way dominating the stage.

CHILDREN'S PLAY LEADS
TO PHYSICAL SCIENCE DISCOVERIES

A subject like physics seems quite outside children's ken. Yet the common phenomena of velocity, leverage, balance, and gravity are observed and investigated by children all the time. Listen to Alfred making his observations about gravity although he may never have heard the word.

"See what I've got," Alfred says, digging into his bulging shirt and producing a collection of old paper plates. "What will happen if I throw them all up at once?" He does so and laughs hilariously. "Ha-ha, they fly right down! I *thought* they would."

Salvatore propels himself downward on a low slide devised from a long board and a sawhorse. Noticing a round coffee can on the ground, he picks it up and puts it on top of the slide, watching intently as the round can rolls down the full length of the board. He smiles broadly and promptly retrieves the can, repeating and studying the downward process seriously. He also experiments with retarding and accelerating the speed by manual propulsion and by introduction of obstacles. Then he lets the can roll down, watching to see how far it will go. He is thrilled when the can rolls onto the pavement after coming down the slide and across a grassy area. When the can whirls at the end of the roll, Salvatore watches it most intently until it comes to a dead stop. Soon several other children want to roll the can down the slide, and they line up for a turn at this activity which, besides being fun, involves investigation of velocity, inertia, speed, and space.

Or watch any two kindergartners of different weights at opposite ends of a seesaw. Both the huskier and the lighter will jiggle forward and back, studying the relation of weight to the distance from the fulcrum until balance is achieved or until they solve the problem by looking for a partner of the same size.

Five-year-olds love handling and using ropes, which of course requires supervision. Using pails and wooden or metal pulleys in experimenting with ropes can help children understand concepts of weight, strength, force, and basic mechanics. Attaching ropes to poles, trees, or other heavy, secure equipment can make the outdoors a place for studying distance and space as children consider ways of reaching or connecting particular areas or points.

Often, children today have more mechanical interest and aptitude than the kindergarten teacher. Six-year-old Miguel (with only a few English words at his command) was given a small spinning top. He instantly began operating the top, quickly learning the technique of spinning, then experimenting with different surfaces, including the flattened palm of his hand, and placing obstacles in the top's path. After a few minutes he discovered a different way of starting the top. He

changed his sitting position to lying prone on the floor in order to watch the area and the direction of the moving top. He gestured excitedly at the change in speed.

What seems clear in Miguel's enthusiastic activity is a child's fascination with controlling and exploring motion. The obvious implication for a teacher of active young children is to make available not only tops but also such different spinning objects as metal jar lids of different sizes, round covers, smooth tops of cans, and so on. A teacher who watches children play with such items might also share their fascination with colors as together they notice that tops change color when in motion.

To provide safe, suitable, and functional mechanical items which children can handle and operate, the teacher can employ ordinary household utensils. Although most teachers of this decade may be users of numerous electrically powered devices, and children may be familiar with plug-in or turn-on equipment, the operation of such equipment only requires the children to be passive onlookers rather than active learners. We are therefore suggesting that household tools and utensils for use with preschool and early school age children be of the manual kind. Manual grinders, graters, sifters, strainers and squeezers, beaters, mashers, and whisks are all fascinating to children for studying construction and mechanical operations. What is even more interesting and facilitates further understanding of particular mechanical function is making some crude utensils: a funnel from paper (like a cornucopia); a strainer from a milk carton with holes in the bottom; sandpaper made by spreading glue on thick paper and coating it with clean sand. And as the children show readiness or interest, the teacher can bring in a silent three-minute egg timer, an exposed ticking mechanism of an old clock, and an alarm clock requiring winding. All these devices lead to firsthand experience with the mechanical measurement of time.

Time is not an easy concept, however. Familiarity with timepieces and use of correct terminology on the part of four- to six-year-olds does not mean that they have a concept of time. The common question "Is today tomorrow?" indicates that "today," "now," the immediate, is understandable and felt, but the unseen "tomorrow" is an abstraction. A sense of time is gained gradually, in the process of living through time spans marked by events. It is valid, nevertheless, for the teacher to have available various practical items that reflect the measurement of time, provided they are not given excessive attention at this stage. Clocks and calendars, interesting items for both children's and teacher's occasional reference, may thus invite some beginning conception of their function. When a teacher hesitated before answering a preschooler's question, "What's a calendar?" another child answered thoughtfully, "A calendar—it tells you when it's every day."

Actually, a large calendar has important personal meaning in the kindergarten. Since all children are obviously interested in birthdays, the calendar can be appropriately marked and thus looked at by children, with attention to days or weeks or months. Or the teacher might see fit to introduce a more advanced experience and make (with the participation of some children) a chronological chart of birthdays. Thus an interest in making charts might evolve! But as with so many aspects of adult life, concrete experiences matter more to children than do sophisticated devices and instruments. (See the section "Using the Body as a Tool" later in this chapter.)

Kindergartners also love playing with magnets, electric lights, switches, bells, and buzzers, all of which can be made available by the teacher who understands their principles and respects a child's level of comprehension. A child who loves ringing an electric bell may simply enjoy pushing the button and hearing the noise. Yet some child may be ready for understanding an electric circuit or for exploring other areas of physical science not discussed here.

COMPENSATORY EXPERIENCES
FOR MODERN CHILDREN

It is a curious paradox that the modern home, a veritable display of scientific advances with its mechanical gadgets and labor-saving devices, actually deprives children of basic learning about sources of common products. Bottled juices, canned seasonings, packaged desserts—all artificially colored—and frozen foods of all kinds give small children no direct and active acquaintance with the sources, processes of preparation, or even distinguishing characteristics of many common edibles. It is therefore particularly valuable for kindergarten teachers to have some preparation of food as part of the science curriculum.

Cooking provides a most valuable source of science learning on many levels and in many areas for children of all ages, but particularly for preschoolers. Cooking has an immediate appeal to all the senses; it arouses curiosity and invariably leads to questioning and investigation, particularly in the field of chemistry; it brings tangible results and personal and social satisfactions for many children. Ingredients can either be purchased at nominal cost or brought by children from home.

In one class of four- to five-year-olds, the teacher suggested that the children bring from home different kinds of vegetables to make a vegetable soup. More than half the children brought fresh vegetables, enough for a large pot of soup.

Examining, Testing, and Observing Changes in Materials

The different vegetables were weighed, washed, scrubbed with a brush, peeled (with fingernails to remove onion peels, and a safe metal peeler—not sharp knives— for carrots). Some vegetables were popped open, some were cut with butter knives and with blunt-edged scissors into slices, cubes, strips, and shreds. All were tasted and even eaten raw. The children had never seen or heard of several common vegetables. No one knew that the large, oddly-shaped, heavy, hard, tan and yellow, mild-tasting Thing was a turnip.

"Turnip? Turn-up. Turn-*up*. Does it turn up?"

It was a delightful surprise to find how many peas fit in a pod, and how different each pea was from the other (disproving the cliché "as alike as two peas in a pod!").

"I found five in mine! Let's see how many in *this* one."

"Eight? Let me count." Lima bean pods were found to be quite tough. "How do you open it?" one boy asked after squeezing with his hand, tearing with his finger, and attempting to bite the lima bean pod. When the teacher cut a red beet in half, a little boy exclaimed, "Look, it's bleeding." Several others echoed him and tinted their fingers. "See the blood." Other children used scissors to cut celery into small chunks, parsley into shreds, and a cabbage leaf into strips and "ribbons." One boy used his fingers to break off layers of an onion. When the teacher noticed his tears, she asked: "Why are you crying?" and the boy was so intrigued by the phenomenon that he was not at all distressed by the minor irritation and continued with the onion to the amusement of the others. One child was especially challenged by the effect of onions and said daringly: "This little onion isn't going to make *me* cry." And oddly enough, no tears appeared to mar his determined glance while he snipped and cut a raw onion. Another child was astonished that a dry potato was wet inside.

Different seasonings were added with spoons and sprinkles and pinches. The soup was cooked on an electric burner. Some children were particularly interested in the cooking itself: watching the pyrex pot with the boiling broth (beef bone, water and seasoning), the globules of fat, the "dancing" bubbles, and the appearance of color with the addition of vegetables. They observed the rising and spreading of the steam as the lid came off and talked about how hot the soup was ("so hot you couldn't touch it"). The nature of heat, the cause of heat, and the danger of heat were mentioned spontaneously by the children and picked up and clarified by the teacher. The soup was ladled, cooled, and eaten. All this took two days: one day to prepare as much as time allowed, including washing and cutting and all incidental investigation, and the other day for final additions, the cooking, and the eating. Not every child did everything of course. The two teachers designated and defined each activity: there is a technique as well as a purpose in tasting which is different from eating; seasoning requires caution and small amounts, different from pouring a pitcherful of water or dumping dozens of rolling peas. The teachers controlled quantities; guarded the necessary safety measures with respect to fire, heat, and use of utensils; and were arbiters in the division of labor.

Making vegetable soup was not a formal lesson or an official class project for the children. The activity, however, unmistakably dominated the classroom because it went on for hours with "workers" coming in shifts all during the two days. A visitor walking into the room would hardly have noticed the block building, water play, or housekeeping play. Although all these other enterprises were going on simultaneously, each child had a chance to play an important part in the big cooking event and to share in the enthusiasm, wonder, and intense curiosity. Similar in objective to the vegetable soup project but less elaborate and messy are recipes for applesauce, cocoa, or jelly. No matter how simple a cooking experience is, it is impressive to young children.

CHILDREN'S UNINHIBITED INTEREST IN PHYSIOLOGY

What could be more familiar to a child or more important than his or her own body with its inexhaustible source of powers and array of tools, even weaponry when the occasion demands? Such activities as the closing of ears to control sound reception, the flexing and boastful inspection of arm muscles, experimental holding of breath and blowing of air, and deliberate tapping of fingers and pounding of feet, all attest to a variety of bodily reactions and illustrate the extent of children's awareness and use of their bodies.

Identifying and Exploring Parts of the Body

Four-year-old Matthew, hearing the familiar folksong about bones (". . . shoulder bones connected to the arm bones/arm bones connected to the hand bones"), became so interested in the anatomical connections and the variety of bones that he persisted in locating all the bones mentioned.

In the same spirit five-year-old Carmella touched the somewhat loose skin of the upper underarm of her teacher. "What's the matter with your skin?" Carmella inquired and gave her own answer. "It's too big on you. It doesn't *fit* you any more."

Although Carmella's approach was certainly not as persistent as Matthew's, she was nevertheless motivated by the same sense of slowly awakening interest in the human body that is typical of kindergartners.

Discovering Body Powers

Children love to test their muscular strength. A group of children find twigs and sticks and a limb in the yard after a storm. With the teacher's help they break the twigs and sticks, employing the strength of their arms and hands. When their arms are not strong enough, they use the strength in their feet and legs, placing branches and stout sticks at an angle for stepping on and for snapping and breaking.

Testing the power of breath is fascinating to all children. This can be done by blowing up balloons for a party or blowing up paper bags for a particularly effective sound or for some experiment with paper and air power. Cooling hot food by blowing on it or warming cold hands by cupping them around one's own warm breathing stimulate personal experimentation and discovery.

Appreciation of the growth and vitality of the body through such activities as occasional measurement of height and weight, or observing the repeated cutting of hair and nails and the healing of cut skin and scraped knees can lead to discussion about growth, health, and general good feeling about one's body.

Using the Body as a Tool

Five-year-old Mark needed a piece of string to make a handle for some paper construction. He indicated vaguely, with the fingers of two hands, the length he wanted. The teacher complied with the child's request and then thought about the children's interest in measurement. At first she was going to bring out a ruler but decided instead to try a more primitive way. When Mark asked for another piece of string, the teacher said, "Let me measure you an arm's length," and she measured out the string against the full length of her stretched arms and chest. Immediately other children found need for string and requested a precise measure. They were delighted to obtain a sizable length of string measured out against their own two arms and chest. Most of the boys and girls in the class were very much impressed with the dimensions of their arms' spread and some noted its relation to a person's height. Some commented on ways to insure uniformity of measure, and one child detected a possible way of "cheating." The entire concept and the practice of such measurement was completely new to these modern children, yet they were clearly ready to try it and enjoy it since it meant use of their own bodies.

The same children showed a similar response when the teacher showed them how to cup their hands to make a water receptacle for washing their hands outdoors, and the teacher poured water out of a pitcher into each child's hands. They all practiced diligently until each one was able to make a fairly leak-proof hand-cup, and to make most use of the rationed water.

Unlike adults, children observe various parts of the body and body products quite uninhibitedly and objectively. This is a typical observation of a five-year-old: "How funny! I drink milk and water and cocoa and tea; but all that comes out of me is tea."[10]

[10] Kornei Chukovsky, *From Two to Five,* trans. Miriam Morton (Berkeley, Calif.: University of California Press, 1974).

CHILDREN'S LEARNING IS SENSORY
AND PERSONAL

Recognizing young children's keen sensory equipment, a teacher can take full advantage of opportunities that allow children to make use of sensory perceptions. There can be simple blindfold games requiring recognition of objects by smell, taste, or hearing alone. Children show surprise over the difference in the sound of tearing paper and tearing cloth, over the distinct odor of pine wood, and over the unique taste of raw potato. Special boxes with materials can be provided to stimulate children's tactile investigations of textures and surfaces. Perceiving metallic hardness, textile roughness, plant smoothness, or animal softness can lead not only to heightened sensory perception but to stimulation of artistic and intellectual perception. An early childhood teacher has an unusual opportunity to see this process.

In Sally Cartwright's school the children, having *heard* the humming of the furnace and having *noticed* strips of paper rising over the register, and then having *felt* the hot air blowing up, were indeed ready to experiment with motion of hot air. With the teacher who shared their curiosity and supplied guidance, the children held paper strips over a hot wood stove and observed the hot air propelling the paper. This led to the conclusion (although not unanimous and final) that hot air rises!

Many scientists have observed that a human is distinguished by the ability (and need) to *think* and learn. We provide a necessary environment and sympathetic, respectful guidance to a point, then trust a child to learn (without compulsory gimmicks) the rest. Thus a teacher must sense when to leave the child, but must not stop listening and must not lose interest.

EXPERIENCE IN BOTANY

Plants usually appear on the kindergarten windowsill to add color and attractiveness to the room. Yet geared to the natural interests of five-year-olds, plants may offer more than mere decoration. Not all teachers are clear about their role in developing such interest.

Mrs. Meyer is very fond of plants. She comes to school early to inspect the buds on the geranium, remove the dry leaves from the sweet potato, and water the tall, branching avocado plant. Later she tells the children that she has already watered the plants and they can do other work. Now and then Mrs. Meyer asks them with real pride, "Isn't the avocado plant growing beautifully?" or "Doesn't the geranium look gorgeous?" She takes the plants home with her during vacation, and in school she often consults other teachers and parents about the plants. But the children are in no way involved.

Miss Sobel, however, made definite plans for planting a real garden with her kindergarten class. She discussed this project on several occasions, and on the day of the planting she checked on the children's readiness.

"What will we have to do first?" she asked. The children knew and answered, "Turn the soil over." The garden had already been plowed and the children knew about raking the ground smooth, gesticulating appropriately as they spoke of it.

"And then we sprinkle seeds in the little ditch," explained Janet, making delicate dancing finger movements to express sprinkling. The teacher collected the tools and seeds and conducted the group to the garden area beyond the playground. The children waited by the wire fence while the teacher inspected the garden. She then explained to them that because of rain the previous night the ground was unusually wet and therefore she would rake the soil and plant the seeds herself. She instructed the children to stand and watch her. They could be in the garden area, but Miss Sobel cautioned them to step only on the paved space so they would not get their shoes muddy.

It was a beautiful, warm day with the ground just the right wetness for planting. The children's eager hands were anxious to finger and manipulate the dark, soft, crumbly, clingy, wet garden earth. But the teacher herself dutifully raked the ground and did not give the children a chance either to enjoy the activity or to feel that good soil. As she was raking, Miss Sobel explained about the ditch she was making. She deliberately called the ditch a furrow, and several children repeated "furrow" with interest.

Then she took a handful of corn seed and said, "Watch. I am going to drop the seeds now."

As an afterthought Miss Sobel handed each child a kernel of corn while she herself planted the corn seed. The children held the corn kernels somewhat self-consciously and crowded tightly on the edge of the garden where the teacher was doing all the work. Because they were either pushed in the crowding or could not resist the temptation, two children from the group of thirty managed to step on the soil. They were told to stand outside the garden area.

Later Miss Sobel explained to a colleague that the children would have been disappointed if the planting had been postponed because of the wet ground, and they could still see *her* planting very well. She concluded that they had learned a great deal from their garden project, and they had also learned the word "furrow." Again, however, the children were not involved.

When Teachers and Children Learn Together

In order for children really to learn from gardening, they must feel that it is *their* garden.

Terrell asks his teacher about planting in school as a result of the story *The Plant Sitter*.[11] Terrell declares he wants to plant a potato seed. At the teacher's suggestion, he brings an entire potato, cuts a chunk, feels the bumpy potential sprouts, and stuffs it into the soil of a deep flower pot. Terrell is possessive about

[11]Gene Zion, *The Plant Sitter* (New York: Harper & Row, Publishers, Inc., 1959). See also, Irma Webber, *Bits That Grow Big* (Reading, Mass.: Addison-Wesley Publishing Co., Inc., 1949) and Ross E. Hutchins, *The Amazing Seeds* (New York: Dodd, Mead & Company, 1965).

the potato. He waters it, looks at it frequently, and tells children and adults confidently that the small piece of potato will grow. Happily enough, a tall, leafy plant does come up, and after a while delicate purplish blossoms emerge. Then the stalks sprawl and seem to weaken and wither. Terrell worries; he peeks to see the roots and makes an exciting discovery—recognizable grape-size potatoes. Terrell looks on with a sense of pride and even a touch of wisdom. "My potato did grow."

Terrell is actually the only one who is completely involved and impressed with the potato, but the other children are all aware and interested and therefore share the experience. Terrell's enthusiasm, his genuine intellectual curiosity, and his independent observations naturally stimulate the children and constitute science learning by contagion, which can be the most effective kind of all. Although Terrell's project was rather individual, the quality of his experience can occur in a group project, too.

Miss Birch brings in a package of string bean seeds. "We will plant them in our new window box," she tells the class.

"Yes! Our new window box!" the children chant.

"I know where it is," one child offers. "I saw it in the closet." The large, empty window box promptly appears on the table. Miss Birch throws the sealed package into it, and about ten children surround the table to take part.

"What's in the package?" some children ask, and some answer, looking at the picture, "String beans." The teacher asks Candy to tear open the package, and the children rush to pick up a hard, white bean.

"These are not string beans. String beans are long and green."

"These are seed beans," the teacher points out.

"Can we eat them?" one child asks, and another promptly bites into a bean and ejects it, making a wry face.

"We could cook these beans and then eat them, but we will plant these seed beans in soil," the teacher explains. "And after they grow, they'll be plants with string beans like those in the picture."

"Let's plant them!" the children say. Practically the whole class of twenty-one children is around the table by this time. The teacher lets five children at a time go out with shovels, empty milk cartons, and coffee cans she had set aside and bring in dark, soft soil. Some children pat it down, making hand impressions, others fluff and raise the soil, still others sift it through their fingers. They moisten the soil, thumb holes, drop a bean in a hole, cover the seed gently, and then water their garden as a final touch to planting. Every one of the children looks curiously at the solid, smooth, dark soil and the picture of string beans which a child has taped to the box at the teacher's instruction. There is an enigmatic expression on their faces.

"Can we see it grow?"

"After a while," the teacher answers. "The sunshine through the window here and the moisture from your watering will help the beans to grow; and in about a week you'll see some green sprouts come out from the dark earth."

The passage of time defies the children's comprehension and tries their patience. Every day they enumerate and name the days of the week, and every day they ask to see the beans grow. The teacher allows them to uncover one or two concealed seeds, and they are impressed to see that they have changed. They continue watering the window box and watch the seeds' slow sprouting and the plants' gradual growth. They are observant of the changes that come with growing, the emergence of the blossoms, and finally the plants' bearing of scrawny pods.

"Look! *Now* there is a bean pod," Candy is the first to notice.

The biological fact of the forceful action of a quite little seed as it pushes, expands, changes, and produces fruit takes on meaning for the children.

"These are real string beans. Taste them . . . they came from the seeds that were in the package. We planted them." So the children have a harvest feast; they cook and eat the beans they grew.

WHAT ELSE IS SCIENCE?

How ready are kindergarten children to understand phenomena in a truly scientific way? One hears them talk about "space docking," "lasers," "cloning," or "organ transplants" with a confidence that seems born of knowledge, but we must not forget that technical knowledge cannot be gleaned through words alone. Yet information they have picked up in distorted form often needs to be corrected.

On a kindergarten field trip, the teacher advised Jenny not to put a plastic bag on her head. Hearing this, Brian added, "Some children died when they put a plastic bag on their face," and John explained. "They suffercated. It means suffer from air." But Brian corrected him: "Suffer without air." The conversation was then interrupted by the exciting appearance of a leaping toad, and the teacher could not comment on the children's observations concerning plastic bags or the use of the word *suffer*. But when she talked with the children about the trip later, she made reference to using plastic bags as containers, and went on to the danger of "suffocating" when the bag is put over the face, trying to be serious without sounding ominous.

When the teacher is confronted with children's mistakes, in contrast to misconceptions or misinformation, she or he has a different responsibility. The teacher needs to be patient, and rather than *show* or instantly point out the error to the child, to give him or her a chance to discover it. Recognition and admission of mistakes is very difficult for young children, and the teacher, of whom they are respectful, must demonstrate her or his own attitude toward recognizing and benefiting from mistakes. Thus, when a teacher forgot the white sugar for a cake recipe calling for two kinds of sugar because she had neglected to check the ingredients, she identified her error to the children, and together they resolved to check the ingredients the next time. The term "to check on" was frequently used after that and became a very important concept in other projects for the rest of the year.

Similarly, teachers must be ready to face their own limitations in knowledge. "I don't know what 'streamlined' is, but we can look it up in a book with pictures and explanations,"[12] the teacher may say, revealing not so much ignorance as the

[12] John Kaufmann, *Streamlined* (New York: Thomas Y. Crowell Company, Inc., 1974).

difficulty of the subject and indicating respect for the child's question. "It's hard for me to explain how birds fly," the teacher might reply to another kind of question, "but if you keep on watching, you might get an idea yourself." Nor do teachers need to understand the engineering of a satellite's orbit or grasp astronomical math in order to stimulate the scientific development of children this age, although they may indicate to the children that scientists do have answers to many questions and that there also are an infinite number *yet unanswered.* What is particularly important for teachers to realize is that they must maintain their own curiosity and courage to find out. They will set an example by looking up information, obtaining materials, and acknowledging their own limitations, all in the scientific spirit.

What is needed in modern science education is the recognition of ignorance and the courage to question, which is more significant than keeping up with technological advances.[13] The teacher will, of course, want to share the important news of these advances with the children, but more to give them a sense of sharing in a larger scientific endeavor than to teach them science per se. Such news has immediate excitement and attraction for children, whether it involves medical discovery, mechanical invention, or space exploration. Yet we must pause before the appearance of potentially frightening information. Discussion of mechanical replacements for body parts threatens the sense of body integrity children must feel; the arguments over nuclear reactors can be very frightening. It is wise to tread carefully in some areas. Children want to know that adults are taking care of things, but they do not necessarily want or need to know details they cannot put in perspective. As in all teaching, some matters must wait.

The fact that words are not the key to growing awareness of scientific fact and concept is beautifully demonstrated by Frances Hawkins in the description of her work with a group of preschool deaf children.[14] Despite hearing and speech handicaps, these children reveal scientific curiosity, intellectual perseverance, and logic in their reactions to the author's selection of appropriately presented materials. Her work is an inspiration to teachers who are interested in a meaningful science readiness program and can't quite tear themselves away from verbalization.

Teachers of young children must strive to be knowledgeable adults attuned to children's concerns and respectful of their abilities and limitations. They must be aware of the opportunities that exist both in everyday living and in classroom activities for prescience experience, to which they must add appropriate materials and guidance to promote scientific readiness. Utilizing children's natural affinity for observation and investigation, as well as the firsthand knowledge they already have, teachers can introduce projects and materials (for work and play) which stimulate such learning and help children cultivate the scientific approach.

When we read in the 1980s of the appalling lack of science teaching in upper grades as well as the general disinterestedness in and fear of science, we are con-

[13]Lewis Thomas, "The Art of Teaching Science," *New York Times Magazine,* March 14, 1982.
[14]Frances Hawkins, *The Logic of Action* (New York: Pantheon Books, Inc., 1974).

vinced that an important remedy for such a "sorry state" of science[15] would be to begin with the kind of fundamental learning and positive approach characteristic of our youngest students—the kindergartners.

REFERENCES AND FURTHER READING

Books and Other Publications for Teachers

BLOUGH, GLENN, and SCHWARTZ, JULIUS. *Elementary School Science and How to Teach It* (5th ed.). New York: Holt, Rinehart and Winston, 1974.

BREARLEY, MOLLY (ed.). *The Teaching of Young Children,* chap. 2, "Science: Expectations, Conjectures, and Validations." New York: Schocken Books, Inc., 1970.

CARIN, ARTHUR, and SUND, ROBERT B. *Teaching Science as Discovery* (3rd ed.).Columbus Ohio: Chas. E.Merrill, 1975.

CHUKOVSKY, KORNEI (trans. Miriam Morton). *From Two to Five.* Berkeley, Calif.: University of California Press, 1974.

CRAIG, GERALD. *Science for the Elementary School Teacher.* Boston, Mass.: Ginn, 1958.

ENGEL, ROSE. "Learning about Common Everyday Things: Snails," *Journal of Nursery Education,* 16, 1 (1960–61).

GALE, FRANK C., and GALE, CLARICE W. *Experiences with Plants for Young Children.* Palo Alto, Calif.: Pacific Books, 1975.

HAWKINS, FRANCES. *The Logic of Action.* New York: Pantheon, 1974.

HOLT, BESS-GENE. *Science with Young Children.* Washington, D.C.: NAEYC, 1977 (plus related pamphlet: "Doing a Workshop with an NAEYC Publication").

HUBLER, H. CLARK. *Science and Children.* New York: Random House, 1974.

HUNTINGTON, HARRIET E. *Let's Go Outdoors.* Garden City, N.Y.: Doubleday, 1959.

LEWIS, JUNE E., and POTTER, IRENE C. *The Teaching of Science in the Elementary School* (2nd ed.). Englewood Cliffs, N.J.: Prentice-Hall, 1970.

MAEROFF, GENE I. "A Science Dean Describes Teaching as in Sorry State," *New York Times,* April 6, 1982.

MOORE, LILIAN. *Lucky Cookbook for Boys and Girls.* Englewood Cliffs, N.J.: Scholastic Book Services, 1970.

NAVARRA, JOHN G. *The Development of Scientific Concepts.* New York: Columbia University Press, 1955.

ROCHE, RUTH L. *The Child and Science.* Washington, D.C.: Association for Childhood International, 1977.

ROUNDS, SUSAN. *Teaching the Young Child,* chap. 6, "Cooking in the Classroom" and chap. 7, "Plants and Animals in the Classroom." New York: Agathon, 1975.

RUDOLPH, MARGUERITA. *From Hand to Head: A Handbook for Teachers of Preschool Programs.* New York: McGraw-Hill, 1973; Schocken Books Paperback, 1977.

RUDOLPH, MARGUERITA. *Should the Children Know?* New York: Schocken Books, Inc., 1978; Schocken Books Paperback, 1981.

[15] Dean Harry Lustig, "A Science Dean Describes Teaching as in Sorry State," interview with Gene I. Maeroff, *New York Times,* April 6, 1982.

THOMAS, LEWIS. "The Art of Teaching Science," *New York Times Magazine,* March 14, 1982.

VICTOR, EDWARD. *Science for the Elementary School* (3rd ed.). New York: Macmillan, 1975.

WATERS, BARBARA S. *Science Can Be Elementary. Discovery-Action Programs for K–3.* New York: Citation, 1973.

Books for Children

BLOUGH, GLENN E. (illus. Jeanne Bendick). *Who Lives at the Seashore.* New York: McGraw-Hill Book Company, 1962.

BOURGEOIS, FLORENCE. *Beachcomber Bobbie.* Garden City, N.Y.: Doubleday, Doran, out of print.

CHRYSTIE, FRANCES N. *Pets* (3rd ed.). Boston: Little, Brown, 1974.

ELLIOTT, ALAN C. *On Sunday the Wind Came.* New York: Morrow, 1980. A book about weather.

GOUDEY, ALICE E. (illus. Adrienne Adams). *Houses from the Sea.* New York: Scribner's, 1959. A book about shells.

HUTCHINS, ROSS E. *The Amazing Seeds.* New York: Dodd, Mead, 1965.

KAUFMANN, JOHN. *Streamlined.* New York: Thomas Y. Crowell, 1974.

KOHN, BERNICE. *The Beachcomber's Book.* New York: Viking, 1970.

SELSAM, MILLICENT. *Eat the Fruit, Plant the Seeds.* New York: Morrow, 1980.

SELSAM, MILLICENT. *How Kittens Grow.* New York: Scholastic Book Services, Four Winds Press, 1973.

WEBBER, IRMA. *Bits That Grow Big.* Reading, Mass.: Addison-Wesley, 1949.

WOLKSTEIN, DIANE (illus. Ed Young). *800,000 Stones: A Chinese Folktale.* New York: Doubleday, 1972. A book about solving problems of weighing.

WYLER, ROSE, and AMES, GERALD. *Secrets in Stones.* New York: Scholastic Book Services, 1970.

ZION, GENE. *The Plant Sitter.* New York: Harper & Row, Pub., 1959.

ZOLA, SELMA WASSERMAN MEGUNDO. *Promoting Thinking in Your Classroom.* Washington, D.C.: Association for Childhood International, 1977. A pamphlet.

A useful source of information for teachers and children is "Ranger Rick's Nature Magazine," a monthly publication of The National Wildlife Federation, 1412 16th St., N.W., Washington, D.C. 20036. They also publish "Ranger Rick's Teacher's Guide."

In addition, free or inexpensive materials on animals are available by writing to the Department of Fish and Game in your state capital. Ask for pictorial information about local wildlife and resource materials for teachers.

12 The Importance of Art for All Children

Although in a broad sense art pertains to creative expression in many media, we shall consider chiefly painting, drawing, and work with clay in this chapter, since these highly malleable materials allow children to express thoughts and feelings with little interference from any structured shape or form. We are not using such terms as *creative expression* and *art* to discuss the special skills or talents of the artistically gifted. Our concern is with the universal human urge for expression and symbolic representation to which we referred in the chapters on language and play. Children delight in exploring color and form, and their work ranges from the most abstract to the most carefully representational, as they draw upon their own subjective reactions to the world to give the materials form. Through the media they can distance themselves from their experience, the better to clarify and appreciate it.

GOALS IN THE USE OF ART MEDIA

For young children the ability to handle feelings and impressions through words is still somewhat limited, and access to nonverbal forms of communication is both necessary and tension reducing. Through the art media, kindergartners can express feelings and perceptions quite beyond their verbal capabilities.

Freedom to use crayons, paint, clay, and other art materials in their own way and on their own terms is therefore vital. Victor Lowenfeld,[1] an authority on children's art, speaks repeatedly of the necessity for personal choice in a young child's expression and use of art materials. This means not only the freedom for children to select their own medium and their own subject, but also freedom from adult standards of realism and techniques.

Yet interference does occur, and often with the best intentions. In a public school kindergarten, where several children are drawing at two tables, the teacher comes along to see what help may be needed, what encouragement may be due, what correction might be called for, or to say a jesting word or two.

"That's nice, Henry. What a lovely picture, Jane." Blue-eyed, long-haired Debby is working away with concentration, forming the image of a little girl with long hair. She adds details, fills in spaces, and emphasizes each space with a particular color she selects from a large assortment. The dominating color in Debby's picture is blue. Blue is the color in the flowery dress, blue are the spots of eyes, and blue is even the color of the hair!

"That's lovely, dear, but tell me: what color hair do people have?" Debby looks puzzled, almost startled, as if she were unprepared either to think or speak about it. She gives no answer. "What color is *your* hair?"

"Brown," Debby answers quietly and knowledgeably, but indicating in no way that she sees any relation between real hair color and the meaning or feeling in the blue hair of her drawing. The teacher now stops near another child and looks at the drawing of a person with rather straggly weak limbs. "Tell me, honey, where do the arms belong? Show me on you! That's *right*. On your shoulder, of course." Still another child shows the teacher a picture with people in it. After praising it the teacher asks cheerfully and humorously, "My goodness—did all their hair fall out?"

"No," the child answers, chagrined, and runs back to the drawing table to put hair on.

While on the surface this teacher's careful realism handed on to the children sounds reasonable, leaders in the field of art teaching find it undesirable and even detrimental. Lowenfeld throws light on the meaning of blue-haired, hairless, and weak-limbed representation of people in the following statements:

> We notice that there is a difference between what the child *sees* and what he *expresses* in his art. A five-year-old child may represent a man by only draw-

[1] Victor Lowenfeld and W. Lambert Brittain, *Your Child and His Art* (New York: Macmillan Inc., 1955).

ing his head and feet. This by no means indicates that a five-year-old child does not know more about a man. He knows perfectly well that a man has arms, hands, even fingernails. In his art work, however, he paints only what is important to him or what stands out in his eyes while he is painting.[2]

Lowenfeld also suggests that

> . . . to look for reality in our children's drawings is one of the most common mistakes. "It does not look real" is the worst thing you can say to a child about his art. That Mary's art does not look real to the adult eye, that it does not look real to you, by no means indicates that it is not real to her. However, the kind of reality is quite different. Reality in appearance does not make things real to your *feelings* and *emotions* . . . If we ask Mary to adjust her painting to our adult concept of reality, we overpower her own sensitive relationships to her experiences only to please ourselves.[3]

And again,

> . . . The child expresses in his art *his* level of growth, which cannot be changed or "corrected" through superficial criticism. Growth is a continuous process, and we cannot force the child into it. Since John is not ready to relate his painting to reality, a criticism which forces him to compare it with reality would only be discouraging. For him it is much more important to establish a relationship between his own *experience* and his creative expression. Reality at this point is inconceivable to him, and since it is out of his reach it would only frustrate him.[4]

APPLYING ADULT STANDARDS
TO CHILDREN'S ART

Charles and Margaret Gaitskill,[5] who studied the art activities of 9,000 children in 425 Canadian kindergartens, demonstrate quite conclusively that when children copy adult drawings or are commanded to draw or paint in a particular way, their artistic imaginativeness is restricted and they have difficulty in thinking up their own ideas. This does not mean, of course, that young children must be left entirely alone or ignored during art sessions in school. As children develop from a manipulative, uncertain stage to more advanced expressive activity with symbolic and representational content, many of them will need guidance. But this guidance need consist of no more than encouraging a child to participate, recognizing effort, making various materials available and attractive, showing respect for the child's in-

[2] Ibid., p. 27.
[3] Ibid., p. 21.
[4] Ibid.
[5] In Rhoda Kellogg, "Understanding Children's Art," in *Readings in Psychology Today*, 2nd ed. (Del Mar, Calif.: CRM Books, 1972).

dividuality, and offering appropriate praise of results. Should a teacher, then, only praise and never criticize a child's art?

In the light of Lowenfeld's and the Gaitskills' insights that the meaning of any young child's picture is purely personal and subjective, what purpose can criticism have? Criticism implies a right and a wrong way. But if there is no "right" way, because no two individuals express quite the same thing, how can we speak of criticism? It is difficult for adults, with their learned feeling for balance, photographic accuracy, and traditional color harmony, to remain undisturbed by children's apparent lack of concern for such features in art. But unless we realize and accept the fact that children's art expression is a personal response and evaluation of what they perceive and feel and not necessarily an objective portrayal, we are tempted to "teach" them. To a child a tree may be significant for its height and not its color; a person for his importance in the composition rather than for his bodily proportions; a house for its inhabitants rather than for its architectural balance. To a child the part frequently stands for the whole; the essence of a subject may not be its external realities. To a young child, mother may be the lady with the "smile and the green pocketbook," and the teacher may be portrayed with her sunglasses larger than her shoes. The time for precision and realistic accuracy comes much later. In the kindergarten it is well to let children use the art materials as they will. We ourselves may like some efforts more than others, but we should not be judges. Now let us look at some of the art activity in detail.

DRAWING

The urge to draw seems to be as old as human consciousness, as cave drawings so eloquently remind us. Perhaps that is because the essential nature of art is to give shape to something experienced. Viewed in this way, art becomes not merely a means of expressing feeling but a way of giving order to the world, even as mathematics and science are ways of creating order. Art seems to fulfill a need to reproduce and imitate that which abounds in the world around. How else can we account for the spontaneous appearance and development of drawing in children of every culture? Whether it is done with a stick in the sand, a piece of charcoal on wood, a pencil on paper, or the most elaborate array of crayons on a variety of textured papers, all children, except those most inhibited by adults, love to draw. Focusing on the image lurking in their minds sharpens the perception of the image and crystallizes it in concrete terms. This is why children's drawings of a person have been used to assess intelligence (how much one perceives) as well as emotional reactions of health or disturbance.

The particular medium children use for drawing can lead to somewhat different possibilities for expressiveness. The pencil, with its thin, fine line, allows for detail of a minute character when children are ready for that; or for sweeping scribbles that do not blot each other out when children are first ready to make any marks at all. Crayons offer a different kind of latitude. Crayons allow children to attain variation in shading by adapting the pressure and tempo of their hand move-ments on the crayon, an aid to small-muscle development as well as to the growth in awareness of differentiation. Magic markers, by contrast, are clean, sharp, and brilliant. They allow no variations, no subtlety, only repetition of their single dimen-sion, brilliance; and their opaque markings can all too easily blot each other out. The tendency to substitute magic markers for crayons, instead of using them as an occasional variation, decreases the opportunity for dealing with degrees and subtle-ties in small-muscle development, aesthetic experience, and expression of feeling and detail. Teachers should give serious thought to the differences in potential of the different media with which children can draw.

PAINTING

It has been observed that painting is a most popular activity in kindergarten.[6] The distinct colors seem to attract children and stimulate their aesthetic sense. The large, empty paper gives them both freedom and the challenge of filling that empty space. The strong brushes allow them a secure grip while they produce strokes, sweeps, and transformation of surface. The material has movement that is easily controlled.

When children enter kindergarten they frequently encounter painting for the first time in their lives. It is therefore very important for them to get acquainted in their own way, at first, with the materials themselves. Then they can be eased into conforming with specific rules of appropriate use of supplies. Kindergartners need to find out for themselves the wetness and drippiness of paint, and that the mere addition of water to a small quantity of paint does not make more paint but makes the small amount drab and unusable. They need to learn from experience about the thinness of paper and how easily it tears, and about the different effects of paint on different kinds of paper. Allowed to experiment and make mistakes, chil-dren will learn how much wet overlay any one kind of paper can withstand. They are bound to find out in the same way that indiscriminate mixing of colors on the paper or in the containers ruins the clear colors and leads to unattractive muddiness.

Teachers are bothered by this kind of experimentation because it seems so costly. Not only does the thrifty soul of an adult squirm at waste that seems the result of pure carelessness, but it is frustrating to have to refill jars that were so recently cleaned and set up. Also, ruined paint may cause too long a delay for the next child's turn, and paint spilled on the floor causes an interruption of other worthwhile activities until it is cleaned up. The cost and frustration need not go on for too long, however, because children can and do indeed learn reasonable care of equipment and supplies. We must, however, distinguish between true learning and wanton destruction. It is one thing to discard a failed attempt and take a fresh piece

[6]Charles and Margaret Gaitskill, *Art Education in the Kindergarten* (Peoria, Ill.: Charles A. Bennett Co., Inc., 1952).

of paper, and quite another to fill a wastebasket with bare beginnings, impatiently discarded. The teacher, by being aware of a child's intent and purpose, can help the child distinguish between using materials and abusing them. In the authors' own experience as well as in more recent findings,[7] children learn appropriate use of materials best when they are involved in all aspects of an activity, including storage of materials, preparation for activity, distribution of paint, protection of work and of product, and necessary clean-up.

The guidelines associated with painting that help children learn from experience are (1) that some kind of protection for their clothing is a realistic precaution; (2) that paint and paint brushes may be used only at the easel or at other designated places; (3) that each brush is returned to the jar from which it was taken unless the practice is to dip a brush into a container of water before applying the next color (a brush for each color, in our opinion, is a more satisfactory approach for the younger kindergarten children); (4) that children may clip their own paper to the easel and remove their paintings when they are finished (obviously, suitable clips and a place for drying must be clearly available); (5) that it helps to wipe a brush at the edges of the paint container if the painter is at all concerned with the control of color strokes (it is not a grave offense if a child forgets to do this!); (6) that a handy sponge or mop can be used to clean up accidental spills.

Patience with still-clumsy hands and caution in imposing stringent instructions too soon will lead children toward the confidence that follows free use of the paints. Responsible and careful attention to the use of materials as the children develop socially through the year is an almost certain result. Do not fret too much about awkwardness at the beginning.

Stages of Development in Using Paints

It should be clear from the foregoing that each child will go through some stage of trial manipulation and exploration before he or she can feel assured in handling materials and attain expression with the paint medium. In *Art through Your Child's Eyes*[8] Ann Allen and Daveen Herley (referring to studies by Kellogg) describe graphically the developmental stages in children's artistic activity and compare those stages to motor development. Just as a child makes random, then controlled, movements and then takes tentative steps and finally walks, so in painting the child makes random, then exploratory, then controlled movements, and finally the same child makes purposeful designs. Somewhat like motor activity, painting follows a natural progression which seems to be influenced by opportunity, approval, and encouragement from adults. It does not require teaching, and it does not require talent or art training on the part of a teacher.

[7]Thelma Harms, *My Art Is Me,* Discussion Guide for the film. (Harold E. Jones Child Study Center, Univ. of California, Berkeley). *My Art Is Me,* film, color, 22 min. (Extension Media Center, 2223 Fulton St., Berkeley, Calif. 94720).

[8]Ann W. Allen with Daveen Herley, *Art through Your Child's Eyes,* photography and design by Barbara J. Wilk (Southampton, N.Y.: Suffolk County Early Childhood Education Council, 1975).

It is interesting to learn that the developmental stages in young children's untutored artwork are the same in different cultures[9] as well as in different historical eras. It is also well to remember, however, that kindergarten children may revert to an earlier manipulative stage after achieving orderly, symbolic, or representational work. The cause of this regression may be physical, such as some illness, a passing emotional disturbance, too rigidly prescribed instruction, or too high and demanding standards. A similar observation about children moving back and forth between stages during artistic development in the early years is made by Judith Danoff in an article in *Children Today.*[10]

But if all goes well, most children will develop noticeably in their painting throughout the year. From simple manipulation of the material for its own sake, the children go on to finding the medium's possibilities. From here it is but a step to producing painting for one's pleasure, satisfying, aesthetically pleasing designs or highly impressionistic representations of the world one knows. An experienced teacher can tell the approximate age of a group of young children by the character of the paintings on the walls.

Since the quality and satisfaction of the children's painting depends to a large extent on the teacher's understanding, let us watch how children in Mrs. Margolis's class paint.

Stimulating Children's Interest in Painting

The setting here is ideal for space, brightness, and general pleasantness, as we see Mrs. Margolis helping four children painting at the easels. She removes finished pictures protectively and sets them carefully to dry on a clothes dryer. She provides requested colors and fastens plastic aprons as she comments to a parent visitor on the originality and completeness of the children's work, their inventiveness, and their satisfaction. One little girl, after working seriously for over fifteen minutes, produces a pleasing pattern of balanced, roundish shapes, then stands watching a long drip running unexpectedly over clear space. Mrs. Margolis does not rush over with either unnecessary words of regret or confusing suggestions for correction. She believes that this thoughtful, well-organized little girl will find a way of incorporating the drip, and indeed the result is a painting of movement and strength with effective color and pattern.

We also see in Mrs. Margolis's class that the strongest impression in the room comes from the children's original paintings on the walls. They are beautiful and distinctive abstract designs, strong rhythmic patterns, paintings that show individuality in composition and color, and one picture of a snowman that has obvious humor. Clearly, Mrs. Margolis is sensitive to the individual child's need for expression and is also genuinely interested in the children's feelings and the results of their artwork. She does not impose her own opinions and standards.

[9]Joseph H. Di Leo, *Children's Drawings as Diagnostic Aids* (New York: Brunner/Mazel, 1973).

[10]Judith Danoff, "Children's Art," *Children Today* (July–August 1975).

Every kindergarten teacher realizes that paint is a rich and universal art medium and that it is generally a favorite activity. Yet sometimes individual children will not care to paint, or there may be very little painting going on in the class as a whole.

How can the teacher stimulate the children's interest in this art medium? Are there ways of encouraging children without curtailing their sense of freedom? Mrs. Brown stumbled on one such way by accident, which may teach us something important about children and about art.

"Not much painting going on in my class. Hardly anyone comes to the easels. There they stand, untouched," Mrs. Brown complained to another teacher. Yet she assured herself each morning that the jars of clear paint were ready and the paint thinned and stirred to the consistency of heavy cream. Fresh paper sat invitingly on the easels and the brushes were clean and handy in a can near the easel. Then suddenly interest was sparked one morning when five-year-old Shirley discovered a discarded scrap of paper with symmetrical strokes of bright primary colors, which the teacher had left after testing the paints. Shirley was fascinated with the idea of testing the colors.

"How did you do it? Let *me!*" she demanded, and immediately laid a sheet of paper flat on the table and eagerly made parallel strokes with each of the primary colors as well as the black and white. She then tested the colors again with a dabbing stroke followed with more elaborate strokes, and quickly filled the paper with a complete, pleasing, rhythmic pattern of "testing colors." The picture excited not only Shirley but several other children who became intrigued by color testing. These children were given a privileged turn each morning to work under the teacher's supervision in stirring, pouring, testing, and if necessary, thinning out paint, inspecting brushes, and checking on paper supply and easel fasteners. Empty jars and fresh spoons were also offered the children so they could make new shades by mixing colors or adding white to ready-made ones. Pastels—lavender, pink, light blue, pale green—appeared and gave the room a lovely spring air. Brown, dark green, gray, purple, and reddish orange were the favorites of other children. After this the painting area became populated, active, interesting. Testing and making colors proved to be the opener these children needed for further artistic activity.

In this case the teacher's own preparations for the children's painting aroused curiosity and interest in the paints, because what the teacher herself does is generally very interesting to children. However, Mrs. Brown might have been as effective if she had introduced a new type of paper, such as construction paper or easel paper in a color rather than white, or if she had left a novel size brush at the easel, a ½-inch brush in addition to the more usual ¾-inch size. She might also have added a new color or a new shade to blend with the season, a holiday, the weather, or just a mood. Sometimes moving a portable easel to another area, after consulting the children, may stimulate an interest.

An occasional use of cheap white paper plates may produce an exciting change in approach to painting by the difference in dimension as well as texture of surface. The use of white plastic trays from sealed store packages will serve a similar purpose. Another stimulating change from the usual newsprint is to use the pages of old newspapers, where there are no pictures and the print is small and uniform. Painting on such paper has a different challenge and different effect. Going on interesting trips will, of course, stimulate ideas and subjects for paintings and drawings.

Stimulating children's sensitivity and awareness and therefore giving them food for expression is certainly valid, provided the teacher does not overpower them with her own intellectual notions about art and thus question children's faith in their own spontaneity. As to the method of stimulation, that depends on the teacher's own resourcefulness and her awareness of the children's interests and experiences.

The Child Who Does Not Paint

But with all this, there are almost always several children in a class who never paint. What does the teacher do for them?

Miss Byrd noted that Greg enjoyed watching others paint without doing it himself, and that he was especially amused by the accidental splatters of paint around the easel. She offered him a chance just to make splatters. Placing a sheet of paper on the top of some oilcloth on the floor, she let Greg select his own jars with paints, which she placed in a secure receptacle (a milk carton with one long side cut out) near the paper. First hesitantly, then with vigor, and finally with unrestrained pleasure, Greg made multicolored splatters and speckles over the entire paper. He enjoyed this so much that he promptly made another splatter painting on the floor. Greg's paintings were loudly admired by his classmates. When the splatters came together, Greg evened them out with the strokes of the brush, and thus started painting in conventional manner, although still on the floor. Several other children who did not paint much at the easel enjoyed painting on the floor in a quadruped position! With adequate newspaper covering, the floor and tables can extend limited easel space for an active class responsive to art materials.

José, a classmate of Greg's, also did not paint, but he did more than watch; he evaluated other children's work, usually favorably, and his critical judgment was sought by other children.

"Come and see my horse, José. Do you like it?"

"Hey, that looks like a horse, only where is his tail?"

"It's on the other side, it doesn't show." José continued looking at the picture, puzzling something out. At that point the teacher suggested that José paint a horse himself and find out about having a tail show. José responded first with agreement, then with criticism. "The paper's too thin," and then, "I have an idea." His idea was to attach thicker construction paper onto the newsprint used at the easel, and thus produce a three-dimensional effect as he painted over different surfaces. It was an experimental venture and did not last long. Apparently it did not really absorb José the way a woodworking project did when he used a board for a base and then with nails and wire, dowels, spools, cardboard, and cloth produced an attractive montage that had dimension and mobility. In her own mind, therefore, the teacher concluded that painting did not suit José particularly for the expression of his feelings or ideas. His interests and feelings were better handled in other media.

According to Allen and Herley,[11] "We . . . do a service to [a child's] development by allowing him or her to *not* paint or draw when not in the mood." But of course, close observation is needed to help a teacher decide when it is wiser to stand back and when it is wise to move in with suggestions and encouragement.

When No One Paints

Sometimes a whole group may ignore a major medium, such as painting, for a few weeks or even months. They may be happy with good dramatic play or may derive special enjoyment from finger paint. Or more important perhaps, the excitement and pleasure from vigorous and creative play with snow, or delight from sunshine and spring breezes outdoors may satisfy them completely. One cannot have time for everything, and painting may be left for a while by a particular child or even by a group without its meaning anything. At such a time the teacher may observe the children's reaction to objects or situations that have an artistic or aesthetic component—for example, sections or cross sections of fruits during snack time, an unusual form or distinctive color of a vegetable brought into class, or a found feather of unique texture and pattern. And, sometimes it is even beneficial to stay away from a much-used material for a while to be able to come back to it with a new approach and fresher energy.

FINGER PAINTING

Let us examine another kind of painting experience that has great appeal to young children. Here is a large group of five-year-olds in a day care center. Three boys come to an oilcloth-covered table made available for finger painting. Later two more boys and a girl take part in this activity. A globby, messy, but smooth mixture of wallpaper paste and water[12] rests in a wide jar. A spoon and some glass sugar shakers with powdered paints in them are also there. Each of the boys puts on a plastic apron, scoops himself a small mound of the base mixture, shakes in some color from one or more of the jars, and mixes it with fingers or palm of the hand, studying and feeling the color hue, the texture, and the consistency. The children work directly on the table surface without paper, which means that in this case they are not making pictures to save; however, this makes the process no less meaningful. The children are absorbed in using their fingers, fingernails, and knuckles. This gives variety to the strokes, the resulting patterns, and the accompanying rhythm. There is a quick tapping with the fingers and a slow sweep when the wrist

[11] Allen and Herley, *Art through Your Child's Eyes*, p. 28.

[12] If one prefers to make finger paint rather than buy it another method is to combine in equal proportions liquid starch and soap powder. Add water and tempera paint and mix to proper consistency.

moves, and the pattern of the picture changes. The children are also fascinated with the color itself. One boy produces orange color from an addition of clear yellow to a solid red, and his face is aglow from this chemical magic. Another child gets a purple hue when he swirls red on blue. A little girl makes green grass with gentle scratchings of yellow and blue. The resulting objects and effects change quickly in such finger painting.

After a half hour the children are through, and they go independently to the sink for sponges to clean the table. This postartistic work appears quite as enjoyable as the finger painting itself, as the children squeeze and smear the sponges, observe the blurring and disappearance of the colors, and seem satisfied by having nothing more than a clean table to show for their effort. (The children also wash their aprons by themselves.)

What was accomplished in that situation? First, the activity involved practical preparation and independent use of the media. Four- to six-year-olds were able to work in an orderly, responsible way while enjoying perfect freedom, as long as the outer limits of where and what is permissible were clearly understood. Each child's style, discovery, and personal pleasure, however, was his or hers to find and enjoy without adult intervention. The teacher reported that although glossy finger paint paper is often used by the children, it was simpler in the afternoon period to have the children use the smooth-covered table surface without the help of a teacher. However, she did need to remind the children to moisten the surface before applying finger paint. Thus, with or without a product to show, there was a sensory and emotional experience with texture, incidental forms, and patterns, no less than experimentation and satisfaction with color. When the children did make pictures on glossy finger paint paper or on good quality shelving,[13] these were carefully laid on newspapers to dry so they would not smear, and finished pictures were saved. Often a child was praised for the delicacy of a painting or for the originality of using paint thickly to make something stand out.

COLLAGES AND ACCESSORY MATERIALS

Collage work, attaching a variety of materials to thick paper or cardboard, stimulates both the teacher's and the children's imagination and observation. There is no limit to the ideas and artistic effects that can come from making collages. A box with a rich assortment of materials may include rough pieces of burlap and sandpaper; tough scraps of leather and rubber; malleable thin wire and straight straws; clear and colored transparent cellophane; smooth bits of silk, velvet, or synthetic fabrics; colored Christmas cards, ribbons, and harder textured materials; dabs of soft cotton; depressable sponges; glossy and brilliant colored paper; delicate old lace; attractive labels and Christmas wrappings; lengths of soft-colored yarn; or

---

[13] According to Rhoda Kellogg, "the best economical paper is meat wrapping, or butcher's, paper which comes either in rolls or flat bundles, cut to desired size."

curly wood shavings. There is literally no limit to the kinds of materials an alert teacher might find and use. But of course, the teacher must not have too many at one time, or making a choice would be overwhelming even for imaginative and un-repressed kindergartners. If collage activity really engages the children's and the teacher's interest, however, one box of materials will not be enough. In that case the teacher would do well to resort to a sorting system suggested by Naomi Pile (although she advises teachers to devise their own). In separate marked containers, she stores

fabrics	transparent items
papers	shiny items
natural materials	patterns
yarn and string	solid colors
buttons and beads	

and so on. She also adds: "It never hurts to have a box of 'miscellaneous' materials to give children for the pleasure of sorting through on their own."[14]

Sharp enough, blunt-edged scissors must be available for the children to cut the material into the sizes and shapes they need. Paste, glue, Scotch tape, and stapler or large needle and thread should be available for collage construction. A hole puncher is also a handy tool. A hole-punched piece of paper pasted on a different color surface gives a surprising effect. Discovery of the variety and the change in materials provides a great deal of sensory stimulation and opportunity for individual selection of materials and method of working.

VARIETY IN ART MATERIALS

The teacher must keep in mind that the children must choose for themselves what appeals to them, but the choice must be genuinely possible. However adequate a supply of collage materials one may have to start with, it is important to examine the box frequently to change and supplement the materials or to make the supply box cleaner and more orderly.

Aesthetic possibilities exist in various objects in nature and in the home. For example, blowing bubbles with a straw from a container of soapy water produces quantities of different-sized spherical, mobile objects that reflect color, invite experimentation, and bring delight to all children, as recorded by Sally Cartwright.

Robin and Ryan blew bubbles at the water table together. They were de-lighted with rainbow colors on the bubbles in the sunlight.

"Look, Robin! Let's paint 'em!" They went together to the wall easel and worked side by side.

"Here's the prettiest red cloud you ever saw," exclaimed Robin. Long si-lence. Then Ryan asked,

[14] Naomi Pile, *Art Experiences for Young Children* (New York: Macmillan, Inc., 1973).

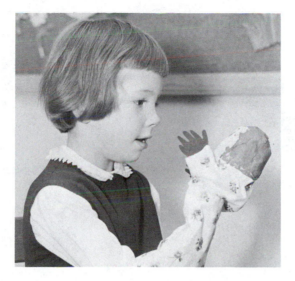

"Does this look like a rainbow to you, Robin?" But the light in their eyes, their shared involvement, their joyous purpose with paint and brush were more eloquent than any words.[15]

A large collection of buttons brought to class soon has children feeling and inspecting them, admiring the beauty of some buttons, choosing favorites, commenting on the variety of sizes and shapes and designs, distinguishing the metal, the leather, and the wooden and plastic materials in the buttons. Buttons prove to be a surprisingly rich and stimulating material. Some of the buttons may be used as effective bits of decoration on small block buildings, some may be used as focal points in a collage, some may be sewn on cloth as a decoration, and some, of course, will be "borrowed" permanently.

Miss Woo uses every opportunity to bring flowers to her class. She not only strives for pleasing arrangements of flowers in vases and effective displays of flowers and foliage in the room, but she always involves children in such activity. Often she gathers the wilted flowers or scattered petals from a withered bouquet and leaves them in an open bowl or basket, lined perhaps with some special cloth or paper, on the children's worktable. The dabs of color and distinct shapes, the little mounds of texture for the children to finger and explore, as well as the noticeable aroma, also offer a distinctly aesthetic experience. There are very few children who are not tempted by Miss Woo's offering; some paste petals as extra decoration on finished drawings, some make rich collage arrangements, and others like a handful to keep, to smell, or to save for taking home.

---

[15]From an unpublished report by Sally Cartwright, Director, Community Nursery School, Tenants Harbor, Me.

CLAY

After the relative lightness and distracting profusion of collage materials, it is interesting to turn to a medium such as clay, which has qualities of solidity and depth. Clay is a rich, natural material that responds readily to the hand. Practically all children enjoy it but need the time and the opportunity to find its special value for themselves.

Taking Time to Know the Medium

At the beginning, a pure hunk of clay without accessories such as sticks or tongue depressors is all children need. They learn to appreciate the heaviness as they pick up a good-sized lump (about the size of a large orange) or help the teacher move the clay crock or galvanized pail in which it is stored. They feel the moisture and like to add water as they work to get the hard-enough, soft-enough consistency that makes the texture just right. They love the pliability, so useful to forceful and even angry pressing and banging, or gentle, sensitive patting. And they play with making, remaking, and unmaking objects. It is wise to provide special surfaces for clay work, such as a 12″ × 12″ board or a large scrap of linoleum that can be scraped fairly clean when work is over. Formica top tables are fine, too.

One preschool child may get carried away just with smoothing a clay surface and making fingerprints, hand prints, and even knuckle depressions. Another may be enthusiastic about extending a clay "snake" to its ultimate length, then do the opposite and compress it to its smallest dimension, an act which, incidentally, helps them understand the permanence of matter. Still another may announce gleefully, "Here is a giant! Now I cut his head off—poof!"

There are some children, however, who are either not experienced or not free enough to handle a natural, malleable material, and they don't know what to do when presented with it. In that case the teacher does not show the child *what to do,* but helps her or him to see its properties and possibilities. Clay, for instance, can be compressed, thinned out, broken into many pieces and stuck together again; it can be stretched by rolling, or cut with a rigid object other than a knife, or sliced with a taut string. All these properties of clay need not be revealed at once. The teacher needs to feel the child's receptivity and readiness while introducing the material in order to stimulate the child's own exploration, which in time will suggest procedures and generate ideas. It is the initial exploration and personal, creative involvement that give children's work with clay an artistic dimension.[16]

Interest in Clay Products

After initial acquaintance with the material and following exploration and experimentation with its potentialities, many kindergartners love to make representative everyday objects with clay. These are often obvious, such as concave-shaped dishes or flat pancakes, or more involved, such as a bird's nest with eggs. Human or animal forms and transportation items are also popular subjects for clay.

Use of Accessories

Later in the year, in order perhaps to stimulate fresh interest or offer additional potential, the teacher can introduce supplementary materials which appeal to the imagination and stimulate the senses. Such accessories can include wire, wood, twigs, feathers, shells, or some other material a child or teacher will suggest. In this case clay is used as a substantial and effective base from which the child reaches out. One child, shaping a small amount of clay, calls it a mountain, then reaches for a twig and plants a tree. He sticks on a dab of cotton with glue and beholds snow on the tree. Another child scoops and extends her clay form until it is a lake for the fish she has created from a scatter of little shells. Thus accessory materials made available to children at the appropriate time can add an extra dimension of enrichment to clay work.

Protection and Care of Products

Although the greatest value of clay as of other artwork is in the meaning to the child and the process of discovery while at work, both teacher and children will want to preserve some finished products. The teacher must set aside one clear shelf

[16] Nancy Langstaff and Adelaide Sproul, in *Exploring with Clay,* ed., Monroe Cohen (Washington, D.C.: Association for Childhood Education International, 1979). A 46-page pamphlet.

on which to keep clay during drying or before it is taken home. (When a child saves clay in his or her cubby or locker it is very apt to get broken.) Some area in the room should also be provided to display clay work, with the display changed often enough that all children have a fair chance to see their work on view.

The child's name must be inscribed on the work with a nail or stick before the clay dries, and the clay piece should then be placed on a paper to dry slowly so it will not crack. When the clay product dries, the children usually love to paint it. Here the teacher needs to explain or demonstrate to the children how fragile a clay figure can be and how to handle it securely in order to prevent disappointment. After a clay product is painted, it may be further enhanced by a coat of clear shellac, which gives it gloss and a finished look. This must be done with a brush which is used only for shellac and later cleaned with denatured alcohol. A simpler way to get the same effect is to put the clay piece in a bowl and pour liquid floor wax over it; lift the product with tongs, place it on paper to dry, and reuse the surplus wax. All such operations are fascinating to children, who quickly learn to respect the time, the place, and the supervision required for the procedure of beautifying their artwork before taking it home.

PLASTICINE AND SALT DOUGH

Plasticine is a pliable, easy-to-store, and relatively inexpensive artificial material that provides a useful medium for manipulative and experimental work. It has the practical advantage of not sticking to surfaces or clothing, and it does not require extensive clean-up. It can therefore be used when there is limited time or limited supervision. To keep plasticine in good, soft condition, a small amount of vaseline may be added. It should be kept covered in a warm place, as it hardens when chilled.

Children enjoy pounding hunks of plasticine with a mallet or fist to make it more pliable, or they knead and press it between their hands. When it is sufficiently smooth, they roll and shape and structure it to suit their fancy. Some teachers find plasticine so convenient that they do not use clay. This is an unfortunate limitation, because clay, being a natural medium, has stronger sensory appeal and challenge to exploration and experimentation. But plasticine does provide a useful and diverting supplementary art material.

Another pliable material which children love is salt dough. This can be made with one part salt to three parts flour mixed with approximately one part water and kneaded until it is of firm and smooth consistency. Many teachers add a small amount of oil for extra smoothness, and others use a substantially smaller amount of salt with satisfactory results. Children are fascinated with the preparation of this material. Food coloring or poster paint may be added to the water to give the dough color. The virtue of this material is that when properly kneaded to the consistency of baker's dough it is very smooth and does not stick to the hands. The children can quickly make various shapes and objects with it, and the products can be left to harden and be painted.

Interestingly, since the material is dough, it naturally suggests cooking and food, and children often use it as dramatic play props, such as "cookies" which are put in the "oven" and "meat" which is sliced and "served" on plates. Children love using various utensils and dishes with play dough, all of which has more utilitarian and imitative value than the more freely expressive value of an art medium, but which is just as important in children's lives.

ART PROJECTS

Although "arts and crafts" seem to be taken for granted (like "salt and pepper" or "meat and potatoes") as being an integral part of children's activities, it may be useful to make a distinction between, and thus increase teachers' awareness of, the *art* and the *craft* components in various projects that engage both teachers and children.

For instance, a teacher sets up a potato (or apple or pear) print project, and the children are given a turn at coloring the cut surface and printing it on paper. The activity is indeed interesting to the children for its surprising result, the demonstrable "picture" that appears instantly, and especially for the easy duplication. But perhaps along with the satisfaction that comes from constructive activity and the introduction to craftwork, there is also the possibility of an artistic dimension beyond the finished product or the technical process itself. This might be achieved if the teacher provides a separate session devoted to discovering the patterns and symmetries found in cross sections of different fruits and vegetables *before* reproducing the design, thus enabling the children, as well as the teacher, to deepen their appreciation of these forms.

In another instance, a teacher brings in a quantity of perfectly shaped, pure white, smooth-surfaced shells. The children are to paint the shells any color or decorate them and take home as gifts. Here, too, the teacher might provide a period of acquaintance and free handling of the shells before they are embellished, giving the children an opportunity to appreciate their unique form, durability, and even function. Without such experience, the children, along with the teacher, might easily miss the kinds of knowledge and feeling that are part of an aesthetic experience and that can add meaning to an art project.

These were some of the considerations as one of the authors observed a tie-dyeing project that took place recently in a kindergarten class. The twenty children in the class were clearly excited about the project and had a general idea about the result, although little, if any, notion about the process.

Each child brought a white t-shirt from home, and the teacher brought packages of commercial dye. The first task for each child was to bunch up and *tie with a rubber band* a section of the garment. How simple, the teacher assumed. But how complicated it proved to be for all but a very few of the children. How difficult for them to coordinate the task of twisting a rubber band to tightly secure a section of the garment! The majority of the children, most of them already six years of age, were not able to operate a rubber band, so it had to be done by an adult. The next operation, dipping the shirt in water and soaking it in a basin of dye, though requiring some help and supervision, appeared to be simpler for the children, who were anxious to get on with the work and see the result.

When the teacher untied and identified the children's shirts, all were thrilled with the transformation from plain white to colored and designed. After the tie-dyed garments were dried on shrubs outside the classroom and each child took her or his own, looking satisfied, the adults reflected while cleaning up.

True, the children kept busy throughout and enjoyed taking something home to show and to wear, even if the expected design was barely discernible on some shirts. But it was clearly evident that the process required a kind of coordination the children hadn't yet developed and a skill they hadn't had a chance to practice. Would the value of this project have been different if the children had been prepared for it? How prepared? They might have first played and experimented with rubber bands to learn the tying function on a small item. They might have also practiced dyeing cloth, or paper, using plain vegetable colors (from beets, blueberries, and so on), thus finding out for themselves, and enjoying the sight of, color changes. Such activity might have been available to the children for a period of weeks, so that, through their own discovery and learning and developing interest, they could have gotten ready for the sophisticated class project. Then they would have been able to work more independently, with discrimination of artistic results, and would have taken pride in the product.

There is certainly a place in the kindergarten for special teacher-directed and teacher-aided craft projects. They can provide considerable social satisfaction as children work together, as well as important skill development and aesthetically pleasing results. However, four- to six-year-olds still need individual acquaintance with basic unstructured materials—and this need should be given priority and become an integral part of a teacher's planning.

CHILDREN'S WORRY ABOUT GETTING DIRTY

Sometimes a child is hesitant, perhaps even fearful, about using spilly paint or sticky, clingy clay; messy finger paint; or even squashable plasticine and dough. To this child there is good reason behind such hesitancy, and the teacher must respect this feeling rather than be disappointed that the child is not producing as everybody else is. Often such children benefit from simple reassurance. They may be concerned about getting paint on their clothing, in which case an adequate smock and reminder (or demonstration) that school paint is washable will serve to allay their concern. If dirty hands bother a child and keep her or him from using clay, show casually how it comes off or provide sticks, such as tongue depressors, with which to poke and cut and smooth clay so that this particular child can prepare for freely using bare hands. Let such hesitant, fearful children have a chance to see how children wash finger paint from their hands. They may well have been overtaught at home to stay clean. Some children may actually fear that the paint or clay covering their hands *will remain*, transforming their hands, and many cover their hands with the medium as though to test the fantasy. This is usually a passing phase.

Sufficient time, a relaxed atmosphere, and no urging usually bring about a change in any hesitant or fearful child in a few months. When that happens, it not only makes the child happy with the new freedom and new activity but brings a real thrill to the patiently waiting teacher. "Alexander painted for the first time today! Isn't it wonderful!" is a common exclamation of a teacher's satisfaction.

WHAT TO DO WITH CHILDREN'S ARTWORK

Although thus far we have been concerned mainly with the intrinsic value of art media, we now need both for practical and educational reasons to be concerned with the care and clearance of products.

Children often work quickly and are apt to produce innumerable paintings, drawings, and other creations in a short time. The teacher is then faced with the problem of saving, displaying, and sending home, as well as judiciously discarding, the variety of products of the entire class, which may include as many as fifty children in two sessions. The teacher needs to be sensitive to the children's feelings about their work, practical about storage, and tactful about sending work home or discarding it.

In placing value on children's artwork, the teacher makes it a point first of all to notice each child's work and protect it. Paintings need to state the child's name and be dried carefully on portable clothes racks, on the tops of unused surfaces, on clothesline fastened with pins, or on guarded floor space. Without provision for drying, paintings can very easily be ruined. When dry, paintings need to be stored. It is good to have some shelves for storing artwork. Some teachers solve the problem by designating a special place on the wall for each child, hanging each child's paintings one over the other in that one place. After a week of having the chance to see what the child did, the teacher may then pick some for display, send some home, and, if there are many similar ones, do some discarding, unless the child wants to take them all home. Some teachers keep a hard-cover scrapbook or ring notebook made from large sheets of oak tag for each child's drawings and paintings.

Displaying Pictures

Matting and framing pictures adds to their beauty and distinctiveness, but even without that, the display of their work by the teacher gives children a wonderful satisfaction about their own handiwork and thus about themselves. Teachers must not keep any one child's work up too long because the display area is necessarily limited. They must take the trouble to display at some time each child's best or most important work. Changing displays regularly allows teachers to do this, and even to include the work of the relatively unexpressive child, who although undramatic, also needs the support of being noticed. Perhaps an uninteresting picture will not be given a prominent spot, but it should be up. It helps the appearance of a room, incidentally, to balance the children's pictures with some attention to the effect of one upon the other as they hang in proximity on the wall.

FAMILY REACTION TO CHILDREN'S ART

Taking art products home often satisfies kindergarten children's practical sense of having something to show for their day in school, and it usually pleases parents and other relatives. A child will often be eager to take as many things home as he or she can. Here the teacher will benefit from some knowledge about how the child's artwork is treated at home. If on the whole the parents accept the child's work kindly, personally, and with genuine appreciation, the kindergartner has a good experience taking artwork home. But if the parents have only perfunctory words ("Those are nice pictures, honey—run along and wash your hands now"), then it may be better for the teacher not to send many pictures home with that child. Perhaps an older sibling jeers at important works of the preschooler ("That's *baby* stuff you do in kindergarten. Look at that scribble-scrabble!"). In that case the teacher may need to bolster the child with extra confidence to take home along with the pictures. Some parents may be critical of the child's art because they do not understand it, especially when representational work is attempted. "This is a girl jumping rope? Where is the *girl?*" they might ask. In this case the parents would benefit from a teacher's brief explanation about children's art. Perhaps the teacher might send home explanatory notes to all parents about young children's artwork or plan a parents' meeting on the topic. Then there would be more of a likelihood that children would at least not be discouraged, even if they did not receive appreciation of their art products and artwork.

Of course, every teacher hates discarding large accumulations of work, yet for the sake of expediency and orderliness, discarding, as well as selecting, is not disastrous and is necessary. Every child can see that out of a number of similar pictures only one or two need to be saved. Many children need to be prolific, but their products are not meant to be permanent.

THE TEACHER'S ARTISTIC TALENT

Will a kindergarten teacher have a more successful art program if she or he has some skill and personal experience with painting or clay modeling? Will she or he have greater understanding of the children's expression and development, and deeper sensitivity to the problems and pleasures of the media after having struggled with them? Emma Sheehy in *Fives and Sixes Go to School*[17] tells about a most creative

[17]Emma Sheehy, *Fives and Sixes Go to School* (New York: Holt, Rinehart and Winston, 1954).

teacher who is not an artist in any specific medium, yet is able to create a classroom environment that encourages freedom of expression and invites artistic activity. This is a more valuable asset for the kindergarten teacher than creative ability. But if a teacher is an artist, experience with art materials, appreciation of form and color, and feeling for originality may make the program, as well as the entire curriculum, that much richer, *provided her or his standards are realistic for young children.* If an artist, the teacher may be more likely to appreciate the similarity between adult art, whether primitive, classical, or modern, and what the child produces naturally. In any case it is the teacher's attitude of encouragement, faith in the validity of a child's expression, offering of variety and suitability of materials, and organization of working areas and boundaries that enable the children to get the most out of the creative media.

The teacher comes to know the children through their artwork, the activity itself, the accompanying behavior, and the changes in the work. All these reveal aspects of the child's development, uniqueness, and growth toward literacy. Kellogg[18] tells us:

> Children who have been free to experiment with and produce abstract esthetic forms have already developed the mental set required for learning symbolic language.

The teacher will see this without "teaching" or testing. The observant teacher may also notice in the child's artwork areas of particular weakness—motor, sensory, or intellectual—and thus be of special help to that child. At the same time the teacher will have many moments of pleasure observing the children's satisfaction with the materials and will also be periodically surprised by some individuals, as we see in the following:

> "Are you finished?" the teacher asked Karl, who stood before an easel and looked passively at his picture with blobs of different colors close to each other and one separate roundish red form. "Is this an apple you painted?" "No, that's the red light, don't you see? I am waiting for it to turn green, so I can get out of the traffic jam."[19]

REFERENCES AND FURTHER READING

ALLEN, ANN WRIGHT, with HERLEY, DAVEEN. *Art through Your Child's Eyes.* Southampton, N.Y.: Suffolk County Early Childhood Education Council, 1975.

BIBER, BARBARA. *Children's Drawings.* New York: Bank Street Publications, 1934.

BLAND, JANE COOPER. *Art of the Young Child.* Museum of Modern Art, New York. Dist. by Doubleday, 1957.

[18] Rhoda Kellogg, "Understanding Children's Art," p. 3.

[19] Marguerita Rudolph, *From Hand to Head* (New York: Schocken Books, Inc., 1977).

BREARLEY, MOLLY, ed. *The Teaching of Young Children.* New York: Schocken Books, 1970. See Chap. 3.

COHEN, DOROTHY H. "Continuity from Prekindergarten to Kindergarten," *Young Children* (May 1971).

COHEN, DOROTHY H., STERN, VIRGINIA, and BALABAN, NANCY. *Observing and Recording the Behavior of Young Children,* Chap. 4, "Recording a Child's Use of Materials." New York: Teachers College Press, Columbia University, 1958; revised ed., 1983.

DANOFF, JUDITH. "Children's Art," *Children Today,* July–August 1975.

DI LEO, JOSEPH H. *Children's Drawings as Diagnostic Aids.* New York: Brunner/ Mazel, 1973.

GAITSKILL, CHARLES, and GAITSKILL, MARGARET. *Art Education in the Kindergarten.* Peoria, Ill.: Chas. A. Bennett Co., Inc., 1952.

HARMS, THELMA. *My Art Is Me* (Discussion Guide for film). Berkeley, Calif.: Harold E. Jones Child Study Center, University of California.

HARTLEY, RUTH E., FRANK, LAWRENCE K., and GOLDENSON, ROBERT M. *Understanding Children's Play.* New York: Columbia University Press, 1952.

KELLOGG, RHODA. *The How of Successful Finger Painting.* San Francisco: Fearon Publishers, Inc., 1958.

KELLOGG, RHODA. "Understanding Children's Art" in *Readings in Psychology Today* (2nd ed.) Del Mar, Calif.: CRM Books, 1972.

GITTER, LENA. *How Art Can Nourish Self-Concepts* (pamphlet). San Rafael, Calif.: Academic Therapy Publications, 1972. A Montessori approach.

LANGSTAFF, NANCY, and SPROUL, ADELAIDE. *Exploring with Clay,* ed. Monroe Cohen. Washington, D.C.: Association for Childhood Education, 1979.

LASKY, LILA, and MUKERJI, ROSE. *Art: Basic for Young Children.* Washington, D.C.: NAEYC Booklet #106, 1980.

LERNER, SHARON. *Orange Is a Color, Square Is a Shape, Straight Is a Line* (3 books). Minneapolis: Lerner Publications Company, 1970.

LOWENFELD, VICTOR, and BRITTAIN, W. LAMBERT. *Creative and Mental Growth* (5th ed.). New York: Macmillan, 1970.

LOWENFELD, VICTOR, and BRITTAIN, W. LAMBERT. *Your Child and His Art.* New York: Macmillan, 1955.

LORD, LOIS. *Collage and Construction in School* (rev. ed.). Worcester, Mass.: Davis Publications, 1970.

PILE, NAOMI. *Art Experience for Young Children.* New York: Macmillan, 1973.

RUDOLPH, MARGUERITA. *From Hand to Head.* New York: Schocken Books, 1977.

SPARLING, JOSEPH J., and SPARLING, MARILYN C. "How to Talk to a Scribbler," *Young Children* (August 1973).

Films

"The Purple Turtle," 13½-minute color film for the National Kindergarten Association, produced by ACI Productions for Association Films Inc., 1108 Jackson St., Dallas, Texas.

"My Art Is Me," 22-minute color film from Extension Media Center, 2223 Fulton St., Berkeley, California 94720.

13 Music and Rhythm in School Life

When we consider the physical powers and creative imagination of kindergarten children, their ready response to rhythm, their advanced coordination as compared with nursery school children, their agility and grace in movement, their fascination with sound (in spite of intolerant adult ears), it is obvious that music and movement should play a vital and influential role in the active kindergarten curriculum. We need only hear children's spontaneous chants and melodic taunts, listen to the strong rhythms and catchy rhymes that go with ritual games, and observe the playfulness and inventive pantomime in original dancing to recognize that children are inherently musical.

This natural delight in rhythm, sound, and movement leads easily into a kindergarten program of personal expression with voice and body, satisfying experience with a variety of sound-producing instruments, and acquaintance with different

(Photo by Tana Hoban)

musical forms. Teachers can avail themselves of many excellent books dealing with appropriate musical programs and materials for four- to six-year-olds. (See bibliography at end of chapter.) Underlying the specific activities and materials, however, must be a philosophy of music and movement education. As in so many other phases of kindergarten learning, teachers look to the spontaneous, individual expression among the children as the starting point for expansion and enrichment of experience. They encourage the children's own creative powers with rhythm, sound, and movement, yet continue to increase their existing store of knowledge from wider experience with musical possibilities.

SONG AND DANCE

To help answer the question of just how one protects and encourages the spontaneous and creative while also feeding known ideas and material to children, let us analyze the several aspects of a good musical experience, or total rhythms program, for young children.

In a broad sense we are dealing with the expression and enjoyment of both movement and sound, and earlier comments about the highly physical character of young children's behavior pertain here, too. The children themselves must see and touch and do again and again in order to crystallize and deepen understanding. This active quality, so intrinsic to their conceptual learning, applies especially to their movement and music experiences. The space surrounding a child is conquered and understood by the movement of his or her own body into it, not by diagrams and charts. *Under* is defined through the sensation of a humped back as one crawls beneath the low roof of a table or bed; *over* is the victorious stretching of a long and crooked limb above an obstacle in one's way; *up* is the sweep of one's neck muscles under a tilted chin as one stares at the top step of the slide; *down* is a sudden, deflating drop into space. Big, small; heavy, light; fast, slow are all learned through the use of one's body.

Older people, and that includes young adults, take their spatial learning for granted. They are no longer so needful of using bodily energy to explore and do not enjoy the possibilities of movement for its own sake. The tastes and aptitudes of the adult include a variety of other developed areas as yet unknown to the young. But growing children feel themselves in their bodies, enjoy victories through the successful use of their bodies, and locate themselves in the world through moving in all directions in all kinds of ways.

CHILDREN LOVE MOVEMENT

Movement is as natural to children as breathing itself. Here, for example, is a boy running after a windblown paper. He is stretching, reaching out, running, stopping, starting, falling. A little girl is enjoying the flapping of the wind on the teacher's scarf. She is given the scarf and runs with it against the wind, delighting in the muscular sensation resulting from the rising and the swelling of the "sail" in her hand; she raises her hand, expands her chest, and finds amusement by elevating herself on her toes. A group of children in the spring of the year go rolling down a grassy hill. There is such boldness as they abandon themselves to the thrilling and dizzying rolling. The shyest and most inhibited children cannot resist the tumbly, bouncy bodily contact with the earth. They do it over and over again. It is exhausting, yet exhilarating. The hats roll off, the jackets slide away, the shoes slip off. The children love the disheveled roughness and the freedom from restrictive movements. "I didn't know where my head was, but I found it," says a child as he rises after rolling down the hill.

"I am a wheel." "I am a ball—watch how fast I go!" "I am a submarine—going way down." "I am a statue."

It is easy to see that such vigorous activities can later be refined, controlled, or intensified with rhythmic, musical direction of pattern by the teacher. But the children's inherent joy in spontaneous movement must first be there.

FROM MOTION TO SONG

Edna Buttolph, a music educator of wide experience, tells us

> The natural sequence with children of nursery and primary years is from motion to song, rather than from song to motion. Full free use of the body not only relaxes the children, but makes them ready and eager for singing time. Yet too often in special music periods, children are gathered in small chairs in a circle, and the very first procedure is the singing of songs. The children's urge to move, almost invariably strong, is criticized by the eager specialist, convinced she has something beautiful to give. She may become annoyed when the children do not give her their immediate and quiet attention, and she creates for herself some totally unnecessary problems.[1]

The observation is a wise one, and successful rhythms periods frequently begin with support by the teacher of the natural, rhythmic movements of the children. By a simple accompaniment such as clapping, beating a drum, or sounding tone bells, a teacher helps the children become aware of the *regularity* of their actions (i.e., the beat and pattern); of the *dynamics* of their actions (i.e., loud and soft); and of the *form* of their actions (i.e., the beginning and the end). Such supportive accompaniment of the children's natural rhythm helps them become aware of the relationship between music and movement, thus fostering greater sensitivity to the rhythmic and dynamic components of music.

By the same token the slightly wild galloping of cowboys who have just dismantled their block ranch and the dizzying spinning and twirling of experimenters in space fall into patterned reliability when the teacher introduces a musical accompaniment that stabilizes an almost out-of-control activity into a solid experience of

---

[1] Edna G. Buttolph, *Music for the Classroom Teacher*, Bank Street College Publication (New York: Bank Street College, 1958).

group unity. And the teacher can terminate it all by the magic of the music whenever deciding to do so. Or rhythms may begin with a teacher's intuitive response to the children's unexpressed need for physical activity. Because the teacher knows the children have been absorbed and quiet for a long stretch before the actual music time, the period opens with jumping or running or stamping.

DISCOVERING POSSIBILITIES WITHIN ONESELF

Whether at the beginning, the middle, or the end of a rhythms period, the teacher is sensitive to the spontaneous, unplanned movements in which children indulge all the time. In addition to picking these up and helping to give them pattern and control, there are ways of deliberately fostering ingenuity and imagination in body movement. To better understand the concepts, a teacher might actually try the suggestions that follow. The space that surrounds each of us offers several levels and planes for body functioning. Let us start with the lowest plane of all, the floor beneath us, and put the body into its flattest position—flat on the back, arms at sides and legs out straight. What can you do in the prescribed space occupied by your body and yet remain on that plane? You can rock from side to side, you can lift one or both legs upward, one or both arms upward, behind you, across your chest. You can lift your head, or lift everything that can be lifted at once. Suppose you remained in the same prescribed space on the floor but turned over on your stomach and chest? What could you do then? Rocking from side to side has a different sensation from this kinesthetic view; lifting limbs and head is also a different experience from the earlier prone position. Can you do anything else without removing yourself from that spot on the floor?

The next plane to consider brings you into a sitting position. With knees drawn up, you can spin around like a top. If you set your legs down, you can sway from side to side, bend forward and back, rest on your arms extended behind you, or do whatever else you can think up. Getting onto your knees, new possibilities open up again. Rooted to one spot, on your knees, what can you do? Your whole torso can bend backwards as one straight rod, with the knees as pivot, or you can fold into a seat on your upturned heels and bounce gently. Now stand up, but remain in one spot on the floor. What can your body do as it stands in space? Notice that we have not yet moved out into space with the more familiar walking, running, skipping activities. Those will come. What we are concentrating on first is the exploration of less obvious kinds of movement within the muscular structure of the body as it relates to a prescribed section in space. Thus, initially, we use no more space than the inches we actually occupy on the floor, although we may begin from a variety of initial postures, such as lying down, sitting on knees or buttocks, or standing. Try offering five-year-olds the opportunity to explore body movement in this way and you will learn that there are possibilities for movement you never could have dreamed up yourself. Help each child not only to an awareness of the possibilities within himself or herself, but let each look at other children's different movements to imitate and build on. That is one way each individual can expand the vocabulary of motion while at the same time feeling pride in what he or she has discovered. This technique may be used on other planes, of course, but one need not go through the gamut—from the floor, upward, and then on to movement across the room—in any one rhythms period. Over time, one explores movement away from the one spot and across the floor. This may be on one's stomach, back, bottom, or knees, on the soles of the feet when squatting low, on the feet when bending over, or on the soles, the heels, and the toes when standing upright and moving out into space. Tempo can be added to these, and variation in pitch. Sometimes we move fast, sometimes slowly, sometimes alternately fast and slowly. Sometimes the teacher's accompaniment is staccato, sometimes smooth and evenly paced. Sometimes it is quiet (for walking on tiptoe), sometimes loud and crashing (for stamping). One not only goes forward and backward into space on different planes, one goes up and down, leaving the floor in little jumps that spring from the ankles or in prances that lift the knees high. In time one moves forward and up into space with leaps, skips, and jumps that take one up and out.

When a teacher understands how varied are the possibilities for body movement and realizes that children take pleasure in the discovery and use of kinesthetic sensation for its own sake, he or she has the basis for encouraging creativity and freedom.

Personality Differences and Body Movement

Not all children are quite ready, however, to reveal themselves without inhibition, and therefore no one should be forced to participate in rhythms.

There are children whose normal urge to movement has been repressed, children who have been told to sit nicely, to be quiet, to stop running, to stop jumping, in short, to stop being children. Such children may need a longer time, perhaps several months, to find the freedom and imagination that will enliven them. To such children one may offer ideas to get them started. Shake your hands floppily, roll your head loosely, and wiggle up and down. Jump up in one spot and stretch your arms and head as high as they will go. Stamp your feet in alternating patterns of fast and slow, loud and soft, even when sitting, just to let the children know that to move with abandon is right and good. Resistant or shy children can accompany other children on percussion instruments.

Much can be learned by observing children's movement.

> Movement is part and parcel of personality, of a child's inner attitude and intention. It can reflect immaturity or precocity, steadiness or hastiness, lethargy or resilience. A teacher can see pride in a child's walk, fear in a child's posture, caution in the head, shoulders and torso.
>
> The body is an extension of self. It exhibits competency or lack of it, because movement is basically a reflection of the development of body control. Children learn better and better mastery of their bodies as they move from unskilled activity to purposeful action.[2]

[2]*Physical Education in the Primary School. Part One: Moving and Growing.* Prepared by the Ministry of Education and Central Office of Information. London: Her Majesty's Stationery Office, 1952.

SPACE

In addition to the exploratory experiences which a teacher guides but allows the children to develop in their own way, there are the common childhood movements that children enjoy. There is *walking*: fast, faster, *very fast*; slow, slower, heavy, and droopy; walking with long steps, tiny steps, ordinary steps; walking on toes, on heels; walking to a song one sings, to a drum, to a piano or record accompaniment; walking alternating with running and then ending perhaps with a jump! *Marching* and *stamping* are variations of walking that allow for different emphases of the arms, the torso, and the head. *Skipping* is a new skill for most five-year-olds, and perhaps not yet accomplished by all of them. They love to skip, alone or with a partner, in little jumpy skips, or high leapy skips. Many settle for hopping. Galloping is learned before skipping, although an occasional child gets the legs mixed up and cannot seem to get the beat and the emphasis quite right. But gallop they do, singly, in pairs (one behind the other and holding hands), or in a threesome (one in front, arms stretched back to the two behind). *Running,* free and yet within limits, is a much loved experience but is possible indoors only if the room is large enough. Then small groups can run in a circle, all going the same way of course. Or one at a time, each child can run catty-corner across the cleared space in the middle, the teacher maintaining a rhythm in the timing of each child's entry into the arena. The teacher can increase the fun and the alertness of the children by introducing signals for stopping and changing actions.

In time children learn to recognize the music that lends itself best to skipping, to galloping, to running, or to marching. They enjoy hearing a familiar accompaniment to such activities, but it is also important to test and strengthen their rhythmic sensibilities by offering them new marches, gallops, and skips from time to time.

DRAMATIZATION

Movement for its own sake and the enjoyment of rhythmic variation and intensity are only some of the possibilities open to children. With their keen eyes and imitative powers, young children take pleasure also in reproducing the movement of animals and machines. They waddle like ducks on their haunches and heels; wiggle like fish on their bellies; leap like kangaroos, frogs, and rabbits; stretch their heads cautiously up and around like turtles; and inch along on hands and flat feet like inchworms. With a salute to their industrial environment, they are equally happy to zoom like airplanes with wide wingspread, swing their hammers up and down, chug along like trains, or bend their backs to become unloading trucks. Some of these dramatizations come from experience outside of school, some result from trips and stories that introduce new ideas, and some are responses to songs that lend themselves well to acting out. Hardly a songbook for children exists that does not have a number of musical dramatizations in it. One portion of the rhythms period could easily include a few of these and still leave room for other activities. While the teacher may or may not suggest a theme, its development should be the children's own. The teacher's major role would be in making it possible for the children to see firsthand the many animals and machines that they will model themselves on so successfully. In some instances, their own simple chants and melodies can be improvised to accompany improvised movements.

Instrumental accompaniment to such dance-dramatization is not always necessary. Consider the following poem, which a teacher can read to children in carefully considered cadence, with properly timed pauses:

cat

The black cat yawns,
Opens her jaws,
Stretches her legs,
And shows her claws.

Then she gets up
And stands on four
Long stiff legs
And yawns some more.

She shows her sharp teeth,
She stretches her lip,
Her slice of a tongue
Turns up at the tip.

Lifting herself
On her delicate toes,
She arches her back
As high as it goes.

She lets herself down
With particular care,
And pads away
With her tail in the air.[3]

In one of the author's own experiences, the following verse on a similar theme was shared with the children and elicited active pantomime from different groups of four- to five-year-olds.

Kitty Can

Kitty can walk
Kitty can stalk
And run
And race
Hold her tail like a sail
And stare into your face.

[3]Mary B. Miller, "Cat," in *Sung under the Silver Umbrella* (Washington, D.C.: Association for Childhood Education International, 1958). Reprinted by permission of the Association for Childhood Education International, 3615 Wisconsin Avenue, N.W., Washington, D.C. Copyright © 1958 by the Association.

Kitty can stretch her back
And hump;
Twirl her whiskers
And do a high jump;
Wash her face
And brush her fur
Partly close her eyes and purr,
Kitty cannot talk like you,
But she hears you, and says, "Mew."
Come, Kitty-kitty. Quick!
Here is food you like to lick:
Fish to chew
And milk to lap
Then curl up
And have a nap.
Wake up! It's a sunny day!
Kitty dashes out to play,
She climbs a tree,
She bats a ball.
She watches
Shadows on the wall.
Kitty can be very friendly
With a child
Or a man.
Kitty can.[4]

Spontaneous, inventive movement can also come from the use of interesting props, such as hoops, as reported by Sally Cartwright.

In rhythms today, after moving with bamboo hoops to music in many different ways, these children spontaneously got into their hoops and each held another's hoop in front, forming a long train. They chuffed around and around the room, with small shuffling steps to "train music" on my accordian. *Every* child joined this hoop train, and when one stumbled or the train broke apart, all waited patiently until the "cars" were hitched and ready to start again.[5]

SOUND

Children are as interested in sound as in movement, and they frequently reproduce and develop cues from the environment. In one class we see each child eager for a turn at the noisy, vibrating electric sander at the workbench, enjoying particularly

[4]Marguerita Rudolph, "Kitty Can," in *Believe and Make Believe,* eds. Lucy Sprague Mitchell and Irma S. Black (New York: E. P. Dutton & Co., Inc., 1961).

[5]From an unpublished report by Sally Cartwright, Director, Community Nursery School, Tenants Harbor, Me.

the noise production, which they all might imitate quite accurately. When using sandpaper on rough wood, children discern the raspy, rubbing sound as much as the rubbing motion and the change in surface. The rhythmic, sharp sound of the saw contributes to the immense popularity of woodworking; the heavy flat whack of a hammer absorbs the children and invites repetition regardless of results. The crashing sound that can be made with pot lids, the clatter with tin cans, the varied tapping with finger and fingernails on different surfaces, the whirring of egg beaters, the popping of balloons, all produce an endless variety of sounds which children enjoy differentiating. This is graphically conveyed in *Max the Music-Maker* as Max discovers the different musical sounds and motions and rhythm in innumerable objects around him—boxes and sticks and kitchen utensils.[6] Playfulness in such "music" making is the dominant note.

Appreciating and allowing such play with sounds by bringing in appropriate materials leads naturally to play instruments such as shakers (boxes or cans filled with pebbles or dry beans, covered securely); drums (large cylindrical cans, boxes, or pails covered tightly with rubber or leather); tambourines (paper plates with attached shaky bottle tops); sanding blocks (two hand-size blocks of wood covered with rough grade sandpaper); a xylophone made with a series of glasses filled with water at different levels so a musical scale is produced; and various other instruments the teacher may know about or invent with the children. These instruments are fun and valuable to make in the class and to keep in the room for the children's inspection, possession, and sound experimentation. However, the teacher must not overlook the fact that the homemade instruments are seldom of high musical quality; they are more in the nature of playthings and, with their limited range, cannot alone satisfy the musical appetite of children or nourish musical discrimination, as real instruments can.

REAL INSTRUMENTS

The musical value of good and expensive instruments will not be lost on kindergarten children. A good drum expertly constructed that responds to palm and fingers; an attractive, well-made tambourine that vibrates with the least turn and jangles gorgeously when shaken; beautiful South American gourds and maracas; metal triangles that have a range from a gentle "ing" to a clear strong "cling"; xylophones with good musical tone and cymbals that vibrate when clashed are all necessary adjuncts to a musical program. Very good drums and xylophones and tambourines may prove to be relatively expensive. In that case purchasing one of each would still enable the children to become acquainted with the nature of the instrument, with its musical range and possibilities, and with the feel of using it. Another common and inexpensive instrument suitable for young children is the bell. There hap-

---

[6]Miriam B. Stecher and Alice S. Kendell, *Max the Music-Maker* (New York: Lothrop, Lee, & Shepard Company, 1980).

pens to be a good variety of bells, each with special form and sound and beauty. There are dainty table bells, tiny jingle bells that can be attached and worn on wrists and ankles, beautifully decorated Indian bells, clay bells from Mexico, old sleigh bells that are lovely to hear, and big, crude cowbells. The reader must be familiar with many others from particular lands, regions, and peoples. In many kindergartens the children successfully handle the autoharp and relish the chords its strings produce. But whatever instruments the teacher collects and keeps, it is important to make them available for the children to use and enjoy individually, before and along with participation in a controlled group ensemble in a formal music period.

THE RHYTHMIC ENSEMBLE

The formal organization of an ensemble must wait on the readiness of the children to work as a group, to have some awareness of the role of a leader in starting and stopping the group, and enough familiarity with how each instrument is handled to free the children for joint effort in making music. For this reason instruments must be freely available to the children for experimentation and guidance in the weeks before an ensemble is formed. They must learn, not be told, that the triangle can sound clearly only when hanging freely from its string, the cymbals resound when clashed in an upward movement rather than flatly against each other, and the drums boom differently when struck by the palm or a padded stick. And they must learn that the vibration of each can be stopped with the touch of one's hands. Some of this can be learned by accompanying each others' movements.

Exploring the possibilities of rhythmic beat enhances the rhythm ensemble. The teacher organizes clapping to names, to drum beats, to known songs, and to deliberately changing rhythms at the piano or on a drum. The teacher adapts the familiar walking and stamping to two-quarter, three-quarter, and four-quarter time in order to heighten the sensitivity to beat that will later make more likely the satisfaction of a shared instrumental rendition. When the children are first given the instruments to use together, as in other experiences of shared group activity, some guidelines are helpful. The instruments stay on lap or floor until the teacher gives the signal. When the music ends, no further playing by individuals goes on; instruments may be exchanged, but in an orderly fashion.

Songs with a chorus can be played by two different groups within the ensemble, the verse part by triangle, bells, and rhythm sticks, and the chorus by drums, cymbals, and tambourines, for example. Children who are familiar with instruments and have had good opportunities for musical experience are often intrigued with the possibilities of arranging a piece of music, with or without words, for their ensemble. In a very simple way they can grasp the concept of organization, and they do very well with it.

LISTENING TO MUSIC

To further acquaint children with musical instruments, the teacher might invite a musical parent, relative, or friend to visit and perform for them in class. The personal quality and directness of such an informal concert are meaningful and impressive to children, and such an occasion provides genuine musical stimulation. Neither teacher nor artist need worry about performing special children's music, although many of the great composers from Bach to Bartok did indeed write especially for children. Any short piece or short portion of a larger composition that has a clearly defined rhythm and definite melodic line and that does not introduce too many musical ideas in too brief a time will be suitable for children. The music, the personal playing, and the instrument itself will all arouse the curiosity and interest of the children and hold the attention of most of them.

The live concert is not as readily available as a concert of recorded music, and the teacher can enhance the children's familiarity with instrumental music by using well-chosen records. Good marches and dances are always favorites, and lullabies can be soothing and appealing.

Many classical composers, especially Mozart and Haydn, wrote pieces that are popular with children, who also respond favorably to some of the lyrical or dramatic works of nineteenth- and twentieth-century composers. Sometimes overlooked is the music written from the fourteenth to eighteenth centuries, which includes many lovely pieces, brief and rhythmically clear, that are readily enjoyed by our twentieth-century children. Finally, there should also be a place in the kindergarten for some of the music that is part of our contemporary culture. What matters is the teacher's open-mindedness, individual preferences, and interest in learning and sharing with the children.

An important category of music which is used liberally in kindergartens is folk music. There are many fine collections (see bibliography) of American and world folk songs. The special qualities of directness and earthiness, free humor, musical use of the absurd, and sometimes the appealing numerical pattern make folk songs very popular with children. A professional or amateur folk singer might come to sing and play folk songs with the children. Children and teacher can pick up songs from the many good recordings available, and if the teacher plays any accompanying instrument and dares to sing, she or he can share with the children any number of choice folk songs from her or his repertoire.

It is also desirable to invite parents and neighbors of varied ethnic back-grounds to share folk music representing their particular heritages. And of course, we must accept the children's interest in the popular music of their teenage brothers and sisters and perhaps invite some of them into the kindergarten to share their offerings with the children, too.

Teachers must acquaint themselves with the recorded offerings of different kinds of music, some of them organized by recording companies in categories of age and grade for best usefulness. But much good music crosses age lines, and in the end it is the teacher's own pleasure in music that will stimulate her or him to share this enjoyment with children.

SINGING

It is a pity that we Americans did not continue the custom of our many forebears of singing at work, while walking, and at play. An Israeli visitor to American kinder-gartens commented on this lack of singing as she described an Israeli kindergarten, "We sing all the time, as we put away, as we clean tables, as we go to the play-ground. Why do you dole songs out so sparingly?"

Perhaps the main reason we Americans do not sing enough lies in our earlier school practice of isolating children who could not carry a tune, thus setting up standards for singing that few teachers feel they themselves can meet. In truth, group singing can carry all the voices, and the satisfaction of lifting one's voice in song is one we should encourage in children and give them opportunities to enjoy. Not all children this age can carry a tune—but then they are not overly concerned because their sensory discrimination is still gross and unrefined. More important is the fact that the ear and the voice are both capable of learning but need continued experiences in discrimination to do so. In other words, singing improves with prac-tice! Teachers certainly contribute more to musical pleasure if they can sing, but if they are not talented vocally, they can still free the children to sing by showing no inhibition and introducing suitable song material.

A very different but equally compelling reason for singing is the support that singing songs gives to general language facility. Musical phrases give practice in using a rhythmic flow of words and promote recall of sound patterns. For the non-English-speaking child, singing is of particular value. Songs suitable for the age group give such children the opportunity to mouth words and phrases in a pleasurable context, thus hastening the process of making the English language their own.

GOOD SONGS FOR KINDERGARTNERS

Perhaps the best way to nurture musical appreciation among children is to choose songs we think will appeal to them from collections that have the approval of musical authorities. There are some things, however, that all teachers can understand. One is that to musicians no one style or period of music is in and of itself the best. Just as in the selection of books, the classics are hardly the whole story. Musicians say there is good and bad classical music, good and bad contemporary music, good and bad jazz, good and bad popular music, and so on. We are therefore not limited to one style or type of music for the kindergarten. Young children themselves have limitations which we must heed. Their attention span is short, they love repetition, they enjoy dramatic quality, they can feel either bold or tender (but actually do feel bold more often than tender), they enjoy the familiar but have a sense of humor about the odd and incongruous, and their voice range is not too great and tends to be higher than adults' but not as high as some children's songbooks seem to imply. Therefore, in selecting a song from a collection, let us bear in mind the following.

A song for kindergartners can be as short as a poem of one verse if each line expresses a different thought or a separate part of a thought, thus making the little piece really quite complex. Or a song can be much longer when a basic chorus is repeated regularly and the story line is developed by a simple change in the main verse. In such songs the repetition carries the children along and the changes are easy to apply. This is not the same as learning a song of many verses, each quite different from the ones before. Examples of such songs would be "There's a Little Wheel-A-Turning"[7] or "Skip to My Lou."[8] Young children adore the dramatic and will appreciate a song with a surprise ending, like

> Jack is quiet
> Down in his box
> Until somebody opens the lid![9]

or a song about a process they can understand, such as,

[7]Beatrice Landeck, *Songs to Grow On* (New York: William Morrow & Co., Inc., 1950).

[8]Ruth C. Seeger, *American Folk Songs* (Garden City, N.Y.: Doubleday & Company, Inc., 1980).

[9]"Jack in the Box," in Satis N. Coleman and Alice G. Thorn, *Another Singing Time* (New York: The John Day Co., 1937).

> Once there were some children in the kitchen,
> 　　　in the kitchen
> Washing, washing apples with their cooking aprons on.
> Once there were some children at the table,
> 　　　at the table
> Eating, eating apples with their cooking aprons off![10]

They also love songs with definite, repetitive rhythms of special character, such as a swinging song, a rocking song, a marching song, or songs that capture the mood of snow or rain, the spirit of a holiday, the ticking of a clock, or the sounds of machines and animals.

Children love to sing, and they should sing not only at the prescribed singing time but while walking in and out of their classroom if it seems right (not as rigid routine), as they work at cleaning up, as some experience reminds teacher or children of an appropriate song, and wherever it is natural and right to express the joy of living in a song.

This means, of course, that teachers must build up a repertoire of suitable songs, which they can do by studying some of the many excellent collections available (also in public libraries). The main task is to overcome that common feeling of "I can't sing" or "My two years of piano lessons are not for showing off." Freedom from inhibition may be even more important than technical skill in a kindergarten teacher. If you cannot play the piano, get a friend to go through some songbooks with you and take the trouble to learn a song or two by heart at each session. The same thing can be accomplished by listening to records. As you start to introduce the songs to the children, you will be repeating them again and again and building a repertoire at the same time. You will find yourself enjoying the pleasure of the music just as much as the children.

TEACHING SONGS TO CHILDREN

When you feel you do know a song well and feel at ease in singing, sing it through for the children so they can get the whole sense of it in one sweep. Sing it through a second time, and the third time start to teach it. Sing a line and have them repeat it, sing the next line and have them repeat that, and so on until the end. Sing the song through again slowly, and let the children follow along as best as they can. Then, and only then, should you make a deliberate try at the song together. Let it go after that, but on another day introduce it again by singing it through as a reminder, and then have the children sing with you. It is also possible to introduce a song by first singing and encouraging the children to participate in singing the chorus of the song, or a repetitive phrase, an echo, or any other simple patterning of the whole song.

[10] "Baking Apples," in Satis N. Coleman and Alice G. Thorn, *Singing Time* (New York: The John Day Company, 1961).

Sometimes children learn a song best by hearing it without the piano accompaniment, which may drown out the words for them. In that case know the song well enough so that you know the tune and do not need to look at the words. You need not sing like an opera star in order to carry a tune. Just about everybody can sing "America" in tune because of the endless repetitions of that song during school years, and yet many people claim they cannot carry a tune. If you are slow at it, try a little more practice with a piano accompaniment or listen to someone else's voice to guide you. The spirit of a kindergarten program is considerably enhanced by lots of good, lusty singing.

MAKING UP THE RHYTHMS PERIOD

Rhythms time in the kindergarten can be planned or spontaneous but should certainly occur with regularity, several times a week if possible. The period can last from ten minutes to thirty, but, in the course of the passing weeks and months, all aspects of the sound and movement experiences we have been describing should be included. A teacher can make up a balanced rhythms period from among the following:

1. Movement
   Free, exploratory movement within one or several planes or in new directions in space (sidewards, backwards while moving away from one spot), including individual experimentation, building in time to a simple composition.

   Movements suggested by the teacher to free inhibited children and give ideas to those afraid to try their own as yet.

   Dramatizations, to song, poems, percussion, piano, or phonograph accompaniment, of imitable animals, machines, workers, and so on.

   Rhythmic responses to clearly defined musical patterns: marches, skips, gallops.
2. Sound
   Singing some familiar songs, learning a new song, making up a song, or making up a new verse to an old one.

   Use of instruments.

   Listening to live or recorded music.
3. Rhythm and Pitch Games
   Rhythm
   clapping:
   children and teacher
   child as leader
   group against group
   variation in beats (teacher- or child-led)
   guessing clapped out songs that are known
   stamping, tapping, stepping:
   similar to clapping, but using heels, when seated, varying with hands beating or tapping on chair, wall, floor, and of course, stamping or stepping around room to different tempos and degrees of loudness or softness.

Pitch

"high and low" games to accompaniment, e.g., "Jack in the Box"

scale songs, using parts of the octave or the whole, and going up and down; for example:

"As-I-climbed-up-the-ap-ple-tree
(c   d   e   f g   a   b   c)
"All-the-ap-ples-fell-down-on-me."
(c   b   a   g   f   e   d   c)

(This one is easily accompanied by gestures, stretching up as high as one can reach on the way up, and slowly lowering arms and body on the way down.)

echo songs, such as

"Echo I can hear you
(hear you, hear you)" or
"Who has the penny?"
"I have the penny . . ."

games of imitating familiar sounds: horns, whistles, cows, ducks.

identifying higher and lower pitch on the piano.

helping children to discover the range of their voices by encouraging them to experiment and explore a variety of effects and expressive qualities in stories and characterizations—e.g., deep, high, or shrill.

4. Organized group singing games simple enough for kindergarten, such as "Muffin Man" or "Looby Loo"

CONTROLLING FOR FREEDOM

An important consideration for the teacher who wants to offer maximum freedom of expression and yet keep inexperienced young children from losing all sense of proportion and going out of control is to establish clearly stated and clearly understood signals by which the group can be brought back to the piano or back to their seats, or can be stopped to just listen by sheer force of conditioned response. Early in the semester, therefore, the teacher acquaints the group with the signals: a particular phrase on the piano that means "Come back to the piano," a special gong for quick silence and attention, a chord at the piano, or perhaps a special clapping rhythm that means "Go sit down at your seats." Such signals are individual, and it does not really matter precisely what they are, although an attractive sound is preferable to a harsh one. The important thing is that a teacher should not have to shout above the noise of excited children to get their attention. Therefore, after introducing the signals early in the year, the teacher must spend time helping the children learn to respond to them automatically. Games similar to musical chairs and musical spots can teach the children that when the music stops, the movement stops. As the children complete an activity on the floor, the signal for returning to the piano or their seats can be given as often as needed to get everybody to respond. Such conditioning is important if young children are to be allowed to be free, because the better judgment and perspective of an adult may suddenly be needed to help them out of a potentially unsafe situation (if they are running in different directions in a small space and are headed for collisions) or to halt contagious behavior before the children find themselves exhausted.

Another important consideration is the balance of active and quiet activities that helps children to catch their breath and relax as necessary. This means concern for what *they* can do comfortably. They cannot come back breathless from mad galloping and start immediately to sing. It would be better for them to flop onto the floor "like a burst balloon" and lie there several seconds before coming for the singing. A teacher must be sensitive to what *quiet* means. Singing a lullaby is not necessarily a quiet activity, since one must use one's breath, although a lullaby itself is quiet in contrast to a gallop. Change of pace, change of mood, and change of muscular involvement all go into the consideration of a balanced rhythms period.

THE TEACHER'S ROLE

If the teacher recognizes that the rhythms experience is encouraging exploration with movement and sound, introducing new material in these areas to the children, allowing for individual and group functioning, and protecting children from both self-consciousness and precocity, while giving them full opportunity to enjoy the elements of music and body movement, then there can be satisfaction that the possibility for lifelong learning in these fields has been opened. But any teacher owes it to the children and to herself or himself to explore the pleasures of motion and song for her or his own enjoyment. Enthusiasm and interest are needed for the building of a repertoire of songs and instrumental selections, for the willingness to explore and learn as well as share these age-old satisfactions with a new generation of youngsters.

REFERENCES AND FURTHER READING

Music and Movement Education

ANDREWS, GLADYS. *Creative Rhythms for Children.* Englewood Cliffs, N.J.: Prentice-Hall, 1954.

BREARLEY, MOLLY (ed.). *The Teaching of Young Children,* Chap. 5. New York: Schocken Books, Inc., 1970.

BROOKS, CHARLES V. W. *Sensory Awareness: The Rediscovery of Experiencing.* New York: Viking, 1974.

BUTTOLPH, EDNA. *Music for the Classroom Teacher.* Bank Street College Publications. New York: Bank Street Publications, 1958.

ENGSTROM, GEORGIANNA (ed.). *The Significance of the Young Child's Motor Development,* #128. Washington, D.C.: National Association for the Education of Young Children, 1971.

JONES, ELIZABETH. *What Is Music for Young Children?* Monograph No. 107 (rev. ed.). Washington, D.C.: National Association of the Education of Young Children, 1969.

JORDON, DIANA. *Body Movement for Children.* Boston: Plays, Inc., 1971.
Physical Education in the Primary School, Part One: Moving and Growing.
Prepared by the Ministry of Education and Central Office of Information.
London: Her Majesty's Stationery Office, 1952.
NORTH, MARION. *Movement Education.* New York: Dutton, 1973.
ROWEN, BETTY. *Learning through Movement.* New York: Teachers College
Press, 1963.
SHEEHY, EMMA. *There's Music in Children.* New York: Holt, Rinehart and Winston, 1952.
STANIFORD, DAVID J. *Natural Movement for Children.* Dubuque, Iowa:
Kendall-Hunt Pub., 1982.
STECHER, MIRIAM B., McELHENY, HUGH, and GREENWOOD, MARION.
Threshold Early Learning Library: Music and Movement Improvisations.
Vol. 4. New York: Macmillan, 1972.

Sourcebooks for Songs and Rhythms

BAILEY, CHARITY. *Sing a Song.* New York: Plymouth Music Co., 1955.
COLEMAN, SATIS N., and THORN, ALICE G. *Singing Time.* New York: The
John Day Company, 1961.
JENKINS, ELLA. *The Ella Jenkins Songbook for Children.* New York: Oak Publications, 1966.
JONES, BESSIE, and LOMAX, BESSIE. *Step It Down, Songs and Games from
Afro-American Heritage.* New York: Harper & Row, Pub., 1972.
LANDECK, BEATRICE. *Children and Music.* New York: William Sloane Assoc.,
1954.
LANDECK, BEATRICE. *Songs to Grow On.* New York: Marks & Sloane, 1950.
And by the same publisher, *More Songs to Grow On,* 1954.
LANDECK, BEATRICE, and CROOK, ELIZABETH. *Wake Up and Sing!* New
York: Morrow, 1969.
MITCHELL, LUCY SPRAGUE, and BLACK, IRMA S. (eds.). *Believe and Make
Believe.* New York: Dutton, 1961.
NELSON, MARY J., and TIPTON, GLADYS. *Music for Early Childhood.* Morristown, N.J.: Silver Burdett Company, 1952.
Pocket Songbooks. Delaware, Ohio: Cooperative Recreation Service. (A series of
inexpensive pamphlets, including African Songs, Amigos Cantandos, Rounds,
etc.)
SEEGER, RUTH. *American Folk Songs for Children.* Garden City, N.Y.: Doubleday, 1980.
STECHER, MIRIAM B., and KENDELL, ALICE S. *Max the Music-Maker.* New
York: Lothrop, Lee & Shepard Company, 1980.
Sung under the Silver Umbrella. Washington, D.C.: Association for Childhood
Education International, 1958.
YURCHENKO, HENRIETTA. *A Fiesta of Folk Songs* (Latin America). New
York: Putnam's, 1967.

Sources for Records

Folkways Scholastic Records, 906 Sylvan Ave., Englewood Cliffs, N.J. 07632
R.C.A. Educational Sales Dept., 1133 Avenue of the Americas, New York, N.Y.
10036
U.N.I.C.E.F., 331 East 38th St., New York, N.Y. 10016
McDONALD, DOROTHY T. *Music in Our Lives: The Early Years.* Washington,
D.C.: National Association for the Education of Young Children, 1979.

14

Exposure to Literature

YOUNG CHILDREN AND LITERATURE

Literature has a prominent position in the landscape of our culture. Children's literature must have the same artistic standards, the same power to affect the spirit, and the same inherent stamina to survive changing generations as does adult literature. The difference is only in the degree of complexity of ideas, of subject, and of language to allow for the children's limited experience and comprehension. Kindergartners have the emotional power, however, to be deeply moved by the feeling and the beauty of literary works, and although they are illiterate they can become acquainted with good literature by being read to. They also have the intellectual capacity to respond to ideas, the facility to learn new words and concepts, and the maturity to follow a story and catch the humor from books properly presented to them. Like art and music, true literature with style, originality, conviction, and valid content illuminated with artistic insight has something vital to say to preschool children who are not yet able to read. We are fortunate to have an abundance of children's literature that increases with each year's literary harvest.

SELECTIVITY

Hundreds of excellent children's books come out annually and hundreds of mediocre ones are just as sure to appear. In addition there is an unlimited amount of printed matter on the market that unfortunately passes for children's books, as well as scores of very good books still available that were published in earlier decades. There are also the classics: some of the traditional, stylized folktales of different times and cultures and the enduring rhymes of Mother Goose.

At first glance so many children's books may seem like a surfeit of goods presenting an insurmountable problem of selection for a conscientious teacher. On second thought, this abundance can be regarded as an advantage; it gives the teacher a personal as well as a professional choice and thus lends individuality to the library of each kindergarten. There can be enough books to appeal to changing moods and curiosity and to provide for the many directions taken by growing minds.

Quality Rather Than Quantity

Kindergarten teachers cannot possibly be expected to be familiar with the entire range of good books available, yet they bear the responsibility of knowing how to evaluate what is good in young children's literature. Desirable as it is to have enough books and sufficient variety in a classroom, we must not succumb to the lure of sheer numbers. Filled book racks and shelves may look impressive but are useless if they contain many unsuitable volumes. It is not uncommon to find books on school shelves that are so uninteresting that neither the teacher nor the children ever pick them up ("It's been here ever since I can remember," is the usual explanation). Children given a steady diet of poor books will be impeded in the development of literary interest and taste. If there is no way immediately to replace unsuitable books, it would certainly be more functional and interesting if those full shelves were only half full. A *few* good books may not satisfy a teacher's standards but the library can be enlarged if necessary by borrowing from the public library, provided the teacher knows what to choose. Let us consider some of the essentials in books of literary merit suitable for young children.

Knowing Children and Appropriate Books

Knowing children means understanding general principles of child development, especially preschoolers' capacities and the directions in which their interests lie as they try to get to know their world.

Charlotte S. Huck indicates the relation between developmental characteristics of children and their interest in books by showing how physical and emotional development affect children's behavior and receptivity to literature.[1] Thus the rapid development of language in preschool children relates to their pleasure in rhymes, nonsense, and repetition that can be found, for example, in *Mother Goose* as well

---

[1] Charlotte S. Huck, *Children's Literature in the Elementary School* (New York: Holt, Rinehart and Winston, 1979), 3rd ed., pp. 31–32.

as in contemporary collections of humorous verse. Curiosity about the world contributes to the interest in everyday experiences as portrayed realistically and imaginatively in books by the Hobans, Arnold Lobel, H. L. Rey, and Richard Scarry,
among others. The young child's developing independence is reflected in many
books including those by M. W. Brown, Ruth Krauss, Maurice Sendak, and Beatrice
de Regniers.

A teacher need not stop, of course, with any prescribed list but can amend it
with personal knowledge, insights about children, and experience and acquaintance
with current literature. Books with "everyday experience," for instance, could
deal with relationships in a divorced family, such as Ron Roy's story *Breakfast with
My Father,* depicting the great sadness of a father moving out and the deep joy of
having him come back once a week.

Knowing children also means knowing the specific children with whom the
teacher is now working. The class may have children with advanced language development and wish to use stories of greater length and complexity than otherwise
would be possible. The class may have children of low language development and
picture books with simple words or brief, dramatic poems may have to be used,
until their language develops more.

The class may have children representing certain minorities, which is especially
true of the growing urban areas, and books that picture the backgrounds or experiences of those children should be included. Fortunately, many fine books which
picture our multiracial, multinational, American society have been published in the
last decade. Beautifully illustrated books about blacks, Hispanics, Chinese, American
Indians, Mexican-Americans, and other ethnic groups are now available in book-
stores, in libraries, and on classroom shelves. (See also the annotated bibliography
at the end of the chapter.)

SELECTION CRITERIA

Aesthetic Values

One of the outstanding values of books is their overall aesthetic appeal. Children respond to the aesthetic, although they may not be able to express their appreciation in words. There are so many books that are beautiful in their entirety,
books that have an inspiring story (whether the plot has development or a repeated
pattern of events), beautiful pictures, attractive design and printing, and appealing
shape, that choice becomes very difficult. In fact, the difficulty is similar to the one
felt by the old man in Wanda Gag's *Millions of Cats* who was seeking the most
beautiful kitten and kept finding another and another with distinctive and different
characteristics of beauty until he selected millions and billions and trillions of cats!

Illustrations and format. Since so much of the beauty of children's books
comes from the illustrations, let us look at several kinds. The words and pictures of
the unusually attractive *Green Eyes* by A. Birnbaum convey harmoniously and with

strong sensory images the *whole* life of a cat, starting with the first impression of the world so analogous to a child's first impression.

In Else H. Minarik's *Little Bear* (and its sequels), illustrated by Maurice Sendak, there is a special kind of humor, whimsy, rhythmic pattern, and spirited depiction both of characters and fantasy themes that contribute to the total impression of Sendak's pictures in the life of a boylike bear. Among numerous other contributions by Maurice Sendak is *The Nutshell Library,* consisting of five small books in a box, each amusing to hold, to listen to, to look through.

Very different from these is the slim little volume by Leo Lionni, *Little Blue and Little Yellow.* Its boldness and simplicity of colored abstract forms are very effective and rather surprising. Children have no difficulty in perceiving Little Blue (a mere roundish blue blob) and Little Yellow (an equally crude roundish yellow shape) as thoroughly animate and important friends, by virtue of their proximity and position.

Still another kind of book is *Brookie and Her Lamb* by M. B. Goffstein. Its shape, artwork, and striking simplicity have an overall sophistication. A book such as *Rain, Rain Rivers* by Shulevitz makes an instant impression with its unique format; poetic, sweeping language; and lovely landscapes.

There is aesthetic stimulation in the variety of artistic styles in illustrations and in the general format and design of books. It is stimulating to have books of different size, shape, and construction; books with durable clothlike soft covers; books with spiral binding that open and close differently from standard ones; books with full-page pictures; and those with little scattered decorations.

When children inspect such books as those by the ingenious Bruno Munari or Eric Carle, they are fascinated by the unique effect of exposing concealed objects and by finding out how the book "works."

Literary Merit

Literary value, intrinsic to the aesthetic character of a book, deserves serious and separate focus. What is the quality we call "literary" when applied to books for the young?

Reality. The reader probably has heard the expression "here and now" but may not have had an opportunity to learn its origin or application to children's literature. The phrase actually originated with Lucy Sprague Mitchell's famous first *Here and Now Story Book* and was reinforced by the second, *Another Here and Now Story Book.* These collections of stories of the familiar and the everyday are actually anthologies of original literary works of different forms, themes, and levels of language reflecting children's own development. The stories deal with the truly significant in a child's life as seen from the child's point of view. The sections dealing with children's language and receptivity to literary forms at different ages are of timeless value.

Contemporary works in the here-and-now tradition take cognizance of children's feelings as well as interests; indeed they take children themselves seriously, too. One of the best-known modern children's writers, the late Margaret Wise Brown, was a student and close associate of Lucy Sprague Mitchell. Experimenting with literary styles, exploring exhaustively all the senses and perceptions, Brown produced many superb stories that continue to be published in new editions. Her many works show great originality and a genius for evoking deep feelings. One of the best known is *The Noisy Book*. The purely sensory element in this book was so loved by children that the author followed it with a whole series of *Noisy Books:* indoor, outdoor, city, country, and even *The Quiet Noisy Book*. The essence of the *Noisy Book* is the fresh awareness of pure sound. Muffin the dog gets a bandage over his eyes after the doctor takes a cinder out, and so he cannot see. But Muffin can hear. Does he know what he hears and who makes the particular noises?

Comprehensible portrayal of struggle.   Although there was a time when only goodness and sweetness were the appropriate subjects for children's books, there is recognition today that young children necessarily face many realities and must resolve frustrations, fears, and conflicts of all kinds. There are many books with either human or animal characters that depict a wide range of realistic struggles—physical, social, and psychological—understandable to young children. In one, *Timothy Turtle*, by Alice Davis, Timothy, a heavy turtle, slides down a river bank, lands upside down, and is unable to turn over. The physical struggle for desirable bodily position by Timothy is very understandable to young children, and when Timothy's condition invites the struggles and unique cooperation of his numerous friends, the children also understand that and share in the ultimate victory.

In another book, *The Carrot Seed,* by Ruth Krauss, struggle of a different kind is experienced by a nameless little boy who plants a carrot seed. In spite of all the doubts and discouragements from every member of the family and the many days when "nothing came up," the little boy persists in watering and weeding. He does not give up, until one day a carrot comes up, "just as the little boy had known it would." And the reader, who most likely also knew it, experiences the same struggle and faith vicariously. In *I Like a Whole One* by Marguerita Rudolph, Arthur's reasonable family keep offering him mere pieces of a fruit. Frustrated and angry, he does not give up striving for "a whole one" and gets what he wants at last, to the surprise of his family. Children identify with Arthur's desire.

In *Benjie on His Own,* the author, Joan M. Lexau, describes the desperate conditions of ghetto life and Benjie's fears, strengths, and struggles as he manages traveling to and from school and caring for his sick grandmother. The same author has other books with realistic themes which she treats with warmth and humor. In *Stevie,* author-artist John Steptoe deals honestly with a child's initial resentment of, and subsequent satisfaction with, a foster brother.

Present-day family life.   As realities in life change, social mores and morality change, too, and with them children's literature undergoes change. Many of the subjects, themes, and illustrations of books published in the later sixties and into the seventies, including books for younger children, reflect the "new reality" and the changed moral atmosphere. For example, the traditional American family portrayed in books written before the sixties now appears side by side with acknowledgment and acceptance of other life styles in present-day society. There is a beautiful book by Eleanor Schick called *City in Winter* about a child who lives with a mother and grandmother only. The mother works and the grandmother is the loving caretaker. In *Ida's Idea,* a mystery story by Wendy Kindred, a strong relationship and unusual communication exist in a family of working mother and a young school girl. *Me Day,* by Joan Lexau, tells about a family that has undergone divorce and a child who wants to be "undivorced." Today's books are saying that differently organized and even disrupted families can still offer family love and protection to their members. Another striking example of this is *Daddy* by Jeannette Caines, illustrated by Ronald Himler, showing the child's side of seeing Daddy on Saturdays only, when they do many things together. The author conveys, through simple prose, tremendous love between father and child, strengthened by realistic pictures of a black family.

Learning about death.   Even death is faced realistically in the new morality. Margaret Wise Brown's *The Dead Bird* was a rarity when it was first published, although its description of the bird as "cold dead and stone still and no heart beating" is as meaningful as ever. But there are quite a few more now, among them Charlotte Zolotow's *My Grandson Lew,* Sandol S. Warburg's sensitive account of the grief of a child facing the approach and then the reality of the death of a beloved dog in *Growing Time,* and Judith Viorst's *The Tenth Good Thing about Barney.* All affirm the importance of life, yet all treat death honestly.

Identification with the literary character.   In their response to literature children, like adults, identify with certain characters. Such characters need not necessarily be representative of the children's own way of life but they must have believable and meaningful experiences and communicate universal human feelings artistically.

Ferdinand, in Munro Leaf's *The Story of Ferdinand,* is a hero of an old storybook which has enjoyed a best-selling career since the 1930s. Although the book has a background of Spanish bullfight ritual and regalia and the hero is a shy, flower-smelling bull (what an unusual subject for American preschool children), it is immediately understood by children; they identify with the idiosyncrasies of the bull and with his being different from the other bulls, and they feel his plight when the very important grown-ups misunderstand him. The direct style and physical, earthy humor and drama, as well as the outstanding illustrations, contribute to the intensity of the children's response.

> He didn't look where he was
> sitting, and instead of sitting
> on the nice cool grass in the
> shade he sat on a bumble bee.

> Well, if you were a bumble bee
> and a bull sat on you, what
> would you do? You would sting
> him. And that is just what this
> bee did to Ferdinand. Wow! Did
> it hurt . . . . .[2]

And the children listening to the story *do* empathize with the gentle Ferdinand in this instance and throughout the story as he resists efforts to turn him into a fierce fighter in the bullring.

Another literary character of great appeal to children is a curious, questioning little raccoon in Margaret Wise Brown's *Wait Till the Moon Is Full.*

> "How dark is the dark tonight?" asked the little raccoon.
> "Not so dark," said his mother. "There is a new moon tonight, thin as the curve of a raccoon's whisker in the sky above the tree tops."
> "Can I see it?" asked the little raccoon.
> "No," said his mother. "You must wait. Wait till the moon is full."
> "How big is the night?" asked the little raccoon.
> "Very big," said his mother.
> "How big is Big?" asked the little raccoon.
> "Wait," said his mother. "Wait till the moon is full."[3]

The children identify with him not because he is a raccoon and lives in the woods but because he expresses the urgent wish to see the hidden, the as yet forbidden; because he has a compelling curiosity and has to endure having to wait for what he wants to know. Children also identify with normally subordinate characters who enjoy finding themselves in a superior position to that of an authority. This happens in Elizabeth Guilfoile's *Nobody Listens to Andrew,* in Claire Bishop's *The Five Chinese Brothers,* and in Benjamin Elkin's *Six Foolish Fishermen.*

Appropriate Fantasy

Many of the books we have referred to in this chapter, as well as others with which the reader must be familiar, have an important element of imagination and fantasy; the old man brings millions of cats as a present for his wife, a little bear takes a trip to the moon, and a raccoon asks questions about the night. Yet the fantasy is within the bounds of real sense. The characters do have genuine physical attributes appropriate to their kind. Animals may talk in human language but what they say is relevant and right for them and for the story. There is some contact

---

[2] From *The Story of Ferdinand* by Munro Leaf. Copyright 1936 by Munro Leaf and Robert Lawson. Copyright © renewed 1964 by Munro Leaf and John W. Boyd. Reprinted by permission of The Viking Press, Inc., and Hamish Hamilton Ltd.

[3] From *Wait Till the Moon Is Full* by Margaret Wise Brown, illus. Garth Williams. Copyright © 1948 by Margaret Wise Brown. Reprinted by permission of Harper & Row, Publishers, Inc.

between the story's fantasy and the world children know as real. Even a story like Sendak's *Where the Wild Things Are,* in which the imagination of the child himself is used, remains rooted in everyday reality. The hero gets carried away by irrational "wild things," has confrontations with monsters and ultimately conquers them, but the listeners can enjoy the element of fright because the story resolves itself in the hero's return to the safety of home and mother. For children who are still unsure about the difference between fantasy and reality, fantasy that creates an entirely new world where nothing is familiar can be an unsettling experience.

In this connection some of the classical fairy tales one always thinks of when talking about fantasy in children's literature may not always be appropriate for kindergartners—at least not in their original versions. The great heroes performing elaborate symbolic deeds in distant places are out of young children's intellectual grasp.

While kindergarten children do appreciate the presence of negative as well as positive feelings in the characters, the envy, greed, anger, and mischief they understand are aspects of more common human behavior and not the epitome of evil as depicted in the sophisticated language of fairy tales in their original form. Yet we are aware of the special appeal fairy tales hold for children of all ages. Why?

Bruno Bettelheim, the child psychoanalyst who wrote *The Uses of Enchantment,* an analysis of fairy tales, contends that they not only nurture imagination but also enable children to cope with fears, relieve a sense of helplessness and insignificance, and inspire hopefulness. Bettelheim further believes that fairy tales exert a moral effect by telling children how problems will be solved and justice will prevail through great struggle and hard work.[4]

The question then is not so much the validity or significance of fairy tales as a literary form, but more specifically their use in the kindergarten classroom. Not only do the language and length of the *originals* seem inappropriate in this setting, but the abbreviated and distorted versions in which they more commonly appear often lack literary or artistic distinction. Fortunately there have been new adaptations in recent years which do have merit (including those published by Scholastic Book Services) and the discerning teacher may find others in collections as well as in separate editions.

Fantasy appropriate for young children is a common ingredient in many modern books. It is quite clear in Beatrice de Regnier's *The Giant Story.* The title alone suggests a removal from, or at least a natural manipulation of, reality. And once established, the book's make-believe is consistent. The once-little-boy-now-giant performs purely gigantic deeds till the end of the day. At that point, to satisfy the young reader who is not too secure in the distinction between a story and the truth, the author has the one-day-giant-now-little-boy get back home to his mother.

The two playful, furry rabbits in Garth Williams' picture book, *The Rabbits' Wedding,* live in a lovely world of hills and fields of flowers. With great simplicity

---

[4] Bruno Bettelheim, *The Uses of Enchantment: The Meaning and Importance of Fairy Tales* (New York: Alfred A. Knopf, Inc., 1976; Random House, Inc., Vintage Books, 1977).

of scene and action, Williams conveys a deep mood, as through easy dialogue he unfolds a pastoral tale of joyous companionship and fulfillment of wishing, of sadness, and of longing, ending with a wedding of the two rabbits wearing golden dandelions in their graceful ears. Of course, the beauty of the story is heightened by the harmonious mood in the illustrations and the soft contrasts in the pictures of the black and white rabbits.

Appreciation of a particular fantasy and the meaning gained from the story will depend on the reader's and listener's imagination and taste. Some may appreciate the poetic form of Thatcher Hurd's *The Quiet Evening*,[5] picturing the serenity before bedtime when the "ocean has wrapped around all its fish and sea monsters" and when "The clock . . . is talking to itself." For a brief excursion into fantasy, one can always resort to the rhyming *Mother Goose* who ventures even beyond the moon.

> There was an old woman tossed in a basket,
> Seventy times as high as the moon.[6]

The folktale.   In the long-lived classic folktales, the fantasy seems well established. It is taken for granted that the three bears are in a faraway, once-upon-a-time place and that the little red hen is not the kind of hen one will ever meet in a barnyard. The fact that these stories are recognizably make-believe frees the children's imagination. The rhythmic refrains of folktales accentuate the magic. "And I can run away from you, I can, I can," fulfills the listener's expectations in Paul Galdone's *Gingerbread Boy*. Slightly different versions of the same story can be found in various folktale collections and in lavishly illustrated (and expensive) editions of single stories. In addition to their fantasy and narrative qualities, folktales often have a strong flavor of humor, as in Esphyr Slobodkina's *Caps for Sale*. Keeping his wares on his head in a precise order of colors, a traveling peddler sits down beneath a tree. On waking, the peddler misses all but one of his caps and naïvely looks for them. When he discovers that the tree is full of monkeys and each monkey is wearing one of his caps, the peddler's anger grows in stages; each stage of anger is expressed with different gestures which are copied by the monkeys. The story is perfect for dramatization. Other folktales too, with simple action, appealing refrain, and repetition are suitable for dramatization by kindergartners or first graders, with easy assistance by the teacher.

Structure and Plot

All good children's stories have an orderly arrangement of content, a satisfying pattern, and a plot intriguing to children. Order is as basic to children's literature as to all art. Let us consider some well-tested and much-demanded stories for the merit of their plots.

---

[5] Thatcher Hurd, *The Quiet Evening* (New York: Greenwillow, 1978).

[6] From *Mother Goose—The Tenggren Tell-It-Again Book*, illus. Gustaf Tenggren (Boston: Little, Brown & Company, 1940).

In Marjory Clark's *Poppy Seed Cakes* the plot springs from the nature of the characters in the separate episodes in the book. Among the characters are a boy who would always rather do something on his own than follow the advice of those who know better; a charming and troublesome goat; and a generous, sympathetic, old country aunt. The boy is unable to resist bouncing on a featherbed, swinging on a garden gate, or wading barefoot in a small stream, all at wrong times, which makes for suspense in the story. But the ever-helpful auntie keeps the consequences of wrongdoing from becoming dire, so in the end a good time is had by all!

In the book *Blueberries for Sal* by Robert McCloskey, the story is built on a background of seasonal activities for people and bears. A very exciting and satisfying balance is created by parallel activities of a human mother followed by her child Sally *picking* blueberries for the winter on one side of the hill, while on the other side a bear mother followed by her bear child are *eating* blueberries to get fat for the winter. Each family group is in happy pursuit of free food from nature; each mother is concerned with the safety of her young. After a suspenseful but temporary mix-up of mothers, each child is delighted to have her own mother back.

Some books reveal structure and suspense in the titles. In Sorche Nic Leodhas's *Always Room for One More,* the reader holds her or his breath each time the door opens for a new arrival at the house. In Joan Lexau's *I Should Have Stayed in Bed,* a story on a slightly older level, the listener follows Sam's disasters of a morning anxiously, though not without a smile. This story has the added attraction of an interracial friendship. Some books may arouse curiosity about their contents by intriguing titles such as *No Fighting, No Biting* by Else Minarik or *A Hippopotamus Ate the Teacher* by Mike Thaler.

Language

Let us focus now on the language of children's literature. No matter what the theme, is not the essential vitality of a literary work conveyed through the artistic language? Literary language is no mere statement of physically accurate fact, no grammatical perfection alone, no artificiality that may pass for style. Literary language springs from an author's original thinking and genuine feeling; it is language in which the words are fresh and important, the meaning clear and interesting. Through the language readers are able to share in the author's special development of mood, action, ideas, and loves; they are able to partake of the author's senses and spirit and style. In *Angelo the Naughty One,* Helen Garrett builds up a scene of dramatic contrasts that young children can follow well.

> He dashed across the yard, through the gate and disappeared.
> The brothers and sisters ran to the gate too.
> But all they saw was a herd of dainty goats tripping downhill to the market.
> And two sleepy donkeys climbing uphill under eNORmous loads of cornstalks.
> Only their little white noses and big ears showed.
> Angelo was gone![7]

[7]From *Angelo the Naughty One* by Helen Garrett. Copyright 1944, © renewed 1972 by Helen Garrett and Leo Politi. Reprinted by permission of The Viking Press, Inc.

Some books on a very young level have emotion and promise as in these lines from *Play with Me* by Marie Hall Ets:

> The sun was up and there was dew on the grass
> And I went to the meadow to play.[8]

There is intense feeling from the start in Ezra Jack Keats's *Whistle for Willie.*

> Oh, how Peter wished he could whistle![9]

Certainly the richness of the English language is felt and made use of by all good writers, and many children's books will arouse curiosity about big words whose meaning will be remembered because of artful treatment. This is true of Duvoisin's *Veronica,* where the words *conspicuous, famous,* and *demolish* are dramatized as an integral part of an amusing story.

In *A Gaggle of Geese* by Eve Merriam, a serious book by a gifted writer, the author writes of the marvels and effectiveness of the current and past English language. It is a fascinating story of words designating *groups* of animals, fish, and birds: flocks and herds and schools and swarms. You say "flights of swallows" and "tribes of goats" just as correctly as you refer to a "husk of jackrabbits" and "a smack of jellyfish." Such a book would indeed expose children, who are eager language appreciators, to the unique flavor of English.

Meeting Children's Emotional Needs

There is a common saying or at least a common understanding that a good book can be your best friend. This also applies to children's literature and to children, particularly if you regard a friend as one who answers your needs. Such an idea requires elaboration, for children have many needs. It also requires discrimination, for books are innumerable, and we may become submerged in the sea of subjects and in the number of needs books may rightly answer.

Concern with family membership and members.   That works of literature can serve children's emotional and intellectual needs should be of great comfort to a kindergarten teacher who is always on call to help an individual child or even the whole class. One of the first interests, and sometimes concerns, of preschool children has to do with their own families. Present four-, five-, or six-year-olds with a grouping of any objects or show them some animals together, and it is likely that they will ask you or tell you which is the mother, the father, the sister, or brother. McCloskey's *Make Way for Ducklings* deals with finding a home, raising a family, and feeding and protecting the children by a careful mother and a daring father. In another animal book, Charlotte Steiner's *Ten in a Family,* the very *number* of

[8]From *Play with Me* by Marie Hall Ets. Copyright © 1955 by Marie Hall Ets. Reprinted by permission of The Viking Press, Inc.

[9]From *Whistle for Willie* by Ezra Jack Keats. Copyright © 1964 by Ezra Jack Keats. Reprinted by permission of The Viking Press, Inc., and The Bodley Head Ltd.

family members is fascinating and involves the reader completely. And the numbers change in this family of ten, adding and multiplying prolifically (as can happen with mice). "Three plus two equals five" is not a mathematical equation but a thrill when twins arrive.

Mother is, of course, most important to young children, and she appears in a large number of stories, as the reader may already have noted. In a Russian folktale, *My Mother Is the Most Beautiful Woman in the World,* by Becky Reyher, mother is the subject of a child's loving idealization; she is in fact a homely peasant woman, proving that "we do not love people because they are beautiful, but they seem beautiful to us because we love them."

A picture story, Norma Simon's *The Daddy Days,* is likely to bring on children's own discussion of what happens on daddy days in their homes. *Martin's Father,* by Margrit Eichler, shows a father in a nurturing relationship with a child, a good example of the changing role of men. Charlotte Zolotow's *William's Doll* deals with this phenomenon in a direct application to a little boy.

Relationships with grandparents also have great meaning, as shown in Helen Buckley's *Grandfather and I* and *Grandmother and I.* Johanna Hurwitz's *Super-Duper Teddy* humorously depicts modern family mores: children question and stubbornly resist their baby-sitting grandparents (saying "no" to everything), then respond enthusiastically to grandfather's storytelling, and a genuine relationship is established.

Family status and new arrivals.   The expectation or arrival of a new family member and the subsequent new family status for the child is of deep interest to young children and can be a cause for unspoken concern. The kindergarten teacher might then find in Nancy Langstaff's *A Tiny Baby for You* an answer to her quest for a helpful book on the subject. This slim and simple book, with photographs that have profound charm in their reality, is large in its total meaning yet not confusing with details. Nor does it belabor the subject as some books do. This book instead helps the child experience brotherhood or sisterhood. More recent books about new members in the family deal more frankly with the troubles as well as the possible benefits that can ensue with the coming of a new addition. In Joan Gill's *Hush Jon,* Jon sees nothing good in a baby sister, who only cries and eats, until she reacts to *him!* Similar in theme is *Nobody Asked Me If I Wanted a Baby Sister* by Martha Alexander.

Relationship with pets.   Not as special as a chosen adopted human member of a family, but of more universal interest to children, is the chosen pet living as a member of the family. The almost classic saga by Lynd Ward, *The Biggest Bear,* tells of a boy's acquisition of a small bear cub and the care and support the boy has to give this unusually demanding pet. The inevitable rapid growth of any pet from babyhood to adulthood is a dramatic process, and it is especially dramatic and near tragic in the case of *The Biggest Bear.* This is a wonderful story which shows the strength of devotion and responsibility a child can have for a pet. A pet animal can be a central character even in a story about family relationships, as in Evaline Ness's *Josefina February,* in which a Haitian girl gives up her pet burro to buy shoes for her grandfather.

Another story of devotion to a pet is *Mr. Turtle's Mystery* by Betty Miles. Nothing like a big bear in the woods, this pet is but a small birthday-present turtle which David keeps in a little tank in the room. David feels a most tender attachment for him, and when Mr. Turtle disappears, there is deep disappointment, which any child can feel over losing a pet. What a relief when Mr. Turtle at long last reappears.

The fact that pets and people living in the same family have different lives is told amusingly in Irma S. Black's *Night Cat.* Not only are the sleeping people unaware of the nocturnal adventures of their pet, but they mistakenly assume that the cat slept home all night.

Problem of being little.   Some writers treat the theme of smallness with understanding and humor while others may moralize and weaken the effect as well as the literary merit. In *The Very Little Girl,* Phyllis Krasilovsky presents the physical proportions of littleness and how it changes; the very little girl seems bigger when compared to the "very very very little baby brother."

A little older and longer book on the trials of being little is *Rosa-Too-Little* by Sue Felt. Five- and six-year-olds would be especially interested in Rosa's struggle and determination to be big enough to take her own books out of the library.

Special interest in growing.   It is very likely among fast-growing kindergartners that a special interest in growing itself will come up. *The Growing Story* by Ruth Krauss would stimulate further interest. The observations as well as the illustrations of the relative rate of growth among vegetables, animals, and children will cause amusement, reflection, and probably inspection of one's own growth. The book conveys to all children the fact that no matter how imperceptibly growth may proceed, they are all growing. In *Happy Birthday, Sam* by Pat Hutchins, a child discovers that the day of the birthday itself doesn't bring the expected growth, but grandpa's birthday present enables him to achieve a measure of independence, which is part of growth.

Difficulty of waiting.   Marjorie Flack's *Wait for William* is an appealing story about the youngest child in the family, who has trouble keeping up with bigger brothers and sisters. *Little Dog Dreaming,* by Edith Thatcher Hurd, deals with the unbearable waiting for the slow but eventual arrival of summer. Taro Yashima's *Umbrella* is a beautiful book about a little Japanese girl living in the United States who is waiting and longing for a rainy day so she can use her new blue umbrella and red boots. All strike responsive chords in any child.

Having disputes.   Having disagreements and arguments and seeking arbitration is an experience with which children working away at friendships are quite familiar. They may get considerable understanding of their own feelings by reading about someone else's problems, particularly when problem situations are presented with the humor of Will and Nicholas in *Finders Keepers.* In a very impressive and serious way the Beims in *Two Is a Team* show children that there are disagreements and quarrels among friends; this is a direct and lively story that has been popular with preschoolers and young school-age children for over thirty years.

Need for privacy.   Among the many books by Beatrice Schenk de Regniers poetically depicting the inner world of childhood, one, *A Little House of Your Own,* deals with children's need for privacy and the many ways in daily life that children try to find it. So does Ramey Bennett's *The Secret Hiding Place,* even though the protagonist is a hippopotamus. In *Six Secret Places,* by Monica De Bruyn, a book on a slightly older level, three children together finally obtain a hiding place.

Coping with fear.   Being frightened, admitting fear, and overcoming it is another part of the inner world of childhood which is treated with artistic insight by writers whose stories help lighten some burdens and confusions that come from fear. Margaret Wise Brown comes straight to the point as she begins her story of the *Little Frightened Tiger.*

> Once there was a little tiger
> who was absolutely scared to death.[10]

And she reveals how differently the little tiger feels when he finds out that all animals have fears. The cat in Phyllis Krasilovsky's *Scaredy Cat* has a similar experience.

Experiencing illness.   Sickness, operations, hospitalization, or medication are matters of daily knowledge to children, who sometimes discuss the subjects among themselves with brutal frankness. Recent children's books on the subject are often scientifically objective or photographically detailed, offering more than the child needs or cares to know; previously such books were often falsely comforting, attempting to evade unpleasantness. Evasions, whether offered by parents, teachers, or authors, are not helpful to young children. But an artistically entertaining and reasonably realistic story very well taken by kindergartners, and no doubt helpful, is *Madeline* by Ludwig Bemelmans. Waking in the night, summoning help, riding in an ambulance, staying in the hospital, getting flowers, receiving visitors and presents, and no less important, showing off her scars, are all part of exciting living for Madeline and, vicariously, for children listening to the story. Also dealing humorously and dramatically with accidents and hospitalization is one of H. A. Rey's stories about George, the insatiably curious monkey, *Curious George Goes to the Hospital.* These tales should not be confused with realistic chronicles of what to expect in the hospital, or at the doctor's, or when being fitted with a hearing aid.

---

[10]From *The Little Frightened Tiger* by Margaret Wise Brown, illus. Leonard Weisgard. Copyright © 1953 by Margaret Wise Brown.

The former is comedy that dissipates fear; the latter is knowledge that clears up confusion.

As is evident from all the books to which we have referred, children's literature reflects feelings and elicits responses to a variety of emotional needs. But there are some books which have a special focus on feelings as such. Books like Norma Simon's *How Do I Feel?* and Janice May Udry's *Let's Be Enemies* are charming, easygoing stories in pictures; others, like Terry Berger's *I Have Feelings* and Joan Fassler's *Don't Worry Dear,* are quite distinctly psychological and explanatory. It is up to the teacher to become acquainted with such books and to determine which book to use for what purpose, or to decide whether to use them at all after assessing the effect. Too much talk about feelings at too early an age can lead to precocity and loss of spontaneity. It is important to safeguard children against becoming verbal about feelings in place of growing deeper in the capacity to feel.

Depicting work. With increasingly sophisticated labor-saving devices in our society, work tends to be denigrated, but young children still find adult work interesting and certainly enjoy the good feelings of accomplishment that come with working away at tasks within their own powers. The worthiness of work needs to be presented as part of the values children can live by, since to be effective through one's own efforts is an important goal that is becoming hard to attain in a highly technological society. To satisfy this need, the teacher should not overlook such a useful old book as *Mike Mulligan and His Steam Shovel* by Virginia Lee Burton. Though old-fashioned in its pace and in the personification of a steam shovel, it still is loved by modern children, as is the companion volume by the same author, *Katy and the Big Snow.*

In a brief story in verse, Irma Simonton Black's *What Is Work?,* Tommy discovers what work is by noticing what goes on around him. The classic Swedish story by Elsa Beskow, *Pell's New Suit,* published in the United States in 1929 and issued in paperback in the 1970s, tells in charming folktale style of the relationship among people's needs, nature, various products, and different kinds of work. In K. Ushinsky's *How a Shirt Grew in the Field,* a Russian classic, a boy observes his whole family's elaborate work and the dramatic transformation of tiny flax seeds into flowering plants, tough fiber, thread, cloth, and finally into a shirt for him. In Marguerita Rudolph's *The Sneaky Machine,* a young schoolboy is involved in work using household machinery, despite other boys deriding it as "mommie's work."

Meeting Children's Need to Know

In looking even briefly at books with predominantly intellectual emphasis, we see again such an abundance of material that the books discussed here can represent only a fraction of the good ones.

Books on transportation. Everybody knows how fascinating transportation is to preschool children and how they enjoy picture books and straight accounts of boats and buses, trains and planes; how they get carried away by travels on land and sea, in air and outer space, attuned to special sounds and super-speeds as only late twentieth-century children can be. There are many informative and engaging books for young children about every means of modern transportation, as the following few titles suggest: *Behind the Wheel* by Edward Koren, *Cars and Trucks and Things That Go* by Richard Scarry, *I Like Trains* by Catherine Wooley, *The Earth Is a Space Ship* by Julius Schwartz, and, of course, *Journey to the Moon* by Erich Fuchs. No doubt, new children's books on space and interplanetary travel will continue to appear.

In the midst of the expert, scientific, travel books, there is a gentle, personal, and very touching one, Barbara Brenner's *Barto Takes the Subway,* about a child's first ride in a city subway. With literary description and moving photographs, the book tells of the intricacies, surprises, special motions and sounds, and interesting information gathered by this child on his ride in the New York City subway.

Science and nature books. Science books often have literary style, artistic design, illustrations, and creative treatment of subject. They serve primarily as an important basis for advancing learning of a subject. For example, *Magnets and How to Use Them,* by Pine and Levine, gives a basic lesson in magnetism.

Various animals and nature in general are subjects of many exciting, informative books for young children. *The Secret World,* by Mary De Ball Kwitz, reveals with verbal and pictorial accuracy the underground lives of various burrowing creatures. Bernice Kohn's *The Beachcomber's Book* is almost an encyclopedia of what can be found, collected, used, and above all enjoyed from the sea. Ruth B. Gross's *What Is That Alligator Saying?* is a first book on how animals communicate and what they communicate about.

A prolific writer of science books for kindergarten and early school-age children is Millicent Selsam. Her numerous books on plants and animals, among them, *Play with Seeds, All about Eggs and How They Change into Animals,* and *All Kinds of Babies,* answer with clarity and scholarship the specific questions children ask on these subjects.

Outstanding in their literary quality as well as in their inspiring knowledge are the many nature books by Alvin Tresselt, usually superbly illustrated by Roger Duvoisin. One such is *Hide and Seek Fog,* in which this writer's inspired prose conveys his dedication to nature in a way that is contagious. Tresselt describes the seasons and gives the rhythms and the reasons behind all the action and drama, the color and form in nature, whether he writes about a tiny snowflake, a glowing sunrise, or the unerring migration of birds. Also informative, poetic, and intriguing is *What Do You See?* by Janina Domanska. *The Web in the Grass,* by Berniece Freshet, is distinctive in text as well as in pictures of nature. Outstanding books for any age are Tana Hoban's *Look Again,* in which illuminating photographs and format reveal shapes, shadows, and changes in the world around us, and *Take Another Look,* which further enlarges one's vision and perspective. In the beautiful *Where Does the Butterfly Go When It Rains?,* May Garelick makes interesting observations on what some animals do when it rains and asks good questions to ponder and speculate upon. In *What's Inside?* the same author tells how baby geese grow in the egg, hatch, and are cared for by their parents.

Living as we do in an era of rapid scientific advances, it is inevitable that many new science books for young children will be published every year. We recommend that teachers consult the librarian periodically for new titles. In addition, look at new issues of children's monthly magazines such as *Cricket, Humpty Dumpty's Magazine, Child Life,* or *Ranger Rick's Nature Magazine* for brief, well-written science stories.

Humor

Although humor is an element in human life everywhere and greatly regarded in literature, it nevertheless remains something elusive; here you have it and now you don't. Humor differs with countries and people, and in books it changes with the reader's moods. The criteria for humor vary with the reader's age, too. Because humor is sought and enjoyed by children as much as by adults, it is universally regarded as an important element of good children's books along with aesthetic and literary qualities.

Humor in children's books is lightness and amusement with various degrees of laughter. It is the element of surprise and delight in many of the books we have already discussed for other reasons but will refer to again at this time.

Munari's *Jimmy Has Lost His Cap* seems thoroughly amusing to children because Jimmy's cap turns out to be on his own head, but neither Jimmy nor the reader knows it until the end.

There is great humor in *Caps for Sale,* perhaps because monkeys with their human weaknesses never fail to amuse human children, who assume they are at least a little superior. This must be the reason in part why Curious George has reappeared in pursuit of work and happiness in a half dozen books since 1941, all reissued in paperback. Children love Curious George and laugh at his antics because they identify with his mischief and yet can appreciate that his predicaments, though a little worrisome at times, are funny.

Roger Duvoisin's *Veronica* is unmistakably funny because the hippo heroine is also in a predicament by being preposterously out of place among people and cars. Somehow preschool children who are still learning about where things belong find obvious misplacements hilariously funny. It is very possible that young children grow able to laugh at obvious incongruity only as their own competency develops and they are no longer threatened by possible failure.

Good illustrations invariably need to carry the humor as it appears in the text in children's books; that is why author-illustrators such as Gag, Duvoisin, and Rey reach artistic success in conveying humor. One of Duvoisin's most popular books is the very funny *Petunia,* who is really a big silly goose. Her head swells with false pride to such proportions that it becomes too big to fit in the page of the book! When children laugh at Petunia, they seem to enjoy their own superiority over such obvious foolishness. "*I* know better than that" they seem to imply.

Preposterously funny deeds in children's books are not peculiar to animals. In Phyllis Krasilovsky's *The Man Who Didn't Wash His Dishes,* it is a grown-up whose ideas and actions are way out of kilter when he uses up all the dishes and eats out of flower pots, ash trays, and such. The reader need not worry that children will take over the man's notion of housekeeping, for the author brings an effective and good resolution to the man's problem. The preposterous humor of bad housekeeping appears also in an old Swedish folktale, *Turnabout,* as told by William Weisner, in which a farmer and his wife exchange jobs, with triumph for the wife and comical disaster for the man.

Another humorous book with a wrongdoing adult who gets into predicaments is Edith Thatcher Hurd's *Hurry Hurry,* in which a conscientious but misguided Miss Mugs hurries herself silly and falls into a manhole. Not heeding a warning that something worse might happen, she continues to hurry and gets stuck in spilled glue. Like the man with the dirty dishes, Miss Mugs gets reformed in the end (only she does it with the help of a child). An unusual, humorous old story, which first appeared in 1922 and shouldn't be overlooked, is *The Wedding Procession of the Rag Doll and the Broom Handle and Who Was in It,* by the famous American poet Carl Sandburg. It has many hilarious characters, such as the Musical Soup Eaters who "whistled and chuzzled and snozzled their soup."

Not infrequently, humorous books do have a moral, or they may at least succeed in having the reader question certain undesirable behavior. However, there is never any deliberate moralizing in a successful humorous book. Gene Zion's *Harry, the Dirty Dog,* is a very funny book in more than name only. Harry's actions in evading washing and finding ways of getting dirty are completely understandable to young children. But dirty Harry appreciates the benefits of becoming a clean dog, although there is a bit of a suggestion that he may not stay that way very long.

As anyone familiar with children knows, they find sure cause for laughter in physical mishaps and in slapstick situations, as do many grown-ups. Falling down, getting squashed, or suddenly getting splashed can be hilarious. Unrestrained physical combat and even violence seem especially funny in verse form, as shown in Mother Goose and in other folk rhymes.

Older kindergarten children can understand paradox in situations that have known and familiar elements. Thus, *Nobody Listens to Andrew* by Elizabeth Guilfoile or Benjamin Elkin's *Six Foolish Fishermen* leave the children chuckling at the foolishness of normally all-knowing adults.

Once in a while you may come across a book that is so unquestionably funny that you can't wait to share it! Such a book is *'Could Be Worse.*[11] The story of Grandpa, whose habitual response to grandchildren's daily troubles is "Could be worse," grows in absurdity. Then Grandpa himself tells the children *his* preposterous nightmare, and they reply—aptly—with his own words: "Could be worse." A just-right punch line!

[11] James Stevenson, *'Could Be Worse* (New York: Greenwillow Books, 1977).

In many books words alone strike a humorous note, as in Ellen Raskin's *Who, Said Sue, Said Whoo?* The teacher can save such special books to savor humor together with the children and to let the experience lighten the mood and brighten their perception of the fascinating English language.

POETRY

Poetry is also prominent in great literature for children. There are ancient lines of poetry in lullabies for infants, in action rhymes for babies, in the timeless verses of old Mother Goose, and in the linguistic frolics of modern humorists. There is musical, imaginative poetry, both old and new, uniquely revealing glimpses of childhood by authors of the past and present, and sensory descriptive poems in the contemporary "here and now" vein.

As with stories, poems must also be suitable for the children who are to hear them. There are several criteria that affect the choice of poems for the young.

Briefness of Form

As a literary form poetry is particularly appealing to young children, provided the subject matter is within their range of comprehension. Many poems are short and direct, so that even a four-line poem can be perfectly complete and attuned to the young child's experience. This is evident in "Snow," by Alice Wilkins, which tells what befell on a winter night.

> The snow fell softly all the night.
> It made a blanket soft and white.
> It covered houses, flowers and ground,
> But did not make a single sound.[12]

And here are four lines by an anonymous poet describing *all* the seasons of the year.

> Spring is showery, flowery, bowery.
> Summer: hoppy, croppy, poppy.
> Autumn: wheezy, sneezy, freezy.
> Winter: slippy, drippy, nippy.

Any teacher can gather a collection of short poems for reading and rereading and keep them handy by typing each favorite on a $3'' \times 5''$ card. Such cards can then be classified and kept in an attractive card file always ready for that unexpected extra minute when a poem is just the thing. Short poems heard again and again encourage memorizing and whet the appetite for more and longer selections.

[12] "Snow" by Alice Wilkins.

Poetic Imagery

The language of poetry has vivid imagery to which children, being imaginative themselves, respond strongly. The teacher must be sure, however, that the imagery in the poems that are read is comprehensible to preschool children. Word pictures must go back to something known or experienced in children's lives so that their imaginations can make the necessary leaps from there. When Alice Wilkins, in the poem "Snow" refers to snow as "a blanket, soft and white," children can understand that, since blankets actually have meaning to them in sensory terms. And in this poem about storms by Dorothy Aldis in *Hello Day,*

> On stormy days
> When the wind is high
> Tall trees are brooms
> Sweeping the sky.[13]

the children can follow the fresh imagery of trees as sweeping brooms because they know well how brooms function and they are familiar with trees, which in their eyes seem to touch the sky. The easiest images for young children to conjure are images that have roots in the physical experiences known with one's eyes, nose, ears, hands, or feet. An unforgettable, amusing image is ". . . a feather is a letter from a bird," which appears in *Something Special* by de Regniers. And some children have even had the kind of experience that makes Carl Sandburg's "Fog," one of his *Chicago Poems,* clearly visible in their mind's eye.

> The fog comes
> On little cat feet.
> It sits looking
> Over harbor and city
> On silent haunches
> And then moves on.[14]

**Expression of Children's Feelings
and Fantasies**

There are many poets who express feelings, fantasies, and reflections which children recognize as their own but which they usually cannot articulate. In her collection *I Would Like To Be a Pony and Other Wishes,* Dorothy Baruch gives reasons for wanting to be something, and whether fanciful or humorous, the reasons are profoundly childlike; the child's reason for "I'd Like to Be a Whale" is to swallow his mother so he could keep her home that night.

---

[13] From *All Together* by Dorothy Aldis. Copyright 1925, 1926, 1927, 1928, 1934, 1939, © 1952 by Dorothy Aldis, renewed. Reprinted by permission of G. P. Putnam's Sons.

[14] From *Chicago Poems* by Carl Sandburg. Copyright 1916 by Holt, Rinehart and Winston; copyright 1944 by Carl Sandburg. Reprinted by permission of Harcourt Brace Jovanovich, Inc.

A. A. Milne, who is read as much now as when his poems first appeared in the twenties, tells of the unique puzzling position of being halfway down the stairs, which isn't at the bottom, and half way up, which isn't up. "It isn't really anywhere!" he says in the poem "Half Way Down" in *When We Were Very Young*. And he tells of the tiresomeness of answering adults' silly questions in the poem "Politeness" in the same book. Milne describes the busyness of being a muffin man, a postman, a bear, and then an elephant with one dizzying "round about" motion after another, in the poem "Busy," in *Now We Are Six*. And he conveys the inordinate pride in achieving six-year-oldness in the poem "The End" in the same collection. Reaching six, the child feels "clever as clever" and decides to remain six "forever and ever." Most of Milne's poems in *When We Were Very Young* and *Now We Are Six* express a child's way of thinking, but some of them can be appreciated more by adults than by children and one must be selective.

Strength and Power of Rhythm

Perhaps the most immediate appeal of poetry to all young children is the physical appeal of rhythm. Children respond to rhythm and balance naturally with a movement of body, a clap, a step, a shout, or a song. Just as they enjoy the balance of a seesaw and the bounce on a board, so they wait for the repeat of any refrain. Perhaps the strong rhythmic quality of the Mother Goose rhymes is one reason for the survival of these verses in spite of the fact that the content of many is strange to modern children. "Jack be nimble, Jack be quick/Jack jump over the candlestick!" has powerful stimulus to keep time and to execute a jump. The same holds for "One for the money/two for the show/three to get ready/and four to go!" Children will say it, breathe it, and move to it without any thought of the meaning of each phrase. The pattern of numbers and of counting occurs often in Mother Goose and other folk rhymes and is quite prevalent in children's poetry. A particularly beautiful children's story poem with a strong rhythm and counting pattern is the familiar *Over in the Meadow* by John Langstaff.

> Over in the meadow,
> In the sand, in the sun,
> Lived an old mother turtle
> And her little turtle one.[15]

Each animal has a different and appropriate function and an increasing number of young, all living "over in the meadow." It has a delightful lilt and is highly conducive to chanting out loud. Also appealing is the rhythmic quality of the descriptive action words in Evelyn Beyer's poem "Jump or Jiggle" describing the styles of locomotion of different animals which jump, hump, wiggle, and jiggle, ending with "lions stalk, but I—walk."

[15] From *Over in the Meadow* by John Langstaff, illus. Feodor Rojankovsky (New York: Harcourt Brace Jovanovich, Inc., 1957). Reprinted by permission of Harcourt Brace Jovanovich, Inc. and World's Work Ltd.

Liveliness of Humor

There are innumerable humorous verses in collections of folk rhymes, in Mother Goose, and in the verses of Edward Lear, who is a specialist in humorous poetry. There are ripples and trickles of humor in much of children's poetry in general because rhyme and humor seem to go especially well together whatever the subject. Of the many amusing alphabet verses, Edward Lear's old one in *The Complete Nonsense Book* is still very funny. Although limericks are generally too subtle for preschoolers, the older kindergartners do appreciate the ridiculous situation in Lear's limerick in the same volume.

> There was an Old Man with a beard
> Who said, "It is just as I feared! —
> Two Owls and a Hen,
> Four Larks and a Wren
> Have all built their nests in my beard.[16]

Laura Richards's collection *Tirra Lirra* has many poems with humorous ideas. In "Talents Differ," a robin boasts of "doing the thing that you cannot do," and a child finally answers in kind. "The Difference" tells what happens when one nose is not enough and the contrary, when one nose is plenty. Many of the poems are amusing plays on words and tongue twisters, such as:

> Once there was an elephant,
> Who tried to use the telephant —
> No! No! I mean the elephone
> Who tried to use the telephone.[17]

Perhaps it is best, in choosing poetry for young children, to think in terms of the way in which children tend to perceive the world, from their own egocentric, sensory view. A poem can be about one's body.

Reflection

> In the mirror I can see
> Lots of things but mostly me.[18]

And it can be about one's body in action.

---

[16]From *The Complete Nonsense Book* by Edward Lear. Reprinted by permission of Dodd, Mead & Co., and Faber & Faber Ltd.

[17]From *Tirra Lirra: Rhymes of the Old and New* by Laura E. Richards, illus. Marguerite Davis. Reprinted by permission of Little, Brown and Company. Copyright 1932 by Laura E. Richards; copyright © renewed 1960 by Hamilton Richards.

[18]From *Wide Awake and Other Poems* by Myra Cohn Livingston, illus. Jacqueline Chwast. Copyright © 1959 by Myra Cohn Livingston. Reprinted by permission of Harcourt Brace Jovanovich, Inc.

Drinking Fountain

When I climb up
To get a drink,
It doesn't work
The way you think.

I turn it up.
The water goes
And hits me right
Upon the nose.

I turn it down
To make it small
And don't get any drink at all.[19]

Animals and insects are always good topics for poems for children.

The Wriggily Worm

I saw a worm
I saw it squirm

I saw it wiggle
I saw it wriggle

Until it found
A hole in the ground.[20]

And certainly there's room for comments and speculations, as in A. A. Milne's quizzical "In the Fashion," with a child's reaction to animals—"They've all got tails but me," or in this poem by Aileen Fisher:

When It Snows

When it snows and blows
do you ever wonder
about bugs and things
that get hidden under?

Perhaps they can dig
and tunnel around
as well in the snow
as they can in the ground.

[19]From *Around and About* by Marchette Chute. Copyright © 1957 by E. P. Dutton & Co., Inc., and reprinted with permission.

[20]"The Wriggily Worm" by Ilo Orleans, from *The Littlest Ones*, by Pelagie Doane. Copyright © 1956 by Pelagie Doane, published by Henry Z. Walck, Inc., a division of David McKay Co., Inc. Reprinted by permission of the publisher.

You'd think they would freeze,
but they must be tough . . .
because in the spring
they seem spry enough. . . .[21]

And there's always room for friendship, as in this poem by Nikki Giovanni, "two friends," from her *Spin a Soft Black Song:*

lydia and shirley have
two pierced ears and
two bare ones
five pigtails
two pair of sneakers
two berets
two smiles
one necklace
one bracelet
lots of stripes and
one good friendship.[22]

This is a poem that can be read slowly and deliberately and lead to dramatic impact in the last simple line.

PROVIDING LITERATURE FOR YOUNG CHILDREN

Variety

Keeping a variety of books and stories is important not only for the development of children's and teachers' tastes but to meet the various needs and the changing interests of the children. There must be some picture books on the shelves for the children to reach and hold and look through by themselves in a leisurely way, books which the teacher periodically inspects, replaces, and changes. There must be well-illustrated content books both on the open shelves for children and on the teacher's private shelves, books used for specific needs and to answer questions pertaining to environment, community, seasons, family, or any subject of current concern to the class. Although preschool children's stories should not be too long because the children's attention span and sitting endurance are short, the teacher must be prepared for the children's developing readiness for longer stories. Such a longer story may be *The Five Chinese Brothers* by Claire Buchet Bishop, in which the plot develops anticipation to such an extent that the children want to listen and find out how it will be resolved.

[21] "When It Snows" by Aileen Fisher, from *Runny Days, Sunny Days* (New York: Abelard-Schuman, 1958). Copyright © 1958 by Aileen Fisher. Reprinted by permission of the author.
[22] From *Spin a Soft Black Song* by Nikki Giovanni. Copyright © 1971 by Nikki Giovanni. Reprinted by permission of Farrar, Straus & Giroux, Inc.

As they acquire more literary experience, the children can develop the adventures of a hero in a still longer story with fuller character development and complexity of relationships and events. A good example of a longer book with chapters is Margery Clark's *The Poppy Seed Cakes,* which has chapters with separate episodes about a boy who would rather do something on his own than follow the advice of his elders. Children show sustained interest in the book; they remember the previous accounts of mischief and look forward to new ones. A more recent book with separate story chapters and the same character throughout is Johanna Hurwitz's *Busybody Nora,* a girl "going on six," who is full of initiative and enviable daring. She thinks up ways of getting to know all of the two hundred residents (some with dogs) in her apartment building.

To insure variety in the kindergarten library, some anthologies of stories and poems are indispensable. *Believe and Make-Believe,* for example, edited by Lucy Sprague Mitchell and Irma S. Black, has a great variety of subjects and styles. Some stories answer urgent questions about the physical world; some are humorous treatments of familiar situations. One poem, "Rain" by Betty Miles, is an elemental expression of communion and union with rain, something that young children sense intensely. Child Study Association's *Read Me Another Story* and *Read Me More Stories* are old collections that still stand up. An especially useful anthology is the large, colorful, and relatively inexpensive book, *The Round the Year Story Book* by Kathryn Jackson, containing ninety-two short tales and verses on a variety of subjects. Variety of another kind can be found in Virginia A. Tashjian's *Juba This and Juba That,* which contains riddles, rhyming games, and stories for telling that invite improvisation by teacher and children.

Among the many poetry collections are May Hill Arbuthnot's *Time for Poetry,* William Cole's *I Went to the Animal Fair, Poems to Read to the Very Young* selected by Josette Frank, and *Poetry and Verse for Urban Children,* edited by Donald J. Bissett.

Sources

Where should the teacher go to look for, borrow, buy, or beg books to start a collection or keep it fresh?

To get a general idea of what books are being published for younger children, teachers can write to publishers for the latest free descriptive catalogues. Better still, they can read reviews of children's books in newspapers, magazines, or professional periodicals. They can also obtain free or for a nominal fee specially selected and annotated lists of recommended books from various educational organizations (see end of chapter). Teachers must make as judicious use of their book budgets as they can and not overlook the new, durable, soft-cover editions of desirable but costly hard-cover books. They can also supplement the necessary supply with library borrowing. The pressure to change library books at stated intervals may even prove to be a special advantage. If library facilities are inadequate and teachers would like to have certain books that are important but unobtainable with limited funds, they could ask their librarians to borrow books from a larger collection or borrow books themselves from other teachers in school. They could also appeal to parents to raise money or perhaps collect a Christmas Gift Fund for the class to buy books with, providing the parents understand how much books are appreciated, used, and needed by the children.

One teacher felt so keenly about having a sufficient library in her class, was so concerned about cultivating children's love of books, that she evolved a unique, practical project: on a child's birthday, celebrated in school very simply and without gifts, the class was presented with an inscribed copy of a book which the child and the parents selected and purchased from a list of known favorites. Besides giving everybody pleasure in acquiring a new book, this gave the birthday child and the parents an interesting experience in selecting a book and offering a birthday gift rather than receiving one, which a five- or a six-year-old can usually appreciate. Furthermore, there is special satisfaction in having one's name written in a book, to be acknowledged by present classmates and future acquaintances or siblings. To carry out such a project, the teacher has to consult with and advise parents, communicating her enthusiasm to them. She also has to be flexible in order to see when some child may rightly not want to give a book away or when some parent may not care to spend money to enrich the kindergarten. But when such a project is successful—in a class of eighteen to twenty-five children, and double that when there are two sessions, with most children having birthdays during the term—a sizable library of good books can be built up over the years.

Care of Books

Having selected and collected a fairly good kindergarten library, the teacher and children can by no means take for granted the continued good functioning of such a library. The teacher's respect for and interest in books are shown in the way in which she or he picks up books, handles them, puts them in place, and calls children's attention to their protection. To facilitate care there must be a definite place for books so they will not be left on the hot radiator, dropped into an obscure, dusty corner, or be lost in some miscellaneous pile. Although wide, slanting shelves for holding and displaying books are best, even clean, painted, proper-sized orange crates with a cleared table and chairs nearby can be quite serviceable if attended to by teacher and children together. The proper way of turning one page of a book at a time, and even the use of a handmade bookmark, can be learned and practiced by children with the teacher's repeated demonstration.

Picking up and putting books away in the right place is a habit that should be cultivated by a teacher and children, but the teacher must do it out of respect for books and not with the righteousness of a compulsive housekeeper. And out of respect for group needs the teacher should keep, with the children, a record of borrowed books and dates for returning. Appreciating the books and recognizing their usefulness and worth, the teacher needs to help children detect damages and share in some simple repairs with transparent or binding tape. Such physical care will not only protect and prolong the life of the books but will further children's appreciation of books. When one takes care of something—whether a pet, a plant, or a book—one comes to love it.

HOW AND WHEN TO READ TO CHILDREN

It is easy to depend so much on the charm of children's books that one may ignore the very important art of reading a story to children. Often the way in which a story is read, as well as the time during the program when it is read, can make the difference between a thoroughly satisfying experience and a routine one. Remember, too, that children may have very different backgrounds of experience with stories and therefore be at different levels of readiness to *listen*—to enjoy complexity or simplicity of plot, length, or brevity of story and of sentences—and readiness *to share the teacher* with other children. Be sure the *theme* of the story suits the age of the children; but also consider whether the *construction* of the story suits the children's prior experience with language and listening.

Knowing the Book and Your Listeners

Just knowing the title of a book is not enough preparation for reading it. *One Kitten Too Many* by Bianca Bradbury, for example, proves to have little to do with cats or children's interest in cats. Instead, it involves the children's feelings about family status and requires the sensitivity of the teacher's inner and outer ear when reading it. The publisher's blurb may also be inadequate for judging a book and even misleading as to age level. A teacher is the best judge of whether a book is too advanced or too simple for her or his class, so knowing the book beforehand is a good idea. You need to have read a book at least once before trying it on others out loud. It is important to be sensitive to the total implications of a story in such a way that your phrasing, pacing, and pauses as you read aloud point to the particular meaning, the narrative flow, and the rhythmic pattern of the words. The matter of what to emphasize is especially pertinent in books of humor, where with the wrong emphasis or no emphasis at all, the humor of a story can elude the children completely. Suspense, excitement, tenderness, anger, surprise, dismay—all these are carried in the reader's voice and heightened by the tempo with which the phrases, or single words sometimes, are offered to the children.

Dramatizing

How, the reader may ask, can the average teacher exercise such fine points of elocution and drama? The answer lies in being an honest amateur actor, using voice and gestures freely. Do not be afraid to chant, hiss, or bray when the dialogue calls for this, and let the children help you out! Children love their stories read with dramatic emphasis, but if you overdo it, some child may curb your exaggeration with a "You look silly when you make a face!"

On the other hand, a teacher's own dramatization may occasionally intrude on some children's individual impression of a particular literary work and inhibit their reaction. At such times the teacher may need to tone down his or her presentation.

Interrupting

What about interruptions in reading? Let us recognize that the teacher often intrudes on the story's flow of words with a brief aside, an explanation, or an illustration that makes the story clearer to follow. In doing so the teacher heightens the satisfaction in the story by using the interruption to enhance, not destroy, the unity of the tale. This often avoids confusions and interrupting questions on the part of the children. However, children will interrupt with comments or questions in any case, and there is no formula for what to do. As with the teacher's comments, enhancement of the story and pleasure in it are the first considerations. And interruptions from the children are not necessarily disrupting influences; interruptions may even help them relate to a story. Williamson contends that responses other than listening serve to cultivate an interest in books and that "young children should be given plenty of opportunities to relate their own lives and experiences to those of characters in literature."[23]

The teacher's decision to curb the children depends more on the situation than on anything else. Experienced children may not be frustrated at all about withholding comments and waiting for discussion until storytime is over. But more often a spontaneous reaction from a child needs to be uttered for its importance to the child, and one has to absorb it and save the story, too. Teachers themselves have different degrees of tolerance for interruptions. A teacher who realizes that she or he is reading to children for *their* sakes can better evaluate whether interruptions are truly important to the children (even if it means not finishing the story, itself an interesting lesson, although *not* a punishment), or whether a gentle reminder that it would be better to let the story proceed is in order.

Kindergartners will adjust to reasonable regulations about interruptions if the teacher has communicated a genuine interest in literature to them. They feel this by the sensitivity with which the teacher reads to them, by the way the teacher tries to embrace the group with her or his eyes, by the way the teacher looks at each child at some point when reading or showing pictures, and by her or his special comments pertinent to one child or to the group.

Story Time

Settling on a good time to read to children cannot be done by formula either. Some teachers may plan a definite time for reading every day and prepare the children for it; others may read sometimes by plan and sometimes when the opportunity presents itself. At no time should one begin a story for which there is not enough time to reach the end, unless of course it is to read a chapter in a continuing

---

[23] Paul M. Williamson, "Literature Goals and Activities for Young Children," *Young Children* (May 1981), 27.

tale. When there is a free minute or two, when waiting to go home, or during the dull quiet of resting time, a teacher can read a short poem or two. Lovely words reaching children's ears for a mere minute can be remembered for hours or days.

TEACHER'S KNOWLEDGE OF, AND FEELING FOR, BOOKS

As the kindergarten teacher becomes responsible for exposure of children to literature, acquires discrimination in selection from the available abundance, and becomes sensitive to children's responses to literary qualities and forms, he or she will be acquiring a personal knowledge of the field of children's literature. Such knowledge will give the teacher maturity in judgment of books and heightened taste.

A teacher who has acquired a feeling for books will know how to read or tell a story to children effectively. Appreciating the material, the teacher will give it intelligent interpretation, convey enthusiasm, and not be inhibited in the proper use of voice and illustrative gestures to give some color and feeling to the presentation.

STORYTELLING

Consideration of children's literature and the lasting influence of beautiful books is not complete without proper recognition of storytelling as a form of literary expression. After all, dramatic-social-artistic communication by means of storytelling goes far back in history. The oral traditions are universal. And storytelling has been a source of inspiration to authors in all regions of the world.

Moreover, storytelling either by children or teacher involves important elements of literature: a creative use of language, an attempt to use narrative skill, a desire to appeal to an audience, and the courage to begin and the willingness to end a story. Any effort put into such activity—whether the result is a success, a challenge, or just a struggle—is apt to increase awareness and appreciation of literature in general.

How can a kindergarten teacher, who is busy enough with customary activities, lacks experience, and may even feel inadequate to "perform," include storytelling in the curriculum? Without further delay or procrastination, the teacher could enroll in some seminar, workshop, or other brief course in storytelling. Such courses are offered at many schools, colleges, and other educational-recreational centers. Or a teacher could attend some storytelling sessions at libraries, parks, or even special festivals. Such pursuit and experience will give the teacher enough preparation to initiate or develop a program of his or her own. But even without professional preparation on the part of the teacher, there can be genuine storytelling activities in the kindergarten.

Storytelling can take place spontaneously when something happens which is of personal interest to the children. For instance, when a student-teacher (or any adult) arrives late because of a traffic tie-up, the adult could sit down, invite the children, and relate a "trouble" story. It could be about the suspected cause, the sound and fury of the motorists around, the worry about being late and the frequent glances at a watch by the teller, and then the actual cause of the problem. Such a story will elicit close sympathetic attention and a desire to contribute to it. Or a child may bring some items from a recent trip to show or to share with the class, and the teacher might encourage the child to relate the event. This may well inspire another child to recall (or invent) a trip she or he has taken. The ideas or subjects for such stories—whether humorous, serious, happy, or sad—come from the personal experience of the teller, and thus have special appeal and authenticity to both teller and audience.

On a more sophisticated and literary level, the teacher can prepare for a story-telling session by choosing, perhaps, a favorite short folktale and learning to relate the plot and portray the characters—all the while focusing on the theme and being mindful of suspense. It is not necessary to memorize the language, except for a particular rhythmic refrain or "chorus line" in which the audience may join. The advantage and challenge of telling a folktale is that one is free to *retell*—do slight alterations or improvisations to suit one's own style or language.

Children, too, may want to retell the same story—and find out how practice brings improvement. Folktales are of course not the only tales for telling. The teacher may have favorites from original literature or those enjoyed in her or his own childhood. But whatever the story, *telling* it, relating to an audience by language with vocal and body expression and without dependence on illustrations, adds an important dimension to the understanding of literature.

LITERATURE CITED IN THIS CHAPTER

ALDIS, DOROTHY (illus. Susan Ilson). *Hello Day.* New York: Putnam's, 1959.

ALEXANDER, MARTHA. *Nobody Asked Me If I Wanted A Baby Sister.* New York: Dial Press, 1971.

ARBUTHNOT, MAY HILL, and ROOT, SHELTON L., SR. (eds.). *Time for Poetry.* New York: Lothrop, Lee & Shepard Company, 1970.

BARUCH, DOROTHY (illus. Mary Chalmers). *I Would Like to Be a Pony and Other Wishes.* New York: Harper & Row, Pub., 1959.

BEIM, L., and BEIM, J. (illus. Ernest Crichlow). *Two Is a Team.* New York: Harcourt Brace Jovanovich, Inc., 1945.

BEMELMANS, LUDWIG. *Madeline.* New York: Viking (hardcover), 1958; Viking, Seafarer Books (paperback), 1969.

BENNETT, RAMEY. *The Secret Hiding Place.* Cleveland: World Publishing Co., 1960.

BERGER, TERRY. *I Have Feelings.* New York: Behavioral Press, 1971.

BESKOW, ELSA. *Pell's New Suit.* New York: Harper & Row, Pub., 1929.

BETTELHEIM, BRUNO. *The Uses of Enchantment: The Meaning and Importance of Fairy Tales.* New York: Knopf, 1976; Random House, Vintage Books, 1977 (paperback).

BEYER, EVELYN. "Jump or Jiggle," in *Very Young Verses,* ed. Barbara Peck Geisner and Antoinette Sutter, illus. Mildred Bronson. Boston: Houghton Mifflin Company, 1945.

BIRNBAUM, A. *Green Eyes*. Racine, Wisconsin: Western Publishing Company, Inc., Golden Press, 1973.

BISHOP, CLAIRE BUCHET. *The Five Chinese Brothers*. New York: Coward, McCann & Geohegan, 1938.

BISSETT, DONALD J. (ed.). *Poetry and Verse for Urban Children*. Book 1, *Poems and Verses to Begin On*; Book 2, *Poems and Verses about Animals*; Book 3, *Poems and Verses about the City*. San Francisco: Chandler Publishing Co., 1968.

BLACK, IRMA SIMONTON. "What Is Work?" in *Believe and Make Believe,* ed. Lucy Sprague Mitchell. New York: Dutton, 1956.

BLACK, IRMA SIMONTON (illus. Paul Galdone). *Night Cat*. New York: Holiday House, 1957.

BRADBURY, BIANCA (illus. Marie Nichols). *One Kitten Too Many*. Boston: Houghton Mifflin Company, 1952.

BRENNER, BARBARA (photographs Sy Katzoff). *Barto Takes the Subway*. New York: Knopf, 1961.

BROWN, MARGARET WISE (illus. Leonard Weisgard). *The Noisy Book*. New York: Harper & Row, Pub., 1939.

BROWN, MARGARET WISE (illus. Garth Williams). *Wait Till the Moon Is Full*. New York: Harper & Row, Pub., 1948.

BROWN, MARGARET WISE (illus. Leonard Weisgard). *The Quiet Noisy Book*. New York: Harper & Row, Pub., 1950.

BROWN, MARGARET WISE (illus. Leonard Weisgard). *The Little Frightened Tiger*. New York: Harper & Row, Pub., 1953.

BROWN, MARGARET WISE (illus. Remy Charlip). *The Dead Bird*. New York: William R. Scott, Inc., 1958.

BROWN, MARGARET WISE (illus. Evaline Ness). *The Steam Roller*. New York: Walker & Company, 1974.

BUCKLEY, HELEN (illus. Paul Galdone). *Grandfather and I*. New York: Lothrop, Lee & Shepard Company, 1959.

BUCKLEY, HELEN (illus. Paul Galdone). *Grandmother and I*. New York: Lothrop, Lee, & Shepard Company, 1971.

BURTON, VIRGINIA LEE. *Mike Mulligan and His Steam Shovel*. Boston: Houghton Mifflin Company, 1939.

BURTON, VIRGINIA LEE. *Katy and the Big Snow*. Boston: Houghton Mifflin Company, 1943.

CAINES, JEANETTE (illus. Ronald Himler). *Daddy*. New York: Harper & Row, Pub., 1977.

CARLE, ERIC. *The Honeybee and the Robber*. New York: Philomel Books, 1981. A moving-picture book.

CHILD STUDY ASSOCIATION (compiler). *Read Me Another Story* (1949) and *Read Me More Stories* (1951) (illus. Barbara Cooney). New York: Thomas Y. Crowell.

CHUTE, MARCHETTE. "Drinking Fountain," in *Rhymes about the City*. New York: Macmillan, 1946.

CLARK, ANN (photographs A. Cohn). *Along Sand Trails*. New York: Viking, 1969.

CLARK, MARGERY (illus. Maud and Miska Petersham). *The Poppy Seed Cakes*. Garden City, N.Y.: Doubleday, 1929.

COLE, WILLIAM (ed.). *I Went to the Animal Fair,* illus. Collett Rosselli. Cleveland: World Publishing Co., 1958.

DAVIS, ALICE (illus. Guy Brown Wiser). *Timothy Turtle*. New York: Harcourt Brace Jovanovich, Inc., 1940.

DE BRUYN, MONICA. *Six Secret Places.* New York: Western Publishing Company, Inc., Whitman Books, 1975.
DE REGNIERS, BEATRICE (illus. Maurice Sendak). *The Giant Story.* New York: Harper & Row, Pub., 1953.
DE REGNIERS, BEATRICE (illus. Irene Haas). *A Little House of Your Own.* New York: Harcourt Brace Jovanovich, Inc., 1955.
DE REGNIERS, BEATRICE (illus. Irene Haas). *Something Special.* New York: Harcourt Brace Jovanovich, Inc., 1958.
DOMANSKA, JANINA. *What Do You See?* New York: Macmillan, 1974.
DUVOISIN, ROGER. *Petunia.* New York: Knopf, 1950.
DUVOISIN, ROGER. *Veronica.* New York: Knopf, 1961.
EICHLER, MARGRIT. *Martin's Father.* Chapel Hill, N.C.: Lollipop Power, Inc., 1977.
ELKIN, BENJAMIN. *Six Foolish Fishermen.* Chicago: Children's Press, 1957.
ETS, MARIE HALL. *Play with Me.* New York: Viking, 1955.
FARJEON, ELEANOR. "Down! Down!" in *Eleanor Farjeon's Poems for Children.* Philadelphia: Lippincott, 1951.
FASSLER, JOAN. *Don't Worry Dear.* New York: Behavioral Publishers, 1971.
FELT, SUE. *Rosa-Too-Little.* Garden City, N.Y.: Doubleday, 1943.
FISHER, AILEEN. "When It Snows" in *Runny Days, Sunny Days.* New York: Abelard-Schuman, 1958.
FLACK, MARJORIE (illus. the author and Richard Halberg). *Wait for William,* Boston: Houghton Mifflin Company, 1935.
FLEISCHMAN, SID (illus. Jay Yang). *The Wooden Cat Man.* Boston: Little, Brown, 1972.
FRANK, JOSETTE (ed.). *Poems to Read to the Very Young,* illus. Dagmar Wilson. New York: Random House, 1961.
FRESHET, BERNIECE (illus. Roger Duvoisin). *The Web in the Grass.* New York: Scribner's, 1972.
FUCHS, ERICH. *Journey to the Moon.* New York: Delacorte Press, 1970.
GAG, WANDA. *Millions of Cats.* New York: Coward, McCann & Geohegan, 1928.
GAG, WANDA. *Nothing at All.* New York: Coward, McCann & Geohegan, 1941.
GALDONE, PAUL. *The Gingerbread Boy.* New York: The Seabury Press, 1975.
GARELICK, MAY (photographs Rena Jakobsen). *What's Inside?* New York: Scholastic Paperbacks, 1960.
GARELICK, MAY (illus. Leonard Weisgard). *Where Does the Butterfly Go When It Rains?* New York: William R. Scott, Inc., 1961.
GARRETT, HELEN. *Angelo the Naughty One.* New York: Viking, 1944.
GILL, JOAN (illus. Tracy Sugarman). *Hush Jon.* Garden City, N.Y.: Doubleday, 1968.
GIOVANNI, NIKKI. "two friends," in *Spin a Soft Black Song.* New York: Farrar, Straus, & Giroux, Inc., 1971.
GOFFSTEIN, M. B. *Brookie and Her Lamb.* New York: Farrar, Straus, & Giroux, 1981.
GROSS, RUTH BELOV (illus. John Hawkinson). *What Is That Alligator Saying?* New York: Hastings House, Publishers, Inc., 1972.
GUILFOILE, ELIZABETH. *Nobody Listens to Andrew.* Chicago: Follett Publishing Co., 1957; Scholastic Paperback, 1964.
HITTE, KATHRYN, and HAYES, W. D. (illus. Anne Rockwell). *Mexicali Soup.* New York: Parents' Magazine Press, 1970.
HOBAN, TANA. *Look Again.* New York: Macmillan, 1971.
HOBAN, TANA. *Take Another Look.* New York: Greenwillow, 1981.

HOBERMAN, MARY ANN (illus. Norman Hoberman). "The King of Umpalazo," in *Hello and Good-bye*. Boston: Little, Brown, 1959.

HURD, EDITH THATCHER (illus. Clement Hurd). *Hurry, Hurry*. New York: Harper & Row, Pub., 1960.

HURD, EDITH THATCHER. *Little Dog Dreaming*. New York: Harper & Row, Pub., 1967.

HURD, THATCHER. *The Quiet Evening*. New York: Greenwillow, 1978.

HURWITZ, JOHANNA (illus. Susan Jescke). *Busybody Nora*. New York: William Morrow, 1976.

HURWITZ, JOHANNA. *Super-Duper Teddy*. New York: Morrow, 1980.

HUTCHINS, PAT. *Happy Birthday, Sam*. New York: Greenwillow, 1978.

JACKSON, KATHRYN. *The Round the Year Story Book*. New York: Western Publishing Co., Inc., Golden Press, 1971.

KEATS, EZRA JACK. *Whistle for Willie*. New York: Viking, 1964.

KINDRED, WENDY. *Ida's Idea*. New York: McGraw-Hill, 1972.

KOHN, BERNICE (illus. A. Wheatley). *The Beachcomber's Book*. New York: Viking, 1970.

KOREN, EDWARD. *Behind the Wheel*. New York: Holt, Rinehart and Winston, 1972.

KRASILOVSKY, PHYLLIS (illus. Barbara Cooney). *The Man Who Didn't Wash His Dishes*. Garden City, N.Y.: Doubleday, 1950.

KRASILOVSKY, PHYLLIS (illus. Ninon). *The Very Little Girl*. Garden City, N.Y.: Doubleday, 1953.

KRASILOVSKY, PHYLLIS. *Scaredy Cat*. New York: Macmillan, 1959.

KRAUSS, RUTH (illus. Crockett Johnson). *The Carrot Seed*. New York: Harper & Row, Pub., 1945; Scholastic Paperback, 1966.

KRAUSS, RUTH (illus. Phyllis Rowand). *The Growing Story*. New York: Harper & Row, Pub., 1947.

KWITZ, MARY DE BALL. *The Secret World*. Chicago: Follett Publishing Co., 1971.

LANGSTAFF, JOHN (illus. Feodor Rojankovsky). *Over in the Meadow*. New York: Harcourt Brace Jovanovich, Inc., 1957; Scholastic Paperback, 1971.

LANGSTAFF, NANCY (photographs Susan Szasz). *A Tiny Baby for You*. New York: Harcourt Brace Jovanovich, Inc., 1955.

LEAF, MUNRO (illus. Robert Lawson). *The Story of Ferdinand*. New York: Viking, 1936.

LEAR, EDWARD. *The Complete Nonsense Book*. New York: Dodd, Mead, 1946.

LEODHAS, SORCHE NIC (illus. Nonny Hogrogian). *Always Room for One More*. New York: Holt, Rinehart and Winston, 1965.

LEXAU, JOAN (illus. Syd Hoff). *I Should Have Stayed in Bed*. New York: Harper & Row, 1965.

LEXAU, JOAN (illus. Don Bolognese). *Benjie on His Own*. New York: The Dial Press, 1970.

LEXAU, JOAN (illus. Robert Weaver). *Me Day*. New York: The Dial Press, 1972.

LIONNI, LEO. *Little Blue and Little Yellow*. New York: Ivan Obolensky, 1959.

LIVINGSTON, MYRA COHN. "Reflections," in *Wide Awake*, illus. Jacqueline Chwast. New York: Harcourt Brace Jovanovich, Inc., 1959.

LIVINGSTON, MYRA COHN. *Listen Children, Listen*. New York: Harcourt Brace Jovanovich, Inc., 1972.

McCLOSKEY, ROBERT. *Make Way for Ducklings*. New York: Viking, 1941.

McCLOSKEY, ROBERT. *Blueberries for Sal*. New York: Viking, 1948.

MEREDITH, JUDITH C. *And Now We Are A Family*. Boston: Beacon Press, 1970.

MERRIAM, EVE (illus. Paul Galdone). *A Gaggle of Geese*. New York: Knopf, 1960.
MILES, BETTY (illus. Jo Lowery). *A House for Everyone*. New York: Knopf, 1958.
MILES, BETTY (illus. Jacqueline Tomes). *Mr. Turtle's Mystery*. New York: Knopf, 1961.
MILNE, A. A. "In the Fashion" in *When We Were Very Young*. New York: Dutton, 1954.
MILNE, A. A. "Busy," in *Now We Are Six,* illus. E. H. Shepard. New York: Dutton, 1954.
MILNE, A. A. "The End," in *Now We Are Six*. (see above.)
MILNE, A. A. "Half Way Down," in *When We Were Very Young,* illus. E. H. Shepard. New York: Dutton, 1954.
MILNE, A. A. "Politeness," in *When We Were Very Young*. (See above.)
MINARIK, ELSE H. (illus. Maurice Sendak). *Little Bear*. New York: Harper & Row, Pub., 1978.
MINARIK, ELSE H. (illus. Maurice Sendak). *No Fighting, No Biting*. New York: Harper & Row, Pub., 1978.
MITCHELL, LUCY SPRAGUE (illus. H. W. Van Loon). *Here and Now Story Book*. New York: Dutton, 1921.
MITCHELL, LUCY SPRAGUE (illus. Rosalie Slocum). *Another Here and Now Story Book*. New York: Dutton, 1937.
MITCHELL, L. S., and BLACK, I. S. *Believe and Make-Believe*. New York: Dutton, 1948.
Mother Goose (illus. Gustaf Tenggren). Boston: Little, Brown, 1940.
MUNARI, BRUNO. *The Birthday Present*. Cleveland: World Publishing, 1959.
MUNARI, BRUNO. *Jimmy Has Lost His Cap*. Cleveland: World Publishing, 1959.
NESS, EVALINE. *Josefina February*. New York: Scribner's, 1963.
ORLEANS, ILO. "The Wriggly Worm," in *The Littlest Ones,* compiled by Pelagie Doane. New York: Henry Z. Walck, Inc., 1956.
PINE, TILLIE, and LEVINE, JOSEPH. *Magnets and How to Use Them*. New York: McGraw-Hill, 1958.
POTTER, BEATRIX. *The Tale of Peter Rabbit*. New York: Frederick Warne and Co., 1903; Scholastic Paperback, 1978.
RASKIN, ELLEN. *Who, Said Sue, Said Whoo?* New York: Atheneum, 1973.
REY, H. A. *Curious George*. Boston: Houghton Mifflin Company, 1941, Scholastic Paperback, 1963.
REY, H. A. *Curious George Goes to the Hospital*. Boston: Houghton Mifflin Company, 1965.
REYHER, BECKY (illus. Ruth Gannett). *My Mother Is the Most Beautiful Woman in the World*. New York: Lothrop, Lee, & Shepard Company, 1945.
RICHARDS, LAURA (illus. Marguerite Davis). *Tirra Lirra: Rhymes of the Old and New*. Boston: Little, Brown, 1955.
RUDOLPH, MARGUERITA (illus. John E. Johnson). *I Like a Whole One*. New York: McGraw-Hill, 1968.
RUDOLPH, MARGUERITA (illus. Linda Edwards). *The Sneaky Machine*. New York: McGraw-Hill, 1974.
SANDBURG, CARL. "Fog," in *Time for Poetry,* compiled by May Hill Arbuthnot and Shelton L. Root, Jr. New York: Lothrop, Lee, & Shepard Company, 1970.
SANDBURG, CARL. *The Wedding Procession of the Rag Doll and the Broom Handle and Who Was in It*. New York: Harcourt Brace Jovanovich, Inc., 1967.

SCARRY, RICHARD. *Cars and Trucks and Things That Go.* New York: Western Publishing Company, Inc., Golden Press, 1975.

SCHICK, ELEANOR. *The City in Winter.* New York: P. F. Collier, 1972.

SCHWARTZ, JULIUS (Illus. Marc Simont). *The Earth Is a Space Ship.* New York: McGraw-Hill, 1963.

SCOTT, ANN H. (illus. Symeon Shimin). *Sam.* New York: McGraw-Hill, 1967.

SELSAM, MILLICENT E. (illus. Helen Ludwig). *All about Eggs and How They Change into Animals.* Reading, Mass.: Addison-Wesley, 1952.

SELSAM, MILLICENT E. (illus. Helen Ludwig). *All Kinds of Babies.* New York: William R. Scott, 1953.

SELSAM, MILLICENT E. (illus. Helen Ludwig). *Play with Seeds.* New York: Morrow, 1957.

SENDAK, MAURICE. *The Nutshell Library.* New York: Harper & Row, Pub., 1962.

SENDAK, MAURICE. *Where the Wild Things Are.* New York: Harper & Row, Pub., 1963.

SEUSS, DR. *Horton Hatches an Egg.* New York: Vanguard Press, 1940.

SHULEVITZ, URI. *Rain, Rain Rivers.* New York: Farrar, Straus, & Giroux, 1969.

SIMON, NORMA (illus. Abner Graboff). *The Daddy Days.* New York: Abelard-Schuman, 1958.

SIMON, NORMA (illus. Joe Lasker). *How Do I Feel?* New York: Western Publishing Company, Inc., Whitman Books, 1970.

SLOBODKINA, ESPHYR. *Caps for Sale.* New York: William R. Scott, 1947: Scholastic Paperback, 1979.

STEINER, CHARLOTTE. *Ten in a Family.* New York: Knopf, 1960.

STEPTOE, JOHN. *Stevie.* New York: Harper & Row, Pub., 1969.

STEVENSON, JAMES. *Could Be Worse.* New York: Greenwillow Books, 1977.

TASHJIAN, VIRGINIA A. (illus. Victoria de Larrea). *Juba This and Juba That.* Boston: Little, Brown, 1969.

THALER, MIKE. *A Hippopotamus Ate the Teacher.* New York: Avon Books, 1981.

THOMAS, DAWN (illus. Harold James). *Mira, Mira.* Philadelphia: Lippincott, 1970.

TIPPETT, JAMES S. *I Live in a City.* New York: Harper & Row, Pub., 1927.

TRESSELT, ALVIN (illus. Roger Duvoisin). *Hide and Seek Fog.* New York: Lothrop, Lee, & Shepard Company, 1965.

UDRY, JANICE (illus. Maurice Sendak). *Let's Be Enemies.* Harper & Row, Pub., 1961.

USHINSKY, K. (trans. Marguerita Rudolph, illus. Yaroslava). *How a Shirt Grew in the Field.* New York: McGraw-Hill, 1967.

VIORST, JUDITH (illus. Erik Blegvad). *The Tenth Good Thing about Barney.* New York: Atheneum, 1971.

WARBURG, SANDOL S. (illus. Leonard Weisgard). *Growing Time.* Boston: Houghton Mifflin Company, Sandpiper Paperback, 1974.

WARD, LYND. *The Biggest Bear.* Boston: Houghton Mifflin Company, 1952.

WIESNER, WILLIAM. *Turnabout.* New York: Seaburg Press, 1972.

WILKINS, ALICE. "Snow," in *Time for Poetry,* compiled by Arbuthnot and Root. (See above.)

WILL and NICHOLAS. *Finders Keepers.* New York: Harcourt Brace Jovanovich, Inc., 1952.

WILLIAMS, GARTH. *The Rabbits' Wedding.* New York: Harper & Row, Pub., 1958.

WOOLEY, CATHERINE (illus. George Fonesca). *I Like Trains*. New York: Harper & Row, Pub., 1965.
YASHIMA, TARO. *Umbrella*. New York: Viking, 1958.
ZION, GENE (illus. Margaret B. Graham). *Harry, the Dirty Dog*. New York: Harper & Row, Pub., 1956.
ZION, GENE (illus. Margaret B. Graham). *No Roses for Harry*. New York: Harper & Row, Pub., 1958.
ZOLOTOW, CHARLOTTE (illus. Wm. Pene Du Bois). *William's Doll*. New York: Harper & Row, Pub., 1972.
ZOLOTOW, CHARLOTTE (illus. Wm. Pene Du Bois). *My Grandson Lew*. New York: Harper & Row, Pub., 1974.

ADDITIONAL TITLES ON SPECIAL ASPECTS OF EXPERIENCE

Family Life and Relationships

BANISH, ROSLYN. *I Want to Tell You about My Baby*. Berkeley, Calif.: Wingbow Press, 1982.
Story with photographs of expecting, witnessing and welcoming arrival of a baby.
CHILD STUDY ASSOCIATION, compiled by Richard Cuffari. *Families Are Like That*. New York: Thomas Y. Crowell, 1974.
Ten different, well-told stories of many kinds of families.
ETS, MARIE. *The Story of a Baby* (rev. ed.). New York: Viking, 1969.
Clear, detailed story with drawings of the baby's beginning and growth inside the mother.
GREENFIELD, ELOISE (illus. John Steptoe). *She Come Bringing Me That Little Baby Girl*. Philadelphia: Lippincott, 1974.
Portrayal of a black family; Kevin is waiting for a baby brother, but eventually accepts his sister.
HAZEN, BARBARA SHOOK (illus. Leigh Grant). *Why Couldn't I Be an Only Child Like You, Wigger?* New York: Atheneum, 1975.
A boy from a big family gives reasons for complaint, but Wigger, an only child, doesn't agree. A revealing story.
HOFFMAN, ROSENKRANS. *Anna Banana*. New York: Knopf, 1975.
An amusing story about a misunderstood preference for a boy baby on the part of each parent. The girl baby is splendid.
HOLLAND, VICKY. *We Are Having a Baby*. New York: Scribner's, 1972.
A child's point of view; honest and sensitive approach.
HURD, EDITH THATCHER (illus. Emily Arnold McCully). *I Dance in My Red Pajamas*. New York: Harper & Row, Pub., 1982.
A child's overnight visit to grandparents provides *shared* activities, learning, and love between generations.
LAPSLEY, SUSAN (illus. Michael Charlton). *I Am Adopted*. New York: Bradbury Press, 1975.
Simple, positive explanations of the social (not biological) means of gaining family membership.

PETERSON, JEANNE WHITEHOUSE (illus. Deborah Ray). *I Have a Sister. My Sister is Deaf.* New York: Harper & Row, Pub., 1977.
Very appealing and realistic.

SKORPEN, LIESEL M. (illus. Joan Sandin). *Michael.* New York: Harper & Row, Pub., 1975.
Distressed by father's scolding him for negligence, Michael finds comfort in companionship with a dog, but a special event brings about an understanding with father.

SONNEBORN, RUTH A. (illus. Emily A. McCully). *Friday Night Is Papa Night.* New York: Viking, 1970.
The special love of waiting for Father, who comes home from work only on Fridays.

STECHER, MIRIAM, and KENDELL, ALICE. *Daddy and Ben Together.* New York: Lothrop, Lee and Shepard, 1980.

VOGEL, ILSE-MARGRET. *Dodo Every Day.* New York: Harper & Row, Pub., 1977.
Love, loyalty, and corrected misunderstandings between a little girl and her grandmother.

Death and Illness

ALIKI. *The Two of Them.* New York: Greenwillow, 1979.
Growth of a little girl and her increasing abilities are parallel to the aging and disabilities of her grandfather. Memories after his death bring life to the story.

CHALMERS, MARY. *Come to the Doctor, Harry.* New York: Harper & Row, Pub., 1981.
Lighthearted story of taking a cat to the doctor.

FASSLER, JOAN. *One Little Girl.* New York: Human Sciences Press, 1969.

FASSLER, JOAN. *My Grandpa Died Today.* New York: Human Sciences Press, 1970.
Uses psychological realism to portray the struggle to understand and accept death and life.

HOWE, JAMES (photographs Mal Warshaw). *The Hospital Book.* New York: Crown Publishers, Inc., 1971.
Preparations, procedures, and important facts of human as well as medical activities in hospital.

LUNDGREN, MAX (illus. Fibben Hald, trans. Ann Pyk). *Matt's Grandfather.* New York: Putnam's, 1972.
Realistic and sympathetic approach to senility.

MILES, MISKA. *Annie and the Old One.* Boston: Little, Brown, 1971.
Text and pictures convey the spirit and the scene of Navajo Indian life through a grandmother.

TRESSELT, ALVIN (illus. Charles Robinson). *The Dead Tree.* New York: Parents' Magazine Press, 1972.
Poetic depiction of the full cycle of life in the forest.

WEBER, ALFONS, M.D. (illus. Jacqueline Blass). *Elizabeth Gets Well.* New York: Thomas Y. Crowell, 1970.
Honest, realistic in detail and experience, and a good story.

YOLEN, JANE (illus. Remy Charlip and Dimitra Raraslis). *The Seeing Stick.* New York: Thomas Y. Crowell, 1977.
An unhappy blind princess learns from a blind old man how to see and enjoy people and objects by touching!

Adjusting to New Experiences

BELPRE, PURA (illus. Symeon Shimin). *Santiago*. New York: Frederick Warne & Co., Inc., 1969.
With his teacher's help a boy overcomes adjustment difficulties after moving to New York City from Puerto Rico.

GRAY, GENEVIEVE (illus. Floyd Sowell). *A Kite for Benny*. New York: McGraw-Hill, 1972.
Realistic depiction of ghetto life, telling how Benny, a black boy, finally flies a kite over rooftops!

HANSON, JOAN. *I Won't Be Afraid*. Minneapolis, Minn.: Carolrhoda Books, Inc., 1975.
A little boy dreams of overcoming his fears when he'll be six years old.

HAYWOOD, CAROLYN. *Here Comes the Bus*. New York: Morrow, 1963.
Adventures on a school bus for a first grader. The importance of this form of transportation is well conveyed.

ISADORA, RACHEL. *The Potter's Kitchen*. New York: Greenwillow, 1977.
Moving from a country house to a city apartment brings sadness of parting, but also pleasures of new experiences to children.

JUSTUS, MAY. *A New Boy in School*. New York: Hastings House, 1973.
The frightening experience of moving from a small Southern town to a big city and coming to a strange school.

MACK, NANCY (illus. and photographs Heinz Kleutmeir). *I'm Not Going*. Milwaukee: Children's Press, Raintree Editions, 1976.
The reluctance of leaving, the strangeness of having everything packed up, the excitement of new places, and other realistic details of moving day are well depicted.

RASKIN, ELLEN. *Spectacles*. New York: Atheneum, 1968.
For Iris, everything seems distorted and difficult to see. And what a marvelous *change* when vision is corrected with spectacles!

SCOTT, ANN HERBERT. *On Mother's Lap*. New York: McGraw-Hill, 1973.
Story of family life, with pictures of people and household objects depicting Eskimo background.

TOBIAS, TOBI (illus. William Pene du Bois). *Moving Day*. New York: Knopf, 1976.
Realistic details and feelings about packing, leaving the familiar, keeping Teddy, arriving in the new home—different but acceptable.

WEBER, BERNARD. *Ira Sleeps Over*. Boston: Houghton Mifflin Company, 1972 and 1975.
Sleeping away from home for the first time is not a casual matter!

WEIR, LA VADA (illus. William Hoey). *Howdy!* Austin, Texas: Steck-Vaughn Company, 1972.
A small, cheerful black boy in cowboy hat greets strangers effectively!

Nonsexist Characters

BALDWIN, ANNE NORRIS (illus. Ann Grifalconi). *Sunflowers for Tina*. New York: Four Winds Press, 1970.
A determined, clever black heroine grows a garden in the middle of the city!

GOFFSTEIN, M. B. *Two Piano Tuners*. New York: Farrar, Straus & Giroux, 1970.
Debbie not only *wants* to do grandfather's work of piano tuning, but has the ability, and succeeds in spite of odds!

SHERMAN, IVAN. *I Am a Giant.* New York: Harcourt Brace Jovanovich, Inc., 1975.
  This convincing fantasy giant (reflecting the modern aspiration of "Women can be anything they want") is actually only a small girl.

Science, Environment, Transportation

CARTWRIGHT, SALLY (illus. Marilyn Hafner). *Water Is Wet.* New York: Coward-McCann & Geoghegan, 1973.
CARTWRIGHT, SALLY (illus. Marilyn Hafner). *Sunlight.* New York: Coward-McCann & Geoghegan, 1974.
CARTWRIGHT, SALLY (illus. Don Madden). *Sand.* New York: Coward, McCann & Geoghegan, 1975.
  How sand is formed and the many practical and playful uses of it.
CREWS, DONALD. *Freight Train.* New York: Greenwillow, 1979.
  A vigorous, clear portrayal of all the different sections and cars and the roads traveled. The works!
DE PAOLA, TOMIE. *Charlie Needs a Cloak.* Englewood Cliffs, N.J.: Prentice-Hall, 1973.
  Clear information of olden days' cloth production, presented attractively for today's children.
GIBBONS, GAIL. *Trucks.* New York: Thomas Y. Crowell, 1981.
  Pictures a variety of trucks.
HOGROGIAN, NONNY. *One Fine Day.* New York: Collier Macmillan International, Inc., paper, 1971.
  A fox loses and retrieves her tail while encountering the interlocking needs of nature. A Caldecott winner with beautiful pictures.
KAUFMANN, JOE. *What Makes It Go?* New York: Western Publishing Company, Inc., Golden Press, 1972.
  For those with technical interest and for the teacher—clear information and pictures on how some hundred common contraptions work: escalators, trains, toilets, lunar modules, musical instruments, etc.
LEAF, MUNRO. *Who Cares? I Do.* Philadelphia: Lippincott, 1971.
  Amusingly informational book about littering. The author is really *mad* at all the spoilers and wreckers.
SCHLEIN, MIRIAM (illus. Ray Cruz). *What's Wrong with Being a Skunk?* New York: Four Winds Press, 1974.
  Clear information on the unique life and special advantages of a generally maligned creature, and on its place in nature, with focus on being biased.
SHULEVITZ, URI. *Rain, Rain Rivers.* New York: Farrar, Straus & Giroux, 1969.

Poetry

ALDIS, DOROTHY. *All Together: A Child's Treasury of Verse* (5th ed.). New York: Putnam's, 1952.
BODECKER, N. M. *It's Raining Said John Twaining.* New York: Atheneum, 1973.
  Fourteen short Danish nursery rhymes, expertly translated and illustrated by a Dane; has humor, rhythm, and poetry not unlike the English Mother Goose.
BREWTON, SARA (compiler). *Birthday Candles Burning Bright.* New York: Macmillan, 1960.
CHUTE, MARCHETTE. *Rhymes about Ourselves.* New York: Macmillan, 1943.

CHUTE, MARCHETTE. *Around and About.* New York: Dutton, 1957.

DE REGNIERS, BEATRICE. *Poems Children Will Sit Still For.* New York: Citation Press, 1969.

FISHER, AILEEN. *Runny Days, Sunny Days.* New York: Abelard-Schuman, 1933.

FISHER, AILEEN. *Up the Windy Hill.* New York: Doubleday, 1946.

FISHER, AILEEN. *Cricket in a Thicket.* New York: Scribner's, 1963.

FISHER, AILEEN (illus. Janina Damanska). *I Like Weather.* New York: Crowell, 1963.

FISHER, AILEEN (illus. Symeon Shimin). *Listen Rabbit.* New York: Crowell, 1964.

HOBERMAN, MARY ANN. *All My Shoes Come in Twos.* Boston: Little, Brown, 1957.

ISSA and others (illus. T. Stubis). *Don't Tell the Sour Crow.* New York: Four Winds Press, 1969.
Thirty-four brief haiku Japanese poems, appropriate for young children, which may invite response in kind.

ITSE, ELIZABETH (ed.) (illus. Susan C. Smith). *Hey, Bug! And Other Poems about Little Things.* New York: McGraw-Hill, 1972.
Thirty poems by several authors, all dealing with tiny lively creatures, on a miniature scale; scientifically accurate drawings.

LIVINGSTON, MYRA COHN (illus. Eric Blegvad). *Happy Birthday.* New York: Harcourt Brace Jovanovich, Inc., 1964.

LIVINGSTON, MYRA COHN (illus. Eric Blegvad). *I'm Waiting.* New York: Harcourt Brace Jovanovich, Inc., 1966.

SANDBURG, CARL (illus. William A. Smith). *Wind Song.* New York: Harcourt Brace Jovanovich, Inc., 1960.

TIPPETT, JAMES. *I Go A-Traveling.* New York: Harper & Row, Pub., 1929.

WITHERS, CARL. *A Rocket in My Pocket.* New York: Scholastic Book Services, 1967.

WYNDHAM, ROBERT (illus. Ed Young). *Chinese Mother Goose Rhymes.* New York: World Publishing, 1968.
An extraordinary volume of traditional, timeless folk poems on a variety of subjects, wise and humorous notions; easy to take, yet pleasantly different.

Bilingual Books—Spanish-English

DANA, DORIS (illus. Antonio Frasconi). *The Elephant and His Secret.* New York: Atheneum, 1974.
A poetic fable of how the elephant came to be; impressive woodcuts.

DE BRUNHOFF, LAURENT. *Babar's Spanish Lessons.* New York: Random House, 1965.
A story of the famous elephant Babar teaching Spanish to children. Told in English, with relevant use of Spanish words and phrases.

FRASCONI, ANTONIO. *The Snow and the Sun (La Nieve y el Sol).* New York: Harcourt Brace Jovanovich, Inc., 1961.
A South American folk rhyme.

LIONNI, LEO. *Suimi.* New York: Random House, 1963.
Spanish translation of *Swimmi,* with identical format and illustrations.

POMERANZ, CHARLOTTE (illus. Byron Barton). *The Tamarindo Puppy and Other Poems.* New York: Greenwillow, 1980.

Lighthearted verses in *combined* English and Spanish that are spontaneous, effective, and fun!

PRIET, MARIANNA (illus. Lee Smith). *A Kite for Carlos.* New York: The John Day Company, 1966.
   Birthday of a Spanish-American boy; his grandfather makes him a kite.

REY, H. A. (trans. Pedro Villa Fernandez). *Jorge el Curioso.* Boston: Houghton Mifflin Company, 1961.
   Spanish translation of *Curious George,* with Spanish-English vocabulary.

SIMON, NORMA. *What Do I Say?* New York: Western Publishing Company, Inc., Whitman Books, 1969.
   Simple story of a Puerto Rican child.

Learning to Read

BAER, EDITH (illus. Karen Gundersheimer). *Words Are Like Faces.* New York: Pantheon, 1980.
   An exploration of words through pictures of different activities.

BERGEN, TERRY. *Ben's ABC Day.* New York: Lothrop, Lee & Shepard Company, 1982.

COHEN, MIRIAM (illus. Lillian Hoban). *When Will I Read?* New York: Greenwillow, 1977.

SCARRY, RICHARD. *Early Words.* New York: Random House, 1976.
   Numerous pictures and labels.

VANGHELI, SPIRODON (trans. Miriam Morton, illus. Trina Schart Hyman). *Meet Guguze.* Reading, Mass.: Addison-Wesley, 1977.
   An engaging story of a Russian village boy, still of preschool age, who is determined to enter school and persists in attempts to gain recognition for his need to do schoolwork at home. And he succeeds!

Collections of Stories and Folktales

BOEGEHOLD, BETTY (illus. Jim Arnosky). *Chipper's Choices.* New York: Coward, McCann & Geoghegan, 1981.
   A collection of humorous stories, rhymes and riddles.

DE REGNIERS, BEATRICE (illus. Margot Tomes). *Everyone Is Good For Something.* New York: Houghton Mifflin Company, Clarion Books, 1980.
   An ingenious adaptation of a Russian tale. After many failures, and believing that he is good for nothing, a boy finds out that he *is* good for something, and life changes for him.

GINSBURG, MIRRA (illus. Jose Aruego and Ariane Dewey). *The Strongest One of All.* New York: Greenwillow, 1977.
   A Caucasian tale on the interrelationships in nature. Beautifully told in the form of intriguing questions by a lamb who wants to know.

KEATS, EZRA. *John Henry.* New York: Pantheon, 1965.
   The black American railroad man of legendary fame. Inspiring artwork.

ROCKWELL, ANNE. *The Old Woman and Her Pig and 10 Other Stories.* New York: Thomas Y. Crowell, 1979.
   Folktales and fables.

STRICKLAND, DOROTHY S. (illus. Leo and Diane Dillan). *Listen Children: An Anthology of Black Literature.* New York: Bantam Books, Inc., 1982.
   A sampling of outstanding black playwrights, poets, and speakers.

Unclassifiable

BULLA, ROBERT CLYDE (illus. Anne Rockwell). *The Stubborn Old Woman.* New York: Thomas Y. Crowell, 1980.
An attractive book with good story of an old woman overcoming extreme stubbornness through the patience and wisdom of a little girl.

GINSBURG, MIRRA (illus. Byron Barton). *Good Morning, Chick.* New York: Greenwillow, 1980.
Bright and strong in spirit and pictures.

GOFFSTEIN, M. B. *Neighbors.* New York: Harper & Row, Pub., 1979.
Very simple things a woman does for a new neighbor—bringing lilacs and staying for breakfast; and with each season a different aspect of the relationship is developed.

HALZENTHALER, JEAN (illus. Nancy Tafuri). *My Hands Can.* New York: Dutton, 1978.
A practical, proud presentation of hand skills.

LIONNI, LEO. *Inch by Inch.* New York: Astor-Honor, Inc., 1980.
A stunning book picturing relative dimensions in nature, measured by a tireless inchworm.

RUKEYSER, MURIEL (illus. Symeon Shimin). *More Night.* New York: Harper & Row, Pub., 1981.
A dreamy, moody book to elicit reflection.

SKORPEN, LIESEL M. (illus. Margot Tomes). *Plenty for Three.* New York: Coward, McCann & Geoghegan, 1971.
Lonely, shy "she" at last joins adventurous two of "them" and attains friendship.

Sources of Information about Children's Books

The reader may well have his or her own sources—such as a children's book review column in a favorite magazine, a library journal or booklet, or particular publishers' catalogs. The following list is a small sample:

BOOKS FOR THE PRE-SCHOOL CHILD and GIFT BOOK LIST. Brooklyn Public Library, Grand Army Plaza, Brooklyn, N.Y. 11238.

GROWING UP WITH BOOKS (compiled by Eleanor B. Widdoes). 1976. R. R. Bowker Co., 1180 Ave. of the Americas, N.Y., N.Y. 10036.

RESOURCE CATALOG. Gryphon House, P. O. Box 275, Mt. Rainier, Md. 20712.

SCHOLASTIC BOOK SERVICES. Catalog of Paperbacks. Scholastic Book Services, 904 Sylvan Ave., Englewood Cliffs, N.J. 07632.

SELECTED CHILDREN'S BOOKLIST. Afro-American Book Center, 532 W. 145th St., N.Y., N.Y. 10031.

15 Reading and Writing

WHY READING HAS NOT BEEN TAUGHT IN KINDERGARTEN

The kindergarten has a long tradition of resisting instruction in reading and writing. From the 1870s on, kindergarten protagonists worried that kindergartens might be coopted into becoming preparation for the grades, instead of influencing the grades toward greater informality and flexibility. Sound reasons for resisting skill learning in kindergarten were spelled out by Kate Douglas Wiggin in a remarkably contemporary-sounding observation of young children published in 1892.

> The child of four or five years is still interested in objects, in the concrete. He wants to see and to hear, to examine and to work with his hands. How absurd then for us to make him fold his arms and keep his active fingers still; or strive to stupefy him with such an opiate as the alphabet. If we can possess

our souls and primers in patience for a while and feed his senses; if we will let him take in living facts and await the result; that result will be that when he has learned to perceive, compare, and construct, he will desire to learn words, for they tell him what others have seen, thought and done. This reading and writing, what is it, after all, but the signs for things and thought? Logically, we must first know things, then thoughts, then their records. The law of human progress is from physical activity to mental power, from Hercules to Shakespeare, and it is as true for each unit of humanity as it is for the race.[1]

The influence of Montessori on American kindergartens did not alter this view. Montessori, who recognized that three- to six-year-olds are particularly responsive to intellectual stimulation and learning, including skill learning, believed that such learning should involve the senses and be in response to a child's readiness. The thrust of her argument was that if a child failed to learn, it was clearly because the child was not ready and the teacher had begun too soon. Throughout most of this century, therefore, the kindergarten in any public school was likely to be a quiet oasis of unpressured, child-oriented activity that older children and adults later remembered with nostalgia.

Change for the kindergartens came during the 1960s, when concern for the school failure of children of poverty backgrounds threw the spotlight on young children and on beginning reading at the same time. It was reasoned by politicians, psychologists, and poverty parents alike that since children who learned to read easily generally recognized letters before they got to first grade, it was logical to teach the ABCs to those who did not and thereby protect them from failure. In the political climate of the time, this view was given extraordinary coverage by the press and strongly influenced public attitudes toward young children's learning. Kindergartens that did not emphasize skill learning were labeled "traditional." At the same time, there seemed to be a simplistic assumption that the bare-bones elements of letters, numbers, and shapes would support intellectual growth, an assumption that still prevails among many parents and among administrators unfamiliar with young children's capacity for learning.

Continued interest in the causes of school failure among poor children led to excessive emphasis on cognitive training as a solution. Commercial firms spent fortunes promoting materials that carried out the "new" emphasis. Television, in the form of *Sesame Street,* stepped in to advance the cause of letters, numbers, and shapes for young children, spreading the gospel far and wide in an entertaining manner that eventually captured all the children and their parents, not only the poor. There was frantic haste to solve the serious problem of school failure, which was and still is a reality. But few paused long enough to consider that success in reading depends on far more than recognizing letters of the alphabet; that children are more complexly put together than a single goal (knowing the ABCs) can satisfy; and that

---

[1] Kate Douglas Wiggin, *Children's Rights: A Book of Nursery Logic* (Boston and New York: Houghton Mifflin Company, 1892), pp. 53–54.

learning is an integrated experience that includes physical, social, and emotional responses as well as mental activity.

Kindergarten teachers, accustomed to responding to the whole child, fought this narrow approach to children's learning. They protested when workbooks were offered their physically active children. They protested when time was taken away from imaginative play, music, arts, trips, and discussions. They did not really know *why* they were against reading in the kindergarten. They responded intuitively, out of their everyday experience with young children, and they *felt* they were right. But they could not explain why skill learning in the kindergarten was premature, and they were overwhelmed by the onslaught from every side. As a result, it is a rare kindergarten and nursery school today that does not, at least in self-defense, give lip service to reading and writing at age five, or even at ages four and three. There are kindergartens today in which children sit in their seats and do paper-and-pencil tasks for much of their brief two-and-one-half hour stay.

What is ironic is that this change in the kindergarten was taking place during a period when the first grade was coming under the influence of the British Infant School movement toward more play materials and informality. Six-year-olds were urged to build with blocks, paint, and use clay in the same school districts where five-year-olds were being given workbooks! Even more ironic is the fact that the experienced British were tending to give up teaching reading at the age of five in favor of a more flexible approach to individualized readiness between five and seven. Yet Americans were in a rush to lower the starting age of formal skill learning from six to five; and the ubiquitous alphabet, in uppercase and lowercase letters, was conspicuous on the walls of preschools everywhere. No one remembered the lesson of the late 1940s when the school entry age was lowered to five-and-a-half in a number of places but had to be raised back to six because too many children suffered from strain and failure. Whether or not to teach reading in the kindergarten is thus as much an issue today as it was in 1870. Many kindergarten teachers with long years of experience are succumbing under pressure, but with regrets. "The children are being turned into robots," some say with feeling. Newer teachers, unaware of the historical development, are teaching skills to four- and five-year-olds in a pioneering spirit, convinced that they are in tune with the times. Meanwhile, Glen Nimnicht, Director of the International Center for Education and Human Development, warns us against too much "basic education."[2] He contends that such a formal emphasis on early reading and writing doesn't provide necessary emotional support or nurture self-concept, which are needed for problem solving and secure learning. Regardless of differing viewpoints, however, all kindergarten teachers must decide each year whether the children are ready for first grade. Yet few kindergarten teachers, principals, or school superintendents have examined the theoretical findings on reading and readiness for reading in order better to understand what affects success in academic learning. This is what we propose to do in this chapter.

[2]Glen Nimnicht, "Back to the Basics: More Loving, Tender Care for Young Children," *Young Children* (September 1981), 4.

WHAT IS READING?

This question is not as simple as it sounds. People at many levels of expertise cannot quite agree on an answer. Gibson and Levin, who spent years studying the *process* of reading (not methods of teaching), define reading as *"extracting information from text."*[3] They mean more than the printed page. "Text" includes combinations of text and pictures, diagrams, graphs, illustrated instructions, and so on. In other words, reading is getting a message from many graphic representations of meaning. While this answer seems reasonable to some, there are experts who describe reading as the decoding process itself, the sounding out of letters and the forming of words from letters.[4] In our view, this difference is really one between ends and means and ought not to be a matter of controversy. But strong commitment to one interpretation without including the other creates sharp divergence on such questions as when to start children learning to read and how to teach them.

There also seems to be a popular confusion about the meaning of reading. Historically, before mass literacy became a fact, reading was associated with being educated and an intellectual, thus giving to reading itself an aura of intellectuality. But it is clear now that knowing how to read does not automatically make a person educated. Neither are the procedures involved in learning how to read intellectual, in the sense that being knowledgeable is intellectual. Although a certain level of intelligence is required for decoding, even retarded children can be taught to decode, even though it takes them longer. Retarded children cannot extract meaning at certain levels of thought that are beyond their understanding, but they can and do learn to read simple material.

This easy association of the process of learning to read with the knowledgeableness that is potentially possible once reading is achieved has diverted many educators, psychologists, and parents from examining objectively *what affects the process.* Instead, methods of teaching have been stressed. But if we understand the process, we can examine the capacities children have at different stages of development for meeting the requirements involved in the process. We could make sensible decisions for large groups of children at a similar stage, and for differing individuals within a stage.

WHAT LEARNING TO READ INVOLVES

As far back as 1908, questions were raised about what actually happens when children learn to read, but these questions were not pursued with seriousness until more than fifty years later. The new body of research that has ensued since the 1960s now makes it very clear that reading is more than a simple sum of separate skills and more than the translating of symbols to sound. The most significant find-

[3] Eleanor Gibson and Harry Levin, *The Psychology of Reading* (Cambridge, Mass.: The M.I.T. Press, 1975), p. 5.

[4] Rudolph Flesch, *Why Johnny Can't Read* (New York: Harper & Row, Publishers, 1955).

ings are that learning to read requires *an internal integration of many developmental capacities and processes* and that *a child must be self-directed and actively involved* in the task. *Training* for the task, without considering the necessary self-involvement by the child, is wasteful. "Reading," say Gibson and Levin, "requires the ability to transfer knowledge of rules and economical strategies to new materials, something a child has to do for himself."[5] Just as in the learning of speech, so in reading children must abstract principles and apply them freshly in new situations if they are to be truly efficient readers.

Self-Involvement

Although to some people this finding will seem to negate the teacher, whose role has been to tell children what to do and how to do it in orderly, sequential fashion, there is a very important and essential place for the teacher in the processes involved in children's learning to read. Some of the teacher's role *is* to create sequence and order in the learning task. But some of what the teacher needs to do with and for the children may not appear on the surface to bear any relationship to the end goal at all. A perfect illustration of this paradox exists in a little-known contradiction: knowing the letters before coming to school is correlated with learning to read; but there is *no* correlation between classroom attempts to *teach* children the letters[6] and learning to read. The reason for this apparent contradiction is likely to be that the internal integration and motivation necessary for learning the letters are the same as for learning to read. Children who learn letters by themselves or after coming to school are revealing a readiness for reading; but *training* to name and produce letters does not affect the internal integration we call readiness. Just knowing letters is not what makes a child ready. Despite the proliferation of letters as a pattern for decorating blocks and crib mobiles, or as a subject for the earliest books, there is no indication that our society is becoming more literate as a result. In fact, a Russian study found that teaching children the names of letters *interfered* with reading![7] Since the really important information about letters in the English language is their sound, and not their names, that may be an additional factor influencing these results. Yet it has been assumed for hundreds of years that teaching children the alphabet helps them to read because it *seems* obvious.

Antecedent Experiences

Complex learning tasks are almost always preceded by activities that look very different from the end result, but without which the desired learning does not occur. For example, learning to read is in part dependent on the ability to recognize

[5] Gibson and Levin, *Psychology of Reading,* p. 11.

[6] R. J. Johnson, "The Effect of Training in Letter Names on Success in Beginning Reading for Children of Differing Abilities" (Paper presented at the American Education Research Association, Anaheim, California, 1970).

[7] D. B. Elkonin in *Comparative Reading,* J. Downing, ed. (New York: Macmillan, 1973), pp. 551–79.

left from right (or right from left). That, in turn, is dependent upon a well-integrated neurological structure which, in its turn, is supported by physical activity. So we could say, quite realistically, that lots of physical activity in early childhood helps children learn to read. Perhaps that is why Kephart, an authority on slow learners, suggests that "we may have to bring into the classroom the equivalent of ladders to climb, fences to walk, or horses to ride and help the child to build up the sensory-motor skills that are required by the more complex activities of reading, writing, and arithmetic."[8] It also explains why five times as many premature children as children born at full term become reading failures.[9] The prematures apparently need more time to catch up on important physiological growth before being asked to learn to read, and they are not generally given that time in our conventional schools.

Old-fashioned kindergartens—that is, those before the era of cognitive pressure—encouraged lots of physical activity, something which the present drive toward seatwork and workbooks is tending to reduce. At the same time, there is greater passivity of young children in general today, most likely because they watch so much television instead of using their bodies in active, physical play.

There is thus good reason to speculate that this decrease in physical activity among young children is a contributing cause of the widespread learning disability we see among beginning readers today. Would training in recognizing letters help that?

WHAT READINESS FOR READING MEANS

Readiness for reading depends first of all upon the merging of such different aspects of growth and experience as basic neurological development, cognitive awareness, and language power.[10] In addition, there are factors like understanding part-to-whole relationships, grasping the meaning of invariance and reversibility, knowing left from right, and so on. To this battery one could add experience in living that provides motivation, feelings about self and significant others (especially in relation to success or failure), ability to meet challenge and not be thrown by it, and much more. Such integration of physical, social, emotional, and intellectual capacities for learning to read is most likely to be achieved by age seven by most children.

It is not a mere matter of chance, therefore, that the developmental studies of Ilg and Ames revealed that almost half of all first-grade children are overplaced, that is, that they are not ready for reading when they enter school.[11] Nor is that

---

[8]N. C. Kephart, *The Slow Learner in the Classroom* (Columbus, Ohio: Charles E. Merrill Publishing Company, 1960).

[9]T. Eames, "Children of Premature and Full Term Birth Who Fail in Reading," *Journal of Education Research,* 38 (March 1954), 506–08.

[10]Frances Ilg and Louise Ames, *School Readiness: Behavior Tests Used at the Gesell Institute* (New York: Harper & Row, Publishers, 1964); also Ames, Louise, *Is Your Child in the Wrong Grade?* (New York: Harper & Row, Publishers, 1967).

[11]Ibid.

finding new. Although it is common knowledge that 25 percent of all children in our country read below grade level, with a heavier distribution of failure among the poor, few people are aware that reading failure is not a recent phenomenon. Between 1915 and 1925 there were such large numbers of complaints about failure in first grade that a good deal of research followed, uncovering the fact that as many as 20 to 40 percent were failing to learn to read in first grade.[12] In 1934 a study showed that children younger than six had some chance of success in reading *only* if they had a mental age of between six and six-and-a-half *and* were sufficiently mature physically, emotionally, and socially.[13] In 1946 a study found many bright children at all school levels failing in reading, indicating that other factors were at work besides I.Q.[14]

The standard answer for reading failure has always been a search for better methods and materials of teaching. Time and again it has been proven that all methods are effective with about 70 percent of all children; with all methods, anywhere from 20 to 40 percent of children fail. The time has come to stop seeking solutions in *methods* of teaching reading (about which we know a good deal), and instead to concentrate on what goes into the reading *process* so that we can assess children's readiness and progress with a reasonable degree of accuracy. This is especially important for kindergarten children. The British percentage of reading failure was very similar to ours during all the years when they taught reading at five and we at six. A British study that reflects school beginnings at five showed that by age seven only 28 to 41 percent of the children surveyed were "good" readers (on grade level), and that social class differences continue to be significant.[15] This is essentially our problem, too. The present tendency to assume that all kindergarten children are ready to learn to read is dangerous.[16] Let us see why.

STRENGTHS NECESSARY FOR READING AND WRITING

A Graphic Sense

The invention of a systematic way of recording spoken language is a tribute to the ingenuity and inventiveness of the human mind. As long as three to four thousand years ago that invention had passed by stages from pictorial representation to the creation of symbols for the sounds of speech. The amazing leap from

[12]Mary Reed, "An Investigation of Practice for the Admission and Promotion of Children from First Grade" (Ph.D., Teachers College, Columbia University, 1927).

[13]Elizabeth Bigelow, "School Progress of Under-Age Children," *Elementary School Journal,* 35 (November 1934), 186–92.

[14]George Thomas, "A Study of Reading Achievement in Terms of Mental Ability," *Elementary School Journal,* 27 (September 1946), 28–33.

[15]Ronald Davie, Neville Butler, and Harvey Goldstein, *From Birth to Seven* (Report of the National Child Development Study) (New York: Longman, Inc., 1972).

[16]Miles E. Tinker, *Bases for Effective Reading* (Minneapolis: University of Minnesota Press, 1965).

spontaneous talk to a graphic representation of talk is made over and over again by fresh generations of children. In all literate societies, children learn quite by themselves to distinguish writing from pictures by the time they are three years old, especially if they've had a chance to make designs and pictures themselves—with brush, or crayon, or a stick on sand or dirt.

Children surrounded by print (especially at home) make their way into the symbol system by trying to reproduce writing before anyone "teaches" them letters, since the physical task of writing is easier than the mental task of reading. Studies of progression in children's spontaneous attempts to write show that without training, children move along in an observable sequence from scribbles to letter formation. As a result of such findings, in 1971 Wheeler undertook to see what would happen if kindergarten children were given notebooks and told they were for writing, but were not given any kind of formal instruction, including not being shown the relation between letters and sounds. As the kindergarten year progressed, the initially large number of scribbles in the notebooks gave way to designs, then pictures, and then letters. Words in isolation, word phrases, words in sentences, and finally, symbols (such as +) followed in that order. Although letters and words were visible in the kindergarten room, the children's efforts were never corrected. The shifts from stage to stage occurred completely by self-correction. The output was different for different children, of course, but for all of them errors decreased during the year, and the errors were largely confusions between similar looking letters, a very normal state for beginning readers.[17] Thus, long before the insistent message on *Sesame Street* made knowledge of letters a matter of honor among preschoolers, most five-year-olds were able to name some letters and many were attempting to write their names. Dolores Durkin, who made a study of children who learned to read before first grade, corroborates the role of writing in the acquisition of reading skills. She writes

> Almost without exception, the starting point of curiosity about written language was an interest in scribbling or drawing. From this developed interest in copying objects and letters of the alphabet. When a child was able to copy letters—and not all children who had the interest developed the skill—the almost inevitable request was, "Show me my name."[18]

Yes, name comes first in the precocious, self-initiated, uncorrected writing of four-year-old Sylvia. The name shows clearly the most practiced and perfected kind of writing.

Besides emphasis on one's name there are other ventures into the world of writing shown in the sample. There are the free phonetic spelling, the random capitalization, and the lack of punctuation, which are all characteristic of children's

---

[17]M. E. Wheeler, *Untutored Acquisition of Writing Skills.* (Ph.D., Cornell University, 1971).

[18]Dolores Durkin, *Children Who Read Early,* quoted in E. Gibson and H. Levin, *The Psychology of Reading* (Cambridge, Mass.: The M.I.T. Press, 1975), p. 555.

By Sylvia Fitchen

The littL Girl 'StoRY
WoNTS Thar Was a littL
Girl She Was Vary littL
her Mother aND Fother
LoKeT Like   Jients To her
But She DidnoT Kayr Bicos WdN
You ARE littL PePel ReaD you StoRis

The END

(Courtesy, Janet M. Fitchen)

experience in writing when they are not yet ready for correction or instruction yet ready to compose a story from direct beginning to graphic end! Her mother tells us

> At age 3, 4, and 5, Sylvia's drawings and easel paintings were usually sprinkled with letters, at first just those of her own name, then of names of family members, and then words to go with the pictures. As Sylvia was turning 5, she was doing a lot of writing of word lists and stories, usually on her own initiative. Sometimes she would ask how to spell a word, but mostly she just sounded them out for herself, syllable by syllable.[19]

In her study of young children's writing experiences Marie Clay states that among children who enter school at age five there are large differences among their abilities to work with language. The differences are due equally to intelligence, experience, and development. The work samples collected by Clay show not only how children gain writing concepts, but also how frequently confusions occur and difficulties in learning left-right and up-down directionals arise. But writing also has special challenge and attraction to the child "if his efforts have been responded to with appreciation."[20]

Much earlier Montessori explained young children's interest in practicing writing by the fact that the period between three and seven years of age covers rapid

[19] Courtesy of Janet M. Fitchen.
[20] Marie M. Clay, *What Did I Write?* (Exeter, N.H.: Heinemann Educational Books, 1981). Reprinted by permission of Heinemann Educational Books and Heinemann Publishers (NZ) Ltd. Copyright 1975 by Marie M. Clay.

physical development and is appropriate for development of sensory activities.[21] Close observer of children that Montessori was, she had also noted that aside from the movement of forming letters, writing requires movement in managing the instrument of writing. "To hold and to manipulate a little stick securely corresponds to the acquisition of a special muscular mechanism which is independent of the writing movement."[22] And this points further to the importance for teachers observing children continuously, of taking nothing for granted.

All of us are familiar with the principle of repetition in learning writing—the practice of forming the same letters or words again and again, line after line or column after column, to gain skill. We all know as well that such practice can be a deadly bore to children as well as adults. In fact, in the not too distant past, the repeated writing of a particular phrase was used as a punishment to go with staying after school. However, for children of kindergarten age, who engage in *self-initiated* writing, repetition presents exciting experimentation, surprising effect, and a sense of accomplishment! This kind of writing is not at all like copying and repeating what a teacher has written. To make a series of shapes on paper or a whole page of similar curves or wiggles or real letters, or best of all, one's actual name—and to have done it all by one's self—is a worthy task to a young child. Worthy of repetition—and more repetition!

The sense of satisfaction from rudimentary writing, which, characteristically, has a natural proximity to drawing, is shown in the next example.[23] The caption speaks for Natasha's self-esteem and pride generated by the experience.

We see then that children's early striving to write—whether connected to drawing, consisting of pretend writing along with rudimentary letter forms, or composed of personally meaningful repetitions—has an intimate link to language development and to self-expression that is essential in early schooling. Clearly such striving is nurtured in kindergarten not by stacks of workbooks and formal instruction but by classroom activities and individual opportunities and encouragements that have direct bearing on, or provide incentive for, learning to write. We see also that experience in writing, especially creative writing (as we shall see later), is *complementary* to experience in reading.

What does this mean to modern kindergarten teachers concerned with advancing the literacy of their students? Because children want to be part of the grown-up world, they will exert spontaneous efforts to practice and learn skills of literacy. But these efforts will vary in timing and intensity from child to child. Some will inevitably need help in focusing their attention on print, because their homes did not include books and newspapers. Yet teaching children from nonliterate homes by rote repetition to recognize and even produce letters without giving them a

---

[21] Maria Montessori, "Teaching Reading and Writing" in *The Montessori Method* (New York: Schocken Books, Inc., 1977). (See also the introduction by J. McV. Hunt.)

[22] Ibid., p. 263.

[23] Marie M. Clay, *What Did I Write?* p. 3.

NATASHA (to mother): What does this say?
MOTHER (sounding out the first line): Sahspno!
NATASHA (thoughtful and satisfied): I did it.

(Courtesy, Heinemann Educational Books)

motive to learn to read is to undermine their chances of becoming readers.[24] Focus on print, for all children, must be meaningful, as in hearing stories read from a book or seeing one's spoken words transformed to written matter which becomes intelligible reading delightful to listen to! And learning to read is then a promising adventure.

A first prerequisite for learning to read is a *graphic sense,* that is, a recognition that writing carries a message. Without this understanding, print remains forever a meaningless jumble. It must have been awareness of the importance of this relationship that caused Montessori to teach reading through writing, a practice followed today in the experience-language approach to reading. Once we clearly understand this, we will surround children with stories they can hear, respond to, and enjoy; write *their* stories on paper for them. This is how Walter created his own special composition:

After listening intently to the teacher reading an unillustrated story in verse,[25] he asked her to "read KITTY CAN again." Familiar with the teacher's postpone-

[24]Dorothy H. Cohen, "The Effect of a Special Program in Literature on Vocabulary and Reading Achievement," *Elementary English* (February 1968).
[25]Marguerita Rudolph, "Kitty Can," in *Believe and Make-Believe,* eds. Lucy Sprague Mitchell and Irma Black (New York: E. P. Dutton & Co., Inc., 1961).

ments, Walter made the request urgent: "Do it *now*!" But when the teacher read the first two lines, "Kitty can walk, Kitty can stalk . . ." he asked her to stop reading. "Now I want to tell you a poem about Jonathan." He dictated carefully but unhesitatingly:

> Jonathan likes to walk
> Jonathan likes to stalk
> But he *mostly* likes to talk!

Walter, almost five years of age, was thrilled with his literary achievement—a "poem" about his two-year-old brother. And along with the feeling of creativity, the interest in the visible marks on paper that the teacher wrote, and the pleasing sound of his story, the experience brought the *connection* between speech and the meaning in reading. We might say it served Walter's graphic sense. Yet graphic sense is only one facet of total readiness.

Awareness of Language Structure

Perhaps because traces on paper can so easily be seen, it is possible for children to grasp the concept that they can have meaning. It is definitely harder for them to realize that spontaneous spoken language, which seems to vanish as it happens, has a structure and a form. Luria, a world-renowned specialist in language development, points out, "Children cannot make *the word itself* the object of awareness, and do not suspect that it has its own existence."[26] They cannot grasp the concept of a sentence either. Children say, "JackandJillwentupthehill," but have no idea that in print it will be "Jack and Jill went up the hill." Words get separated in print because adults know that each word is an entity.[27] Yet the fact that spoken language has structure must be conceivable to a child if the printed form of the language is to make full sense. We might say that Walter *felt* the structure of his spoken language.

When they first learn to speak, children focus on meaning. They absorb the syntax and structure of language by their efforts to fit form to their need and intent, but form by itself has no meaning. Most children become dimly aware of the objective existence of words at approximately four to seven years of age. We can tell this because they begin to "play around" with words as though they have a separate existence. Giving double meaning to words, as in the moron jokes, is one such action. This stage of playing with language is used humorously in a children's book by Mary Elting.[28] In *Q Is for Duck*, an alphabet book, the *fun* of letter

[26] Quoted in Courtney Cazden, "Play with Language and Metalinguistic Awareness: One Dimension of Language Experience," in *Dimensions of Language Experience*, ed. C. Winsor (New York: Agathon Press, Inc., 1978), p. 8.

[27] N. S. Meltzer and R. Herse, "The Boundaries of Written Words as Seen by First Graders," *Journal of Reading Behavior, I,* 1969, pp. 3–14.

[28] Mary Elting and Michael Folsom, *Q Is for Duck*, illus. Jack Kent (Boston: Houghton Mifflin Company, Clarion Books, 1980).

sounds (rather than the focus on conventional spelling) leads children to finding the fun in words.

The capacity to grasp the structure of language increases with age, especially between the second and fourth grades. Nevertheless, even as children grow aware of the existence of sentences and words in sentences, they continue to focus most on the meaning of language. The words they recognize first in reading are the *content* words, especially nouns and verbs. Function words, such as articles, prepositions, and auxiliaries, take longer to learn even though they *look* easier because smaller. There are studies which show the strengths and limitations of most kindergarten children in awareness of language structure. Most, for example, cannot see any correspondence between short and long *spoken* words, for example, "pig" and "elevator," when spoken or *written* on a chart or blackboard. Not only the concept of a word as a unit, but the concept of *length* does not exist for them separate from a specific, concrete example, such as the length of a board they are using or a line they are drawing. Consequently, they cannot visualize length applied to a spoken word nor have they any idea that length can be relative (short and long) or exist in different dimensions, such as in sound, time, distance, or direction. All of this makes sense in terms of Piaget's description of the preoperational stage, during which children find it very difficult to deal with abstractions, which is what words are. Kindergartners can match single letters because their graphic sense develops earlier than their ability to conceptualize something that is not concrete. Matching pairs or groups of letters, however, is not so easy because the distinctive features begin to get too complicated. (This is still difficult for third-grade poor readers.)

Awareness of Units of Sound

Another hurdle in learning to read is understanding that sounds, or phonemes, are concealed in print. Our reading system is based on twenty-six symbols which stand for forty sounds of speech.

Elkonin, a reading specialist, maintains that the development of awareness of the language's phonological aspects represents the most essential precondition for literacy.[29] By phonological aspects Elkonin means the units of sound, that is, words distinctly different from each other, syllables, letter groups, and single letter sounds.

In testing four-, five-, and six-year-old children on their ability to differentiate the various sounds in a spoken word, Liberman found that four-year-olds could not segment words into the smallest sound unit—phonemes. Only 17 percent of the five-year-olds could segment words into phonemes, but by six, 70 percent could identify the number of phonemes. Half the four-year-olds could, however, identify the number of syllables, but by six 90 percent could tap out the correct number of syllables. In general, six-year-olds can, with training, break words down into syllables with ease, but they still cannot segment words into the sounds of individual letters, even though most of them can identify the number of sounds. Yet by age eight, children have enough command of this knowledge to enjoy "Pig Latin," a

[29]Elkonin, in *Comparative Reading*.

language made up by shifting letter-sounds from their usual places in the spoken words, and some teach themselves a backward language ("tac" for "cat," and so on). A good generalization for teachers to remember is that children have probably reached a workable level of mastery within any area of knowledge when they can "play around" (or be creative) with the knowledge.

Since eventually the study of phonics becomes important in learning to read fluently, *children's capacity to deal with segments of speech is a basic requirement for the successful application of phonics learning.* This capacity increases with age. By accepting the reality of stages of development, we will cease to push children into rote learning of phonics before they have the capacity to *apply* their learning in new situations. Premature "learning" may well explain why so many children fail to make the leap, between second and third grade, from *recognition* of letters and sounds into *reading.* A more careful assessment of individual readiness, not in terms of age, grade, or adult anxiety but in terms of the specific kinds of maturity required, could avoid a good deal of reading failure with all the concomitant emotional and social upheaval that goes with such failure.

Kindergarten teachers are in a good position to make such an assessment without formal tests by the middle of the year. They will by then have noticed children's particular struggles and facility with oral language and comprehension, observed their interest in some aspects of reading and writing and indifference to others, and become acquainted with each child's personality and style of learning. The kindergarten teacher will thus be able to convey confidence in each child's direct or indirect pursuit of reading and writing.

Stage of Development and Reading

Piaget's theories of stages, drawn from his interviews with children, help explain why individual assessment is logical and even economical in so important a task as learning to read.

From egocentricity to conservation.   Children's early, basic learning is done through their own bodies. They draw their information about the world from their own sensory experience, and it is completely natural that their understanding is limited to that which they themselves can see, hear, touch, taste, and smell. But they also see themselves as *causing* happenings, partly as a result of this physical involvement, and partly because they do not understand that there are other forces at work causing happenings, forces which they may not see or understand. Thus they interpret all events from their own subjective perception, a viewpoint that persists to some extent throughout our lives.

This state of being unable to see from another's point of view, which Piaget calls *egocentricity*, normally undergoes a serious jolt for most children sometime between the ages of five and seven. As kindergarten teachers well know, egocentricity is still strong among the majority of the children. Yet the major shift in capacity to go beyond self-involved perceiving occurs among some children during the kindergarten year. It is a shift away from being bound to the obvious, or from being *perception bound,* as Piaget puts it. Children come to understand that their personal sensory feedback is not the only information available about the world and that objects and events may have more to them than meets the eye. They are then able to realize, as adults do, that changes in the appearance of things, such as changes of color or shape, do not affect such basic attributes of objects as weight, quantity, volume, or length. Thus, when someone drops a block on their toes, they can at last accept an explanation that it was not deliberately done to hurt *them* but was an accident. They can accept the reality that they received the same number of cookies even though someone is boasting about having more after breaking the cookies up into several pieces. They *know,* and no one can mislead them, that seeing is not the whole story. So they become capable of grasping the concept that *words,* which are not concrete and tangible items, can nevertheless be thought about as though they are. This important cognitive growth spurt is called "conservation" by Piaget. Many psychologists believe there is an important connection between conservation and the capacity to apply principles of phonics in learning to read.

Cognitive Skills

It is generally assumed that there is a strong correlation between I.Q. and learning to read. Yet an I.Q. score does not assess the variety of cognitive skills children must have in order to learn to read. There are poor readers among children of high I.Q.; there are retarded children who learn to read. A number of mental operations quite different from what I.Q. measures need to be developed to a point of usable readiness for the challenges involved in reading.

Perceptual development. "Perceptual factors are most important for initial acquisition of reading skill," say Birch and Belmont in comparing problems of beginning and later readers.[30] According to Gibson and Levin, perception is "the process of extracting information from objects, places or events in the environment."[31] It does not result from *adding on* anything to what a child has or is. Perception is a *pulling out by the child,* an *extraction,* of whatever in objects, events, or situations the child can pull out, or perceive. It is subjective, based on sensory experience, and it is selective. Perception is an organic process that develops internally as a consequence of a combination of genetic, experiential, and psychological factors. There can be no *training* for this or any kind of organic growth, only support and encouragement through appropriate experience.

Perceptual development begins in infancy and proceeds through childhood in three major directions. One of these directions is toward increasing *differentiation,* that is, the noting of distinctive features that distinguish one person from another,

---

[30] H. G. Birch and I. Belmont, "Auditory Visual Integration, Intelligence and Reading Ability in School Children," *Perceptual and Motor Skills, 20,* 1965, 295–305.

[31] Gibson and Levin, *Psychology of Reading.*

one thing from another, one event from another; that distinguish classes from each other, such as persons from animals and things. Another direction is toward identifying characteristics of objects, events, and people which remain stable, or *invariant*. For example, a mother is a mother by day, at night, and in any clothing or mood. A third direction is the growth in capacity to perceive *order*, or a sequence of relationships, in objects, events, and situations. Children thus learn to look for similarities, redundancies, or rules that organize information and make its meaning more quickly and automatically available. This makes it possible, for example, for them to learn by analogy, a more economical way than experiencing everything at first hand.

In learning to read, all these perceptual capacities must be sufficiently developed so that (1) words and letters can be readily differentiated from each other with few mistakes, for instance, M must be seen clearly different from N, (2) the stability or invariance of words and letters can be perceived under differing conditions, as when the letter M is printed in a different size or color yet is sounded the same way, and (3) principles that allow for application of new learning are understood, for example, that the letter M does not change sound when there are two M's together.

Attention and nonattention. Perceptual development helps children to focus and pay attention. But it also makes room for nonattention to that which is *irrelevant*, a most important capacity if one is not to be endlessly distracted. *Attention*, as an aspect of perceptual development, is in part a matter of inborn temperament, in part learned from experience, and in part influenced by maturation. At birth children show varying degrees of attention within a normal range, and this is less related to intelligence or lack of it than to susceptibility to distraction. As children grow, their capacity for attention is heightened by the stability and order they experience in the environment, especially in the relations with significant adults and in orderly contact with the objective world of materials and things. Children whose lives are a kaleidoscope of changing figures and inconsistent responses, for whom things (and people) disappear and fail to reappear with frequency, or whose attention is caught by video games are children likely to be easily distracted.

Computer technology, pervasive in all areas of human endeavor, is now having a significant impact on education, including early schooling. Computers are becoming a familiar part of classrooms at all levels. According to a recent report, there are now fifteen thousand schools (elementary and secondary) using microcomputers as teaching tools.[32] At the Lamplighter School in Dallas, Texas, four-year-olds playing a computer game on a screen pick up such skills as looking at characters from left to right and identifying words that begin with the same letter. However, although several studies are in progress, there is considerable debate as to the merit, efficacy, and *ultimate result* of computerized education, especially in the early years. What effect computers have on *the human process of learning and thinking,* and specifi-

---

[32] Edward B. Fiske, "Computers Alter Lives of Pupils and Teachers," *New York Times,* April 4, 1982, p. 42.

cally on perceptual development, we still don't know. But we do know that perceptual development, like awareness of language structure and sound, is dependent on total development. Normally it improves with age. As with everything else in growth, however, environment plays its part. An environment that is barren, limited in variety of objects, materials, events, and people, does not support growth in differentiation very well. An environment that is constantly changing and unstable can impede growth in invariance. On the other hand, an environment too rich in stimuli for a young child to be able to handle can thwart growth in differentiation and invariance just as well, because the child is too overwhelmed to make sense out of the confusion. Television plays a potentially negative role in this regard. According to one psychiatrist,

> Sesame Street's use of intense visual and auditory patterns to capture attention, its rapid perceptual shifts through the use of zoom lenses and quick dissolve, and its studied avoidance of time lags between messages strongly interfere with the emergence of the perceptual readiness state.[33]

Thus, continuous *under*stimulation or *over*stimulation of children's sensory receptors in early childhood appears to have the same practical effects: interference with perceptual development and eventually with the ability to learn to read. Perceptual problems are rampant among poor readers. The experiences offered young children must be examined carefully with this in mind.

EMOTIONAL ASPECTS OF LEARNING

The youngest children have feelings that they bring to their learning. If they are afraid of failing, they may not try; if they are unrealistic about their capacities and the nature of the task, they may feel let down and withdraw in a confused sense of having failed. If they are competitive or overly anxious to succeed, they may trip over their own toes, or they may succeed at a level of tension that will harm them. If they are too needful of and dependent on adult approval, they will settle for mimicry and parroting. If they are suspicious of new experience, they will hang back. If they are impulsive, they will try anything and everything but without attention or focus. A suitable level of social and emotional maturity is necessary for academic learning.

Motivation

"Children who come from reading homes become readers" was once a proven dictum. It is probably not completely true any more because of several changes in our lives. One is the powerful pull of the visual mode, which is making it harder for

---

[33] Werner I. Halpern, "Turned-on Toddlers," *Journal of the Annenberg School of Communication,* University of Pennsylvania (Fall 1975).

children to extract information from the nonpictorial. Whereas once children listened to stories on records and imagined what was happening, many of today's children grow restless when they listen to something without pictorial accompaniment. Some say plainly that they do not like radio, because "You can't see anything." Print is nonpictorial.

Another factor influencing motivation to read is the negative influence of television entertainment techniques. A third-grade teacher expressed her feelings about this to a TV commentator:

> I cannot change my body into different letters, nor can I change color. But the lessons I consider exciting fall flat because I do not do these phenomenal things.[34]

The result seems to be that many children have a hard time applying themselves to tasks of any kind, including learning to read in first grade.

Still another factor is the common attitude, often promoted by advertising, of scorn for hard work and praise for the easiest way to do anything. Further analysis of obstacles to learning to read comes from Bruno Bettelheim.[35] Bettelheim asserts that a child's unconscious thoughts and feelings may cause difficulties and persistent errors which result in discouraging learning to read. Bettelheim's study also shows that the boring content of American primers not only fails to engage the child's mind but is apt to promote errors and impede progress.

Another negative factor in learning to read comes from lessons which are unrelated to anything that interests children. One such child was Herman. His kindergarten teacher had asked the children to cut pictures out of magazines of things that began with the letter "S" because she believed in an early start. Herman had other things on his mind. Herman and four other children are sitting on the floor with a stack of magazines, cutting anything that appeals to them. They have not understood the point of the activity. Herman keeps wanting to cut out pictures of women in underwear. He keeps tapping the student teacher on the shoulder, exclaiming "Look! Look!" She tells him that it is not a picture of anything that begins with "S." He ignores this. Finally he comes to a picture of a woman in a slip. The teacher tells him he may cut that out because "slip" begins with "S." This does not appear to interest him, but he is anxious to cut. The student teacher helps him. She comes across a sweater, and tells Herman he may cut this out. He ignores her and is already painstakingly cutting out two women in underwear. The student teacher asks him if he thinks sweater begins with S. He continues to ignore her. Finally, he mumbles "no." . . . When he finishes cutting out the women, he holds them up in the air, one in each hand, crying "Look!" to the student teacher, and moves his cutouts, pretending that they are walking as though they were paper dolls.

Although Herman's lesson appears utterly futile, reading lessons *unrelated* to children's interests is not uncommon in our schools.

[34]Communication sent to Eda Le Shan and shared with the authors.

[35]Bruno Bettelheim and Karen Zeldan, *On Learning to Read: The Child's Fascination with Meaning* (New York: Alfred A. Knopf, Inc., 1981).

Children must *want* to learn to read, because without this involvement nothing will happen. Kindergarten teachers can create high motivation for reading by reading interesting stories and poems to children regularly, thus giving them the best support for becoming readers.[36]

SHOULD READING BE TAUGHT IN KINDERGARTEN?

Analysis of the process involved in reading combined with Piaget's findings on the stage of development of kindergarten children and the existence of large-scale reading failure causes us to take a position against the formal teaching of reading in the kindergarten curriculum as premature and therefore risky. There is ample evidence that a *range* of readiness for reading exists in children between five and seven, with the greatest readiness for most children closer to seven than five. A recent study of beginning first graders identified as high risks in reading readiness verifies the existence of a range of normal variations in growth patterns. Three groups of these high-risk children were given some form of remediation: perceptual training, remedial reading, and placebo play. A fourth group (the control) received no special program of any kind. At the end of the treatment period, *there were no differences in level of attainment or amount of gain for any of the groups. All had progressed over the seven months, but the form of help did not matter.*[37] If these high-risk children improved in reading readiness only with time and ordinary experience, does that not indicate that we are labeling many five- to seven-year-olds as failures before they have really gotten started? How important is an early start in reading when it has been shown that between ages eight and ten such early gains no longer matter?[38]

There are undoubtedly children who can learn to read at five (some at four) without strain. In Terman's study of highly selected gifted children, 25 out of 1,000 read before five. In a general population sample Durkin found 49 out of 5,000 who read before first grade. There are undoubtedly more early readers now because of the great pressure for early reading, but they are still a very small percentage of the total child population. In kindergartens catering to children of highly educated, economically favored families, an informal check by the authors shows perhaps five or six out of a class of 25 entering kindergarten as readers; half the children read by late spring, when they are six. Early readers are not harmed by waiting for formal training, since they tend to pick up the skills on their own.[39] If they can already read, they simply read along with other activities. But the vast

---

[36] Dorothy H. Cohen, "Effect of a Special Program in Literature."

[37] Ira Belmont and Herbert Birch, "The Effect of Supplemental Intervention on Children with Low Reading–Readiness Scores," *Journal of Special Education*, 8, *1* (Spring 1974).

[38] P. E. Vernon, M. B. O'Gorman, and P. McClellan, "Comparative Study of Educational Attainment in England and Scotland," *British Journal of Educational Psychology*, 25 (1955), 195–203.

[39] Helen Roche, "Junior Primary in the Van Dyke Level Plan," *Journal of Educational Research*, 55 (February 1962), 232–33.

majority of children under six, and almost half of those under seven, are not likely to have reached the point where they can benefit from formal instruction in reading without strain or failure. Children in Scandinavia and the U.S.S.R.[40] all start reading at seven. They do not show any less capacity for later school achievement as a result.

Instead of pushing the few who are potentially ready it is wiser for teachers to be familiar with normal growth patterns and to learn to identify children likely to have difficulty. Kindergarten is a time for supportive help toward developing the language power, perceptual differentiation, emotional stability, and sound physical skills of all children as a most important contribution to their future academic success. Teachers should therefore evaluate cautiously the barrage of advice coming from many publishers pushing their kits and boxes and tricky folders promoting "Early Skills," and making learning "easy and fun" with the latest (expensive) products. One must resist such tempting products, knowing that in the long run there is no advantage in early acquisition of skills or in striving for *easy* kinds of learning in kindergarten or first grade.

INFORMAL KINDERGARTEN CURRICULUM AND ACADEMIC LEARNING

Much of the research which compares first-grade achievement of children who attended kindergarten (no cognitive training) with those who did not favors the former group.[41]

In a 1949 study Pratt found that children with kindergarten experience ranked higher in reading readiness at the beginning, and significantly higher on the Gates Primary Reading Tests at the end of first grade.[42] Morrison and Harris studied the effect of an informal kindergarten program on the reading of disadvantaged children. The children showed development in social and emotional behavior, expansion of intellectual abilities, and greater ease in oral expression. They learned to share personal experiences and ideas and to listen to stories. At the end of first

[40] See Evangeline Burgess, *Values in Early Childhood Education*, Digest of Elementary, Kindergarten & Nursery Education, Washington, D.C.: NEA, 1965; Chester W. Harris, *The Encyclopedia of Educational Research* (New York: Macmillan, 1960); Mary Mindess and Alice Keliher, *Review of Research Related to the Advantages of Kindergarten* (Washington, D.C.: Bulletin of the Association for Childhood Education International, 1966-67); Nila B. Smith, *Shall We Teach Formal Reading in the Kindergarten?* (Washington, D.C.: Bulletin of the Association for Childhood Education International, 1964).

[41] However, during a September 1982 American Teachers tour, school officials in Moscow and Leningrad informed us that plans have been concluded to lower the school entrance age from seven to six, for the general reason that children are now ready for academic learning by six.

[42] Willis E. Pratt, "A Study of the Differences in the Prediction of Reading Success of Kindergarten and Non-Kindergarten Children," *Journal of Educational Research*, 42 (March 1949), 525-33.

grade, twenty-one grade-equivalent comparisons were made, and all but one favored the kindergarten group.[43]

The Relation of Kindergarten Experience to Academic Readiness

Let us see how and why a kindergarten curriculum based on firsthand, sensory experience and play without stress on academic achievement can nevertheless support later academic success. Mary Moffitt[44] worked out an analysis of the relation between play, play materials, and cognitive learning. She pointed out that such time-honored kindergarten activities as music, rhythms, running, jumping, creeping, painting, block building, manipulating materials, woodworking, steering, and dramatic play require growth in *left-right understanding* (laterality), *directionality, ocular pattern scanning, hand-eye coordination,* and *manipulative skill,* all required in reading. The ability to make associations and comparisons is also learned in play and through the use of play materials. Figure-ground relationships, an important aspect of perceptual development, are strengthened by puzzles, painting, pasting, blocks, and construction of all kinds. The capacity to discriminate among forms, which young children learn best by touch, is supported by floor blocks, table blocks and puzzles. These activities also strengthen the ability to see relationships between parts and wholes.

The relationship between sound awareness and size of vocabulary is strengthened by the language models of teacher, by literature, and by songs. Insensitivity to rhyme, which is related to reading failure,[45] begins to disappear after experiences with the traditional kindergarten rhyming games and exposure to poetry. The use of signs for the children's block building, the labels on their clothing racks, the recording of their dictated stories, the stories they hear read from books, the recipes for cooking, the special dates on the calendar, the shopping lists, notes sent home, and the letters written to absent friends all make clear the relationship between meaning and print. The availability of paper, pencils, and crayons encourages the sequential development from scribbling to writing as small-motor muscles and perceptual awareness join to give children impetus to re-create the symbols of literacy. Children who use paints, paper, pencil, and crayons freely in an environment of print learn to distinguish the variables of graphic information—straightness, curvature, tilt, continuity, closedness, and intersection of lines, all of which must be differentiated for learning to read.[46]

Movement experiences give children a sense of *part to whole* ("shake your wrists" vs. "all of you jump"); *sequence* ("walk on your toes, on your heels, and

[43] Coleman Morrison and Albert J. Harris, "Effect of Kindergarten on the Reading of the Disadvantaged," *Reading Teacher,* 22, *1* (October 1968), 4–9.

[44] Mary Moffitt, "Play as a Medium for Learning," Part 3, *Research and Thought about Children's Play,* Special Issue of *Leisure Today* (Journal of the American Association of Health, Physical Education, and Recreation) June 1972.

[45] Gibson and Levin, *Psychology of Reading,* p. 228.

[46] Ibid.

on your toes again"); *contrast* (fast–slow, tall–short, loud–soft); *space* (small, large; forward, back; around, straight ahead; up, down). Experiences with sound and percussion instruments help develop awareness of patterns in a nonconcrete mode, just as dominoes and design cubes develop awareness of patterns in a concrete mode. Analyzing patterns and perceiving the structure of patterns are both necessary for reading. According to de Hirsch the capacity to perceive patterns is a basic predictor of success in reading.[47]

The use of unit blocks and outdoor hollow blocks and boards encourages a sense of order, skill in classification, and discrimination of shape, size, and weight. Blocks serve also to support the sense of balance needed for laterality and the development of eye-hand coordination so important to writing and reading. The housekeeping corner stimulates language skills, social competence, and self-direction. The workbench helps develop eye-hand coordination as a child swings a hammer to hit a nail on its head, and part-to-whole relationships as wood is cut into pieces and then recombined to form a new whole.

Discriminatory skills of all kinds—visual, tactile, auditory—grow stronger as children use the materials of the kindergarten. The widening of their interests through trips, books, discussions, and other resources gives support to verbal facility and concept building. Games like "Simon Says" or "Follow the Leader" encourage imitation from visual cues and the following of directions from spoken cues. Games like "Looby Loo" and "Hokey Pokey" help differentiate right from left. Guessing games like "What's Missing" or "Hot and Cold" sharpen perception and memory. Another source of language stimulation which is outside the classroom is regional rope-jumping rhymes. These are universally loved and spontaneously learned by young schoolchildren. Their value to children lies in their playful nonsense, rhythm, and humor.

Discussions and planning sessions, storytelling and dramatization, even social conversation at snacktime introduce young children to the variety of purposes to which language is put and cultivate their memory by focusing attention on past events. Most important for future academic success is the encouragement of curiosity in the kindergarten. Children's questions are listened to and answered. Children's interests are followed up and deepened. Children's errors in the course of experimentation and exploration are analyzed or explained, not condemned. *Reasons for learning grow clear.*

Rote learning and memorization of letters cannot do this. Workbooks cannot do this. In fact, children who use workbooks test no higher than children who do not use them.[48]

Seat activities that "look like school" to the uninformed are not necessarily genuine educational experiences. Young children need *general* support of discrimi-

---

[47]Katrina de Hirsch, *Predicting Reading Failure* (New York: Harper & Row, Publishers, 1972).

[48]Milton H. Ploghoff, "Do Reading Readiness Workbooks Promote Readiness?" *Elementary English*, 36 (October 1959), 424–26.

nating abilities and help in noting distinguishing characteristics of anything and everything relevant to child interests rather than specific training in letters and numbers.

According to Tinker, an authority on reading, a kindergarten program that supports reading should provide experiences in verbal facility, concept building, word-recognition skills, left-right orientation, auditory discrimination, comprehension and interpretation, elementary study skills (sequence, duration, persistence, and finishing) and widening of interests, all to be embedded in content that is interesting and offers challenges to young children.[49]

Finally a special note about writing. Although we've demonstrated that young children are ready for the task of writing and the development of the skill at their own pace, they are apt to become discouraged from writing throughout later schooling. A recent article depicts assigned writing as a still-practiced method of discipline and punishment in the United States. Such practice will in no way advance our serious quest for greater literacy in our country.[50]

REFERENCES AND FURTHER READING

AMES, LOUISE BATES. *Is Your Child in the Wrong Grade?* New York: Harper & Row, Pub., 1967.

AMES, LOUISE BATES. *Stop School Failure.* New York: Harper & Row, Pub., 1972.

BECK, HELEN L. *Don't Push Me, I'm No Computer; How Pressures to "Achieve" Harm Preschool Children.* New York: McGraw-Hill, 1973.

BELMONT, I., and BIRCH, H. G. "The Effect of Supplemental Intervention on Children with Low Reading-Readiness Scores," *Journal of Special Education,* 8*I* (Spring 1974).

BERGAMINI, Y., and SWANSON, W. "Does Kindergarten Make a Difference?" *School Executive,* 74 (December 1954), 54–55.

BETTELHEIM, BRUNO, and ZELDAN, KAREN. *On Learning to Read: The Child's Fascination with Meaning.* New York: Knopf, 1981.

BIBER, BARBARA. "Premature Structuring: A Deterrent to Creativity," *American Journal of Orthopsychiatry,* 29, 2 (April 1959).

BIGELOW, ELIZABETH. "School Progress of Under-Age Children," *Elementary School Journal,* 35 (November 1934).

BIRCH, H. G., and BELMONT, I. "Auditory Visual Integration, Intelligence and Reading Ability in School Children," *Perceptual Motor Skills,* 20 (1965).

BLAKELY, W. P., and SHADLE, E. M. "A Study of Two Readiness for Reading Programs in Kindergarten," *Elementary English,* 38 (November 1961), 502–05.

BRUNER, JEROME S. "Nature and Uses of Immaturity," *American Psychologist,* 27, *8* (August 1972), 687–716.

[49] Miles Tinker, *Prepare Your Child for Reading* (New York: Holt, Rinehart and Winston, 1971).

[50] Fred M. Hechinger, "The Evil in Using Writing to Punish," *New York Times,* January 4, 1983.

BURGESS, EVANGELINE. *Values in Early Childhood Education.* Washington, D.C.: Department of Elementary, Kindergarten, and Nursery Education of the National Education Association, 1965.

CAZDEN, COURTNEY. "Play with Language and Metalinguistic Awareness," in *Dimensions of Language Experience,* ed. C. Winsor. New York: Agathon Press, Inc., 1978.

CHOMSKY, CAROL. "Write First. Read Later," *Childhood Education* (March 1971), 296.

CLAY, MARIE M. *What Did I Write?* Exeter, N.H.: Heinemann Educational Books, 1981.

COHEN, DOROTHY H. "The Effect of Literature on Vocabulary and Reading Achievement," *Elementary English* (February 1968).

COHEN, DOROTHY H. "Is TV a Pied Piper?" *Young Children* (November 1974).

DAVIE, RONALD, BUTLER, NEVILLE, and GOLDSTEIN, HARVEY. *From Birth to Seven.* (Report of the National Child Development Study). New York: Longman, 1972.

DE HART, ELLEN. "What's Involved in Being Able to Read?" *Young Children* (March 1968).

DE HIRSCH, KATRINA. *Predicting Reading Failure.* New York: Harper & Row, Pub., 1972.

DURKIN, DOLORES. *Children Who Read Early.* New York: Teachers College Press, 1966.

EAMES, T. "Children of Premature and Full Term Birth Who Fail in Reading," *Journal of Education Research,* 38 (March 1954).

"Eating Well Can Help Your Child Learn Better." International Reading Association, 800 Barksdale Road, P. O. Box 8139, Newark, Delaware, 1971. (A brochure.)

ELKONIN, D. B. in *Comparative Reading,* ed. J. Downing. New York: Macmillan, 1973.

ELTING, MARY, and FOLSOM, MICHAEL (illus. Jack Kent). *Q Is for Duck.* Boston: Houghton Mifflin Company, Clarion Books, 1980.

FISKE, EDWARD B. "Computers Alter Lives of Pupils and Teachers," *New York Times,* April 4, 1982.

FLESCH, RUDOLPH. *Why Johnny Can't Read.* New York: Harper & Row, Pub., 1955.

GIBSON, ELEANOR J., and LEVIN, HARRY. *The Psychology of Reading.* Cambridge, Mass.: The M.I.T. Press, 1975.

HALPERN, WERNER I. "Turned-On Toddlers," *Journal of the Annenberg School of Communication,* University of Pennsylvania, Fall, 1975.

HAMALAINEN, ARTHUR. "Kindergarten-Primary: Entrance Age in Relation to Later School Adjustment," *Elementary School Journal,* 52, 7 (March 1952), 406–11.

HECHINGER, FRED. "The Evils in Using Writing to Punish," *New York Times,* January 4, 1983.

HOLT, JOHN. *How Children Learn* (rev. ed.). New York: Delacorte, 1983; Dell, 1983 (paperback).

ILG, FRANCES, and AMES, LOUISE. *School Readiness: Behavior Tests Used at the Gesell Institute.* New York: Harper & Row, Pub., 1964.

JACOBS, JAMES N. "An Evaluation of the Frostig Visual-Perceptual Training Program," Research Supplement, *Educational Leadership,* 1 (January 1968), 332–40.

JOHNSON, R. J. "The Effect of Training in Letter Names on Success in Beginning Reading for Children of Differing Abilities" (Paper presented at the American Education Research Assoc. in Anaheim, California 1970).

KELLEY, M. L., and CHEN, M. K. "Experimental Study of Formal Reading Instruction at the Kindergarten Level," *Journal of Educational Research,* 60 (January 1967), 224–29.

KEPHART, N. C. *The Slow Learner in the Classroom.* Columbus, Ohio: Chas. E. Merrill, 1960.

KRAUSS, RUTH (illus. Mary Chalmers). *I Write It.* New York: Harper & Row, Pub., 1970. (A children's book dealing with the irresistible urge to write one's name everywhere!)

MELTZER, N. S., and HERSE, R. "The Boundaries of Written Words as Seen by First Graders," *Journal of Reading Behavior, I,* 1969.

MILLER, WILMA H. "Home Prereading Experiences and First Grade Reading Achievement," *Reading Teacher,* 22, 7 (April 1969).

MOFFITT, MARY. "Foundations of Reading and Writing." Campus Film Distributors Corp., 14 Madison Ave., P. O. Box 206, Valhalla, N.Y. 10595. (16 mm sound color educational films)

MOFFITT, MARY. "Play as a Medium for Learning," Part 3, *Research and Thought about Children's Play,* Special Issue of *Leisure Today* (Journal of the American Association of Health, Physical Education and Recreation) June 1972.

MONTESSORI, MARIA. "Teaching Reading and Writing" in *The Montessori Method.* New York: Schocken Books paperback, 1964.

MORRISON, COLEMAN, and HARRIS, ALBERT J. "Effect of Kindergarten on the Reading of the Disadvantaged," *Reading Teacher,* 22, *1* (October 1968), 4.

MOSKOWITZ, S. "Should We Teach Reading in the Kindergarten?" *Elementary English,* 42 (November 1965), 798–804.

NIMNICHT, GLEN. "Back to the Basics: More Tender Loving Care for Young Children," *Young Children* (September 1981).

PAUL, RHEA. "Invented Spelling in Kindergarten," *Young Children* (March 1976).

PFLAUM, SUSANNA WHITNEY. *The Development of Language and Reading in the Young Child.* Columbus, Ohio: Chas. E. Merrill, 1974.

PLOGHOFF, MILTON H. "Do Reading Readiness Workbooks Promote Readiness?" *Elementary English,* 36 (October 1959), 424–26.

PRATT, WILLIS E. "A Study of the Differences in the Prediction of Reading Success of Kindergarten and Non-Kindergarten Children," *Journal of Educational Research,* 42 (March 1949).

RAVEN, RONALD, and SALZER, RICHARD. "Piaget and Reading Instruction," *Reading Teacher,* 24 (April 1971), 630–39.

REED, MARY. "An Investigation of Practice for the Admission and Promotion of Children from First Grade" (Ph.D., Teachers College, Columbia University, 1927).

ROCHE, HELEN. "Junior Primary in the Van Dyke Level Plan," *Journal of Educational Research,* 55 (February 1962).

RUDOLPH, MARGUERITA. "Kitty Can," in *Believe and Make-Believe,* eds. Lucy Sprague Mitchell and Irma Black. New York: Dutton, 1961.

SAMUELS, S. JAY. "Letter-Name Versus Letter-Sound Knowledge in Learning to Read," *Reading Teacher,* 24, 7 (April 1971).

SMITH, NILA BANTON. *Shall We Teach Formal Reading in the Kindergarten?* Washington, D.C.: Association for Childhood Education International, 1964.

SPIEGEL, EDITH. "Yes, 'Sesame Street' Has Its Detractors," *New York Times,* August 5, 1979.

SPRIGLE, HERBERT A. "Who Wants to Live on Sesame Street?" *Young Children* (December 1972), 91–109.

SUTTON, M. H. "Children Who Learned to Read in Kindergarten: A Longitudinal Study," *Reading Teacher,* 22 (April 1969), 596–602.

THOMAS, GEORGE. "A Study of Reading Achievement in Terms of Mental Ability," *Elementary School Journal,* 27 (September 1946).

TINKER, MILES E. *Bases for Effective Reading.* Minneapolis: University of Minnesota Press, 1965.

TINKER, MILES E. *Prepare Your Child for Reading.* New York: Holt, Rinehart and Winston, 1971.

VERNON, P. E., O'GORMAN, M. B., and McCLELLAN, P. "Comparative Study of Educational Attainment in England and Scotland," *British Journal of Educational Psychology,* 25 (1955).

WHEELER, M. E. "Untutored Acquisition of Writing Skills" (Ph.D. diss., Cornell University, 1971).

WIGGIN, KATE DOUGLAS. *Children's Rights: A Book of Nursery Logic.* Boston and New York: Houghton Mifflin Company, 1892.

16 Mathematical Experience in Early Childhood

By contrast with reading, there is a clear and appropriate place for math learning in the kindergarten. Exactly the same strengths and limitations that make formal reading unrealistic for most children at this stage make math experiences and encounters exciting and viable. The reasons for the difference are inherent in the intrinsic natures of reading and mathematics.

Mathematics is essentially a mental operation. Pencil and paper can be an aid, especially at more complex levels, but a grasp of basic mathematical concepts is not dependent on symbols or symbolic rendition. Rather, it involves sensory perception and personal reaction. For instance, *quantitative* difference between a *fraction* (a slice) and a *whole* banana is fully discernible even to a two-year-old; *two* cookies are clearly *more* than (and therefore preferable to) *one;* and any kindergartner could quickly *calculate* that *three chairs* around a table would not *suffice* for the *five people* who came to it, and could figure out how many *additional* chairs would be needed. Reading, on the other hand, calls for dealing directly with a symbol system from the start. A message buried in symbols must be decoded by a separate set of learned skills before the message itself can be dealt with. This difference is most important at the kindergarten level, although it grows less important as children grow older.

THE NEED FOR ORDER

The nature of mathematics is tied in with human need to establish some kind of order in the environment so that people can function on the basis of reasonably reliable guidelines and predictions. The response to this need appears in some kind of mathematical conceptualization about time, space, quantity, number, distance, weight, and volume among all peoples. Actually, it is impossible to function intelligently or safely, with control over one's actions and movements, without some guiding generalizations and categories in these areas. Even animals seem to recognize up to four of their own young, objects, or humans.[1] So it is not surprising that studies of children in preliterate as well as industrial societies indicate that an ability to classify is fundamental to the growing human organism,[2] although *what* is classified and *how* it is classified may vary.

An early sense of mathematical order begins with the response by every human being to basic body rhythms, and then to sequence and pattern of body movement. We are all familiar with infants' and toddlers' responses to rocking, swinging, or repetitive kicking or dropping of objects. From body movement in space, children learn *inside* and *outside, up* and *down, above* and *below, on top* and *underneath, in front* and *behind.* From their parents, children learn about one nose, two eyes, five fingers and five toes; and in short order about numbers used as location finders on television sets, apartment doors, houses, and streets. They are offered half an apple, two cookies, or a whole ice-cream cone. A sense of mathematical conceptualization becomes part of their organization of thought before children arrive in kindergarten. Math learning in the kindergarten, like oral language learning, is thus an extension of natural beginnings, a development in breadth and depth from where children already are. They already know the quantitative value of *more* (mashed potatoes), *bigger* (car), *tiny* (crawling ant), and even the perception of *nothing* (no more) is evident in the reaction to an emptied glass of milk.

MATH CONCEPTS IN PRACTICE

Granted this is somewhat different for different children for reasons explained elsewhere, some sort of basis in body and family experience presents a level of readiness for further learning for all children. Thus kindergarten math learning does not really introduce children to totally unfamiliar processes which most are not ready to use

---

[1] D. R. Price-Williams, "Abstract and Concrete Modes of Classification in a Primitive Society," *British Journal of Educational Psychology,* 32, *962,* 50–61.

[2] K. Lovell, *The Growth of Basic Mathematical and Scientific Concepts in Children,* 3rd ed. (London: University of London Press, Ltd., 1964), p. 30.

effectively, as in reading. That the need to make order out of the environment serves as a continuous impetus to math involvement is clear from the following narrative.

Mrs. Powell, the teacher aide, was working with a group of children whose task it was to hang a line of string across the room on which to dry paper towels that had been used in tie dyeing. A problem intrinsic to the situation soon presented itself. How high should the line be? With much stretching of hands to heights they could reach, the children soon decided that the line must be high enough so that no one's head would hit the string. They had been considering their own heads, but soon realized that adults too had to go under the string. At that point they were a little stymied. Adults are taller than children, but how tall are they? How were they to find this out? The aide suggested a meeting to discuss the problem, and the teacher joined the group to help decide how high the line should be.

"Which teacher is the tallest?" asked Mrs. Perez. "You!" the children shouted.

"We'll let all the teachers stand near each other, and then you will be able to decide," said Mrs. Perez. She called the student teacher over, and she, Mrs. Powell, and Miss Levy stood next to each other in a row. There was a moment of silence as the children stared. Then, suddenly, in voices filled with shock and incredulity, they blurted out, "You're not the tallest, Mrs. Perez!" The adults agreed and allowed the children the time they needed to correct their childlike image of their teacher as the tallest person in the room. Then they and Mrs. Powell set about putting up the line so that the tallest, Miss Levy, could be accommodated along with the others. These egocentric children had begun to break down their naïve conception that height correlates with age and importance.

Sometimes the need for a mathematical solution to a problem is obvious to the children, as in the preceding, although often, as in that case, the answer is complex and they must stretch to grasp it. Just as often, the teacher helps the children recognize hidden math concepts inherent in a situation, as happened when some children collected icicles outdoors in same-sized bowls. When they returned to the classroom, the teacher encouraged them to compare the sizes of the icicles and later, after the icicles had melted, to notice how high up the sides of the bowls the water went. A better defined sense of large and small, high and low followed this experience.

In still another class, a mistake led to math learning. Amanda wanted to make a bed. She sawed two legs, and in her haste to see the bed completed, hammered the legs under the base before sawing the other legs. She measured a third leg from the first two, but her measurement included the base of the bed, and the third leg did not fit as the first two had. She needed help in perceiving that if she hammered the leg on the outside instead of under the base, the height would be the same as the first two. Fortunately, this almost six-year-old was not too fussy about how the bed would look aesthetically. She wanted a bed that stood on the floor, and if it did, her need was satisfied.

In a concise article, "What Math Might Be," the authors describe a number of common objects and point out their mathematical attributes.[3] With a ball there is

---

[3] Leroy C. Callahan and Toni Potenza, "What Math Might Be," *New York Early Education Reporter* (Fall 1979).

counting and *comparing* number of bounces and discerning *sizes* of balls. With a full paper bag there is consideration of *capacity,* the *number* of items the bag holds, and of *weight* that depends on *contents.* A bug, too, could be observed for *structure* and *speed* of movement. The teacher may well have other common objects around, with potential for math learning on the part of children and adults.

SPONTANEOUS LEARNING

The teacher's use of spontaneous events which present mathematical dilemmas or problems is also an important part of math learning in kindergarten. There is room, too, for deliberate use of situations in which the primary problem is not mathematical but from which it is possible to extract math challenges, as happened in the following episodes.

For the task of putting outdoor blocks away, Miss Alonzo has the children sit on piles of three, four, or five blocks until it is their turn to put blocks onto a cart and pull them into the shed. Indoors, Miss Hirsch distributes a few plastic dishpans into which the children may throw all the accessories they used in their floor block play. In go the wedgies (wooden doll-people); the small cars, trucks, buses, planes and trains; the lego pieces; the animals, and whatever else has been used to enrich the block construction. Then when all blocks are back on the shelf, small containers are laid out end to end, and the sorting process begins. All cars go into one box, all planes into another, all animals into another, and so on.

Miss Fitzgerald uses another method for a similar purpose. She is often the recipient of generous quantities of seashells from children back from weekends at the nearby seashore; or she collects and brings in for block accessories quantities of bottle caps, wooden beads, buttons, corks, or whatever she can scavenge from friends or business acquaintances. Before putting the collections out on the shelves, she sections off a table or part of the floor with tape and asks the children, "How would you put these down?" The children are likely to answer, "Big ones and little ones," or, "Coca-cola and Pepsi-cola," or any other obvious classification. Miss Fitzgerald defines spaces with tape for the categories but pushes the thinking further. "Can you think of another way?" she prods. The children struggle happily because they are so ready for this particular kind of challenge.

Math learning that is unplanned but spontaneously adapted, or planned and carefully executed, can indeed be meaningful, provided the teachers are aware of the mathematical implications. Those whose math experiences were heavily confined to paper-and-pencil tests and the right answers tend to block their math knowledge and cannot imagine how to use it with preliterate children. Knowing math as we use it does not necessarily mean being versatile in trigonometry, calculus, or statistics. It does not even necessarily mean always being accurate in the computational skills, although that is of some help. It does mean understanding that mathematics involves *systematic patterns of relationships* and that these patterns and relationships are *concepts,* to be grasped, not formulas, to be memorized.

Mathematical patterns and relationships take many forms, such as sets, one-to-one correspondences; equivalence, near equivalence; cardinal numbers, ordinal numbers; and geometric shapes. Math learning involves organizing, ordering, sequencing, and classifying of fundamental realities such as time, space, quantity, weight, volume, and the rest. The conceptual understanding of patterns and relationships is not nearly as formidable to children mentally ready to grasp them as poor math teaching—that is, mechanical teaching—has made them appear. In fact, it is so much within the realm of possibility for young children to understand many beginning math concepts without the use of words, let alone the use of pencil and paper, that Froebel saw it, too. The Froebelian kindergarten had a circle painted on the floor for games and for the chairs on which the children sat to sing and carry on their finger plays. On the tables were grids on which designs and games could be developed. The dishes and molds in the sand trays were in basic geometric shapes—round, square, triangular, and oval. Froebel's "gifts" (play materials) were spheres and cubes, cylinders and triangular prisms.[4] In 1892, Kate Douglas Wiggin discussed the mathematical properties of the gifts this way:

> The First Gift shows one object, and the children get an idea of one whole; in the second they receive three whole objects again, but of different form; in the third and fourth, the regularly divided cube is seen, and all possible combinations of numbers as far as eight are made (and so on up to the eighth gift).
>
> . . . As to the child's knowledge of form, size and proportion, . . . he knows, not always by name, but by their characteristics, *vertical, horizontal, slanting,* and *curved lines; squares, oblongs; equal sided, blunt and sharp angled triangles; five, six, seven* and *eight sided figures; spheres, cylinders, cubes and prisms.*[5]

LEARNING THROUGH EXPERIENCES

The development of floor blocks by Caroline Pratt decades later represents a continuation of Froebelian awareness of young children's readiness to learn mathematical concepts from the use of construction materials. But Pratt added a new dimension consistent with new knowledge. She released children from a predetermined sequence of learning that was typical of both Froebel and Montessori. Pratt believed in enabling children to discover the principles inherent in the environment through well-thought-out experiences, not through teacher-directed, preplanned lessons. The Pratt blocks, as indicated earlier, are based on a mathematical unit which happens to be a rectangle. The unit is doubled and quadrupled; and it is halved to become squares, pillars, and ramps. Long before the recent "cognitive" vogue that "taught" children shapes through rote recognition of pictures, generations of kindergarten children were gaining a genuine, three-dimensional knowledge of squares, rectangles, triangles, and circles through block play. In addition, they were learning about volume and depth, height and width, and area and space. From handling the blocks, they also learned weight, number, and the relationship of triangles to squares and rectangles, and of squares to rectangles. They learned all this not by *copying* mathematical shapes but as a by-product of building structures about their world. Inevitably, their buildings were based on mathematical relationships, as all architecture is. Piaget has helped us see very clearly that teaching young children abstract concepts without allowing them to see connections with the reality they know, or without allowing them to be actively involved in transforming materials and discovering principles from their operations is not only a waste of children's time but also turns them off from the true content. This is why we are opposed to stressing children's mechanical identification and recitation of numbers and recognition and labeling of shapes, even with musical accompaniment, clowns, and color as in *Sesame Street.* Such activity is not only an inadequate base for continued math learning and interest but a diversion from genuine math learning (aside from creating dependency on being entertained in order to "learn"). *Recognition* of numbers and shapes is not mathematics; understanding numbers and shapes *conceptually* is.

The following incident illustrates the conceptual process, observed by a mother:

> Intrigued with handling a small pile of stones, three-year-old Noel removes a single one and runs to place it on a surface near mother. "It's ONE!" he exclaims, then runs back to the pile, removes another *single* stone and runs to place it next to the first. As he surveys the two, he proclaims: "It's TWO!" As though propelled by an internal force Noel grasps still another single stone from the pile and rushes to lay it next to the first two. Taking a deep breath now as he looks at his work, and flushed with the excitement of fresh understanding, he announces: "It's THREE!" He rushes again to get yet one more stone, but placing it next to the impressive line of three, Noel becomes strangely quiet. He is quite puzzled for a moment. Then, after looking at the THREE and at the additional ONE, he concludes: "It's A LOT!" Noel is thus revealing both the limit of mathematical concept and a unique mathematical solution to a problem he is faced with.

Kindergarten teachers are not able to observe an individual child as closely as Noel's mother did, but they must be clear about what math concepts are and how children learn conceptually. Four- to six-year-olds are all too apt to use a word—e.g., *set,* or *half,* or *triangle*—and not understand the concept behind the word. All children normally engage in an active search for aspects of similarity in objects and events that will allow them to generalize. They can generalize by touch and physical perception long before they know the words for the generalizations they form. For example, when they have physically experienced oranges, balls of all sizes, and other things round, they extract the similarity—roundness—from among the various items that are round but different in color, texture, weight, or smell. When "round" is learned this way, *roundness* is recognized as a characteristic whether it appears in orange, grapefruit, golf ball, or balloon. The *word* "round" becomes useful then for dealing with the concept beyond the physical experiencing of it. Our numerical system is quite easy to master mechanically, and it is tempting for adults to impose their own cognitive structures on children in the effort to teach them math. But unless there is active exploration by children of the features of an object or circumstances so as really to learn the heart of its meaning, they may respond, as many children have when asked to name three things that are round, "A square, a circle, and a triangle." Children must have a physical, experiential base to underpin mathematical learning. For example, a *round* slice of an orange when slit and straightened invariably reveals a whole line of uniform *triangular* shapes; a *square* slice of bread can be cut into two *triangles* for a sandwich.

Let us see how teachers can help children organize and classify their experience. "Who walked to school today?" asks Miss Muzacki, and up come ten hands. "Let's get a unit block (or any other object of which there are many alike) for each child who walked to school, and let's stretch them out here along the floor beginning at this chalk line," says the teacher. The ten children each get a unit block and lay them end to end with precision and dispatch. "Who came to school on the bus?" Fifteen hands go up and fifteen blocks now get laid out on the floor parallel to the first ten and also beginning at the chalk line. "Which is more?" asks Miss Muzacki, and the children gleefully point to the "bus" line. "Yes, there are more blocks there. The line is longer," agrees the teacher. "Now let's make a list of the children who walked and the children who took the bus," she suggests and gets a long sheet of paper. Carefully she writes the name of each child in manuscript in columns headed *walk* and *bus*. Then she allows the children to check the relative lengths of the written lists. They are delighted to find that once again the bus list is longer. Miss Muzacki asks the *Walk* children to stand together at one side of the room and the *Bus* children to stand together at another. A child from each group counts, and then they all have the whole picture. More children rode than walked. Groups of children are those who do the same thing. Groups can be larger and smaller. Groups can have number; fifteen is more than ten; and longer is a variation of more.

Mrs. Johnson was interested in developing concepts of degree as well as of number. She also wanted to help children see the relation between three-dimensional and two-dimensional forms for expressing degree. As she supervised putting away the blocks, she would call out directives and often have the children take turns doing the same. "Build your piles no higher than four." "Take less than six." "Take no more than three to the shelf." "Put seven stacks together over here." "Put all the blocks that are half this size (quadrangle) over here; put all the blocks twice this size (unit) over here." "Can you find two that will make this shape (square)?" She encouraged the children to estimate where there were more blocks at different times during the pick-up—on the shelf or on the floor? Once, when she had asked all the children to make piles of five to bring to the block shelf, some children said, "We want to work together," and she agreed. In a short while four children came up to her and said, "We put away twenty blocks together." Some-what impressed, Mrs. Johnson asked, "How did you figure that out?" "Well," they said, "we know that two fives are ten, right? Like on our hands. So we figured four kids would be two tens and that's twenty, right?"

Perhaps Mrs. Johnson's children had had more math experience than some. Perhaps she had led them far along with her consistent awareness of math concepts. At the juice table, for example, she used stacks of blocks to show how many chil-dren preferred orange juice to apple juice. She then gave the children slips of paper in yellow and brown to tack onto a chart labelled "How many like orange juice?" "How many like apple juice?" The children clearly saw the stacks of blocks and the columns of colored paper that showed their preferences. Mrs. Johnson did the same thing with blocks and paper to chart smells the children preferred, colors they were wearing, or anything else of meaning to the children. But she never used more than two variables for them to deal with. "All the children who have little sisters put a yellow cube in this basket, all the children who have little brothers, put in a green cube. If you have a little brother and a little sister, what will you have to bring?" At one point she decided to let the children keep a record of the weather. She al-lowed every child a chance to crayon in yellow, gray, or blue in the calendar square to indicate sunny, cloudy, or rainy. When all had had a turn, the class looked back to sort out the colors and see how many sunny days they had had and how often it had actually rained during the time they were keeping watch. After months of experience with blocks and paper, Mrs. Johnson decided to use regular graph paper. She made as many vertical rows as there were children in the class and as many horizontal spaces as she needed for the task she had in mind. She gave each child a card with his or her name carefully written out in manuscript (she used the same manuscript style used by the first grades in her school). She asked the children to count the letters in their name, and then helped them order their names on the graph paper according to the number of letters. Jo headed the list, then came Ted, Jon, and Sue; Mary, Dina, and Alan; Scott, Delia; Thomas; Susanna, Beverly, and Antonio and so on up to Christopher. The children blocked in each letter of their names in a square on the graph so that the increasing lengths of names were easy to see. While this was ostensibly math, it worked to support consciousness of word boundaries as well.

Lists are great ways of grouping, which is another way of saying "creating sets." In Mrs. Ginn's class there were lists for lunch set-up; for who would take the wagon into the yard; for snack set-up, including who would pour juice and who would count cookies; for who would count the attendance cards that had been turned over on arrival so as to see how many cookies would be needed and how many children were going to need a place at table; and so on.

By spring the children in Mrs. Ginn's class were so accustomed to dealing with lists of children designated for some specific task, that they wondered if they could put all the lists together somehow. Mrs. Ginn was a bit taken aback by the request, but she put her head to the problem and came up with a job wheel. Around the outside of the wheel were the names of the jobs: lunch, snack, wagon, yard pick-up, calendar, and the rest. An inner wheel that turned had the children's names on its border: Danielle, Alina, Libby, Dimitrius, Todd, Sean, Keisha, and on and on. By now the children had some sense of the invariance of letters and of the look of their own names; they could recognize their names even when they were upside down on the wheel. They turned the wheel of names to match names with jobs, and soon learned to count ahead: "In four days from now it will be my turn to feed the fish," Alina said. "In one day I will be the one to count cookies," said Sean. To their understanding of grouping by task, they added knowledge of sequence and order. They used their counting knowledge appropriately to extend their experience of group living and they enjoyed every moment of it to boot.

In every kindergarten class there are many opportunities to strengthen math concepts. Place cards at lunch or snack are what Miss Avery knew strenthened one-to-one correspondence, and then she had the table arrangers put a cup at each place card to further extend this awareness. At the workbench she set up several lengths of wood periodically as samples, and as the children went for their wood, she asked, "Which size do you think you will want?" "Can you find a piece close to that size?" "Can you saw a piece like that?" "How will you decide if your piece is the same or about the same?"

Cooking, of course, is an endless source of mathematical computation and measurement. How many cups of flour in the recipe? How many cups of milk? How many eggs? Is a handful of nuts the same as a cupful? How many steps in the recipe? Did we take them all? How much did the rice swell and the spinach shrink? How much is left of the two lumps of sugar in Polly's cup of tea? "None." None—that's a very intriguing math concept!

Throughout all these experiences, children of kindergarten age are grappling with important concepts that foretell major shifts in their thinking stage. Do amounts remain the same under all and any conditions? Do length and weight remain the same? Does area? Volume? With the support of the right kinds of experiences, children will develop ability to conserve (to use Piaget's term), which means to recognize that matter remains constant regardless of change in form, shape, or color; and that the concept of number exists separate from the objects a number quantifies. During this period, too, children's constant speculation about mathematical concepts becomes interwoven with science, art, philosophy, logic, and mystery.

In a classroom where the teacher had set up a water basin with some liquid soap in it, two children came to the water table. Louis began to stir the water with an egg beater. To his amazement, lots of bubbles appeared. "Hey, where did the bubbles come from?" he asked aloud. "I wonder how many there are," commented Chris, the other child. Several children sensed the excitement over the bubbles and came to the table to watch. Louis gloated. "Look at all the bubbles!" Hadassah said. "There's infinity bubbles!" Louis answered. "Yeah, infinity is the biggest number." "No, it's not," said Chris. "It's when it goes on and on and on . . ." Louis thought for a moment and then said, *"One* was when the earth was made, *two* was when man came, *three* was when dinosaurs came. And *four* (pause)—we don't know about that yet."

A good math climate in the kindergarten is geared to stimulating inquiry and discussion. It also gives room to the imagination and provides possibilities for children to build concepts through their own activity and experience, through what Piaget calls performing "operations." All children are capable and ready for such involvement. Lovell, the British authority on math in childhood, suggests, however, that math in the kindergarten is best explored in small groups or individually, never as a whole class.

SPECIAL MATERIALS

Teachers may want to know about special math materials, such as the cuisinaire rods, Stern materials, or other systematically developed materials. If these are used by the children in their own style, not imposed by the teacher in formal lessons, they serve the same purpose as all other materials. Teachers must remember that it is easy for children to imitate; they like to please their teachers. But when they do this, it is a cheap victory in the end. Far more reliable for mathematical learning— and always available as a tool—are one's fingers. It is quite natural for children to count, add, and subtract with fingers, and considerable speed and accuracy can be achieved by practice of this ancient method. Another natural physical activity that promotes math learning is measurement (string or cloth) by "arm's length." Such measurement may not be precise, but it entails a *concept* of measuring—and a body concept as well.

There is no hurry about achievement in math; there need be no timetable. The kindergarten year can provide a rich general foundation basic to later specific achievement. In all the skills of the primary grades—reading, writing, and math— kindergarten experiences that use children's true readiness to full advantage work to support the next levels for which the children will be ready as time and experience help them mature.

REFERENCES AND FURTHER READING

BREARLEY, MOLLY (ed.).   *The Teaching of Young Children.* New York: Schocken Books, Inc., 1970.
CHURCHILL, EILEEN M.   *Counting and Measuring.* London: Routledge & Kegan Paul, Ltd., 1966.
CHURCHILL, EILEEN M.   "Young Children's Ideas about Number," in *The First Years in School,* published for the University of London Institute of Education by Geo. G. Harrap and Co., Ltd., 1967.
GLENN, J. A. (ed.).   *Children Learn to Measure; A Handbook for Teachers.* New York: Harper & Row, Pub., 1980. Special focus on "premeasure activities."

LEEB-LUNDBERG, KRISTINA. "The Block-Builder Mathematician," in Elisabeth S. Hirsch (ed.), *The Block Book*. Washington, D.C.: National Association for the Education of Young Children, 1975.

LOVELL, K. *The Growth of Basic Mathematical and Scientific Concepts in Children* (3rd ed.). London: University of London Press, Ltd., 1964.

LOVELL, KENNETH. *The Growth of Understanding in Mathematics: Kindergarten through Grade 3*. New York: Holt, Rinehart and Winston, 1971.

PEEK, MERLE. *Roll Over*. New York: Houghton Mifflin Company, Clarion Books, 1981. A counting book for children, with pictures and music suggesting action. Includes counting backwards.

ZASLAVSKY, CLAUDIA. "It's OK to Count on Your Fingers!" *Teacher* (February 1979). Explanation of technique.

ZASLAVSKY, CLAUDIA. *Preparing Young Children for Math; A Book of Games*. New York: Schocken Books, Inc., 1979. A detailed, instructive book dealing with games, materials, constructions, and familiar and novel activities bearing on mathematical experience.

17 Problems and Pleasures of Outdoor Play

Before discussing the many purposes and pleasures of outdoor play for kindergartners, we need to disavow some of the common misconceptions about the outdoor play period.

1. Playing outdoors is of secondary importance and is generally of incidental value in the total program. As one teacher expressed it, "The children used the playground every day at the beginning of the school year because they weren't able to do more settled work; but now there isn't time to go out, except once in a while."

Yet common sense as well as a medical point of view tells us that however successful the "settled work" in the classroom may be, a day in the life of young children must include the outdoors for their general health and well-being. Children need the fresh air wherever it exists, the physical exercise, the change of pace, and the reorientation in space just as much as they need the productivity of indoor activity. They welcome the general stimulation of the different kinds of play that are possible outdoors. In addition, the children's powers of observation of their environment, especially of nature, are often sharpened by going outside.

2. Children should play outdoors only in the *right* kind of weather—not when it is cold, not when it is hot, and certainly not when it's about to rain, nor when the wind is blowing. Thus, on a snow-bright sunny morning Mrs. Fiddler looks out of the window and says, shivering, "It's bitter out, children. Let's stay in."

But shortly after, Mr. Morrison, also a kindergarten teacher, opens his door onto the playground, sniffs the frosty air; observes the sparkling snow; and says invitingly to the children as he grabs his jacket and scarf, "We are going out!" Mr. Morrison feels the vigor with which the children run through the yard on the soft snow, enjoys seeing the glow on their faces, and loves hearing the joy in their voices as they shout freely after the period of relative confinement indoors.

Apparently some teachers are better able themselves to withstand variations in climate than are others. For reasonably objective criteria, it may be advisable to consult the school nurse or local pediatrician for standards of lowest and highest degrees of temperature bearable, velocity of wind, and the wisdom of play in direct sun during different seasons.

Even if it is too cold to stay out more than twenty minutes, there is still an advantage to the children in the physical release and stimulation of interest which they derive from outdoor play. Sober, stay-on-a-spot adults seem to forget that being active outdoors in the cold weather keeps one warm. Interesting exercises, a variety of races, or such activities as hopping and skipping, tiptoeing and stretching, pushing and pulling, can all be resorted to if the time is too brief for getting out equipment.

On the other hand, when it is very hot outdoors, brief periods in the shade of trees or shelters, use of sun hats, and water activities timed for the least oppressive periods of the day can play a reasonable part in weathering and adjusting to the heat.

But worse than the prejudice toward more than moderate heat or cold is that of parents and teachers toward wetness, mud, and snow. In some schools it is not uncommon for children to arrive at school dressed in raincoats, rain hoods, and boots; carrying umbrellas; and bearing a note for the teacher saying that the child should not go out. Too often no distinction is made between a cold downpour; a gentle, warm drizzle; and a soft, gray mist. The latter two can be very much (and harmlessly) enjoyed by children who are adequately protected.

Teachers often avoid going out if there are visible puddles, even if the children have boots and can put them on themselves. If they do go out, the children are strictly admonished to "stay away from the puddles!" This usually happens in the spring of the year when the air is warm and the shallow puddles could be safely inspected with sticks and certainly could be swept or bailed away by the children. The children themselves, of course, are drawn to these natural phenomena, and if they are not taught how to enjoy them with practical consideration to their health, they will defy adults and mishandle the situation whenever they can.

3. Teachers often have the notion that supervision can relax when children

are outdoors. Not infrequently two kindergarten teachers sharing a yard decide that the two classes can be together outdoors with one teacher only, while the other can use the time for a break or for clerical work. Or, if out together, the time seems a good one to catch up on local gossip and personal news. On the surface this seems reasonable. Is it sound?

Considerations of safety must control the ratio of adults to children, and a really large group needs more than one adult. Teachers of young children must always keep their eyes open for possible or imminent danger requiring quick wits and action. For example, a foolhardy child may be dashing to the top of a high-climbing apparatus, while another may become panicky when not sure how to get down. A mishap may occur when heavy equipment is shoved or shifted, or boisterous play may turn to a quarrel and cause tempers to rise and hands to reach for sticks, stones, or sand scattered on the ground. Children's safety requires no less than full supervision on the playground!

Secondly, children often need help with an outdoor project or problem which may be just as important as one in the classroom. Muriel Ward[1] describes a typical playground incident in which Jackie, pulling a wagon quite easily, takes no notice of a rock on the road and is stumped by his inability to proceed as before. Although persistent, Jackie is unable to understand the problem or the solution. "Shall we let him go on like a nonswimmer floundering in the water?" Miss Ward asks, and in

[1] Muriel Ward, *Young Minds Need Something to Grow On* (New York: Harper & Row, Publishers, 1957), pp. 18-19. Out of print, but worth trying to get at the public or college library.

answer tells how an observant teacher leads Jackie toward perceiving the obstacle. He thereby achieves a solution to the problem and success in his pursuit.

If the teacher is present and attentive during the outdoor period, he or she can find many things to enjoy and observe about the children and can contribute to many kinds of learning. It might be some shy, solitary child, normally inhibited in physical movement indoors, proving to be freer outdoors, even in responses to children, as in chumminess with a whispering partner inside a packing box. The teacher may take part in children's collecting and playing with leaves and seeds in season and may meet their intellectual curiosity about *what, where, and how much* in nature. Or the teacher may take the initiative and bring things to their attention. He or she may observe some children's special bodily skills and courage, and others' fears and hesitancies. The teacher can help the children learn to take turns with equipment and to consider the rights and safety of others under outdoor conditions, which are quite different from those indoors.

It is important to remember that the physical activity of kindergartners helps them gain overall control of their bodies, a control that is basic to their total development. Regular allotment of time for outdoor play must be made, and children should be encouraged to use the time constructively.

PHYSICAL EXERCISE AS AN IMPORTANT "FIRST"

Four-, five-, and six-year-olds must have a chance to exercise their growing muscles. They must have the opportunity to develop coordination and mastery of a variety of activities and skills, because the confidence and satisfaction that follow mastery of one's own body give a child a feeling of adequacy as a coping person.

It is difficult to hold children down when they go out, so eager are they to run and race, to push the heaviest packing case, to reach the highest rung, to balance breathlessly on narrow boards, to hold on tight with straining muscles to a rough, tough rope. Even on a raw, damp day with gray skies and drippy atmosphere, children can, if properly dressed, have an enjoyable, comfortable time in the vigorous exercise of hauling, carrying, and constructing; in tossing a ball; or marching to the rhythm of a drum.

Common playground activities that are hardly noticed by adults provide differentiated muscular activity. A five-year-old boy on a slide *runs* up to it, *climbs* the straight ladder (changing his visual perspective of ground below and around him), *adjusts* his balance, and changes his breathing and vision from the new height. He *lets go* of his whole body, experiencing motion and speed, and comes to a *stop* with a controlled jolt. Then he follows the same steps of running, climbing, sliding, and stopping (perhaps with some improvement) again and again. A little girl walks a straight line across a yard, one foot directly in front of the other with arms extended, and then walks the same distance backward. If we really observe the many activities in which kindergartners engage in a playground we see how essential such physical activity must be.

Observing a Kindergarten "Gym Period"

The kindergarten class in a small, uncrowded suburban public school in New Jersey rushed to the outdoor playground for their allotted twenty to thirty minutes of "gym" time. Instead of the conventional swings, slides, and wheel toys, this playground provided a clear spacious area with portable equipment for vigorous exercise and a variety of attractive items for games to choose from, as we shall see. The one teacher there at once conveyed the impression of being an interested, professional person. She knew how each piece of equipment is used by children, and she knew the individual children. She was also aware of age and of group needs.

First the teacher initiated a total group activity, jogging in line ("no passing!") on a large marked path—around and back. Then everybody chose an activity and changed it at will. The choice consisted of hitting a ball with a bat (the ball perched at a certain height on a pole); hitting a suspended ball with a tennis racket as it swung; hopping on a tick-tack-toe game; doing somersaults, handstands, and headstands on a large gym pad; and waiting for turns (this activity required teacher encouragement or help). In addition there was a good ball for bouncing, which was used by several children for brief periods, and a set of large, colorful plastic hoops for a still different kind of exercise. This was obviously an intense gymnastic period, but one to which the kindergartners responded fully and individually, not competitively. It was an invigorating workout for them!

THE ELEMENTS IN OUTDOOR ACTIVITIES

As was pointed out earlier, children are often admonished by adults to cover up against the wind, dress warmly so as not to feel the cold, and definitely to avoid slush or snow. Yet wind, cold, slush, or snow offers stimulating and valuable possibilities for perfectly healthy physical play and good sensory learning. Protection is needed, but the elements are not merely enemies to be avoided and fought. Of course, we are assuming that any conscientious teacher always checks the children's efficiency in buttoning top buttons, fastening hats, putting on gloves, and managing the latest footwear. With cap or kerchief over the ears and jackets zipped, even wind, if not too strong, can be well endured and put to exciting use. Children can make sails by running with a piece of cloth held high or fly kites, testing the force of the wind by moving with and against it. They can observe the direction of the wind through various kinds of evidence.

Rain can also contribute to children's enjoyment of the outdoors. Immediately after a rain there is apt to be much to do. There is the work (always fun) of wiping slides or bailing water out of the lower part of them, the splashy sweeping of the pavement, and the wiping of rungs and sitting surfaces. If children are allowed, they will discover and explore mud patches, collect worms to watch, gather stray stones to sink, and find floating objects on fresh, shallow puddles.

Snow also holds much fresh and even mysterious appeal for children, especially those who have recently come from a snowless country. It has such rich possibilities for physical activities and poetic experience that it should provide a limitless challenge to a kindergarten teacher. There is the exercise of shoveling or breaking up hard snow, the fun of bashing snowballs against a solid wall, and the joy of packing snow for snow sculpture and snow architecture. Children love seeing their teacher enjoy these adventures with them. But if the teacher regards such play as beneath him or her and merely puts up with it or limits it drastically, the play may have less freedom, energy, spirit, and initiative, and some children may refrain from the activity altogether, sensing the teacher's indifference to it.

THE OUTDOORS AND THE UNEXPECTED

A kindergarten teacher, sensing that the class was ready for a variation in schedule, suggested a walk around the block. As always, she hoped to find something interesting. Halfway around, the class did come upon a spectacular scene of tree pruning. Two strong workmen with noisy power saws and a huge truck were cutting off heavy limbs from a big maple. The smell of fresh wood, the piles of powdery sawdust, and the exposed interiors of the fallen branches fascinated the teacher, the assistant, and the children. The workmen welcomed the visitors and stopped their work to answer questions. The teacher took advantage of the occasion to ask for pieces of the smoothly sawed wood for the class, and the men, glad to be generous with discards, produced a stack of thick circles five inches in diameter. The children came back to their playground with a lasting treasure; the circles became a popular toy in construction and in dramatic play; and the children talked knowingly about the tree, the workmen, and the benefits of pruning. Placed on the block shelves, the circles remained in full use as accessories to building for years, popular with each succeeding class.

THE ATTRACTION OF CITY SIGHTS

From a wire-fenced kindergarten playground facing a city street, children do not see many trees, but they do have exciting moments noticing and playing out city scenes and modern city services. Telephone workers straddling smooth poles, ascending above the street, and perching dangerously while performing with wires; pipe and cable workers crawling into utility holes and disappearing below the street; truck drivers wielding huge steering wheels and manipulating screechy brakes—all these attract and hold the children's attention and stimulate interest in what is going on here and now.

Within the area of a city block or the space surrounding the school building, or even just the paved school yard, children can determine topography (flatness, depression, or rise in surface), they can investigate the surface (cement, stones, or soil), and the teacher can help them see the effects of heat, frost, and moisture on various structures. In their city school yard children can observe plants persevering

and peeking through cracks and crannies and small pockets of soil. They may also get acquainted with such outdoor animals as ants in a bit of earth, worms after rain, ladybugs on shrubs or fences, spiders in a quiet corner, or even the notorious gypsy caterpillar. All such uncelebrated creatures in their natural state can prove to be as interesting and exciting as expensive specimens in a zoo, tamed captives in a pet shop, or caged guests in a classroom. What the teacher must be aware of is the children's unprejudiced attraction and the teacher's own need (and subsequent satisfaction) to learn about such creatures and their environment.

Playing in a school yard almost any time of the year, city children can also get acquainted with birds that inhabit the region. Even in snowbound areas, there are the hardy English sparrows and starlings, the perky pigeons, and often the bright and noisy jays. Occasionally one can catch a glimpse of migrating wild fowl in flying formation passing overhead. In addition, intimate experience with wild birds can come from feeding them in winter. This is a simpler chore than is usually thought but must be maintained responsibly. Bird feeders can be obtained from pet shops or catalogues, or simple ones can be constructed,[2] filled with seeds, suet, or peanut butter, and attached to a tree, a post, a ledge, or a fence in the yard.

However, the teacher must be aware of the conservationist's approach and maintain a feeder once it's started, for birds lured to and dependent on it during winter will suffer if the food supply is removed. Encouraged by the teacher, the children can learn to be disciplined bird watchers. When they discover the empty

[2] Ted S. Petit, *Bird Feeders and Shelters You Can Make* (New York: G. P. Putnam's Sons, 1970).

feeders they will become providers as well. The sight of a bright, busy chickadee; a small, noisy woodpecker; or a nuthatch is worth standing still and silent for.

PLAYGROUND EQUIPMENT

To ensure satisfying outdoor play, it is desirable to have a variety of movable as well as stationary items that can be adapted to the children's ideas. Choices of equipment can be made from standard or newly adopted designs and materials. But in all cases they must serve a purpose children find worthwhile.

Often sedate grown-ups, being instinctively protective toward small, mobile children, feel horrified at seeing children in what appears to be a dangerous position —perching or moving on narrow rungs. But normally developed four- to six-year-olds do have the strength, agility, intelligence, and what is especially important, the reasonable caution to do such climbing. Those children who are at first fearful and inhibited become so fascinated seeing other children climb easily that they persevere until they accomplish the feat! Children gain control and confidence in this exhilarating activity much quicker than adults. And rarely do children attempt what is physically beyond their powers.

Climbing

Climbing is so important and interesting to all young children while they are growing in limbs and stature that equipment for this purpose must be provided. Lucky are the children who have a tree they can climb; but also interesting and challenging for climbing up and down and for straddling is a large log, or better still, several logs, although some may need to be smoothed or covered for safe sitting.

In addition to this natural equipment, it is good to have ladders in two or three heights to accommodate different children and different ranges of reaching. They can be wooden and aluminum ones, illustrating different qualities and weights of materials. Watch the children's professional body motions and expressions while carrying the ladders and placing them in a stable position against walls or fences. Observe, too, the dramatic play that results from the use of even as few as half a dozen ladders in the yard.

A secure wooden fence within the playground that is safe for climbing offers not only physical challenge to boys and girls but can lead to different kinds of dramatic play. If there is a storage house or a playhouse in the yard it is a good idea to have a permanently attached ladder from the ground to the roof. A strong flat roof with a railing is wonderful to climb onto and interesting to climb down from.

Doing It the Hard Way

The standard jungle gym used in many kindergartens is far from a strictly climbing apparatus to imaginative four- to six-year-olds. It is exhilarating to reach the highest point, to learn to stand without holding on, to survey the scene below, to get around the entire circumference, and to climb down, a process which is always surprisingly slower than climbing up. But once children learn to manage this with ease and it ceases to be a challenge, other materials should be made available to expand their use of the jungle gym.

Tommy looks like an ant when he drags a 12-foot walking board to the jungle gym. He attaches this board to the middle rung.

"Why are you using the *walking* board where children are *climbing?*" the student teacher asks Tommy.

"So I can walk into the jungle gym."

"But you can climb on it without attaching the board."

"It's too easy that way. Don't you know?" Tommy walks laboriously up the board, then climbs on higher and slides out of the jungle gym on the board instead of climbing down or using the sliding pole.

The space, stability, and structure of the jungle gym permit a variety of important physical activities. Four- and five-year-olds appreciate their own strength and enjoy lifting and pulling objects. Thus, a child-directed (although probably teacher-guided) game involving hoisting full pails by ropes onto a high shelf placed on the level parallel bars can hold the attention of many children and lead to constructive dramatic play. Filling pails with rocks or pebbles or mud or sticks and discovering the weight differences in materials calls for adjustment in coordination as children haul, pull, and hold heavy objects safely.

Creating a Private World

Children like to make their own special private places right in the midst of public activity, and a jungle gym is apt to be used as a ship, a house, a lodge, or a submarine with the addition of a few boards, perhaps a blanket, and a ladder entrance. Sometimes a few children take possession of it as if they were moving into a special house, a special world. Such a small group can be quite determined about excluding or even fighting off other interested users of the jungle gym. The teacher might be inclined to say to these few that the jungle gym is meant for all the children, that it cannot be monopolized by a few, and that in school we always share. But must we *always?* Can fair concessions not be made in order to allow small group activity, to support children's departure from the usual, and to nurture some independence without really depriving others? This is an important question.

Perhaps a teacher could instead say that the small group may use the jungle gym for a while and then give it up to others. This is quite possible if the teacher has enough other equipment in the yard for climbing, construction, and interesting and vigorous play. One such kind of equipment is cardboard packing boxes that can be obtained free from business establishments or homes. The educational potential of boxes has always been known to early childhood teachers, but a study by Carol Seefeldt brought into sharper focus their social value in inviting cooperative play; the physical and intellectual challenges of construction with boxes; the stimulation of imagination as children transform boxes into vehicles or other functional units;

and the way in which boxes serve to strengthen the developing space relationships of kindergarten-age children.[3] Let us not, therefore, overlook that ordinary box which can sometimes be picked up free from liquor store, grocery, and fruit market. A set of such boxes, sanded and painted, can be a very welcome addition to the large packing boxes that are already in the play yard and is certainly desirable if there are none of the latter. If enough of these boxes are obtained the children stack and build with them. They are good to jump from, and when arranged in a row with space between each, are fun for a stepping-over-space game. If holes are made at the ends of the boxes or hooks screwed in, ropes, leather, or wire can be used for coupling the boxes and making freight cars. A single box can be fitted with soft lining to become a nest.

Boxes also serve as accessories to the hollow outdoor blocks provided in many playgrounds for young children. Available from educational equipment companies, these blocks are large, hollow, and of uniform related sizes. Since they are larger ($5\frac{1}{2}'' \times 5\frac{1}{2}'' \times 11''$; $5\frac{1}{2}'' \times 11'' \times 11''$; $5\frac{1}{2}'' \times 11'' \times 22''$) and require more space for building and storing than the smaller, indoor unit blocks, they are particularly suitable for outdoor use. Being large they lend themselves to quick construction, which immediately stimulates dramatic play. And being relatively heavy, they provide considerable physical exercise and practice in coordination to the children who lift, carry, place, and replace the blocks as they use them. New materials for large-scale construction, such as Tri-Board, are also useful as separate building materials or in conjunction with blocks and boxes.

Swinging

A very common item of playground equipment is a set of swings. They afford satisfaction from rhythmic motion in space and a certain exhilaration from pumping and being pushed to a daring height.

However, the standard swings in a row are often a hazard to young children, who have no judgment about speed-space-motion dynamics and run up to the back of the swing the instant another child is propelled in the air. They often do not hurry to escape the swing on its forceful return. The extra burden this places on the nerves of a conscientious teacher is not always worth the passing pleasure of such swinging.

Therefore, if possible the teacher should provide for some safe swinging activity, such as on a wide-limbed tree or a substitute for the same type of structure. When a rope is flung across a strong limb away from the trunk and an inner tube from an automobile tire is securely attached to it, the children can explore every possibility, style, and technique of swinging. The teacher might also observe that some children show an excessive urge to swing—doing it on and on, oblivious to all else; in which case the teacher's encouragement or help may be needed to lead the child to try other diversions as well.

---

[3] Carol Seefeldt, "Boxes Are to Build—A Curriculum," *Young Children* (October 1972).

Sliding

Another common piece of playground equipment is the slide. Slides are appealing for the experience of momentary exhilaration at the top, the brief fun of swift descent, and the easy use of the whole body. Sliding is often shared fun when a group uses it for a dramatized trip, with rhythmic controlled movements and planned destinations leading to or combining with other activities and sometimes with other equipment. No healthy, lively five-year-olds conform consistently to the necessary safety rules (feet first, no pushing). They may use different ways of reaching the top, may experiment with legs or arms to change the course, may invent difficulties and obstacles, or may add adventure by mere disobedience to a rule. Given a chance and some materials and encouragement, children will often extend the ordinary slide by adding an extra climbing structure to get to it, or they will expand its function by placing a stack of tin cans at the foot. They laugh uproariously at the clatter and scattering of the cans as they come down.

In one class, adventurous kindergartners added excitement to their use of the slide by letting a ball roll off the top, bounce, and continue rolling in an unpredictable direction. Each child would follow a ball on the slide. After a while a wheel was let loose from the top of a slide and with proper precaution to bystanders, a small stone. Then the children observed the relative speed and sound of the large ball, the small wheel, the small stone, and a boy of average size going down the steep incline of a slide!

Providing there is supervision for safety, seesaws and the making of seesaws with boards and sawhorses of different heights enable children to enjoy another dimension of space and experience a sense of balance, of weight, and of gravity. Watch Philip and the part played by the fulcrum of the seesaw in creating balance. He is a restless child who easily gives up anything that seems demanding, and according to his mother and his teacher, he does not concentrate well. Here he is eager to use the seesaw alone. With caution in his approach, arms extended, head inclined, feet moving gingerly, and almost breathless concentration on his face, Philip walks up the grounded side of the seesaw with measured sliding steps until he reaches the precise middle, when the uplifted side is about to go down from the weight of his deliberate tread. Then, catching his breath, he runs down the rest of the slide.

Kenny was tiny compared to many of his husky classmates and had a difficult time straining and pushing in order to make himself heavy enough to go down on a seesaw when any other child sat on the other end. The only time he enjoyed a seesaw ride was when there was a pack of children on either end. He worked on the seesaw alone and made a weighing scale out of it by placing large blocks on one end, then a single block and various objects on the other. He thus had an interesting experience controlling weights and balances, illustrating the variety of purposes to which a piece of equipment can be put when a child is using his head as well as his muscles. (See the section in the science chapter, "Children's Play Leads to Physical Science Discoveries.")

INNOVATIVE OUTDOOR EQUIPMENT

What about the modern equipment that is appearing in playgrounds throughout the land? Ivalee McCord describes imaginative use of natural terrain and of different construction materials such as brick, rope, styrofoam, and wood of different kinds in one such playground.[4] Sculptured jungle gyms, artistic water tables, a sandy area at the end of a ravine with short logs to sit on, and concrete pipes for underground climbing afford activities that are stimulating at many levels. In an illustrated free booklet, "Tires Are Tools for Learning," Mabel Pitts gives clear, simple instructions for making sturdy pull toys, tunnels, supports for bouncing boards or seesaws, and many other items out of tires. The author also discusses storing tires, ways of

---

[4]Ivalee H. McCord, "A Creative Playground," *Young Children* (August 1971). Good photographs show the playground in use.

securing them in place, painting them, and obtaining tires in different sizes for various purposes.[5] A tested and approved playground, including large play animals and made entirely of old tires, can be ordered at relatively low cost from an ingenious builder who recognized the resiliency, safety, and availability of discarded tires and developed a major playground material as a result.[6] Very large inner tubes have been used successfully with handicapped children as stimuli to physical activity and dramatic play.[7]

Major equipment companies are involved in working out new forms and structures that will enable children to venture safely forth and test their strength and coordination. We are at long last leaving behind the static concept of playgrounds, and teachers should be open to the new possibilities. Not everything new will endure, of course, but new equipment is worth examining.

Inviting Travel

Since transportation is an outstanding aspect of our life, young children make important use of actual items of transportation or of props that symbolize transportation for dramatic play. Durable wagons that have loading and passenger capacity are put to ingenious use and can involve several children and different kinds of equipment and materials. A few tricycles in good condition are valuable in the yard for trips, races, stunts, and sometimes for "harnessing" to a wagon. A scooter is fine for practicing balance, propulsion, and self-direction. The wheelbarrow gives children a sense of weight and balance, power of muscle propulsion, and basic power of the wheel.

If an old rowboat can be salvaged for the kindergarten play yard, its constant occupancy can be practically guaranteed. Of course, such an item should be safe from splinters or nails and have a coat of paint; a steering wheel that can turn, securely attached, would add to the boat's usefulness. Children make of it a tug, a rescue ship, an ocean liner, or even a rowboat, especially if oars are provided. In lieu of a real boat, any sturdy, safe, stationary box in which some seating space can be devised will also speedily ply deep and dangerous waters. In one community a parent in a cooperative kindergarten contributed from his place of business two excellent long, deep wooden boxes. These were painted bright colors, and they proved to be most popular for both land and water journeys.

Although children enjoy manageable, testable transportation items, they are also concerned with less concrete and less understandable means of transportation, such as aircraft for celestial navigation and capsules for orbiting through space. But here simple props, including boxes, small boards, perhaps colored chalk for marking the "instrument panel," and helmets or improvised space suits will suffice. The rest of the construction, operation, and success is provided by the children's imagination

---

[5] Mabel P. Pitts, *Tires Are Tools for Learning* (Austin, Texas: State Department of Public Welfare, 1974).

[6] William Weisz, Tirecraft, 475 President Street, Brooklyn, N.Y. 11215.

[7] William T. Taylor, "Tube Play," *Young Children* (September 1969).

as they talk about and play at the most advanced kind of transportation of the moment or at some extraterrestrial travel.

Creating Motion

A ball, which is perhaps *the* universal action toy, is a must for the kindergarten playground. Although a good rubber ball of a size fit for grasping with both hands is very useful for preschoolers, balls that are different in size, color, texture, weight, and composition can also provide exciting exercise. With a ball, children can cause the motions of rolling, twirling, spinning, throwing, falling in various directions, and catching and bouncing at various speeds. Games with balls can be traditional, individual, group, or experimental. Lightweight bicycle wheels or hoops are good for rolling or running with, and they give the children experience in guiding motion. Blown-up inner tubes and old automobile tires are also useful for this purpose, although teachers will need to judge the safety of heavy rolling tires and caution the children accordingly. In this connection spinning tops provide play that goes beyond mere diversion to become an investigation of speed, motion, and visual impression both outdoors and indoors.

Other Attractive Equipment and Activities

A sandbox with equipment for sifting, straining, shaping, measuring, and counting is a must for kindergarten children. The utensils for the sandbox are often better found among kitchen cupboard discards than in a toy store, since kitchen tools are generally sturdier, of better size, and more interesting and durable than commercial sand toys.

When no sandpit or sandbox is available, or even when it is, it is good—very good—to fence or rope off an area for plain digging in the dirt if a little ground space is available. Children two to eight years of age everywhere in the world love to dig. This is different from playing with clean and measured sand. You dig—and never come to the bottom; you fill different containers and holders and feel the weight; you probe the earth with a stick or finger; you make mounds or holes or tunnels and find something alive, as the child does in digging for roots in Chapter 2. Diggers have a relaxed, communal attitude; digging appears with each generation of children. Must we defend the value of this outdoor activity?

Another ordinary item interesting to children is a bag. Bags made of paper, burlap, or other kinds of cloth can be used not only as practical containers but for different kinds of play and investigation outdoors, such as determining strength and durability, volume, and effect of water and weather.

A smooth, clean oil drum with or without a bottom is a challenging and easily manageable piece of equipment, too. So are ropes—once their danger is clearly recognized by adults and children and their use supervised. They are a popular, versatile addition to any play yard. Ropes can be used to separate space, for example, by roping off an area for gardening or a game; to provide pulling power; to connect things by tying them together; and to serve as handles when handles are needed.

Gardening

The oldest activity appropriate for kindergartners is gardening. Either in the yard, if there is room enough, or in earth-filled tubs in the playground or on the roof, children can engage in preparing the soil, handling seeds or tiny seedlings, nurturing and caring for the growing plants, and eventually they can behold the results. Whether the plant is quick-growing lettuce or radishes to eat, bright marigolds to enjoy, or even grass with dandelions to feed an animal, the meaning of gardening will come through to the children. They will sense the mysterious force of growth as they perceive that human responsibility for a plant helps the emergence of flower, fruit, or vegetable. For a fuller discussion of gardening, see the chapter on science.

HANDLING MISHAPS

In addition to being aware of the many possible activities involving playground equipment, the teacher also needs to be aware of possible abuses of equipment. Children and equipment need respect. Occasionally there are mishaps in the playground, and the teacher must be prepared to handle these calmly. In this connection we advise a conveniently located first-aid kit. It should contain tweezers or sterile needle to remove splinters, nonstinging antiseptic solution, sterile cotton to clean a superficial cut or bruise, band-aids for satisfying display as well as hygienic protection, and whatever else may be advised by the school nurse, pediatrician, or principal.

Although an occasional kindergartner may resist any emergency medications from a teacher, most children are pleased by the personal attention and special emergency devices. In one situation a teacher obtained an ice cube for a bump on the head, and the injured child was so intrigued by handling the ice totally aside from its therapeutic use, and so envied by the others, that there was a veritable epidemic of bumped heads for a few days!

That children may enjoy the drama of a minor disaster more than they fear its consequences is well shown by that classic child heroine Madeline, whose appendectomy was the envy of her class. However, while children generally will not attempt to do what they cannot do comfortably, and therefore safely, they do not always use good judgment and may not be sufficiently aware of inherent danger in the tasks they undertake. Teachers must be watchful of potentially dangerous equipment that may be too high, or have hinges that may catch fingers, or be heavy enough to hurt small toes. Without hovering anxiously over children, adults can foresee the consequences of poorly balanced boards or crowded climbing apparatus tumbling or being dropped by children unaware of what or who is below. Children can be taught to be reasonably cautious and considerate without impeding their sense of freedom seriously. We must all be reminded that safety is more effectively taught by practice on the part of both children and adults than by mere admonitions.

Yard Upkeep

What exactly is involved in the upkeep of a play yard? Any yard or play-ground can get messy from the elements overnight and can confront the children on their arrival with slippery slushy snow, splashy puddles, stray objects blown in, and even broken bottles thrown in from the street. The yard can get messy from activities and be full of spilled sand, strewn papers, and forgotten containers. Clearing a yard when this needs to be done can be appealing and interesting to kindergartners. Sweeping the paved part or raking the grass and dirt part, pushing water toward the drain, shoveling snow, and even collecting trash should be initiated by the teacher as a valid school activity demanding a professional attitude. The activity will arouse interest in the proper tools and utensils, provide stimulating large-muscle activity, and give an understanding of various practical problems. It is therefore important to have one of each kind of outdoor clean-up tool and a place to keep them. This does not mean that the teacher and children must take entire responsibility for cleaning the playground. But it does mean that the teacher must recognize the usefulness and interest of such work to children and give them the opportunity and encouragement to do it.

If outdoor equipment needs to be stored, different ways of stacking; fitting and using space; or carrying, rolling, wheeling, or dumping objects can challenge active four-, five-, and six-year-olds.

When a child says, "We put everything away—see!" it is said with pride. Children also like being inspectors and detectors of damaged equipment. "This block has a crack, see, teacher? It can give you a splinter!"

"Thank you, Roscoe, let's put it aside to be fixed."

"Hey, there is a big nail in the red barrel. Tell the teacher we need a hammer to pull it out."

"I saw broken glass in the playhouse. That's dangerous."

Those are typical four-, five-, and six-year-olds' comments, clues to children's readiness for responsibility. Perhaps all teachers need to recognize that saving, repairing, and protecting equipment means "War on waste," an approach that is becoming increasingly widespread as necessity forces us to face the reality of decreasing resources.

BRINGING THE OUTDOORS IN

Once in a while one meets a kindergarten class which has no outdoor period in its program. The reasons may be lack of a play yard close by, reluctance of teachers to curtail important indoor activities, lack of playground equipment to make the outdoors interesting to children, or insufficient help for the teacher to get the class ready to go out. In that case, while efforts are being made to make at least occasional outdoor play possible, the teacher might also try to obtain some appropriate facilities indoors. The classroom automatically precludes certain rough outdoor play, but if the room is large enough there can be a permanently placed piece of climbing apparatus. In one kindergarten with a wide climbing structure yet enough space left for a music period or for dancing, with a large area for table work and blockbuilding and a cozy library corner, the children use the climber all the time for active play, for dramatic games, and for doing "tricks." The teacher reports that the climber does not interfere with the children's interest in or attention to other activities.

Some classrooms have rope-ladders hung unobtrusively in the room, some a fireman's pole for sliding down from a balcony. Some have suitable areas for bouncing a large ball. Some teachers make it a point once in a while to bring in some equipment for physical exercise if the children have to miss vigorous outdoor play because of inclement weather. Such equipment may consist only of some boards and a few strong wooden boxes which can be arranged to allow sliding, jumping, bouncing, balanced walking, or other "tricks." Because all such equipment is unstructured, requiring no formal instruction or rigid organization, the children will use it freely with initiative and ingenuity, developing confidence as well as muscular skill and coordination.

The more we watch children the more we see that whether indoors or out, they need to stretch their growing muscles and feel their budding strength. Early childhood is a *physical* time. Children must have the opportunities they need to strengthen their muscular skills. Besides, physical activity is indispensable for intellectual learning, as was pointed out in Chapter 15. But in addition to outdoor equipment, outdoor elements can be brought indoors for temporary fun and learning: a pail containing rain water, a tray of snow, a pile of windblown seed pods in the fall, freezing-cold icicles in winter, or a limb of a tree broken off by a storm. Such outdoor items can be observed even more closely when brought in. Teachers will surely think of other outdoor items in their localities that would bring adventure and innovation from outdoors in.

REFERENCES AND FURTHER READING

AARON, DAVID, with WINNAUER, BERNICE. *A Creative Approach to Play Spaces for Today's Children.* New York: Harper & Row, Pub., 1965.

BAKER, KATHERINE READ. *Let's Play Outdoors.* Washington, D.C.: NAEYC, 1966.

FRIEDBERG, PAUL. *Handicrafted Playgrounds.* New York: Random House, Vintage Books, 1975.

HEWES, JEREMY. *Build Your Own Playground.* Boston: Houghton Mifflin Company, 1975.

McCORD, IVALEE H. "A Creative Playground," *Young Children* (August 1971).

New York City Board of Education. *Operation New York.* Curriculum Research Report (110 Livingston Street, Brooklyn, N.Y. 11201), 1970.

PETIT, TED S. *Bird Feeders and Shelters You Can Make.* New York: Putnam's, 1970.

PITTS, MABEL P. *Tires Are Tools for Learning.* Austin, Texas: State Department of Public Welfare, 1974.

RUDOLPH, NANCY. *Workyards.* New York: Teachers College, Columbia University and London: London Teachers College Press, 1974.

SEEFELDT, CAROL. "Boxes Are to Build—a Curriculum," *Young Children* (October 1972).

STONE, JEANNETTE GALAMBOS, and RUDOLPH, NANCY. *Play and Playgrounds.* Washington, D.C.: National Association for the Education of Young Children, 1970.

TAYLOR, WILLIAM T. "Tube Play," *Young Children* (September 1969).

WARD, MURIEL. *Young Minds Need Something to Grow On.* New York: Harper & Row, Pub., 1957.

CHILDREN'S
PUMPHOUSE
DAILY
SCHEDULE

8:00 – 9:30 – – – – Free play
9:30 – 10:30 – – – – Group 1
                       Outside play
                       Group 2
10:30 – 11:30 – – – – Group action
                       Group 1
                       Group action
                       Group 2
                       Outside play
11:30 – 12:00 – – – – Clean Up
12:00 – 1:00 – – – – Lunch
1:00 – 2:00 – – – – Story hour
2:00 – 4:00 – – – – Nap time
4:00 – 4:30 – – – – Snack
4:30 – 5:30 – – – – Free play

18 Classroom Management

SCHOOL ENTRY AND ADJUSTMENT

Children's formal introduction to a public kindergarten comes at the initial registration, when their parents produce the certificate of their birth, showing not only the date of a child's entry into the world and their family but his or her legal name—William Henry Howell or Mary Elizabeth McCarthy. Up to this time, a child may have been Billy, Betsey, Ginnie or Junior. Katherine Ann Porter describes the reaction of one little boy to this experience.

> All the children had names like Frances and Evelyn and Agatha and Edward and Martin, and his own name was Stephen. He was not Mama's "Baby," nor Papa's "Old Man"; he was not Uncle David's "Fellow" or Grandma's "Darling" or even Old Janet's "Bad Boy." He was Stephen.[1]

[1] Katherine Ann Porter, "The Downward Path to Wisdom," in *The Leaning Tower* (New York: Harcourt Brace Jovanovich, Inc., 1934), p. 93.

Some schools ask for the child's nickname along with the given name. Even so, there is much that is unfamiliar in the new surroundings, which causes a child some worry. For instance, in a large school, which to a child's eyes seems even larger than it is, there may be many doors to open and go through; sometimes the doors all look alike. What if one opens the wrong door? How can one be sure which is right? Children worry about bathroom facilities that appear unfamiliar or whether they have the right to use all the toys. Worries about getting home safely and finding home and family intact are not uncommon for children of this age. Many kindergarten children have questions which they cannot bring themselves to ask in the early weeks because they do not feel sure yet that they can fully trust the teacher.

Home Visits

A great help in the initial adjustment to school is acquaintance with the teacher beforehand, and this can be accomplished in several ways. One way is for the teacher to visit each child at home in the few days allotted for preparation before the official opening of school. Facing the teacher in one's own home, surrounded by the familiar and protective, a child finds it easier first to fit the teacher into a known and familiar world and then to make the transition to the school world. While time is being allotted to this practice in some schools, it is by no means universally practiced.

Nevertheless it remains desirable for a child to feel close to a teacher in a more intimate fashion than the initial impact of the total class will allow. Therefore, if individual home visits are impractical, small groups of children, and even individuals, can come visiting at the school on a planned schedule before the formal opening. Some schools also encourage such visiting in the spring before admission. Other schools stagger the entry of children during the first week so that the teacher can get acquainted with no more than a handful of fresh and eager faces each day. Closer attention to these few makes them feel especially noted and accepted. However it is done, it is wise to allow for a one-to-one relationship between the teacher and each child before plunging into the overwhelming confusion of faces, materials, and regulations involved in school entry.

Proceeding Slowly

Most children start kindergarten having very little experience with rules, and the teacher's introduction of various necessary class rules may seem confusing to them. It is best during the opening weeks to be gradual in introducing new rules as well as new materials to kindergarten children. They need some time to absorb the first new impressions, new ideas, and new experiences before being confronted with more newness. They will show pride in remembering and chagrin in forgetting what is expected of them. And they are sure to have much experience with both of these feelings!

Adjustment may be slow for some children, painful for others, and no problem at all to still others. In his story "The First Day of School," William Saroyan[2] describes six-year-old Jim, who is fascinated with a child's defiance of the no-gum-chewing rule. He watches the teacher's detection of "the crime," her reaction, and his classmate Hannah's courageous walk to the wastebasket to dispose of the gum. He never dreamed there could be such suspense and confrontation—school wasn't bad after all! But for many children the first day of kindergarten in a regular school is a day of worry and confusion about all the unknowns. When asked by a visitor why he was crying (on the first day of school) a kindergartner blurted out, "I don't know what 'recess' is." Many kindergartners will have anxiety about what's expected of them; and some will panic at separation and cling desperately to the parent. Occasionally, teachers must allow a parent to stay a few days while a hesitant child builds bridges into the new independence.

Some young children may still depend on a special toy to help them adjust. They either bring something from home to hold on to or stake a claim to something attractive on a shelf at school. Such a child likes to have this possession—a little toy horse perhaps, a rubber ball, or a small plastic car—in pocket or hand for security, support, or some private need. At school there are generally rules about where playthings must be kept or rules about not bringing toys from home. But a sensitive teacher can make temporary exception to such rules where it is obvious the child has a definite need for the little inanimate friend. In time, the teacher may tell the child that the toy car, which belongs in school, will be on the shelf for him or her *and* the others, all of whom will eventually take turns. The teacher may in time encourage a child to let others hold and touch the special possession, leading to the eventual suggestion that personal treasures might be left at home to wait for the little owner and brought only if they can readily be shared by all in the way a record or a book can. At the same time, by noting what other materials a child prefers and what use he or she makes of them, the teacher tries to extend the child's field of activity and satisfaction. Adjustment depends not only on age, for there are "young" and "old" kindergartners, but on previous experience with adults, children, materials, and learning. There is no precise time schedule for adjustment of any one individual child, but a sympathetic, helpful teacher can make the period shorter and in some cases smoother. For most groups, two to three months is the reasonable time span in which full, comfortable acquaintance with the program can be realized.

PLANNING THE CURRICULUM

No matter how well-intentioned a teacher may be, the success of her or his curriculum in the long run will depend heavily on the amount and quality of planning invested in the task. Although the role of the teacher has variously been described

---

[2]William Saroyan, "The First Day of School," in *Little Children* (paperback ed.) (London: Faber & Faber, 1964). Also in Robert D. Strom, *Parent and Child in Fiction* (Belmont, Calif.: Wadsworth Publishing Co., Inc., 1977).

as parent substitute, friend, instructor, or guide, we prefer in this chapter to focus on the teacher as *organizer*—organizer of experiences which enable children to grow and learn. Paradoxically, the more we believe that children should function with independence and creativity, the more organizing and planning have to be done.

The ideal kindergarten will look, after a while, as though the children are running it themselves, with the teacher not even obviously in view. But this can only happen when careful provision has been made for the children to get along pretty much on their own, when the stage has been set, so to speak, for the children to work and play productively without excessive dependence on the adult. The authors are guided in their view of classroom organization and management by two underlying assumptions: (1) Children and adults who live together in a limited space for several hours each day must have conditions set up that make the mechanics of living together as comfortable and smooth as possible without denying individual rights to anyone; (2) children's needs must be met if all concerned are to enjoy living together and are to gain from the experience. Consequently, not only must special needs of group living be planned for, but age-level needs and individual needs as well. In addition, the nature of the curriculum, which concerns itself with intellectual growth, social learning, and emotional and physical satisfactions, calls for special provisions other than those involved in the mechanics of sharing space and supplies.

ANTICIPATING LONG-RANGE NEEDS

Before school starts in the fall, a teacher needs to do basic planning and preparation, some of it with the administrator, to underpin the entire year's work. Every child needs a chair to sit on and a spot at a table to work. Every child needs a place to leave clothing and any precious possession he or she wishes to safeguard. Toilet and water facilities must be available, and if not in the room, as is the case in old buildings, a teacher must know exactly where they are and just how the group will have access to them. Storage space for the quantities of materials to be drawn on during the year, as well as storage space for children's work-in-progress, has to be accounted for. Supplies in sufficient quantity and variety, especially of expendable materials, plans for changing supplies throughout the year (perhaps by exchange with another teacher, perhaps by new purchases), and specific locations in the open for supplies likely to be in use each day must all be provided. And of course conditions of health and cleanliness have to be met with proper tools, equipment, and practices. In addition, if the kindergarten is part of a large institution, the teacher must know just how her or his special group is expected to fit into the larger organization of the school: Will they share a yard; is there a set time for recess; does a music teacher come at certain times on certain days; are there areas considered out-of-bounds within the building? Regulations concerning trips and unexpected expenses (as when the goldfish must be replaced or rabbit food is used up), fire-drill regulations, and entrances and exits that the class may use must be determined.

Not until the overall details for the year are settled can a teacher get closer to the daily program and think about the particular details.

Even then, before deciding what to do on the first day and thereafter, there is planning. The neighborhood and school grounds must be familiar to the teacher, for determining what possibilities exist for the children's explorations. The time and nature of arrival and departure, snack and lunch, and rest must all be known so that they can be guides around which to schedule. Is there a piano and space for rhythms in the classroom or must one use the gymnasium at set times? Is the room to be vacated for another teacher in a split-session school, or will the class have complete freedom to use its room in its own way?

Once these basics are determined, a teacher is ready to think about her or his unique role in organizing for the children.

ROOM ARRANGEMENT AND ORGANIZATION

A rather down-to-earth study of physical environments in preschools (including day care centers, Montessori schools, and Head Start programs) points out that

> Irrespective of type of program three dominant factors seemed to relate to the quality of all the preschools observed: (1) the organization and utilization of physical space; (2) the child's access to materials and the ways in which they are used; and (3) the amount and type of adult-child interaction.[3]

Yet there is no single superior arrangement of a kindergarten room, although suggested arrangements abound. Any arrangement will be determined first by the amount and kind of stationary cabinets and other items, then by the size and shape of the room, by the availability and type of portable equipment, and most important of all, by the program the teacher envisions as meeting the needs of four-, five-, and six-year-olds. Since the first few limitations are usually beyond the teacher's power of determination, let us concentrate on the way in which children's needs affect the organization of a room.

Young children are physical; we have been saying this all along. Are there provisions in the room for physical activity? Some kindergartens have climbing apparatus right in the room; some bring outdoor blocks, boards, and ladders into the room during inclement weather; and some have space for running, skipping, and leaping. Others, in confined space, must rely on jumping up and down, stamping, stretching, twisting in place, or using balance boards.

Kindergarten children are social. Are there areas where small groups and larger groups can enjoy companionship? Is there a nook where a child can retreat and be alone? Room arrangements of chairs and tables, and of movable cabinets and screens, set out to provide alcoves or sweeping space will reflect the recognition of changing needs for sociability or solitude.

[3] David E. Day and Robert Sheehan, "Elements of a Better Pre-School," *Young Children* (November 1974), 15.

Young children love to play, to use materials, to make things. Is there provision for this? Where can they build with wood and blocks? Is the woodwork bench sufficiently removed from the library corner that the banging of a hammer does not pound into the ears of a child who wants to look at a book? Are the block cabinets arranged so that several children can have access to the shelves at one time, and is the floor space in front of the cabinets sufficient for several children to build at once? Easels must be near light and if possible water; mops and sponges should be close enough that children working with wet materials (paint, clay, water, finger-paint) do not have to drag these supplies clear across the room and over the block builders' feet in order to use them as needed. Odd materials, such as dress-up clothes, need hooks or shelves or even orange-crate closets—but they must have a place. A "prop box" or two, or an old-fashioned decorated toy chest (to be found in someone's attic), can hold assorted items to enhance the play.[4]

Uniqueness

Thus a room arrangement that is to allow for the fulfilling of children's needs requires careful estimation of just what needs the children who come there have. Then, given the conditions available in a particular school, a teacher adapts these quarters in the best way possible so that the children's physical needs can most comfortably be met. Sometimes the best use of a room is not discovered with the first try at arrangement. A teacher, especially a beginner, has to be prepared in the first weeks of school to watch the children in action to see if changes are necessary. It is true that children enjoy the security of knowing where everything is, but if a change has to be made, a discussion with the class as to what the stumbling blocks and the reasons for the change are will make them feel involved and will hasten their cooperation.

Organizing for Autonomous Behavior

A teacher's attitude toward children and his or her philosophy of education affects the way in which the placement and distribution of materials and supplies are conceived. If the teacher believes that these are little children who are likely to waste supplies, spill liquids, and harm themselves and others, he or she will cautiously dispense all items for their use from a locked cabinet under carefully controlled conditions of supervision. But if the belief is that it is important that children develop competence and efficiency in the handling of materials, and that they need freedom to express and develop feelings and ideas with and through materials, a teacher is more likely to have supplies available in an orderly fashion on open or otherwise accessible shelves. Rules for use—no obvious waste, return what you do not use, no hogging, no misuse of material (clay is not to be stamped underfoot and paint may not be applied to walls or faces)—are certainly in order. But it may cost the loss of some paper, clay, or even a tool before the learning takes full effect.

---

[4]Judith Bender, "Have You Ever Tried a Prop Box?" *Young Children* (January 1971).

Trusting children, albeit spelling out the rules for respectful use of materials, a teacher helps them to take pride in their competency. In time the children actually help each other learn how to share and use constructively the available materials in the classroom. It is far better to accept the challenge of teaching children how to handle materials and allow them free access to these for their individual, creative use than to dispense materials as if doing a child a favor by doling out a piece of drawing paper and a box of crayons and inadvertently teaching stinginess. In the long run the teacher is eventually free of a good deal of unnecessary supervisory concerns if the children are permitted to grow in independence as a result of good instruction at the beginning. They can then function with competence and skill on their own.

ALLOWING FOR MANY CHOICES OF ACTIVITY

Here is a kindergarten in a modern suburban public school. It is the kindergartner's own place to work, play, and learn in a way suitable for five-year-olds.

Although there are no more than twenty-five children in the class, there seem to be many more. It would be difficult to count them accurately during this main work period, for they are in many places and are performing many different activities. There is a variety of lively sounds in the room—a discussion at a table with construction materials, the sound of a saw and of sandpapering, and mock yelping of a little "dog" reprimanded by its "mistress."

Mrs. Higher, the teacher of this lively kindergarten, is a pleasant and relaxed older woman. Although she is keeping an eye on what goes on in all the areas, she is not intrusive. It is close to the spring of the year, and Mrs. Higher's knowledge of the children, and their own knowledge of what to do, are such that not much supervision is required. A good deal more help, stricter supervision, and more encouragement was given by Mrs. Higher earlier to prepare the children for the independence and competence they now show.

There is quiet intermittent conversation around the easels where three children are painting seriously and beautifully. Mrs. Higher is actually not near those children or watching them. But she has checked earlier on the consistency and sufficiency of paints in the containers, and although the children themselves put their paintings on the drying rack, Mrs. Higher comes over later on to affix the names and dates. When one child tells her about "clouds in the sky" she adds the notation to the picture; this is important to the child and interesting to the teacher.

In the farthest corner of the class there is special liveliness. This area is almost like a little room in itself, with half walls and a door. There is clanking of dishes in that little room, with explosive domestic talk, banging of doors, and dressing up in odd-fitting, gaudy grown-up clothes. These children, too, are getting along without a teacher, except that a modern, medically conscious member of the "family" rushes over with an urgent request. "Mrs. Higher! We need some pills for the sick daddy! Would you give us some pills!" The teacher recognizes the need for "medication" (with which children of our era are quite familiar), and she turns to the supply of dry cereal usually used for that purpose. They work!

What appears to be the central activity in the class is an impressive block-building project. The blocks are held up by intricate balance and external supports. There is an interior structure into which the children are peering from above and peeking from a small side opening. Earnest consultation among the builders can be heard.

"I don't want the roof to fall down!" one child asserts.

"But people will bump it when the roof sticks out," another explains.

"We have to finish it," insists a third. Hearing this, the teacher offers some construction material for the roof and helps to make a requested sign for the finished building.

Relaxing somewhat from her involvement in the complicated building project, the teacher watches the profound absorption of a pensive, poetic little girl, as she slowly turns the pages of a book. This expression of concentration and feeling on a child's face is a beautiful sight to any teacher.

In Mrs. Higher's kindergarten class the children are free to choose from a variety of appropriate activities and materials. Some go to the mechanical tools and the muscular action of woodworking; some like the fluid paint and the feel of color as they put it on blank paper; some are ready to be involved in intimate groups as they play out creatively and dramatically various relations; another enjoys solitude with a puzzle or a book. In this class children are free to follow their tastes and preferences, to use initiative and independence. True freedom of choice in both materials and companions can be easily destroyed, however, under the guise of organization when the teacher's concern over equitable distribution of space and materials causes her to assign people in "fair" fashion, but without regard to individual needs. It is important to understand that some children may need to spend weeks at the sandbox or to block build instead of paint, and some may need to stay with the same companion for a long time in order to learn how to play at all. Freedom of choice must mean just that, except where waiting for a turn becomes necessary. In this case a child should still have freedom of choice—to wait or to turn to something else. Naturally all freedom of choice is curtailed by reality. There may be only one workbench, for example. But it should not also be curtailed by arbitrary assignment of all children to all activities in turn.

Real freedom of choice for the children is possible in Mrs. Higher's class because Mrs. Higher has set the stage for it. She has seen to it that the tools and materials are in working order, safe and accessible, and the room arrangement is such that a variety of activities can be carried on without confusion. She knows that when children are planning some paper construction, they need paper, scissors for cutting, perhaps string for tying, rubber bands and clips for holding things in place, or crayons for marking and decorating. If they are to carry out their purpose with relative efficiency they need to know where such things are, learn to use them, and learn also the importance of putting them back for later use.

When a simple cooking project, such as making jello, is carried out in this class, the teacher initiates and supervises an orderly arrangement of bowls, stirring spoons, measuring cups, eating spoons, and a potholder for the pot with boiling water. She plans for time to read directions, time for chilling the jello, and the most rewarding or appropriate time for eating. Although perhaps all this planning cannot always be discerned, the resulting orderliness can be felt in the atmosphere of the class, and this orderliness is absorbed by the children. The teacher also sees to it that the activities are maintained on a satisfying and constructive level; neither damage nor interference is tolerated.

ORDERLY AND FLEXIBLE ORGANIZATION

Mrs. Lu is a teacher of a kindergarten of sixteen five-and-a-half-year-olds housed in a small room which is first arranged for work, then adapted for lunch, then re-arranged for nap, and again set up for informal snacks. Although one does not hear any orders from Mrs. Lu, one is attracted by her knowing, confident, yet particularly gentle manner. The room is full of children's mobiles, framed pictures, displays of clay work, and pots, cans, and jars of germinating, rooting, and budding plants. At lunch time the teacher is seated among the tables with children, attending to serving. The children also help themselves in a casual and orderly fashion. There is lively table conversation that at once suggests informality, good relations, and a sensible attitude toward eating and food. Children clear and stack their plates independently. They are so relaxed that when a visitor appears and Mrs. Lu suggests that they introduce themselves to her, each child tells the visitor his or her name without any interruption in the meal. As some of the children were eating their dessert, others clearing the tables, and the teacher attending to the finishing touches and general supervision, a father of one of the children came in to take his child home for a special reason. He immediately attracted a great deal of happy attention, especially from his son, and for about fifteen minutes most of the children sat or stood around and talked to the man about baseball, traffic, and birthdays. The teacher was aware of the slight delay in the routines, but she was equally aware and respectful of the visiting father. She did not rush him away or nag the children about getting their cots; she simply reminded them softly and worked with them, and in a few minutes the room was rearranged and quieted for napping.

Thus, it is entirely possible to have a room in which routines are respected by the children and consistently supervised by the teacher, in which flexibility absorbs the unexpected, and extra social pleasures can take place. In spite of the fact that Mrs. Lu happened to lack both supplies and space, thus limiting some activities, her orderly use of what she did have and her strong sense of organization carried over to the children and created a room in which children had adventure as well as stability.

ALLOWING CHILDREN TO PARTICIPATE
IN ORGANIZATION

Attending to the many chores connected with group living involves much real work, which kindergarten children can and should share with the adults. Considering the subject of children's work broadly, we might say that there is moral value in a child's acquiring respect and admiration for some kind of work through good early experiences. But there is economy, too, when able, energetic four-, five-, and six-year-old children attend to tasks with healthy independence and even with some appreciable skills. Work is at the core of the adult world, and children live in a world of adults. They depend on and want to be part of this world. Work means grown-up responsibility; it is something real, as compared to exclusively playful activities or make-believe. It carries prestige and social satisfaction through recognition gained from other children as well as grown-ups. Work is a challenge to various skills and entails learning. It can therefore be exciting to young children, who are such avid learners.

But work must come into the school life of young children in relation to the school environment and their needs. What does it consist of? We will begin with what might be thought of as the more mundane areas of responsibility.

Cleaning

If there is an invisible custodian attending to the entire work when the class is not in session, or if most of the children have servants at home to do all the cleaning, the children may hold cleaning in low esteem. The teacher must be aware of this as well as of her own values. However, whatever the children's backgrounds, their eager response and interest will be stimulated by the understanding that the classroom is theirs, and that together with the teacher (as well as the custodian) they can take some responsibility.

First, there are the tools and equipment that go with cleaning and that are attractive to young children. These include floppy mops, tough brushes, absorbent sponges, stiff brooms, and soft rags, all kept in proper places and in good condition, and replaced when necessary. To use a suitable size mop on the classroom floor when spills occur is an acceptable job to any young child. The necessary use of a broom and dustpan and brush makes good sense to practical-minded kindergartners. If such children's work commands the teacher's respect and is accompanied by the teacher's own readiness to be equally involved, the kindergartners can enjoy the physical activity of cleaning and creating order and not take it for granted as if it were done by fairies and elves.

Scrubbing

Scrubbing tables with soap and brush or cleanser and cloth and making them shiny is satisfying to any child. The splashing of water, the sprinkling of cleanser, the different uses of brush and sponge and cloth are actually fun to children. In fact, they are likely to get carried away with the fun, and the teacher may need to remind them of their original purpose.

Children are generally fascinated by seeing any surface transformed. Thus, in one class, the most popular job was scrubbing, on hands and knees, a large piece of oilcloth that was kept under the standing easel and was speckled with paint. All the children enjoyed seeing it conspicuously clean as much as they enjoyed the process of scrubbing.

The same class became negligent in the routine care of the bathroom. Faucets were left running, used paper towels were strewn on the floor, and objects were left in wash bowls. The teacher called a special meeting and said that she noticed wrong things in the bathroom and asked who else noticed anything wrong. Several children mentioned noticing things out of place. When asked by the teacher, they also had an idea of what could be done. The teacher then suggested that one child have charge of checking the bathroom before the end of the session. Six volunteers responded at once. The enthusiasm for checking the bathroom lasted for several weeks with these four-and-a-half to five-year-old children. The floor was indeed spick-and-span and the sinks actually shining. They enjoyed the responsibility, the activity, and the results. There was no scolding or nagging on the part of the teacher, only relevant attention to an immediate need and, of course, recognition of whatever positive response came from the children. Scrubbing sinks with scouring powder and special brushes or mops, polishing mirrors, or even washing and wiping a window until it is shiny, when it is an accepted or shared rather than an imposed task, is dignified and even delightful labor, bringing a sense of self-sufficiency to any child.

There are classrooms, however, where there are children so underdeveloped that the normal vigor and effectiveness just described comes hard to them. A teacher who had such a class described them this way:

> Keeping the room clean is extremely difficult. Marisol is the only one who has put together the coordination for sweeping. Manuel and Leonard try, but end up swinging the dirt and scraps around with the broom. As for washing the tables, again Marisol, sometimes Manuel and Leonard, can wash the tables thoroughly. The others don't have the strength or coordination to wash paste and paint off the tables. They are content to squirt on the soap and water.

Such children should be encouraged to participate. But obviously one cannot hold them to the same standards as one could put forth for better coordinated children. Nevertheless, it is important for them to be helped to focus on the tasks and to try.

"Dirty Work"

Attention to the wastebasket or trash can may be considered just "dirty work," but it is something important. If the place for emptying classroom trash is reasonably accessible, children enjoy, as an occasional if not a daily job, carrying a heavy trash can, emptying it into a large can, and clapping the lid. If in the process they should encounter the "real garbage man" (who is called "sanitation worker") and perhaps even the garbage truck, so much the better.

In planning for classroom cleaning the teacher needs to do some self-examining. Is she or he inclined to be fastidious rather than simply orderly? Does she or he feel disgusted when there is "an awful mess" during children's work or play or during clean-up itself? As long as the mess does not endanger safety (wet floors, broken objects, obstructions in necessary passages, in which case the teacher must be alert, prompt, and efficient), the teacher must aim to be casual and must either ask the children for constructive suggestions or offer them. A teacher's disgust with a mess can discourage an interest in cleaning. The teacher must also check on the standards held for the children's work. Children's abilities and interests vary not only among individuals but with home experience. Furthermore, children may well become tired and bored, and the teacher will need to provide change, variety, and perhaps some attraction. A colorful dustpan, a new brush, a different kind or shape of cloth, a design on the mop handle, or a sign (perhaps made or decorated by a child) can serve to stimulate or maintain regard for cleaning.

Putting Things Away

Putting things away should be required and *expected* by a helpful teacher, but not made compulsory in authoritarian fashion. This may sound contradictory, but what it means is that young children, who are still learning, should have expectations set before them. Realistically, however, a teacher does not expect full acquiescence. One must not, however, succumb to the amorality of children who ask, after they clean up, "Are you going to reward me?" Learning to be cooperative for its social value is important.

Putting things away marks a transition between activities, and transitions are often confusing and frustrating to many young children. To ease the situation the teacher needs to know the extent of the children's involvement and give them warning or offer help accordingly.[5] It may seem more efficient to have the children obey a signal and perform instantly (as may be necessary under emergency conditions); but for daily living it is more human to be helpful and flexible. The teacher must be a guide, not an officer demanding obedience.

It must not be forgotten by the teacher that working materials are put away to maintain the welfare of the entire group, and as such the task is social in implication. It is a meaningful activity which may lag at times or be uneven in tempo and result, but which need not deteriorate into a mechanical act of compliance for which, with effort, kindergarten children can be trained. We must also avoid giving children a common adult notion that work is something we suffer through and therefore get done and over with expediently. There are satisfactions in work well done. And certainly it is not done for the sake of fostering individual virtue or for children to ingratiate themselves with the teacher.

Let us consider separate areas in the work of putting things away. Blocks must not be shoved off the floor to some out-of-the-way spot, as so often happens. They must also not be dumped in a basket, stuffed into some chest or container, or piled and squeezed on shelves haphazardly. Such procedures bring confusion and have no place in good work practices for children. Order and purpose must be observed in putting blocks away on sufficient shelves of proper dimensions, stacked

---

[5] Elisabeth Hirsch, *Transition Periods: Stumbling Blocks of Education* (New York: Early Childhood Education Council).

according to shape, distributed with some eye for balance and in such a way that they are particularly handy to take out for use. A common error consists of stacking blocks so close to the top that they become wedged in and difficult to remove. All accessory materials also need to be put away where they can be attractive and accessible.

Elisabeth Hirsch describes how some teachers give prearranged signals (such as a chord on the piano) for putting things away, but she reports, too, that serious builders need to be reminded several times.[6]

Putting away painting materials usually has special appeal. This includes disposal of unusable paint, washing of brushes, scrubbing of jars, and cleaning of easels, all of which provides a good deal of sensory satisfaction and often calls for ideas for improvement. Ways of putting things away and ways of keeping materials can provide interest and stimulate responsibility. Clay must be kept moist to be usable. Crayons must not be stored near heat. Boxes or baskets or cans with materials must be sorted and labeled with some symbolic designation as well as the teacher's writing. Not only cubbies and closets, but earthenware crocks, tin canisters, wooden buckets, aluminum pails, plastic containers, string and drawstring bags, cellophane bags, paper bags, and gunny sack bags, all lend interest and are useful.

Interesting and suitable receptacles, planning and organizing *with* the children, and fairness in dividing responsibility are all important in establishing effective and meaningful routines for clean-up and general order.

Caring for Plants and Animals

Taking care of plants and animals is closely related to the enjoyment and learning which children derive from living and growing things. Children frequently observe unusual conditions and changes while doing these chores, and these should be capitalized upon by the teacher.

Here is a group around a fish tank. It was Peter's turn to feed the fish that whole week. This was the third day and he had already distinguished the different appearance, behavior, and even disposition of each of the three goldfish. "This is Firstie; he's always the first one to take a nibble of the food, and *he* is Snoopie; he snoops around and waits. I don't know what he's waiting for . . ."

"Maybe he's finding out if it smells good."

"Can fishes smell?"

"Of course, you dope . . ." Now the teacher is consulted, the goldfish book is looked at, and an encyclopedia referred to. Another child calls Peter's attention to the water level in the tank. Peter then checks with the teacher and replenishes the

[6] Elisabeth Hirsch, "Block Building—Practical Considerations for the Classroom Teacher," in *The Block Book* (Washington, D.C.: National Association for the Education of Children, 1974), p. 95.

tank with bottled water of room temperature. He does this slowly, watching the stirring in the tank, the movements of each fish, and the precise rise in water level.

Betsy was attending to the watering of the potted avocado plant on the windowsill. On close inspection she had noticed a strange leaf on the tall stem. What was it? Well, Horace had played a trick and attached a green cut-out paper leaf with scotch tape right onto the real stem. Betsy soon discovered the "fakeness" and the culprit, and since that time she became particularly interested in inspecting the leaves when attending to the watering. This time it was her luck to notice something strange. One leaf was all rolled up into a little tube.

"Did you do that to the leaf, Horace? Who did it? Why is this leaf rolled up?" On further most careful inspection Betsy discovered a caterpillar in some cozy wrappings turning over as Betsy rudely moved in on him. At this point Betsy's excited, high-pitched voice rose even more than usual, and her normally keen eyes blazed. She pleaded urgently to be the one responsible for the avocado plant for "another few days. Just a few, please!" The teacher decided in this situation that fairness in the strict sense had to be abandoned. The avocado plant, conspicuously enriched by its moth guest, had to be in Betsy's possessive charge until, some ten days later, a pale, slight, feeble common moth emerged. To Betsy this common moth, in its magical transformation from a crawly grounded caterpillar to a mobile winged creature, departing and ascending, might well have been an angel.

To some children work seems to constitute an important kind of unique expression. These are children who often seem shy and unsure with conventional, teacher-controlled materials and directed activities but may show enthusiasm, vigor, and confident communication in a work task. Perhaps such children have had wise encouragement, or perhaps they have been accustomed to helping at home, or possibly they simply have a bent for work. It's nice to know such children! But alas, there are also children who learned to take the easiest way out and resist effort. Teachers must recognize the social nature of clean-up activities and give all kinds of children suitable guidance toward carrying their share of a social responsibility.

It is also true, however, that teachers cannot count on a steady performance of chores by most kindergarten children. Watering plants, taking turns feeding animals, or helping regularly with cleaning a cage, all bring proud and desired responsibility. But alas, four-, five-, and even six-year-olds are easily diverted, and they may forget their chores completely as their interest is captured elsewhere. Although they can work with real care, children this young cannot be held to full responsibility. Teacher reminders are much in order. Even charts allowing for changing names and jobs cannot do the entire job of reminding kindergartners. Intrigued as the children are by charts and changing tasks, they do forget. Nevertheless, it is worth encouraging responsibility, making sure that the standards for quality of work relate to age as well as particular interest. It helps when the teacher also takes some share in the children's work and does not just supervise. For the kindergarten child, work should be neither punishment nor reward, but a normal and necessary part of living, with its own inherent difficulties and pleasures.

SELF-CARE ROUTINES

Dressing and Undressing

In the fall of the school year children in most parts of the country come to school without heavy outer clothing, and dressing and undressing does not seem a problem at all. But when seasonal changes bring heavy clothing and perhaps layers of it, the program schedule has to be altered to allow time for sweaters, boots, jackets, hats, scarves, mittens, and possibly raincoats. As in all other phases of development, groups of children vary somewhat in independent handling of dressing and undressing. In general, poorer children learn this kind of independence earlier than middle-class children, but all are quite capable of dressing and undressing themselves during the kindergarten year. They do need help in the *group* phases of the task: How many, and in what order, shall go to the clothing closets? How shall they come to the teacher for last-minute touches without overwhelming her? How can the teacher expedite techniques for slipping into snow pants, sweater, and boots for large groups of individuals who are still awkward at this?

The aim in this mundane task is, of course, efficiency and reasonable speed, so that the group can get on to more interesting activities. But for many children this simple routine is still a challenge, especially if they have had too much protection at home. For some it is a matter of real indifference whether boots or mittens match or whether collars are turned in or out. To still others it is almost traumatic to misplace a boot or mitten or to leave with a hat that is not properly buttoned. These are the personal meanings of dressing and undressing, meanings of competency and independence or helplessness and dependence; fear of adult censure for awkwardness or security with adults no matter what; responsibility for personal possessions or disinterest in them. Therefore, although the teacher helps each child find a place in the hustle and bustle of a large-scale operation by establishing suitable regulations to expedite movement and avoid confusion, she or he also remains aware of the individual meaning which this simple operation can have. For the sake of the parents' peace of mind the teacher should also make a quick check of the collars, ties on hats, mittens, boots, and scarves to see that each child leaves properly dressed for the weather and wearing home what he or she came with. If the children's things are labeled at home, much confusion can be avoided. It is heartening and helpful for a teacher to see how a more competent child is usually glad to help another who is having difficulty. This whole matter of helping individuals help themselves in a group situation is a suitable topic to discuss at an early parent meeting, but it should be done with a bit of humor.

Resting

The rest periods automatically included in every kindergarten program call for fresh appraisal, or they may deteriorate into the hardly restful battle that teachers can have with children. Just why and how resting came into the kindergarten program to begin with is not known. We believe that it is good and even necessary for children (and adults, too) to relax between sessions of hard work. We also believe that it is possible for children to relax completely and thoroughly without necessarily stretching out on rugs or mats with eyes closed tight. Scheduled rest is often unnecessary and a waste of time in a short program. Therefore we do not believe relaxation ought to be legislated into a program and tyrannically enforced.

The key to relaxation in a morning or afternoon kindergarten session lies in the balance of activities. Common sense tells us not to have a rhythms period, go on a trip for several blocks, come back to the gym for some exercise, and then run relay races. Ordinarily a program should include a listening time (story or records), a crafts time which demands little exertion, table games, opportunity to look at books and pictures, and woven throughout, the chance for an individual youngster to withdraw briefly and relax with a game, toy, book, instrument, or just slouch on the floor and watch others. Good programs definitely intersperse quiet activities with vigorous ones. By five most children have outgrown their need for a regular nap, and their bodies are accommodated to a sunrise-to-sunset schedule of wakefulness. Living in a group, however, can be a tiring experience, especially at the beginning of the year. The noise, conflicts of views, and continuous exercise of control over impulses certainly can affect one's equilibrium. It may be quite necessary, therefore, for a teacher to plan for times when all noise ceases, times when the intensity of preoccupation and the intrusion of discord come to a brief stop. But this does not necessarily mean sitting or lying in a particular position, such as heads on table or flat on one's back. Above all it does not mean to *reward* "good resters" with special treats—a fairly common technique. It is easy to see how resting can thus become an ingratiating behavior for some children instead of a natural and desirable condition.

Children do need to relax, especially those who by temperament tend to become overintense. And sometimes they need to be taught how to relax and enjoy it. In no case, though, need the resting time become a battle between the "I-know-what's-good-for-you" teacher and the "You-can't-make-me" child.

Planning for a period of cessation of noise and discord may mean a story time or a record time, with everyone sprawled comfortably on the floor. One teacher collected a wide assortment of small gadgets, mechanical and magnetic toys, locks and keys, pipe cleaners, erasers and colored pencils, small pencil sharpeners, shoe polish, fingernail polish, and whatever else normally appears first in kitchen catch-all drawers and later in children's pockets. These were kept in several boxes which were constantly refilled with new items as she found them and cleared temporarily of old ones. At rest time the children could take one thing they wanted from these boxes, or a puzzle or book, to their cots. For the forty-five-minute rest in this all-day school, the children played quietly for part of the time, stretched out peacefully for a short while, and heard a story or music for the remainder of the time. They got up from rest quite toned down, as was evident from the quiet, relaxed conversation that accompanied the putting away of cots.

When we see a teacher start her two-hour afternoon session with a one-half-hour rest, however ("They come in tired"), we cannot help but wonder how necessary this is. We have also been in schools where the children are undernourished, share a bed with several siblings at home, and are kept awake at night by adult activity in crowded quarters with no privacy. These children need their rest just as they need a good hot lunch, and provision should be made for both. Well-fed, healthy youngsters who come to kindergarten for two or three hours will probably manage quite nicely with the balance of quiet and action planned by the teacher and the individual choice of restful sprawling as they feel the need. Except for special occasions, such as the return from a trip or a high pitch of excitement sustained all through play, the rest break need not be more formal than indicated.

Toileting

There is one constant routine in the kindergarten class which needs to be looked at separately because it still has much personal meaning for four- and five-year-olds, and that is the toileting associated with special terminology that differs among families and ethnic groups. Fours and fives are generally quite capable of handling their own needs, although many absorbed in play, overestimate their holding capacity. "Accidents," although not too common, still do occur, to the intense humiliation of the child, let alone the discomfort of the teacher and the fascination of the rest of the class. In some school buildings the kindergarten room is quite close to bathrooms and in the newest buildings the bathroom is in the classroom, so that a child may follow individually determined habits and leave the group at will. This is not possible everywhere, however, as in many schools the bathrooms are at the end of one or more long corridors and perhaps down a flight of stairs. In this event a teacher is justifiably reluctant to allow a young child complete freedom so far from her watchful eye, and she may be compelled to arrange for the entire group to take a daily trip to the toilets. This exodus has to be planned with concern for time and in compliance with the conditions that prevail. Perhaps at some point in the year, the teacher can institute a "buddy" system, with two children at a time looking after each other.

Even within this framework, however, it is important for a teacher to understand that toileting may still carry overtones of emotional significance to individual youngsters. Some children are quite inhibited about using public toilets and will suffer tortures rather than do so, teacher or no teacher. Some are more prone than others to tease and peek, to the acute discomfort of others. For some children the disclosure of each other in a partial state of undress is a stimulus to sexual curiosity and play. Kindergarten teachers must face realistically the fact that the emphasis on group practices in this regard may have the effect of heightening symptoms of immature behavior, since the experience cannot be casual and of minor matter under the circumstances, as it normally should. It therefore is important to recognize that children's individual differences in need and attitude must be respected and understood, even under the trying circumstances of regimentation.

The first question many a new kindergartner asks his or her parent is "Where is the bathroom?" It is probably a good idea for the teacher to take the class to the bathroom as an initial school orientation experience and to point to the difference between an individual, closed room at home and a multicubicled, perhaps different-looking structure at school. Asking the children what the differences are may bring forth surprising observations on the strength and length of the flush, the difference in mechanism of the flush, the special smell of disinfectant, the unique type of faucet at the sink, perhaps the absence of hot water, certainly the fascinating little receptacle for liquid or powdered soap, and the novel way of dispensing towels. Reassurance about the differences can readily lead to discussion of suitable behavior —protecting the privacy of each individual, avoiding the misuse of equipment, not lingering for play when the whole group is waiting. Since this is an independent activity and usually without the teacher's direct supervision, the children's faith in the teacher who shows understanding leads to the comfortable sense of trust children still must feel with adults to be better able to bring problems in this area to them. It goes without saying that the child who does have an accident will need real comforting and face-saving. Having learned control and pride in control quite recently, kindergartners have no humor about their mistakes. (They are, however, very ready to laugh in relief at others in distress!)

Teachers must also know that children may develop diarrhea at the start of an illness as well as when under tension; they may wet themselves because they are afraid to use the school toilet and cannot hold out, as well as moisten underpants because they cannot bear to leave exciting play. These events are to be expected and indeed still appear in first grade. Readiness on the teacher's part to handle them with sympathetic efficiency protects the child from unnecessary shame and guilt. In the course of a happy and fulfilling school year the children mature, and their growth is reflected in this area, too.

EMERGENCIES

The best-run class is bound to be confronted with the unexpected at one time or another. A kindergarten teacher of a private school walked into her classroom one Monday morning together with a group of children who had arrived early, and beheld with horror a broken window and glass strewn all over the otherwise clean and well-prepared room. But in spite of her shock and distress the teacher did not overlook the children and their impression and interest. The teacher felt she should have the children take part in the problem all the way. Physical safety was, of course, the first concern, and the teacher indicated the small area in the room and the hall which the children could occupy. That was understandable to them. Second, proper report of the accident and immediate help had to be obtained. "Tell the office," suggested Larry. The teacher sent a note with three children, which resulted in having the secretary and another teacher come in with a large broom. Two of the children served as guards, telling all the arrivals not to go into the "dangerous" place until the adults finished the sweeping. Then the children were assigned to jobs as "inspectors." They examined with closest attention every area for "small, almost invisible specks of glass." Then they commented how cold the room was, and the teacher explained that a man would come in later to fix the broken window.

"But can't we cover up the hole now?" After some discussion, the hole was covered up with a piece of cardboard. So the problem of physical safety and protection was attended to with sufficient understanding and security for the children. The teacher had gained cooperation from the children easily enough in a moment of need; they had also shown responsibility and given necessary help. But the episode led to the serious question of cause, which in turn led to the moral issue of wrongdoing which was involved in the broken window.

"How did the window get broken?" several children asked of the teacher right away.

"I am not sure. Have you any idea?" Fantastic answers of jets and bombs and flying saucers came from those four- to five-year-olds, showing what children are thinking about. Some thought the break came from a ball.

"Maybe a boy was playing, and he didn't *know* the ball was going to hit the window." Consideration of cause brought to mind responsibility and the possibility of someone's guilt.

"Maybe a *bigger* boy did it."

"I didn't do it." This was said very seriously, and a hush of consternation settled over the group of children.

"I know you didn't," the teacher said confidently, relieving the hush.

"Maybe a pussycat did!" This child wanted to be funny and succeeded. Everybody laughed and made pawing motions of breaking a window. The laughter and movement served to relieve the children's tension. Then a little girl said, "Whoever did it, should clean up."

"But it's already cleaned up." They were thus back to the concrete solution, and the teacher ended the discussion at this point.

SCHEDULING

Kindergarten Units

Many curriculum bulletins and syllabi suggest specific themes around which to organize the activities of the children, with attention to their general interests. Thus, one might find a teacher organizing class experiences around the seasons, holidays, or major community events like the circus, and see carefully prepared lessons in language arts, music, art, and mathematical concepts related to the specific theme of the week. In many traditional kindergartens one finds jack-o-lanterns in October, turkey pictures on the wall in November, Christmas trimmings in December, snow in January, valentines in February, daffodil cutouts in March, pictures of rabbits on the windows in April, and flowers in May, with appropriate accompanying activities. We have tried throughout this book to develop an approach to curriculum for kindergarten children that will take them further afield into stimulating intellectual learning than the traditional projects alone allow. Consequently, we suggest that units and projects be allowed to grow out of the children's interests and concerns for the most part, or out of the teacher's insight into what might be meaningful to them. If one listens carefully, one will hear the many questions children have that can lead to exploration and study. Many of these leads are not relevant to the conventional curriculum at all. Young children are very much interested in how things happen, how they change, even why they happen and why they change. But they can only understand how and why in relation to concrete phenomena. They need to see for themselves, touch, hear, taste, and smell. They want to learn, they are eager for information, but they must learn in their own style for the learning to be effective. The introduction of such important aspects of our culture as the traditional holidays, or high points of seasonal change, should therefore be more casual and take up less time than is usually the case. There is great comfort to a teacher to plan in advance a number of projects likely to interest little children. But too heavy reliance on projects planned and conceived by adults and introduced into groups that may or may not be ready for them does not necessarily lead to valuable learning. It is important that units and projects developed by the teacher satisfy the curiosity and keen interests of the children. The interests of young children change fairly rapidly; they are interested in everything but do not stay interested long enough to study anything in depth. We must realize that topics like the weather and the seasons, even the farm, are leftovers from the agricultural era in our country, when they had greater reality for adults and could be related to adult life by children. Today they are better dealt with at a later stage of schooling. Kindergarten curriculum must be closer to the lives the children actually lead.

Individual variations in concentration span also exist, and the patience to stay with an activity because the whole group is doing it is not as strong as it will become later. Time blocks must be planned with these developmental characteristics in mind.

The project that is carefully organized ahead of time may be a necessary support for children lacking in ideas and experience, but even then it is important that the experiences offered for their enlightenment be of the kind that stimulates further inquiry and exploration. When this is so, units flow out of each other, as children are really thinking, and this is the fun of creative curriculum building.

In any case kindergarten children do not always need to be on a unit. The fluid and divergent range of their interests speaks against too formal an organization. Although all the experiences we have described—trips, science, literature, discussion, blocks, woodwork, art, and music—are necessary for their growth, these do not need to be so limited by specific themes as to discourage exploration and discovery by the children themselves of totally unexpected areas. Introducing children to the traditions of our culture is after all only one part of their education, much of which they get outside of school. At school we should be concerned with the stretching of minds and enrichment of intellectual experience. Kindergarten teachers can feel quite comfortable about pursuing the leads gleaned from the children or suggested by the environment, without worrying about how carefully organized these are into neatly laid out, continuous units. The place of skill learning in the kindergarten curriculum is discussed at length in Chapters 15 and 16.

Building Up Experiences

The rapidly changing attention of kindergartners and the brevity of the kindergarten day does mean that one has to plan for a *cumulative* effect from repeated, brief experiences, incorporating repetition of certain kinds into the schedule. Music is one of these, and since time does not allow for music every day, although that is desirable, then an experience once or twice a week will add up at the end of the year to a repertoire of songs and competence with instruments. But the once or twice a week must be scheduled. Stories, on the other hand, give a child a basis for appreciating books, an important part of the preparation for reading, and story or poem time should be included every day, however short the time. Science need not be deliberately scheduled on a regular basis but it must be intrinsic to the program through the availability and restocking of materials and through the constant awareness of the challenges of scientific exploration that lie in the immediate world. We have shown this often in the accounts of various classrooms throughout this book.

The Daily Schedule

Scheduling for kindergarten is best done broadly, allowing sizable periods of time each day for a work period, a five- to twenty-minute story time, at least half an hour each for outdoor, snack, and toileting time, and ample time for dressing and undressing, which is not a speedy operation for most children under seven. Discussion time must be included but might be part of the snack period, an opener for the day, or scheduled twice a week once the framework of basically unchangeable activity is set. Subjects for discussion may be ones brought up by the children and jotted down by the teacher during the week or thought of by the teacher in response to activities within the class or outside of it.

The daily program is often built on activities of the day before, and unexpected interruptions (the new litter of white mice, or a sudden snowstorm) must be built into the curriculum, too. Compared with the formal programming of the upper grades, the kindergarten program may seem too amorphous for a person who must know ahead of time what each hour will bring and who must follow a "lesson plan." But such people are not counting on the children. With plenty of materials and well-utilized space, children will offer many clues for teachers to pursue. They must be on their toes and ready to be resource persons and guides. Teachers must prepare materials and know the song they will teach. But while they know in broad terms how their day with the kindergartners will go, one of the pleasures in working with young children is the excitement of exploring new paths opened by any new group of children. This is what keeps teachers themselves learners and what gives teaching its spark and zest.

Planning the Work Period

During a work period or free play, as it is called to distinguish it from a teacher-controlled and directed program, children may enjoy one or several activities. The organization of this basic aspect of the kindergarten curriculum must allow for time to make up one's mind, time to get involved, perhaps time to change one's mind and try something else, and time to put away materials and products. Usually this period lasts from forty-five minutes to an hour and a half, depending on the maturity of the children, and therefore must be scheduled so that latitude of ten to fifteen minutes will not be affected by prescribed yard time, going home time, or anything else that is unchangeable.

In many kindergartens it is the first experience of the day, with children entering and immediately picking their activities and friends with zest. In other situations scheduled activities like assembly, music, and outdoor yard allotment mean postponing this period until later in the morning. At the beginning one can start with the shorter work period (forty-five minutes) and watch to see how it is going; then the time can be extended to what seems reasonable for a group, without going beyond their powers of comfortable endurance (one and a half hours). The work period should be part of every day's program unless the children will be away all morning on a trip or other special activity. The important thing is that the children do not feel hurried and frustrated too soon after they have become absorbed and fascinated by what they are doing. At the other end is the teacher's sensitivity in timing to fatigue, high-pitched excitement, and peak of endeavor. Energy and time must still be available for putting things away, and ending on a note of positive achievement is more desirable than ending with a sense of letdown because one did not know when to stop. Play has a way of petering out. It should be stopped before this happens.

EVALUATION

In addition to the many tasks of organizing and running a program, there is the final task of evaluating the children's growth and development throughout the year. Evaluation at this stage must not be interpreted as passing judgment. Young children are still in process, and the rate of growth, pace, and pattern varies in individual children. The same behavior can mean quite different things when looked at in the light of a child's total growth rather than from an arbitrary standard applied undiscriminatingly to all. Thus, *hitting* may at one point be a positive step forward for a child who has been withdrawn; it may express a residue of unhappiness in a child who has suffered; it may indicate self-sufficiency but poor social techniques; or it may mean frustration and despair. Yet in adult eyes, all and any hitting could be judged improper and the child labeled as hostile and aggressive. Realistic evaluation of children will show a composite view of how they are functioning compared not only to long-range goals but to achievable performance at kindergarten age, with individual variations noted and accounted for.

Records

End-of-year evaluations are more likely to be accurate and fair when they are based on records a teacher has been keeping throughout the year. Three kinds of records are involved: those a teacher keeps for understanding, planning, and conferring with parents; those that form a part of the total administrative records and add to the long-range view of a child's life at school; and the standardized testing that has begun to be part of the assessment of young children's development and which the teacher may be called upon to administer.

Records of the inner life of the class.   Here the records are of two types: those of individual children and those showing the dynamics of group interaction. Records of individual children should reveal their uniqueness, their stage-relatedness, and their behavior in response to others in the group. The manual *Observing and Recording the Behavior of Young Children*[7] deals in detail with the practical techniques of taking the kinds of notes on individuals that are useful in gaining a reasonably full, objective picture of a child.

For the group as a whole, there are somewhat different guidelines, a few of them mentioned in the manual. To understand the dynamics of a group, one would look at it with the following questions in mind:

> Are there subgroups? Who belongs to them? What holds them together? What is the relationship of the subgroups to the group as a whole? Who are their leaders?
>
> Does the group as a whole have cohesion? Who seem to be leaders? Do they emerge as natural leaders or does the group make them function as leaders? Who are the isolates? The children on the fringe? Are any children rejected? Are any scapegoated? By whom?
>
> Who are the instigators of ideas or initiators of discussion? Which children pick up the ideas and carry them forward? Are there children who act in opposition? Any who are neutral? Is there competition or cooperation among the instigators of ideas, the initiators, the leaders?
>
> How does the group react to newcomers? How does it react to new situations? Does the group as a whole gang up on one person? How does the group react when certain leaders are absent? Does the group (or certain sections of it) wait for reactions of certain individuals before giving its own reactions? Are there boy-girl friendships as well as boy-boy, girl-girl?
>
> How would you describe the emotional climate of the group?

A careful evaluation of how children in a group are interacting tells something about individuals that helps the teacher guide the group toward constructive interaction.

[7]Dorothy H. Cohen, Virginia Stern, and Nancy Balaban, *Observing and Recording the Behavior of Young Children* (New York: Teachers College, 1958; revised ed. 1983).

Group records of curriculum. To ascertain how a group is functioning in terms of curriculum, some teachers keep a log or diary in order to have a check on what has happened. It is amazing how much can be forgotten by Christmas of what happened in September. Reviewing the development of curriculum this way makes a teacher considerably more sensitive to the subtleties of growth in group life. There are also checklists a teacher can make to keep track of the activities and of the frequency with which individuals are involved in the use of materials. Spot-checking on a regular basis during free-play time and keeping note of where each child is and what the child is doing will give a profile of each child's use of available opportunities, as well as an overview of the whole class. Valuable as such notes are, however, they are not records in depth as individual observations are.

Records for the administration. The larger school administration has a somewhat different perspective from the teacher's. It needs facts and figures to do its own kind of evaluation and satisfy local and state requirements that certain procedures established by law are actually being carried out at the school. A teacher thus has to fill out and return to the administration a variety of forms relating to his or her program and schedule; the health and attendance of the children; reports to, and conferences with, parents; trips away from the building; budget data pertaining to supplies and equipment; and classroom collections of funds. These often become quite a chore, and it is tempting to attend to them during the times when children are quietly at play. These happen to be the best times for observing the children and getting to know them better, so that often administrative efficiency interferes with genuine teacher competency. Requirements vary from school to school, and not all forms need immediate attention. Part of a teacher's planning, then, should include an allotment of time for attention to the clerical aspects of the job, which, if planned for, could probably be handled with a minimum of time taken from the children themselves.

The time with the children is the most valuable time and should be safeguarded by teachers and administrators alike. The planning and organizing aspects of the job come before and after the time with the children. The more carefully these are attended to, the smoother will be the time spent with children in action.

Large-Scale Evaluation

There has been a tendency in recent years to do large-scale screening of kindergarten children in order to find those who are in need of remedial work that will save them from failure in learning to read. Testing of this kind, although well intentioned, must be regarded with caution by teachers. The extraordinary pressure for achievement, which has focused on early reading for children, has merged with the appropriate concern about the learning problems of children from impoverished backgrounds to create a climate of anxiety about children's learning. Large-scale testing turns up the children with normal but slow growth, the children with developmental lags, and the children with neurological problems that will interfere with learning to read. Thus, although only 10 percent to 15 percent fall into the last category, about 30 percent are swept up in the testing process, because the tests do not discriminate between developmental lag and genuine disability. Furthermore, some of the large-scale tests look more for what unknowing adults think children *should* be capable of than for what they *are* capable of. This is due to the "deficit" model perpetrated on children of poverty and from which it is hard for testers to shift in order to study children objectively without judging them. This shortcoming is at last being recognized by leading psychologists, and questions have already been raised, for example, about the validity of large-scale testing of early childhood programs. It is therefore more important than ever that teachers know their children well and keep some records of their activities and relationships. They may be called upon to fill out the picture of more than one child who tests poorly but who the teacher knows is growing steadily.

LENGTH OF THE SCHOOL DAY

In many school districts, as well as in private schools, the kindergarten session lasts from two and one-half to three hours for each group of children, with double sessions each day for the teacher. In other places, the kindergarten session may be comparable to that for the elementary grades and run from 9 to 3, with an hour for lunch either at school or at home. Kindergartens may also be included in day care programs and last from 8 A.M. to 6 P.M., with a hot meal and a long nap. Obviously, the length of the session must affect scheduling. With a longer day, the work period can be fuller with more on-going projects and flexible transitions. There can be more frequent enjoyment of music and movement, trips and books. There may need to be a greater variety of materials to counter boredom, and there must be serious consideration of children's fatigue that results from group living. Provision must be made for relaxed yet smoothly running routines such as eating and resting. It is important that these be personalized in order to avoid the feeling of an institutionalized setting. A plus for the day-long session is that teachers have more intimate contact with the children and perhaps closer relationships with parents. But it is essential that teachers have a regular break if they are to remain fresh through a long day.

We may wish that the practice of scheduling the length of the kindergarten day were the result of careful research into what is best for young children. But realistically the length of the session is usually dictated by other considerations. It may be in answer to community needs (as in the case of day care centers serving working mothers); or the education budget (it is more economical to have short double sessions in one classroom and claim to serve upward of fifty children). Focused on academic achievement in the grades, few of those in a position to expend funds have asked, "What is good for the youngest children?"

A short two-and-one-half-hour session, often further shortened by attention to winter clothing and chores, allows the barest minimum for developing a good, unhurried, intellectually varied and stimulating program that is satisfying to four-to six-year-olds. When that brief time is usurped by an emphasis on training in skills, the loss to the children is even greater. In a short session the teacher is bound to skimp on trips or outdoor play and to encourage brief encounters with play materials in an effort to include variety of experience. Far from feeling unpressured, the teacher becomes an anxious clock watcher. When short sessions also mean double sessions, the teacher is held responsible for two separate groups of twenty-five to forty children daily, the only teacher in the elementary hierarchy to be so taxed. She cannot possibly get to know all the children well or plan for their needs in any depth. It should be obvious that a teacher with one group of children in a longer session can offer children much more to enhance their learning, a benefit in the end to them, their parents, and the community.

Ideally, therefore, kindergartens should be longer than the present minimum. When they run to full days, as in the day care centers, it is essential that overlapping staffs resist slipping into mechanical, routine approaches to curriculum development as a consequence of the very long hours. It is penny wise and pound foolish, however, to consider the nonacademic preschool experience a less significant part of the educational experience than the grades.

As a result of community interest, 37 percent of school districts in New York State have now extended the usual two-and-a-half-hour kindergarten session to four or five hours. Although some educators and parents expressed concern that a prolonged school day is too confining and tiring for five-year-olds, the proponents contended that five-year-olds are capable of more learning and development than is possible in a shorter session.[8]

A more recent report on studies of the kindergarten day[9] cites continued growth of full-time kindergartens throughout the country, doubling since 1970. The basic reasons for favoring the extended kindergarten day, from the point of view of educators and parents, are need for extended appropriate learning for five-year-olds, need for a longer school day when both parents are away from home, and a belief that a full-day kindergarten teacher knows her children better and is therefore a more effective teacher. Proponents of the shorter day on the other hand contend that it is a strain on the young child to be away from home that long and be subjected to demands of group living and supervision; and that a shorter day therefore is educationally sufficient and psychologically preferable.

ACCOMMODATING NEW CHILDREN

In some schools, children may be arriving throughout the year although for rather different reasons. Some school districts allow children to enter kindergarten any time after their fifth birthday, a practice children and parents find logical. In some

[8]Rona Kavee, "A Kindergarten Day: Should It Be Longer?" *New York Times,* May 3, 1981.

[9]Virginia Satkowski, "The Kindergarten Is Going Full Time," *New York Times,* Winter Survey of Education, January 9, 1983.

communities there is much turnover. There may be frequent arrivals of immigrants; or, in others, migrant children may enter school according to patterns of seasonal work. Faced with such additions to the class, the teacher must be flexible enough about the schedule and program to accommodate a new child who is likely to be confused by the unfamiliar busyness and to feel isolated by the ease of communication and friendships already established in the class. The teacher must take time to become acquainted with such children and provide ways by which the "regulars" can befriend the newcomers. The teacher will need to recognize which children in the class are likely to test or tease a new child and which can be counted on to be protective or helpful. The teacher and the children can together decide the best seat or the most suitable job for the newcomers and thus make them feel welcome and wanted. A most effective kind of help is to make it possible for new children to contribute in some way to the class. A child may offer the class some words in another language, an item from another cultural context, a beloved book or record, a piece of fabric for the dress corner, a visit from a parent with a special skill. A new child who can make a contribution becomes part of the class faster than a child who remains at the receiving end only.

REFERENCES AND FURTHER READING

Association for Childhood Education International. *Housing for Early Childhood Education,* 1968.

Association for Childhood Education International. *When Children Move.* 3615 Wisconsin Ave., N.W., Washington, D.C., 1972.

Austin Association for the Education of Young Children. *The Idea Box.* Washington, D.C.: National Association for the Education of Young Children, 1973.

BAKER, KATHERINE READ. *Ideas that Work with Young Children,* Bulletin No. 304. Washington, D.C.: National Association for the Education of Young Children, 1972.

BENDER, JUDITH. "Have You Ever Tried a Prop Box?" *Young Children* (January 1971).

BENTLEY, ROBERT J., WASHINGTON, ERNEST D., and YOUNG, JAMES. "Judging the Educational Progress of Young Children, Some Cautions," *Young Children* (November 1973).

BURKE, MARIE. "The Boxes in My Basement," *New York Early Education Reporter,* Winter 1982.

COHEN, DOROTHY H. "Dependence and Class Size," *Childhood Education* (1966).

COHEN, DOROTHY H., and STERN, VIRGINIA. *Observing and Recording the Behavior of Young Children.* New York: Teachers College, 1958; revised ed. 1978.

DAY, DAVID E., and SHEEHAN, ROBERT. "Elements of a Better Pre-School," *Young Children* (November 1974).

DEAN, JOAN. *Room to Learn: Working Space; A Place to Paint; and Language Areas.* New York: Scholastic Book Services, Citation Press, 1973.

Early Childhood Education Study. *A List of Classroom Items That Can Be Scrounged or Purchased.* Newton, Mass.: Education Development Council, 55 Chapel St. (A very useful, free, 17-page booklet.)

HIRSCH, ELISABETH (ed.). "Block Building—Practical Considerations for the Classroom Teacher," in *The Block Book*, Washington, D.C.: National Association for the Education of Young Children, 1974.

HIRSCH, ELISABETH. *Transition Periods: Stumbling Blocks of Education.* New York: Early Childhood Education Council of New York, 66 Leroy St., New York City.

KRITCHEVSKY, SYBIL, and PRESCOTT, ELIZABETH. "Planning Environments for Young Children: Physical Space." Washington, D.C.: National Association for Education of Young Children, 1977.

MACKLER, BERNARD, and HOLMAN, DANA. "Assessing, Packaging, and Delivery: Tests, Testing, and Race," *Young Children* (July 1976).

MINDESS, DAVID, and MINDESS, MARY. *Guide to an Effective Kindergarten Program.* West Nyack, N.Y.: Parker Publishing Co., 1972.

MITCHELL, EDNA. "The Learning of Sex Roles through Toys and Books: A Woman's Point of View," *Young Children* (April 1973).

OVITT, JEAN M. "What about the School Bus?" *Young Children* (May 1970).

PFLUGER, LUTHER, and ZOLA, JESSIE M. "A Room Planned by Children," *Young Children* (September 1969).

ROUNDS, SUSAN. *Teaching the Young Child,* Chap. 4, "Record-Keeping and Planning." New York: Agathon Press, dist. by Schocken Books, Inc., 1975.

SHAPIRO, EDNA. "Educational Evaluation: Rethinking the Criteria of Competence," *School Review,* 81, 4 (August 1973).

SPRUNG, BARBARA. *Guide to Non-Sexist Early Childhood Education.* New York: Women's Action Alliance, 1974.

STROM, ROBERT D. *Parent and Child in Fiction.* Belmont, Calif.: Wadsworth Publishing Co., Inc., 1977.

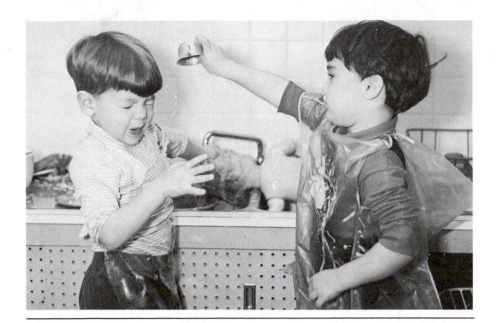

19 The Meaning of Discipline

For centuries authoritarian relationships among people were accepted without question in many cultures and countries, and relationships within the home and school reflected the practices of society at large. We in the United States have challenged all kinds of long-standing customs and attitudes in human relationships: the right of the upper classes only to education and opportunity; the right of the majority religious, ethnic, or racial group to suppress minority rights; the right of men to dominate women solely because of their social position. And we have questioned the right of parents or teachers to dominate and control children without regard for the children's feelings. A number of things contributed to the last, such as the concept of respect for the individual, regardless of position in life; the new knowledge that children are not little adults but subject to laws of development consistent with age and maturation; and the greater opportunity with increased leisure time to share pleasures with children. All these contributed to the breakdown of authoritarianism in the home and the school, while at the same time a search began for ways of functioning in interpersonal relationships that would encompass the rights of all individuals regardless of rank, status, position, or age. This view of human relationships based on greater sensitivity toward the rights of individuals in society was bound to affect disciplinary practices. Few Americans today can or do consciously accept the authoritarianism of the past, although a debate on corporal punishment in public schools still takes place.

But new forms of behavior do not always develop logically. Often they come as a reaction *against* the old instead of striking out toward fresh paths. Consequently many parents and teachers who are against authoritarianism are not at all clear what they are *for*. Such people may give up any and all control in order to avoid being overcontrolling, as though no limits and no controls were the only alternative to unfeeling and very strict control. Adults who allow themselves to be dominated by children (ostensibly so they will not themselves dominate the children) are often simply perpetuating their own childhood relationships. Having been dominated by parents and teachers as children, they continue to be dominated as adults, but now by children. In reality, by failing to exercise necessary controls over children, they abdicate their responsibility toward them as adults. Such extremists, although in the minority, have done much to shape the popular view that permissiveness means license.

The absence of definite limits or controls is as harmful to children as we know harsh and severe punishment to be. Neither license nor excessive punishment takes into account children's needs, stage of development, and readiness for learning; nor is either conducive to building inner discipline that will work when adults are not around. And neither builds relationships between adults and children of the kind that will be most satisfying to both.

Confusion still exists about the difference between *authoritative* and *authoritarian*. The authoritative teacher reacts on the basis of knowledge, skill, and experience to support the interests of the less experienced, less skilled, and less knowing. The authoritarian teacher demands conformity to her wishes by virtue of power that comes from being bigger, stronger, or in a position of status. Authoritative adults are concerned about the feelings of those who depend upon them, and are therefore likely to be fair. Authoritarian adults are subjective and therefore often unfair. So the issue is not "to control or not to control." The issue really revolves around the question of which criteria adults use to help them decide where, when, and how limits on behavior are to be set for children and where, when, and how children should be allowed the freedom to learn from their own mistakes without adults stopping them.

It should be obvious that our position is clearly affirmative for discipline in the education of young children; it is necessary to the successful functioning of a kindergarten class. But good discipline, as we see it, incorporates affectionate acceptance and understanding of children at their stage of development; respect for individual and group needs; order and sufficient supervision so all can feel safe; and a satisfying range of interesting things to do without unduly repressing individuals. But words have a way of remaining words. Let us look in on disciplinary situations with young children.

BEHAVIOR THAT CALLS FOR DISCIPLINE

Sh! Be Quiet

A bugaboo held over from authoritarian days is that children should be quiet. An elementary school principal made this clear to a group of nursery school children who had come with their teacher to visit the kindergarten which they would attend the next term.

"Good morning, boys and girls! How do you like our *nice, quiet* school? Now remember, when you come to kindergarten next fall, *you* are going to be nice and quiet, too."

The children stood and stared for a moment in silence. But one irrepressible four-year-old broke through the silence: "I am going to be in the second grade." (Safe distance away from the quiet kindergarten, he figured.)

In a classroom in that school, a little boy begins to whistle while children are finishing up work and clearing away systematically. "Who was whistling?" the teacher asks in a tone of unmistakable criticism. Several children's glances are directed at the boy. "I didn't do it," comes a self-protective remark from one. "We don't whistle in class—you know that," says this teacher, who was so intent on keeping her room quiet that she overlooked the pleasure of whistling while you work, as well as the special triumph whistling represents to a five-year-old who achieves this enviable accomplishment.

The Need for Quiet

No good teacher would question quiet in relation to something meaningful for all the children. When a teacher requires quiet so that her or his own or a child's talking, or a story, or music may be heard, such a request makes sense to the children and they can be expected to exercise control. The kind of talk and the type of story and music will have something to do with the length of time children can be expected to be quiet or sit still, however, since young children do have their limits for sitting quietly.

"Good" vs. "Bad" Noise

When a kindergarten is not quiet, what are the sounds we hear? During the work period in Mrs. Gilson's classroom there is laughter in the housekeeping corner; full conversation at the clay table; some indescribable, human machine noises emanating from the sandbox; some experimental scraping sounds coming from the workbench; the sound of humming in many areas; and lively skipping here and there. Mrs. Gilson does not admonish the children to be quiet, for she believes in few restrictions on children's spontaneity during the main work period in the session. She announces clean-up by speaking personally to several groups in the room and sending messengers to others. She addresses the group when it is necessary to have attention, as "boys and girls" or "people" and the children do listen. (A quiet voice aimed directly at eyes and ears is more effective than loud shouting that goes over children's heads and envelops them in meaningless noise.) During clean-up she does not act as a supervisor but goes *among* the children, helping, encouraging, or reminding as needed without undue praise or irritable scolding. While some children are still cleaning up, five children who have finished their task organize a lively song and dance game. Mrs. Gilson notices, but does not interfere. She realizes that it is a good way for the small group to enjoy music without really disturbing the class.

"It seems chaotic sometimes but it doesn't really hurt the children," Mrs. Gilson says. "Some of the kindergarten teachers have the getting-dressed-to-go-home time very organized and quiet, but I can't stop these children from talking."

It is true that following an exciting music period with singing, acting, dancing, and impromptu composition, the children are still noisy. They are not wild, however, and are quite efficient and independent about dressing. But they speak freely to each other, and several children try to speak to Mrs. Gilson at the same time. Mrs. Gilson puts her hands to her ears and shakes her head with mock distress. She does try to hear each one and exchanges pleasantries with many.

Mrs. Gilson's room is perhaps too noisy for some, but all the sounds are natural and relate to the activities and to the children's communication. This is a distinction we must bear in mind. Activity is inevitably accompanied by noise, but it is not the same kind of noise as uncontrolled, useless expenditure of energy in sound which grows out of boredom, confusion, or simple immaturity. In the one case sounds accompanying production need to be recognized and adjusted to with some grace. In the second instance the children need guidance and help in attaining constructive outlets for their energies.

Teacher tolerance for noise must certainly be considered, too, but teachers will be able to find a reasonable compromise once they accept the reality that some noise is inevitable in a busy kindergarten. The larger the kindergarten class, the higher will be the volume of sound. And certainly there will be times when children will need reminders to lower their voices because there are so many people saying so many things at once. But how else does language develop except by use?

Rebellion in the Ranks

There are twenty children in this next class, many of whom are a month or two short of five. It is a bright, crisp day and the teacher and the aide both feel that the first part of the session should be spent outdoors by *all* the children, including those who often resist going outdoors. As the children gradually arrive, they are informed: "We are playing outdoors first today." In response they all run out eagerly where the aide is already in charge. The other teacher is inside waiting for the last arrivals. As anticipated, three children who at the moment constitute a special, intimate group within the class conspire to rebel; in addition to these there is Nancy, who is a determined nonconformist. She also protests the teacher's definite announcement.

"We want to stay in," says Miriam, spokesperson for the rebels, now numbering five.

"I know," the teacher grants, "you like to play in the doll corner; but you can use the play house outdoors. You'll have a good time outside."

"It's too cold out," another child answers.

"No, the weather is fine," the teacher states.

"But *we* don't like to go out! *Do* we?" offers another child, upholding the solidarity of the group.

"Even so, today we are *all* going out first and there will be no teacher in the room. You will play indoors later." Plainly, the teacher was not just arbitrarily denying them an immediate pleasure, but neither was she backing down.

"But we don't need any teacher. We'll play by ourselves," explains the spokesperson rationally.

"No, a teacher must always be in the room with children in case someone does need help. That's a school rule. Come, I'll hold the door open," the teacher says confidently and with finality, making clear that *she* is in charge. And the rebels come out agreeably, all except Nancy, the determined nonconformist. "No! I already played outdoors this morning at home. So I had enough fresh air. My *mother* even said so," Nancy protests, pitting parental authority against the teacher's.

"Well, it is nice, sunshiny weather," the teacher answers placidly enough, "and *all* of us are going out," she adds, firmly, reasserting teacher control for Nancy's benefit.

"I am staying in." Nancy at this point does not want to lose face by giving in and wants to have the last word. "Anyway, other days I stayed in," she says, offering consistency as her last argument.

"Those days we had three teachers (student-teacher), so one was in the room," the teacher explains matter-of-factly. "Come!" she calls, invitingly, "See the jump-off bridge the children built!" The teacher is now interested in appealing to Nancy's curiosity rather than carrying the argument further; she is sure of her position and she is giving Nancy an out.

Outdoors, Nancy is perfectly cheerful and enjoys the bridge, playing on it cooperatively with a group of several children. The other four all enjoy jumping and climbing and hiding in packing boxes. After a while Miriam, speaker for the resistance, says, "We were outside long enough. Can't we come in now?"

"Five more minutes," answers the teacher cheerfully, and in five more minutes she goes in with children who had been out forty minutes already (excluding Nancy).

We see here that the teacher has deliberately exercised control of the situation. Yet the children felt free to question and test the control until they understood and accepted the whole situation, convinced of the teacher's unmistakable authority to exercise supervision and protection on their behalf. The teacher, for her part, did not moralize; rather, she answered each argument in such a way as to help the children understand the reasons for school rules. (The authoritarian demands obedience because he or she says so and does not feel at all impelled to give reasons or tolerate questions.) Despite the expressions of assertiveness and resistance from the children, the adult authoritative statements were not offered either as punishment or bargaining on the part of the teacher, nor was there unquestioned submission or lasting resentment on the part of the children. Thus, discipline exercised with consideration of the children's needs and with confident control on the part of the teacher resulted in a change in attitude and behavior on the part of the children.

While there may be times when absolute, unquestioning obedience is in order, as in a fire drill or while crossing the street, generally it is possible to let children in on the reasons for necessary controls. This acts in the long run to give them a basis for judgment when they must make their own decisions. Discipline clearly based on the well-being and safety of the group helps individuals control their wishes and conform to class regulations with a sense of the larger, social necessity that tempers the frustration of individual denial.

Following the outdoor period Nancy's teacher noticed her standing by the easel and watching Miriam mixing paints. "Did you see how Miriam made that beautiful purple with red and blue?" she asked other children, and she soon gathered a group of articulate admirers who, far from disturbing the artist, encouraged her to heights of inventiveness. Nancy, herself a good painter, was able to become absorbed in another child's creativity and by her strength of generous feeling, to draw others to the scene. The teacher wondered if Nancy's self-assertion could perhaps be seen as springing from the same source of positive conviction about her feelings that led her to both a warm appreciation of Miriam's work and to insistence on having her own way in regard to the outdoor play period. Yet the teacher, by holding her ground with equal conviction but broader reason, helped Nancy accept realistic, socially based inhibitions on her will, without questioning her right to hold strong convictions. Often what a child does in one situation makes better sense when the teacher notes how that child behaves in a variety of situations.

Bad Language

When four-and-a-half-year-old Martin burst out with an explosive "Shut up, shut up!" which he flung around indiscriminately at children and adults, the teacher controlled her irritation, postponed judgment, and listened calmly for a while. Knowing Martin, she realized that he was experimenting with rebelling and with shocking people. She did not forget Martin's otherwise excellent vocabulary and his ability to talk reasonably most times; she therefore did not judge this outburst to be deliberate rudeness. She was able to speak to Martin quietly, saying in effect that it was tiresome to hear the same phrase over and over again and that it was time for a change. To this Martin responded by talking casually about a new subject!

In Chris's case, the situation was different. Chris was a child of the streets, and "bad" language was *the* language of communication, as far as he was concerned. Chris needed broadening of vocabulary and experience; Chris needed to trust adults and relate to them around interesting activities. So the teacher did not scold him or otherwise comment on his endless stream of invective. But she worked hard to get and keep his attention on materials and activities; she accompanied her actions and his with simple but appropriate language; she listened to his meaning and not to his words. Eventually she was able to say, "Chris, try telling us straight, just what you mean," and he understood her. He did not change his verbal style overnight, but the percentage of foul and abusive language in relation to the whole output did decrease, and that was a real victory for Chris and his teacher.

Neither child's unsocial behavior was overlooked by the adult. They were both given a chance to change their behavior without being humiliated or belittled. This is important, for the aim of discipline is the attainment of self-discipline, not obedience out of fear.

Behavior Related to Total Personality Need

Tyrone, almost five, has shown special concern about being "a big boy now." He asked the teacher, "Guess how old I am going to be on my birthday?" and without waiting for an answer he stated powerfully, "Ten." When questioned soberly by other children, he adjusted this number to eight but apparently wanted to be a bigger boy still. "I went with my daddy and he let me drive the car. Then pop! we had a flat tire and I got out and changed the flat tire, because I know how." Then he concentrated on making a "big building." He built and built till he was satisfied that the building was bigger than himself, bigger than the teacher, a building bigger than any other child had made that day. But that same day he threw another child's hat over the fence. It was a wild gesture. The other child was upset by Tyrone's "meanness" and received comfort and help from the teacher. The teacher called to Tyrone, but he eluded her approaches. "I can't hear what you're saying," he said defiantly, holding both hands to his ears. When the teacher picked Tyrone up bodily to bring him inside for discussion in private, he resisted her control by kicking and then crying. The "big boy" was reduced to a crying, kicking baby and subsided only in the teacher's arms.

Growing up was far from easy for Tyrone. He worked so hard at bigness he could not take it any more. He was tired, and so crumpled to littleness and even to a temper tantrum. At that moment the teacher could not possibly have asked him to "act like a big boy" or "stop the nonsense." She simply protected him as well as others, leaving him safely alone till he regained his composure and self-respect. At an appropriate time she tried to direct him to relaxing and releasing activities. And the other children, taking the cue from the teacher, asked sympathetically as well as cautiously, "Is Tyrone all right now?" They learned that a little boy in trouble will get help and will be "all right."

DISAGREEMENTS

Among kindergartners, as among any children, arguments may spark up a hot quarrel, and this in turn can lead to hurt feelings. Two boys, almost six years old, are arguing about the creation of the world.

"... God made the whole world, and he made the people and everything *in* the world, every single thing. *God* did it!" Terrell asserts passionately, addressing Evan. The teacher, who is clearing a table nearby, listens without comment as Terrell's friend Evan answers with a bold, cold statement: "God didn't make the world." Evan then offers a learned reference to biological origins. Terrell interrupts him with even greater passion: "God *did* make everything!"

"But how could God make *different* things at the same time?" Evan asks analytically, and adds with finality, "That's silly." Terrell's voice quavers, his mouth drops, and he flounders with distress. Evan hurts him further by taunting him for his belief. Terrell's frustration and pain are clearly seen in the bitter tears rolling down his cheeks. At this point the teacher states her position clearly to Evan. "It's all right to talk about your idea of how the world was made. But it's *not* all right to tease Terrell about *his* idea."

"I didn't do anything to him," Evan defends himself.

"You were *hurting* Terrell by teasing him. You may disagree with people, but you may not tease. That hurts people's feelings."

The teacher did not attempt to reconcile the difference in beliefs or presume to be on the side of one or another child in the argument, for the children's was a personal discussion. They needed to express themselves and to hear each other out. But when one child inflicts pain on another, whether psychological or physical, a teacher's sensibility as a mature person and responsibility as a teacher require stopping such undesirable behavior and discouraging bad relationships.

In another situation two girls choose the same book from the library shelf. Each claims to be the first to have chosen the book and each pulls on the book and on the other's hand. The teacher sees that no solution to the struggle is imminent, and furthermore, that the book, if not the girls, is certainly about to be damaged.

"I'll take that book, please," the teacher commands. "We can't let our books get torn!" Putting the book away the teacher tells the quarreling children that they should decide by *talking* whether one, the other, or both together should look at the desired book. The teacher refrains from any moral pressure such as "Shame on you, girls! Can't you just be friends?" because that does not really tackle the issue at hand. Instead, she appeals to their common sense and the logic called for by the situation itself, and the girls respond. In a few minutes they make their decision, ask the teacher politely for the book, and sit down to look at it together.

Fighting

Arguing that leads to physical blows is not uncommon among young children. It comes naturally to them to use physical means to attain ends, and they must painfully learn to control hands and feet and use words instead. Lauretta Bender,[1] studying aggression in disturbed children, found that normally developing children, by contrast with the disturbed, went through a stage of *saying* they must not hit before they acted on the prohibition. Such verbal understanding before the actual performance is typical of young children. By five a good deal of internal assimilation of the words has taken place—in comparison to age three. But the assimilation is not yet perfect and certainly is not the same for all children. More fives than threes express verbal injunctions against hitting. But as a group fives are not yet completely reliable. Individual differences in temperament and experience affect this development of control.

When children have difficulty controlling direct physical outbursts of anger and irritation, a kindergarten teacher must first get over the shock of witnessing primitive behavior, which is not to be unexpected at ages four to six, and then get into the situation to guide it. First, the teacher must honestly and fairly try to understand the children's own appraisal of the situation. Although they may be wrong, they do not know this yet; unless the teacher sees the issue with their eyes, there is no real approach to them. On the other hand, children might be right but may nevertheless have a poor way of dealing with people. Something impels them to act, and the teacher must see things as the children see them in order to understand their problem. Only by sympathetic awareness of what really bothers a child or what he or she is trying to do can the teacher hope to communicate an altered perspective or more suitable techniques. Words and fists are after all only different means for handling feeling. Feelings are universal and therefore must be understandable to teachers. Techniques of handling feeling have to be learned in childhood, and they are learned from adults. Recognizing the validity of a child's feeling (even if he or she does not like what is seen), the teacher shows the child socially acceptable methods for coping with feelings.

Kindergarten teachers also need to know that children may receive very different kinds of training at home in regard to fighting. Some children are taught never to fight under any circumstances but to come and tell an adult. Others are taught to fight back when hit but not to start a fight themselves. Still others are taught by life on the street, if not directly by an adult, that the way to avoid possible attack is to hit the other person first, before that person makes a move. Consider the differences in experience that lead to these different views. Favored children, whose mothers sit on the park bench while they play nearby, grow accustomed to having their mothers step in with guidance, admonition, or protection at the first sign of troubled relations with other children. They not only hear what their mothers say but watch their mothers in action and learn from them. They

[1] Lauretta Bender, *Aggression, Hostility and Anxiety in Children* (Springfield, Ill.: Charles C. Thomas, 1953).

expect the same involvement from their teachers. But what happens to the child of an overburdened, harried mother who sends her toddler outdoors alone or with an older child because she cannot take care of her large family under difficult circumstances and give individual attention to each child? This little one, confronted with the sink-or-swim philosophy of children left early in life to their own devices, learns either to fight for survival or stay indoors. Both kinds of children come to the same public school kindergarten. But they feel very differently about this matter of fighting. The teacher is likely to support the home views of some of the children, but the others will hear a point of view that is incomprehensible to them in view of their experience. For the less protected children in particular, the teacher who says "Talk it over" is contradicting the evidence of their own eyes.

Angry, Impulsive Children

Although fighting is very common among children in our culture, and usually not too serious, there are children whose hostile, aggressive fighting goes far beyond any "norm" we might find acceptable. In searching for reasons for so much anger in so many children, several conditions in the larger society come to mind. One is the tension and anxiety among increasing numbers of parents that we know exists not only from normal interactions between teachers and parents but from reports of child abuse coming to public attention. A second condition may well be the prevalence of violence in television programs for children.[2] Since children of kindergarten age are still struggling to distinguish fantasy from reality, and are prone to imitate what they see, it is not uncommon for some to act out TV violence.[3]

In one school the teachers noticed the preschoolers' unusually wild behavior. "When they were yelling "Batman" or doing karate kicks, what they had seen on television was evident." Then the entire staff decided to send a letter of alarm to the parents. The parents in this case responded by curbing TV watching at home and instituting selectivity of programs. And everyone appreciated the results.[4]

Another demonstration of needed reform in TV viewing by young children comes from a rare source, a TV executive.

> Television did have an effect on me right from the beginning. In first grade, I was a member of a four-kid gang that went around imitating TV Westerns. We'd disrupt class to play out scenes, picking up chairs and hitting people over the head with them—except, unlike on TV, the chairs didn't break, the kids did. Finally, the teacher called my parents in and said, "Obviously, he's being influenced by these TV shows, and if he is to continue in this class, you've got to agree not to let him watch television any more." So, from first

---

[2] Robert W. Liebert, John M. Neal, and Emily Davidson, *The Early Window: Effects of Television on Children and Youth* (Elmsford, N.Y.: Pergamon Press, Inc., 1973).

[3] Dorothy H. Cohen, "Television and the Child Under Six," *Television Awareness Training: A Viewer's Guide* (Media Action Research Center, Inc., 417 Riverside Dr., N.Y. 10027, 1979).

[4] Nadine Brozan, "Film and TV Violence: A Nursery School Takes a Stand," *New York Times,* June 3, 1975, p. 28.

to second grade there was a dark period during which I didn't watch TV at all. And I calmed down and the gang broke up.[5]

The above was recounted during an interview by Brandon Tartikoff, president of NBC.

We can see then that a teacher's discipline and guidance in the case of disruptive behavior due to television can be effective. However, uncontrollable, hostile behavior on the part of some children is beyond a teacher's understanding and is really more than a teacher can cope with in a full group of youngsters. Children so hurt and so undeveloped tend to be "touchy" children, reacting with violence to any slight accidental push, someone's calling them a name, someone's taking their chair, or for reasons the teacher cannot always see. Such children have difficulty listening, focusing, and sustaining interest or contact. They do not have a sense of order, either of time or space. They expect punishment, they are suspicious of praise. They tend to be overactive and impulsive. It is therefore understandable that in some settings there are special classes for such children—small, well equipped, and well staffed. These children need much individual attention and yet must learn to be acceptable members of a group.

Destructiveness

In many groups of children there may be some who are destructive for the distorted satisfaction destruction brings to them. They mishandle materials and tools, destroy children's work, smash clay, and kick down block buildings. While all young children take some pleasure in seeing things crash and even in deliberately causing a crash, it is not the usual pattern of healthy children; it occurs sporadically and then as a kind of unexpected outburst. Children who are consistently destructive must be looked at carefully. Their strong and misdirected anger will probably be apparent in their behavior toward people as well as with materials. When children occasionally delight in crashing a building with a kind of guilty joy in this absolute breakdown of the control they have come to accept in their daily lives, one can sympathize with the escape from controls which this represents and can recognize the behavior as a safety valve. It is when destructiveness is continuous, deliberate, and perhaps even tinged with malice that one should feel alarmed. In such a case destructiveness is a symptom of some disturbance and the task of soothing and reeducating a sorely troubled child may be beyond the teacher. She can only hope to give such a child safe outlets, such as water play, clay, and carefully supervised woodwork, where he or she can destroy with impunity. At the same time a teacher must continuously make clear to such a child the restrictions on destroying other people's things, which protect the aggressor as well as the other children.

Intentional destructiveness must also be distinguished from accidental destructiveness that comes with inexperience and from the misuse of materials for experimental purposes. A child who breaks a vase, snaps off the leaf of a plant while

[5]Tony Schwartz, "Do the Networks Need Violence?" *New York Times,* May 16, 1982.

watering it, drops a pile of blocks on someone's toes, or spills paint on someone's picture while filling a jar may only be showing signs of inadequate attention to normal precautions which have to be learned with experience. Such destructiveness must be taken in stride, and to a certain extent, expected, especially at the beginning of the school year.

In any case destructiveness, like so many other aspects of behavior, may have different causes and different meaning. The *meaning*—exuberant defiance of bounds, malice and hate, inexperience and poor coordination—will influence the nature and extent of the treatment. Often special help is needed.

Low Tolerance for Frustration

Children have always found it hard to make choices among two or more desirable attractions, to be patient, and to see the relationship between a present chore and future outcome. In part this is the consequence of their normal egocentricity, in part the response to a very human desire not to feel pain or discomfort. Good teachers help children over these hurdles of growing, largely by their responsible behavior in keeping promises and presenting order and sequence in the daily program. It is possible for children to be assured of the value of waiting, or trying, or choosing by successfully overcoming difficulties in the attainment of goals important to them.

This particular task is harder for today's teachers, because the message of "instant gratification" is a loud one in our culture. Tolerance for frustration of any kind is harder than ever for many children. They haven't the patience to do several steps in a process of work but want the pinwheel or potholder or block building or clay object to be instantly created without much effort on their part. They find the time lapse between their desire and its fulfillment irritating; they may whine and cry or withdraw from productive work to sulk or wander aimlessly.

Teachers must recognize this for what it is, and work to help children learn the satisfaction of being effective through their own efforts. They must also help them see the difference between realistic impediments and fear of struggle. Young children's awareness hovers between the real and the wished for. It is a painful process to learn duration of time, to follow a step-by-step sequence toward a finished production, to deny oneself an immediate pleasure for a future goal. Yet life demands that we all know this, and we must help children learn it even if they find such learning hard.

The "Hyperactive" Child

Increasingly teachers are talking about children who are restless and overactive, who are not necessarily hostile or unpleasant but are unable to concentrate, and who spent much of their time in aimless wandering or running around. Many reasons have been advanced for such behavior including poor home guidance and inadequate school curriculum.

Two very different possibilities have recently been suggested. One is that food coloring and sugar create hyperactivity in some children and that a corrected diet brings them back to normal activity and the capacity to concentrate.[6] Although there is no conclusive evidence yet, studies on the subject are continuing.[7] At an annual conference of the National Association for the Education of Young Children, Jane Goldman, of the Human Development Center, University of Connecticut, reported on a wide range of pediatric and nutritional studies of the effect of food dyes on behavior and on findings that young children especially are prone to have sensitivity to food dyes.[8] The other possibility affecting hyperactivity is that children who watch too much television develop symptoms of hyperactivity and restlessness.

Before condemning either hyperactive children or their parents, teachers might suggest that parents have such children diagnosed for their reactions to food coloring and sugar, reexamine the number of hours the children watch television, and note which programs they watch. While all this may still not be the answer for certain children, we must recognize that in simpler cultures than ours the phenomenon of hyperactivity is not a common one. Let us not forget, especially with difficult children, that *all behavior is caused.* Young children may be helpless victims of factors beyond their control or understanding. Even though such children are difficult for teachers to deal with, they need proper diagnosis, not punishment.

GUIDANCE AS OPPOSED TO DOMINATION

There is ample evidence from research that punishment for wrongdoing does not work as effectively as praise for doing the right thing. Children need limits set on their behavior, but room must be left for initiative, choice, and self-direction.

Seeing Others' Motivation

Appel[9] studied the causes for fighting in low-income and middle-income preschool centers. In the first, children fought mainly over possessions; in the second, over leadership. In the first center the teachers employed "stopping" techniques ("No more fighting!" and "Both of you sit down!") The number of fights did not decrease. But in the other center the teachers tried to help the children understand their own and other children's motivations. ("You thought he would break your building, but he was only reaching for that board which he needs for his building.") The number of incidents decreased as the children themselves came to apply this

[6] Ben Feingold, M.D., *Why Your Child is Hyperactive* (New York: Random House, 1975).
[7] Frederick J. Stare, "Diet and Hyperactivity: Is There a Relationship?" *Pediatrics*, 66, no. 4 (October 1980).
[8] Jane A. Goldman, *Food and Behavior.* Paper presented at the NAEYC Conference, Washington, D.C., November 13, 1982.
[9] M. H. Appel, "Aggressive Behavior of Nursery School Children and Adult Procedures in Dealing with Such Behavior," *Journal of Experimental Education*, Vol. II (1942), 185–99.

same kind of probing for causes to the solution of their differences. There is a correlation between teachers' seeking causes and children doing so.

"Strict" and "Permissive"

Adults must offer guidance and even a firm "no" when necessary. How they say "yes" or "no" will depend on how they see their own roles in relation to children.

The strict or traditional approach seems to be built on an assumption that children will not know what to do without continuous and careful direction. Whether out of protectiveness and love or anger and fear, restrictions are set up in all areas of children's lives. They are deliberately made dependent on the wisdom and judgment of the adult, and their freedom to think or act independently is curtailed more by the adults' values of right and wrong than by their awareness of the urges to growth that propel a child to action and thought. Excessive strictness may be kind or unkind. Either way its effect is to limit the possibilities for approved independent action by the child.

The more permissive approach, on the other hand, seems to depend more on *watching* carefully but allowing more opportunity for children to learn many things through their own efforts, even at the risk of making mistakes and often of temporarily contradicting such adult values as thrift, cleanliness, manners, and appearance. Limitations are clearly stated and imposed when safety, health, other people's property and feelings, or long-range irreversible consequences are involved. The criteria are rational and based on faith in a child's capacity to learn from mistakes, if the conditions of learning include commonsense precautions and adult supervision when necessary. The very strict approach probably is more heavily based on fear that children will get into trouble if they are not carefully directed into known, safe, and proper channels; the permissive approach is more trusting of the children's capacity to handle themselves and learn from their own experience, with the condition that the watchful adult will limit potentially dangerous behavior. The less one trusts children (and oneself), the more it seems that control is imposed. Yet inadequate knowledge of children's real limitations may lead people who are permissive to overtrust children and allow them liberties they are not able to handle. This can also be dangerous. Obviously, the more strictly brought up children (but not the ones treated with severity and harshness) are easier for teachers to deal with. They have been taught to obey adults without question. Yet adults who are secure in themselves and in their own power to control if they have to, may find the child who asks questions, even to the point of questioning adults with a confidence that verges on brashness, a delightful challenge. Such a teacher will not hesitate to ask for conformity when necessary, as Nancy's teacher did. But adults who are insecure about their role feel safest when holding the reins tightly, since they are afraid of not being able to take hold again if they once let go. This complete and dominating control by adults may be easier in some ways, but life with children is far more stimulating and enriching for adults and certainly for children when youngsters can test their powers without fear of reprisal. At the same time they must be secure in the knowledge that they will definitely be stopped if their actions go beyond the bounds of safety, health, and consideration for others or lead to irreversible, far-reaching consequences.

FACTORS AFFECTING DISCIPLINE

Teachers as People

Where do a teacher's ideas on discipline come from? A school superintendent made the following rueful remark: "When I interview a candidate, she gives me all the correct theories about children that she learned at school. But when I observe her in the classroom she acts toward the children just as her mother did toward her!" This is not far from the truth. Almost everyone, lay or professional, has ideas about how children should behave and how they should be disciplined. These ideas come from the upbringing we ourselves received, which some of us copy slavishly and others of us reject out of hand, sending us to an opposite extreme.

Ideas on discipline differ with class and ethnic background. Studies suggest that middle-class families expect more inner control of their children earlier, use words as mediators between feeling and approval, and discipline according to standards of behavior that will be useful in society later on. Lower-class parents are more likely to be immediately annoyed, punish physically, and expect their children to use physical means of defense when necessary, which many use on children without compunction. Teachers, on the whole, follow middle-class ideas on discipline, which may bring them into conflict with working-class children and parents or with families of other cultures. Many a teacher has stood speechless before a well-intentioned parent who said earnestly, "Hit him, teacher, if he's not good. Hit him. He *must* mind."

Every teacher is a product of his or her own class and especially own family. Ideas about good and bad behavior are learned early and learned emotionally, so that years later a reaction to what a child does may not be an objective reaction at all, but a spontaneous response to what one learned early to approve or disapprove of. Let us take as an example learned attitudes about what boys and girls may or may not do. Boys are not supposed to cry, even when little. They should be brave, defend girls, and never hit them. Girls may be tomboys and get away with it, but boys pay a heavy price for gentleness and nonaggressive attitudes. Are teachers guided by these old-fashioned standards, learned in childhood, when they judge the actions of boys and girls? Are teachers likely to be furious when a sturdy little boy hits just as sturdy a little girl in absolutely justifiable anger, because *gentlemen do not hit ladies?* Or can she be impartial regardless of a child's sex?

What is learned early in life becomes part of us and influences our attitudes toward "good" and "bad" behavior in children. For this reason, difficult as it is, teachers must make an effort to understand the sources of their own reactions. Discipline is more than a bag of tricks and should not be governed by such questions as, "Is it better to put children in the corner or outside the door, when they misbehave?"

Interdependence.   In supervising student-teachers one of the authors found that again and again the core of the disciplinary relationship with children lay in the innermost feeling of the fledgling teacher concerning the right to be the authority, the controlling adult, instead of the child. Teaching for most people begins at just about the time that they are in the process of achieving final emotional independence from their own parents. The more prolonged the struggle for autonomy at home, the more difficult it seems for the student to take over a class with a conviction of being able to handle those now dependent on him or her. Not yet in complete control of themselves, student-teachers seem to fear most losing control of a class. Discipline is the most popular topic of discussion in seminars and coffee breaks term after term, among experienced teachers and novices alike.

Readiness for authority.   The beginning, then, of any disciplinary relationship between teacher and children must be an examination of the meaning that being an authority has for the individual teacher. Is this at long last a chance to hold the upper hand? Is this a chance to treat other children the way one would have wanted to be treated oneself? Is there a fear that children will not like you if you say "no" to them, and is it so important to be liked that you will not do anything to jeopardize this? Are you determined to teach children all the "right" things because you believe so strongly that children are little animals and it is your job to civilize them? Are you reluctant to use your "power" to teach the children right from wrong?

These are not idle questions. Under every professional veneer of objectivity is the human being who was once a child and who grew to adulthood with learned convictions about right and wrong. Are these so overpowering that they blot out the fact that young children are only just learning right from wrong and need more help than censure? Or is a teacher so opposed to his or her own upbringing that he or she is reluctant to offer any guidance to children for fear of imposing values on them?

The influence of feelings on actions.   The following story about Kevin, a generally quiet, serious, and quite tense child, is a story about a teacher as well.

Kevin was apparently the kind of five-year-old who was always pushing his curiosity into strange nooks and crannies with some degree of providence. But one time he went to inspect the teacher's purse while she was not in the room, removed a dollar bill, and left the purse wide open. The teacher soon learned that her money was missing and promptly took the law into her hands. She commanded everyone to attention and demanded that the guilty one give herself or himself up. None of the children admitted guilt. Like a police officer and with a spirit of wrath and vengeance, the teacher searched each child's pockets, and sure enough, discovered the money in Kevin's. Silent, frightened Kevin was then brought to the front of the class as a bona fide thief. And to make sure that the "lesson" would not escape the kindergartners, the teacher informed them of the consequences of stealing. "You go to jail for it." So righteous did the teacher feel that she unhesitatingly reported to Kevin's mother both the offense and the details of her own action. The mother acknowledged the news curtly and took the weeping child home. He was inconsolable. That evening he had fever and remained ill for several days.

Was the teacher acting as she did only out of a rational desire to help Kevin learn not to steal? Before answering, let us look at another incident of stealing in the kindergarten. In this case the teacher reluctantly admitted to her principal that the depletion of scissors in her classroom was the result of the children's helping themselves. "They don't have any scissors at home," she pleaded. "I feel so sorry for them. How can I scold them when they are just little children who love scissors and are too poor to buy them?"

In both these instances the teachers believed that what they were doing was best for the children. Yet both teachers were far too motivated by their own emotions of indignation in one case and pity in the other to recognize clearly what the children's real learning had to be. Both Kevin and the children in the other class were five-year-olds. This meant that their consciences were hardly developed enough to restrain them from following their impulses, even though verbally they might repeat, "Stealing is wrong." Because understanding is relatively superficial at this age, such behavior is hardly unusual. Therefore, stealing at ages four, five, and six should never be given the weight that is given to behavior of the same type by fully grown men and women. However, no one can develop a conscience and a clear sense of right and wrong unless taught; and children learn best of all when taught by someone who respects and understands their problem. Both teachers, therefore, failed in their responsibility to help the children learn. The first teacher, in her fury, gave Kevin a burden of guilt he was far too young to carry, such as the teacher herself had probably once experienced. And the second teacher literally taught her children that it is all right to take what does not belong to you if you want it badly enough. Control must be accompanied by understanding if it is to be meaningful control.

Accepting "unacceptable" behavior. Little children have not been around long enough to have picked up perfectly the good manners and accepted graces that we call civilized behavior. There is a simple directness of expression, a quick response to the urgency of feeling, and a tendency to *do* first and *think* later, that can make them seem uncouth and even barbaric at times. The same children are, of course, quite capable of charm, sweetness, tenderness, and even charity to others. Adults who have never worked with young children generally have a way of finding the graces absolutely to be expected and the crudities a bit of a shock and a surprise. Perhaps the second major learning of the kindergarten teacher, after working out her or his leadership role, is to learn to be shockproof. Anything can happen in a kindergarten and usually does. Although most children are usually nicely behaved, the rawness of early physical reactions to life is not too remote. Frustration, anger, envy, rivalry—all human, if not pretty—can cause a child to do quite uncivilized things. Illness, fatigue, insecurity, feelings of rejection can also cause unhappy behavior. The teacher who has finally, and more or less painfully over the years, learned to control her or his emotions and handle body processes with dispatch and even indifference, may have a long way back to go in acceptance of what is normal if she or he is to live comfortably with children who are on their way to civilized living but backslide once in a while.

Fairness to all and bias toward none.   Let us carry the matter of learned standards into another realm. Do we not all find certain kinds of children more attractive than others? Blond ones perhaps, or snub-nosed, or coffee-colored, or ones with long braids? Bright ones, shy ones, easygoing ones, perky ones? Clean ones, nicely dressed ones, nonsmelly, carefully brought up ones?

We have mentioned the acceptance of individuals before, but perhaps in discussing discipline it is pertinent to raise the question again. People do have favorites, and they do find some children more appealing than others. It is not too hard to forgive a child you like for some transgression you then consider minor and see the same act as major in a child whom you do not like. Studies show that teachers at the upper levels of school tend to grade girls higher than boys; studies of juvenile law show adolescents punished more severely than much older adults for the same crimes; a child with a reputation for being bad is expected by each new teacher to be bad. We cannot condone these things as being human and therefore to be expected. It is an absolutely necessary part of the professional growth of anyone in an interpersonal profession to recognize his or her particular prejudices, no matter what they are, so that he or she can give to each child the fairness that all children are entitled to when they need disciplining and guidance. Teachers, no less than other members of the population, may make scapegoats of certain children. Children often tell their parents that one child is picked on by the teacher and that the children do not know why because *they* accept each other pretty much as they are. We have said before that no one can be expected to love every child. But a teacher must *respect* every child and offer him and her an equal chance with others to grow. Certainly not race, religion, ethnic background, socioeconomic class, or individual idiosyncrasies should be a barrier to full acceptance. This is a right guaranteed to each child by our democratic principle of respect for the individual.

Ability to understand some children more readily than others.   Miss Kane was an outstanding teacher who had a way of establishing a group long before anyone else. No one in her class remained on the outskirts. In one way or another all were made to feel welcome and to find a place. But Miss Kane was talking to a fellow teacher one day when five-year-old Ellen edged near, and with great curiosity, obviously listened in on the conversation between the adults. Miss Kane became ruffled. "Go back to work, Ellen," she said. "I want to talk to Miss Duggan in private." Ellen skipped off and was soon in the midst of an active group of youngsters, apparently unbothered by the reprimand. But Miss Kane continued to muse about her. "There is something about that child I can't stand," she said. "She reminds me of the girls at college who were 'in,' and who treated me as if I didn't exist. She doesn't really do anything wrong; it's just that she always knows what's going on, and has a finger in every pie. Somehow, that type doesn't appeal to me."

Miss Kane could not see as any outsider could that her maneuvering to include all the children reflected her own feelings about being left out, and her feeling for Ellen was certainly affected by her former envy of the girls who were so easily "in."

Discipline is often affected by this kind of identification with a child. More than one teacher takes secret pleasure in acts of aggression that cause another teacher to wince in remembered fear. When people become teachers they do not cease to be the people they always were. They must face their feelings if they are to offer children the guidance children do need.

Tolerance.   It is evident that teachers differ considerably from each other, not only in teaching techniques but in personal tolerances for various kinds of behavior. Each teacher must understand her or his own level of tolerance. How much noise can you take without getting irritable? How do you really feel about messy, sloppy, sticky hands and tables?

What is the point at which sassiness ceases to be cute and becomes obnoxious instead? Or is sassiness something that makes your blood boil? How many times does it take to say the same thing before you feel ready to explode? How much disorder can you stand while children are at work? How much resistance can you take from children without losing your temper? And perhaps we should ask, too, what are your physical tolerances? Are there times when you get headaches, or cramps, or otherwise feel so miserable that you are likely to let the nearest victims feel the impact of your irritability?

There is no reason why you cannot tell children honestly, "You are not doing anything wrong, but I can't stand so much noise today." And although you might not say, "I guess I am a bit cross because I stayed up late last night watching a show," you have to face this truth within yourself. It is not fair to give children the feeling that what *they* do is the cause of their teacher's displeasure, when it is really the teacher who is having the problem.

What we are saying in all the above is that teachers are people and subject to the same range of human feelings as all others. Because they have chosen to work with other human beings they have a responsibility to be as fair and objective as they can be when they apply limits, controls, censure, or whatever is needed to help children grow in social maturity. Teachers may not indulge in personal whims, prejudices, squeamishness, or other forms of personal bias allowed to the average citizen. Precisely because they are teachers and can influence the lives of young children for better or for worse, they must face themselves and at least be *aware* of what it is in the adult-child relationship that they are not able to handle with objectivity. Awareness may not mean an immediate change in attitudes. But awareness will put a teacher on guard and eventually influence her or his attitudes. Immediately, the teacher will at least question the application of disciplinary measures on the basis of a blind feeling that what she or he is doing is right, hopefully using intelligence and training to make the wisest and most helpful decision for any child or group of children.

One little episode that occurred in a college teacher-education class bears repeating here. Barbara Atkin, a lively and devoted education student, insisted vociferously in a class discussion on discipline that the thing to do with fractious children was to put them in a separate room and let them think things over. "Barbara," her teacher asked her, "is this what your mother did to you?" "Yes," Barbara answered righteously. "And did you think things over?" There was a long pause before Barbara meekly answered, "No. I did not."

Group Effects on Discipline

In all fairness, we must point out that the teacher's personal responses are not always the major cause of disciplinary problems. The most mature teacher, the most patient, understanding, and wise person may have a group that has more than its share of individual problems, or there may be a particular set of children who react to each other so poorly that, try as the teacher will, there is no unifying them as a group. Fritz Redl discusses this fully in the excellent pamphlet *Discipline for Today's Children and Youth.*[10] Although he refers to older children generally, the dynamics of group life operate in the kindergarten, too. It may happen that in one community the children coming to kindergarten are almost all quite immature, and the size of the group will be too large for children who still require large doses of individual attention. A group may have more than its share of badly treated children who are hostile to adults and perhaps to each other. Many physically charged, highly active children may make it difficult to plan for anything but the shortest periods of focused activity. On the positive side, regardless of group composition, is the fact that kindergartners are predisposed to love school. And the kindergarten teacher, with recognition of the limitations as well as the assets of any particular group, can, by being flexible about curriculum, usually win them over to more mature social behavior. But it is important to recognize that groups come with different backgrounds of experience and that some are more ready than others to share a teacher, to sit still for a story, to take turns with equipment, to handle tools and materials competently. If a teacher has a stereotyped notion of how children should behave and a standard program of exactly the same stories, songs, trips, and materials for *each* class, that teacher may be involved in discipline problems because of failure to recognize that differences in groups call for differences in such things as time allotments for specific activities and long-range learning, differences in how directions and instructions are offered, and even differences in degree and kind of supervision.

[10]George V. Sheviakov, F. Redl, and S. K. Richardson, *Discipline for Today's Children and Youth,* rev. ed. (Washington, D.C.: National Education Association, 1956).

The group as opposed to the individual.   One last important aspect of group life is discussed with great insight by Redl, and that is the persistent conflict between the interests of the group and the needs or interests of individuals. It is easy enough to agree that one tries to achieve the satisfaction of all individual needs and that this will take care of the group. But it happens that sometimes an individual interferes too seriously with group life, or, conversely, that a group gangs up against an individual. Occasionally there is a child in a group who has more serious problems than even the best teacher can cope with in a school setting. Redl then suggests his principle of "marginal antisepsis," which he defines as action taken by the teacher to protect the group, *but which is not harmful to the individual,* or action taken for the individual, *which is not harmful to the group.* One kindergarten teacher pitted the group against an individual when she went out of her way to ease the entry into school of a recently arrived little Japanese girl. She praised the child lavishly, displayed her work prominently, took every opportunity to mention her virtues to the class, and showed her own affection overtly and unrestrainedly. The class reacted as one to make life as miserable as they could for this child. The harder the teacher tried to win acceptance for her, the more intolerable her position became. In despair the teacher called for a conference with the class. From the children themselves she finally got the clues. Befriending the Japanese child in the way she did caused the rest of the class to feel that she did not care as much about them, which was certainly not her intention. So action taken for an individual must at the least not be harmful to the group, and vice versa. When children must be isolated from the group, teacher and class should not stand as a solid unit against them. No matter how much they deserve isolation, they should always feel that they are members of the group, even though they must conform to group standards to be liked. Their *participation* may be curtailed, but not their *membership.* Unless they feel they belong, the chances of helping them are completely eliminated.

Curriculum Effects on Discipline

Because groups vary it should be obvious that curriculum which does not meet the needs of a particular group may be the cause for restlessness and quarreling in the kindergarten. Inadequate supplies; materials too hard or too easy to use; reliance on the same program and materials day after day; unawareness of effects of weather, seasons, and illness on children; too many group-controlled activities and not enough opportunities for individual experimentation; unrealistic standards for achievement—all these may cause more disciplinary interference than might otherwise be called for. Interesting, stimulating activity leads to greater satisfactions among children and therefore to greater readiness to cooperate and enjoy a good life with each other.

When visitors ask, "How do you discipline the children when you allow them to initiate their own activities?" I say, "Just watch those kids." Their own creative purpose, the discipline of the learning itself, and the *very momentum of the group process!* . . . these, along with my faith in the children's self-direction, my implicit trust in each child's striving to learn (in our environment) maintain the children's constructive behavior.[11]

DISCIPLINE AS TEACHING

Of the many definitions of the word "discipline," perhaps the most popularly accepted is the interpretation of discipline as punishment. While it is true that there are occasions when punishment (to fit the crime) is in order, it is even truer that the best interpretation of discipline is that of teaching. If we see the child-adult relationship as the child's lifeline to socialization, then the teacher's role as disciplinarian is primarily a role of guidance, support for effort, and clarity of standards for right and wrong. It is easiest to function in this capacity if we recognize that children are born totally unaware of the standards which any society upholds and are dependent on adults for learning what these standards are. There is no reason to scold and censure for what they have not learned at all or may not yet have learned thoroughly. Five-year-olds are old enough that one can reason with them and appeal to their burgeoning need for group participation and acceptance. But they are still young enough to be struggling with growth of inner controls without which a social being does not develop. They need help in controlling their impulses and they need instruction in suitable techniques for group living, *and* they need a minimum of censure for the normal mistakes which they are sure to make while they are learning how to behave in a civilized society.

REFERENCES AND FURTHER READING

APPEL, M. H., "Aggressive Behavior of Nursery School Children and Adult Procedures in Dealing with Such Behavior," *Journal of Experimental Education,* Vol. 11 (1942).

BREARLEY, MOLLY (ed.). *The Teaching of Young Children,* Ch. 8 "Morality: Values and Reasons." New York: Schocken Books, Inc., 1970.

FEINGOLD, BEN. *Why Your Child Is Hyperactive.* New York: Random House, 1975.

GOLDMAN, JANE A. *Food and Behavior.* Paper presented at the National Association for the Education of Young Children Conference, Washington, D.C., November 13, 1982.

NEWMAN, RUTH G. *Groups in Schools.* New York: Simon & Schuster, 1974.

SHEVIAKOV, GEORGE V., REDL, FRITZ, and RICHARDSON, SYBIL K. *Discipline for Today's Children and Youth* (rev. ed.). Washington, D.C.: National Education Association, 1956.

SINGER, D. G., and SINGER, J. L. *Getting Involved: Your Child and TV.* Washington, D.C.: Head Start Bureau, Administration for Children, Youth, and Families, 1982.

---

[11] From an unpublished report by Sally Cartwright, Director, Community Nursery School, Tenants Harbor, Me.

SINGER, J. L., and SINGER, D. G.   *Television, Imagination and Aggression: A Study of Preschoolers.* Hillsdale, N.J.: Erlbaum, 1981.

STARE, FREDERICK J.   "Diet and Hyperactivity: Is There a Relationship?" *Pediatrics* (October 1980).

STONE, JEANETTE GALAMBOS.   *A Guide to Discipline* (rev. ed.). Washington, D.C.: National Association for the Education of Young Children, 1978.

20 Parents and Teachers Can Learn from Each Other

Every child entering kindergarten comes on her or his own terms as a unique individual. Even though all children bring something of the manners, attitudes, and language of their parents with them, a teacher responds to each as an independent person. As time goes on, most teachers need help in understanding certain phases of individual children's behavior, and so they turn to the parents for help in testing their initial reactions.

DIFFERENT PERCEPTIONS

Teachers and parents have somewhat different perceptions of the child whose rearing they share, since their experiences emphasize different although overlapping aspects of a child's behavior. Parents know their children's detailed history from

(Photos by Ken Heyman)

birth, remember special events and their effects, and know just how the children will react to certain kinds of people and happenings. Most mothers, regardless of social, ethnic, or economic background, are fully cognizant of their child's unique-ness from long, intense, and intimate association, although they may interpret what they see differently from the teacher. However, most parents do not know clearly how their children act among strangers and friends without familiar faces nearby; how they react to an authority who is not a parent; in short, how they behave when they are on their own. Nor do parents know how their child compares with others of the same age in skills and aptitudes of all kinds or how the association with peers affects their child's behavior.

The teacher, on the other hand, knows how each child fits into a group, what his or her social techniques are, and how he or she takes to learning. But she or he may have no idea what the children's fears are, the effects which illness may have had on them, or the successes and frustrations they may face each day before and after coming to school. Nor is the teacher likely to know how the family's customs and values differ from the school's and thus confuse children. Some mothers tell their children at the kindergarten door "to behave"; other mothers tell them "to learn" or "do as the teacher tells you"; hoping that the child will not incur disfavor or reflect unfavorably on the mother; and many mothers seem uncertain of what to tell their children about school.

THE WHOLE CHILD

Despite the differing perceptions of teacher and parent, children remain themselves throughout. They do not leave parts of themselves inside or outside the schoolroom door. What happens at home comes to school; what happens at school goes home. It follows logically that parent and teacher do well to know how the two parts they observe quite separately merge in the one child. Sharing and comparing their per-ceptions, teacher and parents together can be most effective in providing for the child. For this a relationship of mutual trust and friendship must be established as far as is possible.

In so heterogeneous a society as ours, such trust must often grow out of teachers' acceptance of life styles different from their own. They must recognize that children's earliest associations influence their responses both to them and to school and that these responses are culturally as well as individually determined. Parents and teachers do have a common meeting ground—the child—but they come to the child from different vantage points.

Parents may fear that the teacher cannot possibly take an interest in each child when there are so many to look after and that their particular child may be the one to miss out. A mother may be learning quite a big lesson when she relin-quishes some of her jurisdiction over her child to a teacher and then sees that the teacher can be friendly and fair to her child and many others at the same time.

The teacher may worry that the parents are going to be critical and that they must be impressed with results as soon as possible. Young teachers in particular face a peculiarly sensitive relationship which only time and experience can alter. Barely out of a dependency relationship with their own parents, they may project onto parents in general feelings not quite resolved within themselves. Thus some very competent teachers are afraid of the parents, afraid that all parents will be condemning and critical; others resent parents because they seem to threaten the teacher's independence of action. Still other young teachers are not sure how they are to talk to an older person now that they are themselves in authority.

Thus a common obstacle to the establishment of good rapport right from the beginning is the possibility of prejudgment on either side. Sometimes the teacher assumes that the parent does not know much about his or her own child or the educational process, often because the parent's expressed goals and values for the child seem somewhat different from the teacher's. Conversely, some parents judge a teacher by hearsay: "I hear the teacher in Room 13 is a horror—everybody says so." Or some mothers may feel that they are entrusting their children to people intellectually or socially their inferior. On the other hand, some teachers are barely tolerant of parents of unfamiliar ethnic, racial, or religious background. With all these possibilities, school people face a real responsibility for getting across a message of consideration and concern, especially to culturally different or uneducated parents.

It is important for all parents to be assured early in the year that the teacher's training and professional awareness prepare him or her to plan in such a way as to be able to supervise different activities and notice special conditions at the same time, thus making it possible to pay attention to every child. Yet assurance that the children will be carefully attended to and individually valued is sometimes difficult to communicate to parents whose language or different styles of expressing concern are unfamiliar. Often such parents are even more apprehensive than others about their children's being noticed and cared for precisely because the barriers to communication make them feel isolated. It is all too easy for them to believe that the school does not have the child's best interest at heart when they see their own values apparently ignored. It is up to the teacher to take the lead in bridging such gaps by becoming familiar with at least the dominant cultural styles in the community so that the teacher can help parents learn about the expectations of the school.

Obstacles to communication can also arise when teachers, filled with pride and conscientiousness in their role, become possessive toward "their" children. The parent is even seen as a rival whom one would gladly dispense with so as to avoid any interference. All too frequently, committed teachers take the side of the child against the parent and fail to see parents as people with a point of view and needs of their own.

Listen to what a kindergarten teacher heard outside her door, and see if, after you feel for the child, you can feel for his mother, too. The child is a five-year-old who has been wetting himself and needing changes of clothing.

George arrives with his mother, who appears to be in a hurry and speaks to George in an angry voice: "Hurry up! Take your things off! You made me late for work already! Come on!" The child standing half inside his cubby, looks at his mother and doesn't move.

Angry at the child's lack of response, the mother turns away and starts to walk out. At this point, George leaves his perch and runs after his mother whining, "Ma, Ma. I wanna kiss. I wanna kiss goodbye." In response the mother, retrieving her coat from the child's grasp, bends down to receive his kiss, but not without an admonition: "Don't let me hear you wetted on yourself again or you gonna get it. . . . Now you be good and don't you make me no trouble, y'hear!"

How much can the teachers do? To whom should they listen first?

Parent-teacher relationships inevitably evoke a variety of feelings, and honest self-evaluation helps to put them in perspective. Teachers must understand that parents also have feelings, and they have more to lose or gain from the success or failure of their children than teachers do. Accepting the reality of the human elements in the relationship, and keeping in mind the welfare of the child as the central objective, the teacher must take the first step to make contact and all the necessary steps to continue this contact. By voice and manner the teacher implies assurance that the communication is not an occasion for attack but for sharing. When a teacher establishes a climate of acceptance, parents, even unhappy ones, are better able to meet a teacher half way. Problems that arise can then be worked out much more readily. The hard-pressed mother in the episode above needed help, not condemnation.

ORIENTING PARENTS TO SCHOOL

Some schools have an orientation program in the spring of the year when the next fall's kindergarten children and their parents are invited to the class for short visits in small groups. On such visits the parents may be a little awed by the big room and uniform furnishings, and they may worry that their own child will feel lost. However, they also notice how the children function without being prodded to perform in this or that activity. They are impressed that little kindergartners can be so self-reliant, as was Mrs. Albert in Chapter 2. Parents are also likely to observe equipment and materials that are new to them.

After the visit to the kindergarten, at a meeting of the parents with the teacher, meaningful questions are apt to be asked pertaining to health, social requirements, and learning in the kindergarten, and the teacher has a chance to give parents advance knowledge about regulations and procedure. All of this contributes to mutual understanding and friendliness, if it is given in a spirit of trust and acceptance.

Making arrangements for visits and meetings takes both time and interest on the part of the teacher, the principal, and often a representative group of parents as well. However, when there is goodwill and active cooperation (not mere politeness), arrangements for early visits and meetings can be successful, and the school year can begin with a head start toward good adjustment.

GETTING TO KNOW PARENTS

In order to establish rapport with parents, the teacher needs from the very start of school to be willing to face them: to exchange brief greetings or pleasantries with those who escort children to school, to get in touch with those whose children require special attention, and to plan for some informal get-together with the group of parents. If the teacher is responsible for double sessions, it would be advisable not to meet all parents at once, for she or he will only behold a sea of faces and be unable to recall individuals.

Sometimes an informal social meeting can be arranged at the beginning of the year when refreshments add to the expression of hospitable welcome and some friendly conversation takes place. Questions of common interest may be discussed according to plan or may be allowed to come up spontaneously. At such a meeting the teacher might convey special pleasure in kindergarten teaching and share thoughts about the forthcoming year. She or he might relate the importance of kindergarten to later school experience or discuss the nature of adjustment to school at this age. The teacher would listen to parents' comments, questions, or practical suggestions and, of course, invite their cooperation in carrying out regulations pertaining to health and orderliness in the class. She or he would encourage the development of closer relationships with the school. The teacher may be asked some questions about curriculum or discipline that cause discomfort. Rather than regard such questions as a confrontation, she or he would do well to describe plans for the children's learning and progress toward later schooling. She or he might also, then and there, decide to hold a special meeting at another time on the topics in question if there is general interest or arrange to speak individually to a concerned parent.

CONDUCTING PARENTS' MEETINGS

General meetings with small or large groups of parents are an important aspect of the teacher's job. They involve learning for both teacher and parent. But the planning, preparation, and aims of the group parent meeting are different from those of the individual parent-teacher conference, which we will discuss later.

The number of teacher-parent meetings per year varies. If the school is a private cooperative with parent participation in the classroom, meetings may be held as frequently as once a month because of the need to interpret the program and evaluate the techniques of parent participation. In day care centers or other schools where teachers have limited time and parents limited availability, two or three meetings a year may be all that can be arranged.

Schools that are eager for parent-teacher relationships have tried various techniques to encourage parent attendance at class or school meetings. At one school with a large number of working mothers, the administration arranged for a box-supper meeting right after work, with parents and teachers arriving in work clothes.

Coffee was served by the school and the meeting got off to an early enough start for parents to be home in time to see their youngsters to bed. At another school, located near a new housing development teeming with young mothers and baby carriages, it was realized that provision would have to be made for the toddler and infant brothers and sisters of their kindergarten children if the mothers were to come. An after-school meeting was arranged with baby-sitters from among parents of older grades and a contribution of toys and play materials from the kindergarten. At still another school with a large percentage of foreign-born parents, the business of the meeting was always translated on the spot by a willing bilingual parent interpreter. Many a seemingly knotty problem can be solved with the assistance of those parents who have already established their relationship with the school and who are only too happy to be of assistance in drawing new parents closer to the school community.

Sometimes, however, even after careful thinking and extensive planning, the meetings do not fulfill the teacher's expectations for attendance, and she or he asks, "How do you get parents to come? Those who do get to the meeting appreciate it and are glad they came, but how do you get *everybody* to come?" Often teachers say that it is the very parents who *should* come who do not, and they are baffled, even resentful.

There are many, sometimes surprising, reasons why parents do not come to school meetings. The easiest assumption is that the parents are not sufficiently interested in their children or the school to make the effort, but it is the rare parent who falls into that category. Most parents care very much about their children's welfare; but they may not come to a meeting because they cannot get a baby-sitter or perhaps cannot afford one. Fathers or mothers or both may get home late for dinner and be too tired to go out. During the winter months there can be weeks of illness in a family, as one child gets out of bed only for another to get in! Differences in language, clothing, customs, and values cause feelings of discomfort among some parents, and they are self-conscious about appearing at school meetings if they feel inferior because they speak with an accent, have not had much of an education themselves, or are otherwise different from the school personnel. Well-educated parents, on the other hand, sometimes feel that school meetings are repetitions of what they already know and no longer interesting. Big-city parents are often afraid to go out at night.

Then there are the parents who have not set foot in an elementary school since the day they themselves were graduated. Depending on their own childhood experience as pupils, they may approach reentry into the school in their new capacity as parents with the same feelings of awe, fear, dislike, or nostalgia they had as children. These feelings are often like the feelings with which a student-teacher first meets as colleagues and peers the teachers whom he or she has revered, respected, or feared as a student.

The last group of reasons for poor attendance has to do with the meetings themselves—their nature and character and the spirit in which they are planned.

No one enjoys long-winded speeches or being preached to, and parents are no different from other people in this respect. Meetings can and should be interesting, not last too long (forty-five minutes to an hour and a half), and allow for two-way communication. If a topic is to be explored with the help of a speaker, a film and moderator, a dramatic presentation, or a group discussion, the topic must be one that has meaning and appeal to most parents in that group and not be selected because the teachers feel it is *good* for the parents. That's patronizing! Finally, replying to the question of why parents don't come to parents' meetings a teacher states candidly: "Perhaps, most simply, they don't appreciate the importance or purpose of such meetings. It is up to teachers or administrators to clarify this in the beginning. (I suspect that most teachers resent having to hold meetings and parents resent having to come—all out of ignorance.)"

Resource people for meetings exist in most communities among the professional personnel (doctors, social workers, psychologists, teachers), in film libraries of universities or state departments of education, and, of course, the parents and teachers themselves have much to offer. Expertise does not always carry a conventional credential, although it may.

CONTENT OF GROUP MEETINGS

The most important first item in planning meetings is neither the speaker nor the special film, helpful as these are, but the pertinence of the topic for the group for which it is intended. Only a topic of genuine interest to parents will assure their interested involvement in the meeting. Meetings can deal with a range of goals from the purely social one of establishing rapport to the more specifically directed ones of acquainting parents with new programs and the school philosophy or sharing child development information. The last would include many topics which have to do with the development and behavior of preschool children and which absorb young parents. Yet these topics may bore mothers of third and fourth children who have been through it all before. At the same time, one group might want to talk about how children of five can be helped to become more independent, whereas another may need to explore the question of limits for their self-sufficient but much-too-daring five-year-olds. One group may need help in handling brother-sister conflicts at home that are spilling over into school behavior, another may welcome guidance in the selection of good books and play materials for Christmas presents. Uses and values of creative and scientific materials and activities at school, books children enjoy, pursuit of interests through trips and other experiences, discipline at school as opposed to discipline at home, changing sex roles, how young children learn—all these are good topics only to the extent that they are perceived by the group as useful.

By observing the children at school, listening to the questions parents ask, recognizing differences in school and home outlook and what these stem from, a teacher can tailor a meeting to fit the needs of the parent group. As a further aid it may be helpful to a teacher to sound out parent representatives before making a final decision on choice of topic.

Topics of Persistent Interest

Many kindergarten parents are strongly interested in three particular aspects of kindergarten life—discipline, reading, and play—each of which has proven to be a controversial topic, and for good reason. As parents participate more fully in their children's schools, the varying child-rearing values of a pluralistic population play a part in the concerns and criticisms. Mirra Komarovsky[1] points out that blue-collar families value obedience, neatness, and respect for adults, whereas professional people are more likely to want their children to be happy, to confide in them, and to be eager to learn. Black psychiatrists are explaining that the harsh conditions of life for blacks caused them in the past to rear their children to cope with harshness and that many black parents still have a strong tendency toward excessive strictness and corporal punishment as a result.[2] Educated young parents often express pleasure in spontaneity, self-expressiveness, nondifferentiated sex roles, and even communal living. In addition, a significant number of parents are concerned with the effect of divorce and separation on their young children.

Where does the kindergarten teacher stand, and how can the views of those parents who think differently be reconciled? Meetings have to be very carefully planned if they are to be productive.

PROCESS AND PROCEDURE OF GROUP MEETINGS

Once a specific topic has been determined, the process by which parents will become involved must be considered. Group process can range from spontaneous talk over refreshments to discussion following a prepared speaker, film, panel, or play. Process can also mean workshops in which parents participate in certain activities, learning more from the doing than from talk.

The question of process must be determined by consideration of how people can best learn in a particular area. For example, common behavior problems of young children are often best clarified by discussions among parents in response to such simple questions as, "What does your child do to make you mad?" or "What do you do when your child acts up?" rather than by a professional lecture. Parents' feelings of being the only ones with children who misbehave are relieved, new alternatives are opened to them as they share the experience of other parents, and they can move ahead in their parenting. On the other hand, awareness about what goes into learning to read may be best developed by putting parents themselves

[1] Mirra Komarovsky, *Blue Collar Marriage* (New York: Random House, 1964).

[2] James P. Comer and Alvin Poussaint, *Black Child Care* (New York: Simon and Schuster, 1975).

through the paces of learning to read with a made-up alphabet. When the experience is then crystallized through a discussion led by a knowledgeable person, the issues of how, why, and when reading is best taught are clarified. For a meeting on sex education, on the other hand, a good film or lecture on reproduction may be an excellent starter, since it offers concrete, factual information that parents may not have and that they will need in order to use good judgment.

Whatever the decision, content and process must both be made to fit the needs of a specific group. Group meetings challenge every teacher to provide experience through which adults can learn without feeling patronized.

Discussion Meetings

Topics that involve serious differences in values between teachers and parents or among the parents are best worked out in *discussion* meetings. These have proven to be among the most valuable techniques, and they work with all kinds of parents.

The technique of discussion groups is basically a simple one: The teacher does not "teach" or feel impelled to reach conclusions. She or he asks questions and guides discussions that allow all participants to feel comfortable about stating, explaining, clarifying, questioning, or challenging their own or others' views.

Out of informal, unpressured discussions many things happen. For one, teachers learn how parents teach their children, what parents value, and what their hopes, expectations, and fears are. For another, the exchange among parents of even the same background reveals individual differences. Third, as the group examines, argues perhaps, and rationalizes its views, its members, the teacher included, may move to a realistic resolution of their differences as these affect the children's life at school. And fourth, as parents experience satisfaction in presenting an idea or in discussing issues affecting their children, they grow in self-respect.

Children need parents who have self-respect, and an important outcome of parent relations with the school should be the strengthening of the parents' own self-concept. This teachers can do to the extent that they realize the educational role parents play in their children's lives. Parents and teachers may not always see eye-to-eye on what to do with children, but they are generally in complete agreement on end goals. Both want children to become productive, happy, successful human beings, although teachers and parents may interpret productive, happy, and successful in culturally determined, and therefore different, ways.

The last decades of this century may well be an especially difficult time in which to bring up children. The pressures for physical and psychological survival which many people face are greatest of all for parents, who must offer guidelines to their children in a period of tremendous change and uncertainty. The special problems of the poor and of the poorly integrated minority peoples are particularly pressing, as are those of the single-parent family, and call for warm and sympathetic responses from teachers. Differences in values have to be examined with the parents in a spirit of openness and concern for the children. When teachers are clear about their own values, they can better differentiate between those parental attitudes which reflect inadequate information about child development and those which are deeply ingrained in a cultural pattern that must be respected. Examples of the first exist among many black parents who despair over the failure of the schools to help their children become successful learners in the academic realm, although they are perfectly capable children outside of school. A typical solution among such parents has been to get their children started in the skills very early in order to overcome the handicaps they will face later. On the face of it, this is a sensible solution, but it is not supported by experience and actually opens up the probability of creating fresh, otherwise avoidable problems. One such possibility is the creation of excessive anxiety in the children, a serious deterrent to learning. Even more important, given the parents' goals, is the possibility of truly inadequate preparation for an academic future when the parents' emphasis on the prereading requisites is so limited that really good readers and avid learners cannot result. This makes it imperative that kindergarten teachers know the reading process and children's learning styles enough to reassure parents at the level of the parents' realistic concerns. Parents need solid information about how reading is supported in early childhood. Neither platitudes about how everything will turn out all right nor capitulation to practices that are doomed to be disappointing will do. (See Chapters 15 and 16 for help in this regard.)

The matter of ingrained cultural attitudes is something else again. When Christmastime rolls around, the sparkling, colorful Christmas tree is assumed to be a joy to all Americans as they celebrate a common holiday. Yet, aside from Jewish children, most of whom do not celebrate Christmas, there are the Mexican-Americans, who break a piñata full of gifts instead of trimming a tree, and American Indians, who have a totally different background of belief and may not have incorporated a lit-up tree into their customs. There is no right or wrong here, just difference of custom, and this has to be respected by the teacher whether or not the custom is his or hers. Relations with the parents and the curriculum itself should both reflect that respect.

Meetings on Special Situations

There may have to be still another kind of parents' meeting in case of an unexpected event that involves a teacher's important decision and parents' values or traditions. Such an event might be damage to premises requiring temporary relocation; departure of a teacher and his or her replacement; new admission of handicapped children; or a death in a kindergartner's family. The teacher would then be responsible for informing the children honestly of the event and providing guidance appropriate to those children. In addition, the teacher would need to know the parents' point of view. Sharing ideas and feelings with parents would provide guidance to the teacher. Such a parents' meeting, called on the death of a five-year-old member of the class, was led by one of the authors.[3]

[3] Marguerita Rudolph, "Tell Them Rachel Moved," Chap. 1 in *Should the Children Know? Encounters with Death in the Lives of Children* (New York: Schocken Books, Inc., 1978, paper 1980).

All the parents came when summoned on the phone, and all indicated concern and uncertainty as to what to say to the children, expecting the teacher to advise them. The teacher, however, needed to hear first what the parents had to say. What she heard most was a desire to *protect* the children from stressful knowledge. ("Tell them Rachel moved.") This was followed by a teacher-led discussion on how children can tell when you are withholding important facts. The teacher made it clear that she would be honest with the children about the facts and feelings connected with Rachel's death. But, although the parents on the whole were responsive to the teacher, a different note was sounded by a clergyman father. He offered what appeared to be an irrefutable answer to all the questions raised so far. The event, this father advised, presented an opportunity for religious guidance: the children should be told that Rachel had gone to Heaven. In response, no parent deemed it proper to object to Heaven. But the teacher—after deferring to the families' religious beliefs and practices—explained that her responsibility was different from that of the parents or the theologian. She had to consider the children's level of understanding and their way of learning about events on earth as well as in Heaven. Her care and guidance of the children had to be different, as she shared the tragic event with the children.

This parent-teacher meeting proved to be indeed relevant, thought-provoking, and educational to all. It also presented a challenging and difficult process of communication for all, especially for the teacher.

BUILDING OVERALL COMMUNICATION

The quality of the school's relationships with parents permeates all forms of communication, written as well as oral.

Announcements of meetings can be genuinely inviting or dutifully correct and uninspiring. For example, a letter to parents which says: "Would you like to know what your children talk about? Then come to hear a report on 'Children's Conversations and Discussions in the Kindergarten'" is more inviting than an announcement that says "The subject of tonight's parent meeting is a talk on Children's Language."

One teacher, in planning her workshop meeting for the year, was able to have the school secretary type all the invitations to the parents on postcards (they could easily have been run off on a ditto machine or even written out by helpers from an older grade). Then she told the class of five-year-olds about the meeting at which their parents would use the children's materials, and to their great interest the teacher read aloud all the parents' names and addresses on the postcards. Then the class went to the nearby post office and each child dropped a card in the mail slot. As the teacher expected, this resulted in the children's concern with the meeting, which in turn produced strong pressures: "You *have* to come to the meeting, daddy —I sent you a letter." The teacher attributed the unusually good attendance—some 90 percent—to the children's persuasion.

Some teachers help the children prepare a snack for the evening meeting and, of course, let the parents know about it in the notice. Other teachers arrange to have a committee of parents attend to the invitations and reminders, sometimes by means of a telephone chain. But whatever method is used to summon parents, it must be remembered that tricks to gain attendance do not lead to *consistent* effect. Only sincerity of purpose and the actual development of suitable programs can do that.

Professional Terms vs. Everyday Speech

It is well to remember that sincerity can often be misunderstood when a teacher's language is so laden with professional terms that it is understood only by the initiated. Words and phrases like "social maturity," "language arts," "impulsive behavior," and even "adjustment" mean special things to early childhood practitioners but may represent a whole new world of words, attitudes, and practices to the average parent, including the well-educated parent, who is not likely to be educated in the special vocabulary of early childhood education. To the uninitiated parent, such language, or "jargon" can seem patronizing and can increase distance, something teachers do not want to see happen.

Maintaining Home-School Relations by Mail and Telephone

Home-school communication so often has to do with problems that it is helpful to the relationship if teachers can make time to send notes home about the positive days at school. "Joshua loved doing his share of washing the brushes today." "Nicole built a wonderful house out of blocks." "Tracy adored the story *One-Mitten Lewis.*" Teachers cannot do this every day for every child, but parents love every indication that their child is real to the teacher. In writing notes to tell about something negative or to give an instruction, remember that written language is easily misinterpreted. One teacher, for example, wrote hastily to forewarn a mother, "Dawn threw up today." She put the note in Dawn's hand and ran off to a meeting, leaving Dawn with the paraprofessional. The teacher had written the note with complete compassion, but when the mother read it, she was painfully embarrassed. Her child had created a mess! What did everyone think? With a little more thought, the teacher could just as easily have written, "Dawn threw up today. I hope she's not getting sick. Please let me know how she is." Mother and teacher would then have been *sharing* the child's mishap as a matter of common concern, and all other feelings would have been alleviated.

It is desirable to maintain communication with a child during a prolonged absence, and an effective and expressive way is a letter or card written by the teacher or by the children under the teacher's guidance. Some children might prefer to send a drawing, some to dictate a proper, "How are you? Hope you'll get well soon," and others to tell some news, like "Mike the turtle got lost again" or "Guess what happened to Verne—she lost a tooth." But whatever the content of the letter, the teacher-initiated communication between school and home speaks to the parents of personal interest.

Telephoning has a place in communication between teacher and parent, but not for anything really important if one can help it. In any serious conversation with a parent, teachers need to be alert to facial expressions, gestures, or tone of voice betraying anxiety, anger, resentment, or fear as well as anything else which indicates feelings that need reassurance or which reflects inadequate communication. Over the telephone, much can be concealed or missed. Better to use the telephone for quick uncomplicated messages or for setting up appointments or conferences than for real issues. Incidentally, it is in the teacher's best interests to protect his or her private life at home so as to find renewal each day for the next day's tasks. Thus, although teachers ought to be available to parents, they need not be endlessly at the mercy of parents who cannot wait, who are unreasonably demanding, or who use the telephone on impulse. Teachers must clarify this to themselves and to parents even as they offer their numbers for emergency.

The Class Report

Some teachers like to maintain contact with parents by sending a comprehensive report to all the parents on a regular basis. In such a report, they can discuss what has been happening in the classroom during the period of time involved. One teacher included in a class report a brief paragraph relating to specific interests or strengths of children associated with any specific program described in the class report. One such notation was, "Alvin asked many questions about the horse on the farm trip and enjoyed books about horses." Also, "Alexis has recently become interested in painting, and is now often the first one at the easel." This is concrete evidence of meaningful activity for that child and adds a personal quality to the class report. But even without the individual statement, the objective report in black and white would enable the parents to find out what kind of activity and learning there is in the kindergarten and perhaps clarify some random report from the child. If photographs of children in action could be attached, the report would be that much more vivid. This type of class report could be from one to five pages in length, depending on the style of writing. It may be in outline form, organized statements or description, or short essays. If after receipt of this the parents also meet to discuss the report and to ask questions of the teacher, they should really have a chance to learn the facts as well as the values in their children's education. As far as the teacher is concerned, preparing such a report would require conscious awareness about her or his own work and would help the teacher focus on what would be significant to parents.

If such a class report seems unrealistic to a teacher burdened by other, official, reports and by numerous professional obligations, another kind can be devised, perhaps a monthly or bimonthly brief newsletter; topics for it may even be suggested by the children. This may be quite short—yet the regular attention to it will give the teacher and children an objective appreciation of their class.

VISITING THE HOME

Still another way of communicating with parents, aside from written and oral reports, group meetings, and individual conferences, is a home visit by the teacher. In some situations this might serve as an initial acquaintance, as when the teacher is allowed a certain number of days before school starts officially to call on each of her or his new kindergarten children for a brief greeting to the child and the family. Such visits can give the teacher an insight into how mother and child interact; how the child responds to siblings; where, with what, and with whom the child plays; and the general context within which the child grows. Such visits help in later communication with child and parents after school starts. It goes without saying that a teacher enters a parent's home as a guest, not as a critic or judge. Observations, which are inevitable, are motivated by concern for understanding the child's environment so as to understand the child better, not to get details for gossip, awe, or pity.

However desirable home visits are, they are practical only when special time is provided, where groups are not overwhelmingly large, and in communities where the visits are acceptable and welcome. Fortunately, the involvement of parents in Headstart programs has extended the traditional cooperativeness of parents and teachers in middle-class nursery schools to include all parents of preschool children, and the concept of home visits is no longer strange to most teachers and perhaps not to parents either. Teacher experiences have on the whole been good, and teachers generally find the visits valuable. But one must also be prepared for the occasional surprise. For example, one teacher who called on a child of a poor family was regarded with suspicion as if she were an investigator from the Welfare Department. Another, calling on the child of a very well-to-do family, was "entertained" by the servant. But these are not typical.

Sometimes a teacher visits a child's home at the invitation of the child or mother, or both. This is an individual social visit, for lunch, perhaps, or tea, or even supper, and it usually takes place in the middle of the year when it can be particularly important to the child. By that time all the children know their teacher well enough to want him or her to come to their house. They are apt to assume that if the teacher is willing to come he or she not only likes them but the whole family! Of course the teacher would not have time for many such visits nor be likely to get invitations from all the children in the class. But the few social visits that could be made would give the teacher and the parents the opportunity to improve communication and relationships.

A rather special purpose served by a home visit is the possibility of alleviating a troubled situation at school. If a teacher feels by the middle of the year that he or she is not reaching a child, is not able to cope with a child's apparent tensions or aggressions or unhappiness, and is not successful in establishing good communication with the parents, the teacher might well improve things by making a friendly call. He or she may gain understanding of the parents' total responsibilities or some other special insight into how the child's life affects him or her, even though the visit is social.

Still another helpful purpose served by visiting is keeping the contact with children who have been out of school for a long while. Young children out of school for a lengthy period because of ill health respond with pride and pleasure at being remembered and included in the still novel position of school membership. The consideration and thoughtfulness expressed in this gesture to an isolated child affects later ability to find the way back again with security and ease.

VISITING THE SCHOOL

Let us now briefly consider visits moving in another direction, *from* the home *to* the school. Coming into the kindergarten, mothers and fathers can observe how the child actually fares. They can see the child's special associates, sense the atmosphere of work and play of which their child is part, discern the requirements demanded by being a member of a group, and discover the way the teacher treats different individuals and situations. The mother and father can be asked to help out in specific ways or they may remain informal visitors—not just standing around but participating here and there if they are comfortable doing it. They may be urged to focus on special facets of child life so as to broaden their understanding of their child's stage of development.

Fewer fathers than mothers are able to visit school despite the increase in working mothers. Those men whose occupations permit them to bring the child into the kindergarten, or who can take time for an hour's visit, find themselves especially appreciated not only by their own child but by the entire class. And if the father is also able to *do* something in the kindergarten—to show or demonstrate the tools or products of his trade or profession—whether he happens to be a fireman, farmer, plumber, manufacturer, doctor, lobsterman, musician, or whatever—then his status and that of his child will rise to great heights among the kindergarten people. This happened to Javier, whose father came to demonstrate weight-lifting when the class was studying the circus. Not only did the six-foot-four-inches tall father explain the different combination of weights and how to lift them, but he also created a small set of six-pound weights for the children to try. Javier was regarded with very respectful eyes from then on.

In another kindergarten a mother was able to come in twice a month regularly to cook with the children. It was a completely different and very pleasurable day for the children when she came, fully appreciated by the teacher, who was always glad to learn something herself and maintained a flexible schedule. The mother also learned a good deal from her activity in behalf of and with the children and from her cooperative relationship with the children and the teacher.

IMPORTANCE OF THE WHOLE FAMILY

Other members of the child's family may have an opportunity to visit and an interest in visiting the kindergarten, too, and they may make their contribution. Grandparents, whether young or elderly, can bring a special affection or friendship;

sometimes they bring items or language of a different culture from the one prevailing in the immediate community. Grandparents, like parents, may be people of special skills, hobbies, or talents that could be of interest and perhaps even assistance to the class. In more than one school, questionnaires to grandparents inquiring into their abilities, interests, and available time for help in the kindergarten have brought substantial responses. Grandparents have come into the kindergarten classroom to read to children, sew doll's clothes, help with children's clothing, play the piano, and help the teacher with materials.

Visits from older brothers or sisters, if occasion permits, are also meaningful home-school communication as far as the kindergarten child and teacher are concerned. An informal, sincere welcome from the teacher invariably helps the older child to feel at home and to enjoy surveying or trying out kindergarten play materials, which always appeal to the bigger children. Then, when the older child says, "You are lucky to have such nice things to play with!" the younger ones feel happy and privileged.

FAMILY PETS

Sometimes family pets can visit the kindergarten. When Sheila showed envy of another child who legitimately held attention and admiration from the group, the teacher allowed her to bring her new pet kitten to school. The mother had to bring the kitten and then return to take it home, but it proved to be so important to Sheila that the teacher allowed the kitten to be brought a second time. The children gave loving and undivided attention to the lively, cuddly kitten, and Sheila was as pleased as if the attention had been given all to her.

Thus, going to kindergarten need not mean to children a sharp break with their past and their home at all, but can signify a continuity and extension of the world they know. When the school invites parents for something pleasant and does not summon them only for problems, children enjoy their family's participation and feel secure in the knowledge that all concerned have a strong interest in them.

CONFERENCES

Communication between parents and teachers continues throughout the year, beyond the establishment of rapport and communication in groups. Parents and teachers need to stop and take account of how a child is growing—how she handles materials, how he takes to those demands necessary for group functioning, what kinds of satisfactions she finds, and what he cannot cope with—because without a realistic look at the child they share, they cannot successfully guide growth.

Good written reports are so difficult to produce that most kindergartens do not send them out at all, relying instead on personal conferences as a means of communicating with parents. In many school systems, time is set aside for such conferences because they lend themselves best of all methods to the two-way exchange so essential to real communication. A great deal has been written on the techniques, the value, and the problems of parent-teacher conferences. All writers stress the dynamic nature of the give-and-take involved, the necessary restraint and empathy needed in good listening, and the importance of sharing knowledge on the one hand and learning the point of view of the parents on the other. The ultimate purpose of a conference is for a teacher and a parent to explore and exchange their thoughts and feelings about a child in a relaxed and open-minded fashion. Teachers should not be too determined or set in advance about the outcome. Human beings are full of surprises, and one can never be too sure that one's understanding of another, including understanding of a child, is totally correct. Foregone conclusions and pat assumptions may close off the possibility of learning something really vital about a child or the parent's relations with the child. In an informal conference lasting from twenty minutes to an hour, the parent can gain assurance of the teacher's genuine concern for the child, knowledge of the child's status in the group, awareness of areas of needed help and areas of special satisfaction to the child.

The teacher can learn how children report their school experience at home, about their play life outside of school, and about their physical needs, history, or important family events. One teacher learned from a conference that there was an invalid uncle living with the family, which helped her to understand the child's preoccupation with certain medical matters in his play. Another teacher realized that the mother's anxiety about doing a good job as a parent was causing her to be overly demanding, and the child's tension could reasonably be traced to this. A teacher who regarded a child as fairly average in personality and ability extended her conception when she heard from the parents about the importance of this child within the family.

A common difficulty for a teacher in facing a parent during a conference is a sense of guilt or uncertainty if she or he does not happen to like that particular parent's child as much as the other children. Every teacher might ask, "Can I, or anyone, really love *all* children, and love them equally?" The truthful answer is "no." There may well be children in the class who do not arouse a teacher's love. As indicated earlier, there may be a nagging one, one with unpleasant mannerisms, an irritating bully, a tiresome whiner, or a sulky or a sneaky one. Such children may be a challenge and even arouse sympathy, but not affection. Yet the teacher, both by virtue of being a teacher and because she or he is an adult, must be *fair* to such a child, must look at him or her objectively (a teacher can do that better than a parent can), and by all means must notice whatever good qualities and constructive interests the child might have. In this way the teacher can gain some understanding of the child's positive drives as well as the occasions or causes of distress. Then a teacher may share such observations and understanding with the parent, to whom they can be of vital interest. The teacher may also learn of the mother's worry or interest, impatience, and even burden concerning this child and gain some realization of the life this mother has with the child. The teacher might acquire a special respect or regard for the mother or father, and hence added insight into the child.

Or the teacher might come out of the conference with added sympathy and respect for the child whom she or he sees as being in a very tough spot at home.

Such experiences cause us to wonder whether the standards by which a teacher judges a child are ever sufficiently inclusive! In any case, when teachers and parents think together on children's behalf, their mutual, increased understanding is bound to benefit the children and even make them more lovable! Good communication in a conference invariably affects the teacher's and parents' positive attitude toward the child and thus enhances the child's self-esteem.

KNOWING THE CHILD

Conferences are helped considerably by a teacher's specific knowledge of a child, which is more useful than an impressionistic "She's a charmer," or an emotional, "He's such a sad little thing." She needs to know how a child copes with the reality of school, down to the smallest detail. Who are his friends and how does he relate to them? How does she react in an emergency? What play materials does he like best? Which activities does she shun? What are the child's capabilities as seen in action? In which areas of school life does the child show confusion, unreadiness, or awkwardness?

Information for the conference is gained by observation and keeping records, as indicated in Chapter 3. While the initial purpose of record keeping is to help the teacher know the children better so as to plan for them as individuals and as members of the group, the objective, unbiased descriptions of how a child acts under certain conditions and circumstances are most valuable to parents, too. They indicate immediately that a teacher knows a child, which assures the parent of the teacher's concern. Records also give the parent real content to respond to instead of such vague generalities as "He's just fine," or such ambiguities as "She's insecure," or "She's immature." Parents are hungry for details of their children's lives away from home. It was not too long before kindergarten entry that the parent knew every aspect of the child's experience, so close was the relationship. Parents want their children to grow away from them in independent functioning, but they most definitely want to stay in touch. They are grateful to teachers who cue them in.

GIVING ADVICE

One of the common and confusing challenges to a teacher is the matter of giving advice to parents: should you, should you not, and if you do, how much? It is common knowledge that advice is easier to give than to take, and in the parent-teacher relation this is no less true than in human relations in general. Yet parents ask for advice, and a teacher is often besieged with pleas for specific help: "How do you punish a child? What do you do about stubbornness?" "He keeps asking how to spell words. Shall I tell him?" "Exactly what shall I say when he asks . . . ?" Looking with common sense at this matter, we see that people do not as a rule take advice because the advice may not exactly fit their own perception of the situation, may not really answer their underlying question behind their obvious one, or may represent a solution impossible to fulfill for that person at that time. The teacher, in giving advice, gives the parent the end result of his or her learning and experience, but the answer may enter the parent's ears as a formula to be applied without understanding or flexibility. Very few teachers would presume to dictate to a parent, but few teachers enjoy disappointing a parent, and fewer still like to have it appear that they do not know how to solve the parents' dilemma. It is human to take pleasure in revealing wisdom and knowledge to those who look to us for such leadership. True leadership, however, takes into account the ways by which those led can be helped to grow in understanding themselves. It is wise, therefore, in response to requests for direct and specific advice, to try to involve parents in solving the problem so that they can themselves see the reasoning behind the solution.

Let us suppose, for example, that a parent asks a teacher for a list of good children's books to read to the child. An experienced teacher could easily compile a list of favorites and might even have one readily available for all the parents. The parent would feel safe in the choices, and there would be a kind of minimum guarantee that the child would gain from the selections. But suppose that in addition to supplying a list the teacher asked the parent to browse among the books in the classroom, talked a little about the subjects in children's books, the style of writing illustrated in several of the classroom samples, and the particular child's interests and preferences. In this way the parent might discover some values in good literature for young children and would be able to add to the list by using a new-found understanding of what to look for.

Or a parent might ask advice about a suitable trip. In that case, along with giving the name and address of a place, the teacher could invite the mother or father to join a class trip and in this way help her or him to see firsthand how children respond to well-planned trips.

The more complicated question "How do I deal with his stubbornness?" is worthy of more than a technique. For one thing, what does a certain mother mean by *stubbornness*? What might she be doing that is causing the child to resist her so strongly? Is her concern truly justified? Does the matter call for a shift in the relationship between the two? Only as the mother can look at the problem with the teacher, only as they pull it apart together, can they reach a decision that the mother will be capable of carrying out.

A common method of giving advice is to recommend suitable adult reading. Too often we see well-read parents become less and less spontaneous, natural, and effective as parents. There must be self-awareness and conviction along with reading if the books are to become a supplement and stimulation to, but not the chief source of, guidance to parents.

SPECIAL PROBLEMS, SPECIAL TECHNIQUES

The content of most conferences falls into the common variety of growth and coping problems which are part of every human being's struggle to be a participating member of family and society. Children must be socialized, and they do not always like the conflicts socialization entails; parents must guide their children, and in these changing times, they are too often unsure as to which direction is best. When the teacher's concern and objectivity meet with the parents' undisputed commitment and intimate knowledge of their child, possible solutions to these common problems are more likely than not to result from the joint thinking.

But occasionally a teacher meets children whose problems, or whose parents, do not lend themselves to the goodwill, devoted effort, and careful approaches that are normally helpful. These may include children who are abused and need the community's help; children who cannot cope and must undergo further examination and analysis outside of school; and, especially important in the 1980s, children with physical and mental handicaps who have a legal right to a place in a regular class. They may include parents who are so overwhelmed by life that they have escaped into untenable solutions for themselves to the detriment of their children, or parents who feel overwhelmed by handicapped or adopted children, or parents who are raising a child alone and find it hard to manage without support.

Many of these problems give way before the rational and supportive efforts of knowledgeable teachers. But some do not, and teachers feel helpless. It is important to know that teachers cannot solve every problem they encounter and that this is not a mark against them. For the teacher to continue to function as a good teacher, he or she must learn to understand what is beyond his or her powers or training and consider how best to get help for a child or family. Such decisions are not to be made lightly. They must be based on careful observations of the child at school, on honest effort to enlist the parent, and on evaluation by the teacher of his or her own motives and state of knowledgeableness as well. Beginning teachers especially must be sensitive to what they cannot do, recognizing that it is more important to help a child than to preserve their own pride.

The first hurdle to be faced and overcome is the realization that, try as the teacher will, the child is not responding. The teacher must have the evidence for this that only careful and objective records give. The second hurdle is to acquaint the parent with the problem. It goes without saying that a teacher need not expect to offer a diagnosis to a parent. In all too many cases where a child is not responding to teacher efforts—whether the problem involves emotional, physical, or intellectual behavior—it takes more skill than a teacher has to uncover the nature and causes of the difficulty. An objective description, however, with supporting illustrations given without judgment, will speak for itself. What must also come across is that the teacher is clearly interested in the child's welfare and is not passing judgment on either the child or the parent. Identifying with the parent's feelings of pain makes it easier for the teacher to withstand whatever defensive reactions the parent may fall back on when she or he first hears the teacher's assessment. Reporting bad news is very difficult for teachers because they do not enjoy being the bearers of news that causes another person anguish. Yet parents are more often grateful than not for the consideration and thoughtfulness that alerts them to the need for further examination and diagnosis of their child. While many parents deny the possibility that something is wrong with their child, many more respond after the initial impact with "What can we do?" In fact, they are helped toward such a response by the knowledge that they are not alone in facing an unpleasant reality. The teacher's professional awareness helps to relieve what would otherwise be a sense of aloneness. In every school or community there is someone who is well informed concerning the various health, social, and psychological agencies and organizations that can support families in need. Teachers must know who these people are for the parents' sake.

THE DIFFICULT PARENT

The really difficult parent is another problem. Parents are people, and to the degree that their lives are satisfactory, they are more likely to be pleasant and agreeable people. But life is not equally desirable for all people. In addition, we live in a time of great stress, when all kinds of customs and relationships are changing. No one, for example, accepts inferior status any more or the inevitable power of authority. The drive to self-assertion is strong among many who once accepted traditional relationships without question. This is generally healthy but can produce specific individuals who are angry, belligerent, suspicious, defensive, or otherwise unreasonable. It helps always to remember that conditions create behavior and that the teacher who faces a parent who is hostile, resentful, or who makes false accusations faces a hurt person whom life has taught to be distrustful. The teacher is really being perceived as a societal representative, and not as an individual. It is helpful to teachers to realize this and not feel personally attacked or threatened. Patience, the effort to understand what the parent is trying to say (and saying so poorly), interest, and time often help to reduce the passions and open the parent to a more helpful level of communication. And effective communication between parents and teachers depends to a large extent on the teachers' interest and initiative.

LOOKING FORWARD

Although we cannot help being aware of the steady rise in the breakup of the traditional family through divorce and other forms of separation, we must not overlook the positive aspects of the changes in family structure taking place in our society.

One conspicuous change is in the practice and the concept of parenthood, which consists of the expanding role of the father, whether married or single. One evidence is the prevalence and popularity of movies and some popular television programs which deal with a father finding challenge and fulfillment in the daily care of a young child.

Although not in large numbers yet, men are requesting paternity leave with the birth of a child in the family; and some men are exchanging the customary role of provider for that of househusband, which includes care of young children.[4] Some schools and colleges are offering courses on fathering that clearly aim to help fathers become active in child rearing and in general encourage men to take on nurturing roles.[5]

Among more innovative fatherhood courses was an elective offered to sixth-grade boys in a private school on infant care.[6] Although at first skeptical and even scornful, the boys learn to actually handle and enjoy real babies (including diapering), and in the end the boys recognize that the course gives them not only handy knowledge for babysitting, but is actually *preparation for fatherhood.*

There are now many publications dealing with the psychological-educational-practical aspects of the phenomenon of modern fatherhood (see bibliography at the end of this chapter).

Such expansion of the fatherhood function means more than mere economic expediency or just another social change in a democratic society. Dr. Philip Cowan, clinical psychologist at the University of California, reports from a study of one hundred couples that men chose to become fathers not only to pass on the family name but also "to be taught about the world in terms of a child's spontaneity and feelings."

With signs of appreciation of childhood and a caring attitude, the modern father stands in sharp contrast to the old-fashioned, authoritarian disciplinarian and masculine provider. And thus, when one contemplates *the future achievements* of fathers in the educational and even political arenas, they are worth looking forward to.

Another social phenomenon expanding the field of parenting is the increasing number of older persons who are functional grandparents. Contrary to the myth that aging is inevitably accompanied by disability, illness, and dependency, most people of retirement age are competent, contributing citizens and can be important family members or associates (if they live separately from the family). We are not making full use of their abilities, talents, and especially experience. However, some communities are introducing adult helpers from senior citizens' groups, and some schools carry on a program of individual help to special students, with the help of volunteer older teachers. A hospital in California employs a "professional grandmother" to counsel and to provide actual assistance to new parents.[7]

What a tremendous human resource for many social and educational endeavors grandparents can be! And what lasting influence they can exert on the young—

[4] Jane Merrill Filstrup with Dorothy W. Gross, "House Husband," Chap. 2 in *Monday through Friday: Day Care Alternatives* (New York: Teachers College Press, 1982).

[5] *Bank Street News,* Fall 1981 (New York: Bank Street College).

[6] Alison Cragin and Jane Lawrence Mali (photographs Katrina Thomas) *Oh, Boy! Babies!* (Boston: Little, Brown and Company, 1980).

[7] "Grandparents: The New Profession," *Newsletter* of the Early Childhood Education Council of New York City (October 1980).

if there is contact between them! With increased opportunities for sharing both burdens and joys of the new generation, grandparents can make a difference in the parenting constellation of mother-father-grandparents—whether the grandparents arrive at such status biologically or by function and cultivation.

REFERENCES AND FURTHER READING

Styles of Parenting

ANDREWS, J. D. (ed.). *One Child Indivisible.* Washington, D.C.: National Association for the Education of Young Children, 1975.
COLLINS, GLENN. "Paternity Leave: A New Role for Fathers," *New York Times,* December 7, 1981.
CRAGIN, ALISON and MALI, JANE LAWRENCE (photographs by Katrina Thomas). *Oh, Boy! Babies!* Boston: Little, Brown, 1980.
DULLEA, GEORGIA. "Fatherhood: Expanding Role and Expanding Joys," *New York Times,* June 20, 1982.
EIDUSON, BERNICE T. "Looking at Children in Emergent Family Styles," *Children Today,* U.S. Dept. of Health, Education and Welfare, 3, 4 (July-August 1974).
FILSTRUP, JANE MERRILL with DOROTHY W. GROSS. *Monday through Friday: Day Care Alternatives.* New York: Teachers College Press, 1982.
GREENBERG, KENNETH R. *Tiger by the Tail: Parenting in a Troubled Society.* Chicago: Nelson-Hall, Inc., 1974.
HERZOG, ELIZABETH, and SUDIA, CECILIA. "Families without Fathers," *Childhood Education,* 48 (1972), 175–81.
KLEIN, CAROLE. *The Single Parent Experience.* New York: Avon Books, 1973.
LEVINE, JAMES A. *Who Will Raise the Children?* Philadelphia: Lippincott, 1976.
LYNN, DAVID B. *The Father: His Role in Child Development.* Monterey, Calif.: Brooks/Cole, 1974.
POGREBIN, LETTY COTTIN. *Growing Up Free; Raising Your Child in the '80s.* New York: McGraw-Hill, 1981.
STEVENS, JOSEPH H. and MATHEWS, MARILYN, (eds.). *Mother/Child, Father/Child Relationships.* Washington, D.C.: National Association for Education of Young Children, 1978.
UNICEF. *Father and Child,* photographic calendar. New York: UN Publications, 1982.

Techniques of Working with Parents

AUERBACH, ALINE B. *Parents Learn through Discussion: Principles and Practice of Parent Education.* New York: John Wiley, 1967.
AUERBACH, ALINE B., and ROCHE, SANDRA. *Creating a Preschool Center: Parent Development in an Integrated Neighborhood Project.* New York: John Wiley, 1971.
CHILMAN, CATHERINE. "Recent Trends in Parent Education and Participation," in *Review of Child Development Research,* vol. 3, eds. B. Caldwell and H. Ricutti. Chicago: University of Chicago Press, 1972.
COHEN, DOROTHY H. *Working with Parents in Low-Income Areas.* Bank Street Publication No. 11. Bank St. College, 610 W. 112th St., New York 10025.

HONIG, ALICE. *Parent Involvement in Early Childhood Education.* Washington, D.C.: National Association for the Education of Young Children, 1975.
HYMES, JAMES L., JR. *Effective Home-School Relations.* Englewood Cliffs, N.J.: Prentice-Hall, 1953.
NEWMAN, SYLVIA. *Guidelines to Parent-Teacher Cooperation in Early Childhood.* 1972. Book Lab, Inc., 1449 37th Street, Brooklyn, New York 11218.
TAYLOR, KATHERINE WHITESIDE. *Parents and Teachers Learn Together* (3rd ed.). New York: Teachers College Press, 1981.

Readings for Parents

AMES, LOUISE, and CHASE, JOAN A. *Don't Push Your Preschooler* (rev. ed.). New York: Harper & Row, Pub., 1980.
ANDERSON, LULEEN S. "When a Child Begins School," *Children Today,* 5, 4 (July-August 1976), pp. 16–19.
BANK STREET COLLEGE FACULTY. *The Pleasure of Their Company: How to Have More Fun with Your Children.* Radnor, Pa.: Chilton Book Company, 1981.
CARTER, LANIE. *Congratulations, You Are Going to Be a Grandmother!* San Diego: Oak Tree Publications, 1980.
COHEN, DOROTHY H. *The Learning Child.* New York: Pantheon, 1972.
COMER, JAMES P., and POUSSAINT, ALVIN F. *Black Child Care.* New York: Simon & Schuster, 1975.
HARRISON-ROSS, PHYLLIS, and WEYDEN, BARBARA. *The Black Child: A Parents' Guide.* New York: D. McKay, 1973.
KELLY, MARGUERITE, and PARSONS, ELIA. *The Mother's Almanac.* New York: Doubleday, 1975.
PINES, MAYA. "Baby, You're Incredible," *Psychology Today* (February 1982).

Special Problems:
Child Abuse, Neglect, Exceptional Children

FONTANA, VINCENT J. *Somewhere a Child Is Crying.* New York: Macmillan, 1973.
HEISSLER, VERDA. *A Handicapped Child in the Family: A Guide for Parents.* New York: Grune & Stratton, 1972.
KEMPE, C., HELFER, HENRY, and HELFER, RAY. *Helping the Battered Child and His Family.* Philadelphia: Lippincott, 1972.
KVARACEUS, W. C., and HAYES, E. N. *If Your Child Is Handicapped.* Boston: Porter Sargent, 1969. Personal accounts by parents of children with various handicaps.
LEWIS, ELEANORE GRATER. "The Case for Special Children," *Young Children* (August 1973).
PAVENSTEDT, E. (ed.). *The Drifters.* New York: Little, Brown, 1967.
SMITH, B. K. *Your Nonlearning Child: His World Upside Down.* Boston: Beacon Press, 1968. For parents of the learning disabled.
SPOCK, B., and LERRIGO, M. O. *Caring for Your Disabled Child.* New York: Crowell, Collier and Macmillan, Inc., 1965. For parents of the physically handicapped.
STEIN, LISA. "Techniques for Parent Discussion in Disadvantaged Areas," *Young Children,* 22, 4 (March 1967), 210–17.

Sources of Publications for Parents and Teachers

American Social Health Association
1740 Broadway
New York, N.Y. 10019

Bank Street Publications
Bank Street College Bookstore
610 W. 112th Street
New York, N.Y. 10025

Early Childhood Education Council of New York City
66 Leroy St.
New York, N.Y. 10014

Highlights for Children
(*Parenting,* a monthly newsletter)
2300 W. Fifth Ave.
P.O. Box 2505
Columbus, Ohio 43216

Hogg Foundation for Mental Health
University of Texas
Austin, Texas 18712

Human Development News
(published eight times a year)
U.S. Department of Health and Human Services
200 Independence Ave. S.W.
Rm. 356-G, HHH Bldg.
Washington, D.C. 20201

Metropolitan Life Insurance Co.
1 Madison Ave.
New York, N.Y. 10010

National Congress of Parents and Teachers
(Monthly National Congress Bulletin
and official PTA Magazine, *The National Parent Teacher*)
600 South Michigan Blvd.
Chicago, Illinois 60605

Parent's Institute
52 Vanderbilt Ave.
New York, N.Y. 10017

Parents' Campaign for Handicapped Children
(*Closer Look,* a quarterly publication)
1201 16th St. N.W.
Washington, D.C. 20036

Public Affairs Pamphlets
381 Park Ave. South
New York, N.Y. 10010

Salk Letter
(A monthly publication from Dr. Lee Salk,
Professor of Psychology and Pediatrics)
941 Park Ave.
New York, N.Y. 10028

Science Research Associates
259 E. Erie Street
Chicago, Illinois 60611

State Education Departments
of your own and other state governments

Teachers College, Columbia University
Bureau of Publications
1234 Amsterdam Ave.
New York, N.Y. 10027

Sources of Equipment and Materials

Childcraft
155 East 23rd Street
New York, N.Y. 10010

Community Playthings
Rifton, N.Y. 12471

Constructive Playthings
1040 East 85th Street
Kansas City, Mo. 64131

Creative Playthings
1 East 53rd Street
New York, N.Y. 10021

J. L. Hammett Co.
2393 Vauxhall Road
Union City, N.J. 07083

N.Y.T. Teaching Resources
100 Boylston Street
Boston, Mass. 02116

Selective Educational Equipment
3 Budge Street
Newton, Mass. 02195

We close our book with a reminder from the great educator
to whose memory it is dedicated.

Children Need Time to Grow

You cannot hurry human growth,
It is slow and quiet,
Quiet and slow
As the growth of a tree.

Only when its roots go deep,
Deep within the earth that nourishes it—
Its own earth
Its own soil—
Will its branches spread wide
Wide as the earth is wide.

Agnes Snyder

Reprinted with permission of the Association for Childhood Education International, 3615 Wisconsin Ave., N.W., Washington, D.C. Copyright © 1973 by the Association.

Index